A GUIDE TO CRITICAL REVIEWS

Part I: *American Drama, 1909-1982.* 3d ed. 1984.

Part II: *The Musical, 1909-1989.* 3d ed. 1991.

Part III: *Foreign Drama, 1909-1977.* 2d ed. 1979.

Part IV: *The Screenplay from "The Jazz Singer" to "Dr. Strangelove."* 2 vols. 1971.

Part IV: *The Screenplay, Supplement One: 1963-1980.* 1982.

176.50

A Guide to Critical Reviews:

Part II:
The Musical, 1909-1989

Third Edition

by

JAMES M. SALEM

The Scarecrow Press, Inc.
Metuchen, N.J., & London
1991

British Library Cataloguing-in-Publication data available

Library of Congress Cataloging-in-Publication Data

(Revised for vol. 2)
Salem, James M.
   A guide to critical reviews.

   Includes bibliographical references and indexes.
   Contents: pt. 1. American drama, 1909-1982 --
pt. 2. The musical, 1909-1989.
   1. Theater--New York (N.Y.)--Reviews--Indexes.
2. Motion pictures--United States--Reviews--Indexes.
3. Musicals--Reviews--Indexes.   I. Title.
Z5781.S16 1984 [PN2266] 016.8092   84-1370
ISBN 0-8108-1690-3 (v. 1)
ISBN 0-8108-2387-X (v. 2)

CONTENTS

FOREWORD

The purpose of Part II of A Guide to Critical Reviews: The Musical (third edition) is to provide a bibliography of critical reviews of 2,149 musicals on the New York stage from 1909 to the 1988-1989 theater season. The 2,669 productions listed are, for the most part, Broadway shows, though Off-Broadway productions have been included when accurate statistical data could be obtained. In addition, selected Off-Off-Broadway presentations are included, as well as some musicals that closed during their pre-Broadway tryouts. The key source for production data of this kind is, of course, The Best Plays of the Year series, begun by Burns Mantle and currently directed by Otis L. Guernsey and Jeffrey Sweet.

Musical revues have been included in this volume, one (wo)man shows, and musical extravaganzas, spectacles, burlesques--even a musical described as a "Fragment from France in two explosions, seven splinters, and a short gas attack" (The Better 'Ole, Season of 1918-19). And while I have excluded most operas and operettas, the shows of Jerome Kern, Sigmund Romberg, and Vincent Youmans are here, along with the works of Marc Blitzstein, Gian-Carlo Menotti, and Leonard Bernstein's Trouble in Tahiti.

The reviews cited in this volume are those which appeared in general circulation American and Canadian periodicals and in the New York Times. With the exception of some now defunct dramatic magazines, such as Dramatic Mirror and New York Clipper, most of the reviews should be available in college and public libraries. Reviews in other New York newspapers have not been indexed, but New York Theatre Critics' Reviews has been cited for plays produced since that publication began in 1940, when reviews were reprinted from the New York Journal-American, Daily News,

Post, Mirror, World Telegram and Sun, Herald Tribune, and Times. Currently, this valuable reference tool also reprints reviews from Wall Street Journal, Time, Women's Wear Daily, WABC-TV, USA Today, Christian Science Monitor, Newsweek, and New York Newsday.

The organization of this volume is alphabetical, by title, with liberal cross-referencing. While I have omitted the English articles "A," "An," and "The" in alphabetizing titles, I have yielded to the indexing practice of retaining "La," "Les," "Los," and "Der" as beginning words in foreign titles. The three indexes at the end will enable the user to track down Authors, Composers, and Lyricists; Directors, Designers, and Choreographers; and the titles and original authors of novels, plays, movies, biographies, comic strips, and stories upon which many musicals are based. I have also included listings of Long Run Musicals (more than 500 performances), and those which have won a Pulitzer Prize, Tony Award, or a New York Drama Critics' Circle Award.

Two symbols are used throughout to indicate incomplete data. For early plays, the number of performances enclosed by parentheses ( ) denotes that the play probably had a longer run than the number of performances given. For the most recent productions, an asterisk (*) denotes that the musical was still running on June 1, 1989.

I should like to acknowledge a debt of gratitude to Lauren Bielecki, Larry Harbin, Ingrid Nelson, Donna Salem, Tim Salem, Jennifer Santoyo, Rebecca Simpson, Margaret Vines, and Jennifer Wallace--all of whom assisted me in the research or production of this volume.

James M. Salem
University of Alabama
Tuscaloosa, AL
September 1990

MUSICALS

A La Broadway (Presented with Hello, Paris, 1911)
>   book: William Le Baron
>   music: Harold Orlob
>   lyrics: William Le Baron and M. H. Hollins
Productions:
>   Opened September 22, 1911 for 8 performances
Reviews:
>   Life (New York) 96:35, Dec 5, 1930

A La Carte
>   book: Rosalie Stewart
>   sketches: George Kelly
>   music: Herman Hupfeld, Louis Atter, Norma Gregg,
>   Paul Lannin and Creamer and Johnson
>   staging: George Kelly
Productions:
>   Opened August 17, 1927 for 45 performances
Reviews:
>   Life (New York) 90:19, Sep 8, 1927
>   Theatre Magazine 46:23, Oct 1927
>   Vogue 70: 97, Oct 15, 1927

A ... My Name Is Alice
>   conceived: Joan Micklin Silver and Julianne Boyd
>   songs: Various authors and composers
>   staging: Joan Micklin Silver and Julianne Boyd
>   sets: Ray Recht
>   costumes: Ruth Morley
>   choreography: Edward Love
Productions:
>   (Off-Broadway) Opened February 24 and April 8, 1984 for 353
>   performances
Reviews:
>   New York 17: 93- 4, Apr 23, 1984
>   New York Times III, page 14, Feb 27, 1984
>   II, page 5, Mar 11, 1984
>   III, page 15, May 7, 1984

Above the Clouds
>   book: Will B. Johnstone

```
music:          Tom Johnstone
lyrics:         Will B. Johnstone
Productions:
    Opened January 9, 1922 for 89 performances
No Reviews.
```

Absolutely Free
```
    music/lyrics:    Frank Zappa
Productions:
    (Off-Broadway) Opened May 24, 1967 for 208 performances
Reviews:
    New York Times page 58, May 25, 1967
```

The Act
```
    book:           George Furth
    music:          John Kander
    lyrics:         Fred Ebb
    staging:        Martin Scorsese
    sets:           Tony Walton
    costumes:       Halston
    choreography:   Ron Lewis
Productions:
    Opened October 29, 1977 for 240 performances
Reviews:
    America 137:423, Dec 10, 1977
    Los Angeles 22:232+, Oct 1977
    New York 10:89+, Nov 14, 1977
    New York Theatre Critics' Reviews 1977:151
    New York Times page 39, Oct 31, 1977
                    II, page 3, Nov 6, 1977
    New Yorker 53:103, Nov 7, 1977
    Newsweek 90:49, Sep 5, 1977
                    90:99, Nov 14, 1977
    Saturday Review 5:44, Oct 1, 1977
    Time 110:61, Nov 14, 1977
```

Adele
```
    book:           Paul Herve; English version by Adolf Philipp
                    and Edward A. Paulton
    music:          Jean Briquet
    staging:        Ben Teal
Productions:
    Opened August 28, 1913 for 196 performances
Reviews:
    Dramatic Mirror 70:6, Sep 3, 1913; 70:2+, Oct 22, 1913
    Green Book 10:769-70, Nov 1913; 11:524, Mar 1914
    Munsey 50:290-3, Nov 1913
    New York Dramatic News 58:20-1, Sep 6, 1913
    New York Times page 9, Aug 29, 1913
                    III, page 4, Jun 14, 1914
    Theatre Arts 18:xi, Oct 1913; 18:117, Oct 1913
    Theatre Magazine 18:127, Oct 1913; 20:283, Dec 1914
```

Adolph Green (see A Party with Betty Comden and Adolph Green)

Adrienne
book: A. Seymour Brown; from a story by Frances
                      Bryant and William Stone
music: Albert Von Tilzer
lyrics: A. Seymour Brown
staging: Edgar J. MacGregor
Productions:
Opened May 28, 1923 for (24) performances
Reviews:
Life (New York) 81:18, Jun 21, 1923
New York Clipper 71:14, Jun 6, 1923
New York Times page 10, May 29, 1923
Theatre Magazine 38:16, Aug 1923

Aesop's Fables
book: Jon Swan; based on Aesop's Fables
music: William Russo
lyrics: Jon Swan
staging: William Russo
sets: Vanessa James
Productions:
(Off-Broadway) Opened August 16, 1972 for 58 performances
No Reviews.

Afgar
book: Fred Thompson and Worton David
music: Charles Cuvillier
lyrics: Douglas Furber
staging: Frank Collins
Productions:
Opened November 8, 1920 for 171 performances
Reviews:
Dramatic Mirror page 895, Nov 13, 1920
                 page 1218, Dec 25, 1920
Life (New York) 76:960, Nov 25, 1920
New York Clipper 68:3, Nov 17, 1920
New York Times page 13, Nov 9, 1920
                 VI, page 1, Nov 14, 1920
Theatre Magazine 33:11+, Jan 1921; 33:74, Jan 1921

Africana
music: Donald Heyward
lyrics: Donald Heyward
staging: Louis Douglas
Productions:
Opened July 11, 1927 for 72 performances
Reviews:
Life (New York) 90:19, Aug 18, 1927
New York Times page 29, Jul 12, 1927
                 VII, page 1, Sep 4, 1927

After Stardrive

book:	Kathleen Kramer and O-Lan Shepard
music and lyrics:	Kathleen Kramer and O-Lan Shepard
staging:	Bevya Rosten
sets:	Linda Hartinian
costumes:	Linda Hartinian

Productions:
   (Off-Off-Broadway) Opened May 8, 1981
Reviews:
   Los Angeles 28:46, Aug 1983
   New York Times page 15, May 16, 1981
   New Yorker 57:115-16, May 25, 1981

Ah, Men

by:	Paul Shyre
songs:	Will Holt
staging:	Paul Shyre
sets:	Eldon Elder
costumes:	Eldon Elder

Productions:
   (Off Broadway) Opened May 11, 1981 for 14 performances
No Reviews.

Ain't Misbehavin'

conceived:	Murray Horwitz and Richard Maltby, Jr.
music:	Fats Waller
lyrics:	Various authors
staging:	Richard Maltby, Jr.
sets:	John Lee Beatty
costumes:	Randy Barcelo
choreography:	Arthur Faria

Productions:
   Opened May 9, 1978 for 1,604 performances
   Opened August 15, 1988 for 176 performances
Reviews:
   America 159:346, Nov 5, 1988
   Down Beat 45:14, Nov 2, 1978
   Encore 7:34, Jun 5, 1978
   Harper's 257:77, Dec 1978
   Horizon 21:88-93, Sep 1978
   Los Angeles 25:234+, Feb 1980
   Nation 226:645, May 27, 1978
   New Republic 179:28, Jul 8, 1978
   New West 5:65, Jan 14, 1980
   New York 11:111-12, May 22, 1978
                21:59, Aug 29, 1988
   New York Theatre Critics' Reviews 1978:288
                                     1988:204
   New York Times III, page 13, Feb 20, 1978
                   III, page 19, May 10, 1978

II, page 7, May 14, 1978
XXI, page 19, Jul 11, 1982
XI, page 2, Jan 8, 1983
XXXIII, page 27, May 25, 1986
II, page 5, Aug 14, 1988
III, page 15, Aug 16, 1988
New Yorker 54:91, May 22, 1978
  64:89, Sep 5, 1988
Newsweek 91:71, May 22, 1978
Saturday Review 5:24, Jul 8, 1978
  5:40, Aug 1978
Theatre Crafts 20:25+, May 1986
Time 111:58, Feb 27, 1978
  111:70-1, Jun 5, 1978
  132:75, Aug 29, 1988

Ain't Supposed to Die a Natural Death (Tunes from Blackness)
  book: Melvin Van Peebles
  music: Melvin Van Peebles
  lyrics: Melvin Van Peebles
  staging: Gilbert Moses
  sets: Kert Lundell
  costumes: Bernard Johnson
Productions:
  Opened October 20, 1971 for 325 performances
Reviews:
  Nation 213:476-7, Nov 8, 1971
  New York Theatre Critics' Reviews 1971:229
  New York Times page 55, Oct 21, 1971
          II, page 3, Oct 31, 1971
          II, page 1, Nov 7, 1971
          II, page 28, Apr 16, 1972
          page 13, Jul 29, 1972
  New Yorker 47:101-2, Oct 30, 1971
  Newsweek 78:85-6, Nov 1, 1971
  Saturday Review 54:10+, Nov 13, 1971
  Time 98:95, Nov 1, 1971

Alice
  book: Vinnette Carroll, based on Lewis Carroll's Alice
               in Wonderland and Through the Looking Glass
  music: Micki Grant
  lyrics: Micki Grant
  staging: Vinnette Carroll
  sets: Douglas W. Schmidt
  costumes: Nancy Potts
  choreography: Talley Beatty
Productions:
  Closed prior to Broadway opening (Philadelphia, May 1978)
Reviews:
  Texas Monthly 7:228, Nov 1979

Alice in Concert
>book: Elizabeth Swados, based on Lewis Carroll's Alice
>   in Wonderland and Through the Looking Glass
>music: Elizabeth Swados
>lyrics: Elizabeth Swados
>staging: Joseph Papp
>sets: Michael H. Yeargan
>costumes: Theoni V. Aldredge
>choreography: Graciela Daniele

Productions:
>(Off-Broadway) Opened December 29, 1980 for 32 performances

Reviews:
>New York 14:38, Jan 19, 1981
>New York Theatre Critics' Reviews 1981:359
>New York Times III, page 17, Jan 8, 1981
>New Yorker 56:90-1, Jan 19, 1981
>Newsweek 97:87, Jan 19, 1981
>Time 117:77, Jan 19, 1981

Alive and Kicking
>sketches: Ray Golden, I. A. Diamond, Henry Morgan,
>   Jerome Chodorov, Joseph Stein, Will Glickman,
>   Mike Stuart
>music: Hal Borne, Irma Jurist and Sammy Fain
>lyrics: Paul Francis Webster and Ray Golden
>additional
>   music/lyrics: Sonny Burke, Leonard Gershe, Billy Kyle, Sid
>   Kuller
>special music
>   and lyrics: Harold Rome
>staging: Robert H. Gordon
>sets: Raoul Pene du Bois
>costumes: Raoul Pene du Bois
>choreography: Jack Cole

Productions:
>Opened January 17, 1950 for 46 performances

Reviews:
>New York Theatre Critics' Reviews 1950:390+
>New York Times page 25, Jan 18, 1950
>Newsweek 35:66, Jan 30, 1950
>Theatre Arts 34:16, May 1950
>Time 55:40, Jan 30, 1950

All Aboard
>book: Mark Swan
>music: E. Ray Goetz and Malvin Franklin
>lyrics: E. Ray Goetz
>staging: William J. Wilson and W. H. Post

Productions:
>Opened June 5, 1913 for 108 performances

Reviews:
>Blue Book 17:876-80, Sep 1913

Book News 32:255-6, Jan 1914
Dramatic Mirror 69:15, Jun 11, 1913
Green Book 10:433-5, Sep 1913
New York Dramatic News 57:18, Jun 14, 1913
New York Times page 11, Jun 6, 1913
Theatre Magazine 18:xx, Jul 1913

All American

book:	Mel Brooks, based on Robert Lewis Taylor's Professor Fodorski
music:	Charles Strouse
lyrics:	Lee Adams
staging:	Joshua Logan
sets:	Jo Mielziner
costumes:	Patton Campbell
choreography:	Danny Daniels

Productions:
Opened March 19, 1962 for 86 performances
Reviews:
America 107:278-9, May 19, 1962
New York Theatre Critics' Reviews 1962:318+
New York Times page 44, Mar 20, 1962
page 29, May 24, 1962
New Yorker 38:104-6, Mar 31, 1962
Newsweek 59:58, Apr 2, 1962
Theatre Arts 46:58, May 1962
Time 79:46, Mar 30, 1962

All by Myself

sketches:	Anna Russell
music/lyrics:	Anna Russell
staging:	Kurt Cerf
sets:	Robert E. Darling
costumes:	Stephanya

Productions:
(Off-Broadway) Opened June 15, 1964 for 40 performances
Reviews:
New York Times page 47, Jun 16, 1964

All for Love

sketches:	Max Shulman and others
music/lyrics:	Alan Roberts and Lester Lee
staging:	Edward Reveaux
sets:	Edward Gilbert
costumes:	Billy Livingston
choreography:	Eric Victor

Productions:
Opened January 22, 1949 for 141 performances
Reviews:
Commonweal 49:447, Feb 11, 1949
New York Theatre Critics' Reviews 1949:377+

New York Times page 16, Jan 24, 1949
New Yorker 24:42, Jan 29, 1949
Newsweek 33:71, Jan 31, 1949
Time 53:44, Jan 31, 1949
          53:63-4, May 2, 1949

All for the Ladies
book: Henry Blossom
music: Alfred C. Robyn
lyrics: Henry Blossom
costumes: Melville Ellis
Productions:
Opened December 30, 1912 for 112 performances
Reviews:
Blue Book 16:1137-40, Apr 1913
Book News 32:180, Nov 1913
Dramatic Mirror 69:6, Jan 8, 1913
Red Book 21:317+, Jun 1913
Theatre Magazine 17:34+, Feb 1913
                 17:xii, Feb 1913

All in Fun
book: Virginia Faulkner and Everett Marcy
music/lyrics: Baldwin Bergersen, June Sillman, John Rox,
                 Irvin Graham, Will Irwin, Pembroke Davenport,
                 S. K. Russell
staging: Leonard Sillman
sets: Edward Gilbert
costumes: Irene Sharaff
choreography: Marjorie Fielding
Productions:
Opened December 27, 1940 for 3 performances
Reviews:
New York Theatre Critics' Reviews 1940:167+
New York Times page 26, Nov 22, 1940
                 page 11, Dec 28, 1940
Stage 1:6, Dec 1940

All in Love
book: Bruce Geller, based on Sheridan's The Rivals
music: Jacques Urbont
lyrics: Bruce Geller
staging: Tom Brennan
sets: Charles Lisanby
costumes: Charles Lisanby
choreography: Jack Beaber
Productions:
(Off-Broadway) Opened November 10, 1961 for 141 performances
(Off-Broadway) Opened Season of 1966-1967 for 14 performances
Reviews:
Commonweal 75:389, Jan 5, 1962

New York Times page 15, Nov 11, 1961
New Yorker 37:96+, Nov 18, 1961

All in One   (see Trouble in Tahiti)

All Kinds of Giants
    book: Tom Whedon
    music: Stan Pottle
    lyrics: Tom Whedon
    staging: Peter Conlow
Productions:
    (Off Broadway) Opened December 18, 1961 for 16 performances
Reviews:
    New York Times page 40, Dec 19, 1961
    New Yorker 37:58-9, Jan 6, 1962

The All Night Strut!
    conceived: Fran Charnas
    music: Various composers
    lyrics: Various authors
    staging: Fran Charnas
    costumes: Celia Eller
    choreography: Fran Charnas
Productions:
    (Off-Broadway) Opened October 4, 1979 for 6 performances
Reviews:
    New York Times III, page 3, Oct 5, 1979

All Star Gambol   (see Marie Dressler's All Star Gambol)

All-Star Literary Genius Expatriate Revue   (see Paris Lights)

All the King's Horses
    book: Frederick Herendeen
    music: Edward A. Horan
    lyrics: Frederick Herendeen
    staging: Jose Ruben
    sets: Herbert Ward
Productions:
    Opened January 30, 1934 for 120 performances
Reviews:
    Catholic World 138:734, Mar 1934
    New Outlook 163:32, Mar 1934
    New York Times page 21, Jan 31, 1934
    Review of Reviews 89:58, Apr 1934

All the King's Men
    book: Vinnette Carroll: adapted from Robert Penn War-
                       ren's novel
    music: Malcolm Dodds
    lyrics: Malcolm Dodds
    staging: Vinnette Carroll

Productions:
    (Off-Off-Broadway) Opened May 14, 1974
No Reviews.

Allah Be Praised!
    book: George Marion, Jr.
    music: Don Walker and Baldwin Bergersen
    lyrics: George Marion, Jr.
    staging: Robert H. Gordon and Jack Small
    sets: George Jenkins
    costumes: Miles White
    choreography: Jack Cole
Productions:
    Opened April 20, 1944 for 20 performances
Reviews:
    New York Theatre Critics' Reviews 1944:207+
    New York Times page 14, Apr 21, 1944
    New Yorker 20:46, Apr 29, 1944
    Newsweek 23:78, May 1, 1944
    Time 43:58, May 1, 1944

Allegro
    book: Oscar Hammerstein II
    music: Richard Rodgers
    lyrics: Oscar Hammerstein II
    staging: Lawrence Langner and Theresa Helburn
    sets: Jo Mielziner
    costumes: Lucinda Ballard
    choreography: Agnes de Mille
Productions:
    Opened October 10, 1947 for 315 performances
    (Off-Off-Broadway) Opened January 12, 1978
Reviews:
    Catholic World 166:167, Nov 1947
    Collier's 120:20-1+, Oct 25, 1947
    Commonweal 47:70-1, Oct 31, 1947
    Forum 109:23-4, Jan 1948
    Life 23:70-2, Oct 13, 1947
    Nation 165:567-8, Nov 22, 1947
    New Republic 117:35, Oct 27, 1947
    New York Theatre Critics' Reviews 1947:300+
    New York Times II, page 2, Oct 5, 1947
                   page 10, Oct 11, 1947
                   II, page 1, Nov 2, 1947
                   II, page 6, Nov 9, 1947
                   II, page 1, Nov 16, 1947
                   II, page 3, Jan 18, 1948
                   page 36, Sep 18, 1952
                   page 47, Jan 15, 1978
    New Yorker 23:55-6, Oct 18, 1947
    Newsweek 30:86, Oct 20, 1947

Saturday Review 30:30-3, Nov 8, 1947
        30:59, Nov 29, 1947
School and Society 67:476, Jun 26, 1948
Theatre Arts 31:23, Oct 1947
        31:13-15, Nov 1947
Time 50:66-8+, Oct 20, 1947
Vogue 110:191, Nov 15, 1947

Allez-Oop
    sketches: J. P. McEvoy
    music: Philip Charig and Richard Myers
    lyrics: Leo Robin
    staging: Carl Hemmer
Productions:
Opened August 2, 1927 for 120 performances
Reviews:
Life (New York) 90:10, Aug 18, 1927
New York Times page 29, Aug 3, 1927
Theatre Magazine 46:23, Oct 1927
Vogue 70:84-5, Oct 1, 1927

Alma, Where Do You Live?
    book: George V. Hobart; from the French of Paul Herve
    music: Jean Briquet
    staging: Joe Weber
Productions:
Opened September 26, 1910 for 232 performances
Reviews:
Blue Book 12:652-3, Feb 1911
Life 56:565, Oct 6, 1910
Metropolitan Magazine 33:402-3, Dec 1910
Stage 13:58, Aug 1936
Theatre Magazine 12:159, Nov 1910

Almanac (1929) (see Murray Anderson's Almanac)

Almanac (1953) (see John Murray Anderson's Almanac)

Almost Crazy
    sketches: James Shelton, Hal Hackady, and Robert A.
                   Bernstein
    music: Portia Nelson, Raymond Taylor and James
                   Shelton
    lyrics: Portia Nelson, Raymond Taylor and James
                   Shelton
    staging: Lew Kesler
    sets: John Robert Lloyd
    costumes: Stanley Simmons
    choreography: William Skipper
Productions:
Opened June 20, 1955 for 16 performances

Reviews:
    America 93:378-9, Jul 9, 1955
    New York Theatre Critics' Reviews 1955:298+
    New York Times page 37, June 21, 1955
    Theatre Arts 39:16, Sep 1955

Along Fifth Avenue

sketches:	Charles Sherman and Nat Hiken
music:	Gordon Jenkins
lyrics:	Tom Adair
additional music and lyrics:	Richard Stutz, Milton Pascal, Nat Hiken
sets:	Oliver Smith
costumes:	David Ffolkes
choreography:	Robert Sidney

Productions:
    Opened January 13, 1949 for 180 performances
Reviews:
    Catholic World 168:481, May 1949
    New Republic 120:29, Jan 31, 1949
    New York Theatre Critics' Reviews 1949:392+
    New York Times page 28, Jan 14, 1949
    New Yorker 24:44, Jan 22, 1949
    Newsweek 33:70, Jan 24, 1949
    Time 53:52, Jan 24, 1949
    Theatre Arts 33:16-17+, Mar 1949

Always You

book:	Oscar Hammerstein II
music:	Herbert P. Stothart
lyrics:	Oscar Hammerstein II

Productions:
    Opened January 5, 1920 for 66 performances
Reviews:
    Dramatic Mirror 82:57, Jan 15, 1920
    New York Clipper 67:25, Jan 14, 1920
    New York Times page 18, Jan 6, 1920
    Theatre Magazine 31:184, Mar 1920

Ambassador

book:	Don Ettlinger and Anna Marie Barlow; based on Henry James' novel The Ambassadors
music:	Don Gohman
lyrics:	Hal Hackady
staging:	Stone Widney
sets:	Peter Rice
costumes:	Peter Rice
choreography:	Joyce Trisler

Productions:
    Opened November 19, 1972 for 19 performances
Reviews:
    New York Theatre Critics' Reviews 1972:177

New York Times page 46, Nov 20, 1972
              page 53, Nov 28, 1972
New Yorker 48:123, Dec 2, 1972

The Amber Express
    book: Marc Connelly
    music: Zoel Parenteau
    lyrics: Marc Connelly
    staging: George Marion
Productions:
Opened September 19, 1916 for 15 performances
Reviews:
    Dramatic Mirror 76:7, Sep 30, 1916
    Munsey 59:498, Dec 1916
    New York Dramatic News 63:2, Sep 30, 1916
    New York Times page 7, Sep 20, 1916
    Theatre Magazine 24:281-2, Nov 1916

Amen Corner
    book: Philip Rose and Peter Udell, based on the play
                     The Amen Corner by James Baldwin
    music: Garry Sherman
    lyrics: Peter Udell
    staging: Philip Rose
    sets: Karl Eigsti
    costumes: Felix E. Cochren
    choreography: Al Perryman
Productions:
Opened November 10, 1983 for 29 performances
Reviews:
    New York 16:68, Nov 21, 1983
    New York Theatre Critics' Reviews 1983:132
    New York Times III, page 3, Nov 11, 1983
    New Yorker 59:208-9, Nov 21, 1983

America (1913)
    conceived: Arthur Voegtlin
    music: Manuel Klein
    lyrics: Manuel Klein
    staging: William J. Wilson
Productions:
Opened August 30, 1913 for 360 performances
Reviews:
    Dramatic Mirror 70:7, Sep 3, 1913
                    70:2, Dec 24, 1913
    Leslie's Weekly 117:275, Sep 18, 1913
    New York Dramatic News 58:20, Sep 6, 1913
    Theatre Magazine 18:xiv, Oct 1913
                    18:129, Oct 1913

America (1981)
    conceived: Robert F. Jani

```
     original music
         and lyrics:     Tom Bahler and Mark Vieha
         staging:        Robert F. Jani
         sets:           Robert Guerra
         costumes:       Michael Casey
         choreography:   Violet Holmes, Linda Lemac, and Frank Wagner
Productions:
     Opened March 13, 1981 for 264 performances
Reviews:
     New York Times III, page 7, Mar 17, 1981
```

The American Ballad Singers

```
     arranged:       Elie Siegmeister
     staging:        Elie Siegmeister
Productions:
     Opened February 6, 1944 for 2 performances
No Reviews.
```

American Legend

```
     book:           Paul Green's "Saturday Night" and E. P. Conkle's
                     "Minnie Field"
     staging:        Baldwin Bergersen
     sets:           John Pratt and Hugh Laing
     choreography:   Agnes de Mille
Productions:
     (Off-Broadway)  Opened April 28, 1941
No Reviews.
```

American Passion

```
     book:           Fred Burch
     music:          Willie Fong Young
     lyrics:         Willie Fong Young and Fred Burch
     staging:        Patricia Birch
     sets:           Heidi Landesman
     costumes:       William Ivey Long
     choreography:   Patricia Birch
Productions:
     (Off-Broadway)  Opened July 10, 1983 for one performance
Reviews:
     Dance Magazine 57:72-3, Jun 1983
     New York Times III, page 11, Jul 11, 1983
```

Americana (1926)

```
     book:           J. P. McEvoy
     music:          Con Conrad and Henry Souvaine; additional music
                     by George Gershwin, Philip Charig, Ira Gershwin
                     and  Morrie Ryskind
     staging:        Allen Dinehart and Larry Ceballos
Productions:
     Opened July 26, 1926 for 224 performances
Reviews:
     Life (New York) 88:21, Sep 9, 1926
```

New York Times page 15, Jul 27, 1926
Theatre Magazine 44:14-15, Oct 1926
Vogue 68:124, Oct 1, 1926
Woman's Home Companion 54:130, Feb 1927

Americana (1928)
    book: J. P. McEvoy
    music: Roger Wolfe Kahn
    lyrics: J. P. McEvoy and Irving Caesar
    staging: J. P. McEvoy
Productions:
    Opened October 30, 1928 for 12 performances
Reviews:
    New York Times X, page 1, Oct 14, 1928
                        page 28, Oct 31, 1928
                        page 34, Nov 6, 1928

Americana (1932)
    book: J. P. McEvoy
    music: Jay Gorney, Harold Arlen, Herman Hupfeld,
                          Richard Meyers
    lyrics: E. Y. Harburg
    staging: Harold Johnsrud
    sets: Albert R. Johnson
Productions:
    Opened October 5, 1932 for 77 performances
Reviews:
    Catholic World 136:210, Nov 1932
    New York Times IX, page 1, Sep 23, 1932
                     page 19, Oct 6, 1932
    Stage 10:49, Dec 15, 1932
    Theatre Arts 16:863+, Nov-Dec 1932

America's Musical Legend (see Satchmo: America's Musical Legend)

America's Sweetheart
    book: Herbert Fields
    music: Richard Rodgers
    lyrics: Lorenz Hart
    staging: Bobby Connelly and Monty Woolley
Productions:
    Opened February 10, 1931 for 135 performances
Reviews:
    New York Times VIII, page 2, Jan 25, 1931
                      page 23, Feb 11, 1931
    Theatre Magazine 53:25, Apr 1931
    Vogue 77:116, Apr 1, 1931

The Amorous Flea
    book: Jerry Devine; based on Moliere's School for
                      Wives

music: Bruce Montgomery
lyrics: Bruce Montgomery
staging: Jack Sydow
sets: Bill Hargate
costumes: Donald Brooks
Productions:
   (Off Broadway) Opened February 17, 1964 for 93 performances
Reviews:
   New York Times page 26, Feb 18, 1964
                  page 34, May 4, 1964
   New Yorker 40:108-9, Feb 29, 1964

And I Ain't Finished Yet
   by: Eve Merriam
   staging: Sheldon Epps
   sets: Kate Edmunds
   costumes: Judy Dearing
Productions:
   (Off-Off-Broadway) December 1, 1981 for 24+ performances
Reviews:
   New York Times III, page 9, Dec 28, 1981
   New Yorker 57:98-9, Dec 21, 1981

...And in This Corner
   conceived: Michael McWhinney and Rod Warren
   staging: Jonathan Lucas
   costumes: Baba
Productions:
   (Off-Broadway) Opened February 12, 1964 for 410 performances
No Reviews.

Anderson, John Murray   (see John Murray Anderson and Murray
   Anderson)

André Charlot's Revue of 1924
   book: André Charlot and R. Jeans
   staging: André Charlot
Productions:
   Opened January 9, 1924 for (173) performances
Reviews:
   New Republic 38:73, Mar 12, 1924
   New York Times page 18, Jan 10, 1924
                  page 22, Mar 20, 1924
   Theatre Magazine 39:16, Mar 1924
                    39:18, Mar 1924

Angel
   book: Ketti Frings and Peter Udell, from the Ketti
                    Frings play Look Homeward, Angel, based on the
                    novel by Thomas Wolfe
   music: Gary Geld

lyrics:	Peter Udell
staging:	Philip Rose
sets:	Ming Cho Lee
costumes:	Pearl Somner
choreography:	Robert Tucker

Productions:
  Opened March 10, 1978 for 5 performances
Reviews:
  New York Theatre Critics' Reviews 1978:284
  New York Times III, page 17, May 11, 1978
  New Yorker 54:91, May 22, 1978

Angel Face

book:	Harry B. Smith
music:	Victor Herbert
lyrics:	Robert B. Smith
staging:	George W. Lederer
choreography:	Julian Alfred

Productions:
  Opened December 29, 1919 for 57 performances
Reviews:
  Dramatic Mirror 82:7, Jan 8, 1920
  New York Clipper 67:12, Jan 7, 1920
  New York Times page 18, Dec 30, 1919
  Theatre Magazine 31:101+, Feb 1920

Angel in the Wings

sketches:	Ted Luce, Hank Ladd, Grace Hartman, Paul Hartman
music:	Carl Sigman
lyrics:	Bob Hilliard
staging:	John Kennedy
sets:	Donald Oenslager
costumes:	Julia Sze
choreography:	Edward Noll

Productions:
  Opened December 11, 1947 for 300 performances
Reviews:
  Catholic World 166:456, Feb 1948
  Commonweal 47:277, Dec 26, 1947
  Forum 109:155, Mar 1948
  Life 24:35-7, Jan 5, 1948
  New Republic 117:37, Dec 29, 1947
  New York Theatre Critics' Reviews 1947:238+
  New York Times page 36, Dec 12, 1947
                  II, page 3, Dec 21, 1947
                  II, page 2, Feb 8, 1948
                  II, page 1, Aug 29, 1948
  New Yorker 23:48, Dec 20, 1947
  Newsweek 30:76, Dec 22, 1947
  Time 50:72, Dec 22, 1947
  Vogue 111:151+, Apr 1, 1948

Angry Housewives
book: A. M. Collins
music: Chad Henry
lyrics: Chad Henry
staging: Mitchell Maxwell
sets: David Jenkins
costumes: Martha Hally
choreography: Wayne Cilento
Productions:
(Off-Broadway) Opened September 7, 1986 for 137 performances
Reviews:
New York Times III, page 18, Sep 8, 1986

Animal Crackers
book: George S. Kaufman and Morrie Ryskind
music: Harry Ruby
lyrics: Bert Kalmar
Productions:
Opened October 23, 1928 for 191 performances
Reviews:
Life (New York) 92:14, Nov 16, 1928
New Republic 56:351-2, Nov 14, 1928
New York Times page 26, Oct 24, 1928
            page 26, Apr 7, 1929
Theatre Magazine 52:47, Nov 1930

Ankles Aweigh
book: Guy Bolton and Eddie Davis
music: Sammy Fain
lyrics: Dan Shapiro
staging: Fred F. Finklehoffe
sets: George Jenkins
costumes: Miles White
choreography: Tony Charmoli
Productions:
Opened April 18, 1955 for 176 performances
Reviews:
Catholic World 181:228, Jun 1955
Commonweal 62:330, Jul 1, 1955
New York Theatre Critics' Reviews 1955:329+
New York Times page 27, Apr 19, 1955
New Yorker 31:71-2, Apr 30, 1955
Theatre Arts 39:16, 88, Jul 1955
Time 65:78, May 2, 1955

Ann Reinking ... Music Moves Me
written: Larry Grossman
music: Larry Grossman and various composers
lyrics: Ellen Fitzhugh and various authors
staging: Alan Johnson
sets: Thomas Lynch

costumes: Albert Wolsky
choreography: Alan Johnson and Stephen Jay
Productions:
  (Off-Broadway) Opened December 23, 1984 for 16 performances
Reviews:
  New York Times III, page 3, Dec 28, 1984

Anna Russell's Little Show
  music: Anna Russell
  lyrics: Anna Russell
  staging: Arthur Klein
Productions:
  Opened September 7, 1953 for 16 performances
Reviews:
  America 89:629, Sep 26, 1953
  American Magazine 155:55, Apr 1953
  Commonweal 58:634, Oct 2, 1953
  New York Theatre Critics' Reviews 1953:289
  New Yorker 29:75, Sep 19, 1953
  Theatre Arts 37:20, Nov 1953

Anne of Green Gables
  adapted: Donald Harron; from the novel by L. M. Mont-
                 gomery
  music: Norman Campbell
  lyrics: Donald Harron and Norman Campbell
  staging: Alan Lund
  costumes: Marie Day
  choreography: Alan Lund
Productions:
  Opened December 21, 1971 for 16 performances
Reviews:
  New York Times page 30, Dec 22, 1971
                 II, page 1, Jan 2, 1972

Annie
  book: Thomas Meehan
  music: Charles Strouse
  lyrics: Martin Charnin
  staging: Martin Charnin
  sets: David Mitchell
  costumes: Theoni V. Aldredge
  choreography: Peter Gennaro
Productions:
  Opened April 21, 1977 for 2,377 performances
Reviews:
  America 136:467, May 21, 1977
  Dance Magazine 51:20, Aug 1977
  Los Angeles 23:377+, Dec 1978
  Nation 224:602, May 14, 1977
  New West 3:124, Nov 3, 1978

New York 10:62+, May 9, 1977
New York Theatre Critics' Reviews 1977:258
New York Times III, page 3, Apr 22, 1977
    II, page 5, May 1, 1977
    XXI, page 23, Apr 10, 1983
    XI, page 2, Oct 2, 1983
    XXIII, page 15, Dec 9, 1984
    XXII, page 37, Dec 21, 1986
New York Times Magazine page 39, May 15, 1977
New Yorker 53:89-91, May 2, 1977A
Newsweek 89:112, Apr 11, 1977
    89:52-3, May 2, 1977
Parent's Magazine 52:40-1+, Aug 1977
Saturday Review 4:48-9, Jun 11, 1977
Time 109:87-8, May 2, 1977

Annie Dear
 book: Clare Kummer
 music: Sigmund Romberg and Clare Kummer
 lyrics: Clifford Grey and Clare Kummer
 staging: Edward Royce
Productions:
 Opened November 4, 1924 for 103 performances
Reviews:
 New York Times page 25, Nov 5, 1924
 Theatre Magazine 41:22, Jan 1925

Annie Get Your Gun
 book: Herbert Fields and Dorothy Fields
 music: Irving Berlin
 lyrics: Irving Berlin
 staging: Joshua Logan
 sets: Jo Mielziner
 costumes: Lucinda Ballard
 choreography: Helen Tamiris
Productions:
 Opened May 16, 1946 for 1,147 performances
 Opened February 19, 1958 for 16 performances
 Opened May 31, 1966 for 47 performances
 Opened September 21, 1966 for 78 performances
 (Off-Off-Broadway) Opened May 8, 1980
Reviews:
 America 98:677, Mar 8, 1958
    114:882, Jun 25, 1966
 Catholic World 163:359, Jul 1946
    187:146-7, May 1958
 Commonweal 84:393-4, Jun 24, 1966
 Dance Magazine 40:27+, Jul 1966
 Life 20:89-94, Jun 3, 1946
   60:47, Jun 10, 1966
 Los Angeles 22:244+, Aug 1977

Modern Music 23 no. 2:144, Apr 1946
New West 2:SC-19, Aug 1, 1977
New York Theatre Critics' Reviews 1946: 382+
New York Times page 18, Mar 29, 1946
     page 14, May 17, 1946
     II, page 1, May 26, 1946
     II, page 1, Jul 21, 1946
     II, page 1, Sep 29, 1946
     VI, page 25, Sep 29, 1946
     II, page 3, Dec 15, 1946
     page 63, Jun 8, 1947
     page 26, Jun 9, 1947
     page 10, Oct 4, 1947
     page 35, May 11, 1949
     page 35, May 3, 1950
     page 18, Feb 28, 1957
     page 18, Aug 31, 1957
     page 15, Mar 9, 1957
     page 29, Feb 20, 1958
     page 42, Jun 1, 1966
     page 40, Jul 1, 1966
     page 59, Nov 21, 1966
     page 63, Mar 20, 1967
     III, page 15, Jun 30, 1978
     page 27, Jul 3, 1978
     page 13, May 10, 1980
     XXIII, page 25, Nov 14, 1982
     XI, page 16, May 31, 1987
     III, page 26, Jun 10, 1987
New Yorker 22: 42+, May 25, 1946
Newsweek 27:84-5, May 27, 1946
Saturday Review 29:30-2, Jun 15, 1946
Time 47:66, May 27, 1946

Another Evening with Harry Stoones
 sketches: Jeff Harris
 music: Jeff Harris
 lyrics: Jeff Harris
 staging: G. Adam Jordon
Productions:
 (Off-Broadway) Opened October 21, 1961 for one performance
Reviews:
 New York Times page 22, Oct 23, 1961
       page 31, Oct 25, 1961
 New Yorker 37:132, Nov 4, 1961

Antiques
 music: Alan Greene and Laura Manning
 lyrics: Alan Greene and Laura Manning
 special
  material: Dore Schary

staging: Marco Martone
sets: Bruno C. Scordino
costumes: William Christians
choreography: Jeffrey K. Neill
Productions:
   (Off-Broadway) Opened June 19, 1973 for 8 performances
Reviews:
   New York Times page 33, Jun 20, 1973
                page 83, Jun 21, 1973

Anyone Can Whistle
   book: Arthur Laurents
   music: Stephen Sondheim
   lyrics: Stephen Sondheim
   staging: Arthur Laurents
   sets: William and Jean Eckart
   costumes: Theoni V. Aldredge
   choreography: Herbert Ross
Productions:
   Opened April 4, 1964 for 9 performances
Reviews:
   New York Theatre Critics' Reviews 1964:301+
   New York Times page 36, Apr 6, 1964
                page 17, Apr 11, 1964

Anything Goes
   book: Guy Bolton, P. G. Wodehouse, Howard Lindsay
              and Russel Crouse
   music: Cole Porter
   lyrics: Cole Porter
   staging: Howard Lindsay
   sets: Donald Oenslager
   choreography: Robert Alton
Productions:
   Opened November 21, 1934 for 420 performances
   (Off-Broadway) Opened May 15, 1962 for 239 performances
   (Off-Off-Broadway) Opened October 15, 1977
   (Off-Off-Broadway) Opened March 12, 1981
   Opened October 19, 1987 for *675 performances (still running
   6/1/89)
Reviews:
   Catholic World 140:469-70, Jan 1935
   Dance Magazine 36:26, Jul 1962
                62:52-7, Jan 1988
   Literary Digest 118:18, Dec 8, 1934
   Nation 245:570-2, Nov 14, 1987
   New Leader 70:22, Nov 16, 1987
   New Republic 81:131, Dec 12, 1934
              197:28-9, Dec 21, 1987
   New York 20:111, Nov 2, 1987
   New York Theatre Critics' Reviews 1987:151

New York Times IX, page 1, Nov 18, 1934
page 26, Nov 22, 1934
IX, page 3, Nov 25, 1934
page 20, Jun 15, 1935
X, page 1, Jul 28, 1935
IX, page 1, Aug 18, 1935
IX, page 1, Sep 15, 1935
page 23, Aug 17, 1937
page 24, Aug 26, 1937
page 35, May 16, 1962
XXIII, page 14, Feb 22, 1981
page 59, Mar 22, 1981
XXI, page 17, Nov 25, 1983
XI, page 12, Mar 1, 1987
III, page 17, Oct 20, 1987
II, page 45, Nov 1, 1987
New York Times Magazine pages 22-4+, Jan 24, 1988
New Yorker 38:92-3, May 26, 1962
57:62+, Mar 30, 1981
63:146, Nov 2, 1987
Newsweek 4:23, Dec 1, 1934
Theatre Arts 19:19, Jan 1935
46:59, Aug 1962
Time 24:24, Dec 3, 1934
130:95, Nov 2, 1987

Aphrodite
book: Pierre Frondaie and George C. Hazleton: adapted from Pierre Louys' novel
music: Henri Fevrier and Anselm Goetzl
staging: E. Lyall Swete
Productions:
Opened November 24, 1919 for 148 performances
Reviews:
Dramatic Mirror 80:1901+, Dec 11, 1919
Dramatist 11:1000-1, Apr 1920
Forum 63:111-12, Jan 1920
Life (New York) 74:1024, Dec 18, 1919
New York Times IV, page 7, Oct 26, 1919
page 11, Dec 2, 1919
IX, page 2, Dec 7, 1919
Theatre Magazine 31:16, Jan 1920
31:61, Jan 1920

Applause
book: Betty Comden and Adolph Green; based on the film All About Eve and the original story by Mary Orr
music: Charles Strouse
lyrics: Lee Adams
staging: Ron Field

```
sets:            Robert Randolph
costumes:        Ray Aghayan
choreography:    Ron Field
```
Productions:
  Opened March 30, 1970 for 896 performances
  (Off-Off-Broadway) Opened May 13, 1982
Reviews:
  Commentary 51:79, Feb 1971
  Dance Magazine 44:84-5, Jun 1970
  Life 68:54A-54D, Apr 3, 1970
  Nation 210:473-4+, Apr 20, 1970
  New Republic 162:20+, May 23, 1970
  New York Theatre Critics' Reviews 1970:316
  New York Times II, page 1, Mar 22, 1970
                  page 35, Mar 31, 1970
                  page 36, Apr 1, 1970
                  II, page 1, Apr 26, 1970
                  page 24, Jul 27, 1971
                  II, page 1, Aug 22, 1971
                  page 53, May 24, 1972
                  page 42, Nov 17, 1972
                  page 47, May 23, 1982
                  XII, page 23, Sep 18, 1988
  New Yorker 46:81, Apr 11, 1970
  Newsweek 75:83, Apr 13, 1970
  Saturday Review 53:26, Apr 18, 1970
  Time 95:97, Apr 18, 1970

Apple Blossoms
```
book:     William Le Baron
music:    Fritz Kreisler and Victor Jacobi
lyrics:   William Le Baron
```
Productions:
  Opened October 7, 1919 for 256 performances
Reviews:
  Dramatic Mirror 80:1652, Oct 23, 1919
  New York Times page 22, Oct 8, 1919
  Theatre Magazine 30:350, Nov 1919

Apple Pie
```
book:            Myrna Lamb
music:           Nicholas Meyers
staging:         Rae Allen
sets:            David Mitchell
costumes:        Milo Morrow
choreography:    Baayork Lee
```
Productions:
  Opened March 23, 1975 for 10 performances
  (Off-Broadway) Opened January 27, 1976 for 64 performances
Reviews:
  New York 9:60, Mar 1, 1976

New York Theatre Critics' Reviews 1976: 340
New York Times page 18, Feb 13, 1976
                II, page 7, Feb 22, 1976
New Yorker 52:82, Feb 23, 1976

The Apple Tree

book:	Sheldon Harnick and Jerry Bock; based on The Diary of Adam and Eve by Mark Twain, The Lady or the Tiger? by Frank R. Stockton, and Passionella by Jules Feiffer; additional book material by Jerome Coppersmith
music:	Jerry Bock
lyrics:	Sheldon Harnick
staging:	Mike Nichols
sets:	Tony Walton
costumes:	Tony Walton
choreography:	Lee Theodore

Productions:
   Opened October 18, 1966 for 463 performances
Reviews:
   America 115:786, Dec 10, 1966
   Christian Century 84:144, Feb 1, 1967
   Commonweal 85:167, Nov 11, 1966
   Dance Magazine 41:22, Feb 1967
   Nation 203:493-4, Nov 7, 1966
   New York Theatre Critics' Reviews 1966:262
   New York Times page 53, Oct 19, 1966
                   II, page 1, Oct 30, 1966
                   page 56, Oct 12, 1967
                   page 61, Nov 4, 1967
                   page 61, Nov 10, 1967
   New Yorker 42:95, Oct 29, 1966
   Newsweek 68:98, Oct 31, 1966
   Saturday Review 49:47, Nov 5, 1966
   Time 88:90, Oct 28, 1966
   Vogue 148:161, Dec 1966

Arabesque

book:	Cloyd Head and Eunice Tietjens
music:	Ruth Warfield
staging:	Norman-Bel Geddes

Productions:
   Opened October 20, 1925 for 23 performances
Reviews:
   New Republic 44:305-6, Nov 11, 1925
   New York Times page 20, Oct 21, 1925
   Theatre Arts 10:33-4, Jan 1926
   Theatre Magazine 42:44, Dec 1925
                    43:32, Mar 1926

The Arcadians

book:	Mark Ambient and A. M. Thompson

music: Lionel Monckton and Howard Talbot
lyrics: Arthur Wimperis
staging: Thomas Reynolds
Productions:
   Opened January 17, 1910 for 136 performances
Reviews:
   American Mercury 70:110, May 1910
   Burr McIntosh Monthly 22:322, Apr 1910
   Everybody's 22:700, May 1910
   Hampton 24:566-7, Apr 1910
   Leslie's Weekly 110:591, Jun 18, 1910
                110:640, Jun 30, 1910
   Metropolitan Magazine 32:256-7, May 1910
   Munsey 41:902-5, Sep 1909
   New York Dramatic News 63:6, Jan 29, 1910
   Theatre Magazine 11:xi, Mar 1910
                 11:70, Mar 1910
                 11:94, Mar 1910
                 11:96, Mar 1910
                 12:74, Sep 1910
                 12:114, Oct 1910

Are You With It?

book: Sam Perrin and George Balzer, adapted from
                 George Malcolm-Smith's Slightly Perfect
music: Harry Revel
lyrics: Arnold B. Horwitt
staging: Edward Reveaux
sets: George Jenkins
costumes: Raoul Pene du Bois
Productions:
   Opened November 10, 1945 for 267 performances
Reviews:
   Catholic World 162:359, Jan 1946
   Collier's 117:14-15, Feb 2, 1946
   Commonweal 43:169, Nov 30, 1945
   Life 19:97-100, Nov 26, 1945
   Nation 161:604, Dec 1, 1945
   New York Theatre Critics' Reviews 1945:113+
   New York Times page 17, Nov 12, 1945
                   II, page 1, Feb 3, 1946
                   II, page 1, Apr 28, 1946
   New Yorker 21:50+, Nov 24, 1945
   Newsweek 26:96, Nov 26, 1945
   Theatre Arts 30:14, Jan 1946
   Time 46:64, Nov 19, 1945
   Vogue 106:145, Dec 1, 1945

Ari

book: Leon Uris; based on his novel Exodus
music: Walt Smith

lyrics: Leon Uris
staging: Lucia Victor
sets: Robert Randolf
costumes: Sara Brock
choreography: Talley Beatty
Productions:
Opened January 15, 1971 for 19 performances
Reviews:
New York Theatre Critics' Reviews 1971:386
New York Times page 16, Jan 16, 1971
                page 29, Jan 27, 1971
New Yorker 46:66, Jan 23, 1971

Arlen, Harold (see Harold Arlen)

Arms and the Girl
book: Herbert and Dorothy Fields, Rouben Mamoulian,
                based on Lawrence Langner and Armina Marshall's
                play The Pursuit of Happiness
music: Morton Gould
lyrics: Dorothy Fields
staging: Rouben Mamoulian
sets: Horace Armistead
costumes: Audre
Productions:
Opened February 2, 1950 for 134 performances
Reviews:
Catholic World 171:67, Apr 1950
New York Theatre Critics' Reviews 1950:356+
New York Times II, page 1, Jan 28, 1950
                page 28, Feb 3, 1950
New Yorker 25:46-7, Feb 11, 1950
Newsweek 35:80, Feb 13, 1950
Theatre Arts 34:17, Apr 1950
Time 55:53-4, Feb 13, 1950

Around the Map
book: C. M. S. McLellan
music: Herman Finck
lyrics: C. M. S. McLellan
staging: Herbert Gresham
choreography: Julian Mitchell
Productions:
Opened November 1, 1915 for 104 performances
Reviews:
Dramatic Mirror 74:8, Nov 6, 1915
                 74:2, Nov 20, 1915
                 74:2, Dec 4, 1915
Green Book 15:26, Jan 1916
Munsey 56:617, Jan 1916
         57:324, Mar 1916

New York Dramatic News 61:17, Nov 6, 1915
New York Times page 11, Nov 2, 1915
            VI, page 8, Nov 7, 1915
Opera Magazine 2:28-30, Dec 1915
Theatre Magazine 22:278-9+, Dec 1915

Around the World (1911)
book: Carroll Fleming
music: Manuel Klein
lyrics: Manuel Klein
staging: Carroll Fleming
Productions:
Opened September 2, 1911 for 445 performances
Reviews:
Theatre Magazine 14:125, Oct 1911
              14:128, Oct 1911

Around the World (1946)
book: Orson Welles from Jules Verne's Around the World in Eighty Days
music: Cole Porter
lyrics: Cole Porter
staging: Orson Welles
sets: Robert Davison
costumes: Alvin Colt
choreography: Nelson Barclift
Productions:
Opened May 31, 1946 for 75 performances
Reviews:
Catholic World 163:359-60, Jul 1946
Commonweal 44:238, Jun 21, 1946
Life 20:74-6, Jun 17, 1946
New York Theatre Critics' Reviews 1946:375+
New York Times page 9, Jun 1, 1946
          II, page 1, Jun 9, 1946
New Yorker 22:48+, Jun 8, 1946
Newsweek 27:87, Jun 10, 1946
Theatre Arts 30:473, Aug 1946
Time 47:64, Jun 3, 1946
     47:67, Jun 10, 1946

Around the World in 80 Days
book: Sig Herzig; based on the novel by Jules Verne
music: Sammy Fain; additional music by Victor Young
lyrics: Harold Adamson
production
  supervised: Arnold Spector
staging: June Taylor
sets: George Jenkins
costumes: Winn Morton
choreography: June Taylor

Productions:
    (Off-Broadway)   Opened June 22, 1963 for 73 performances
    (Off-Broadway)   Opened June 27, 1964 for 70 performances
Reviews:
    America 109:122, Aug 3, 1963
    New York Times page 22, Jun 24, 1963
                   page 33, Jun 29, 1964

Artists and Models (1923)
    staging: Larry Wagstaff Gribble and Francis Weldon
Productions:
    Opened August 20, 1923 for 312 performances
Reviews:
    New York Times page 12, Aug 21, 1923

Artists and Models (1924)
    sketches: Harry Wagstaff Gribble
    music: Sigmund Romberg and J. Fred Coots
    lyrics: Clifford Grey and Sam Coslow
    staging: J. J. Shubert
Productions:
    Opened October 15, 1924 for 261 performances
Reviews:
    New York Times page 33, Oct 16, 1924
                   page 16, Jun 17, 1925
                   page 16, Jun 25, 1925
    Theatre Magazine 40:64, Dec 1924

Artists and Models (1925)
    sketches: Harold Atteridge and Harry Wagstaff Gribble
    music: Alfred Goodman, J. Fred Coots, and Maurie
                      Rubens
    lyrics: Clifford Grey
    staging: J. J. Shubert
Productions:
    Opened June 24, 1925 for 411 performances
Reviews:
    New York Times page 16, Jun 17, 1925
                   page 16, Jun 25, 1925
    Survey 55:632, Mar 1, 1926
    Theatre Magazine 42:3, Sep 1925
                        42:15, Sep 1925

Artists and Models (1927)
    music: Harry Akst and Maurie Rubens
    lyrics: Benny Davis; additional lyrics by J. Keirn
                    Brennan, Jack Osterman and Ted Lewis
    staging: J. C. Huffman
Productions:
    Opened November 15, 1927 for 151 performances
Reviews:
    Life (New York) 90:21, Dec 8, 1927

New Republic 54:246-7, Apr 11, 1928
New York Times page 28, Nov 16, 1927
Theatre Magazine 47:40, Feb 1928

Artists and Models (1930)
    book: adapted from the English musical comedy Dear
                         Love
    music: Harold Stern
    lyrics: Ernie Golden
    staging: Frank Smithson and Pal'mere Brandeaux
Productions:
    Opened June 10, 1930 for 55 performances
Reviews:
    Life (New York) 95:16, Jul 11, 1930
    New York Times page 33, Jun 11, 1930
    Theatre Magazine 52:25, Aug 1930

Artists and Models (1943)
    assembled: Lou Walters
    dialogue: Lou Walters, Don Ross, Frank Luther
    music: Dan Shapiro, Milton Pascal, Phil Charig
    lyrics: Dan Shapiro, Milton Pascal, Phil Charig
    staging: Lou Walters
    sets: Watson Barratt
    costumes: Kathryn Kuhn
    choreography: Natalie Kamarova and Laurette Jefferson
Productions:
    Opened November 5, 1943 for 28 performances
Reviews:
    New York Theatre Critics' Reviews 1943:239+
    New York Times page 16, Nov 6, 1943
                      II, page 1, Nov 21, 1943

As the Girls Go
    book: William Roos
    music: Jimmy McHugh
    lyrics: Harold Adamson
    staging: Howard Bay
    sets: Howard Bay
    costumes: Oleg Cassini
    choreography: Hermes Pan
Productions:
    Opened November 13, 1938 for 420 performances
Reviews:
    Catholic World 168:324, Jan 1949
    Commonweal 49:231, Dec 10, 1948
    Life 25:89-90+, Nov 29, 1948
    New Republic 119:37, Dec 6, 1948
    New York Theatre Critics' Reviews 1948:159+
    New York Times page 21, Nov 15, 1948
                      II, page 2, Jan 2, 1949

New Yorker 24:58, Nov 20, 1948
Newsweek 32:80, Nov 22, 1948
Theatre Arts 33:18, Jan 1949
Time 52:85, Nov 22, 1948
Vogue 113:114, Jan 1949

As Thousands Cheer
 book: Irving Berlin and Moss Hart
 music: Edward Heyman and Richard Meyers
 lyrics: Edward Heyman and Richard Meyers
 staging: Hassard Short
 sets: Albert Johnson
 choreography: Charles Weidman
Productions:
 Opened September 30, 1933 for 400 performances
Reviews:
 Canadian Forum 15:274, Apr 1935
 Catholic World 138:337, Dec 1933
 Collier's 94:17+, Aug 18, 1934
 Commonweal 18:591-2, Oct 20, 1933
 Literary Digest 116:18, Oct 21, 1933
 New Outlook 162:42, Nov 1933
 New Republic 76:279, Oct 18, 1933
 New York Times II, page 5, Sep 10, 1933
        page 22, Oct 2, 1933
        IX, page 1, Oct 15, 1933
        page 26, Mar 20, 1934
        page 24, Jul 10, 1934
        IX, page 1, Nov 11, 1934
 Review of Reviews 89:40, Feb 1934
 Stage 11:12-17, Oct 1933
   11:13, Nov 1933
 Theatre Arts 17:919, Dec 1933
 Time 22:27, Oct 9, 1933
 Vanity Fair 41:42, Dec 1933

As You Like It
 book: Dran and Tani Seitz, adapted from Shakespeare's
        comedy
 music: John Balamos
 lyrics: Dran and Tani Seitz
 staging: Val Forslund
 choreography: Joe Nelson
Productions:
 (Off-Off-Broadway) Opened October 27, 1964 for one performance
 (Off-Off-Broadway) Opened January 18, 1980
Reviews:
 New York Theatre Critics' Reviews 1974:166
 New York Times III, page 3, Jan 25, 1980

As You Wait
>> book: Arthur Williams and Lois Dengrove
    music: Jay Woody
Productions:
    (Off-Off-Broadway) Season of 1973-1974
No Reviews.

As You Were
>> book: Arthur Wimperis
    music: Herman Darewski
Productions:
    Opened January 27, 1920 for 143 performances
Reviews:
    Forum 63:317-2, Mar 1920
    New York Clipper 67:25, Feb 4, 1920
    New York Times page 22, Jan 28, 1920
                     VIII, page 2, Feb 8, 1920
    Theatre Magazine 31:185, Mar 1920

At Home Abroad
>> dialogue: Thomas Mitchell
    songs: Howard Dietz and Arthur Schwartz
    staging: Vincente Minnelli
    sets: Vincente Minnelli
    choreography: Gene Snyder and Harry Losee
Productions:
    Opened September 19, 1935 for 198 performances
Reviews:
    Catholic World 142:472, Jan 1936
    Literary Digest 120:18, Nov 2, 1935
    Nation 141:392, Oct 2, 1935
    New York Times page 22, Sep 4, 1935
                     IX, page 1, Sep 8, 1935
                     page 17, Sep 20, 1935
                     XI, page 2, Oct 6, 1935
                     IX, page 1, Oct 27, 1935
                     IX, page 8, Oct 27, 1935
    Newsweek 6:28-9, Sep 28, 1935
    Stage 12:16-17, Sep 1935
          13:57, Oct 1935
          14:61-3, Dec 1936
    Theatre Arts 19:818+, Nov 1935
    Time 26:22, Sep 30, 1935
    Vanity Fair 45:69, Nov 1935
    Vogue 86:57, Nov 15, 1935

At Home at the Palace   (see Judy Garland at Home at the Palace)

At Home with Ethel Waters
>> songs: W. C. Handy, Hoagy Carmichael, Irving Berlin,
                   Ira and George Gershwin, and others

staging: Richard Barr
sets: Oliver Smith
costumes: Robert Mackintosh
Productions:
  Opened September 22, 1953 for 23 performances
Reviews:
  America 90:54, Oct 10, 1953
  Catholic World 178:148, Nov 1953
  Commonweal 59:38, Oct 16, 1953
  Nation 177:298, Oct 10, 1953
  New Republic 129:20, Oct 26, 1953
  New York Times page 36, Sep 23, 1953
  New Yorker 29:80, Oct 3, 1953
  Saturday Review 36:30-2, Oct 10, 1953
  Theatre Arts 37:22-3, Nov 1953
  Time 62:78, Oct 5, 1953

At the Palace   (see Shirley MacLaine at the Palace)

The Athenian Touch
    book: Arthur Goodman and J. Albert Fracht
    music: Willard Straight
    lyrics: David Eddy
    staging: Alex Palermo
    sets: Robert T. Williams
    costumes: Don Foote
    choreography: Alex Palermo
Productions:
  (Off-Broadway) Opened January 14, 1964 for one performance
Reviews:
  New York Times page 25, Jan 15, 1964
                  page 30, Jan 30, 1964

The Atlantic Crossing
    book: Charles Mingus III
    songs: Charles Mingus III and Paul Jeffrey
    music: Gunter Hampel
    staging: Lee Kissman
Productions:
  (Off-Off-Broadway)   Opened July 27, 1972
No Reviews.

Atta Boy
    by: F. Tinney, J. B. Walsh, B. Macdonald, N. Os-
                    borne
    staging: Jack Mason
Productions:
  Opened December 23, 1918 for 24 performances
Reviews:
  Dramatic Mirror 80:9, Jan 4, 1919
  New York Times page 7, Dec 24, 1918

Audition
       book: Steven Holt
       music: John Braden
       staging: Suzanna Foster
Productions:
       (Off-Off-Broadway) Opened November 8, 1972
No Reviews.

Autumn's Here!
       book: Norman Dean; based on Washington Irving's
                          Legend of Sleepy Hollow
       music: Norman Dean
       lyrics: Norman Dean
       staging: Hal LeRoy
       sets: Robert Conley
       costumes: Eve Henriksen
       choreography: Hal LeRoy
Productions:
       (Off-Broadway) Opened October 25, 1966 for 80 performances
Reviews:
       New York Times page 40, Oct 26, 1966
                       page 18, Dec 29, 1966

Aznavour (concert performance)
       music: Charles Aznavour
       lyrics: Charles Aznavour
Productions:
       Opened March 14, 1983 for 14 performances
No Reviews.

Aznavour, Charles (see Aznavour, Charles Aznavour, and The
       World of Charles Aznavour)

                              -B-

Babalooney
       sketches: Improvisation by the company
       original music: Larry Schanker and the Practical Theater Co.
       staging: Brad Hal
       sets: Louis DiCrescenzo
       costumes: Iwo Jima and Jen Crawford
Productions:
       (Off-Broadway) Opened February 15, 1984 for 24 performances
Reviews:
       New York Times III, page 22, Feb 16, 1984

Babes in Arms
       book: Lorenz Hart
       music: Richard Rodgers
       lyrics: Lorenz Hart

staging: Robert Sinclair
sets: Raymond Sovey
costumes: Helene Pons
choreography: George Balanchine
Productions:
  Opened April 14, 1937 for 289 performances
  (Off-Broadway) Season of 1950-51
  (Off-Broadway) Opened October 20, 1967 for 15 performances
  Closed prior to Broadway opening (Tarrytown, NY, June 26, 1985)
Reviews:
  Catholic World 145:343, Jun 1937
  Commonweal 26:48, May 7, 1937
  New York Times page 18, Apr 15, 1937
                  page 7, Mar 10, 1951
                  XXII, page 18, Jun 30, 1985
                  XXII, page 12, Jul 21, 1985
  Newsweek 9:20+, Apr 24, 1937
  Theatre Arts 21:424-5, Jun 1937
  Time 29:26+, Apr 26, 1937

Babes in the Wood
  book, music
    and lyrics: Rick Besoyan; adapted from Shakespeare's A
                  Midsummer Night's Dream
  staging: Rick Besoyan
  sets: Paul Morrison
  costumes: Howard Barker
  choreography: Ralph Beaumont
Productions:
  (Off-Broadway) Opened December 28, 1964 for 45 performances
Reviews:
  New York Times page 21, December 29, 1964
  New Yorker 40:84, Jan 9, 1965
  Time 85:32, Jan 8, 1965

Baby
  book: Sybille Pearson, based on a story developed by
                  Susan Yankowitz
  music: David Shire
  lyrics: Richard Maltby Jr.
  staging: Richard Maltby Jr.
  sets: John Lee Beatty
  costumes: Jennifer Von Mayrhauser
  choreography: Wayne Cilento
Productions:
  Opened December 4, 1983 for 241 performances
Reviews:
  Atlantic 255:39-40, Jan 1985
  Dance Magazine 58:84, Mar 1984
  New York 16:87-9, Dec 19, 1983
  New York Theatre Critics' Reviews 1983:96

New York Times III, page 13, Dec 5, 1983
Newsweek 102:64, Dec 19, 1983
Theatre Crafts 19:23+, May 1985
Time 122:71, Dec 19, 1983

The Bachelor Belles

words:	Harry B. Smith
music:	Raymond Hubbell
staging:	Julian Mitchell

Productions:
    Opened November 7, 1910 for 32 performances
Reviews:
    Blue Book 12:657-60, Feb 1911
    Metropolitan Magazine 33:668-9, Feb 1911
    Munsey 44:562, Jan 1911
    Theatre Magazine 12:xxi, Dec 1910

Bad Habits of 1926

music:	Manning Sherwin
lyrics:	Arthur Herzog

Productions:
    Opened April 30, 1926 for 19 performances
Reviews:
    New York Times page 11, May 1, 1926
    Theatre Magazine 44:16, Jul 1926

Bagels and Yox

songs:	Sholom Secunda and Hy Jacobson

Productions:
    Opened September 12, 1951 for 208 performances
Reviews:
    Catholic World 174:149, Nov 1951
    Commonweal 54:596, Sep 28, 1951
    New Republic 125:21, Oct 1, 1951
    New York Theatre Critics' Reviews 1951:238
    New York Times page 38, Sep 13, 1951
    Theatre Arts 35:6, Nov 1951

Bajour

book:	Ernest Kinoy, based on Joseph Mitchell's New Yorker stories
music:	Walter Marks
lyrics:	Ernest Kinoy
staging:	Lawrence Kasha
sets:	Oliver Smith
costumes:	Freddy Wittop
choreography:	Peter Gennaro and Wally Seibert

Productions:
    Opened November 23, 1964 for 232 performances
Reviews:
    America 112:25, Jan 2, 1965

Commonweal 81: 422-3, Dec 18, 1964
Dance Magazine 39:19-20, Jan 1965
New York Theatre Critics' Reviews 1964:132+
New York Times page 42, Nov 24, 1964
New Yorker 40:88, Dec 5, 1964
Newsweek 64:94, Dec 7, 1964
Time 84:88, Dec 4, 1964

Baker, Josephine (see Josephine Baker and Evening With Josephine
    Baker)

Baker Street
    book: Jerome Coopersmith, adapted from Sir Arthur
                       Conan Doyle's stories
    music: Marion Grudeff and Raymond Jessel
    lyrics: Marion Grudeff and Raymond Jessel
    staging: Harold Prince
    sets: Oliver Smith
    costumes: Motley
    choreography: Lee Becker Theodore
Productions:
    Opened February 16, 1965 for 311 performances
Reviews:
    America 112:589, Apr 17, 1965
    Commonweal 82:21-2, Mar 26, 1965
    Dance Magazine 39:18-19, Apr 1965
    Life 58:133-4, Apr 2, 1965
    National Review 17:561, Jun 29, 1965
    New York Theatre Critics' Reviews 1965:374+
    New York Times page 36, Feb 17, 1965
                   II, page 1, Feb 28, 1965
    New Yorker 41:94+, Feb 27, 1965
    Newsweek 65:84, Mar 1, 1965
    Saturday Review 48:22, Mar 6, 1965
    Time 85:78, Feb 26, 1965
    Vogue 145:100, Apr 1, 1965

Baker's Dozen
    conceived: Julius Monk
    staging: Frank Wagner
    costumes: Bill Belew
    choreography: Frank Wagner
Productions:
    (Off-Broadway) Opened January 9, 1964 for 469 performances
Reviews:
    Newsweek 63:57, Jan 20, 1964

Baker's Wife
    book: Joseph Stein, based on the play and film La
                       Femme du Boulanger by Marcel Pagnol and Jean
                       Giono

music: Stephen Schwartz
lyrics: Stephen Schwartz
staging: John Berry
sets: Jo Mielziner
costumes: Theoni V. Aldredge
choreography: Robert Tucker
Productions:
Closed prior to Broadway opening (Washington, D.C., May to November 1976)
Reviews:
Los Angeles 21:166+, Jun 1976
Texas Monthly 8:161+, Mar 1980

The Balkan Princess
book: Frederick Lonsdale and Frank Curzon
music: Paul A. Rubens
lyrics: Paul A. Rubens and Arthur Wimperis
Productions:
Opened February 9, 1911 for 108 performances
Reviews:
Blue Book 13:25-7, May 1911
Columbian 4:349+, May 1911
Dramatic Mirror 65:15, Jan 25, 1911
                65:10, Feb 15, 1911
                65:2, May 31, 1911
                67:2, Jan 31, 1912
Green Book Album 5:694-5, Apr 1911
Metropolitan Magazine 34:221-2, May 1911
Stage 13:58, Aug 1936
Theatre Magazine 13:ix, Mar 1911
                13:74, Mar 1911

Ballad for a Firing Squad
book: Jerome Coopersmith
music: Edward Thomas
lyrics: Martin Charnin
staging: Martin Charnin
sets: James Tilton
costumes: Theoni V. Aldredge
choreography: Alan Johnson
Productions:
(Off-Broadway) Opened December 13, 1968 for 7 performances
Reviews:
New York Times page 44, Oct 4, 1968
                page 64, Dec 12, 1968
                page 56, Dec 18, 1968
New Yorker 44:65, Dec 21, 1968

Ballad for Bimshire
book: Irving Burgie and Loften Mitchell
music: Irving Burgie

lyrics:	Irving Burgie
staging:	Ed Cambridge
sets:	Donald Ryder
costumes:	Mozelle Forte
choreography:	Talley Beatty

Productions:
   (Off-Broadway) Opened October 15, 1963 for 74 performances
Reviews:
   America 109:643, Nov 16, 1963
   New York Times page 54, Oct 15, 1963
   New Yorker 39:113-14, Oct 26, 1963

The Ballad of Johnny Pot

book:	Carolyn Richter
music:	Clinton Ballard
lyrics:	Carolyn Richter
staging:	Joshua Shelly
sets:	Lloyd Burlingame
costumes:	Alvin Colt
choreography:	Jay Norman

Productions:
   (Off-Broadway) Opened April 26, 1971 for 16 performances
Reviews:
   New York Times page 52, Apr 27, 1971

Ballard, Kaye   (see Hey, Ma ... Kaye Ballard and Kaye Ballard:
   Working 42nd Street at Last!)

Ballet Ballads   (Susanna and the Elders, Willie the Weeper, and
                  The Eccentricities of Davy Crockett)

music:	Jerome Moross
lyrics:	John Latouche
staging:	Mary Hunter
choreography:	Katherine Litz, Paul Godkin, Hanya Holm

Productions:
   Opened May 9, 1948 for 69 performances
Reviews:
   Life 24:135-6+, Jun 7, 1948
   Musical Courier 138:20, Jul 1948
   New Republic 118:34, May 31, 1948
   New York Times page 25, May 10, 1948
               II, page 1, May 16, 1948
               II, page 1, Jun 6, 1948
   Saturday Review 31:28-30, Jun 5, 1948
   School and Society 67:476-7, Jun 26, 1948
   Theatre Arts 32:16, Summer of 1948

Ballet of Niagra   (see The International Cup, the Ballet of Niagra
   and the Earthquake)

Ballroom
   book: Jerome Kass

music: Billy Goldenberg
lyrics: Alan and Marilyn Bergman
staging: Michael Bennett
sets: Robin Wagner
costumes: Theoni V. Aldredge
choreography: Michael Bennett and Bob Avian
Productions:
    Opened December 14, 1978 for 116 performances
Reviews:
    America 140:36, Jan 20, 1979
    Dance Magazine 53:60-2, Feb 1979
    Encore 7:32-3, Jan 15, 1979
    New Leader 62:21, Jan 1, 1979
    New Republic 180:25, Jan 27, 1979
    New York 12:64-5, Jan 8, 1979
    New York Theatre Critics' Reviews 1978:158
    New York Times III, page 3, December 15, 1978
                  II, page 3, December 24, 1978
    Newsweek 93:56, Jan 1, 1979
    Saturday Review 6:52, Feb 17, 1979
    Time 112:83, Dec 25, 1978

Ballyhoo (1930)
    book: Harry Ruskin and Leighton K. Brill
    music: Louis Alter
    lyrics: Harry Ruskin and Leighton K. Brill
    staging: Reginald Hammerstein
    choreography: Earl Lindsey
Productions:
    Opened December 22, 1930 for 68 performances
Reviews:
    Nation 132:24-5, Jan 7, 1931
    New York Times IX, page 3, Dec 14, 1930
                  page 24, Dec 23, 1930
                  page 26, Jan 9, 1931
    Theatre Magazine 53:26, Feb 1931
    Vogue 77:102, Feb 15, 1931

Ballyhoo of 1932
    book: Norman B. Anthony
    music: Lewis E. Gensler
    lyrics: E. Y. Harburg
    staging: Norman B. Anthony, Lewis E. Gensler, Bobby
                         Connelly, Russell Patterson
    sets: Russell Patterson
Productions:
    Opened September 6, 1932 for 95 performances
Reviews:
    Nation 135:266, Sep 21, 1932
    New York Times page 14, Sep 7, 1932
                  page 23, Nov 29, 1932

Stage 10:10-11, Oct 1932
Vogue 80:100, Oct 15, 1932

Bamboola
  book: D. Frank Marcus
  music: D. Frank Marcus and Bernard Maltin
  lyrics: D. Frank Marcus
  staging: Sam Rose
Productions:
Opened June 26, 1929 for 34 performances
Reviews:
New York Times page 17, Jun 27, 1929

The Band Wagon
  book: George S. Kaufman and Howart Dietz
  music: Arthur Schwartz
  lyrics: George S. Kaufman and Howard Dietz
  staging: Hassard Short
  choreography: Albertina Rasch
Productions:
Opened June 3, 1931 for 260 performances
Reviews:
Bookman 73:633-4, Aug 1931
Catholic World 133:463-4, Jul 1931
Life (New York) 97:18, Jun 19, 1931
New York Times VIII, page 3, May 17, 1931
             page 31, Jun 4, 1931
             VIII, page 8, Jun 7, 1931
             VIII, page 1, Jun 14, 1931
             VIII, page 2, Jun 14, 1931
             page 28, Dec 21, 1931
Outlook 158:219, Jun 17, 1931
Theatre Arts 15:625+, Aug 1931
Theatre Guild Magazine 8:18-19, Aug 1931

Banjo Dancing: The 48th Annual Squitters Mountain Song Dance
  Folklore Convention and Banjo Contest ... And How I Lost
  devised: Stephen Wade with Milton Kramer
  staging: Milton Kramer
  sets: David Emmons
Productions:
Opened October 21, 1980 for 38 performances
Reviews:
New York Theatre Critics' Reviews 1980:141
New York Times III, page 21, Oct 22, 1980
Time 113:75, Jun 25, 1979

Banjo Eyes
  book: Joe Quillan and Izzy Elinson from John Cecil
                 Holm and George Abbott's Three Men on a Horse
  music: Vernon Duke

lyrics: John LaTouche and Harold Adamson
staging: Hassard Short
sets: Harry Horner
costumes: Irene Sharaff
choreography: Charles Walters

Productions:
 Opened December 25, 1941 for 126 performances
Reviews:
 Catholic World 154:731, Mar 1942
 Life 12: 62-3, Feb 23, 1942
 New York Theatre Critics' Reviews 1941:164+
 New York Times page 10, Nov 8, 1941
       page 20, Dec 26, 1941
       page 17, Apr 16, 1942
 New Yorker 17:28, Jan 3, 1942
 Theatre Arts 26:155, Mar 1942
 Time 39:47, Jan 5, 1942

The Banker's Daughter
 book: Edward Eliscu; based on Boucicault's Streets
       of New York
 music: Sol Kaplan
 lyrics: Edward Eliscu
 staging: David Brooks
 sets: Kim Swados
 costumes: Peter Joseph
Productions:
 (Off-Broadway) Opened January 21, 1962 for 68 performances
Reviews:
 America 106:633, Feb 10, 1962
 New York Times page 37, Jan 23, 1962
       page 42, Mar 20, 1962
 New Yorker 37:70+, Feb 3, 1962

The Bar That Never Closes
 book: Louisa Rose
 sketches: Marco Vassi
 music: Tom Mandel
 lyrics: Louisa Rose
 staging: John Braswell
 sets: Susan Haskins
Productions:
 (Off-Broadway) Opened December 3, 1972 for 33 performances
Reviews:
 New York 6:66, Jan 15, 1973
 New York Times page 55, Dec 4, 1972
 (Also see Everything for Anybody)

Barbara Cook: A Concert for the Theater (one-woman show)
 music: Wally Harper and various composers
 lyrics: David Zippel and various authors

sets: John Falabella
costumes: Joseph G. Aulisi
Productions:
Opened April 15, 1987 for 13 performances
Reviews:
New York 20:139-40, Apr 27, 1987
New York Theatre Critics' Reviews 1987:282
New Yorker 63:127, May 4, 1987

Bare Facts of 1926
sketches: Stuart Hamill
music: Charles M. Schwab
lyrics: Henry Myers
staging: Kathleen Kirkwood
Productions:
Opened July 16, 1926 for 107 performances
Reviews:
New York Times page 7, Jul 17, 1926
               page 13, Jul 19, 1926
               page 27, Aug 17, 1927

Barefoot Boy with Cheek
book: Max Shulman, from his novel Barefoot Boy with
                    Cheek
music: Sidney Lippman
lyrics: Sylvia Dee
staging: George Abbott
sets: Jo Mielziner
costumes: Alvin Colt
choreography: Richard Barstow
Productions:
Opened April 3, 1947 for 108 performances
Reviews:
Catholic World 165:169, May 1947
Commonweal 46:16, Apr 18, 1947
New Republic 116:37, Apr 21, 1947
New York Theatre Critics' Reviews 1947:402+
New York Times page 20, Apr 4, 1947
               II, page 1, May 4, 1947
New Yorker 23:46, Apr 12, 1947
Newsweek 29:86, Apr 14, 1947
Theatre Arts 31:41, Jun 1947
Time 49:70, Apr 14, 1947

Barnes, Billie   (see Billie Barnes and Billy Barnes)

Barnum
book: Mark Bramble
music: Cy Coleman
lyrics: Michael Stewart
staging: Joe Layton

sets: David Mitchell
costumes: Theoni V. Aldredge

Productions:
Opened April 30, 1980 for 854 performances
Reviews:
American Record Guide 43:11+, Sep 1980
Dance Magazine 54:94, Jul 1980
Nation 230:637, May 24, 1980
New York 13:59, May 12, 1980
          13:45+, May 19, 1980
New York Theatre Critics' Reviews 1980:261
New York Times II, page 1, Apr 27, 1980
          III, page 17, May 1, 1980
          II, page 7, May 11, 1980
People 15:53-4+, May 11, 1981
Theatre Crafts 14:16-17+, Oct 1980
          21:30-2+, Jan 1987
Time 115:83, May 12, 1980

Baron Trenck

libretto: A. M. Willner and R. Rodansky; English version
               by Henry Blossom
music: Felix Albini
lyrics: Frederick F. Schrader
staging: Al Holbrook
Productions:
Opened March 11, 1912 for 40 performances
Reviews:
Blue Book 15:26-8, May 1912
Dramatic Mirror 67:7, Mar 13, 1912
Green Book 7:1100-3+, Jun 1912
Hampton 28:295, May 1912
New York Dramatic News 55:14, Mar 16, 1912
Theatre Magazine 15:xiii, Apr 1912
                15:105, Apr 1912

The Barrier

book: Langston Hughes
music: Jan Meyerowitz
lyrics: Langston Hughes
staging: Doris Humphrey
sets: H. A. Condell
choreography: Charles Weidman and Doris Humphrey
Productions:
Opened November, 1950 for 4 performances
(Off-Broadway) Season of 1952-53
Reviews:
Christian Science Monitor Magazine page 8, Nov 11, 1950
Commonweal 53:172, Nov 24, 1950
Musical America 70:244, Feb 1950
New York Theatre Critics' Reviews 1950:218+

New York Times page 34, Jan 19, 1950
            page 32, Nov 3, 1950
            page 24, Mar 9, 1953
New Yorker 25:71, Jan 28, 1950
        26:79-81, Nov 11, 1950
Newsweek 35:68, Jan 30, 1950
School and Society 71:120, Feb 25, 1950
Theatre Arts 35:12, Jan 1951
Time 55:68+, Jan 30, 1950

Barry Manilow at the Gershwin
conceived: Ernie Chambers, Jack Feldman, Roberta Kent,
                Barry Manilow, and Bruce Sussman
written: Ken and Mitzie Welch, Roberta Kent and Barry
                Manilow
songs: Various authors and composers
staging: Kevin Carlisle
design: Jeremy Railton
Productions:
Opened April 18, 1989 for *36 performances (still running 6/1/89)
No Reviews.

Battling Buttler
adapted by: Ballard MacDonald; from the original of Bright-
                man, Melford and Furber
music: Walter L. Rosemont
staging: Guy Bragdon
Productions:
Opened October 8, 1923 for (288) performances
Reviews:
New York Times page 17, Oct 9, 1923

Be Kind to People Week
book: Jack Bussins and Ellsworth Olin
music: Jack Bussins and Ellsworth Olin
lyrics: Jack Bussins and Ellsworth Olin
staging: Quinton Raines
sets: Bruce Monroe
choreography: Bobby Lee
Productions:
(Off-Broadway) Opened March 23, 1975 for 100 performances
Reviews:
New York Times page 40, Mar 24, 1975

Be Yourself
book: George S. Kaufman and Marc Connelly
music: Lewis Gensler and Milton Schwarzwald
staging: William Collier
Productions:
Opened September 3, 1924 for 93 performances

Reviews:
    New York Times page 13, Sep 4, 1924
                  page 24, Oct 1, 1924
    Theatre Magazine 40:19, Nov 1924

The Beast in Me
conceived by:	Haila Stoddard, based on James Thurber's Fables for Our Time
book:	adapted by James Costigan
music:	Don Elliott
lyrics:	James Costigan
staging:	John Lehne
sets:	Jean Rosenthal
costumes:	Leo Van Witsen
choreography:	John Butler

Productions:
    Opened May 16, 1963 for 4 performances
Reviews:
    New York Theatre Critics' Reviews 1963:324+
    New York Times II, page 1, May 12, 1963
                  page 29, May 17, 1963
    New Yorker 39:57, May 25, 1963
    Newsweek 61:93, May 27, 1963

Beat the Band
book:	George Marion, Jr. and George Abbott
music:	John Green
lyrics:	George Marion, Jr. and George Abbott
staging:	George Abbott
sets:	Sam Leve
costumes:	Freddy Wittop
choreography:	David Lichine

Productions:
    Opened October 14, 1942 for 68 performances
Reviews:
    Catholic World 156:337, Dec 1942
    Nation 155:458, Oct 31, 1942
    New York Theatre Critics' Reviews 1942:204+
    New York Times VIII, page 8, Oct 4, 1942
                  page 26, Oct 15, 1942
    Newsweek 20:87, Oct 26, 1942
    Theatre Arts 26:742, Dec 1942
    Time 40:54, Oct 26, 1942

Beatlemania
conceived:	Steven Leber, David Krebs and Jules Fisher
book:	Robert Rabinowitz, Bob Gill and Lynda Obst
songs:	John Lennon, Paul McCartney and George Harrison
staging:	Jules Fisher
sets:	Robert D. Mitchell

Productions:
  Opened May 31, 1977 for 920 performances
Reviews:
  New York Times III, page 3, Jun 17, 1977
  Rolling Stone pages 11+, May 18, 1978
  Theatre Crafts 12:16-19+, Jan 1978
  Time 110:54-5, Aug 8, 1977

Beautiful Dreamer
  book: William Engvick; based on the life of Stephen
                 Foster
  music: William Engvick
  lyrics: William Engvick
Productions:
  (Off-Broadway) Season of 1960-1961
Reviews:
  New York Times page 22, Dec 28, 1960

The Beauty and the Beast
  book: Oswald Rodriquez; adapted from the fairy tale
  music: Joseph Blunt
  staging: Oswald Rodriquez
Productions:
  (Off-Off-Broadway) Opened January 4, 1973
No Reviews.

The Beauty Shop
  book: Channing Pollock and Rennold Wolf
  music: Charles J. Gebest
  lyrics: Channing Pollock and Rennold Wolf
  staging: R. H. Burnside
Productions:
  Opened April 13, 1914 for 88 performances
Reviews:
  Blue Book 18:426-9, Jan 1914
  Dramatic Mirror 71:13, Apr 15, 1914
  Green Book 12:106, Jul 1914
  New York Dramatic News 59:20, Apr 8, 1914
  New York Times page 11, Apr 14, 1914
  Theatre Magazine 19:282, Jun 1914
                   19:289, Jun 1914

Becaud, Gilbert   (see Gilbert Becaud)

Becoming
  by: Gail Edwards and Sam Harris
  staging: John Mineo
  sets: Dan Leigh
  costumes: Dee Dee Fote
  choreography: John Mineo
Productions:
  (Off-Broadway) Opened June 15, 1976 for 2 performances

Reviews:
New York Times page 30, Jun 17, 1976

Beehive
conceived:	Larry Gallagher
written:	Larry Gallagher
songs:	Various authors and composers of the 1960s
staging:	Larry Gallagher
sets:	John Hickey
costumes:	David Dille
choreography:	Leslie Dockery

Productions:
   (Off-Broadway) Opened March 30, 1986 for 600 performances
Reviews:
Dance Magazine 60:103, Mar 1986
Los Angeles 21:179, Sep 1976
Ms. 15:17, Nov 1986
New York Times II, page 5, Apr 27, 1986
People 26:53-4, Jul 14, 1986
Time 128:86+, Sep 15, 1986

Beg, Borrow or Steal
book:	Bud Freeman, from a story by Marvin Seiger and Bud Freeman
music:	Leon Prober
lyrics:	Bud Freeman
staging:	Billy Matthews
sets:	Carter Morningstar
costumes:	Carter Morningstar
choreography:	Peter Hamilton

Productions:
Opened February 10, 1960 for 5 performances
Reviews:
New York Theatre Critics' Reviews 1960: 370+
New York Times page 39, Feb 11, 1960
                page 22, Feb 12, 1960
New Yorker 36:101-2, Feb 20, 1960

Beggar's Holiday
book:	John Latouche, adapted from John Gay's The Beggar's Opera
music:	Duke Ellington
lyrics:	John Latouche
staging:	Nicholas Ray
sets:	Oliver Smith
costumes:	Walter Florell
choreography:	Valerie Bettis

Productions:
Opened December 26, 1936 for 108 performances
Reviews:
Catholic World 164:455-6, Feb 1947

Commonweal 45:351-2, Jan 17, 1947
Life 22:75, Feb 24, 1947
New York Theatre Critics' Reviews 1946:204+
New York Times II, page 3, Dec 22, 1946
                page 13, Dec 27, 1946
                II, page 1, Jan 26, 1947
                II, page 3, Feb 2, 1947
New Yorker 22:46-7, Jan 4, 1947
Newsweek 29:64, Jan 6, 1947
School and Society 65:252, Apr 5, 1947
Theatre Arts 31:16-17, Mar 1947
              31:27, Mar 1947
Time 49:57, Jan 6, 1947

Bei Mir Bist Du Schoen
    book: Louis Freiman
    music: Sholom Secunda
    lyrics: Jacob Jacobs
    staging: Leo Fuchs
Productions:
    (Off-Broadway) Opened October 21, 1961 for 88 performances
Reviews:
    New York Times page 22, Oct 23, 1961
                   page 17, Dec 26, 1961

The Believers
    book: Josephine Jackson and Joseph A. Walker
    music and
      lyrics: Benjamin Carter, Dorothy Dinroe, Josephine
                  Jackson, Anje Ray and Ron Steward
    staging: Barbara Ann Teer
    sets: Joseph A. Walker
    costumes: Robert Pusilo
Productions:
    (Off-Broadway) Opened May 9, 1968 for 310 performances
Reviews:
    New York Times page 57, May 10, 1968
                   page 33, Jul 15, 1968
    New Yorker 44:75, May 18, 1968

Bella
    book: Tom O'Malley and Lance Barklie
    music: Jane Douglas
    lyrics: Tom O'Malley
    staging: Richard C. Shank
Productions:
    (Off-Broadway) Opened November 16, 1961 for 6 performances
Reviews:
    New York Times page 40, Nov 17, 1961
                   page 14, Nov 18, 1961
    New Yorker 37:95-6, Nov 25, 1961

The Belle of Bond Street
  book: Owen Hall and Harold Atteridge, based on The
                 Girl from Kay's
  music: Ivan Caryll and Lionel Monckton
  lyrics: Adrian Ross and Claude Aveling
  staging: Edwin T. Emery
Productions:
  Opened March 30, 1914 for 48 performances
Reviews:
  Dramatic Mirror 71:13, Apr 1, 1914
                  71:2, Apr 15, 1914
  Green Book 11:1020, Jun 1914
             12:94-6, Jul 1914
  Life (New York) 63:655, Apr 9, 1914
  New York Dramatic News 59:21, Apr 4, 1914
  New York Times page 11, Mar 31, 1914
  Theatre Magazine 19:261, May 1914
                   19:279, Jun 1914
                   19:298, Jun 1914

The Belle of Brittany
  book: Leedham Bantock, P. J. Barron and Percy Green-
                 bank
  music: Howard Talbot and Marie Horne
  staging: Frank Smithson
Productions:
  Opened November 8, 1909 for 72 performances
Reviews:
  Hampton 24:134-5, Jan 1910
  Harper's Weekly 53:24, Dec 4, 1909
  Leslie's Weekly 109:545, Dec 2, 1909
  Metropolitan Magazine 31:826-7, Mar 1910
  New York Dramatic News page 5, Nov 20, 1909
  Theatre Magazine 10:v, Dec 1909
                   10:vii, Dec 1909

Belle Paree, La (see La Belle Paree)

Bells Are Ringing
  book: Betty Comden and Adolph Green
  music: Jule Styne
  lyrics: Betty Comden and Adolph Green
  staging: Jerome Robbins
  sets: Raoul Pene du Bois
  costumes: Raoul Pene du Bois
  choreography: Jerome Robbins and Bob Fosse
Productions:
  Opened November 29, 1956 for 924 performances
Reviews:
  America 96:742, Mar 30, 1957
  Catholic World 184:386-7, Feb 1957

Commonweal 65:408, Jan 18, 1957
Life 42:69-70+, Feb 11, 1957
Nation 183:526, Dec 15, 1956
New York Theatre Critics' Reviews 1956:182+
New York Times VI, page 29, Sep 16, 1956
　　　　　　　　VI, page 29, Nov 4, 1956
　　　　　　　　page 18, Nov 30, 1956
　　　　　　　　II, page 3, Dec 16, 1956
　　　　　　　　page 37, Nov 15, 1957
New Yorker 32:88+, Dec 1956
Newsweek 48:77, Dec 10, 1956
Reporter 16:35, Jan 24, 1957
Saturday Review 39:25, Dec 29, 1956
Theatre Arts 40:76-8, Dec 1956
　　　　　　　41:15-16, Feb 1957
　　　　　　　41:27-8+, Mar 1957
Time 68:70, Dec 10, 1956

Belmont Varieties
　　book:　　　　　　Helen and Nolan Leary and Sam Bernard II
　　music and
　　　lyrics:　　　　Serge Walter, Alvin Kaufman, Charles Kenny,
　　　　　　　　　　Henry Lloyd, Mildred Kaufman, Robert Burk
　　staging:　　　　Max Scheck and Sam Bernard II
Productions:
　　Opened September 26, 1932 for 8 performances
No Reviews.

Below the Belt
　　conceived:　　　Rod Warren
　　staging:　　　　Sandra Devlin
Productions:
　　(Off-Broadway) Opened June 21, 1966 for 186 performances
No Reviews.

Ben Franklin in Paris
　　book:　　　　　　Sidney Michaels
　　music:　　　　　Mark Sandrich, Jr.
　　lyrics:　　　　　Sidney Michaels
　　staging:　　　　Michael Kidd
　　sets:　　　　　　Oliver Smith
　　costumes:　　　　Motley
　　choreography:　　Michael Kidd
Productions:
　　Opened October 27, 1964 for 215 performances
Reviews:
　　America 111:758, Dec 5, 1964
　　Commonweal 81:423, Dec 18, 1964
　　Dance Magazine 38:16, Dec 1964
　　New York Theatre Critics' Reviews 1964:181+
　　New York Times page 52, Oct 28, 1964

Newsweek 64:92, Nov 9, 1964
Saturday Review 47:53, Nov 14, 1964
Senior Scholastic 86:21, Mar 4, 1965
Time 84:52, Nov 6, 1964

Berlin to Broadway with Kurt Weill
    music: Kurt Weill
    lyrics: Maxwell Anderson, Marc Blitzstein, Bertolt
                        Brecht, Jacques Deval, Michael Feingold, Ira
                        Gershwin, Paul Green, Langston Hughes, Alan
                        Jay Lerner, Ogden Nash, George Tabori and
                        Arnold Weinstein
    staging: Donald Saddler
    sets: Herbert Senn and Helen Pond
    costumes: Frank Thompson
Productions:
    (Off-Broadway) Opened October 1, 1972 for 152 performances
Reviews:
    America 127:323, Oct 21, 1972
    Dance Magazine 46:78, Nov 1972
    Los Angeles 30:42, Apr 1985
               30:44, Dec 1985
    New Republic 167:18+, Nov 11, 1972
    New York Theatre Critics' Reviews 1972:170
    New York Times page 43, Oct 2, 1972
                   II, page 1, Oct 8, 1972
    New Yorker 48:125, Oct 14, 1972
    Playboy 20:34, Feb 1973
    Time 100:56, Oct 16, 1972

Bernstein, Leonard (see Leonard Bernstein)

Best Foot Forward
    book: John Cecil Holm
    music: Hugh Martin and Ralph Blane
    lyrics: Hugh Martin and Ralph Blane
    staging: George Abbott
    sets: Jo Mielziner
    costumes: Miles White
    choreography: Gene Kelly
Productions:
    Opened October 1, 1941 for 326 performances
    (Off-Broadway) Opened April 2, 1963 for 224 performances
Reviews:
    America 108:594, Apr 20, 1963
    Catholic World 154:213, Nov 1941
    Life 11:91-2+, Oct 12, 1941
        12:63, Feb 23, 1942
    New York Theatre Critics' Reviews 1941:286+
    New York Times page 24, Sep 12, 1941
                page 28, Oct 2, 1941

IX, page 1, Oct 26, 1941
page 43, Apr 3, 1963
VI, page 104, May 5, 1963
New Yorker 17:44, Oct 11, 1941
39:140, Apr 13, 1963
Newsweek 18:68, Oct 13, 1941
Players Magazine 18:14, Feb 1942
Theatre Arts 25:868+, Dec 1941
26:18, Jan 1942
47:12-13+, Jun 1963
Time 38:67, Oct 13, 1941

The Best Little Whorehouse in Texas
 book: Larry L. King and Peter Masterson
 music: Carol Hall
 lyrics: Carol Hall
 staging: Peter Masterson and Tommy Tune
 sets: Marjorie Kellogg
 costumes: Ann Roth
 choreography: Tommy Tune
Productions:
 (Off-Off-Broadway) Opened November 1977
 (Off-Broadway) Opened April 17, 1978 for 64 performances
 Opened June 19, 1978 for 1,639 performances
Reviews:
 Fortune 106:37, Jul 12, 1982
 Los Angeles 25:292+, Nov 1980
 New York 11:83+, May 8, 1978
 New York Theatre Critics' Reviews 1978:232
 New York Times II, page 6, Apr 9, 1978
 New Yorker 54:67, May 1, 1978
 Newsweek 91:74, May 1, 1978
 Texas Monthly 6:132, Jun 1978
       7:166+, Apr 1979
 Time 111:95-6, May 1, 1978

Betsy (1911)
 book: H. Kellett Chambers, based on An American
        Widow
 music: Alexander Johnstone
 lyrics: W. B. Johnstone
 staging: Edward Elsner
Productions:
 Opened December 11, 1911 for 32 performances
Reviews:
 Dramatic Mirror 66:7, Dec 13, 1911
        66:8, Dec 27, 1911
 Life (New York) pp. 1134-5, Dec 21, 1911
 New York Times page 9, Dec 12, 1911
 Theatre Magazine 15:xii, Jan 1912

Betsy (1926)
    book: Irving Caesar and David Freedman
    music: Richard Rodgers
    lyrics: Lorenz Hart
    staging: William Anthony McGuire and Sammy Lee
Productions:
    Opened December 28, 1926 for 39 performances
Reviews:
    New York Times page 24, Dec 29, 1926

Bette Midler's Clams on the Half Shell Revue (see Clams on the
    Half Shell Revue with Bette Midler)

The Better 'Ole
    book: Captain Bruce Bairnsfather and Captain Arthur
                  Elliott
    music: Herman Darewski and Percival Knight
    staging: Percival Knight
Productions:
    Opened October 19, 1918 for 353 performances
Reviews:
    Dramatic Mirror 79:651, Nov 2, 1918
                  79:827, Dec 7, 1918
    New York Dramatic News 65:6, Dec 28, 1918
    New York Times page 13, Oct 21, 1918
                  IV, page 2, Oct 27, 1918
    Theatre Magazine 28:344-5, Dec 1918

Better Times
    book: R. H. Burnside
    music: Raymond Hubbell
    staging: R. H. Burnside
Productions:
    Opened September 2, 1922 for 409 performances
Reviews:
    Current Opinion 73:625, Nov 1922
    New York Times page 14, Sep 4, 1922
    Theatre Magazine 36:377, Dec 1922
                  36:383, Dec 1922

Betty
    book: Frederick Lonsdale and Gladys Unger
    music: Paul A. Rubens
    lyrics: Adrian Ross and Paul A. Rubens
    staging: Edward Royce
Productions:
    Opened October 3, 1916 for 63 performances
Reviews:
    Dramatic Mirror 76:7, Oct 14, 1916
    Greek Book 16:976+, Dec 1916
    Life (New York) 68:272-3, Oct 19, 1916

Munsey 59:668, Jan 1917
New York Dramatic News 63:11, Oct 7, 1916
New York Times page 11, Oct 4, 1916
Opera Magazine 3:26-7, Nov 1916
Theatre Magazine 24:284, Nov 1916

Betty Be Good
  book: Harry B. Smith; adapted from a French vaude-
                     ville by Scribe
  music: Hugo Reisenfeld
  lyrics: Harry B. Smith
  staging: David Bennett
Productions:
  Opened May 4, 1920 for 31 performances
Reviews:
  Dramatic Mirror 82:311, Feb 21, 1920
                  82:889, May 8, 1920
  New York Clipper 68:17, May 12, 1920
  New York Times page 14, May 5, 1920
  Theatre Magazine 31:505, Jun 1920
                   31:525, Jun 1920

Betty Comden and Adolph Green (see A Party with Betty Comden
  and Adolph Green)

Betty Lee
  book: Otto Harbach
  music: Louis Hirsch and Con Conrad
  lyrics: Irving Caesar and Otto Harbach
  staging: David Bennett
Productions:
  Opened December 25, 1924 for 111 performances
Reviews:
  New York Times page 18, Dec 26, 1924

Between the Devil
  book: Howard Dietz
  music: Arthur Schwartz
  lyrics: Howard Dietz
  staging: Hassard Short and John Hayden
  sets: Albert Johnson
  costumes: Kiviette
  choreography: Robert Alton
Productions:
  Opened December 22, 1937 for 93 performances
Reviews:
  Nation 146:754, Jan 1, 1938
  New York Times page 19, Oct 15, 1937
                   XI, page 2, Oct 24, 1937
                   page 24, Dec 23, 1937
  One Act Play Magazine 1:849, Jan 1938

Stage 15:52-3, Feb 1938
Time 31:22, Jan 3, 1938

The Bible Salesman (with The Oldest Trick in the World, billed as
    Double Entry)
    book: Jay Thompson
    music: Jay Thompson
    lyrics: Jay Thompson
    staging: Bill Penn
    sets: Howard Becknell
Productions:
    (Off-Broadway) Opened February 20, 1961 for 56 performances
Reviews:
    New York Times page 40, Feb 21, 1961
    New Yorker 37:115-16, Mar 11, 1961

Biff! Bang!
    book: Philip Dunning, Robert Cohen, and William
                       Israel
    music: William Schroeder
Productions:
    Opened May 30, 1918 for 16 performances
Reviews:
    New York Times page 15, May 31, 1918
                     page 9, Jun 3, 1918
                     page 11, June 4, 1918
    Theatre Magazine 28:23-4, Jul 1918
                     28:96, Aug 1918

Big Bad Burlesque
    by: Don Brockett
    staging: Celeste Hall
    sets: Charles Vanderpool
    choreography: Don Brockett
Productions:
    (Off-Broadway) Opened August 14, 1979 for 112 performances
Reviews:
    New York Times III, page 18, Aug 15, 1979

Big Boy
    book: Harold Atteridge
    music: James F. Hanley and Joseph Meyer
    lyrics: Bud G. DeSylva
    staging: J. C. Huffman
Productions:
    Opened January 7, 1925 for 48 performances
    Opened August 24, 1925 for 120 performances
Reviews:
    New York Times page 28, Jan 8, 1925
                     page 9, Jan 10, 1925
                     page 15, Jan 12, 1925

                    page 19, Jan 21, 1925
                    page 17, Jan 26, 1925
                    page 20, Feb 10, 1925
                    page 17, Mar 16, 1925
                    page 14, Aug 18, 1925
                    page 12, Aug 25, 1925
                    page 16, Jan 27, 1926
                    page 13, Feb 7, 1926
                    page 20, Feb 10, 1926
      Theatre Magazine 40:19, Mar 1925
                    40:62, Mar 1925

Big Deal
    book: Bob Fosse, based on the film Big Deal on Madonna Street
    music: Various composers
    lyrics: Various authors
    staging: Bob Fosse
    sets: Peter Larkin
    costumes: Patricia Zipprodt
    choreography: Bob Fosse
Productions:
    Opened April 10, 1986 for 70 performances
Reviews:
    America 154:475, Jun 7, 1986
    Dance Magazine 60:60, Jul 1986
                    60:34-9, Aug 1986
    Essence 17:44, May 1986
    Jet 69:16, Mar 17, 1986
        70:60, May 12, 1986
    New York 19:50-7, Apr 7, 1986
            19:95-6, Apr 21, 1986
    New York Theatre Critics' Reviews 1986:327
    New York Times III, page 3, Apr 11, 1986
    New Yorker 62:106-7, Apr 21, 1986
    Newsweek 107:83, Apr 21, 1986
    Theatre Crafts 20:24-5+, Aug/Sep 1986
    Time 127:85, Apr 21, 1986
    Vogue 176:76, Apr 1986

Big River: The Adventures of Huckleberry Finn
    book: William Hauptman, based on the novel by Mark Twain
    music: Roger Miller
    lyrics: Roger Miller
    staging: Des McAnuff
    sets: Heidi Landesman
    costumes: Patricia McGourty
    choreography: Janet Watson
Productions:
    Opened April 25, 1985 for 1,005 performances

Reviews:
    America 152:456, Jun 1, 1985
    Horizon 28:21- 4, Nov 1985
    Nation 240:682- 4, Jun 1, 1985
    New Leader 68:21, Apr 8, 1985
    New York 18:91, May 6, 1985
    New York Theatre Critics' Reviews 1985:302
    New York Times III, page 3, Apr 26, 1985
                    II, page 3, May 5, 1985
                    III, page 11, Jul 16, 1985
    New Yorker 61:128, May 13, 1985
    Newsweek 105:74, May 6, 1985
    Theatre Crafts 19:30- 7+, Aug/Sep 1985

The Big Show
    book: R. H. Burnside
    music: Raymond Hubbell
    lyrics: John L. Golden
    staging: R. H. Burnside
Productions:
    Opened August 31, 1916 for 425 performances
Reviews:
    New York Times page 7, Sep 1, 1916
    Theatre Magazine 24:246, Oct 1916
                     24:275, Nov 1916

Big Time Buck White   (see Buck White)

Billie
    book: George M. Cohan, adapted from his play Broad-
                    way Jones
    music: George M. Cohan
    lyrics: George M. Cohan
    staging: Edward Royce and Sam Forrest
Productions:
    Opened October 1, 1928 for 112 performances
Reviews:
    New York Times page 34, Oct 2, 1928
    Theatre Magazine 49:60, Jan 1929

The Billie Barnes People
    sketches: Bob Rodgers
    music: Billy Barnes
    lyrics: Billy Barnes
    staging: Bob Rodgers
    sets: Spencer Davies
    costumes: Grady Hunt
Productions:
    Opened June 13, 1961 for 7 performances
Reviews:
    New York Theatre Critics' Reviews 1961:276+
    New York Times page 10, Jun 14, 1961

Billion Dollar Baby
book:	Betty Comden and Adolph Green
music:	Morton Gould
lyrics:	Betty Comden and Adolph Green
staging:	George Abbott
sets:	Oliver Smith
costumes:	Irene Sharaff
choreography:	Jerome Robbins

Productions:
Opened December 21, 1945 for 220 performances
Reviews:
Catholic World 162:458, Feb 1946
Harper's 80:106, Jan 1946
Life 20:67+, Jan 21, 1946
Modern Music 23 no. 2:145, Apr 1946
New York Theatre Critics' Reviews 1945:61+
New York Times page 17, Dec 22, 1945
        II, page 1, Dec 30, 1945
        II, page 1, Feb 10, 1946
New Yorker 21:40, Jan 5, 1946
Newsweek 26:78, Dec 31, 1945
Theatre Arts 30:80-1, Feb 1946
Time 46:64, Dec 31, 1945
Vogue 107:170-1, Feb 1, 1946

Billy
book:	Stephen Glassman; suggested by Herman Melville's Billy Budd
music:	Ron Dante and Gene Allan
lyrics:	Ron Dante and Gene Allan
staging:	Arthur A. Seidelman
sets:	Ming Cho Lee
costumes:	Theoni V. Aldredge
choreography:	Grover Dale

Productions:
Opened March 22, 1969 for one performance
Reviews:
New York Theatre Critics' Reviews 1969:316
New York Times page 56, Mar 24, 1969
New Yorker 45:99, Mar 29, 1969

Billy Barnes Revue
sketches:	Bob Rodgers
dialogue:	Bob Rodgers
music:	Billy Barnes
lyrics:	Billy Barnes
staging:	Bob Rodgers
sets:	Glen Holse
costumes:	Peggy Morrison

Productions:
Opened August 4, 1959 for 87 performances
(Off-Broadway) Season of 1959-60

Reviews:
    Dance Magazine 33:13, Sep 1959
    New York Times page 42, Jun 10, 1959
                    page 21, Jul 22, 1959
                    II, page 1, Aug 30, 1959
                    page 47, Oct 15, 1959
                    page 19, Nov 25, 1959
    Saturday Review 42:33, Oct 10, 1959

Billy Bishop Goes to War
    book: John Gray
    music: John Gray
    lyrics: John Gray
    staging: John Gray
    sets: David Gropman
Productions:
    Opened May 29, 1980 for 12 performances
    (Off-Broadway) Opened June 17, 1980 for 78 performances
    (Off-Off-Broadway) Opened February 19, 1987
Reviews:
    New York Theatre Critics' Reviews 1980:225
    New York Times III, page 20, Mar 13, 1980
                    III, page 3, May 30, 1980
                    XI, page 12, Mar 1, 1987

Billy Noname
    book: William Wellington Mackey
    music: Johnny Brandon
    lyrics: Johnny Brandon
    staging: Lucia Victor
    sets: Jack Brown
    costumes: Pearl Somner
    choreography: Talley Beatty
Productions:
    (Off-Broadway) Opened March 2, 1970 for 48 performances
Reviews:
    Dance Magazine 44:89-91, May 1970
    New York Theatre Critics' Reviews 1970:285
    New York Times page 37, Mar 3, 1970
    New Yorker 46:122, Mar 14, 1970

Billy Rose's Crazy Quilt
    assembled by: Billy Rose
    music: Harry Warren, Ned Lehak, Louis Alter
    lyrics: Bud Green, Edward Eliscu, Billy Rose, Mort
                    Dixon, E. Y. Harburg
    staging: Billy Rose
Productions:
    Opened May 19, 1931 for 79 performances
Reviews:
    New York Times VIII, page 2, May 3, 1931

VIII, page 2, May 31, 1931
Stage 9:13, May 1932

Birds of Paradise
  book: Winnie Holzman and David Evans
  music: David Evans
  lyrics: Winnie Holzman
  staging: Arthur Laurents
  sets: Philipp Jung
  costumes: David Murin
  choreography: Linda Haberman
Productions:
  (Off-Broadway) Opened October 26, 1987 for 24 performances
Reviews:
  New York Times III, page 18, October 27, 1987
  New Yorker 63:131-2, Nov 9, 1987

A Bistro Car on the CNR
  dialogue: D. R. Andersen
  music: Patrick Rose
  lyrics: Merv Campone and Richard Ouzounian
  staging: Richard Ouzounian
  sets: John Falabella
  costumes: John Falabella
  choreography: Lynne Gannaway
Productions:
  (Off-Broadway) Opened March 23, 1978 for 61 performances
Reviews:
  New York Times III, page 3, Mar 24, 1978
  New Yorker 54:112, Apr 3, 1978

Bits and Pieces XIV
  conceived: Julius Monk
  staging: Julius Monk
  costumes: Bill Belew
  choreography: Frank Wagner
Productions:
  (Off-Broadway) Opened October 6, 1964 for 426 performances
No Reviews.

Bittersuite (see also Bittersuite--One More Time)
  music: Elliot Weiss
  lyrics: Michael Champagne
  staging: Michael Champagne
Productions:
  (Off-Off-Broadway) Opened January 20, 1984 for 23 performances
  (Off-Broadway) Opened October 5, 1987 for 211 performances
Reviews:
  New York Times III, page 21, Feb 15, 1984
              III, page 15, Apr 13, 1987

Bittersuite--One More Time (new edition of Bittersuite, above)
    music: Elliot Weiss
    lyrics: Michael Champagne
    staging: Michael Champagne
Productions:
    (Off-Broadway) Opened May 16, 1988 for 18 performances
No Reviews.

Black and Blue
    conceived: Claudio Segovia and Hector Orezzoli
    songs: Various authors and composers
    staging: Claudio Segovia and Hector Orezzoli
    sets: Claudio Segovia and Hector Orezzoli
    costumes: Claudio Segovia and Hector Orezzoli
    choreography: Cholly Atkins, Henry LeTang, Frankie Manning,
                    and Fayard Nicholas
Productions:
    Opened January 26, 1989 for *144 performances (still running
    6/1/89)
Reviews:
    America 160:153+, Feb 18, 1989
    Dance Magazine 63:69-70, Jun 1989
    Jet 76:52-3, Apr 10, 1989
        76:52, May 22, 1989
    Nation 248:281-2, Feb 27, 1989
    New Leader 72:22-3, Mar 6, 1989
    New York 22:37-40, Jan 2, 1989
        22:92 Feb 6, 1989
    New York Theatre Critics' Reviews 1989:386
    New York Times III, page 13, Jan 3, 1989
        III, page 3, Jan 27, 1989
        II, page 3, Apr 2, 1989
        II, page 26, May 21, 1989
    New Yorker 64:73-4, Feb 6, 1989
    Time 133:80, Feb 6, 1989
    Vogue 176:484-5+, Mar 1986
        179:192-3, Jan 1989

Black Broadway
    songs: Harold Arlen, Irving Berlin, Eubie Blake, Irving
                    Caesar, Benny Carter, Bob Cole, Vernon Duke,
                    Duke Ellington, Dorothy Fields, Lemuel Fowler,
                    George Gershwin, Ira Gershwin, James P. John-
                    son, James Weldon Johnson, John Rosamond
                    Johnson, Joe Jordan, Ted Koehler, John Latouche,
                    Jimmy McHugh, Johnny Mercer, Maceo Pinkard,
                    Cole Porter, Andy Razaf, Noble Sissle, Chris
                    Smith, Fats Waller, George Walker and Bert
                    Williams
    design: Leo Gambacorta
Productions:
    Opened May 4, 1980 for 25 performances

Reviews:
    New York Theatre Critics' Reviews 1980:253
    New York Times III, page 14, May 5, 1980
    Newsweek 95:81+, May 26, 1980
    Time 115:52, May 19, 1980

The Black Light Theater of Prague
    book: Jiri Srnec and Frantisek Kratochvil
    music: Jiri Srnec
    lyrics: Jiri Srnec and Frantisek Kratochvil
    staging: Jiri Srnec
    sets: Jiri Srnec and Frantisek Kratochvil
Productions:
    Opened September 27, 1971 for 10 performances
Reviews:
    New York Theatre Critics' Reviews 1971:251

Black Nativity
    book: Langston Hughes
    music: Langston Hughes
    lyrics: Langston Hughes
    staging: Vinnette Carroll
Productions:
    (Off-Broadway) Opened December 11, 1961 for 57 performances
Reviews:
    Ebony 37:63+, Apr 1982
    New York Times page 54, Dec 12, 1961
                   page 38, Jan 23, 1962
                   page 37, Aug 15, 1962
    New Yorker 37:57, Dec 23, 1961

Black Picture Show
    book: Bill Gunn
    music: Sam Waymon
    lyrics: Sam Waymon
    staging: Bill Gunn
    sets: Peter Harvey
    costumes: Judy Dearing
Productions:
    Opened January 6, 1975 for 41 performances
Reviews:
    Essence 6:12, May 1975
    New York 8:51, Jan 27, 1975
    New York Theatre Critics' Reviews 1975:386
    New York Times page 28, Jan 7, 1975
                   II, page 7, Jan 19, 1975

Black Rhythm
    book: Donald Heywood
    music: Donald Heywood
    lyrics: Donald Heywood
    staging: Earl Dancer and Donald Heywood

Productions:
    Opened December 19, 1936 for 6 performances
Reviews:
    New York Times page 19, Dec 21, 1936

Black Sea Follies
    conceived: Stanley Silverman
    written: Paul Schmidt
    music: Dmitri Shostakovich and other Russians, adapted
                        by Stanley Silverman
    lyrics: Translated by Paul Schmidt
    staging: Stanley Silverman
    sets: John Arnone
    costumes: David C. Woolard
Productions:
    (Off-Broadway) Opened December 16, 1986 for 31 performances
Reviews:
    High Fidelity (Musical America edition) 36:MA18-MA19, Dec 1986
    New York 20:49-50, Jan 12, 1987
    New York Times II, page 23, Nov 23, 1986
                    III, page 28, Dec 17, 1986
                    I, page 3, Jan 1, 1987
    New Yorker 62:79, Dec 29, 1986

Blackberries of 1932
    assembled by: Lee Posner
    book: Eddie Green
    music: Donald Heywood and Tom Peluso
    lyrics: Donald Heywood and Tom Peluso
    staging: Ben Bernard
Productions:
    Opened April 4, 1932 for 24 performances
Reviews:
    New York Times page 27, Apr 5, 1932

Blackbirds   (see Lew Leslie's Blackbirds)

Blackouts of 1949   (see Ken Murray's Blackouts of 1949)

Blackstone
    magic: Harry Blackstone
    original music: Michael Valenti
    staging: Kevin Carlisle
    sets: Peter Wolf
    costumes: Winn Morton
    choreography: Kevin Carlisle
Productions:
    Opened May 19, 1980 for 104 performances
Reviews:
    New York Theatre Critics' Reviews 1980:234
    New York Times III, page 10, May 20, 1980

Blame It on the Movies!
conceived: Ron Abel, Billy Barnes and David Galligan,
                   from an original idea by Franklin R. Levy
original songs: Billy Barnes
staging: David Galligan
sets: Fred Duer
costumes: Bonnie Stauch
choreography: Larry Hyman
Productions:
(Off-Broadway)   Opened May 16, 1989 for 3 performances
Reviews:
Los Angeles 33:262+, Nov 1988
New York Times III, page 22, May 18, 1989

Bless You All
sketches: Arnold Auerbach
music: Harold Rome
lyrics: Harold Rome
staging: John C. Wilson
sets: Oliver Smith
costumes: Miles White
choreography: Helen Tamiris
Productions:
Opened December 14, 1950 for 84 performances
Reviews:
Catholic World 172:387, Feb 1951
Christian Science Monitor Magazine page 7, Dec 23, 1950
Commonweal 53:327, Jan 5, 1951
Life 30:58+, Jan 22, 1951
Nation 171:709, Dec 30, 1950
New Republic 124:22, Jan 8, 1951
New York Theatre Critics' Reviews 1950:170+
New York Times VI, page 62, Dec 10, 1950
                  page 42, Dec 15, 1950
New Yorker 26:40, Dec 23, 1950
Newsweek 36:59, Dec 25, 1950
Theatre Arts 35:18, Feb 1951
Time 56:47, Dec 25, 1950

Blitzstein!
music: Marc Blitzstein
lyrics: Marc Blitzstein
staging: Ellen Pahl
sets: Cynthia Bernardi
Productions:
(Off-Broadway)   Opened November 30, 1966 for 7 performances
Reviews:
New York Times page 37, Nov 11, 1966
                page 58, Dec 1, 1966
                page 54, Dec 7, 1966

The Blonde Sinner
          book: Leon De Costa
          staging: Edwin Vail
Productions:
    Opened July 14, 1926 for 173 performances
Reviews:
    New York Times page 21, Jul 15, 1926

Blood Red Roses
          book: John Lewin
          music: Michael Valenti
          lyrics: John Lewin
          staging: Alan Schneider
          sets: Ed Wittstein
          costumes: Deidre Cartier
          choreography: Larry Fuller
Productions:
    Opened March 22, 1970 for one performance
Reviews:
    New York Theatre Critics' Reviews 1970:332
    New York Times page 48, Mar 23, 1970
                   page 20, Mar 27, 1970
    New Yorker 46:82+, Mar 28, 1970

Bloomer Girl
          book: Sig Herzig and Fred Saidy, based on a play by
                          Lilith and Dan James
          music: Harold Arlen
          lyrics: E. Y. Harburg
          staging: E. Y. Harburg
          sets: Lemuel Ayers
          costumes: Miles White
          choreography: Agnes de Mille
Productions:
    Opened October 5, 1944 for 654 performances
    Opened January 6, 1947 for 48 performances
Reviews:
    Catholic World 160:168, Nov 1944
                   164:455, Feb 1947
    Collier's 114:12-13+, Dec 9, 1944
    Commonweal 41:37, Oct 27, 1944
    Harper's 78:81, Dec 1944
    Life 17:67-70, Nov 6, 1944
    Nation 159:483, Oct 21, 1944
    New Republic 111:521, Oct 23, 1944
    New York Theatre Critics' Reviews 1944:118+
    New York Times VI, page 16, Sep 24, 1944
                   page 18, Oct 6, 1944
                   II, page 1, Oct 8, 1944
                   VI, page 52, Nov 19, 1944
                   II, page 6, Dec 17, 1944

II, page 1, Feb 24, 1946
II, page 3, Jan 5, 1947
page 33, Jan 7, 1947
page 19, Feb 15, 1947
New York Times Magazine pages 16-17, Sep 24, 1944
New Yorker 20:41, Oct 14, 1944
Newsweek 24:85-6, Oct 16, 1944
Theatre Arts 28:643-5, Nov 1944
29:78, Feb 1945
29:652, Nov 1945
Time 44:52, Oct 16, 1944

Blossom Time
book: Dorothy Donnelly, adapted from the German
              Das Dreimädlerhaus
music: Sigmund Romberg, derived from Franz Schubert
              themes
lyrics: Dorothy Donnelly
Productions:
Opened September 29, 1921 for 592 performances
Opened May 19, 1924 for 24 performances
Opened March 8, 1926 for 16 performances
Opened March 4, 1931 for 29 performances
Opened December 26, 1938 for 19 performances
Opened September 4, 1943 for 47 performances
Reviews:
Dramatic Mirror 84:520, Oct 8, 1921
Life (New York) 78:18, Oct 20, 1921
New York Clipper 69:17, Oct 12, 1921
New York Theatre Critics' Reviews 1943:286+
New York Times page 10, Sep 30, 1921
VI, page 1, Oct 9, 1921
page 26, Aug 8, 1922
page 14, May 22, 1923
page 22, May 16, 1924
page 15, May 20, 1924
VIII, page 8, Mar 7, 1926
page 32, Mar 5, 1931
VIII, page 4, Mar 22, 1931
page 12, Dec 27, 1938
page 21, Sep 6, 1943
Theatre Magazine 34:367, Dec 1921
34:388, Dec 1921

The Blue Bird (see Seeniaya Ptitza)

Blue Eyes
book: LeRoy Clemens and Leon Gordon
music: I. B. Kornblum and Z. Meyers
lyrics: LeRoy Clemens and Leon Gordon
staging: Clifford Brooke

Productions:
    Opened February 21, 1921 for 56 performances
Reviews:
    Dramatic Mirror 83:385-8, Feb 26, 1921
    New York Clipper 69:19, Mar 2, 1921
    New York Times page 11, Feb 22, 1921
    Theatre Magazine 33:340-41, May 1921

Blue Holiday
songs:	Duke Ellington, E. Y. Harburg, Earl Robinson
music:	Al Moritz
lyrics:	Al Moritz
staging:	Moe Hack
sets:	Perry Watkins
choreography:	Katherine Dunham

Productions:
    Opened May 21, 1945 for 8 performances
Reviews:
    New York Theatre Critics' Reviews 1945:216
    New York Times page 13, May 22, 1945

The Blue Kitten
book:	Otto Harbach and William Cary Duncan, adapted from Le Chasseur de Chez Maxim's
music:	Rudolf Friml
lyrics:	Otto Harbach and William Cary Duncan
staging:	Edgar Selwyn, Leon Errol, Julian Mitchell

Productions:
    Opened January 13, 1922 for 140 performances
Reviews:
    Dramatic Mirror 95:63, Mar 1922
    Life (New York) 79:18, Feb 2, 1922
    New York Clipper 69:20, Jan 11, 1922
    New York Times page 9, Jan 14, 1922
    Theatre Magazine 35:264, Apr 1922

The Blue Paradise
book:	Edgar Smith; based on a Viennese operetta by Leo Stein and Bela Jenbasch
music:	Edmund Eysler; additional numbers by Sigmund Romberg
lyrics:	Herbert Reynolds
staging:	J. H. Benrimo
choreography:	Ed Hutchinson

Productions:
    Opened August 5, 1915 for 356 performances
Reviews:
    Dramatic Mirror 74:8, Aug 11, 1915
                    74:2, Sep 1, 1915
                    75:1, Apr 1, 1916
    Green Book 14:623, Oct 1915

Nation 101:212, Aug 12, 1915
Opera Magazine 2:25+, Oct 1915
Theatre Magazine 22:113+, Sep 1915

Blue Plate Special
  book: Tom Edwards
  music: Harris Wheeler
  lyrics: Mary L. Fisher
  staging: Art Wolff
  sets: David Jenkins
  costumes: David Murin
  choreography: Douglas Norwick
Productions:
  (Off-Broadway) Opened October 18, 1983 for 48 performances
Reviews:
  New York 16:108+, Nov 28, 1983
  New York Times III, page 26, Nov 16, 1983

Blues, Ballads, and Sin-Songs (see Libby Holman's Blues, Ballads,
  and Sin-Songs)

Blues in the Night
  conceived: Sheldon Epps
  music: Bessie Smith and various composers
  lyrics: Bessie Smith and various authors
  staging: Sheldon Epps
  sets: John Falabella
  costumes: David Murin
Productions:
  (Off-Broadway) Opened March 26, 1980 for 51 performances
  Opened June 2, 1982 for 53 performances
  (Off-Broadway) Opened September 14, 1988 for 45 performances
Reviews:
  New York 15:71-2, Jun 14, 1982
           21:131-2, Sep 26, 1988
  New York Theatre Critics' Reviews 1982:254
  New York Times page 14, Apr 5, 1980
           III, page 17, Jun 3, 1982
           III, page 23, Sep 15, 1988
  New Yorker 58:106, Jun 14, 1982
           64:79, Sep 26, 1988

The Blushing Bride
  book: Cyrus Wood, based on a play by Edward Clark
  music: Sigmund Romberg
  lyrics: Cyrus Wood
  staging: Frank Smithson
Productions:
  Opened February 6, 1922 for 144 performances
Reviews:
  New York Clipper 70:20, Feb 15, 1922

New York Times page 12, Feb 7, 1922
Theatre Magazine 35:262, Apr 1922

Boccaccio
    book: Kenneth Cavander, based on stories from The
                        Decameron by Giovanni Boccaccio
    music: Richard Peaslee
    lyrics: Kenneth Cavander
    staging: Warren Enters
    sets: Robert U. Taylor
    costumes: Linda Fisher
Productions:
    Opened November 24, 1975 for 7 performances
Reviews:
    New York 8:103, Dec 15, 1975
    New York Theatre Critics' Reviews 1975:145
    New York Times page 42, Nov 25, 1975
    New Yorker 51:119-20, Dec 8, 1975

The Body Beautiful
    book: Joseph Stein and Will Glickman
    music: Jerry Bock
    lyrics: Sheldon Harnick
    staging: George Schaefer
    sets: Jean and William Eckart
    costumes: Noel Taylor
    choreography: Herbert Ross
Productions:
    Opened January 23, 1958 for 60 performances
Reviews:
    America 98:677, Mar 8, 1958
    Catholic World 187:70, Apr 1958
    Dance Magazine 32:15, Mar 1958
    New York Theatre Critics' Reviews 1958:386+
    New York Times page 15, Jan 24, 1958
    New Yorker 33:54-6, Feb 1, 1958
    Newsweek 51:55, Feb 3, 1958
    Saturday Review 41:28, Feb 15, 1958
    Theatre Arts 42:17-18, Apr 1958
    Time 71:78, Feb 3, 1958

Body Indian
    book: Hanay Geoigamah
    music: Ed Wapp
Productions:
    (Off-Off-Broadway) Opened October 25, 1972
Reviews:
    New York Times page 69, Oct 29, 1972

Bombo
    book: Harold Atteridge

music: Sigmund Romberg
lyrics: Harold Atteridge
staging: J. C. Huffman
Productions:
    Opened October 6, 1921 for 219 performances
Reviews:
    Dramatic Mirror 84:556, Oct 15, 1921
    New York Clipper 69:26, Oct 12, 1921
    New York Times page 20, Oct 7, 1921
                    VI, page 1, Oct 30, 1921
                    page 22, May 15, 1923
    Theatre Magazine 34:424, Dec 1921

Boom Boom
    book: Fanny Todd Mitchell, adapted from Louis Verneuil's
                    Mlle. Ma Mere
    music: Werner Janssen
    lyrics: Mann Holiner and J. Keirn Brennan
    staging: George Marion
Productions:
    Opened January 28, 1929 for 72 performances
Reviews:
    New York Times page 26, Jan 29, 1929
    Theatre Magazine 49:47, May 1929

Borge, Victor   (see Comedy in Music)

Borscht Capades
    staging: Mickey Katz
    sets: Charles Elson
Productions:
    Opened September 17, 1951 for 99 performances
Reviews:
    Catholic World 174:149, Nov 1951
    New Republic 125:21, Oct 1, 1951
    New York Theatre Critics' Reviews 1951:235
    New York Times page 38, Sep 18, 1951
    New Yorker 27:64, Sep 29, 1951
    Theatre Arts 35:8, Nov 1951

Bottomland
    book: Clarence Williams
    music: Clarence Williams
Productions:
    Opened June 27, 1927 for 21 performances
Reviews:
    New York Times page 29, Jun 28, 1927

The Boy Friend
    book: Sandy Wilson
    music: Sandy Wilson

lyrics: Sandy Wilson
staging: Vida Hope
sets: Reginald Woolley
costumes: Reginald Woolley
choreography: John Heawood

Productions:
  Opened September 30, 1954 for 485 performances
  (Off-Broadway) Season of 1957-58 for 763 performances
  (Off-Broadway) Opened February 4, 1966 for 17 performances
  Opened April 14, 1970 for 119 performances
  (Off-Off-Broadway) Opened November 7, 1974

Reviews:
  America 92:138, Oct 30, 1954
        122:54-5, May 9, 1970
  Catholic World 180:226, Dec 1954
  Commonweal 61:93, Oct 29, 1954
  Dance Magazine 32:17, May 1958
        44:84, Jun 1970
  Life 37:113-14+, Oct 25, 1954
  Mademoiselle 40:142, Nov 1954
  Nation 179:349, Oct 16, 1954
        210:574, May 11, 1970
  New Republic 131:23, Nov 1, 1954
  New York Theatre Critics' Reviews 1954:299+
        1970:277
  New York Times II, page 1, Sep 26, 1954
        page 20, Oct 1, 1954
        II, page 1, Oct 10, 1954
        VI, page 33, Nov 21, 1954
        II, page 5, Dec 23, 1956
        page 24, Jan 27, 1958
        II, page 1, Jan 25, 1959
        page 54, Apr 15, 1970
        II, page 5, Apr 26, 1970
        page 18, Jul 17, 1970
        page 42, Nov 11, 1974
  New Yorker 29:69, Feb 6, 1954
        30:58+, Oct 9, 1954
        46:95, Apr 25, 1970
  Newsweek 44:56, Oct 11, 1954
        75:64, Apr 27, 1970
  Saturday Review 37:24, Sep 18, 1954
        37:29, Oct 16, 1954
  Theatre Arts 38:18-19+, Dec 1954
  Time 64:93, Oct 11, 1954
        95:59, Apr 27, 1970
  Vogue 124:125, Oct 1, 1954

Boy Meets Boy
  book: Billy Solly and Donald Ward
  music: Billy Solly

lyrics: Billy Solly
staging: Ron Troutman
sets: David Sackeroff
costumes: Sherry Buchs
choreography: James Fradrich
Productions:
  (Off-Broadway) Opened September 17, 1975 for 295 performances
Reviews:
  Los Angeles 21:132, Mar 1976
  New York 8:69, Oct 6, 1975
  New York Times page 49, Sep 18, 1975

Boys and Girls Together
  book: Ed Wynn and Pat C. Flick
  music: Sammy Fain
  lyrics: Jack Yellen and Irving Kahal
  staging: Ed Wynn
  sets: William Oden Waller
  costumes: Irene Sharaff and Veronica
  choreography: Albertina Rasch
Productions:
  Opened October 1, 1940 for 191 performances
Reviews:
  Catholic World 152:218-19, Nov 1940
  Life 9:57-8+, Oct 7, 1940
  Nation 151:345, Oct 12, 1940
  New Republic 103:526, Oct 14, 1940
  New York Theatre Critics' Reviews 1940:266+
                                    1941:475+
  New York Times page 28, Sep 5, 1940
               IX, page 1, Sep 15, 1940
               page 19, Oct 2, 1940
               IX, page 1, Oct 13, 1940
  Newsweek 16:74, Oct 14, 1940
  Stage 1:8, Nov 1940
        1:42-3, Nov 1940
        1:7, Dec 1940
  Theatre Arts 24:773-4, Nov 1940
  Time 36:62, Oct 4, 1940

The Boys from Syracuse
  book: George Abbott, based on Shakespeare's The
                 Comedy of Errors
  music: Richard Rodgers
  lyrics: Lorenz Hart
  staging: George Abbott
  sets: Jo Mielziner
  costumes: Irene Sharaff
  choreography: George Balanchine
Productions:
  Opened November 23, 1938 for 235 performances

(Off-Broadway) Opened April 15, 1963 for 469 performances
(Off-Off-Broadway) Opened December 2, 1976
Reviews:
    Catholic World 148:474-6, Jan 1939
    Commonweal 29:190, Dec 9, 1938
    Life 5:43-4, Dec 12, 1938
    Nation 147:638, Dec 10, 1938
    New Republic 97:173, Dec 14, 1938
    New York Times IX, page 2, Nov 13, 1938
               page 36, Nov 24, 1938
               X, page 5, Dec 4, 1938
               page 31, Apr 16, 1963
               VI, page 106, May 5, 1963
               II, page 1, Jun 2, 1963
               page 14, Nov 9, 1963
               page 37, Jun 19, 1964
               III, page 17, May 30, 1984
    New Yorker 39:84, Apr 27, 1963
    North American Review 247 no. 1:159-60, Mar 1939
    Saturday Review 46:33, Aug 10, 1963
    Theatre Arts 23:10-11, Jan 1939
           47:13, Jun 1963
           47:14-15, Jun 1963
    Time 32:35, Sep 26, 1938
        32:44, Dec 5, 1938

Bravo! (see El Bravo!)

Bravo Giovanni
    book: A. J. Russell, adapted from Howard Shaw's
                    The Crime of Giovanni Venturi
    music: Milton Schafer
    lyrics: Ronny Graham
    staging: Stanley Prager
    sets: Robert Randolph
    costumes: Ed Wittstein
    choreography: Carol Haney and Buzz Miller
Productions:
    Opened May 19, 1962 for 76 performances
Reviews:
    America 107:429-30, Jun 23, 1962
    Commonweal 76:304, Jun 15, 1962
    New York Theatre Critics' Reviews 1962:276+
    New York Times page 41, May 21, 1962
               II, page 1, May 27, 1962
               page 34, Sep 12, 1962
    New Yorker 38:91-2, May 26, 1962
    Newsweek 59:65, Jun 4, 1962
    Saturday Review 45:24, Jun 2, 1962
    Theatre Arts 46:67-9, Jul 1962
    Time 79:83, Jun 1, 1962

Brel, Jacques   (see Jacques Brel)

Brigadoon
    book: Alan Jay Lerner
    music: Frederick Loewe
    lyrics: Alan Jay Lerner
    staging: Robert Lewis
    sets: Oliver Smith
    costumes: David Ffolkes
    choreography: Agnes de Mille
Productions:
    Opened March 13, 1947 for 581 performances
    Opened May 2, 1950 for 24 performances
    Opened March 27, 1957 for 47 performances
    Opened May 30, 1962 for 16 performances
    Opened January 30, 1963 for 16 performances
    Opened December 23, 1964 for 17 performances
    Opened December 13, 1967 for 23 performances
    Opened October 16, 1980 for 133 performances
Reviews:
    Catholic World 165:73, Apr 1947
                   185:227, Jun 1957
    Commonweal 45:593, Mar 28, 1947
               66:128, May 3, 1957
    Dance Magazine 55:104, Jan 1981
    Harper's 81:174, May 1947
    Life 23:57-60, Jul 21, 1947
    Nation 231:489-91, Nov 8, 1980
    New Republic 116:38, Mar 31, 1947
    New York 13:74-6, Nov 3, 1980
             19:70+, Mar 17, 1986
    New York Theatre Critics' Reviews 1947:427+
                                      1957:305+
                                      1980:144
                                      1986:352
    New York Times II, page 1, Mar 9, 1947
                   VI, page 32, Mar 9, 1947
                   page 28, Mar 14, 1947
                   II, page 1, Mar 23, 1947
                   II, page 1, Apr 6, 1947
                   II, page 1, Jun 22, 1947
                   page 11, Apr 16, 1949
                   page 36, May 3, 1950
                   II, page 3, May 21, 1950
                   II, page 1, Dec 31, 1950
                   page 37, Mar 28, 1957
                   II, page 1, Apr 7, 1957
                   page 21, May 31, 1962
                   page 6, Feb 1, 1963
                   page 9, Dec 24, 1964
                   page 59, Dec 14, 1967

III, page 3, Oct 17, 1980
II, page 1, Oct 26, 1980
New Yorker 23:54+, Mar 22, 1947
56:156, Oct 27, 1980
62:114, Mar 10, 1986
Newsweek 29:84, Mar 24, 1947
96:123, Oct 27, 1980
Saturday Review 30:24-6, Apr 5, 1947
School and Society 66:245-7, Sep 27, 1947
68:386, Dec 4, 1948
Theatre Arts 31:21, May 1947
31:41, Jun 1947
41:18, Jun 1957
46:58-9, Aug 1962
47:64-5, Mar 1963
Theatre Crafts 15:30-3+, Jan 1981
Time 49:66, Mar 24, 1947
116:99, Oct 27, 1980

Bright Eyes
book: Charles Dickson; adapted from Mistakes Will
Happen by Charles Dickson and Grant Stewart
music: Karl Hoschna
lyrics: Otto A. Hauerbach
Productions:
Opened February 28, 1910 for 40 performances
Reviews:
Cosmopolitan 49:81, Jun 1910
Dramatic Mirror 63:6, Mar 12, 1910
Hampton 24:700-1, May 1910
Metropolitan Magazine 32:404, Jun 1910
Theatre Magazine 11:127, Apr 1910

Bright Lights of 1944
book: Norman Anthony and Charles Sherman (additional
dialogue by Joseph Erens)
music: Jerry Livingston
lyrics: Mack David
staging: Dan Eckley
sets: Perry Watkins
costumes: Perry Watkins
choreography: Truly McGee
Productions:
Opened September 16, 1943 for 4 performances
Reviews:
New York Theatre Critics' Reviews 1943:276+
New York Times page 27, Sep 17, 1943
II, page 1, Sep 26, 1943
Theatre Arts 27:647-8, Nov 1943

Bring Back Birdie
conceived: Joe Layton

book: Michael Stewart
music: Charles Strouse
lyrics: Lee Adams
staging: Joe Layton
sets: David Mitchell
costumes: Fred Voelpel
choreography: Daniel Troob
Productions:
Opened March 5, 1981 for 4 performances
Reviews:
New York Theatre Critics' Reviews 1981:324
New York Times III, page 4, Mar 6, 1981

Bringing Up Father
book: Nat Leroy; based on George McManus's cartoon
music: Seymour Furth
lyrics: R. F. Carroll
staging: Richard F. Carroll
Productions:
Opened April 6, 1925 for 24 performances
No Reviews.

Broadway Dandies (cabaret revue)
staging: Robert Johnnene
sets: Wilfred Surita
costumes: Cheena Lee
choreography: Henry Lee Tang
Productions:
(Off-Broadway) Opened December 17, 1974 for 8 performances
No reviews.

Broadway Follies
conceived: Donald Driver
music: Walter Marks
lyrics: Walter Marks
staging: Donald Driver
sets: Peter Larkin
costumes: Alvin Colt
choreography: Arthur Faria
Productions:
Opened March 15, 1981 for one performance
Reviews:
New York Theatre Critics' Reviews 1981:318
New York Times III, page 13, Mar 16, 1981
New Yorker 57:62, Mar 30, 1981

A Broadway Musical
book: William F. Brown
music: Charles Strouse
lyrics: Lee Adams
staging: Gower Champion

```
sets:              Peter Wexler
costumes:          Randy Barcelo
choreography:      Donald Johnston and George Bunt
```
Productions:
(Off-Broadway) Opened October 10, 1978 for 26 performances
Opened December 21, 1978 for one performance
Reviews:
New York Theatre Critics' Reviews 1978:150
New York Times III, page 3, Dec 22, 1978

Broadway Nights
```
music:             Sam Timberg, Lee David, Maurice Rubens
lyrics:            Moe Jaffe
staging:           Busby Berkeley and Stanley Logan
```
Productions:
Opened July 15, 1929 for 40 performances
Reviews:
New York Times page 23, Jul 16, 1929
Outlook 152:595, Aug 7, 1929
Theatre Magazine 50:41, Sep 1929

Broadway Sho-Window
```
sketches:          Eugene Conrad
lyrics:            Eugene Conrad
sets:              Clark Robinson
choreography:      Bill Powers
```
Productions:
(Off-Broadway) Opened April 12, 1936
Reviews:
New York Times page 14, Apr 13, 1936

Broadway to Paris
```
book:              George Bronson Howard and Harold Atteridge
music:             Max Hoffman; additional numbers by Anatol
                   Friedland
lyrics:            George Bronson Howard and Harold Atteridge
staging:           Ned Wayburn
```
Productions:
Opened November 20, 1912 for 77 performances
Reviews:
Theatre Magazine 17:5, Jan 1913
                  17:6, Jan 1913

The Broadway Whirl
```
music:             Harry Tierney and George Gershwin
lyrics:            Joseph McCarthy, Richard Carle, B. G. DeSylva
                   and John Henry Mears
```
Productions:
Opened June 8, 1921 for (8) performances
Reviews:
New York Clipper 69:29, Jun 15, 1921

New York Times page 10, Jun 9, 1921
Theatre Magazine 34:98, Aug 1921

A Broken Idol
    book: Hal Stephens
    music: Egbert Van Alsteyne
    lyrics: Harry Williams
    staging: Gus Sohlke
Productions:
    Opened August 16, 1909 for 40 performances
Reviews:
    Dramatic Mirror 62:7, Aug 28, 1909
    Metropolitan Magazine 31:128-9, Oct 1909
    Theatre Magazine 19:iii+, Oct 1909

Broken Toys
    book: Keith Berger
    music: Keith Berger
    lyrics: Keith Berger
    staging: Carl Haber
    sets: Lisa Beck
    costumes: Mara Lonner and Karen Dusenbury
Productions:
    (Off-Broadway) Opened July 16, 1982 for 29 performances
No reviews.

The Brooklyn Bridge
    book: Dorothy Chansky
    music: Scott MacLarty
    lyrics: Dorothy Chansky
    staging: Marjorie Melnick
    sets: Terry Bennett
    costumes: Karen Gerson
    choreography: Missy Whitchurch
Productions:
    (Off-Broadway) Opened August 17, 1983 for 28 performances
Reviews:
    New York Times I, page 60, Aug 28, 1983

Brown Buddies
    book: Carl Rickman
    music: Joe Jordan and Millard Thomas
    lyrics: Carl Rickman
Productions:
    Opened October 7, 1930 for 111 performances
Reviews:
    New York Times page 29, Oct 8, 1930

Brown, Oscar (see Worlds of Oscar Brown)

Brownstone
    book: Josh Rubins and Andrew Cadiff

music: Peter Larson and Josh Rubins
lyrics: Peter Larson and Josh Rubins
staging: Andrew Cadiff
sets: Loren Sherman
costumes: Ann Emonts
choreography: Don Bondi
Productions:
  (Off-Off-Broadway) Opened May 23, 1984
  (Off-Broadway) Opened October 8, 1986 for 69 performances
Reviews:
  New York 17:83, Jun 18, 1984
           19:119-20, Nov 17, 1986
  New York Times I, page 68, Jun 10, 1984
                 III, page 3, Nov 7, 1986
  New Yorker 60:89, Jun 18, 1984
             62:126, Nov 17, 1986

Bubbling Brown Sugar

book: Loften Mitchell, based on a concept by Rosetta
                     LeNoire
music: Various composers
lyrics: Various authors
original music: Danny Holgate, Emme Kemp and Lillian Lopez
staging: Robert M. Cooper
sets: Clarke Dunham
costumes: Bernard Johnson
choreography: Billy Wilson
Productions:
  Opened March 2, 1976 for 766 performances
Reviews:
  Dance Magazine 50:45-6, Jun 1976
  Ebony 31:124-6+, Feb 1976
  Essence 6:28, Jan 1976
          7:125, Aug 1976
  Los Angeles 22:238+, May 1977
  Nation 222:381-2, Mar 27, 1976
  New West 2:SC20, Mar 14, 1977
  New York 9:64+, Mar 22, 1976
  New York Theatre Critics' Reviews 1976:352
  New York Times page 30, Mar 3, 1976
  New Yorker 52:51, Mar 15, 1976
  Time 107:79, Mar 22, 1976

Buck White

book: Oscar Brown Jr.; based on the play Big Time
                     Buck White by Joseph Dolan Tuotti
music: Oscar Brown Jr.
lyrics: Oscar Brown Jr.
staging: Oscar Brown Jr. and Jean Pace
sets: Edward Burbridge
costumes: Jean Pace

Productions:
  Opened December 2, 1969 for 7 performances
Reviews:
  New York Theatre Critics' Reviews 1969:170
  New York Times page 56, Oct 30, 1969
                  II, page 1, Nov 23, 1969
                  page 42, Nov 29, 1969
                  VI, page 32, Nov 30, 1969
                  page 63, Dec 3, 1969
                  page 54, Dec 5, 1969
                  II, page 5, Dec 7, 1969

Buddies
  book: George V. Hobart
  music: B. C. Hilliam
  lyrics: B. C. Hilliam
Productions:
  Opened October 27, 1919 for 259 performances
Reviews:
  Independent 101:86, Jan 17, 1920
  New York Times page 11, Oct 29, 1919
  Theatre Magazine 31:18, Jan 1920

Buddy Hackett (see Eddie Fisher-Buddy Hackett at the Palace)

The Bunch and Judy
  book: Anne Caldwell and Hugh Ford
  music: Jerome Kern
  lyrics: Anne Caldwell
  staging: Fred G. Latham
Productions:
  Opened November 28, 1922 for 63 performances
Reviews:
  New York Clipper 70:20, Dec 6, 1922
  New York Times VIII, page 6, Nov 12, 1922
                  page 20, Nov 29, 1922
  Theatre Magazine 37:20, Feb 1923

A Bundle of Nerves
  conceived: Brian Lasser
  music: Brian Lasser
  lyrics: Geoff Leon and Edward Dunn
  staging: Arthur Faria
  sets: Barry Arnold
  costumes: David Toser
  choreography: Arthur Faria
Productions:
  (Off-Broadway) Opened March 13, 1983 for 33 performances
Reviews:
  New York Times III, page 22, Mar 17, 1983

Bunk of 1926
  sketches: Gene Lockhart and Percy Waxman

music: Gene Lockhart
lyrics: Gene Lockhart and Percy Waxman
Productions:
    Opened February 16, 1926 for 104 performances
Reviews:
    Life (New York) 87:21, Jun 24, 1926
    New York Times page 12, Feb 17, 1926
                     page 25, Apr 23, 1926
    Theatre Magazine 43:14, May 1926
                     43:18, May 1926

But Never Jam Today
    book: Vinnette Carroll and Bob Larimer, adapted from
                        the works of Lewis Carroll
    music: Bert Keyes and Bob Larimer
    lyrics: Bob Larimer
    staging: Vinnette Carroll
    sets: William Schroder
    costumes: William Schroder
    choreography: Talley Beatty
Productions:
    (Off-Off-Broadway) Opened August 1978 for 12 performances
    Opened July 31, 1979 for 8 performances
Reviews:
    New York 12:82-3, Aug 13, 1979
    New York Theatre Critics' Reviews 1979:168
    New York Times page 107, Sep 12, 1978
                     III, page 18, Aug 1, 1979

Buttrio Square
    book: Billy Gilbert and Gen Genovese, based on a play
                        by Hal Cranton from an original story by Gen
                        Genovese
    music: Arthur Jones and Fred Stamer
    lyrics: Gen Genovese
    staging: Eugene Loring
    sets: Samuel Leve
    costumes: Sal Anthony
    choreography: Eugene Loring
Productions:
    Opened October 14, 1952 for 7 performances
Reviews:
    New York Theatre Critics' Reviews 1952:238+
    New York Times page 40, Oct 15, 1952
    New Yorker 28:30, Oct 25, 1952
    Time 60:76, Oct 27, 1952

Buy Bonds, Buster!
    book: Jack Holmes; based on an original concept by
                        Bob Miller and Billy Conklin
    music: Jack Holmes

lyrics: M. B. Miller
staging: John Bishop
sets: William Pitkin
choreography: Bick Goss
Productions:
(Off-Broadway)   Opened June 4, 1972 for one performance
Reviews:
New York Times page 41, Jun 5, 1972

By Bernstein
conceived: Betty Comden and Adolph Green with Michael
               Bawtree, Norman L. Berman and the Chelsea
               Theater Center
book: Betty Comden and Adolph Green
music: Leonard Bernstein
lyrics: Leonard Bernstein, Betty Comden and Adolph
               Green, John Latouche, Jerry Leiber, and Stephen
               Sondheim
staging: Michael Bawtree
sets: Lawrence King, Michael H. Yeargan
costumes: Lawrence King, Michael H. Yeargan
Productions:
(Off-Broadway)   Opened November 23, 1975 for 17 performances
Reviews:
New York 8:101, Dec 8, 1975
New York Theatre Critics' Reviews 1975: 97
New York Times page 31, Nov 24, 1975
               II, page 5, Dec 7, 1975
New Yorker 51:120-1, Dec 8, 1975

By Jupiter
book: Richard Rodgers and Lorenz Hart, based on
               Julian F. Thompson's The Warrior's Husband
music: Richard Rodgers
lyrics: Lorenz Hart
staging: Joshua Logan
sets: Jo Mielziner
costumes: Irene Sharaff
choreography: Robert Alton
Productions:
Opened June 3, 1942 for 427 performances
(Off-Off-Broadway)   Opened February 12, 1965 for 14 per-
formances
(Off-Broadway)   Opened January 19, 1967 for 118 performances
Reviews:
America 116:264, Feb 18, 1967
Catholic World 155:472-3, Jul 1942
Commonweal 36:255-6, Jul 3, 1942
Independent Woman 22:155, May 1943
Life 12:82-5, Jun 1, 1942
Nation 154:693, Jun 13, 1942

New York Theatre Critics' Reviews 1942:274+
New York Times page 22, Jun 4, 1942
                VIII, page 1, Aug 30, 1942
                page 28, Jan 20, 1967
                page 52, Apr 20, 1967
New Yorker 18:36, Jun 13, 1942
           42:46+, Jan 28, 1967
Newsweek 19:70-1, Jun 15, 1942
Theatre Arts 26:607, Oct 1942
Time 39:66, Jun 15, 1942

By Strouse
    book: Charles Strouse
    music: Charles Strouse
    lyrics: Lee Adams and Martin Charnin
    staging: Charles Strouse
    sets: Connie and Peter Wexler
    choreography: Mary Kyte
Productions:
    (Off-Broadway) Opened February 1, 1978 for 156 performances
Reviews:
    Horizon 21:59, May 1978

By the Beautiful Sea
    book: Herbert and Dorothy Fields
    music: Arthur Schwartz
    lyrics: Dorothy Fields
    staging: Marshall Jamison
    sets: Jo Mielziner
    costumes: Irene Sharaff
    choreography: Helen Tamiris
Productions:
    Opened April 8, 1954 for 270 performances
Reviews:
    America 91:171-2, May 8, 1954
    Catholic World 179:225, Jun 1954
    Commonweal 60:95-6, Apr 30, 1954
    Life 36:109-10, May 17, 1954
    Mademoiselle 38:125, Apr 1954
    Nation 178:370, Apr 24, 1954
    New York Theatre Critics' Reviews 1954:335+
    New York Times page 20, Apr 9, 1954
                    II, page 1, Apr 18, 1954
    New Yorker 30:64-6, Apr 17, 1954
    Newsweek 43:66, Apr 19, 1954
    Saturday Review 37:32, May 1, 1954
    Theatre Arts 38:18-19, Jun 1954
    Time 63:85, Apr 19, 1954

By the Way
    book: Ronald Jeans and Harold Simpson

music: Vivian Ellis
lyrics: Graham John
staging: Jack Hulbert
Productions:
    Opened December 28, 1925 for 176 performances
Reviews:
    New York Times page 20, Dec 29, 1925
                    VIII, page 1, Apr 4, 1926
                    page 20, Apr 16, 1926

Bye, Bye, Barbara
    book: Sidney Toler and Alonzo Price
    music: Carlo and Sanders
Productions:
    Opened August 25, 1924 for 16 performances
Reviews:
    New York Times page 6, Aug 26, 1924

Bye Bye Birdie
    book: Michael Stewart
    music: Charles Strouse
    lyrics: Lee Adams
    staging: Gower Champion
    sets: Robert Randolph
    costumes: Miles White
    choreography: Gower Champion
Productions:
    Opened April 14, 1960 for 607 performances
Reviews:
    Life 48:143+, May 23, 1960
    Nation 190:390, Apr 30, 1960
    New York Theatre Critics' Reviews 1960:296+
    New York Times VI, page 90, Mar 27, 1960
                    page 13, Apr 15, 1960
                    page 13, Jun 17, 1960
    New Yorker 36:116-18, Apr 23, 1960
    Newsweek 55:100, Apr 25, 1960
    Saturday Review 43:26, Apr 30, 1960
    Time 75:50, Apr 25, 1960

Bye, Bye, Bonnie
    book: Louis Simon and Bide Dudley
    staging: Edgar McGregor
Productions:
    Opened January 13, 1927 for 125 performances
Reviews:
    New York Times page 15, Jan 14, 1927

-C-

Cabalgata (A Night in Spain)
material:	Iberian folksongs
staging:	Daniel Cordoba
sets:	Luis Marquez
costumes:	Daniel Cordoba

Productions:
Opened July 7, 1949 for 76 performances
Reviews:
Catholic World 169:467, Sep 1949
New York Theatre Critics' Reviews 1949:284
New York Times page 14, Jul 8, 1949
II, page 1, Aug 28, 1949

Cabaret
book:	Joe Masteroff; based on John Van Druten's play I Am a Camera and stories by Christopher Isherwood
music:	John Kander
lyrics:	Fred Ebb
staging:	Harold Prince
sets:	Boris Aronson
costumes:	Patricia Zipprodt
choreography:	Ronald Field

Productions:
Opened November 20, 1966 for 1,165 performances
(Off-Off-Broadway) Opened April 22, 1985 for 3 performances
Opened October 22, 1987 for 262 performances
Reviews:
America 116:25, Jan 7, 1967
158:42, Jan 16, 1988
Christian Century 84:1071-2, Aug 23, 1967
Commonweal 85:326, Dec 16, 1967
Dance Magazine 41:26+, Jan 1967
61:66-7, Oct 1987
62:73-4, Jan 1988
Harper's Bazaar 120:134-5, Jun 1987
Life 62:16, Jan 13, 1967
62:82-3, Jan 13, 1967
Look 31:72-4+, Mar 7, 1967
Los Angeles 32:306+, Aug 1987
Mademoiselle 64:186-7, Mar 1967
Nation 203:651-2, Dec 12, 1966
245:571-2, Nov 14, 1987
New Leader 70:19, Dec 28, 1987
New York 20:112, Nov 2, 1987
New York Theatre Critics' Reviews 1966:240
1987:146
New York Times VI, page 128, Nov 20, 1966
page 62, Nov 21, 1966

II, page 5, Dec 4, 1966
II, page 1, Feb 26, 1967
page 19, Jan 12, 1968
page 32, Mar 1, 1968
page 74, Feb 2, 1969
page 30, Sep 5, 1969
XI, page 10, Jul 5, 1987
III, page 3, Oct 23, 1987
II, page 5, Nov 15, 1987
New Yorker 42:155-6, Dec 3, 1966
63:148-9, Nov 2, 1987
Newsweek 68:96, Dec 5, 1966
Reporter 36:49, Mar 9, 1967
Saturday Review 49:64, Dec 10, 1966
Time 88:84, Dec 2, 1966
130:95, Nov 2, 1987
Vogue 149:52, Jan 1, 1967
177:128, Oct 1987

Cabin in the Sky

book: Lynn Root
music: Vernon Duke
lyrics: John La Touche
staging: George Balanchine
sets: Boris Aronson
costumes: Boris Aronson
Productions:
    Opened October 25, 1940 for 156 performances
    (Off-Broadway) Opened January 21, 1964 for 47 performances
Reviews:
    America 110:239, Feb 15, 1964
    Catholic World 152:333-4, Dec 1940
    Commonweal 33:80, Nov 8, 1940
    Life 9:63+, Dec 9, 1940
    Nation 151:458, Nov 9, 1940
    New Republic 103:661, Nov 11, 1940
    New York Theatre Critics' Reviews 1940:242+
                                      1941:463+
    New York Times page 19, Oct 26, 1940
                   IX, page 3, Nov 10, 1940
                   page 32, Jan 22, 1964
                   page 12, Feb 29, 1964
    Newsweek 16:62, Nov 4, 1940
    Stage 1:24-5, Dec 1940
    Theatre Arts 24:841-2+, Dec 1940
    Time 36:51, Nov 4, 1940

Cafe Crown

book: Hy Kraft, based on his play
music: Albert Hague
lyrics: Marty Brill

staging: Jerome Eskow
sets: Sam Leve
costumes: Ruth Morley
choreography: Ronald Field
Productions:
Opened April 17, 1964 for 3 performances
Reviews:
Dance Magazine 38:26-7, May 1964
New York Theatre Critics' Reviews 1964:284+
New York Times page 32, Apr 18, 1964
      page 83, Apr 19, 1964
New Yorker 40:130, Apr 25, 1964

Cage aux Folles, La (see La Cage aux Folles)

Call Me Charlie
 book: Michael Moran
 music: Sam Burtis and Jane Blackstone
 lyrics: Sam Burtis and Jane Blackstone
Productions:
(Off-Off-Broadway) Opened April 1974
(Off-Off-Broadway) Opened May 11, 1974
Reviews:
New York Times page 46, Apr 2, 1974

Call Me Madam
 book: Howard Lindsay and Russel Crouse
 music: Irving Berlin
 lyrics: Irving Berlin
 staging: George Abbott
 sets: Raoul Pene du Bois
 costumes: Raoul Pene du Bois
 choreography: Jerome Robbins
Productions:
Opened October 12, 1950 for 644 performances
(Off-Off-Broadway) Opened November 8, 1973
Reviews:
Catholic World 172:225, Dec 1950
Christian Science Monitor Magazine page 6, Oct 21, 1950
Collier's 126:22-3+, Oct 21, 1950
Commonweal 53:94, Nov 3, 1950
Life 29:117-18+, Oct 30, 1950
Nation 171:370, Oct 21, 1950
New Republic 123:23, Nov 6, 1950
New York Theatre Critics' Reviews 1950:243+
New York Times II, page 1, Sep 3, 1950
     VI, page 24, Oct 1, 1950
     II, page 1, Oct 8, 1950
     page 25, Oct 13, 1950
     II, page 1, Oct 22, 1950
     II, page 1, Apr 29, 1951

                    page 84, Mar 16, 1952
                    page 17, Mar 17, 1952
                    II, page 3, Apr 13, 1952
                    page 35, May 6, 1952
                    page 44, Dec 16, 1952
    New Yorker 26:55, Oct 21, 1950
    Newsweek 36:84, Oct 23, 1950
    Saturday Review 33:49-50, Sep 30, 1950
                    33:42-4, Oct 28, 1950
    Theatre Arts 34:16-17, Nov 1950
                    34:15, Dec 1950
    Time 56:58, Oct 23, 1950

Call Me Mister
    book: Arnold Auerbach and Arnold B. Horwitt
    music: Harold Rome
    lyrics: Harold Rome
    staging: Robert H. Gordon
    sets: Lester Polokov
    costumes: Grace Houston
    choreography: John Wray
Productions:
    Opened April 18, 1946 for 734 performances
Reviews:
    Catholic World 163:264, Jun 1946
    Collier's 117:22-3, May 18, 1946
    Commonweal 44:72, May 3, 1946
    Forum 105:938-9, Jun 1946
    Life 20:131-2+, May 27, 1946
    Modern Music 23 No. 3:223, Jul 1946
    New Republic 114:662, May 6, 1946
    New York Theatre Critics' Reviews 1946:403+
    New York Times VI, page 26, Apr 7, 1946
                    II, page 1, Apr 14, 1946
                    II, page 1, Apr 18, 1946
                    page 26, Apr 19, 1946
                    II, page 1, Aug 4, 1946
                    II, page 3, Apr 13, 1947
                    II, page 1, June 29, 1947
                    II, page 1, Oct 12, 1947
                    II, page 3, Dec 14, 1947
    New York Times Magazine pages 26-7, Apr 7, 1946
    New Yorker 22:42, Apr 27, 1946
    Newsweek 27:80, Apr 29, 1946
    Saturday Review 29:24-6, May 18, 1946
    Theatre Arts 30:322, Jun 1946
    Time 47:68+, Apr 29, 1946
        47:70, May 6, 1946

Calling All Stars
    sketches: Lew Brown

music: Harry Akst
lyrics: Lew Brown
staging: Lew Brown and Thomas Mitchell
sets: Nat Karson
choreography: Sara Mildred Strauss
Productions:
  Opened December 13, 1934 for 36 performances
Reviews:
  New York Times page 28, Dec 14, 1934
  Time 24:13, Dec 24, 1934

Cambridge Circus
  sketches: Tim Brooke-Taylor, Graham Chapman, John
                       Cleese, David Hatch, Jo Kendall, Jonathan Lynn,
                       Bill Oddie, and others
  music: Bill Oddie, Hugh MacDonald, David Palmer
  staging: Humphrey Barclay
  sets: Stephen Mullin
  costumes: Judy Birdwood
Productions:
  Opened October 6, 1964 for 23 performances
Reviews:
  Dance Magazine 38:16-17, Dec 1964
  Nation 199:286, Oct 26, 1964
  New York Theatre Critics' Reviews 1964:201+
  New York Times page 53, Oct 7, 1964
                page 44, Oct 27, 1964
  Time 84:77, Oct 16, 1964

Camelot
  book: Alan Jay Lerner, based on T. H. White's The
                       Once and Future King
  music: Frederick Loewe
  lyrics: Alan Jay Lerner
  staging: Moss Hart
  sets: Oliver Smith
  costumes: Adrian and Tony Duquette
  choreography: Hanya Holm
Productions:
  Opened December 3, 1960 for 873 performances
  Opened July 8, 1980 for 56 performances
  Opened November 15, 1981 for 48 performances
Reviews:
  America 104:546, Jan 21, 1961
  Commonweal 74:379, Jul 7, 1961
  Coronet 50:15, May 1961
  Dance Magazine 35:16, Feb 1961
                54:108-9, Sep 1980
  Horizon 3:102-4, May 1961
  Life 49:90-3, Dec 19, 1960
  Los Angeles 20:102B+, Oct 1975

26:318, May 1981
26:238+, Jun 1981
Maclean's 93:54, Jun 23, 1980
Musical America 81:264, Jan 1961
Nation 191:510, Dec 24, 1960
National Review 10:224-5, Apr 8, 1961
New York 13:50-1, Jul 21, 1980
      14:89, Nov 30, 1981
New York Theatre Critics' Reviews 1960:154+
                    1980:202
                    1981:114
New York Times VI, page 4, Oct 2, 1960
              page 35, Oct 3, 1960
              VI, page 68, Oct 16, 1960
              II, page 1, Nov 27, 1960
              page 42, Dec 5, 1960
              II, page 5, Dec 11, 1960
              VI, pages 26-27, Dec 11, 1960
              page 20, Aug 7, 1961
              VI, page 34, Dec 3, 1961
              page 5, Jan 5, 1963
              page 34, Aug 20, 1964
              III, page 15, Jul 9, 1980
              III, page 16, Nov 16, 1981
New York Times Magazine pages 18-19, Sep 18, 1960
                    pages 12-16+, Jul 6, 1980
New Yorker 36:95, Dec 10, 1960
          56:81, Jul 21, 1980
Newsweek 56:104-5, Dec 5, 1960
        56:94, Dec 12, 1960
        96:83, Jul 21, 1980
Saturday Review 43:30, Dec 24, 1960
Theatre Arts 44:25-6, Dec 1960
             45:8-9, Feb 1961
Time 76:78, Oct 17, 1960
     76:64-6+, Nov 14, 1960
     76:63, Dec 19, 1960
     116:71, Jul 21, 1980
Vogue 137:116-17, Feb 15, 1961

Can-Can
   book: Abe Burrows
   music: Cole Porter
   lyrics: Cole Porter
   staging: Abe Burrows
   sets: Jo Mielziner
   costumes: Motley
   choreography: Michael Kidd
Productions:
   Opened May 7, 1953 for 892 performances
   Opened May 16, 1962 for 16 performances

(Off-Off-Broadway) Opened November 16, 1978
Opened April 30, 1981 for 5 performances
Reviews:
America 89:228, May 23, 1953
107:361, Jun 2, 1962
Catholic World 177:308-9, Jul 1953
Commonweal 58:200, May 29, 1953
Dance Magazine 62:72-3, Sep 1988
Life 34:59-60+, Jun 1, 1953
Look 17:36-8, May 19, 1953
Nation 176:441-2, May 23, 1953
New York 14:58 May 11, 1981
New York Theatre Critics' Reviews 1953:304+
1981:251
New York Times VI, page 68, Apr 26, 1953
page 28, May 8, 1953
II, page 1, May 17, 1953
II, page 3, Oct 24, 1954
page 32, May 17, 1962
page 87, Nov 19, 1978
III, page 3, May 1, 1981
New York Times Magazine pages 68-9, Apr 26, 1953
New Yorker 29:59, May 16, 1953
57:71, May 11, 1981
Saturday Review 36:28, May 23, 1953
Theatre Arts 37:14, Jul 1953
Time 61:69, May 18, 1953
Vogue 121:86-7, Apr 15, 1953

The Canary
book: based on the French of Georges Barr and Louis
               Vernevil
music: Ivan Caryll, Irving Berlin and Harry Tierney
staging: Fred G. Latham and Edward Royce
Productions:
Opened November 4, 1918 for 152 performances
Reviews:
Dramatic Mirror 79:507, Oct 5, 1918
79:795, Nov 30, 1918
79:899, Dec 21, 1918
New York Dramatic News 65:10, Nov 9, 1918
New York Times page 11, Nov 5, 1918
Theatre Magazine 28:378, Dec 1918
29:37, Jan 1919

Canary Cottage
book: Oliver Morosco and Elmer Harris
music: Earl Carroll
lyrics: Earl Carroll
choreography: Frank Stammers and Frank Rainger
Productions:
Opened February 5, 1917 for 112 performances

Reviews:
Dramatic Mirror 75:16, Jun 10, 1916
77:7+, Feb 10, 1917
77:9, Feb 24, 1917
Green Book 17:592-3, Apr 1917
Life (New York) 69:268, Feb 15, 1917
New York Dramatic News 63:6, Feb 10, 1917
New York Times page 9, Feb 5, 1917
Theatre Magazine 25:150, Mar 1917
25:153, Mar 1917

Candide
book: Lillian Hellman, based on Voltaire's satire
music: Leonard Bernstein
lyrics: Richard Wilbur, John LaTouche, Dorothy Parker
staging: Tyrone Guthrie
sets: Oliver Smith
costumes: Irene Sharaff
Productions:
Opened December 1, 1956 for 73 performances
(Off-Broadway) Opened December 11, 1973 for 48 performances
Opened March 10, 1974 for 740 performances
Reviews:
America 130:262, Apr 6, 1974
Catholic World 184:384-5, Feb 1957
Commentary 57:78, Jun 1974
Commonweal 65:333-4, Dec 28, 1956
Dance Magazine 49:91, Apr 1975
High Fidelity 33:MA31, Apr 1974
33:MA22-MA24, Feb 1983
Maclean's 98:53, Feb 4, 1985
Musical America 76:26, Dec 15, 1956
Nation 183:527, Dec 15, 1956
National Review 26:1049, Sep 13, 1974
New Republic 135:30-1, Dec 17, 1956
170:16+, Mar 30, 1974
187:28-9, Dec 13, 1982
New York 7:66, Jan 14, 1974
7:80, Mar 25, 1974
7:100+, Oct 21, 1974
15:80, Oct 25, 1982
15:106, Nov 15, 1982
New York Theatre Critics' Reviews 1956:176+
1973:138
1974:337
New York Times VI, page 28, Nov 4, 1956
II, page 1, Nov 18, 1956
page 40, Dec 3, 1956
II, page 5, Dec 9, 1956
II, page 9, Dec 16, 1956
page 47, Dec 21, 1973

II, page 1, Dec 30, 1973
page 34, Mar 12, 1974
page 49, Mar 23, 1975
New Yorker 32:52+, Dec 15, 1956
58:152-3, Nov 1, 1982
Newsweek 48:77, Dec 10, 1956
100:102, Nov 8, 1982
Opera News 38:33, Feb 9, 1974
47:37-8, Jan 1, 1983
51:44-5, Nov 1986
Playboy 21:50+, May 1974
Reporter 16:35, Jan 24, 1957
Saturday Review 39:34, Dec 22, 1956
Texas Monthly 5:150, Dec 1977
Time 68:70, Dec 10, 1956
103:75, Mar 25, 1974

Canterbury Tales
book: Martin Starkie and Nevill Coghill; based on the
                work by Geoffrey Chaucer
music: Richard Hill and John Hawkins
lyrics: Nevill Coghill
staging: Martin Starkie
sets: Derek Cousins
costumes: Loudon Saintill
choreography: Sammy Bayes and Bert Michaels
Productions:
Opened February 3, 1969 for 121 performances
(Off-Off-Broadway) Opened November 29, 1979
Opened February 12, 1980 for 16 performances
Reviews:
America 120:316, Mar 15, 1969
Dance Magazine 43:26+, May 1969
National Review 21:918, Sep 9, 1969
New York Theatre Critics' Review 1969:368
1980:371
New York Times page 34, Feb 4, 1969
II, page 10, Feb 16, 1969
page 19, May 17, 1969
III, page 23, Dec 5, 1979
III, page 19, Feb 13, 1980
New Yorker 44:90, Feb 15, 1969
Newsweek 73:113, Feb 17, 1969
Time 91:68, Apr 12, 1968
93:62, Feb 14, 1969
Vogue 153:42, Mar 15, 1969

Canticle
book: Michael Champagne
music: William Penn
lyrics: Michael Champagne

Productions:
(Off-Off-Broadway)   Season of 1973-1974
No Reviews

Cape Cod Follies
    book: Stewart Baird
    music: Alexander Fogarty
    lyrics: Stewart Baird
    staging: Stewart Baird
    choreography: John Lonergan
Productions:
Opened September 18, 1929 for 30 performances
Reviews:
New York Times page 37, Sep 19, 1929
Outlook 153:192, Oct 2, 1929

Captain Jinks
    book: Frank Mandel and Laurence Schwab; based on the
                     play by Clyde Fitch
    music: Lewis E. Gensler and Stephen Jones
    lyrics: B. G. DeSylva
    staging: Edgar MacGregor
Productions:
Opened September 8, 1925 for 167 performances
Reviews:
New York Times page 22, Sep 9, 1925
Theatre Magazine 42:16, Nov 1925

Carib Song
    book: William Archibald
    music: Baldwin Bergersen
    lyrics: William Archibald
    staging: Katherine Dunham and Mary Hunter
    sets: Jo Mielziner
    costumes: Motley
    choreography: Katherine Dunham
Productions:
Opened September 27, 1945 for 36 performances
Reviews:
Catholic World 162:167, Nov 1945
Commonweal 43:17, Oct 19, 1945
New York Theatre Critics' Reviews 1945:157+
New York Times page 17, Sep 28, 1945
New Yorker 21:50, Oct 6, 1945
Theatre Arts 29:624+, Nov 1945
Time 46:78, Oct 8, 1945

Caribbean Carnival
    book: Samuel L. Manning and Adolph Thenstead
    music: Samuel L. Manning and Adolph Thenstead
    lyrics: Samuel L. Manning and Adolph Thenstead

staging: Samuel L. Manning and John Hirshman
costumes: Lou Eisele
choreography: Pearl Primus and Claude Marchant
Productions:
  Opened December 5, 1947 for 11 performances
Reviews:
  New York Theatre Critics' Reviews 1947:246+
  New York Times page 12, Dec 6, 1947
                page 34, Dec 15, 1947

Carmelina

book: Alan Jay Lerner and Joseph Stein
music: Burton Lane
lyrics: Alan Jay Lerner
staging: Jose Ferrer
sets: Oliver Smith
costumes: Donald Brooks
choreography: Peter Gennaro
Productions:
  Opened April 8, 1979 for 17 performances
Reviews:
  Esquire 91:88-9, Apr 24, 1979
  New York 12:70-1, Apr 23, 1979
  New York Theatre Critics' Reviews 1979:292
  New York Times III, page 13, Apr 9, 1979
             II, page 7, Apr 22, 1979
  New Yorker 55:115, Apr 16, 1979
  Time 113:50, Apr 23, 1979

Carmen (see La Tragedie de Carmen)

Carmen Jones

book: Oscar Hammerstein II, based on Meilhac and
                Halevy's adaptation of Prosper Merimee's Carmen
                (Georges Bizet and Prosper Merimee)
music: Georges Bizet, arranged by Robert Russell
lyrics: Oscar Hammerstein II
staging: Hassard Short
sets: Howard Bay
costumes: Raoul Pene du Bois
choreography: Eugene Loring
Productions:
  Opened December 2, 1943 for 503 performances
  Opened May 2, 1945 for 21 performances
  Opened April 7, 1946 for 32 performances
  Opened May 31, 1956 for 24 performances
Reviews:
  America 95:290-2, Jun 16, 1956
  Catholic World 158:394, Jan 1944
                183:311, Jul 1956
  Collier's 113:14-15+, Jan 15, 1944

Commonweal 39:231-2, Dec 17, 1943
Life 15:111-12+, Dec 20, 1943
   16:70-4, May 8, 1944
Nation 157:740, Dec 18, 1943
New Republic 109:885, Dec 20, 1943
New York Theatre Critics' Reviews 1943:207+
New York Times page 17, Oct 20, 1943
             page 29, Oct 28, 1943
             II, page 1, Nov 28, 1943
             page 26, Dec 3, 1943
             II, page 3, Dec 12, 1943
             II, page 9, Dec 19, 1943
             II, page 1, Jun 18, 1944
             page 26, May 3, 1945
             II, page 1, Apr 7, 1946
             page 32, Apr 8, 1946
             page 8, Sep 22, 1951
             page 28, Jun 1, 1956
             II, page 1, Jun 10, 1956
             page 25, Aug 18, 1959
Newsweek 22:91-2, Dec 13, 1943
Theatre Arts 28:69-73, Feb 1944
        28:154-63, Mar 1944
        40:19, Aug 1956
Time 42:44, Dec 13, 1943
Vogue 103:80-1, Mar 15, 1944

Carmilla
   music: Ben Johnston
   staging: Wilford Leach and John Braswell
Productions:
   (Off-Off-Broadway) Opened February 2, 1973
   (Off-Off-Broadway) Opened March 1976
   (Off-Off-Broadway) Opened March 27, 1978
Reviews:
   New York Times III, page 25, May 14, 1976
   Texas Monthly 6:210+, Oct 1978

Carnival!
   book: Michael Stewart, based on material by Helen
                      Deutsch
   music: Bob Merrill
   lyrics: Bob Merrill
   staging: Gower Champion
   sets: Will Steven Armstrong
   costumes: Freddy Wittop
   choreography: Gower Champion
Productions:
   Opened April 13, 1961 for 719 performances
   Opened December 12, 1968 for 30 performances
   (Off-Off-Broadway) Opened November 3, 1977

Reviews:
    America 105:410, Jun 3, 1961
    Catholic World 193:271-2, Jul 1961
    Commonweal 74:327-8, Jun 23, 1961
    Coronet 50:10, Aug 1961
    Dance Magazine 35:15, Jun 1961
    Life 50:85-6+, May 5, 1961
    Musical America 81:25-6, Jul 1961
    Nation 192:378, Apr 29, 1961
    New York Theatre Critics' Reviews 1961:304+
    New York Times II, page 1, Apr 9, 1961
               page 22, Apr 14, 1961
               II, page 1, Apr 23, 1961
               VI, page 16, Apr 23, 1961
               page 37, Jun 6, 1962
               page 5, Jan 5, 1963
               page 58, Dec 13, 1968
               page 69, Nov 6, 1977
    New Yorker 37:116+, Apr 22, 1961
    Newsweek 57:90, Apr 24, 1961
    Saturday Review 44:22, Apr 29, 1961
    Theatre Arts 45:29+, Jun 1961
    Time 77:60, Apr 21, 1961

Carnival in Flanders
    book: Preston Sturges, based on La Kermesse Heroique
                      by C. Spaak, J. Feyder and B. Zimmer
    music: James Van Heusen
    lyrics: Johnny Burke
    staging: Preston Sturges
    sets: Oliver Smith
    costumes: Lucinda Ballard
    choreography: Helen Tamiris
Productions:
    Opened September 8, 1953 for 6 performances
Reviews:
    America 89:629, Sep 26, 1953
    Commonweal 58:634, Oct 2, 1953
    New York Theatre Critics' Reviews 1953:286+
    New York Times page 38, Sep 9, 1953
    New Yorker 29:74, Sep 19, 1953
    Theatre Arts 37:18, Nov 1953

Caroline
    book: Harry B. Smith and E. Kunneke; adapted from
                      the original by Herman Haller and Edward Ride-
                      amus
    music: Edward Rideamus and Alfred Goodman
    staging: Charles Sinclair
Productions:
    Opened January 31, 1923 for (149) performances

Reviews:
   New York Clipper 71:14, Feb 7, 1923
   New York Times page 13, Feb 1, 1923
   Theatre Magazine 37:19, Apr 1923

<u>Carousel</u>
   book: Benjamin F. Glazer and Oscar Hammerstein II,
                     adapted from Ferenc Molnar's play <u>Liliom</u>
   music: Richard Rodgers
   lyrics: Oscar Hammerstein II
   staging: Rouben Mamoulian
   sets: Jo Mielziner
   costumes: Miles White
   choreography: Agnes de Mille
Productions:
   Opened April 19, 1945 for 890 performances
   Opened June 2, 1954 for 79 performances
   Opened September 11, 1957 for 24 performances
   (Off-Broadway) Season of 1959-60
   Opened August 10, 1965 for 48 performances
   Opened December 15, 1966 for 22 performances
   (Off-Off-Broadway) Opened June 22, 1973
   (Off-Off-Broadway) Opened February 7, 1974
Reviews:
   America 91:367, Jul 3, 1954
           98:27, Oct 5, 1957
           113:266-7, Sep 11, 1965
   Catholic World 161:260, Jun 1945
                  168:481, Mar 1949
                  179:308, Jul 1954
   Christian Science Monitor Magazine page 7, Jun 24, 1950
   Collier's 115:18-19+, May 26, 1945
   Commonweal 42:70, May 4, 1945
   Dance Magazine 39:16-17, Oct 1965
                  41:25, Feb 1967
   Life 18:67-70+, May 14, 1945
   Nation 160:525, May 5, 1945
          178:550, Jun 26, 1954
   New Republic 112:644, May 7, 1945
   New York Theatre Critics' Reviews 1945:226+
   New York Times II, page 1, Apr 15, 1945
                  page 24, Apr 20, 1945
                  II, page 1, Apr 29, 1945
                  II, page 1, May 6, 1945
                  II, page 1, Apr 7, 1946
                  II, page 11, Dec 29, 1946
                  page 28, Jan 26, 1949
                  page 14, Jan 31, 1949
                  II, page 1, Feb 6, 1949
                  page 37, Jun 8, 1950
                  page 85, Oct 14, 1951

                    page 38, May 6, 1953
                    II, page 3, May 30, 1954
                    page 32, Jun 3, 1954
                    II, page 1, Jun 13, 1954
                    page 38, Sep 12, 1957
                    page 39, Aug 11, 1965
                    page 56, Dec 16, 1966
                    page 68, Jun 27, 1973
                    page 32, Feb 18, 1974
                    page 23, May 16, 1975
    New Yorker 21:38, Apr 28, 1945
               24:52, Feb 5, 1949
    Newsweek 25:87, Apr 30, 1945
    Saturday Review 28:18-19, May 5, 1945
    Theatre Arts 29:328-30, Jun 1945
               30:41, Jan 1946
               41:18-19, Nov 1957
    Time 45:56, Apr 30, 1945

Carrie
    book: Lawrence D. Cohen, based on the novel by
                        Stephen King
    music: Michael Gore
    lyrics: Dean Pitchford
    staging: Terry Hands
    sets: Ralph Kotai
    costumes: Alexander Reid
    choreography: Debbie Allen
Productions:
    Opened May 12, 1988 for 5 performances
Reviews:
    Nation 246:803-4, Jun 4, 1988
    New York 21:60-1, May 23, 1988
    New York Theatre Critics' Reviews 1988:266
    New York Times III, page 15, Mar 2, 1988
                    III, page 3, May 13, 1988
    New Yorker 64:85, May 23, 1988
    Newsweek 111:72+, May 23, 1988
    Time 131:80, May 23, 1988
        131:65, May 30, 1988
    Vogue 178:88, Apr 1988

Carroll, Earl   (see Earl Carroll)

Castaways
    book: Anthony Stimac, Dennis Anderson, and Ron Whyte,
                        based on the play She Would Be a Soldier by
                        Mordecai Noah
    music: Don Pippin
    lyrics: Steve Brown
    staging: Tony Tanner

sets: Scott Johnson
costumes: Pat McGourty
Productions:
    (Off-Broadway) Opened February 7, 1977 for one performance
Reviews:
    New York 10:62, Feb 21, 1977
    New York Times page 24, Feb 8, 1977
    New Yorker 53:78, Feb 21, 1977

Castles in the Air
book: Raymond W. Peck
music: Percy Wenrich
lyrics: Raymond W. Peck
staging: James W. Elliott
choreography: John Boyle
Productions:
    Opened September 6, 1926 for 160 performances
Reviews:
    Life (New York) 88:23, Oct 7, 1926
    New York Times page 19, Sep 7, 1926
    Theatre Magazine 44:68, Nov 1926

The Cat and the Fiddle
book: Otto Harbach
music: Jerome Kern
lyrics: Otto Harbach
staging: Jose Ruben
Productions:
    Opened October 15, 1931 for 395 performances
    (Off-Off-Broadway) Opened May 6, 1976
Reviews:
    Catholic World 134:335-6, Dec 1931
    Life 98:18, Nov 6, 1931
    New Statesman 3:330-1, Mar 12, 1932
    New York Times VIII, page 3, Sep 27, 1931
                       page 26, Oct 16, 1931
                       VIII, page 2, Oct 18, 1931
                       page 17, Aug 4, 1932
    Vogue 78:102, Dec 15, 1931

Catch A Star!
sketches: Danny and Neil Simon
music: Sammy Fain and Phil Charig
lyrics: Paul Webster and Ray Golden
staging: Ray Golden
sets: Ralph Alswang
costumes: Thomas Becher
choreography: Lee Sherman
Productions:
    Opened September 6, 1955 for 23 performances
Reviews:
    America 93:629, Sep 24, 1955

New York Theatre Critics' Reviews 1955:290+
New York Times page 35, Sep 7, 1955
New Yorker 31:72+, Sep 17, 1955
Theatre Arts 39:17, Nov 1955
Time 66:52, Sep 19, 1955

Cats
    book: Andrew Lloyd Webber, based on Old Possum's
                      Book of Practical Cats by T. S. Eliot
    music: Andrew Lloyd Webber
    lyrics: T. S. Eliot; additional lyrics by Trevor Nunn
                      and Richard Stilgoe
    staging: Trevor Nunn
    sets: John Napier
    costumes: John Napier
    choreography: Gillian Lynne
Productions:
    Opened October 7, 1982 for *2,777 performances (still running
    6/1/89)
Reviews:
    America 147:313, Nov 20, 1982
    Christian Century 99:534-7, May 5, 1982
    Dance Magazine 56:92-7, Dec 1982
                   57:104, Jul 1983
                   59:80, Apr 1985
                   59:101, Sep 1985
    Harper's Bazaar 115:344-5+, Sep 1982
    Horizon 25:41-6, Sep 1982
    Los Angeles 28:60+, Apr 1983
                30:46+, Mar 1985
    Maclean's 98:62, Mar 25, 1985
    Nation 235:442+, Oct 30, 1982
    New Leader 65:18, Nov 1, 1982
    New Republic 187:23-4, Nov 15, 1982
    New York 15:38-9, Sep 20, 1982
    New York Theatre Critics' Reviews 1982:191
    New York Times III, page 3, Oct 8, 1982
                  II, page 5, Oct 17, 1982
    New Yorker 57:81, Aug 10, 1981
                58:158, Oct 18, 1982
    Newsweek 100:80-4+, Oct 11, 1982
    People 18:85-8, Oct 25, 1982
    Smithsonian 13:80-4+, Sep 1982
    Theatre Crafts 17:16-21+, Jan 1983
                   19:14, Feb 1985
    Time 117:47-8, Jun 22, 1981
         120:74-5, Sep 27, 1982
         120:86-7, Oct 18, 1982

Caviar
    book: Leo Randole

```
music:            Harden Church
lyrics:           Edward Heyman
staging:          Clifford Brooke
sets:             Steele Savage
choreography:     John Lonergan
```
Productions:
Opened June 7, 1934 for 20 performances
Reviews:
New York Times page 19, Jun 8, 1934

Celebration
```
book:             Tom Jones
music:            Harvey Schmidt
lyrics:           Tom Jones
staging:          Tom Jones
sets:             Ed Wittstein
costumes:         Ed Wittstein
choreography:     Vernon Lusby
```
Productions:
Opened January 22, 1969 for 109 performances
Reviews:
America 120:315, Mar 15, 1969
Dance Magazine 43:71, Mar 1969
Life 66:82-4+, Mar 14, 1969
New York Theatre Critics' Reviews 1969:383
New York Times page 55, Jan 23, 1969
        II, page 3, Feb 2, 1969
New Yorker 44:49, Feb 1, 1969
Time 93:72, Jan 31, 1969

Censored Scenes From King Kong
```
book:             Howard Schuman
music:            Andy Roberts
lyrics:           Howard Schuman
staging:          Colin Bucksey
sets:             Mike Porter
costumes:         Jennifer Von Mayrhauser
choreography:     David Toguri
```
Productions:
Opened March 6, 1980 for 5 performances
Reviews:
New York Theatre Critics' Reviews 1980:318
New York Times III, page 3, Mar 7, 1980

The Century Girl
```
music:            Victor Herbert and Irving Berlin
```
Productions:
Opened November 6, 1916 for 200 performances
Reviews:
Dramatic Mirror 76:7, Nov 18, 1916
Green Book 17:13+, Jan 1917

Leslie's Weekly 124:128, Feb 1, 1917
Life (New York) 68:904, Nov 23, 1916
New Republic 9:154, Dec 9, 1916
New York Times page 9, Nov 7, 1916
Theatre Magazine 24:392, Dec 1916
                  25:10, Jan 1917
                  25:12, Jan 1917

A Certain Party
    book: Robert Hood Bowers
    staging: William Collier
Productions:
    Opened April 24, 1911 for 24 performances
Reviews:
    Dramatic Mirror 65:7, Apr 26, 1911
                     65:2+, May 3, 1911
    Green Book Album 6:20-3, Jul 1911
    Harper's Weekly 55:19, May 13, 1911
    Red Book 17:573+, Jul 1911
    Theatre Magazine 12:10, Jul 1910
                     13:183, Jun 1911
                     13:196, Jun 1911

Chaim to Life, L'   (see L'Chaim to Life)

Change Your Luck
    book: Garland Howard
    music: J. C. Johnson
    lyrics: Garland Howard
    staging: Cleon Throckmorton
    choreography: Lawrence Deas and Speedy Smith
Productions:
    Opened June 6, 1930 for 17 performances
Reviews:
    New Republic 63:150-1, Jun 25, 1930
    New York Times page 10, Jun 7, 1930

Changes
    conceived: Dorothy Love
    music: Addy Fieger
    lyrics: Danny Apolinar
    staging: Dorothy Love
    sets: Don Jensen
    costumes: Miles White
    choreography: Ron Forella
Productions:
    (Off-Broadway) Opened February 19, 1980 for 7 performances
Reviews:
    New York Times III, page 19, Feb 20, 1980

Chaplin
    book: Anthony Newley and Stanley Ralph Ross

music:	Anthony Newley and Stanley Ralph Ross
lyrics:	Anthony Newley and Stanley Ralph Ross
staging:	Michael Smuin
sets:	Douglas W. Schmidt
costumes:	Willa Kim
choreography:	Michael Smuin

Productions:
  Closed prior to Broadway opening (Los Angeles, August 1983)
Reviews:
  California 8:143+, Oct 1983
  Harper's Bazaar 116:212-13+, Oct 1983
  Los Angeles 28:58+, Oct 1983
  Theatre Crafts 18:4+, Feb 1984

The Charity Girl

libretto:	Edward Peple; added lyrics by Melville Alexander
music:	Victor Hollaender
staging:	George W. Lederer

Productions:
  Opened October 2, 1912 for 21 performances
Reviews:
  Blue Book 15:1138-43, Oct 1912
  Dramatic Mirror 68:10, Jul 31, 1912
                 68:11, Aug 7, 1912
                 68:7, Oct 9, 1912
  Harper's Weekly 56:20, Oct 12, 1912
  New York Dramatic News 56:18, Aug 10, 1912
                         56:25, Oct 12, 1912
  Theatre Magazine 16:xii, Nov 1912

Charles Aznavour

songs by:	Charles Aznavour

Productions:
  Opened February 4, 1970 for 23 performances
Reviews:
  New York Times page 32, Feb 5, 1970

Charles Aznavour (also see Aznavour and The World of Charles Aznavour)

Charlie and Algernon

book:	David Rogers, based on Flowers for Algernon by Daniel Keyes
music:	Charles Strouse
lyrics:	David Rogers
staging:	Louis W. Scheeder
sets:	Kate Edmunds
costumes:	Jess Goldstein
choreography:	Virginia Freeman

Productions:
  Opened September 14, 1980 for 17 performances

Reviews:
  Los Angeles 28:130, Jan 1983
  New York 13:44+, Sep 29, 1980
  New York Theatre Critics' Reviews 1980:168
  New York Times III, page 23, Mar 12, 1980
            III, page 17, Sep 15, 1980
  New Yorker 56:76, Sep 22, 1980

Charlot, André   (see André Charlot's Revue of 1924)

Charlotte Sweet
  book: Michael Colby
  music: Gerald Jay Markoe
  lyrics: Michael Colby
  staging: Edward Stone
  sets: Holmes Easley
  costumes: Michele Reisch
  choreography: Dennis Dennehy
Productions:
  (Off-Broadway) Opened August 12, 1982 for 102 performances
Reviews:
  New York 15:82+, Aug 23, 1982
  New York Theatre Critics' Reviews 1982:234
  New York Times III, page 17, May 3, 1982
  Time 120:84, Aug 30, 1982

Chase a Rainbow
  book: Harry Stone
  music: Harry Stone
  lyrics: Harry Stone
  staging: Sue Lawless
  sets: Michael Rizzo
  costumes: Rita Watson
  choreography: Bick Goss
Productions:
  (Off-Broadway) Opened June 12, 1980 for 6 performances
Reviews:
  New York Times page 13, Jun 14, 1980

Chauve-Souris 1943
  assembled: M. Nikita Balieff
  music: Gleb Yellin
  lyrics: (English) Irving Florman
  staging: Michel Michon
  sets: Serge Soudeikine
  costumes: Serge Soudeikine
  choreography: Vecheslav Swoboda and Boris Romanoff
Productions:
  Opened August 12, 1943 for 12 performances
Reviews:
  New York Theatre Critics' Reviews 1943:298

New York Times page 13, Aug 13, 1943
Newsweek 22:86, Aug 23, 1943
Time 42:64, Aug 23, 1943

Chee-Chee
    book: Lew Fields
    music: Richard Rodgers
    lyrics: Lorenz Hart
    staging: Alexander Leftwich and Jack Haskell
Productions:
   Opened September 25, 1928 for 31 performances
Reviews:
   Life (New York) 92:19, Oct 28, 1928
   New York Times page 25, Sep 26, 1928

Cheer Up
    book: R. H. Burnside
    music: Raymond Hubbell
    lyrics: John L. Golden
    staging: R. H. Burnside
Productions:
   Opened August 23, 1917 for 456 performances
Reviews:
   Dramatic Mirror 77:7, Sep 1, 1917
                    77:7, Sep 22, 1917
   Life (New York) 70:424, Sep 13, 1917
   New Republic 13:23, Nov 3, 1917
   New York Dramatic News 64:2, Sep 1, 1917
   New York Times page 9, Aug 24, 1917
                   IV, page 5, Sep 2, 1917
   Theatre Magazine 26:242, Oct 1917
                   26:287, Nov 1917

Cherry Blossoms
    book: Harry B. Smith, adapted from Benrimo and Harrison Rhodes' The Willow Tree
    music: Sigmund Romberg
    lyrics: Harry B. Smith
    staging: Lew Morton
Productions:
   Opened March 28, 1927 for 56 performances
Reviews:
   New York Times page 22, Mar 29, 1927

Chess
    book: Richard Nelson, based on an idea by Tim Rice
    music: Benny Andersson and Bjorn Ulvaeus
    lyrics: Tim Rice
    staging: Trevor Nunn
    sets: Robin Wagner

costumes: Theoni V. Aldredge
choreography: Lynne Taylor-Corbett
Productions:
Opened April 28, 1988 for 68 performances
Reviews:
America 158:536, May 21, 1988
Los Angeles 33:161+, Jul 1988
Nation 246:726, May 21, 1988
New Leader 71:22-3, Jun 27, 1988
New York 21:34, May 9, 1988
          21:87-8, May 9, 1988
New York Theatre Critics' Reviews 1988:288
New York Times III, page 3, Apr 29, 1988
               II, page 3, May 8, 1988
New Yorker 64:100, May 9, 1988
Newsweek 109:64-5, Mar 30, 1987
         111:73, May 9, 1988
Saturday Review 12:52-3, Jan/Feb 1986
Theatre Crafts 22:70-8, Oct 1988
Time 125:72, Mar 18, 1985
     131:80, May 9, 1988
Vogue 178:94, Apr 1988

Chevalier, Maurice (see Maurice Chevalier)

Chicago
book: Fred Ebb and Bob Fosse, based on the play by
                 Maurine Dallas Watkins
music: John Kander
lyrics: Fred Ebb
staging: Bob Fosse
sets: Tony Walton
costumes: Patricia Zipprodt
choreography: Bob Fosse
Productions:
Opened June 3, 1975 for 898 performances
Reviews:
Dance Magazine 49:38-41, Nov 1975
Essence 6:9, Oct 1975
Los Angeles 23:220, Jun 1978
New York 8:64, Jun 16, 1975
         10:114, Jun 27, 1977
New York Theatre Critics' Reviews 1975:231
New York Times page 23, Jun 4, 1975
               II, page 1, Jun 8, 1975
               II, page 1, Jul 20, 1975
               II, page 5, Aug 3, 1975
               page 26, Aug 15, 1975
               III, page 4, Apr 1, 1977
New Yorker 51:50, Jun 16, 1975
           51:81-2, Aug 25, 1975
Newsweek 85:81, Jun 16, 1975

Playboy 22:30, Sep 1975
Time 105:68, Jun 16, 1975

The Chiffon Girl
    book: George Murray
    music: Carlo and Sanders
    lyrics: Carlo and Sanders
Productions:
    Opened February 19, 1924 for 103 performances
Reviews:
    New York Times page 15, Feb 26, 1924

Children of Adam
    conceived: John Driver
    words: Stan Satlin
    songs: Stan Satlin
    staging: John Driver
    sets: Ernest Allen Smith
    costumes: Polly P. Smith
    choreography: Ruella Frank
Productions:
    (Off-Off-Broadway) Opened March 1977
    (Off-Broadway) Opened August 17, 1977 for 69 performances
Reviews:
    New York Times III, page 13, Aug 19, 1977

Chin-Chin
    book: Anne Caldwell and R. H. Burnside
    music: Ivan Caryll
    lyrics: Anne Caldwell and James O'Dea
    staging: R. H. Burnside
Productions:
    Opened October 20, 1914 for 295 performances
Reviews:
    Colliers 54:14-15, Jan 2, 1915
    Dramatic Mirror 72:9, Oct 28, 1914
    Green Book 13:123-4, Jan 1915
    New York Dramatic News 60:17, Oct 13, 1914
    New York Times page 11, Oct 21, 1914
                    VII, page 8, Nov 8, 1914
                    page 13, Jun 2, 1915
                    page 9, Aug 17, 1915
    Theatre Magazine 20:265, Dec 1914
                    20:304, Dec 1914
                    21:238-9, May 1915
                    21:305, Jun 1915

Chinese Love
    book: Clare Kummer
    staging: W. L. Gilmore
Productions:
    Opened February 28, 1921 for 5 matinees

Reviews:
    Dramatic Mirror 83:408+, Mar 5, 1921
    New York Times page 18, Mar 1, 1921
    Theatre Magazine 33:342, May 1921

The Chocolate Dandies
    book: Noble Sissle and Lew Payton
    music: Noble Sissle and Eubie Blake
    lyrics: Noble Sissle and Eubie Blake
Productions:
    Opened September 1, 1924 for 96 performances
Reviews:
    New York Times page 22, Sep 2, 1924
    Theatre Magazine 40:70, Nov 1924

A Chorus Line
    conceived: Michael Bennett
    book: James Kirkwood and Nicholas Dante
    music: Marvin Hamlisch
    lyrics: Edward Kleban
    staging: Michael Bennett
    sets: Robin Wagner
    costumes: Theoni V. Aldredge
    choreography: Michael Bennett and Bob Avian
Productions:
    (Off-Broadway) Opened April 15, 1975 for 101 performances
    Opened July 25, 1975 for *5,756 performances (still running
    6/1/89)
Reviews:
    America 134:40, Jan 17, 1976
    Dance Magazine 49:62-5, Jun 1975
                   57:102, Nov 1983
    Intellectual Digest 104:531, Apr 1976
    Los Angeles 21:140+, Jul 1976
                22:197, Aug 1976
    Mademoiselle 81:98-9, Jul 1975
    Nation 220:734, Jun 14, 1975
    New Republic 172:20+, Jun 21, 1975
    New York 8:68+, Jun 9, 1975
             8:83+, Nov 3, 1975
             16:92-3, Oct 17, 1983
    New York Theatre Critics' Reviews 1975:238
    New York Times page 32, May 22, 1975
                   II, page 1, Jun 1, 1975
                   II, page 1, Jul 20, 1975
                   page 44, Oct 20, 1975
                   II, page 1, Oct 26, 1975
                   page 17, Dec 18, 1976
                   III, page 12, Aug 11, 1987
    New York Times Magazine pages 18-20+, May 2, 1976
    New Yorker 51:84, Jun 2, 1975
               51:78+, Aug 25, 1975

Newsweek 85:49, Jun 2, 1975
      85:85-6, Jun 9, 1975
      86:68, Nov 3, 1975
      86:66-70, Dec 1, 1975
People 20:34-41, Oct 17, 1983
Playboy 22:30, Sep 1975
Saturday Review 2:16-19, Jul 26, 1975
      2:50, Aug 9, 1975
      4:50, Oct 16, 1976
Theatre Crafts 19:10, Nov 1985
Time 105:60, Jun 2, 1975
    106:47-8, Jul 28, 1975
Vogue 165:120-3+, Aug 1975

The Chosen

book: Chaim Potok, based on the novel The Chosen by Chaim Potok
music: Philip Springer
lyrics: Mitchell Bernard
staging: Mitchell Maxwell
sets: Ben Edwards
costumes: Ruth Morley
choreography: Richard Levi

Productions:
(Off-Broadway) Opened January 6, 1988 for 6 performances
Reviews:
Nation 246:176, Feb 6, 1988
New York 21:84, Jan 18, 1988
New York Times III, page 22, Jan 7, 1988
New Yorker 63:74, Jan 18, 1988

Christine

book: Pearl S. Buck and Charles K. Peck, Jr., adapted from Hilda Wernher's My Indian Family
music: Sammy Fain
lyrics: Paul Francis Webster
sets: Jo Mielziner
costumes: Alvin Colt
choreography: Hanya Holm

Productions:
Opened April 28, 1960 for 12 performances
Reviews:
America 103:267, May 14, 1960
New York Theatre Critics' Reviews 1960:272+
New York Times page 27, Apr 29, 1960
New Yorker 36:114+, May 7, 1960
Saturday Review 43:28, May 14, 1960
Time 75:56, May 9, 1960

Christmas Rappings

text: Al Carmines, adapted from the New Testament

music: Al Carmines
staging: Al Carmines
Productions:
  (Off-Off-Broadway) Opened December 15, 1972
  (Off-Broadway) Season of 1971-1972
Reviews:
  New York Times page 22, Dec 18, 1971

Christmas Spectacular (see Magnificent Christmas Spectacular)

Christy
  book: Bernie Spiro, based on John Millington Synge's
                  The Playboy of the Western World
  music: Lawrence J. Blank
  lyrics: Bernie Spiro
  staging: Peter David Heth
  sets: Peter David Heth
  choreography: Jack Estes
Productions:
  (Off-Broadway) Opened October 14, 1975 for 40 performances
Reviews:
  New York Times page 44, Oct 16, 1975

Chu Chem
  book: Ted Allen
  music: Mitch Leigh
  lyrics: Jim Haines and Jack Wohl
  staging: Albert Marre
  sets: Robert Mitchell
  costumes: Kenneth M. Yount
Productions:
  Opened March 17, 1989 for 44 performances
Reviews:
  New York Theatre Critics' Reviews 1989:301
  New York Times III, page 28, Dec 23, 1988

Chu Chin Chow
  book: Oscar Asche
  music: Frederick Norton
  staging: E. Lyle Swete
Productions:
  Opened October 22, 1917 for 208 performances
Reviews:
  Dramatic Mirror 77:7, Nov 3, 1917
                  77:4, Dec 29, 1917
  Green Book 19:12-16, Jan 1918
  Hearst 33:118-20+, Feb 1918
  Nation 103:448, Nov 9, 1916
  New York Dramatic News 64:7, Oct 27, 1917
  New York Times page 14, Oct 23, 1917
                  VIII, page 6, Oct 28, 1917

Theatre Magazine 26:198+, Oct 1917
27:337, Dec 1917
27:392, Dec 1917
41:36+, May 1925

Cinderella on Broadway
    book: Harold Atteridge
    music: Bert Grant and Al Goodman
    staging: J. C. Huffman
Productions:
    Opened June 24, 1920 for 126 performances
Reviews:
    Dramatic Mirror page 9, Jul 3, 1920
    New York Clipper 68:19, Jun 30, 1920
    New York Times page 18, Jun 25, 1920
    Theatre Magazine 32:106, Sep 1920

Cinders
    book: Edward Clark
    music: Rudolf Friml
    lyrics: Edward Clark
    staging: Edward Royce
Productions:
    Opened April 3, 1923 for 31 performances
Reviews:
    New York Clipper 71:14, Apr 11, 1923
    New York Times page 22, Apr 4, 1923

Cindy
    book: Joe Sauter and Mike Sawyer
    music: Johnny Brandon
    lyrics: Johnny Brandon
    staging: Marvin Gordon
    sets: Robert T. Williams
    costumes: Patricia Quinn Stuart
    choreography: Marvin Gordon
Productions:
    (Off-Broadway) Opened March 19, 1964 for 110 performances
    (Off-Broadway) Opened September 24, 1964 for 94 performances
    (Off-Broadway) Opened January 19, 1965 for 114 performances
Reviews:
    New York Times page 24, Mar 20, 1964
               page 33, Sep 25, 1964
    New Yorker 40:136, Mar 28, 1964

The Circus Princess
    music: Emmerich Kalman
    staging: J. C. Huffman
Productions:
    Opened April 25, 1927 for 192 performances
Reviews:
    Bookman 65:576, Jul 1927

Life (New York) 89:23, May 19, 1927
Theatre Magazine 46:20, Jul 1927
Vanity Fair 28:76, Jun 1927
Vogue 69:100, Jun 15, 1927

The City Chap
    book: James Montgomery, adapted from Winchell Smith's
                   The Fortune Hunter
    music: Jerome Kern
    lyrics: Anne Caldwell
    staging: R. H. Burnside
Productions:
    Opened October 26, 1925 for 72 performances
Reviews:
    New York Times page 21, Oct 27, 1925

City of Light
    conceived: John Dodd
    music: John Herbert McDowell and Terence Thomas
    staging: John Dodd
Productions:
    (Off-Off-Broadway) Opened January 5, 1973
No Reviews.

Clams on the Half Shell Revue with Bette Midler
    staging: Joe Layton
    sets: Tony Walton
    costumes: Tony Walton
    choreography: Joe Layton
Productions:
    Opened April 17, 1975 for 88 performances
Reviews:
    Nation 220:605-6, May 17, 1975
    New Republic 173:25-8, Aug 2, 1975
    New York 8:94, May 1975
    New York Theatre Critics' Reviews 1975:268
    New York Times page 20, Apr 18, 1975
                    II, page 5, Apr 27, 1975
    New Yorker 51:81, Apr 28, 1975
    Newsweek 85:85, Apr 28, 1975
    Playboy 22:20+, Jul 1975
    Rolling Stone 187:18, May 22, 1975

Cleavage
    book: Buddy and David Sheffield
    music: Buddy Sheffield
    lyrics: Buddy Sheffield
    staging: Rita Baker
    sets: Morris Taylor
    costumes: James M. Miller
    choreography: Alton Geno

Productions:
Opened June 23, 1982 for one performance
Reviews:
Nation 235:92-3, Jul 24-31, 1982

The Clinging Vine
book: Zelda Sears
music: Harold Levey
staging: Ira Hards
Productions:
Opened December 25, 1922 for 184 performances
Reviews:
New York Clipper 70:20, Jan 3, 1923
New York Times page 20, Dec 25, 1922
                VII, page 1, Dec 31, 1922
Theatre Arts 32:40, Fall 1948
Theatre Magazine 37:19, Mar 1928
                 40:24, Sep 1924
Woman's Home Companion 51:48, Feb 1924

The Club
book: Eve Merriam
songs: Various authors and composers
staging: Tommy Tune
sets: Kate Carmel
costumes: Kate Carmel
Productions:
(Off-Broadway) Opened October 14, 1976 for 674 performances
Reviews:
America 135:373, Nov 27, 1976
Mademoiselle 83:142-3+, Feb 1977
Ms. 5:34+, Mar 1977
New York 9:75, Nov 1, 1976
New York Theatre Critics' Reviews 1976:122
New York Times III, page 10, Oct 15, 1976
               III, page 21, Nov 17, 1976
New Yorker 52:64, Oct 25, 1976

Coca-Cola Grande, El   (see El Grande de Coca-Cola)

The Cockeyed Tiger
book: Eric Blau
original music
   and lyrics: Nicholas Meyers and Eric Blau
musical score: Bert Kalmar and Harry Ruby
staging: Eric Blau
sets: Donald Jensen
costumes: Donald Jensen
choreography: Gemze de Lappe and Buzz Miller
Productions:
(Off-Broadway) Opened January 13, 1977 for 5 performances

Reviews:
    New York Times III, page 4, Jan 14, 1977
    New Yorker 52:65, Jan 24, 1977

Coco
    book: Alan Jay Lerner
    music: Andre Previn
    lyrics: Alan Jay Lerner
    staging: Michael Benthall
    sets: Cecil Beaton
    costumes: Cecil Beaton
    choreography: Michael Bennett
Productions:
    Opened December 18, 1969 for 332 performances
Reviews:
    America 122:54-5, Jan 17, 1970
    Commonweal 91:558-9, Feb 20, 1970
    Dance Magazine 44:72-8, Feb 1970
                    44:84-5, Mar 1970
    Life 68:12, Jan 30, 1970
    Nation 210:61, Jan 19, 1970
    National Review 22:370-1, Apr 7, 1970
    New York Theatre Critics' Reviews 1969:151
    New York Times page 28, Aug 6, 1969
                    page 52, Oct 14, 1969
                    page 36, Oct 15, 1969
                    page 50, Nov 25, 1969
                    page 59, Dec 19, 1969
                    page 66, Dec 19, 1969
                    II, page 1, Dec 28, 1969
                    page 38, Jul 16, 1970
                    page 28, Aug 7, 1970
                    page 52, Oct 1, 1970
    New Yorker 45:38, Dec 27, 1969
    Newsweek 74:75-9, Nov 10, 1969
                74:58, Dec 29, 1969
    Saturday Review 53:88, Jan 10, 1970
    Time 94:86-7, Nov 7, 1969
            94:35, Dec 26, 1969

The Cocoanuts
    book: George S. Kaufman
    music: Irving Berlin
    lyrics: Irving Berlin
    staging: Sammy Lee and Oscar Eagle
Productions:
    Opened December 8, 1925 for 377 performances
Reviews:
    Dial 80:166-7, Feb 1926
    New York Times page 30, Dec 9, 1925
                    IX, page 1, Dec 13, 1925

VIII, page 1, Apr 18, 1926
page 27, May 17, 1927
Vogue 67:61+, Feb 1, 1926

The Cohan Revue of 1916
    book: George M. Cohan
    music: George M. Cohan
    lyrics: George M. Cohan
    staging: George M. Cohan
    choreography: James Gorman
Productions:
Opened February 9, 1916 for 165 performances
Reviews:
    Dramatic Mirror 75:8, Feb 19, 1916
                   75:2, Feb 26, 1916
                   75:2, Mar 4, 1916
    Green Book 15:658+, Apr 1916
    Harper's Weekly 62:206, Feb 26, 1916
    Life (New York) 67:352-3, Feb 24, 1916
    Munsey 58:314, Jul 1916
    New York Dramatic News 62:17, Feb 19, 1916
    New York Times page 9, Feb 10, 1916
                 II, page 7, Feb 20, 1916
    Theatre Magazine 23:124, Mar 1916
                  23:164, Mar 1916

The Cohan Revue of 1918
    book: George M. Cohan
    music: Irving Berlin and George M. Cohan
    lyrics: Irving Berlin and George M. Cohan
    staging: George M. Cohan
    choreography: Jack Mason and James Gorman
Productions:
Opened December 31, 1917 for 96 performances
Reviews:
    Dramatic Mirror 78:7, Jan 12, 1918
    New York Times page 15, Jan 1, 1918
               IV, page 6, Jan 27, 1918
    Theatre Magazine 27:87, Feb 1918
                  27:137, Mar 1918
                  27:235, Apr 1918

Cole Porter (see The Decline and Fall of the Entire World as Seen
    through the Eyes of Cole Porter) (Also see New Cole Porter
    Revue)

Colette
    book: Elinor Jones; adapted from Earthly Paradise,
                   the Robert Phelps collection of Colette's auto-
                   biographical writings
    music: Harvey Schmidt

lyrics: Tom Jones
staging: Gerald Freedman
sets: David Mitchell
costumes: Theoni V. Aldredge
Productions:
  (Off-Broadway) Opened May 6, 1970 for 101 performances
  (Off-Broadway) Opened October 14, 1970 for 7 performances
Reviews:
  New York Theatre Critics' Reviews 1970:228
  New York Times page 60, May 7, 1970
                  II, page 1, May 17, 1970
                  page 34, Jun 2, 1970
                  page 58, Oct 15, 1970
                  page 40, Oct 21, 1970

The Collected Works of Billy the Kid
  book: Michael Ondaatje
  music: Alan Laing
  lyrics: Michael Ondaatje
  staging: John Wood
  sets: John Ferguson
Productions:
  (Off-Broadway) Opened October 13, 1975 for 10 performances
Reviews:
  Los Angeles 27:270, Sep 1982
  New York 8:71, Oct 27, 1975
  New York Times page 34, Oct 15, 1975

Comden, Betty (see A Party with Betty Comden and Adolph Green)

Come Along
  book: Bide Dudley
  music: John L. Nelson
  lyrics: John L. Nelson
  staging: Edward Royce
Productions:
  Opened April 8, 1919 for 47 performances
Reviews:
  New York Times page 9, Apr 9, 1919
  Theatre Magazine 29:276+, May 1919

Come Summer
  book: Will Holt; based on Rainbow on the Road by
                  Esther Forbes
  music: David Baker
  lyrics: Will Holt
  staging: Agnes de Mille
  sets: Oliver Smith
  costumes: Stanley Simmons
  choreography: Milton Rosenstock
Productions:
  Opened March 18, 1969 for 7 performances

Reviews:
  New York Theatre Critics' Reviews 1969:319
  New York Times page 43, Mar 19, 1969
                  page 43, Mar 21, 1969
  New Yorker 45:99, Mar 29, 1969

Come to Bohemia
  book: George S. Chappell
  music: Kenneth M. Murchinson
  lyrics: George S. Chappell
  staging: Jacques Coini
Productions:
  Opened April 27, 1916 for 20 performances
Reviews:
  Dramatic Mirror 75:8, May 6, 1916
                  75:2, May 20, 1916
  Life (New York) 67:602-3, May 11, 1916
  New York Dramatic News 62:7, May 6, 1916
  Theatre Magazine 23:329, Jun 1916
                   23:366, Jun 1916

Comedy in Music (Victor Borge's One-Man Show)
  material: Victor Borge
Productions:
  Opened October 2, 1953 for 849 performances
Reviews:
  American Magazine 158:50, Sep 1954
  Catholic World 178:230, Dec 1953
  Commonweal 59:119, Nov 6, 1953
  Coronet 35:29-34, Apr 1954
  Cosmopolitan 137:110-17, Oct 1954
  Etude 73:9+, Feb 1955
  Holiday 16:56-7, Sep 1954
  House and Garden 106:116-17+, Dec 1954
  Life 35:87, Dec 7, 1953
  Nation 177:337-8, Oct 24, 1953
  New York Times page 15, Oct 3, 1953
                  page 10, Oct 1, 1955
  New Yorker 29:34-5, Nov 7, 1953
  Newsweek 41:94, Mar 23, 1953
           44:82, Oct 4, 1954
  Saturday Review 36:37, Oct 17, 1953
                  37:5-8, Apr 24, 1954
  Theatre Arts 37:17, Dec 1953
  Time 62:49, Oct 12, 1953

Comedy in Music, Opus 2
  created: Victor Borge
  sets: Ralph Alswang
Productions:
  Opened November 9, 1964 for 192 performances

Reviews:
    America 111:758, Dec 5, 1964
    Commonweal 81:354, Dec 4, 1964
    New York Theatre Critics' Reviews 1964:164
    New York Times II, page 3, Nov 8, 1964
                   page 54, Nov 10, 1964
    Saturday Review 48:32, Jan 2, 1965
    Time 84:81, Nov 20, 1964

Comedy of Errors   (see Oh, Brother!)

Comedy With Music
    by: Victor Borge
    design: Neil Peter Jampolis
Productions:
    Opened October 3, 1977 for 66 performances
Reviews:
    New York Theatre Critics' Reviews 1977:187
    New York Times page 49, Oct 4, 1977
                   II, page 5, Oct 16, 1977
    New Yorker 53:93-4, Oct 17, 1977

Comin' Uptown
    book: Philip Rose and Peter Udell, based on A Christmas
                   Carol by Charles Dickens
    music: Garry Sherman
    lyrics: Peter Udell
    staging: Philip Rose
    sets: Robin Wagner
    costumes: Ann Emonts
    choreography: Michael Peters
Productions:
    Opened December 20, 1979 for 45 performances
Reviews:
    Encore 9:38, Jan 1980
    New York Theatre Critics' Reviews 1979:58
    New York Times III, page 5, Dec 21, 1979
    New Yorker 55:57, Jan 7, 1980

Company
    book: George Furth
    music: Stephen Sondheim
    lyrics: Stephen Sondheim
    staging: Harold Prince
    sets: Boris Aronson
    costumes: D. D. Ryan
    choreography: Michael Bennett
Productions:
    Opened April 26, 1970 for 705 performances
    (Off-Off-Broadway) Opened May 4, 1978
    (Off-Off-Broadway) Opened March 8, 1980
    (Off-Off-Broadway) Opened October 23, 1987

Reviews:
America 122:568, May 23, 1970
Commentary 51:79, Feb 1971
Dance Magazine 44:85-6+, Jun 1970
Life 68:20, Jun 26, 1970
Los Angeles 26:312+, May 1981
National Review 22:905-6, Aug 25, 1970
Nation 210:572-3, May 11, 1970
New Republic 162:20, May 23, 1970
New York Theatre Critics' Reviews 1970:260
New York Times page 40, Apr 27, 1970
    page 50, Apr 28, 1970
    II, page 1, May 3, 1970
    II, page 1, May 10, 1970
    page 31, Jul 29, 1970
    II, page 21, Nov 1, 1970
    II, page 1, Jun 27, 1971
    page 21, Dec 29, 1971
    page 22, Jan 24, 1972
    III, page 18, May 8, 1978
    III, page 28, Mar 26, 1980
    III, page 15, Nov 3, 1987
New Yorker 46:83, May 22, 1970
    63:148, Nov 16, 1987
Newsweek 75:79, May 11, 1970
Saturday Review 53:4-5, May 9, 1970
Time 95:62, May 11, 1970

A Connecticut Yankee
  book: Herbert Fields, adapted from Mark Twain's novel
                 A Connecticut Yankee in King Arthur's Court
  music: Richard Rodgers
  lyrics: Lorenz Hart
  staging: Alexander Leftwich
Productions:
Opened November 3, 1927 for 418 performances
Opened November 17, 1943 for 135 performances
Reviews:
Catholic World 158:395, Jun 1944
Life (New York) 90:23, Nov 24, 1927
New York Theatre Critics' Reviews 1943:219+
New York Times VIII, page 1, Oct 9, 1927
    page 24, Nov 4, 1927
    VIII, page 2, Jun 10, 1928
    page 30, Nov 18, 1943
    II, page 1, Nov 21, 1943
Theatre Arts 28:17-18, Jan 1944
Theatre Magazine 47:49, Feb 1928

The Conquering Hero
  book: Larry Gelbart, based on Preston Sturges' Hail,
                 The Conquering Hero

music: Moose Charlap
lyrics: Norman Gimbel
sets: Jean Rosenthal and William Pitkin
costumes: Patton Campbell
Productions:
Opened January 16, 1961 for 8 performances
Reviews:
   New York Theatre Critics' Reviews 1961:388+
   New York Times page 40, Jan 17, 1961
                    page 29, Jan 18, 1961
   New Yorker 36:64, Jan 28, 1961

The Consul
   book: Gian-Carlo Menotti
   music: Gian-Carlo Menotti
   lyrics: Gian-Carlo Menotti
   staging: Gian-Carlo Menotti
   sets: Horace Armistead
   costumes: Grace Houston
   choreography: John Butler
Productions:
   Opened March 15, 1950 for 269 performances
   Opened March 17, 1966 for 3 performances
   Opened October 6, 1966 for 2 performances
Reviews:
   Catholic World 171:148, May 1950
   Christian Science Monitor Magazine page 5, Mar 25, 1950
   Commonweal 51:677, Apr 7, 1950
   Life 28:61-3, Apr 10, 1950
   Musical America 70:7, Mar 1950
                    71:90, Apr 1951
                    71:6, Oct 1951
                    72:12, Jul 1952
   Musical Quarterly 36:447-50, Jul 1950
   Nation 170:305, Apr 1, 1950
          170:557-8, Jun 3, 1950
   New Republic 122:21-2, Apr 10, 1950
   New York Theatre Critics' Reviews 1950:329+
   New York Times page 32, Mar 2, 1950
                    II, page 1, Mar 12, 1950
                    page 41, Mar 16, 1950
                    II, page 1, Mar 26, 1950
                    II, page 7, Apr 2, 1950
                    II, page 1, May 21, 1950
                    page 24, Jan 23, 1951
                    II, page 7, Jan 28, 1951
                    page 26, Feb 8, 1951
                    page 9, Sep 8, 1951
                    page 40, Oct 9, 1952
                    page 41, Oct 30, 1952
                    page 30, Apr 17, 1953

New Yorker 26:54+, Mar 25, 1950
28:149, Oct 18, 1952
Saturday Review 33:28-30, Apr 22, 1950
School and Society 72:183, Sep 16, 1950
Theatre Arts 34:28-9, Mar 1950
34:17, May 1950

Continental Varieties
    material: A. Selwyn and H. B. Franklin
Productions:
    Opened October 3, 1934 for 77 performances
Reviews:
    New York Times page 18, Oct 4, 1934
                    page 24, Nov 15, 1934
    Stage 12:9-10, Nov 1934

The Contrast
    book: Anthony Stimac; based on the play by Royall
                      Tyler
    music: Don Pippin
    lyrics: Steve Brown
    staging: Anthony Stimac
    sets: David Chapman
    costumes: Robert Pusilo
    choreography: Bill Guske
Productions:
    (Off-Broadway) Opened November 28, 1972 for 24 performances
Reviews:
    Nation 215:637, Dec 18, 1972
    New York Times page 51, Nov 28, 1972
                    II, page 7, Dec 24, 1972

Conversations With Don B
    words: Adapted from the writings of Donald Barthelme
    music: John Rubins
    staging: Caymichael Patten
    sets: John Wulp
    costumes: Willa Kim
Productions:
    (Off-Broadway) Opened January 23, 1976 for 12 performances
Reviews:
    New York Times page 22, Feb 3, 1976
    New Yorker 51:52, Feb 16, 1976

Cooler Near the Lake
    music: Fred Kaz
    staging: Barnard Sahlins
    choreography: Mel Spinney
Productions:
    (Off-Broadway) Opened February 7, 1971 for 26 performances
No Reviews.

The Coolest Cat in Town

book:	William Gleason
music:	Diane Leslie
lyrics:	William Gleason
staging:	Frank Carucci
sets:	Bill Mikeulewicz
costumes:	Bennett and Faded Glory
choreography:	Mary Lou Crivello

Productions:
 (Off-Off-Broadway) Opened February 23, 1978
 (Off-Broadway) Opened June 22, 1978 for 37 performances
Reviews:
 New York Times III, page 11, Jun 30, 1978

Copper and Brass

book:	Ellen Violett and David Craig
music:	David Baker
lyrics:	David Craig
staging:	Marc Daniels
sets:	William and Jean Eckart
costumes:	Alvin Colt
choreography:	Anna Sokolow

Productions:
 Opened October 17, 1957 for 36 performances
Reviews:
 Dance Magazine 31:13, Dec 1957
 Nation 185:310, Nov 2, 1957
 New York Theatre Critics' Reviews 1957:216+
 New York Times VI, page 20, Aug 25, 1957
  page 19, Oct 18, 1957
 New Yorker 33:98-100, Oct 26, 1957
 Theatre Arts 41:26-7, Dec 1957
 Time 70:92, Oct 28, 1957

Copperfield

book:	Al Kasha and Joel Hirschhorn, based on Charles Dickens' David Copperfield
music:	Al Kasha and Joel Hirschhorn
lyrics:	Al Kasha and Joel Hirschhorn
staging:	Rob Iscove
sets:	Tony Straiges
costumes:	John David Ridge
choreography:	Rob Iscove

Productions:
 Opened April 13, 1981 for 13 performances
Reviews:
 New York 14:60-1, Apr 27, 1981
 New York Theatre Critics' Reviews 1981:286
 New York Times III, page 3, Apr 17, 1981
  II, page 3, Apr 26, 1981
 New Yorker 57:143, Apr 27, 1981

Corn
  book: Charles Ludlam
  music: Virgil Young
  lyrics: Virgil Young
  staging: Charles Ludlam
Productions:
  (Off-Off-Broadway) Opened November 23, 1972
Reviews:
  New York Times page 43, Nov 24, 1972

Cosmo Vanities   (see Belmont Varieties)

Cotton Patch Gospel
  book: Tom Key and Russell Treyz, based on The Cotton
                   Patch Version of Matthew and John by Clarence
                   Jordan
  music: Harry Chapin
  lyrics: Harry Chapin
  staging: Russell Treyz
  sets: John Falabella
  costumes: John Falabella
Productions:
  (Off-Broadway) Opened October 21, 1981 for 193 performances
Reviews:
  Christian Century 99:515, Apr 28, 1982
  Christianity Today 26:44, Feb 19, 1982
  Los Angeles 31:44, Jan 1986
  New York Times III, page 17, Oct 22, 1981

Count Me In
  book: Walter Kerr, Leo Brady, Nancy Hamilton
  music: Ann Ronell and Will Irwin
  lyrics: Walter Kerr, Leo Brady, Nancy Hamilton
  staging: Robert Ross
  sets: Howard Bay
  costumes: Irene Sharaff
  choreography: Robert Alton
Productions:
  Opened October 8, 1942 for 61 performances
Reviews:
  New York Theatre Critics' Reviews 1942:214+
  New York Times page 24, Oct 9, 1942
  Newsweek 20:76, Oct 19, 1942
  Theatre Arts 26:742, Dec 1942

The Count of Luxembourg
  book: Glen MacDonough, adapted from the original of
                   Willner and Bodansky
  music: Franz Lehar
  lyrics: Adrian Ross and Basil Hood
  staging: Herbert Gresham

Productions:
    Opened September 16, 1912 for 120 performances
    Opened Febraury 17, 1930 for 16 performances
Reviews:
    Blue Book 16:474-7, Jan 1913
    Dramatic Mirror 68:7, Sep 18, 1912
                   68:2, Oct 9, 1912
    Green Book 8:936-8+, Dec 1912
    Harper's Weekly 56:21, Oct 12, 1912
    Munsey 48:353, Nov 1912
    New York Dramatic News 56:19, Aug 31, 1912
                           56:13, Sep 21, 1912
                           57:29, Dec 28, 1912
    New York Times page 28, Feb 18, 1930
    Red Book 20:508-12, Jan 1913
    Theatre Magazine 16:xiii-iv, Oct 1912
                     16:157, Nov 1912
                     51:74, Apr 1930

Countess Maritza
    book: Harry B. Smith, adapted from the original of
                    Julius Brammer and Alfred Grunwald
    music: Emmerich Kalman
    lyrics: Harry B. Smith
    staging: J. J. Shubert
Productions:
    Opened September 18, 1926 for 318 performances
    Opened April 9, 1928 for 16 performances
Reviews:
    Life (New York) 88:23, Oct 27, 1916
    Nation 23:330, Oct 6, 1926
    New York Times page 28, Sep 19, 1926
                    page 21, Sep 20, 1926
                    page 32, Apr 10, 1928
    Theatre Magazine 44:15+, Nov 1926
    Vanity Fair 27:56, Nov 1926
    Vogue 68:110, Nov 15, 1926

A Country Girl
    book: James T. Tanner
    lyrics: Adrian Ross; additional lyrics and numbers by
                    Paul Rubens
Productions:
    Opened May 29, 1911 for 32 performances
Reviews:
    Blue Book 13:905-7, Sep 1911
    Dramatic Mirror 65:7, Jun 7, 1911
                   65:9, Jun 14, 1911
                   65:4, Jun 21, 1911
    Green Book Album 6:237-40, Aug 1911
    New York Times page 11, May 30, 1911

Red Book 17:765-8, Aug 1911
Theatre Magazine 14:iii, Jul 1911

Courtin' Time
    book: William Roos, based on Eden Phillpott's play The
                    Farmer's Wife
    music: Don Walker
    lyrics: Jack Lawrence
    staging: Alfred Drake
    sets: Ralph Alswang
    costumes: Saul Bolsani
    choreography: George Balanchine
Productions:
    Opened June 13, 1951 for 37 performances
Reviews:
    Catholic World 173: 386-7, Aug 1951
    Commonweal 54:285, Jun 29, 1951
    Nation 172:594, Jun 23, 1951
    New York Theatre Critics' Reviews 1951:254+
    New York Times page 30, Jun 14, 1951
                    II, page 1, Jun 17, 1951
                    II, page 1, Jul 1, 1951
                    II, page 9, Jul 1, 1951
    New Yorker 27:45, Jun 23, 1951
    Newsweek 37:72, Jun 25, 1951
    Theatre Arts 35:6, Sep 1951
    Time 57:73, Jun 25, 1951

Coward, Noel (see Noel Coward)

Cowboy Jack Street
    written: Joan Tewkesbury
    music and
      lyrics: Tony Berg and Ted Neely
    additional
      music: Michael Barry Greer
    staged: Joan Tewkesbury
    sets: Judie Juracek
    costumes: Judie Jracek
Productions:
    (Off-Off-Broadway) Opened November 25, 1977 for 16 performances
Reviews:
    New York Times III, page 3, Dec 9, 1977
                    page 54, Dec 13, 1977

The Cowgirl and the Tiger
    book: Wallace Gray
    music: Hank Beebe
    lyrics: Hank Beebe
    staging: Howard Lipson

Productions:
   (Off-Off-Broadway) Opened 1973-1974
No Reviews.

The Cradle Will Rock
   book: Marc Blitzstein
   music: Marc Blitzstein
   lyrics: Marc Blitzstein
   staging: Marc Blitzstein
Productions:
   Opened January 3, 1938 for 108 performances
   (Off-Broadway) Season of 1936-37
   (Off-Broadway) Season of 1937-38 for 19 performances
   (Off-Broadway) Season of 1938-39 for one performance
   (Off-Broadway) Opened January 15, 1939
   Opened November 24, 1947 for 2 performances
   Opened December 26, 1947 for 21 performances
   (Off-Broadway) Season of 1959-60
   (Off-Broadway) Opened November 8, 1964 for 82 performances
   (Off-Broadway) Opened May 9, 1983 for 24 performances
Reviews:
   Catholic World 146:598-9, Feb 1938
   Commonweal 47:350, Jan 16, 1948
   Current History 48:53, Apr 1938
   Forum 109:156, Mar 1948
   Literary Digest 125:34, Jan 1, 1938
   Magazine of Art 32:356-7+, Jun 1939
   Nation 146:107, Jan 22, 1938
         190:236, Mar 12, 1960
   New Republic 93:310, Jan 19, 1938
             117:35-6, Dec 22, 1947
   New York Theatre Critics' Reviews 1947:229+
   New York Times page 19, Dec 6, 1937
              page 19, Jan 4, 1938
              II, page 7, Nov 23, 1947
              page 38, Nov 25, 1947
              II, page 9, Feb 7, 1960
              page 23, Feb 12, 1960
              II, page 9, Feb 21, 1960
              page 40, Nov 9, 1964
              page 35, Jan 6, 1965
              page 14, May 13, 1978
              III, page 11, May 10, 1983
   New Yorker 23:45, Jan 10, 1948
          36:142-3, Feb 20, 1960
   Newsweek 10:20-1, Jul 3, 1937
         30:78, Dec 7, 1948
         64:102, Nov 23, 1964
   Reporter 30:46+, May 21, 1964
   Saturday Review 31:22-4, Jan 17, 1948
   Scribner's Magazine 103:70-1, Mar 1938

Stage 15:54, Feb 1938
Theatre Arts 22:98-9, Feb 1938
Time 29:46+, Jun 28, 1937
    30:57, Dec 13, 1937
    51:64, Jan 5, 1948

Cranks
book:	John Cranko
music:	John Addison
lyrics:	John Cranko
staging:	John Cranko

Productions:
Opened November 26, 1956 for 40 performances
Reviews:
Christian Century 74:172, Feb 6, 1957
Nation 183:526, Dec 15, 1956
New York Theatre Critics' Reviews 1956:185+
New York Times page 23, May 14, 1956
             page 32, Nov 27, 1956
New Yorker 32:90-1, Dec 8, 1956
        32:25, Dec 15, 1956
Saturday Review 39:26, Dec 15, 1956
Theatre Arts 41:19, Feb 1957
Time 68:70, Dec 10, 1956

Crawford, Joan (see Evening With Joan Crawford)

Crazy Now
book:	Richard Smithies and Maura Cavanagh
music:	Norman Sachs
lyrics:	Richard Smithies and Maura Cavanagh
staging:	Voight Kempson
choreography:	Voight Kempson

Productions:
(Off-Broadway) Opened September 17, 1972 for one performance
Reviews:
New York Times page 45, Sep 11, 1972

Crazy Quilt (see Billy Rose's Crazy Quilt)

Crazy with the Heat
sketches:	Sam E. Werris, Arthur Sheekman, Mack Davis, Max Liebman, Don Herold
music:	Irvin Graham, Dana Suesse, Rudi Revil
lyrics:	Irvin Graham, Dana Suesse, Rudi Revil
staging:	Kurt Kasznar
sets:	Albert Johnson
costumes:	Lester Polakov and Marie Humans
choreography:	Catherine Littlefield

Productions:
Opened January 14, 1941 for 99 performances

Reviews:
     Catholic World 152:728, Mar 1941
     Nation 152:137, Feb 1, 1941
     New York Theatre Critics' Reviews 1941:410+
     New York Times page 18, Jan 15, 1941
                    page 25, Jan 16, 1941
                    page 15, Jan 31, 1941
     Theatre Arts 25:257+, Apr 1941

The Crinoline Girl
     book: Otto Harbach
     music: Percy Wenrich
     lyrics: Julian Eltinge
     staging: John Emerson
Productions:
     Opened March 16, 1914 for 88 performances
Reviews:
     Dramatic Mirror 71:6, Mar 18, 1914
                    71:2, Apr 1, 1914
     Green Book 11:976, Jun 1914
                11:1019-20, Jun 1914
     New York Dramatic News 59:14, Mar 21, 1914
     New York Times page 11, Mar 17, 1914
     Theatre Magazine 19:227, May 1914
                    19:240, May 1914

Criss Cross
     book: Otto Harbach and Anne Caldwell
     music: Jerome Kern
     lyrics: Otto Harbach and Anne Caldwell
     staging: R. H. Burnside
Productions:
     Opened October 12, 1926 for 206 performances
Reviews:
     New York Times page 20, Oct 13, 1926

Croesus and the Witch
     music: Micki Grant; based on a fable
     lyrics: Micki Grant
     staging: Vinnette Carroll
     sets: Richard A. Miller
     choreography: Talley Beatty
Productions:
     (Off-Broadway) Opened August 24, 1971
Reviews:
     New York Times page 18, Aug 27, 1971
     New Yorker 47:54, Sep 4, 1971

Cross My Heart
     book: Daniel Kusell
     music: Harry Tierney

lyrics: Joseph McCarthy
staging: Sammy Lee
Productions:
Opened September 17, 1928 for 64 performances
Reviews:
New York Times page 32, Sep 18, 1928
Theatre Magazine 48:48, Nov 1928

The Crucible
    book: Based on the play by Arthur Miller
    music: Robert Ward
    lyrics: Bernard Stambler
    words: Bernard Stambler
    staging: Allen Fletcher
    sets: Paul Sylbert
    costumes: Ruth Morley
Productions:
(Off-Broadway) Opened October 26, 1961 for 3 performances
No Reviews.

Cry For Us All
    book: William Alfred and Albert Marre; based on William
                  Alfred's play Hogan's Goat
    music: Mitch Leigh
    lyrics: William Alfred and Phyllis Robinson
    staging: Albert Marre
    sets: Howard Bay
    costumes: Robert Fletcher
    choreography: Todd Bolender
Productions:
Opened April 8, 1970 for 9 performances
Reviews:
New York Theatre Critics' Reviews 1970:304
New York Times page 48, Apr 9, 1970
New Yorker 46:79-80, Apr 18, 1970
Time 95:51, Apr 20, 1970

The Crystal Heart
    book: William Archibald
    music: Baldwin Bergersen
    lyrics: William Archibald
    staging: William Archibald
    sets: Richard Casler
    costumes: Ted Van Griethuysen
    choreography: William Archibald
Productions:
(Off-Broadway) Opened February 15, 1960 for 9 performances
Reviews:
New York Times page 31, Feb 16, 1960
                page 40, Feb 24, 1960
New Yorker 36:104-6, Feb 27, 1960

Curley McDimple
  book: Mary Boylan and Robert Dahdah
  music: Robert Dahdah
  lyrics: Robert Dahdah
  staging: Robert Dahdah
  sets: Richard Jackson
  costumes: John Hirsch
  choreography: Larry Stevens
Productions:
  (Off-Broadway) Opened November 22, 1967 for 931 performances
Reviews:
  New York Times page 59, Nov 23, 1967
                  page 52, May 9, 1968
                  page 53, Nov 14, 1968
                  page 53, Nov 25, 1969

Cybele
  book: Mario Fratti; based on Sundays and Cybele
  music: Paul Dick
  lyrics: Paul Dick
  staging: Amy Saltz
Productions:
  (Off-Broadway) Opened 1971-1972
No Reviews.

Cyrano
  book: Anthony Burgess; adapted from Edmund Rostand's
                         Cyrano de Bergerac
  music: Michael J. Lewis
  lyrics: Anthony Burgess
  staging: Michael Kidd
  sets: John Jenson
  costumes: Desmond Heeley
Productions:
  Opened May 13, 1973 for 49 performances
Reviews:
  America 128:538, Jun 9, 1973
  Harper's 106:153, Mar 1973
          106:98+, Apr 1973
  Nation 216:731, Jun 4, 1973
  New York 6:74, May 28, 1973
  New York Theatre Critics' Reviews 1973:272
  New York Times page 37, May 14, 1973
                 page 52, May 17, 1973
                 II, page 1, May 20, 1973
  New Yorker 49:54, May 26, 1973
  Newsweek 81:83, May 28, 1973
  Playboy 20:39, Aug 1973
  Time 101:55, May 28, 1973

-D-

Daffy Dill
book: Guy Bolton and Oscar Hammerstein II
music: Herbert Stothart
lyrics: Oscar Hammerstein II
staging: Julian Mitchell
Productions:
Opened August 22, 1922 for 71 performances
Reviews:
New York Clipper 70:20, Aug 30, 1922
New York Times page 14, Aug 23, 1922
Theatre Magazine 36:228, Oct 1922

Dakota
book: Tom Hill
music: Frances Ziffer, Hortense Belson and Hardy
Wieder
Productions:
(Off-Broadway) Opened 1952-1953
No Reviews.

Dames at Sea
book: George Haimsohn and Robin Miller
music: Jim Wise
lyrics: George Haimsohn and Robin Miller
staging: Neal Kenyon
sets: Peter Harvey
costumes: Peter Harvey
choreography: Neal Kenyon
Productions:
(Off-Broadway) Opened December 20, 1968 for 575 performances
(Off-Broadway) Opened September 23, 1970 for 170 performances
(Off-Broadway) Opened June 12, 1985 for 278 performances
Reviews:
Commonweal 89:735-6, Mar 14, 1969
Dance Magazine 43:70-1, Mar 1969
Life 66:8, Mar 7, 1969
Nation 208:109, Feb 10, 1969
New York Theatre Critics' Reviews 1968:126
1985:220
New York Times page 46, Dec 21, 1968
II, page 1, Jan 5, 1969
II, page 3, Feb 9, 1969
page 24, Aug 29, 1969
page 46, Jan 5, 1970
page 44, Aug 27, 1970
page 60, Sep 24, 1970
III, page 33, Jun 13, 1985
XI, page 16, Jun 30, 1985
New Yorker 44:60-1, Jan 4, 1969

Newsweek 73:86, Jan 13, 1969
Saturday Review 52:74, Jan 11, 1969
Time 93:65, Jan 3, 1969

Damn Yankees

book:	George Abbott and Douglass Wallop, based on Douglass Wallop's novel The Year the Yankees Lost the Pennant
music:	Richard Adler and Jerry Ross
lyrics:	Richard Adler and Jerry Ross
staging:	George Abbott
sets:	William and Jean Eckart
costumes:	William and Jean Eckart
choreography:	Bob Fosse

Productions:
Opened May 5, 1955 for 1,019 performances
(Off-Broadway) Season of 1966-67 for 14 performances
(Off-Off-Broadway) Opened June 30, 1981

Reviews:
America 93:278, Jun 4, 1955
Catholic World 181:307, Jul 1955
Commonweal 62:329, Jul 1, 1955
Life 38:163-71, May 16, 1955
Look 19:64+, Jul 12, 1955
Nation 180:449, May 21, 1955
New York Theatre Critics' Reviews 1955:310+
New York Times VI, page 67, Apr 17, 1955
            II, page 1, May 1, 1955
            page 17, May 6, 1955
            II, page 1, Apr 1, 1956
            II, page 1, May 13, 1956
            page 15, Mar 29, 1957
            III, page 11, Jul 2, 1981
            XXI, page 2, Aug 9, 1981
New York Times Magazine page 67, Apr 17, 1955
New Yorker 31:132+, May 14, 1955
Newsweek 45:96, May 16, 1955
Saturday Review 38:44, May 21, 1955
            39:12, Sep 15, 1956
Theatre Arts 39:20-2, Jul 1955
Time 65:104, May 16, 1955
Vogue 125:77, May 15, 1955

Dance a Little Closer

book:	Alan Jay Lerner, based on Idiot's Delight by Robert E. Sherwood
music:	Charles Strouse
lyrics:	Alan Jay Lerner
staging:	Alan Jay Lerner
sets:	David Mitchell
costumes:	Donald Brooks
choreography:	Billy Wilson

Productions:
  Opened May 11, 1983 for one performance
Reviews:
  Harper's Bazaar 116:38, May 1983
  New York 16:94-5, May 23, 1983
  New York Theatre Critics' Reviews 1983:248
  New York Times III, page 18, May 12, 1983
           II, page 8, Jun 12, 1983

Dance Me a Song
  sketches: Jimmy Kirkwood and Lee Goodman, George Oppen-
                 heimer and Vincente Minnelli, Marya Mannes,
                 Robert Anderson, James Shelton and Wally Cox
  songs: James Shelton, Herman Hupfeld, Albert Hague,
                 Maurice Valency and Bud Gregg
  staging: James Shelton
  sets: Jo Mielziner
  costumes: Irene Sharaff
  choreography: Robert Sidney
Productions:
  Opened January 20, 1950 for 35 performances
Reviews:
  New York Theatre Critics' Reviews 1950:380+
  New York Times page 10, Jan 21, 1950
  New Yorker 25:48, Jan 28, 1950
  Newsweek 35:66, Jan 30, 1950
  Theatre Arts 34:19, Mar 1950
  Time 55:40, Jan 30, 1950

Dance On a Country Grave
  book: Kelly Hamilton, based on Thomas Hardy's Return
                 of the Native
  music: Kelly Hamilton
  lyrics: Kelly Hamilton
  staging: Robert Brewer
Productions:
  (Off-Off-Broadway) Opened April 21, 1977
Reviews:
  New York Times page 47, Apr 26, 1977

Dancin'
  conceived: Bob Fosse
  music and
    lyrics: Johann Sebastian Bach, Ralph Burns, George M.
                 Cohan, Neil Diamond, Bob Haggart, Ray Bauduc,
                 Gil Rodin and Bob Crosby, Jerry Leiber and
                 Mike Stoller, Johnny Mercer and Harry Warren,
                 Louis Prima, John Philip Sousa, Carol Bayer
                 Sager and Melissa Manchester, Barry Mann and
                 Cynthia Weil, Felix Powell and George Asaf, Cat
                 Stevens, Edgard Varese and Jerry Jeff Walker.

```
staging:          Bob Fosse
sets:             Peter Larkin
costumes:         Willa Kim
choreography:     Bob Fosse
```
Productions:
  Opened March 27, 1978 for 1,774 performances
Reviews:
  America 138:349, Apr 29, 1978
  Dance Magazine 52:21+, Aug 1978
  Horizon 21:22-7, Apr 1978
  Los Angeles 24:237, Jul 1979
  New West 4:69, Jul 30, 1979
  New York 11:74, Apr 10, 1978
  New York Theatre Critics' Reviews 1978:316
  New York Times page 48, Mar 28, 1978
                 II, page 5, Apr 9, 1978
  New Yorker 54:91, Apr 10, 1978
            54:149-52, Apr 24, 1978
  Newsweek 91:62-3, Apr 10, 1978
  Saturday Review 5:42, May 27, 1978
  Time 111:94, Apr 10, 1978

Dancing Around
```
    dialogue:        Harold Atteridge
    music:           Sigmund Romberg and Harry Carroll
    lyrics:          Harold Atteridge
    staging:         J. C. Huffman
    choreography:    Jack Mason
```
Productions:
  Opened October 10, 1914 for 145 performances
Reviews:
  Dramatic Mirror 72:8, Oct 21, 1914
                  72:2, Nov 11, 1914
  Munsey 53:558, Dec 1914
  New York Times III, page 3, Oct 11, 1914
  Theatre Magazine 20:255, Nov 1914
                   20:259, Dec 1914

The Dancing Duchess
```
    book:            C. V. Kerr and R. H. Burnside
    music:           Milton Lusk
    lyrics:          C. V. Kerr and R. H. Burnside
    staging:         R. H. Burnside
```
Productions:
  Opened August 19, 1914 for 13 performances
Reviews:
  Dramatic Mirror 72:6, Aug 26, 1914
  Green Book 12:901, Nov 1914
  New York Times page 9, Aug 21, 1914
  Theatre Magazine 20:95, Sep 1914

The Dancing Girl
    book: Harold Atteridge
    music: Sigmund Romberg and Alfred Goodman
    lyrics: Harold Atteridge
    staging: J. C. Huffman
Productions:
    Opened January 24, 1923 for 126 performances
Reviews:
    New York Clipper 71:14, Feb 7, 1923
    New York Times page 16, Jan 25, 1923

Dark of the Moon
    book: Howard Richardson and William Berney
    music: Walter Hendl
    staging: Robert E. Perry
    sets: George Jenkins
    choreography: Esther Junger
Productions:
    Opened March 14, 1945 for 320 performances
Reviews:
    Life 17:55-7, Sep 11, 1944
    Musical Courier 132:13, Oct 15, 1945
    Nation 160:370, Mar 31, 1945
    New Republic 112:447, Apr 2, 1945
    New York Theatre Critics' Reviews 1945:252
    New York Times VI, page 24, Mar 11, 1945
                   page 27, Mar 15, 1945
                   II, page 1, Mar 25, 1945
    Newsweek 25:88, Mar 26, 1945
    Player's Magazine 22:14, Nov-Dec 1945
    Theatre Arts 29:262+, May 1945
    Time 45:70, Mar 26, 1945

Darling of the Day
    book: Nunnally Johnson; based on Arnold Bennett's
                   Buried Alive
    music: Jule Styne
    lyrics: E. Y. Harburg
    staging: Noel Willman
    sets: Oliver Smith
    costumes: Raoul Péne du Bois
    choreography: Lee Theodore
Productions:
    Opened January 27, 1968 for 33 performances
Reviews:
    Dance Magazine 42:27-8, Apr 1968
    New York Theatre Critics' Reviews 1968:359
                            1968:370
    New York Times page 26, Jan 29, 1968
                   II, page 3, Feb 11, 1968
                   page 45, Feb 23, 1968

                        page 42, Feb 26, 1968
      New Yorker 43:77-8, Feb 3, 1968

Darwin's Theories
      book: Darwin Venneri
      music: Darwin Venneri
      lyrics: Darwin Venneri
Productions:
      (Off-Broadway)   Season of 1960-1961
Reviews:
      New York Times   page 40, Sep 6, 1960
                       page 53, Oct 19, 1960
                       page 28, Oct 21, 1960

The Day Before Spring
      book: Alan Jay Lerner
      music: Frederick Loewe
      lyrics: Alan Jay Lerner
      staging: John C. Wilson
      sets: Robert Davison
      costumes: Miles White
      choreography: Antony Tudor
Productions:
      Opened November 22, 1945 for 165 performances
Reviews:
      Catholic World 162:360, Jan 1946
      Commonweal 43:238, Dec 14, 1945
      Harpers 79:128, Dec 1945
      Life 19:85-6+, Dec 17, 1945
      New York Theatre Critics' Reviews 1945:92+
      New York Times page 27, Nov 23, 1945
                       II, page 1, Dec 2, 1945
      New Yorker 21:52, Dec 1, 1945
      Newsweek 26:92, Dec 3, 1945
      Theatre Arts 30:14, Jan 1946
      Time 46:68, Dec 3, 1945

A Day in Hollywood/A Night in the Ukraine
      book: Dick Vosburgh
      music: Frank Lazarus and various composers
      lyrics: Dick Vosburgh and various authors
      staging: Tommy Tune
      sets: Tony Walton
      costumes: Michel Stuart
      choreography: Tommy Tune and Thommie Walsh
Productions:
      Opened May 1, 1980 for 588 performances
Reviews:
      American Record Guide 43:10, Sep 1980
      Fortune 104:50, Nov 16, 1981
      Los Angeles 27:232+, Mar 1982

New York 13:58, May 19, 1980
New York Theatre Critics' Reviews 1980:256
New York Times II, page 1, Apr 27, 1980
                III, page 3, May 2, 1980
                II, page 7, May 11, 1980
                II, page 3, Jul 6, 1980
New Yorker 56:70+, May 12, 1980
Newsweek 95:109, May 12, 1980
Theatre Crafts 14:18-19+, Oct 1980
Time 115:83, May 12, 1980

A Day in the Life of Just About Everyone
    book: Earl Wilson Jr.; additional dialogue by Michael
                    Sawyer
    music: Earl Wilson Jr.
    lyrics: Earl Wilson Jr.
    staging: Tom Panko
    sets: Andrew Greenhut
    costumes: Miles White
Productions:
    (Off-Broadway) Opened March 9, 1971 for 8 performances
Reviews:
    New York Times page 31, Mar 10, 1971
    New Yorker 47:96, Mar 20, 1971

The Deacon and the Lady
    book: George Totten Smith
    music: Alfred E. Aarons
    staging: Alfred E. Aarons
Productions:
    Opened October 4, 1910 for 16 performances
Reviews:
    Blue Book 12:443-5, Jan 1911
    Metropolitan Magazine 33:530, Jan 1911
    Theatre Magazine 12:x, Nov 1910

Dear Oscar
    book: Caryl Gabrielle Young, based on the life of
                    Oscar Wilde
    music: Addy O. Fieger
    lyrics: Caryl Gabrielle Young
    staging: John Allen
    sets: William Pitkin
    costumes: Mary McKinley
Productions:
    Opened November 16, 1972 for 5 performances
Reviews:
    New York Theatre Critics' Reviews 1972:179
    New York Times page 37, Nov 17, 1972

Dear Piaf
    conceived: Ken Guilmartin

music: Various composers, adapted by Ken Guilmartin
lyrics: Various authors, translated and adapted by
                  Lucia Victor
staging: Dorothy Chernuck
sets: T. Winberry
costumes: Adri
Productions:
  (Off-Broadway) Opened December 19, 1975 for 74 performances
  (Off-Off-Broadway) Opened December 1975
No Reviews.

Dear Sir
  book: Edgar Selwyn
  music: Jerome Kern
  lyrics: Howard Dietz
Productions:
  Opened September 23, 1924 for 15 performances
Reviews:
  New York Times page 21, Sep 24, 1924

Dear World
  book: Jerome Lawrence and Robert E. Lee; based on
                  The Madwoman of Chaillot by Jean Giraudoux,
                  as adapted by Maurice Valency
  music: Jerry Herman
  lyrics: Jerry Herman
  staging: Joe Layton
  sets: Oliver Smith
  costumes: Freddy Wittop
  choreography: Dorothea Freitage
Productions:
  Opened February 6, 1969 for 132 performances
Reviews:
  America 120:512, Apr 26, 1969
  Christian Century 86:483-4, Apr 9, 1969
  Dance Magazine 43:20+, Apr 1969
  New York Theatre Critics' Reviews 1969:363
  New York Times page 33, Feb 7, 1969
                  II, page 1, Feb 16, 1969
                  II, page 25, May 11, 1969
                  page 19, May 17, 1969
  New Yorker 44:90, Feb 15, 1969
  Newsweek 73:113, Feb 17, 1969

Dearest Enemy
  book: Herbert Fields
  music: Richard Rodgers
  lyrics: Lorenz Hart
  staging: John Murray Anderson
Productions:
  Opened September 18, 1925 for 286 performances

Reviews:
  Literary Digest 87:31-2, Oct 19, 1925
  New York Times page 9, Sep 19, 1925
  Theatre Magazine 42:44, Dec 1925

The Death of Von Richtofen as Witnessed from Earth
  book: Des McAnuff
  music: Des McAnuff
  lyrics: Des McAnuff
  staging: Des McAnuff
  sets: Douglas W. Schmidt
  costumes: Patricia McGourty
  choreography: Jennifer Muller
Productions:
  (Off-Broadway) Opened July 29, 1982 for 45 performances
Reviews:
  New York 15:42, Aug 9, 1982
  New York Theatre Critics' Reviews 1982:223
  New York Times III, page 3, Jul 30, 1982
  Newsweek 100:68, Aug 9, 1982
  Time 120:74, Aug 9, 1982

Debbie
  songs: Various authors and composers
  staging: Ron Lewis
  sets: Billy Morris
  costumes: Bob Mackie
  choreography: Ron Lewis
Productions:
  Opened September 16, 1976 for 14 performances
Reviews:
  New York Theatre Critics' Reviews 1976:196
  New York Times III, page 4, Sep 17, 1976

The Decameron
  book: Yvonne Tarr, based on Boccaccio
  music: Edward Earle
  lyrics: Yvonne Tarr
Productions:
  (Off-Broadway) Season of 1960-1961
Reviews:
  New York Times page 32, Apr 13, 1961

The Decline and Fall of the Entire World as Seen through the Eyes
  of Cole Porter, revisited
  continuity: Bud McCreery
  songs: Cole Porter
  staging: Ben Bagley
  sets: Shirley Kaplan
  costumes: Charles Fatone
Productions:
  (Off-Broadway) Opened March 30, 1965 for 273 performances

Reviews:
    Life 59:12, Jul 30, 1965
    National Review 17:561, Jun 25, 1965
    New York Times page 24, Mar 31, 1965
                  page 20, Dec 23, 1965
    Newsweek 65:98, Apr 12, 1965
    Saturday Review 48:44, Apr 17, 1965

Deep Harlem
    book: Salem Whitney and Homer Tutt
    music: Joe Jordan
    lyrics: Homer Tutt and Henry Creamer
    staging: Henry Creamer
Productions:
    Opened January 7, 1929 for 8 performances
No Reviews.

Deep River
    book: Laurence Stallings
    music: Frank Harling
    lyrics: Laurence Stallings
    staging: Arthur Hopkins
Productions:
    Opened October 4, 1926 for 32 performances
Reviews:
    American Mercury 9:500-01, Dec 1926
    Dial 81:524, Dec 1926
    Life (New York) 88:23, Oct 21, 1926
    Literary Digest 91:26-7, Oct 23, 1926
    Musical Courier 93:24, Oct 14, 1926
    Nation 123:409, Oct 20, 1926
    Theatre Arts 10:814-15, Dec 1926
    Theatre Magazine 44:18, Dec 1926
    Vogue 68:78-9, Dec 15, 1926

A Delightful Season
    book, music
      and lyrics: Don Allan Clayton, based on Oscar Wilde's
                     Lady Windermere's Fan
Productions:
    (Off-Broadway)   Season of 1960-1961
Reviews:
    New York Times page 30, Sep 29, 1960
                  page 49, Oct 4, 1960

Delmar's Revels
    sketches: William K. Wells
    music: Jimmy Monaco, Jesse Greer and Lester Lee
    lyrics: Billy Rose and Ballard MacDonald
    staging: Harry Delmar

Productions:
  Opened November 28, 1927 for 112 performances
No Reviews.

Der Ring Gott Farblonjet
  book: Charles Ludlam, based on various versions of
                 the Volsung saga (including those of Wagner,
                 Ibsen and Nietzsche)
  music: Jack McElwaine
  staging: Charles Ludlam
  Productions:
  (Off-Broadway) Opened April 27, 1977 for 78 performances
  Reviews:
  New York 10:74, May 16, 1977
  New York Times III, page 3, Apr 29, 1977

The Desert Song
  book: Otto Harbach, Oscar Hammerstein II, and Frank
                 Mandel
  music: Sigmund Romberg
  staging: Arthur Hurley and Robert Connelly
  Productions:
  Opened November 30, 1926 for 471 performances
  Opened January 8, 1946 for 45 performances
  Opened September 5, 1973 for 15 performances
  (Off-Broadway) Opened October 22, 1980 for 35 performances
  (Off-Off-Broadway) Opened August 10, 1983
  (Off-Off-Broadway) Opened March 14, 1984
  (Off-Off-Broadway) Opened March 16, 1988
  Reviews:
  Bookman 65:73-4, Mar 1927
  Life (New York) 88:19, Dec 16, 1926
  New York 6:74, Sep 10, 1973
  New York Theatre Critics' Reviews 1973:236
  New York Times VII, page 1, May 8, 1927
              VIII, page 4, Feb 5, 1928
              II, page 1, Jan 6, 1946
              page 20, Jan 9, 1946
              page 56, Aug 12, 1973
              page 44, Sep 6, 1973
              II, page 1, Sep 16, 1973
              page 38, Sep 19, 1973
              page 52, May 21, 1978
              page 77, Nov 2, 1980
              XI, page 2, May 20, 1984
  New Yorker 21:46, Jan 26, 1946
  Newsweek 82:90, Sep 17, 1973
  Theatre Magazine 49:28, Feb 1929
  Vogue 69:73, Feb 1, 1927

Design for Laughter
  book: William Michkin and John Francis

music: Alexander Maissel
Productions:
   (Off-Broadway) Opened November 29, 1944
No Reviews:

Destry Rides Again
   book: Leonard Gershe, based on a story by Max Brand
   music: Harold Rome
   lyrics: Harold Rome
   staging: Michael Kidd
   sets: Oliver Smith
   costumes: Alvin Colt
   choreography: Michael Kidd
Productions:
   Opened April 23, 1959 for 472 performances
Reviews:
   America 101:479, Jun 27, 1959
   Catholic World 189:320, Jul 1959
   Commonweal 70:328, Jun 26, 1959
   Dance Magazine 33:17, Jun 1959
   Life 46:49-54, May 25, 1959
   New Republic 140:20, May 11, 1959
   New York Theatre Critics' Reviews 1959:314+
   New York Times II, page 1, Apr 19, 1959
                    page 24, Apr 24, 1959
                    II, page 1, May 3, 1959
                    page 37, Jun 16, 1960
   New Yorker 35:95-7, May 2, 1959
   Newsweek 53:57, May 4, 1959
   Saturday Review 42:22, May 9, 1959
   Theatre Arts 43:22-4, Jun 1959
                43:9-10, Jul 1959
   Time 73:74, May 4, 1959

The Devil and Daniel Webster
   book: Douglas Moore, based on Stephen Vincent Benet's
                    short story
   music: Douglas Moore
   lyrics: Douglas Moore
   staging: John Houseman
   sets: Robert Edmund Jones
   choreography: Eugene Loring
Productions:
   Opened May 18, 1939 for 6 performances
Reviews:
   Commonweal 30:160, Jun 2, 1939
   Life 6:37-8+, Jun 12, 1939
   Musical Courier 119:7, Jun 1, 1939
   New Republic 99:131, Jun 7, 1939
   New York Times page 26, May 19, 1939
                    X, page 1, May 21, 1939

Newsweek 13:34, Jun 5, 1939
Saturday Review 20:10, May 20, 1939
20:8, May 27, 1939
Time 33:40, May 29, 1939

Dew Drops Inn

book:	Walter DeLeon and Edward Delaney Dunn
music:	Alfred Goodman
lyrics:	Cyrus Wood
staging:	J. J. Shubert

Productions:
Opened May 17, 1923 for (37) performances
Reviews:
New York Clipper 71:14, May 23, 1923
New York Times page 26, May 18, 1923
page 12, Jul 31, 1923
Theatre Magazine 38:16, Jul 1923

Diamond Studs

book:	Jim Wann, based on the life of Jesse James
music:	Bland Simpson and Jim Wann
lyrics:	Bland Simpson and Jim Wann
staging:	John L. Haber
choreography:	Patricia Birch

Productions:
(Off-Broadway) Opened January 14, 1975 for 232 performances
Reviews:
New York 8:65, Feb 3, 1975
New York Theatre Critics' Reviews 1975:345
New York Times page 50, Jan 15, 1975
New Yorker 50:70, Jan 27, 1975
Newsweek 85:69, Jan 27, 1975
Saturday Review 2:39, Mar 22, 1975

Diamonds

sketches:	Various authors
songs:	Various authors and composers
staging:	Harold Prince
sets:	Tony Straiges
costumes:	Judith Dolan
choreography:	Theodore Pappas

Productions:
(Off-Broadway) Opened December 16, 1984 for 122 performances
Reviews:
Horizon 28:48-9, Sep 1985
New York 18:54-5, Jan 7, 1985
New York Theatre Critics' Reviews 1984:122
New York Times III, page 12, Dec 17, 1984
New Yorker 60:56, Dec 31, 1984
Theatre Crafts 19:10, Feb 1985

Diana Ross   (see Evening With Diana Ross)

Different Times
    book: Michael Brown
    music: Michael Brown
    lyrics: Michael Brown
    staging: Michael Brown
    sets: David Guthrie
    costumes: David Guthrie
    choreography: Tod Jackson
Productions:
    Opened May 1, 1972 for 24 performances
Reviews:
    New York Theatre Critics' Reviews 1972: 286
    New York Times page 50, May 2, 1972
                 page 18, May 20, 1972

The Difficult Woman
    book: Adapted and translated by Ruth C. Gillespie and
                    Malcolm Stuart Boylan; based on a play by Con-
                    rado Nale Roxlo
    music: Dick Frietas
    lyrics: Morty Neff and George Mysels; additional material
                    and dialogue by Maurice Alevy
    staging: Maurice Alevy
Productions:
    (Off-Broadway) Opened April 25, 1962 for 3 performances
Reviews:
    New York Times page 22, Apr 26, 1962

Digging for Apples
    book: James E. Butler and Robert Bowers
    music: James E. Butler and Robert Bowers
    lyrics: James E. Butler and Robert Bowers
    staging: James E. Butler and Robert Bowers
    sets: Gerald E. Proctor
    choreography: Gretchen Vanaken and Bob Cotton
Productions:
    (Off-Broadway) Opened September 27, 1962 for 28 performances
Reviews:
    New York Times page 29, Sep 28, 1962

Dime A Dozen
    conceived: Julius Monk
    staging: Frank Wagner
    costumes: Donald Brooks
    choreography: Frank Wagner
Productions:
    (Off-Broadway) Opened October 18, 1962 for 728 performances
No Reviews.

Dinah! Queen of the Blues
by: Sasha Dalton and Ernest McCarty, based on the life of Dinah Washington
songs: Various authors and composers
staging: Woodie King Jr.
sets: Llewellyn Harrison
costumes: Judy Dearing
Productions:
(Off-Broadway) Opened January 11, 1984 for 7 performances
Reviews:
New York Times III, page 32, Jan 12, 1984

Dispatches
book: Elizabeth Swados, based on the book by Michael Herr
songs: Elizabeth Swados
staging: Elizabeth Swados
sets: Patricia Woodbridge
costumes: Hilary Rosenfeld
Productions:
(Off-Broadway) Opened April 18, 1979 for 63 performances
Reviews:
New York 12:85, May 7, 1979
New York Times III, page 17, Apr 19, 1979
New Yorker 55:95-6, Apr 30, 1979
Newsweek 93:98, Apr 30, 1979

The Disposal
book: William Inge
music: Anthony Caldarella
lyrics: Judith Gero
staging: Barry Feinstein
Productions:
(Off-Off-Broadway) Opened September 22, 1973
No Reviews.

Dixie to Broadway
book: Walter DeLeon, Tom Howard, Lew Leslie and Sidney Lazarus
music: George W. Meyer and Arthur Johnstone
lyrics: Grant Clarke and Roy Turk
Productions:
Opened October 29, 1924 for 77 performances
Reviews:
New York Times page 22, Oct 30, 1924

Do Black Patent Leather Shoes Really Reflect Up?
book: John R. Powers, based on his novel
music: James Quinn and Alaric Jans
lyrics: James Quinn and Alaric Jans
staging: Mike Nussbaum

sets: James Maronek
costumes: Nancy Potts
choreography: Thommie Walsh
Productions:
  Opened May 27, 1982 for 5 performances
Reviews:
  Chicago 28:14+, Jun 1979
  New York 15:62+, Jun 7, 1982
  New York Theatre Critics' Reviews 1982:257
  New York Times III, page 3, May 28, 1982
  New Yorker 58:112+, Jun 7, 1982

Do I Hear a Waltz?

book: Arthur Laurents, based on his play The Time of
                the Cuckoo
music: Richard Rodgers
lyrics: Stephen Sondheim
staging: John Dexter
sets: Beni Montresor
costumes: Beni Montresor
choreography: Herbert Ross
Productions:
  Opened March 18, 1965 for 220 performances
  (Off-Off-Broadway) Opened March 6, 1975
Reviews:
  America 112:590-1, Apr 17, 1965
  Commonweal 82:85-6, Apr 9, 1965
  Dance Magazine 39:28-9, May 1965
  New York Theatre Critics' Reviews 1965:357+
  New York Times page 29, Nov 6, 1964
                page 40, Feb 16, 1965
                page 28, Mar 19, 1965
                II, page 1, Mar 28, 1965
                page 53, Mar 16, 1975
  New Yorker 41:144, Mar 27, 1965
  Newsweek 65:82, Mar 29, 1965
  Saturday Review 48:36, Apr 3, 1965
  Time 85:60, Mar 26, 1965

Do It Again!

conceived: Bert Convy
music: George Gershwin
lyrics: Ira Gershwin
staging: Bert Convy
sets: Barry Arnold
Productions:
  (Off-Broadway) Opened February 18, 1971 for 14 performances
Reviews:
  New York Times page 27, Feb 19, 1971

Do Re Mi

book: Garson Kanin

music:	Jule Styne
lyrics:	Betty Comden and Adolph Green
staging:	Garson Kanin
sets:	Boris Aronson
costumes:	Irene Sharaff
choreography:	Marc Breaux and Deedee Wood

Productions:
Opened December 26, 1960 for 400 performances
Reviews:
America 104:549, Jan 21, 1961
Commonweal 73:509, Feb 10, 1961
Coronet 49:16, Apr 1961
Dance Magazine 35:16-17, Feb 1961
Life 50:53-4+, Feb 10, 1961
Nation 192:39, Jan 14, 1961
New York Theatre Critics' Reviews 1960:129+
New York Times II, page 3, Dec 25, 1960
page 23, Dec 27, 1960
II, page 1, Jan 8, 1961
page 27, Oct 13, 1961
New Yorker 36:88, Jan 14, 1961
Newsweek 57:52, Jan 9, 1961
Saturday Review 44:28, Jan 14, 1961
Time 77:51, Jan 6, 1961

Dr. DeLuxe
book:	Otto Hauerbach and Karl Hoschna
staging:	Frank Smithson

Productions:
Opened April 17, 1911 for 32 performances
Reviews:
Blue Book 13:695-8, Aug 1911
Dramatic Mirror 65:7, Apr 19, 1911
65:2, Apr 26, 1911
65:4, May 10, 1911
67:31, Jan 31, 1912
Green Book Album 6:16-18, Jul 1911
Leslie's Weekly 112:507, May 4, 1911
Life (New York) 57:286, May 4, 1911
Red Book 17:572+, Jul 1911
Theatre Magazine 13:x, May 1911
13:144, May 1911

Doctor Jazz
book:	Buster Davis
music and lyrics:	Buster Davis; additional music and lyrics by King Oliver, Howard Melrose, Jack Coogan, J. L. Morgan, Eubie Blake, E. Ray Goetz, Harry von Tilzer, A. J. Piron, Swanstone, McCarren and Morgan
staging:	Donald McKayle, supervised by John Berry
sets:	Raoul Pene du Bois

    costumes: Raoul Pene du Bois
    choreography: Donald McKayle
Productions:
    Opened March 19, 1975 for 5 performances
Reviews:
    New York 8:69, Mar 10, 1975
    New York Theatre Critics' Reviews 1975:294
    New York Times page 46, Mar 20, 1975

Dr. Magico (see The Magic Show of Dr. Magico)

Doctor Selavy's Magic Theater (The Mental Cure)
    conceived: Richard Foreman
    music: Stanley Silverman
    lyrics: Tom Hendry
    staging: Richard Foreman
Productions:
    (Off-Broadway) Opened November 23, 1972 for 144 performances
    (Off-Off-Broadway) Opened January 1984
Reviews:
    High Fidelity 23:ma 27-8, Mar 1973
    Nation 215:597, Dec 11, 1972
    New York 6:66, Jan 15, 1973
    New York Times page 20, Aug 8, 1972
                    II, page 1, Aug 20, 1972
                    page 47, Nov 24, 1972
                    II, page 32, Dec 3, 1972
                    II, page 21, Dec 17, 1972
                    II, page 15, Jan 21, 1973
                    II, page 18, Jan 21, 1973
                    I, page 41, Jan 29, 1984
    New Yorker 48:109, Dec 9, 1972
    Newsweek 80:70, Dec 4, 1972
    Playboy 20:36, Mar 1973

Dogs
    book: James Stewart Bennett and Charles G. Horne
    music: James Stewart Bennett
    lyrics: James Stewart Bennett
    staging: Charles G. Horne
    sets: Jack Kelly
    costumes: Jack Kelly and Peyton Smith
Productions:
    (Off-Broadway) Opened August 10, 1983 for 6 performances
Reviews:
    New York Times III, page 4, Aug 12, 1983

Doing Our Bit
    dialogue: Harold Atteridge
    music: Sigmund Romberg and Herman Timberg
    lyrics: Harold Atteridge
    staging: J. C. Huffman and J. J. Shubert

Productions:
 Opened October 18, 1917 for 130 performances
Reviews:
 Dramatic Mirror 77:7, Oct 27, 1917
 Green Book 19:5+, Jan 1918
 New York Dramatic News 64:7, Oct 27, 1917
 New York Times page 11, Oct 19, 1917
 Theatre Magazine 26:343, Dec 1917
                 26:392, Dec 1917

The Doll Girl
 book: Leo Stein and A. M. Willner; English version by
                Harry B. Smith
 music: Leo Fall
Productions:
 Opened August 25, 1913 for 88 performances
Reviews:
 Dramatic Mirror 70:6, Aug 27, 1913
                 70:4, Sep 3, 1913
 Munsey 50:288-90, Nov 1913
 New York Times page 19, Aug 26, 1913
 Theatre Magazine 18:xiii, Oct 1913
                 18:114, Oct 1913

The Dollar Princess
 book: Messrs. Willner and Grunbaum; adapted by
                George Grossmith Jr.
 music: Leo Fall
 staging: A. E. Malone
Productions:
 Opened September 6, 1909 for 288 performances
Reviews:
 American Mercury 70:105, May 1910
 Green Book Album 2:1017, Nov 1909
 Hampton 23:694-5, Nov 1909
 Harper's Weekly 54:24, Apr 30, 1910
 Leslie's Weekly 109:318, Sep 20, 1909
                 109:391, Oct 21, 1909
                 110:136, Feb 10, 1910
 Metropolitan Magazine 31:260-1, Nov 1909
 Theatre Magazine 10:xii, Sep 1909
                 10:157, Oct 1909
                 10:163, Oct 1909
 Vanity Fair 6:198-9, Nov 1909

The $ Value of Man
 written: Christopher Knowles and Robert Wilson
 music: Michael Galasso
 staging: Christopher Knowles and Robert Wilson
 sets: Gregory Payne, Terrence Chambers, Charles
                Dennis

costumes: Richard Roth
choreography: Andrew De Groat
Productions:
   (Off-Broadway) Opened May 9, 1975 for 8 performances
Reviews:
   New York 8: 75, May 26, 1975
   New York Times page 44, May 11, 1975

A Doll's Life

book: Betty Comden and Adolph Green
music: Larry Grossman
lyrics: Betty Comden and Adolph Green
staging: Harold Prince
sets: Timothy O'Brien and Tazeena Firth
costumes: Florence Klotz
choreography: Larry Fuller
Productions:
   Opened September 23, 1982 for 5 performances
Reviews:
   America 147: 235, Oct 23, 1982
   Harper's 267: 69-74, Aug 1983
   Nation 235:378-80, Oct 16, 1982
   New York 15: 91-2, Oct 4, 1982
   New York Theatre Critics' Reviews 1982: 207
   New York Times III, page 3, Sep 24, 1982
               II, page 3, Oct 3, 1982
   New Yorker 58: 122, Oct 4, 1982
   Theatre Crafts 16:22-3+, Nov/Dec 1982

Donnybrook!

book: Robert E. McEnroe, based on Maurice Walsh's
               The Quiet Man
music: Johnny Burke
lyrics: Johnny Burke
staging: Jack Cole
sets: Rouben Ter-Arutunian
costumes: Rouben Ter-Arutunian
choreography: Jack Cole
Productions:
   Opened May 18, 1961 for 68 performances
Reviews:
   America 105:532, Jul 15, 1961
   Dance Magazine 35:20, Jul 1961
   New York Theatre Critics' Reviews 1961:292+
   New York Times II, page 1, May 14, 1961
             page 23, May 19, 1961
             II, page 1, May 28, 1961
             page 26, Jul 10, 1961
             page 13, Jul 14, 1961
   New Yorker 37:72+, May 27, 1961

Saturday Review 44:51, Jun 17, 1961
Theatre Arts 45:9-10, Jul 1961
Time 77:79, May 26, 1961

Don't Bother Me, I Can't Cope
conceived: Vinnette Carroll
songs: Micki Grant and others
sketches: Micki Grant and others
staging: Vinnette Carroll
sets: Richard A. Miller
costumes: Edna Watson
choreography: George Faison
Productions:
Opened April 19, 1972 for 1,065 performances
Reviews:
America 126:515, May 13, 1972
Ebony 28:100-2+, Feb 1973
Nation 214:604, May 8, 1972
New York Theatre Critics' Reviews 1972:304
New York Times page 51, Apr 20, 1972
            II, page 30, Apr 30, 1972
            II, page 1, May 7, 1972
            page 147, Dec 3, 1972
New Yorker 48:104, Apr 29, 1972
Time 99:75, May 8, 1972

Don't Get Started
conceived: Ron Milner and Barry Hankerson
book: Ron Milner
music: Marvin Winans
lyrics: Marvin Winans
staging: Ron Milner
sets: Llewellyn Harrison
costumes: Victor Shaffer
Productions:
Opened October 29, 1987 for 86 performances
Reviews:
Nation 245:694-5, Dec 5, 1987
New York Theatre Critics' Reviews 1987:141
New York Times I, page 12, Oct 31, 1987

Don't Play Us Cheap!
book: Melvin Van Peebles
music: Melvin Van Peebles
lyrics: Melvin Van Peebles
staging: Melvin Van Peebles
sets: Kert Lundell
costumes: Bernard Johnson
Productions:
Opened May 16, 1972 for 164 performances
Reviews:
New York Theatre Critics' Reviews 1972:279

New York Times page 39, May 17, 1972
             II, page 1, May 28, 1972
New Yorker 48:82, May 27, 1972
Newsweek 79:75, May 29, 1972

Don't Step on My Olive Branch
conceived:	Jonathon Karmon
book:	Harvey Jacobs
music:	Ron Eliran
lyrics:	Ron Eliran
staging:	Jonathon Karmon
sets:	James Tilton
costumes:	Pierre D'Alby
choreography:	Jonathon Karmon

Productions:
Opened November 1, 1976 for 16 performances
Reviews:
New York Theatre Critics' Reviews 1976:119
New York Times page 27, Nov 2, 1976

Don't Walk on the Clouds
book:	Marvin Gordon
music:	John Aman
lyrics:	John Aman

Productions:
(Off-Broadway) Season of 1971-1972
Reviews:
New York Times page 83, Dec 5, 1971

Doodle Dandy of the U.S.A.
book:	Saul Lancourt
music:	Elie Siegmeister
staging:	Saul Lancourt
choreography:	Elie Siegmeister

Productions:
(Off-Broadway) Opened December 26, 1942
Reviews:
New York Times page 15, Oct 19, 1942
                 page 26, Dec 21, 1942
                 page 36, Dec 27, 1942
                 page 22, Dec 30, 1942
Newsweek 20:74, Dec 28, 1942

Doonesbury
book:	Garry Trudeau, based on his comic strip Doonesbury
music:	Elizabeth Swados
lyrics:	Garry Trudeau
staging:	Jacques Levy
sets:	Peter Larkin
costumes:	Patricia McGourty
choreography:	Margo Sappington

Productions:
  Opened November 21, 1983 for 104 performances
Reviews:
  America 149:435, Dec 31, 1983
  Dance Magazine 58:91-2, Feb 1984
  Horizon 26:53-5, Nov/Dec 1983
  New York 16:149, Dec 5, 1983
  New York Theatre Critics' Reviews 1983: 112
  New York Times III, page 14, Nov 22, 1983
                 II, page 3, Nov 27, 1983
  New Yorker 59:180, Dec 5, 1983
  Newsweek 102:102, Dec 5, 1983
  Time 122:90, Dec 5, 1983

Double Entry (see The Bible Salesman and The Oldest Trick in the
  World)

Double Feature
  book: Jeffrey Moss
  music: Jeffrey Moss
  lyrics: Jeffrey Moss
  staging: Sheldon Larry
  sets: Stuart Wurtzel
  costumes: Patricia Von Brandenstein
  choreography: Adam Grammis
Productions:
  (Off-Broadway) Opened October 8, 1981 for 7 performances
Reviews:
  New York Times III, page 3, Oct 9, 1981
  New Yorker 57:141, Oct 19, 1981

Down in the Valley
  libretto: Arnold Sundgaard
  music: Kurt Weill
  costumes: Bob Nichols
Productions:
  (Off-Broadway) Opened Season of 1952-53
  (Off-Broadway) Opened June 5, 1962 for 16 performances
  (Off-Broadway) Opened April 23, 1965 for 14 performances
No Reviews.

Drat!
  book: Fred Bluth
  music: Steven Metcalf
  lyrics: Fred Bluth
  staging: Fred Bluth
  sets: Christian Thee
  costumes: Tamianne Wiley
Productions:
  (Off-Broadway) Opened October 18, 1971 for one performance
Reviews:
  New York Times page 53, Oct 19, 1971

Drat! The Cat!

book:	Ira Levin
music:	Milton Schafer
lyrics:	Ira Levin
staging:	Joe Layton
sets:	David Hays
costumes:	Fred Voelpel
choreography:	Joe Layton

Productions:
Opened October 10, 1965 for 8 performances
Reviews:
Dance Magazine 39:138, Dec 1965
New York Theatre Critics' Reviews 1965:319
New York Times page 54, Oct 11, 1965
Saturday Review 48:74, Oct 30, 1965

The Dream Girl

book:	Rida Johnson Young and Harold Atteridge
music:	Victor Herbert
lyrics:	Rida Johnson Young and Harold Atteridge

Productions:
Opened August 20, 1924 for 117 performances
Reviews:
New York Times page 12, Aug 21, 1924
Theatre Magazine 40:16, Oct 1924

Dream with Music

book:	Sidney Sheldon, Dorothy Kilgallen, Ben Roberts
music:	Clay Warnick
lyrics:	Edward Eager
staging:	Richard Kollmar
sets:	Stewart Chaney
costumes:	Miles White
choreography:	George Balanchine and Henry LeTang

Productions:
Opened May 18, 1944 for 28 performances
Reviews:
Commonweal 40:156, Jun 2, 1944
Nation 158:688, Jun 10, 1944
New York Theatre Critics' Reviews 1944:188+
New York Times page 15, May 19, 1944
New Yorker 20:40, May 27, 1944
Newsweek 23:91, May 29, 1944

Dreamgirls

book:	Tom Eyen
music:	Henry Krieger
lyrics:	Tom Eyen
staging:	Michael Bennett
sets:	Robin Wagner
costumes:	Theoni V. Aldredge
choreography:	Michael Bennett, Michael Peters

Productions:
 Opened December 20, 1981 for 1,522 performances
 Opened June 28, 1987 for 168 performances
Reviews:
 America 146:73, Jan 30, 1982
  157:88+, Aug 15-22, 1987
 Dance Magazine 56:107, Mar 1982
  57:121-2, Dec 1983
 Ebony 37: 90-2+, May 1982
  38:74-6+, Apr 1983
 Essence 13:15+, May 1982
 Jet 66:54-7, Jun 11, 1984
  72:59, Jul 20, 1987
 Los Angeles 28:56, Jun 1983
 Ms. 11:89-90+, Jul/Aug 1982
 Nation 245:174-5, Aug 29, 1987
 New Leader 65:21, Feb 8, 1982
 New Republic 186:25-7, Jan 27, 1982
 New York 14:43-5, Dec 14, 1981
  15:52, Jan 11, 1982
  20:62-3, Jul 13, 1987
 New York Theatre Critics' Reviews 1981:55
  1987:212
 New York Times III, page 11, Dec 21, 1981
  III, page 3, Jan 3, 1982
  III, page 31, Feb 11, 1982
  III, page 14, Jun 29, 1987
 New Yorker 57:53, Jan 4, 1982
 Newsweek 99:65+, Jan 4, 1982
 People 18-21, Jan 10, 1983
 Saturday Review 8:38+, Dec 1981
  9:50, Feb 1982
 Theatre Crafts 6:2-3+, May 1982
 Time 119:76, Jan 4, 1982

Dressler, Marie (see Marie Dressler)

A Drifter, the Grifter & Heather McBride
 book: John Gallagher
 music: Bruce Petsche
 lyrics: John Gallagher
 staging: Dick Sasso
 sets: Michael Sharp
 costumes: Michael Sharp
 choreography: George Bunt
Productions:
 (Off-Broadway) Opened June 20, 1982 for 9 performances
Reviews:
 New York Times page 46, Jun 27, 1982

Drood (see Mystery of Edwin Drood)

The Drunkard
    book: Bro Herrod; based on the play by W. H. S.
                     Smith
    music: Barry Manilow
    lyrics: Barry Manilow
    staging: Bro Herrod
    costumes: Carol Luiken
    choreography: Carveth Wells
Productions:
    (Off-Broadway)   Opened April 13, 1970 for 48 performances
    (Off-Broadway)   Opened August 6, 1986 for 21 performances
Reviews:
    New York Times page 54, Apr 14, 1970
    New Yorker 46:97, Apr 25, 1970

DuBarry Was a Lady
    book: B. G. DeSylva and Herbert Fields
    music: Cole Porter
    lyrics: Cole Porter
    staging: Edgar McGregor
    sets: Raoul Pene duBois
    costumes: Raoul Pene duBois
    choreography: Robert Alton
Productions:
    Opened December 6, 1939 for 408 performances
    (Off-Broadway) Opened May 4, 1972
Reviews:
    Commonweal 31:227, Dec 29, 1939
    Life 7:58-63, Dec 11, 1939
    Nation 149:716, Dec 23, 1939
    New York Theatre Critics' Reviews 1940:439+
    New York Times X, page 3, Nov 19, 1939
                    page 34, Dec 7, 1939
                    IX, page 1, Dec 24, 1939
                    page 29, Apr 10, 1941
                    VIII, page 2, Nov 1, 1942
                    page 27, May 12, 1972
    Newsweek 14:35, Dec 18, 1939
    Theatre Arts 24:39-49, Jan 1940
                 24:92-3, Feb 1940
    Time 34:45, Dec 18, 1939

Dubliners   (see James Joyce's Dubliners)

The Duchess
    book: Joseph Herbert and Harry B. Smith
    music: Victor Herbert
    staging: J. C. Huffman
Productions:
    Opened October 16, 1911 for 24 performances

Reviews:
  Dramatic Mirror 66:10, Oct 18, 1911
  Theatre Magazine 14:xiv, Dec 1911

The Duchess Misbehaves

book:	Gladys Shelly
music:	Frank Black
lyrics:	Gladys Shelly
staging:	Martin Manulis
sets:	A. A. Ostrander
costumes:	Willa Kim
choreography:	George Tapps

Productions:
  Opened February 13, 1946 for 5 performances
Reviews:
  New York Theatre Critics' Reviews 1946:456+
  New York Times page 32, Feb 14, 1946
              page 10, Feb 16, 1946
  New Yorker 22:44+, Feb 23, 1946

Dude (The Highway Life)

book:	Gerome Ragni
music:	Galt MacDermot
lyrics:	Gerome Ragni
staging:	Tom O'Horgan
sets:	Roger Morgan
costumes:	Randy Barcelo

Productions:
  Opened October 9, 1972 for 16 performances
Reviews:
  Nation 215:410, Oct 30, 1972
  New York Theatre Critics' Reviews 1972:222
  New York Times page 24, Aug 3, 1972
              page 54, Oct 10, 1972
              II, page 1, Oct 22, 1972
              page 39, Oct 26, 1972
              II, page 7, Nov 12, 1972
  Newsweek 80:111, Oct 30, 1972
  New Yorker 48:30, Sep 23, 1972
            48:76, Oct 21, 1972
  Time 100:81, Oct 23, 1972
  Vogue 160:86-7, Oct 15, 1972

Dunbar

conceived:	Ayanna
written:	Ron Stacker Thompson, from Ayanna's adaptation
music:	Quitman Fludd III, Lonnie Hewitt, and Paul E. Smith
lyrics:	Paul Laurence Dunbar; additional lyrics by Quitman Fludd III
staging:	Ron Stacker Thompson

sets:	Giles Hogya
costumes:	Jeffrey N. Mazor
choreography:	Joseph J. Cohen

Productions:
  (Off-Off-Broadway) Opened February 14, 1980 for 12 performances
Reviews:
  Encore 9:44-5, May 1980
  New York Times page 10, Mar 1, 1980

Dynamite Tonite
  libretto: Arnold Weinstein
  music: William Bolcom
  staging: Paul Stills and Arnold Weinstein
  sets: Willa Kim
Productions:
  (Off-Broadway) Opened March 15, 1967 for 7 performances
Reviews:
  Commonweal 86:126, Apr 14, 1967
               86:152-4, Apr 21, 1967
  New York Times page 52, Mar 16, 1967

-E-

Earl Carroll Sketch Book (1929)
  book: Eddie Cantor and E. Y. Harburg
  music: Jay Gorney and Vincent Rose
  lyrics: E. Y. Harburg, Charles and Harry Tobias
  staging: Earl Carroll, Edgar MacGregor, Leroy Prinz
Productions:
  Opened July 1, 1929 for 400 performances
Reviews:
  New Republic 59:262, Jul 24, 1929
  New York Times page 33, Jul 2, 1929
  Outlook 152:471, Jul 17, 1929
  Theatre Magazine 50:39, Sep 1929

Earl Carroll Sketch Book (1935)
  sketches: Eugene Conrad and Charles Sherman
  music and
    lyrics: Charles Tobias, Murray Mencher, Charles New-
                     man, Norman Zeno, Will Irwin
  staging: Earl Carroll
  sets: Clark Robinson
  choreography: Boots McKenna
Productions:
  Opened June 4, 1935 for 207 performances
Reviews:
  Nation 140:724, Jun 19, 1935
  New York Times page 22, Jun 5, 1935

Earl Carroll Vanities (1923)
    songs: Earl Carroll
    staging: Earl Carroll
    costumes: Paul Arlington and R. Reid MacQuire
    choreography: Sammy Lee and Renoff
Productions:
Opened July 5, 1923 for 204 performances
Reviews:
    New York Clipper 71:14, Jul 11, 1923
    New York Times page 8, Jul 6, 1923
                  VIII, page 2, Oct 14, 1923
    Theatre Magazine 38:15, Sep 1923

Earl Carroll Vanities (1924)
    songs: Earl Carroll and others
    staging: Earl Carroll
    sets: Max Ree
    choreography: Sammy Lee
Productions:
Opened September 10, 1924 for 133 performances
Reviews:
    Life (New York) 84:20, Oct 2, 1924
    New York Times page 23, Sep 11, 1924

Earl Carroll Vanities (1925)
    dialogue: William A. Grew; additional sketches by Jimmy
                    Duffy, Arthur ("Bugs") Baer, Blanche Merrill
                    and others
    songs: Clarence Gaskill, Ray Klages, Louis Alter, Fred
                    Phillips, Irving Bilbo, Owen Murphy, Jay Gorney
    staging: Earl Carroll
    sets: Willy Pogany
    costumes: Charles LeMaire
    choreography: Dave Bennett and Sonia Gluck
Productions:
Opened July 6, 1925 for 390 performances
Reviews:
    New York Times page 24, Jul 27, 1925
                  page 10, Aug 24, 1926
                  page 19, Aug 25, 1926
    Theatre Magazine 42:15, Sep 1925

Earl Carroll Vanities (1926-1927)
    sketches: Stanley Rauh and Wm. A. Grew
    music: Grace Henry and Morris Hamilton
    lyrics: Grace Henry and Morris Hamilton
    staging: Earl Carroll
    choreography: David Bennett
Productions:
Opened August 24, 1926 for 440 performances
Reviews:
    Life (New York) 88:21, Sep 9, 1926

89:19, Feb 3, 1927
New York Times page 10, Aug 24, 1926
page 19, Aug 25, 1926
page 18, Jan 5, 1927
page 19, Feb 22, 1927
Vogue 68:142, Oct 15, 1926

Earl Carroll Vanities (1928)
assembled by: Earl Carroll
music: Louis Alter, Jesse Greer, Richard Whiting
lyrics: Ray Klages and Joe Burke
staging: Earl Carroll
Productions:
Opened August 6, 1928 for 203 performances
Reviews:
Life (New York) 92:12, Aug 23, 1928
New Republic 56:21-2, Aug 22, 1928
New York Times page 25, Aug 7, 1928
Outlook 149:670, Aug 22, 1928
Vogue 72:66, Sep 29, 1928

Earl Carroll Vanities (1930)
assembled by: Earl Carroll
music: Harold Arlen and Ted Koehler
lyrics: E. Y. Harburg
staging: Earl Carroll, Priestly Morrison, LeRoy Prinz
Productions:
Opened July 1, 1930 for 215 performances
Reviews:
New York Times page 28, Jul 2, 1930
Theatre Magazine 52:24, Aug 1930

Earl Carroll Vanities (1931)
sketches: Ralph Spence and Eddie Welch
music: Burton Lane
lyrics: Harold Adamson
staging: Earl Carroll
Productions:
Opened August 27, 1931 for 278 performances
Reviews:
New Republic 68:127-8, Sep 16, 1931
New York Times page 28, Aug 11, 1931
VIII, page 1, Aug 16, 1931
page 18, Aug 28, 1931
VIII, page 1, Sep 6, 1931
Outlook 159:55, Sep 9, 1931
159:570, Dec 30, 1931
Vogue 78:79+, Oct 15, 1931

Earl Carroll Vanities (1932)
book: Jack McGowan

music: Harold Arlen
lyrics: Ted Koehler
staging: Earl Carroll
sets: Vincente Minnelli
Productions:
Opened September 27, 1932 for 87 performances
Reviews:
Nation 135: 375, Oct 19, 1932
New Outlook 161:46, Dec 1932
New York Times IX, page 2, Sep 18, 1932
                 page 22, Sep 28, 1932

Earl Carroll Vanities (1940)
assembled by: Earl Carroll
music: Charles Rosoff and Peter deRose
lyrics: Dorcas Cochran and Mitchell Parrish
staging: Earl Carroll
sets: Jean LeSeyeux
costumes: Jean LeSeyeux
choreography: Eddie Prinz
Productions:
Opened January 13, 1940 for 25 performances
Reviews:
New York Theatre Critics' Reviews 1940:418+
New York Times page 1, Jan 15, 1940

Earl of Ruston
book: C. C. Courtney and Ragan Courtney
music: Peter Link
lyrics: C. C. Courtney and Ragan Courtney
staging: C. C. Courtney
sets: Neil Peter
Productions:
Opened May 5, 1971 for 5 performances
Reviews:
New York Theatre Critics' Reviews 1971:289
New York Times page 38, Apr 27, 1971
                 page 55, May 6, 1971
                 II, page 14, May 16, 1971
New Yorker 47:102+, May 15, 1971

Early to Bed
book: George Marion, Jr.
music: Thomas Waller
lyrics: George Marion, Jr.
staging: Alfred Bloomingdale
sets: George Jenkins
costumes: Miles White
choreography: Robert Alton
Productions:
Opened June 17, 1943 for 382 performances

Reviews:
Catholic World 157:522, Aug 1943
Commonweal 38:274, Jul 2, 1943
Life 15:54, Aug 30, 1943
New York Theatre Critics' Reviews 1943:314+
New York Times page 16, Jun 18, 1943
New Yorker 19:33, Jun 26, 1943
Newsweek 21:108+, Jun 28, 1943
Theatre Arts 27:573, Oct 1943
Time 41:94, Jun 28, 1943

Earthlight
    book: Allan Mann and the Earthlight Ensemble
    music: Pure Love and Pleasure
    staging: Allan Mann
    sets: Ron Tannis
    choreography: Peggy Chiereska
Productions:
    (Off-Broadway) Opened January 17, 1971 for 56 performances
Reviews:
New York Times page 38, Nov 4, 1970
                   page 27, Jan 21, 1971

Earthquake (see The International Cup, the Ballet of Niagra and the Earthquake)

East Wind
    book: Oscar Hammerstein II and Frank Mandel
    music: Sigmund Romberg
    lyrics: Oscar Hammerstein II
    staging: Oscar Hammerstein II
    choreography: Bobby Connelly
Productions:
Opened October 27, 1931 for 23 performances
Reviews:
New York Times page 18, Oct 28, 1931

The Eccentricities of Davy Crockett (see Ballet Ballads)

The Echo
    book: William Le Baron
    music: Deems Taylor
    staging: Fred G. Latham
Productions:
Opened August 17, 1910 for 53 performances
Reviews:
Cosmopolitan 49:736, Nov 1910
             50:62, Dec 1910
Dramatic Mirror 64:7, Aug 27, 1910
Life (New York) 56:398, Sep 8, 1910
Metropolitan Magazine 33:116-17, Oct 1910

Munsey 44:136, Oct 1910
Theatre Magazine 12:xiii, Oct 1910

Ed Wynn Carnival
   dialogue: Ed Wynn
   songs: Ed Wynn
Productions:
Opened April 5, 1920 for 64 performances
Reviews:
New York Clipper 68:14, Apr 14, 1920
New York Times page 18, Apr 6, 1920
           VI, page 2, Apr 18, 1920
Theatre Magazine 31:403+, May 1920

Eddie Fisher at the Winter Garden
   songs: Gordon Jenkins, Sammy Cahn and Jimmy Van
                 Heusen, and others
   staging: John Fearnley
   sets: Oliver Smith
   choreography: Tony Charmoli
Productions:
Opened October 2, 1962 for 40 performances
Reviews:
New York Theatre Critics' Reviews 1962:264
New York Times page 47, Oct 3, 1962

Eddie Fisher-Buddy Hackett at the Palace
   staging: Colin Romoff
Productions:
Opened August 28, 1967 for 42 performances
Reviews:
New York Times page 54, Mar 15, 1967
               page 26, Aug 29, 1967

Edith Piaf
   assembled: Edith Piaf
   staging: Edward Lewis
Productions:
Opened October 30, 1947 for 44 performances
Reviews:
New Republic 117:33, Nov 17, 1947
New Yorker 23:52+, Nov 8, 1947
          23:26-7, Nov 15, 1947
Newsweek 30:76, Nov 10, 1947

The Education of H*Y*M*A*N K*A*P*L*A*N
   book: Benjamin Bernard Zavin; based on the stories by
               Leo Rosten
   music: Paul Nassau and Oscar Brand
   lyrics: Paul Nassau and Oscar Brand
   staging: George Abbott

sets: William and Jean Eckart
costumes: Winn Morton
choreography: Jaime Rogers
Productions:
Opened April 4, 1968 for 28 performances
Reviews:
Dance Magazine 42:29, Jun 1968
New York Theatre Critics' Reviews 1968:307+
New York Times page 57, Apr 5, 1968
      II, page 1, Apr 14, 1968
      page 38, Apr 26, 1968
New Yorker 44:114, Apr 13, 1968
Time 91:68, Apr 12, 1968

El Bravo!
book: Jose Fernandez and Thom Shiera, based on a
        story by Jose Fernandez and Kenneth Waissman
music: John Clifton
lyrics: John Clifton
staging: Patricia Birch
sets: Tom Lynch
costumes: Carrie F. Robbins
choreography: Patricia Birch
Productions:
(Off-Broadway) Opened June 16, 1981 for 48 performances
Reviews:
New York Times III, page 23, Jun 17, 1981

El Grande de Coca-Cola (El Coca-Cola Grande)
conceived: Ron House and Diz White
written: Ron House, Diz White and others
choreography: Anna Nygh
Productions:
(Off-Broadway) Opened February 13, 1973 for 1,114 performances
(Off-Broadway) Opened January 22, 1986 for 86 performances
Reviews:
New York 6:66, Mar 5, 1973
New York Theatre Critics' Reviews 1973:311
New York Times page 26, Feb 14, 1973
      II, page 16, Apr 8, 1973
      III, page 24, Jan 23, 1986
New Yorker 49:81, Feb 24, 1973
Newsweek 81:90, Feb 26, 1973
Playboy 20:52, May 1973
Time 101:68, Feb 26, 1973

Elisabeth Welch: Time to Start Living
created: Elisabeth Welch, based on her career
songs: Various authors and composers
staging: Peter Howard
sets: Leo Myer

Productions:
(Off-Broadway) Opened March 23, 1986 for 19 performances
Reviews:
New York Times III, page 5, Mar 21, 1986

Elizabeth and Essex
book: Michael Stewart and Mark Bramble, based on Maxwell Anderson's Elizabeth the Queen
music: Doug Katsaros
lyrics: Richard Enquist
staging: Nancy Rhodes
Productions:
(Off-Off-Broadway) Opened January 31, 1980 for 25 performances
(Off-Off-Broadway) Opened May 17, 1984
Reviews:
New York 13:67, Mar 24, 1980
New York Theatre Critics' Reviews 1980:331
New York Times III, page 15, Feb 25, 1980
III, page 13, May 29, 1984

Elsa Lanchester--Herself
Productions:
(Off-Broadway) Season of 1960-1961
Reviews:
New York Times page 28, Feb 6, 1961
page 29, Apr 3, 1961

Elsie
book: Charles W. Bell
music: Sissle and Blake, Carlo and Sanders
lyrics: Sissle and Blake, Carlo and Sanders
staging: Edgar MacGregor
Productions:
Opened April 2, 1923 for 40 performances
Reviews:
New York Clipper 71:14, Apr 11, 1923
New York Times page 26, Apr 3, 1923

Elsie Janis and Her Gang
book: Elsie Janis
songs: William Kernell, Richard Fechheimer, B. C. Hilliam and Elsie Janis
staging: Elsie Janis
costumes: Charles LeMaire
Productions:
Opened December 1, 1919 for 55 performances
Reviews:
New York Clipper 69:20, Jan 25, 1922
New York Times page 11, Dec 2, 1919

Elvis Mania (Elvis Presley impersonation)
by: Johnny Seaton

songs: Various authors and composers
staging: Leslie Irons
sets: Paul Malec
costumes: Jeffery Wallach
Productions:
(Off-Broadway) Opened September 4, 1984 for 18 performances
Reviews:
New York Times III, page 21, Sep 5, 1984

Enchanted Isle
book: Ida Hoyt Chamberlain
music: Ida Hoyt Chamberlain
lyrics: Ida Hoyt Chamberlain
staging: Oscar Eagle
Productions:
Opened September 19, 1927 for 32 performances
Reviews:
New York Times page 33, Sep 20, 1927

Enchanting Melody
book: Itzik Manger
music: Henock Kon
staging: David Licht
sets: Marvin Gingold
costumes: Dina Harris
choreography: Yehudith and Felix Fibich
Productions:
(Off-Broadway) Opened November 24, 1964 for 84 performances
Reviews:
New York Times page 40, Nov 25, 1964

The Enchantress
book: Fred DeGresac and Harry B. Smith
music: Victor Herbert
lyrics: Fred DeGresac and Harry B. Smith
staging: Frederick G. Latham
Productions:
Opened October 19, 1911 for 72 performances
Reviews:
Blue Book 14:683-5, Feb 1912
Delineator 79:174, Mar 1912
Dramatic Mirror 66:7+, Oct 25, 1911
              67:2, Jan 3, 1912
Green Book 7:8-9+, Jan 1912
Leslie's Weekly 113:529, Nov 9, 1911
Munsey 46:430, Dec 1911
Red Book 18:573-6, Jan 1912
Theatre Magazine 14:xiv, Dec 1911
              14:217, Dec 1911

Encore
music: Various composers

lyrics: Various authors
staging: Robert F. Jani
sets: Charles Lisanby
costumes: Michael Casey
choreography: Adam Grammis, Geoffrey Holder, Violet Holmes,
                 Linda Lemac, Shozo Nakano and Frank Wagner
Productions:
   Opened March 26, 1982 for 288 performances
Reviews:
   New York Times III, page 20, Mar 29, 1982

Ernest in Love
   book: Anne Croswell; based on Oscar Wilde's The Im-
                 portance of Being Earnest
   music: Lee Pockriss
   lyrics: Anne Croswell
   staging: Harold Stone
   sets: Peter Dahanos
   costumes: Ann Roth
   choreography: Frank Derbas
Productions:
   (Off-Broadway) Opened May 4, 1960 for 103 performances
   (Off-Off-Broadway) Opened November 20, 1964
Reviews:
   New York Times page 39, May 5, 1960
                 page 19, Jul 25, 1960
   New Yorker 36:117, May 21, 1960
   Time 75:70, Jun 6, 1960

The Establishment (1962-1963)
   written: Peter Cook and others
   music and
   lyrics: Christopher Logue, Stanley Myers, John Bird,
                 Patrick Gowers and Tony Kinsey
   staging: Nicholas Garland
Productions:
   (Off-Broadway) Opened January 19, 1963 for 192 performances
Reviews:
   America 108:237, Feb 16, 1963
   Nation 196:186-7, Mar 2, 1963
   New Republic 148:28-9, Feb 23, 1963
   Reporter 28:48+, Feb 14, 1963

The Establishment (1963-1964)
   written: Peter Cook, Peter Shaffer, Peter Lewis, John
                 Brine and Charles Lawson
   songs: Stephen Vinaver
   music: Carl Davis
   staging: Peter Cook and Bill Francisco
   costumes: Robert Leader
Productions:
   (Off-Broadway) Opened October 31, 1963 for 260 performances

Reviews:
    Newsweek 62:76, Nov 11, 1963

Ethel Waters   (see At Home with Ethel Waters)

Eubie!
    conceived: Julianne Boyd
    music: Eubie Blake
    lyrics: Noble Sissle, Andy Razaf, Johnny Brandon, F. E.
                        Miller, and Jim Europe
    staging: Julianne Boyd
    sets: Karl Eigsti
    costumes: Bernard Johnson
    choreography: Billy Wilson and Henry LeTang
Productions:
    Opened September 20, 1978 for 439 performances
Reviews:
    America 139:269, Oct 21, 1978
    Horizon 21:92-3, Sep 1978
    New West 5:SC-27, Jan 28, 1980
    New York 11:124+, Oct 9, 1978
    New York Theatre Critics' Reviews 1978:215
    New York Times page 90, Sep 22, 1978
                    page 54, Nov 6, 1978
    New Yorker 54:111, Oct 2, 1978
    Newsweek 92:89, Oct 2, 1978
    Time 112:73, Oct 2, 1978

Eva
    book: Glen MacDonough; based upon the original of
                        Willner and Bodansky
    music: Franz Lehar
    staging: Herbert Gresham
    choreography: Julian Mitchell
Productions:
    Opened December 30, 1912 for 24 performances
Reviews:
    Dramatic Mirror 69:2, Jan 1, 1913
                    69:6, Jan 8, 1913
    Green Book 9:499, Mar 1913
    Harper's Weekly 57:19, Jan 8, 1913
    New York Dramatic News 57:20, Jan 4, 1913
    Theatre Magazine 17:xxii, Jan 1913
                    17:34+, Feb 1913

An Evening With Diana Ross
    songs: Various authors and composers
    special
      material: Bill Goldenberg and Bill Dyer
    additional
      material: Bruce Vilanch
    staging: Joe Layton

Productions:
Opened June 14, 1976 for 24 performances
Reviews:
New York Theatre Critics' Reviews 1976:221

An Evening With Joan Crawford
    conceived: Julian Neil, based on the original characteriza-
                        tion by Lee Sparks
    music and
      lyrics: Joseph Church and Nick Branch
    staging: Julian Neil
    sets: J. Patrick Mann
    costumes: Barbara Gerard
    choreography: Sydney Smith
Productions:
    (Off-Broadway) Opened January 28, 1981 for 15 performances
Reviews:
New York Times III, page 8, Jan 30, 1981

An Evening with Josephine Baker
    by: George Adams
    staging: Ernestine M. Johnston
Productions:
    (Off-Off-Broadway) Opened March 1980
Reviews:
New York Times III, page 10, Apr 22, 1980

An Evening with Max Morath at the Turn of the Century
    compiled: Max Morath
    staging: Max Morath
    sets: Dennis Dougherty
Productions:
    (Off-Broadway) Opened February 17, 1969 for 140 performances
Reviews:
New York Times page 38, Jun 13, 1969
New Yorker 45:96-7, Mar 8, 1969

Evening with Romberg
    songs: Sigmund Romberg
    staging: Jeffrey B. Moss
Productions:
    Closed prior to Broadway opening (October, 1976)
Reviews:
New York Times page 84, Oct 5, 1975

An Evening with Sue and Pugh
    songs: Sue Lawless and Ted Pugh
    sketches: Sue Lawless and Ted Pugh
Productions:
    (Off-Broadway) Opened January 16, 1967 for 3 performances
No Reviews.

An Evening with the Times Square Two
   music: Mycroft Partner and Andrew i.
   staging: Saul Gottlieb
Productions:
   (Off-Broadway) Opened May 19, 1967 for 10 performances
No Reviews.

An Evening with Yves Montand
   staging: Y. Montand
Productions:
   Opened October 24, 1961 for 55 performances
Reviews:
   New York Theatre Critics' Reviews 1961:202
   New York Times page 30, Oct 25, 1961
                    page 39, Nov 17, 1961
   Newsweek 58:69, Nov 6, 1961
   Theatre Arts 46:15, Jan 1962
   Time 78:44, Nov 3, 1961

Everybody's Gettin' Into the Act
   words: Bob Ost
   music: Bob Ost
   lyrics: various authors
   staging: Darwin Knight
   sets: Frank J. Boros
   costumes: Dianne Finn Chapman
Productions:
   (Off-Broadway) Opened September 27, 1981 for 33 performances
Reviews:
   New York Times III, page 7, Sep 29, 1981

Everybody's Welcome
   book: Harold Atteridge, based on Frances Goodrich and
                     Albert Hackett's Up Pops the Devil
   music: Sammy Fain
   lyrics: Irving Kahal
   staging: William Mollison
Productions:
   Opened October 13, 1931 for 139 performances
Reviews:
   New York Times VIII, page 3, Sep 20, 1931
                    page 26, Oct 14, 1931

Everyman at La Mama
   written: Geraldine Fitzgerald and Brother Jonathan
   music: Jimmy Justice
   staging: Geraldine Fitzgerald and Brother Jonathan
Productions:
   (Off-Off-Broadway) Opened September 7, 1972
No Reviews.

Everything
    book: R. H. Burnside
    music: John Philip Sousa, Irving Berlin and others
    lyrics: John L. Golden and others
    staging: R. H. Burnside
Productions:
    Opened August 22, 1918 for 461 performances
Reviews:
    Dramatic Mirror 79:360, Sep 7, 1918
    New York Times page 7, Aug 23, 1918
               page 5, Sep 7, 1918
               page 11, Jan 27, 1919
    Theatre Magazine 28:199, Oct 1918
                 28:212, Oct 1918

Everything for Anybody (The Bar That Never Closes)
    book: Louisa Rose
    fables: Marco Vassi
    music: Tommy Mandel
    staging: John Broswell
Productions:
    (Off-Off-Broadway) Opened September 9, 1972
Reviews:
    New York Times page 65, Sep 19, 1972
(Also see The Bar That Never Closes)

Evita
    music: Andrew Lloyd Webber
    lyrics: Tim Rice
    staging: Harold Prince
    sets: Timothy O'Brien
    costumes: Timothy O'Brien
    choreography: Larry Fuller
Productions:
    Opened September 25, 1979 for 1,567 performances
Reviews:
    America 141:237, Oct 27, 1979
    American Record Guide 43:34+, Dec 1979
    Chicago 29:170+, Dec 1980
    Commonweal 107:596, Oct 24, 1980
    Los Angeles 25:220, Mar 1980
                  36:274, Sep 1981
    Ms. 8:28+, Sep 1979
    Nation 229:381-2, Oct 20, 1979
    New Republic 181:25-6, Nov 10, 1979
    New West 4:SC-35+, Jun 4, 1979
    New York 12:98+, Oct 8, 1979
    New York Theatre Critics' Reviews 1979:149
    New York Times III, page 19, Sep 26, 1979
    New Yorker 55:100, Oct 8, 1979
    Newsweek 94:105+, Oct 8, 1979

Saturday Review 6:49-50, Nov 24, 1979
Theatre Crafts 13:14-19+, Nov 1979
19:20+, May 1985
Time 114:84, Oct 8, 1979

Exchange
dialogue: Eric Levy
music and
lyrics: Mike Brandt, Michael Knight and Robert J.
Lowery
staging: Sondra Lee
sets: Peter Harvey
costumes: Stanley Simmons
Productions:
(Off-Braodway) Opened February 8, 1970 for one performance
Reviews:
New York Times page 47, Feb 9, 1970

Experience
book: George V. Hobart
music: Max Bendix
songs: Silvio Hein
staging: George V. Hobart
Productions:
Opened October 27, 1914 for 255 performances
Opened January 22, 1918 for 23 performances
Reviews:
American Playwright 3:377-8, Nov 1914
Book News 34:525-6, Aug 1916
Bookman 40:417, Dec 1914
Dramatic Mirror 72:8-9, Nov 4, 1914
73:2, Feb 17, 1915
73:1, Mar 10, 1915
Green Book 13:107-8+, Jan 1915
Hearst 27:198-205, Feb 1915
Life (New York) 64:860, Nov 12, 1914
Munsey 53:795-9, Jan 1915
Nation 99:561, Nov 5, 1915
New England Magazine 53:239, Sep 1915
New York Dramatic News 60:16, Nov 7, 1914
61:4, Apr 3, 1915
New York Times page 13, Oct 28, 1914
VIII, page 9, Nov 1, 1914
Strand 48:414-5, Apr 1915
Theatre Magazine 20:264-6, Dec 1914

-F-

F. Jasmine Addams
book: Carson McCullers, G. Wood and Theodore Mann;

based on Carson McCullers' The Member of the
Wedding
music: G. Wood
lyrics: G. Wood
staging: Theodore Mann
sets: Marsha Louis Eck
costumes: Joseph G. Aulisi
choreography: Patricia Birch
Productions:
  (Off-Broadway)   Opened October 27, 1971 for 6 performances
Reviews:
  America 125:427, Nov 20, 1971
  New York Times page 49, Oct 28, 1971
                   II, page 6, Nov 7, 1971
  New Yorker 47:115-16, Nov 6, 1971

Fable
  book: Jean-Claude van Itallie
  music: Richard Peaslee
  staging: Joseph Chaikin
Productions:
  (Off-Off-Broadway) Opened October 1975
Reviews:
  New York Times page 26, Oct 28, 1975
                   II, page 5, Nov 30, 1975

Face the Music
  book: Moss Hart
  music: Irving Berlin
  lyrics: Irving Berlin
  staging: Hassard Short and George S. Kaufman
  choreography: Albertina Rasch
Productions:
  Opened February 17, 1932 for 165 performances
  Opened January 31, 1933 for 32 performances
Reviews:
  Art and Decoration 36:45+, Apr 1932
  Bookman 74:666, Mar 1932
  Catholic World 135:75-6, Apr 1932
  Commonweal 15:495, Mar 2, 1932
  Nation 134:294, Mar 9, 1932
  New Outlook 161:48, Mar 1933
  New Republic 70:97, Mar 9, 1932
  New York Times page 25, Feb 4, 1932
                   page 24, Feb 18, 1932
                   VIII, page 1, Mar 20, 1932
                   page 13, Feb 1, 1933
  Outlook 160:189, Mar 1932
  Theatre Guild Magazine 9:28-30, Mar 1932
                         9:23, Apr 1932
  Vogue 79:56+, Apr 15, 1932

Fade Out--Fade In

book:	Betty Comden and Adolph Green
music:	Jule Styne
lyrics:	Betty Comden and Adolph Green
staging:	George Abbott
sets:	William and Jean Eckart
costumes:	Donald Brooks
choreography:	Ernest Flatt

Productions:
Opened May 26, 1964 for 271 performances
Reviews:
America 111:114-15, Aug 1, 1964
Dance Magazine 38:17, Aug 1964
Life 57:30, Sep 25, 1964
Nation 198:611, Jun 15, 1964
New York Theatre Critics' Reviews 1964:248+
New York Times page 45, May 27, 1964
                    page 42, May 28, 1964
                    II, page 1, Jun 7, 1964
                    page 56, Nov 10, 1964
                    page 34, Apr 14, 1965
Newsweek 63:69, Jun 8, 1964
Saturday Review 47:28, Jun 20, 1964
Time 83:75, Jun 5, 1964

Fads and Fancies

book:	Glen MacDonough
music:	Raymond Hubbell
lyrics:	Glen MacDonough
staging:	Herbert Gresham
choreography:	Julian Mitchell

Productions:
Opened March 8, 1915 for 48 performances
Reviews:
Dramatic Mirror 73:8, Mar 17, 1915
                  73:2, Mar 24, 1915
Green Book 13:1150-1, Jun 1915
Life (New York) 65:467, Mar 18, 1915
Munsey 55:111, Jun 1915
New York Dramatic News 60:17, Mar 13, 1915
New York Times page 9, Mar 9, 1915
Theatre Magazine 21:167, Apr 1915
                     21:170, Apr 1915

The Faggot

words:	Al Carmines
music:	Al Carmines
staging:	Al Carmines
sets:	T. E. Mason
costumes:	T. E. Mason
choreography:	David Vaughan

Productions:
  (Off-Off-Broadway) Opened April 13, 1973
  (Off-Broadway) Opened June 18, 1973 for 182 performances
Reviews:
  National Review 25:1125-6, Oct 12, 1973
  New Republic 169:20+, Aug 11, 1973
  New York 6:94, May 14, 1973
         6:64, Jul 9, 1973
  New York Theatre Critics' Reviews 1973:247
  New York Times page 50, Apr 16, 1973
               page 30, Jun 19, 1973
               II, page 1, Jul 1, 1973
               II, page 1, Jul 22, 1973
               II, page 12, Jul 29, 1973

A Family Affair
  book: James Goldman, John Kander, William Goldman
  music: James Goldman, John Kander, William Goldman
  lyrics: James Goldman, John Kander, William Goldman
  staging: Harold Prince
  sets: David Hays
  costumes: Robert Fletcher
  choreography: John Butler
Productions:
  Opened January 27, 1962 for 65 performances
Reviews:
  America 106:737, Mar 3, 1962
  New York Theatre Critics' Reviews 1962:374+
  New York Times page 17, Jan 29, 1962
               page 36, Mar 26, 1962
  Theatre Arts 46:58-9, Apr 1962
  Time 79:61, Feb 9, 1962

Fancy Free
  book: Dorothy Donnelly and Edgar Smith
  music: Augustus Barratt
  lyrics: Augustus Barratt
  staging: J. C. Huffman
Productions:
  Opened April 11, 1918 for 116 performances
Reviews:
  Dramatic Mirror 78:549, Apr 20, 1918
               78:584, Apr 27, 1918
  Green Book 20:200+, Aug 1918
  Life (New York) 71:682, Apr 25, 1918
  New York Times page 11, Apr 12, 1918
  Theatre Magazine 27:316, May 1918

Fanny
  book: S. N. Behrman and Joshua Logan, based on
                 Marcel Pagnol's "Marius," "Fanny," and "Cesar"

music: Harold Rome
lyrics: Harold Rome
staging: Joshua Logan
sets: Jo Mielziner
costumes: Alvin Colt
choreography: Helen Tamiris
Productions:
Opened November 4, 1954 for 888 performances
Reviews:
America 92:305, Dec 11, 1954
Catholic World 180:307-8, Jan 1955
Commonweal 61:288, Dec 10, 1954
Life 37:117-20, Nov 29, 1954
Look 18:56-60, Nov 16, 1954
Mademoiselle 40:142, Nov 1954
Nation 179:451, Nov 20, 1954
New Republic 131:22-3, Nov 29, 1954
New York Theatre Critics' Reviews 1954:256+
New York Times VI, page 64, Oct 31, 1954
                page 16, Nov 5, 1954
                II, page 1, Nov 21, 1954
                VI, page 23, Jan 16, 1955
                II, page 1, Oct 30, 1955
                page 19, Dec 17, 1955
                page 17, Nov 17, 1956
                II, page 3, Dec 2, 1956
New York Times Magazine pages 64-5, Oct 31, 1954
New Yorker 30:104, Nov 13, 1954
Newsweek 44:98, Nov 15, 1954
Saturday Review 37:30, Nov 20, 1954
                38:5, 23, Jan 8, 1955
                38:23, Feb 5, 1955
                39:13, Sep 15, 1956
Theatre Arts 39:17-18, 20-1, Jan 1955
Time 64:62, Nov 15, 1954

A Fantastic Fricassee
    staging: Andre Chotin
Productions:
Opened September 11, 1922 for 112 performances
Reviews:
New York Clipper 70:20, Sep 27, 1922
New York Times page 24, Sep 12, 1922

The Fantasticks
    book: Tom Jones; based on Edmund Rostand's Les
                    Romantiques
    music: Harvey Schmidt
    lyrics: Tom Jones
    staging: Word Baker
    sets: Ed Wittstein

Productions:
  (Off-Broadway) Opened May 3, 1960 for *12,106 performances
  (still running 6/1/89)
Reviews:
  Catholic World 194:128, Nov 1961
  Essence 6:21, Dec 1975
  Horizon 30:64-5, Oct 1987
  Life 57:75-6+, Oct 16, 1964
  New York Times page 55, May 4, 1960
              page 36, Sep 8, 1961
              page 15, Nov 24, 1962
              page 14, Feb 1, 1964
              II, page 3, May 3, 1964
              II, page 19, Oct 18, 1964
              page 67, Oct 19, 1964
              page 41, May 3, 1965
              page 50, May 3, 1966
              II, page 3, Jul 31, 1966
              page 23, Aug 4, 1966
              page 21, Nov 5, 1966
              page 20, Jan 7, 1967
              page 32, Jan 7, 1967
              page 32, Jan 19, 1968
              page 42, May 3, 1968
              page 73, May 20, 1968
              page 53, May 5, 1969
              page 49, May 4, 1970
              II, page 24, May 2, 1971
              page 50, May 1, 1973
  New Yorker 36:96-7, May 14, 1960
  Newsweek 95:12, Jun 2, 1980
  People 25:96+, Jun 23, 1986
  Saturday Review 43:33, May 21, 1960
  Stereo Review 43:54, Nov 1979
  Theatre Arts 46:9, Nov 1962
  Vogue 174:90, May 1984

Farina, Richard (see Richard Farina)

The Fascinating Widow
  book: Otto Hauerbach
  staging: George Marion
Productions:
  Opened September 11, 1911 for 56 performances
Reviews:
  Blue Book 12:648-51, Feb 1911
  Dramatic Mirror 66:13, Sep 13, 1911
  Green Book Album 5:246-8+, Feb 1911
  Munsey 46:282-3, Nov 1911
  Theatre Magazine 14:113, Oct 1911

Fashion
    book: Anthony Stimac; based on the play by Anna
                      Cora Mowatt
    music: Don Pippin
    lyrics: Steve Brown
    staging: Anthony Stimac
Productions:
    (Off-Off-Broadway) Opened December 6, 1973
    (Off-Broadway) Opened February 18, 1974 for 94 performances
Reviews:
    New York 7:62, Mar 4, 1974
    New York Theatre Critics' Reviews 1974:294
    New York Times page 61, Dec 6, 1973
                   page 25, Feb 19, 1974
                   II, page 3, Mar 3, 1974
    New Yorker 50:68-9, Mar 4, 1974
    Playboy 21:48, Jun 1974
    Time 103:104, Mar 11, 1974

Fashions of 1924
    music: Ted Snyder
    lyrics: Harry B. Smith
    staging: Alexander Leftwich
Productions:
    Opened July 18, 1923 for 13 performances
Reviews:
    Life (New York) 82:18, Aug 8, 1923
    New York Times page 18, Jul 19, 1923
                   page 12, Jul 31, 1923
    Theatre Magazine 38:15, Sep 1923

Fast and Furious
    assembled by: Forbes Randolph
    music: Joe Jordan and Harry Revel
    lyrics: Rosamond Johnson, Mack Gordon, Harold Adamson
    staging: Forbes Randolph
Productions:
    Opened September 15, 1931 for 7 performances
Reviews:
    New York Times page 15, Sep 16, 1931

Fearless Frank
    book: Andrew Davies
    music: Dave Brown
    lyrics: Andrew Davies
    staging: Robert Gillespie
    sets: Martin Tilley
    costumes: Carrie F. Robbins
    choreography: Michael Vernon
Productions:
    Opened June 15, 1980 for 12 performances

Reviews:
  New York 13:49-50, Jun 30, 1980
  New York Theatre Critics' Reviews 1980:212
  New York Times III, page 13, Jun 16, 1980
  New Yorker 56:55, Jun 30, 1980

Feinstein, Michael   (see Michael Feinstein in Concert)

Festival
  book: Stephen Downs and Randal Martin, based on the
                   chantefable Aucussin Niccolette
  music: Stephen Downs
  lyrics: Stephen Downs and Randal Martin
  special
    material: Bruce Vilanch
  staging: Wayne Bryan
  sets: George Gizienski
  costumes: Madeleine Ann Graneto
  choreography: Stan Mazin
Productions:
  (Off-Broadway) Opened May 16, 1979 for 5 performances
Reviews:
  New York Times III, page 3, May 18, 1979

Feunte Ovehuna
  book: Lope de Vega
  music: Guy Strobel
  staging: Alan Holzman
Productions:
  (Off-Off-Broadway) Opened October 12, 1972
No Reviews.

Fiddler on the Roof
  book: Joseph Stein, based on the stories of Sholom
                   Aleichem
  music: Jerry Bock
  lyrics: Sheldon Harnick
  staging: Jerome Robbins
  sets: Boris Aronson
  costumes: Patricia Zipprodt
  choreography: Jerome Robbins
Productions:
  Opened September 22, 1964 for 3,242 performances
  Opened December 28, 1976 for 167 performances
  Opened July 9, 1981 for 53 performances
Reviews:
  America 112:25, Jan 2, 1965
  Commentary 38:73-5, Nov 1964
            39:12+, Apr 1965
  Commonweal 81:100, Oct 16, 1964
  Dance Magazine 38:24-5+, Nov 1964
                54:36-8+, Oct 1980

Life 57:104-5+, Dec 4, 1964
Nation 199:229-30, Oct 12, 1964
        224:61-2, Jan 15, 1977
National Review 29:394-5, Apr 1, 1977
New Republic 151:31+, Oct 17, 1964
New York 10:50, Jan 17, 1977
New York Theatre Critics' Reviews 1964:214+
                                  1976:47
                                  1981:206
New York Times page 10, Aug 8, 1964
                page 56, Sep 23, 1964
                page 47, Sep 24, 1964
                II, page 1, Oct 4, 1964
                page 36, Oct 6, 1964
                page 14, Jan 23, 1965
                page 40, Jun 9, 1965
                II, page 2, Aug 15, 1965
                page 35, Jan 23, 1966
                page 39, Sep 2, 1966
                page 54, Sep 22, 1966
                page 40, Dec 22, 1966
                page 50, Feb 17, 1967
                page 29, Jun 30, 1967
                page 25, Sep 4, 1967
                page 50, Sep 7, 1967
                page 59, Sep 28, 1967
                page 61, Nov 16, 1967
                page 28, Feb 2, 1968
                page 36, Feb 22, 1968
                page 36, Feb 26, 1969
                page 47, Jun 26, 1969
                page 82, Nov 16, 1969
                page 20, Feb 28, 1970
                page 34, Jul 8, 1970
                page 39, Sep 22, 1970
                II, page 40, Dec 27, 1970
                II, page 16, Apr 18, 1971
                II page 3, Jul 18, 1971
                page 16, Jul 21, 1971
                page 35, Aug 23, 1971
                page 54, Dec 7, 1971
                page 47, Jan 13, 1972
                II, page 14, Jan 16, 1972
                page 28, Jun 17, 1972
                page 1, Jun 18, 1972
                page 7, Jul 3, 1972
                page 11, May 29, 1973
                page 42, Jul 1, 1974
                page 12, Dec 30, 1976
                II, page 3, Jan 16, 1977
                XXII, page 20, Apr 12, 1981

XXIII, page 26, May 17, 1981
III, page 3, Jul 10, 1981
III, page 16, Jul 20, 1981
New Yorker 40:96, Oct 3, 1964
52:76, Jan 10, 1977
Newsweek 64:106, Oct 5, 1964
89:66, Jan 10, 1977
Saturday Review 47:33, Oct 10, 1964
Theatre Crafts 20:28-9+, May 1986
Time 84:82, Oct 2, 1964
Vogue 144:66, Nov 1, 1964

Fiesta in Madrid

book:	Tito Capobianco; adapted from Thomas Breton's La Verbena de La Paloma
music:	Tito Capobianco
lyrics:	Tito Capobianco
staging:	Tito Capobianco
sets:	Jose Varona
costumes:	Jose Varona
choreography:	Teresa

Productions:
Opened May 28, 1969 for 23 performances
Reviews:
Dance Magazine 43:71, Aug 1969
New York Times page 49, May 29, 1969
Newsweek 73:95-6, Jun 9, 1969
Saturday Review 52:46, Jun 14, 1969

The 5th Season

book:	Luba Kadison, based on the play by Sylvia Regan
music:	Dick Manning
lyrics:	Dick Manning
staging:	Joseph Buloff
sets:	Jeffrey B. Moss
costumes:	Jeffrey B. Moss

Productions:
Opened October 12, 1975 for 122 performances
Reviews:
New York Times page 37, Oct 13, 1975

Fifty-Fifty, Ltd.

book:	Margaret Michael and William Lennox; based on William Gillette's All the Comforts of Home
music:	Leon De Costa
lyrics:	Leon De Costa

Productions:
Opened October 27, 1919 for 40 performances
Reviews:
New York Times page 14, Oct 28, 1919
VIII, page 2, Oct 19, 1919

Fifty Million Frenchmen
      book: Herbert Fields
      music: Cole Porter
      lyrics: Cole Porter
      staging: Edgar M. Woolley (Monty Woolley)
      choreography: Larry Ceballos
Productions:
   Opened November 27, 1929 for 254 performances
Reviews:
   Nation 129:756-8, Dec 18, 1929
   New York Times page 34, Nov 28, 1929
                     X, page 1, Dec 8, 1929
                     VIII, page 1, Jan 5, 1930
   Theatre Magazine 51:49, Jan 1930
   Vogue 75:100, Jan 18, 1930

The Fig Leaves Are Falling
      book: Allan Sherman
      music: Albert Hague
      lyrics: Allan Sherman
      staging: George Abbott
      sets: William and Jean Eckart
      costumes: Robert Mackintosh
      choreography: Eddie Gasper
Productions:
   Opened January 2, 1969 for 4 performances
Reviews:
   New York Theatre Critics' Reviews 1969:397
   New York Times page 19, Jan 3, 1969
                     page 32, Jan 4, 1969
   New Yorker 44:56, Jan 11, 1969
   Newsweek 73:86, Jan 13, 1969

Fine and Dandy
      book: Donald Ogden Stewart
      music: Kay Swift
      lyrics: Paul James
      staging: Morris Green, Frank McCoy, David Gould, Tom
                       Nip
Productions:
   Opened September 23, 1930 for 255 performances
Reviews:
   Bookman 72:411, Dec 1930
   Commonweal 12:583, Oct 8, 1930
   Life (New York) 96:18, Oct 10, 1930
   Nation 131:422, Oct 15, 1930
   New York Times IX, page 2, Sep 7, 1930
                     page 26, Sep 24, 1930
                     IX, page 1, Oct 5, 1930
   Outlook 156:233, Oct 8, 1930
   Theatre Magazine 52:64, Dec 1930
   Vogue 76:116, Nov 10, 1930

Finian's Rainbow
     book: E. Y. Harburg and Fred Saidy
     music: Burton Lane
     lyrics: E. Y. Harburg
     staging: Bretaigne Windust
     sets: Jo Mielziner
     costumes: Eleanor Goldsmith
     choreography: Michael Kidd
Productions:
     Opened January 10, 1947 for 725 performances
     (Off-Broadway) Season of 1952-53
     Opened May 18, 1955 for 18 performances
     (Off-Broadway) Season of 1959-60
     Opened April 27, 1960 for 27 performances
     Opened April 5, 1967 for 23 performances
     (Off-Off-Broadway) Opened June 30, 1977
Reviews:
     Catholic World 164:453-4, Feb 1947
                    181:308, Jul 1955
     Collier's 120:14-15, Aug 2, 1947
     Commonweal 45:446, Feb 14, 1947
     Dance Magazine 41:26, May 1967
     Harper's 81:174, May 1947
     Life 22:76-7, Feb 24, 1947
     New Republic 116:43, Feb 3, 1947
     New York Theatre Critics' Reviews 1947:486+
                                       1960:279+
     New York Times VI, page 28, Jan 5, 1947
                    page 23, Jan 11, 1947
                    II, page 1, Jan 26, 1947
                    II, page 3, Feb 2, 1947
                    II, page 1, Apr 6, 1947
                    II, page 1, Jul 13, 1947
                    II, page 1, Aug 17, 1947
                    page 38, Oct 22, 1947
                    II, page 3, Nov 9, 1947
                    II, page 1, Aug 29, 1948
                    page 36, Oct 19, 1949
                    page 13, Mar 17, 1953
                    page 19, Sep 25, 1953
                    page 25, May 17, 1955
                    page 31, Apr 28, 1960
                    page 44, Apr 6, 1967
                    page 25, Jul 5, 1977
     New Yorker 22:46+, Jan 18, 1947
     Newsweek 29:84, Jan 20, 1947
              30:78, Nov 3, 1947
     Saturday Review 30:28-30, Feb 15, 1947
     Theatre Arts 31:8, 15, 23, Mar 1947
                  32:49, Feb 1948
     Time 49:69, Jan 20, 1947
     Vogue 109:148, Feb 15, 1947

Fiorello!
    book: Jerome Weidman and George Abbott
    music: Jerry Bock
    lyrics: Sheldon Harnick
    staging: George Abbott
    sets: William and Jean Eckart
    costumes: William and Jean Eckart
    choreography: Peter Gennaro
Productions:
    Opened November 23, 1959 for 795 performances
    Opened June 13, 1962 for 16 performances
    (Off-Off-Broadway) Opened October 14, 1976
    (Off-Off-Broadway) Opened October 27, 1988
Reviews:
    America 102:594, Feb 13, 1960
    Christian Century 76:1506, Dec 23, 1959
    Commonweal 71:422, Jan 8, 1960
    Life 48:55-7, Jan 18, 1960
    Nation 189:475, Dec 19, 1959
    New York Theatre Critics' Reviews 1959:219+
    New York Times VI, page 18, Nov 8, 1959
                    II, page 1, Nov 22, 1959
                    page 45, Nov 24, 1959
                    page 19, Nov 25, 1959
                    II, page 1, Nov 29, 1959
                    page 12, Oct 28, 1961
                    page 24, Jun 14, 1962
                    page 60, Oct 10, 1962
                    III, page 20, Oct 15, 1976
                    III, page 16, Oct 31, 1988
    New Yorker 35:95-7, Dec 5, 1959
    Newsweek 54:96, Dec 7, 1959
    Saturday Review 42:26-7, Dec 12, 1959
                    43:75, Jan 16, 1960
    Time 74:54+, Dec 7, 1959

Fioretta
    book: Earl Carroll, adapted by Charlton Andrews
    music: George Babgy and G. Romilli
    lyrics: George Babgy and G. Romilli
    staging: Earl Carroll
Productions:
    Opened February 5, 1929 for 111 performances
Reviews:
    Life (New York) 93:24, Mar 15, 1929
    New York Times VIII, page 4, Jan 6, 1929
                    page 30, Feb 6, 1929
    Theatre Magazine 49:46, Apr 1929

Fire of Flowers
    words: Peter Copani

music: Peter Copani, David McHugh, Lawrence Pitilli,
                      Christian Staudt, Bob Tuthill and Ed Vogel
lyrics: Peter Copani
staging: Don Signore
sets: Richard Harper
Productions:
  (Off-Off-Broadway) Opened January 1976
  (Off-Broadway) Opened January 29, 1976 for 38 performances
Reviews:
  New York Times page 20, Jan 30, 1976

The Firebrand of Florence
  book: Edwin Justus Mayer and Ira Gershwin, based on
                      The Firebrand by Edwin Justus Mayer
  music: Kurt Weill
  lyrics: Edwin Justus Mayer and Ira Gershwin
  staging: John Murray Anderson
  sets: Jo Mielziner
  costumes: Raoul Pene du Bois
  choreography: Catherine Littlefield
Productions:
  Opened March 22, 1945 for 43 performances
Reviews:
  Catholic World 161:167, May 1945
  New York Theatre Critics' Reviews 1945:241+
  New York Times page 13, Mar 23, 1945
  New Yorker 21:42, Mar 3, 1945
  Newsweek 25:84, Apr 2, 1945
  Theatre Arts 29:271, May 1945
  Time 45:60, Apr 2, 1945

The Firefly
  book: Otto Hauerbach
  music: Rudolf Friml
  lyrics: Otto Hauerbach
  staging: Frederick G. Latham
Productions:
  Opened December 30, 1912 for 120 performances
  Opened November 30, 1931 for 8 performances
Reviews:
  Dramatic Mirror 68:6, Dec 4, 1912
                   68:2, Dec 18, 1912
  Green Book 9:196-7+, Feb 1913
  Harper's Weekly page 18, Feb 1, 1913
  Munsey 48:844, Feb 1913
  New York Dramatic News 56:19, Dec 7, 1912
  Red Book 20:894-6, Mar 1913
  Theatre Magazine 17:3, Jan 1913

The Fireman's Flame
  book: John Van Antwerp

```
music:          Richard Lewine
lyrics:         Ted Fetter
staging:        John and Jerrold Krimsky
sets:           Eugene Dunkel
costumes:       Kermit Love
choreography:   Morgan Lewis
```
Productions:
Opened October 9, 1937 for 204 performances
Reviews:
Life 3:62-5, Dec 27, 1937
New York Times XI, page 3, Oct 3, 1937
                page 26, Oct 10, 1937

The First
```
book:           Joel Siegel with Martin Charnin, based on the
                life of Jackie Robinson
music:          Bob Brush
lyrics:         Martin Charnin
staging:        Martin Charnin
sets:           David Chapman
costumes:       Carrie F. Robbins
choreography:   Alan Johnson
```
Productions:
Opened November 17, 1981 for 37 performances
Reviews:
Dance Magazine 56:98, Feb 1982
New York 14:88, Nov 30, 1981
New York Theatre Critics' Reviews 1981:110
New York Times III, page 25, Nov 18, 1981
                II, page 3, Dec 13, 1981
New Yorker 57:110, Dec 7, 1981
Newsweek 98:109, Nov 30, 1981
Sports Illustrated 55:96, Nov 30, 1981

First Impressions
```
book:           Abe Burrows, based on Jane Austen's Pride and
                Prejudice and the play by Helen Jerome
music:          Robert Goldman, Glenn Paxton, George Weiss
lyrics:         Robert Goldman, Glenn Paxton, George Weiss
staging:        Abe Burrows
sets:           Peter Larkin
costumes:       Alvin Colt
choreography:   Jonathan Lucas
```
Productions:
Opened March 19, 1959 for 92 performances
Reviews:
Catholic World 189:241-2, Jun 1959
Commonweal 70:57-8, Apr 10, 1959
Dance Magazine 33:16, Jun 1959
New York Theatre Critics' Reviews 1959:336+
New York Times page 28, Mar 20, 1959

II, page 1, Mar 29, 1959
page 31, May 26, 1959
New Yorker 35:89, Mar 28, 1959
Saturday Review 42:28, Apr 4, 1959
Theatre Arts 42:23-4, May 1959
Time 73:43, Mar 30, 1959

First Reader (see Gertrude Stein's First Reader)

Fisher, Eddie (see Eddie Fisher)

5 O'Clock Girl
    book: Guy Bolton and Fred Thompson
    music: Bert Kalmar and Harry Ruby
    lyrics: Bert Kalmar and Harry Ruby
    staging: Philip Goodman
Productions:
  Opened October 10, 1927 for 280 performances
  Opened January 28, 1981 for 14 performances
Reviews:
  Life (New York) 90:23, Nov 3, 1927
  New York 12:57, Jul 30, 1979
             14:46, Feb 9, 1981
  New York Theatre Critics' Reviews 1981:372
  New York Times page 26, Oct 11, 1927
               XXIII, page 32, Dec 14, 1980
               III, page 13, Jan 29, 1981
               II, page 3, Feb 9, 1981
  New Yorker 56:106, Feb 8, 1981
  Time 117:63, Feb 9, 1981
  Vogue 70:116, Dec 15, 1927

Five-Six-Seven-Eight...Dance!
    by: Bruce Vilanch
    original songs: David Zippel and Wally Harper
    music: Various composers
    lyrics: Various authors
    staging: Ron Field
    sets: Tom H. John
    costumes: Lindsay W. Davis
    choreography: Ron Field
Productions:
  Opened June 15, 1983 for 156 performances
Reviews:
  Dance Magazine 57:88, Sep 1983
  New York 16:73, Jun 27, 1983
  New York Theatre Critics' Reviews 1983:199
  New York Times III, page 1, Jun 17, 1983

Fixed
    conceived: Anita L. Thomas and George Faison

book: Robert Maurice Riley
music and
   lyrics: Gene Bone and Howard Fenton
additional
   lyrics: Langston Hughes
staging: George Faison
sets: David Chapman
costumes: Victor Capecce
Productions:
   (Off-Off-Broadway) Opened November 26, 1977 for 28 performances
Reviews:
   New York Times III, page 15, Dec 21, 1977

Flahooley
book: E. Y. Harburg and Fred Saidy
music: Sammy Fain
lyrics: E. Y. Harburg
staging: E. Y. Harburg and Fred Saidy
sets: Howard Bay
costumes: David Ffolkes
choreography: Helen Tamiris
Productions:
   Opened May 14, 1951 for 40 performances
   (Off-Off-Broadway) Opened April 25, 1964 for 8 performances
Reviews:
   Catholic World 173:307, Jul 1951
   Commonweal 54:189, Jun 1, 1951
   New York Theatre Critics' Reviews 1951:264+
   New York Times II, page 1, May 13, 1951
                page 39, May 15, 1951
                II, page 1, May 20, 1951
                page 17, Aug 13, 1952
   New Yorker 27:48+, May 26, 1951
   Newsweek 37:58, May 28, 1951
   Theatre Arts 35:5, Sep 1951
   Time 57:78, May 28, 1951

Flamenco Puro
conceived: Claudio Segovia and Hector Orezzoli
music: Flamenco songs and instrumentals
staging: Claudio Segovia and Hector Orezzoli
design: Claudio Segovia and Hector Orezzoli
Productions:
   Opened October 19, 1986 for 40 performances
Reviews:
   New York Theatre Critics' Reviews 1986:180
   New York Times II, page 1, Oct 19, 1986

Flo-Flo
book: Fred de Gresac
music: Silvio Hein

lyrics: E. Paulton and Fred de Gresac
staging: Walter Brooks
Productions:
Opened December 20, 1917 for 220 performances
Reviews:
Dramatic Mirror 77:7, Dec 29, 1917
Green Book 20:208-10, Aug 1918
Life (New York) 71:22, Jan 3, 1918
New York Times page 9, Dec 20, 1917
Theatre Magazine 27:87, Feb 1918
                  27:93, Feb 1918

Flora, the Red Menace
book: George Abbott and Robert Russell, based on
                  Lester Atwell's Love Is Just Around the Corner
music: John Kander
lyrics: Fred Ebb
staging: George Abbott
sets: William and Jean Eckart
costumes: Donald Brooks
choreography: Lee Theodore
Productions:
Opened May 11, 1965 for 87 performances
Reviews:
America 113:121-2, Jul 31, 1965
Dance Magazine 39:23, Jul 1965
National Review 17:561-2, Jun 29, 1965
New York Theatre Critics' Reviews 1965:330+
New York Times page 31, Mar 2, 1965
               page 41, May 12, 1965
New Yorker 41:114, May 22, 1965
Newsweek 65:99, May 24, 1965
Saturday Review 48:50, May 8, 1965
Time 85:69, May 21, 1965
Vogue 146:38, Jul 1965

Floradora
book: Owen Hall
music: Leslie Stuart
lyrics: E. Boyd Jones and Paul Rubens
staging: Lewis Morton
Productions:
Opened April 5, 1920 for 64 performances
Reviews:
Dramatic Mirror 82:572-3, Mar 27, 1920
               82:680, Apr 10, 1920
Green Book 8:102-10, Jul 1912
Life (New York) 75:752, Apr 22, 1920
New York Clipper 68:14, Apr 14, 1920
New York Times page 18, Apr 6, 1920
               VI, page 2, Apr 18, 1920

Stage 14:88, Aug 1937
Theatre Arts 29:456, Aug 1945
Theatre Magazine 31:573, Jun 1920
40:52, Oct 1924

Florida Girl
book: Paul Porter, Benjamin Hapgood Burt and William
A. Grew
music: Milton Suskind
lyrics: Paul Porter, Benjamin Hapgood Burt and William
A. Grew
staging: Frederick Stanhope
Productions:
Opened November 2, 1925 for 40 performances
Reviews:
New York Times page 34, Nov 3, 1925

Flossie
book: Armand Robi
music: Armand Robi
lyrics: Ralph Murphey
Productions:
Opened June 3, 1924 for (16) performances
Reviews:
New York Times page 25, Jun 4, 1924
Theatre Magazine 40:15, Aug 1924

Flower Drum Song
book: Oscar Hammerstein II and Joseph Fields, based on
the novel by C. Y. Lee
music: Richard Rodgers
lyrics: Oscar Hammerstein II
staging: Gene Kelly
sets: Oliver Smith
costumes: Irene Sharaff
choreography: Carol Haney
Productions:
Opened December 1, 1958 for 600 performances
Reviews:
America 100:438, Jan 10, 1959
Catholic World 188:420, Feb 1959
Commonweal 70:426-7, Apr 14, 1959
Dance Magazine 33:16-17, Jan 1959
Life 45:77-8+, Dec 22, 1958
New Republic 139:23, Dec 22, 1958
New York Theatre Critics' Reviews 1958:187+
New York Times VI, pages 16-17, Nov 23, 1958
page 44, Dec 2, 1958
II, page 5, Dec 7, 1958
page 20, Mar 25, 1960
New Yorker 34:104+, Dec 13, 1958

Newsweek 52:53-6, Dec 1, 1958
    52:63, Dec 15, 1958
Saturday Review 41:33, Dec 20, 1958
Theatre Arts 43:10, Feb 1959
Time 72:44, Dec 15, 1958
    72:42-4+, Dec 22, 1958
Vogue 133:95, Jan 1, 1959

Fly Blackbird

book:	C. Jackson and James Hatch
music:	C. Jackson and James Hatch
lyrics:	C. Jackson and James Hatch
staging:	Jerome Eskow
sets:	Robert Soule
costumes:	Robby Campbell
choreography:	Talley Beatty

Productions:
    (Off-Broadway) Opened February 5, 1962 for 127 performances
Reviews:
    America 106:773-4, Mar 10, 1962
    Nation 194:201, Mar 3, 1962
    New York Times page 26, Feb 6, 1962
    New Yorker 37:94-5, Feb 17, 1962
    Theatre Arts 46:61-3, May 1962

Flying Colors

book:	Howard Dietz
music:	Arthur Schwartz
lyrics:	Howard Dietz
staging:	Howard Dietz
sets:	Norman Bel-Geddes

Productions:
    Opened September 15, 1932 for 188 performances
Reviews:
    Arts and Decoration 38:45+, Nov 1932
    Catholic World 136:210-11, Nov 1932
    New Outlook 161:47, Jan 1933
    Nation 135:318, Oct 5, 1932
    New York Times page 24, Sep 16, 1932
    Stage 10:11, Oct 1932
        10:18-21, Nov 1932
    Theatre Arts 16:873, Nov 1932
    Vogue 80:89, Nov 1, 1932

Flying High

book:	B. G. DeSylva, John McGowan
music:	Ray Henderson
lyrics:	B. G. DeSylva and Lew Brown
staging:	Edward Clark Lilley
choreography:	Bobby Connelly

Productions:
    Opened March 3, 1930 for 357 performances

Reviews:
  Life (New York) 95:18, Mar 28, 1930
  New York Times VIII, page 4, Feb 9, 1930
                  page 24, Mar 4, 1930
                  VIII, page 4, Mar 30, 1930
  Outlook 155:29, May 7, 1930
  Theatre Magazine 51:43, May 1930
  Vogue 75:126, May 10, 1930

Folies Bergère
  book: Paul Derval
  music: Henri Betti, additional music by Phillippe Gerard
  staging: Michel Gyarmathy
  sets: Michel Gyarmathy
  costumes: Michel Gyarmathy
  choreography: George Reich
Productions:
  Opened June 2, 1964 for 191 performances
Reviews:
  New York Theatre Critics' Reviews 1964:242+
  New York Times page 52, May 13, 1964
                  II, page 1, May 31, 1964
                  page 36, Jun 3, 1964
                  II, page 1, Jun 21, 1964
                  page 53, Sep 17, 1964
                  page 18, Sep 19, 1964

Follies   (see also Ziegfeld Follies)

Follies
  book: James Goldman
  music: Stephen Sondheim
  lyrics: Stephen Sondheim
  staging: Harold Prince and Michael Bennett
  sets: Boris Aronson
  costumes: Florence Klotz
  choreography: Michael Bennett
Productions:
  Opened April 4, 1971 for 521 performances
  (Off-Off-Broadway) Opened May 6, 1976
  Opened September 6, 1985 for 2 performances
Reviews:
  America 124:615, Jun 12, 1971
  Commonweal 94:239-40, May 14, 1971
  Dance Magazine 45:81-2, Jun 1971
  Los Angeles 30:46, Nov 1985
  National Review 23:1129-30, Oct 8, 1971
  Nation 212:509-10, Apr 19, 1971
  New Republic 164:24+, May 8, 1971
  New York 18:77-8, Sep 30, 1985
  New York Theatre Critics' Reviews 1971:309

New York Times II, page 1, Apr 4, 1971
       page 44, Apr 5, 1971
       page 20, Apr 9, 1971
       II, page 1, Apr 11, 1971
       II, page 1, Apr 25, 1971
       page 26, May 16, 1971
       II, page 32, Nov 14, 1971
       III, page 2, May 14, 1976
       III, page 16, Sep 9, 1985
       II, page 1, Sep 15, 1985
New Yorker 47:67, Apr 10, 1971
Newsweek 77:121, Apr 12, 1971
People 24:78-9, Sep 23, 1985
Saturday Review 54:16+, May 1, 1971
Time 97:78, Apr 12, 1971
   97:70-4, May 3, 1971
Video 12:59, Aug 1988
Vogue 157:154-5, May 1971

Follies Burlesque '67
   book: Stanley Richman
   music: Sol Richman
   lyrics: Sol Richman
   staging: Dick Richards
   costumes: S. Binder
   choreography: Paul Morokoff
Productions:
   (Off-Broadway)   Opened May 3, 1967 for 16 performances
No Reviews.

Follow Me
   book: Based on the original of Felix Doermann and Leo
          Ascher
   music: Sigmund Romberg
   lyrics: Robert B. Smith
   staging: J. H. Benrimo
   choreography: Jack Mason and Allen K. Foster
Productions:
   Opened November 29, 1916 for 78 performances
Reviews:
   Dramatic Mirror 76:7-8, Dec 9, 1916
          77:4, Jan 13, 1917
   New York Times page 11, Nov 30, 1916
   Theatre Magazine 25:20, Jan 1917
          25:24, Jan 1917

Follow the Girl
   book: Henry Blossom and Zoel Parenteau
   staging: J. C. Huffman
Productions:
   Opened March 2, 1918 for 25 performances

Reviews:
    Dramatic Mirror 78:5, Mar 16, 1918
    New York Times page 9, Mar 4, 1918
    Theatre Magazine 27:216, Apr 1918
                  27:220, Apr 1918

Follow the Girls

book:	Guy Bolton and Eddie Davis, with dialogue by Fred Thompson
music:	Dan Shapiro, Milton Pascal, Phil Charig
lyrics:	Dan Shapiro, Milton Pascal, Phil Charig
staging:	Harry Delmar
sets:	Howard Bay
costumes:	Lou Eisele
choreography:	Catherine Littlefield

Productions:
    Opened April 8, 1944 for 882 performances
Reviews:
    Commonweal 40:38-9, Apr 28, 1944
    Life 16:115-18+, Apr 24, 1944
    New York Theatre Critics' Reviews 1944:222+
    New York Times page 15, Apr 10, 1944
                  II, page 1, Apr 16, 1944
    Newsweek 23:106, Apr 17, 1944

Follow Thru

book:	Laurence Schwab and B. G. DeSylva
music:	Ray Henderson
lyrics:	B. G. DeSylva and Lew Brown
staging:	Edgar MacGregor and Donald Oenslager

Productions:
    Opened January 9, 1929 for 403 performances
Reviews:
    Theatre Magazine 49:51, Mar 1929
    Vogue 73:72, Mar 2, 1929

Footlights

book:	Roland Oliver
staging:	Bunny Weldon

Productions:
    Opened August 19, 1927 for 43 performances
Reviews:
    Life (New York) 90:19, Sep 8, 1927
    New York Times page 8, Aug 20, 1927

For Goodness Sake

book:	Fred Jackson
music:	William Daly and Paul Lannin
lyrics:	Arthur Jackson
staging:	Priestly Morrison and Allen K. Foster

Productions:
    Opened February 20, 1922 for 103 performances

Reviews:
New York Clipper 70:22, Mar 8, 1922
New York Times page 13, Feb 22, 1922
Theatre Magazine 35:334, May 1922

Forbidden Broadway (1982)
conceived: Gerard Alessandrini
music: Various composers
lyrics: Gerard Alessandrini
staging: Jeff Martin
Productions:
(Off-Off-Broadway) Opened January 15, 1982
(Off-Broadway) Opened May 4, 1982 for 2,332 performances
(Revised [1984] version opened October 27, 1983)
(Revised [1985] version opened January 1, 1985)
Reviews:
Harper's Bazaar 117:134-5, Jul 1984
Los Angeles 28:62, Jun 1983
New Leader 66:22, Nov 14, 1983
New York Times III, page 9, Feb 14, 1982
               III, page 1, Nov 19, 1982
               III, page 14, Mar 29, 1983
               III, page 4, Oct 28, 1983
               III, page 13, Feb 5, 1985
               III, page 22, Jun 19, 1986
New Yorker 58:178, Nov 22, 1982
Newsweek 100:75, Jul 19, 1982
         102:105, Dec 5, 1983
People 17:100+, May 31, 1982
Time 121:80, Jan 24, 1983

Forbidden Broadway 1988 (later 1989)
conceived: Gerard Alessandrini
music: Various composers
lyrics: Various authors
original songs: Gerard Alessandrini
staging: Gerard Alessandrini
costumes: Erika Dyson
choreography: Roxie Lucas
Productions:
(Off-Broadway) Opened September 15, 1988 for *296 performances
(still running 6/1/89)
Reviews:
New York 19:59, Jul 28, 1986
         21:131, Sep 26, 1988
New York Theatre Critics' Reviews 1988:163
New York Times II, page 3, Sep 4, 1988
               III, page 3, Sep 16, 1988
               II, page 7, Apr 16, 1989
New Yorker 64:79, Sep 26, 1988
Newsweek 112:58, Oct 3, 1988

Forbidden Melody
----
   book: Otto Harbach
   music: Sigmund Romberg
   lyrics: Otto Harbach
   staging: Macklin Megley
   sets: Sergei Soudeikine
   costumes: Ten Eyck
Productions:
   Opened November 2, 1936 for 32 performances
Reviews:
   New York Times page 30, Oct 13, 1936

Fortuna
----
   book: Arnold Weinstein; adapted from a drama by
                   Eduardo de Filippo and Armando Curcio
   music: Francis Thorne
   lyrics: Arnold Weinstein
   staging: Glen Tetley
Productions:
   (Off-Broadway) Opened January 3, 1962 for 5 performances
Reviews:
   New York Times page 26, Jan 4, 1962
                  page 12, Jan 6, 1962
   New Yorker 37:67, Jan 13, 1962

48th Annual Squitters Mountain Song Dance Folklore Convention and Benjo Contest ... And How I Lost (see Banjo Dancing)

45 Minutes from Broadway
----
   book: George M. Cohan
   music: George M. Cohan
   lyrics: George M. Cohan
   staging: George M. Cohan
Productions:
   Opened January 1, 1906 for 90 performances
   Opened March 14, 1912 for 36 performances
Reviews:
   Blue Book 15:228-32, Jun 1912
   Dramatic Mirror 67:6, Mar 20, 1912
                   67:4, Apr 10, 1912
   Theatre Magazine 6:26+, Feb 1906

42nd Street
----
   book: Michael Stewart and Mark Bramble, based on the
                   novel by Bradford Ropes
   music: Harry Warren and Al Dubin
   lyrics: Harry Warren and Al Dubin
   additional
   lyrics: Johnny Mercer and Mort Dixon
   staging: Gower Champion
   sets: Robin Wagner

```
costumes:        Theoni V. Aldredge
choreography:    Gower Champion
```
Productions:
Opened August 25, 1980 for 3,486 performances
Reviews:
America 143:212, Oct 11, 1980
Dance Magazine 54:56-9, Oct 1980
50 Plus 20:40-4, Nov 1980
Los Angeles 29:46, Mar 1984
New Republic 183:25-6, Nov 1, 1980
New York 13:12+, Sep 8, 1980
        13:75-6, Sep 8, 1980
New York Theatre Critics' Reviews 1980:172
New York Times III, page 7, Aug 26, 1980
New Yorker 56:100, Sep 8, 1980
Newsweek 96:85, Sep 8, 1980
Saturday Review 7:88, Dec 1980
Seventeen 40:164-9, Apr 1981
Theatre Crafts 14:28-31+, Nov/Dec 1980
Time 116:54-5, Sep 8, 1980

Four Saints in Three Acts
```
book:           Gertrude Stein
music:          Virgil Thomson
lyrics:         Gertrude Stein
staging:        Maurice Grosser
sets:           Paul Morrison
costumes:       Paul Morrison
choreography    William Dollar
```
Productions:
Opened April 16, 1952 for 15 performances
Reviews:
Catholic World 178:228, Jun 1952
Commonweal 56:116, May 9, 1952
Musical America 72:7, May 1952
New York Theatre Critics' Reviews 1952:312
New York Times page 35, Apr 17, 1952
New Yorker 28:122-4, Apr 26, 1952
Newsweek 39:52, Apr 28, 1952
Saturday Review 35:33, May 3, 1952
School and Society 75:393-4, Jun 21, 1952
Theatre Arts 36:19, Jun 1952
Time 59:42, Apr 28, 1952

4th Avenue North
```
sketches:       George Allan, Michael Batterberry, Shippen Geer,
                Murray Grand, Cy Walter and others
music, lyrics:  George Allan, Michael Batterberry, Shippen Geer,
                Murray Grand, Cy Walter and others
staging:        Michael Batterberry
```
Productions:
(Off-Broadway) Opened September 27, 1961 for 2 performances

Reviews:
    New York Times page 50, Sep 28, 1961

Fourtune
    book: Bill Russell
    music: Ronald Melrose
    lyrics: Bill Russell
    staging: Ron Troutman
    sets: Harry Silverglat
    costumes: Joan Culkin
    choreography: Troy Garza
Productions:
    (Off-Broadway) Opened April 27, 1980 for 241 performances
Reviews:
    New York 13:42, Aug 4, 1980
    New York Times III, page 8, Apr 29, 1980

Foxfire
    book: Susan Cooper and Hume Cronyn, based on ma-
                     terials from the Foxfire books
    music: Jonathan Holtzman
    lyrics: Susan Cooper, Hume Cronyn and Jonathan Holtz-
                     man
    staging: David Trainer
    sets: David Mitchell
    costumes: Linda Fisher
Productions:
    Opened November 11, 1982 for 213 performances
Reviews:
    America 148:56, Jan 22, 1983
    Los Angeles 31:40, Jan 1986
    Nation 235:600+, Dec 4, 1982
    New Leader 65:21-2, Dec 27, 1982
    New Republic 188 Spring Issue:26, Jan 3, 1983
    New York 15:77, Nov 22, 1982
    New York Theatre Critics' Reviews 1982:141
    New York Times III, page 3, Nov 12, 1982
                    II, page 3, Nov 21, 1982
    New Yorker 58:176, Nov 22, 1982
    Newsweek 100:123, Nov 22, 1982
    Time 120:105, Nov 22, 1982

Foxy
    book: Ian McLellan Hunter and Ring Lardner, Jr.,
                     suggested by Ben Jonson's Volpone
    music: Robert Emmett Dolan
    lyrics: Johnny Mercer
    staging: Robert Lewis
    sets: Robert Randolph
    costumes: Robert Fletcher
    choreography: Jack Cole

Productions:
  Opened February 16, 1964 for 72 performances
Reviews:
  America 110:465, Mar 28, 1964
  Commonweal 79:723, Mar 13, 1964
  New York Theatre Critics' Reviews 1964:349+
  New York Times page 26, Feb 17, 1964
                 page 30, Mar 20, 1964
                 page 33, Apr 14, 1964
  New Yorker 40:106, Feb 29, 1964
  Newsweek 63:56, Mar 2, 1964
  Saturday Review 47:23, Mar 7, 1964
  Time 83:61, Feb 28, 1964

Francis
  book: Joseph Leonardo
  music: Steve Jankowski
  lyrics: Kenny Morris
  staging: Frank Martin
  sets: Neil Bierbower
  costumes: Martha Kelly
Productions:
  (Off-Broadway) Opened December 22, 1981 for 30 performances
Reviews:
  New York Times page 60, Dec 27, 1981

Frank Merriwell, or Honor Challenged
  book: Skip Redwine, Larry Frank and Heywood Gould
  music: Skip Redwine and Larry Frank
  lyrics: Skip Redwine and Larry Frank
  staging: Neal Kenyon
  sets: Tom John
  costumes: Frank Thompson
  choreography: Neal Kenyon
Productions:
  Opened April 24, 1971 for one performance
Reviews:
  New York Theatre Critics' Reviews 1971:296
  New York Times II, page 1, Mar 14, 1971
                 page 40, Apr 26, 1971
                 II, page 1, May 9, 1971
  New Yorker 47:94, May 1, 1971

Frankie and Johnny
  book: John Huston
  songs: Hilda Taylor and Eddie Safranski
  incidental
  music: Irwin A. Bazelon
Productions:
  (Off-Broadway) Opened October 28, 1952 for 2 performances
Reviews:
  New York Times page 37, Oct 29, 1952

Free for All
   book: Oscar Hammerstein II and Laurence Schwab
   music: Richard A. Whiting
   lyrics: Oscar Hammerstein II
   staging: Oscar Hammerstein II
   choreography: Bobby Connelly
Productions:
   Opened September 8, 1931 for 15 performances
Reviews:
   Arts and Decoration 36:73, Nov 1931
   New York Times VIII, page 1, Aug 16, 1931
   Outlook 159:119, Sep 23, 1931

Freedom
   book: C. Lewis Hind and E. Lyall Swete
   music: Norman O'Neill
Productions:
   Opened October 19, 1918 for 33 performances
Reviews:
   Dramatic Mirror 79:687, Nov 9, 1918
   New York Times page 9, Oct 28, 1918
                         page 11, Dec 9, 1918
   Theatre Magazine 28:339, Dec 1918
                        28:345, Dec 1918

Frère Jacques
   music: Gerard Singer
   staging: Richard Palin
Productions:
   (Off-Broadway) Opened June 6, 1968 for 13 performances
Reviews:
   New York Times page 23, Jun 8, 1968

Frimbo
   book: John L. Haber, adapted from All Aboard With
                       E. M. Frimbo by Rogers E. M. Whitaker and
                       Anthony Hiss
   music: Howard Harris
   lyrics: Jim Wann
   staging: John L. Haber
   sets: Karl Eigsti with Fred Buchholz
   costumes: Patricia McGourty
Productions:
   (Off-Broadway) Opened November 9, 1980 for one performance
Reviews:
   New York Times III, page 20, Nov 10, 1980

Frivolities of 1920
   sketches: William Anthony McGuire
   music: William B. Friedlander
   lyrics: William B. Friedlander

additional
songs: Harry Auracher and Tom Johnstone
Productions:
Opened January 8, 1920 for 61 performances
Reviews:
New York Clipper 67:25, Jan 14, 1920
New York Times page 22, Jan 9, 1920

From A to Z
sketches: Woody Allen, Herbert Farjeon, Mark Epstein and
Christopher Hewett, Nina Warner Hook
music and
lyrics: Jerry Herman, Jay Thompson, Dickson Hughes
and Everett Sloane, Jack Holmes, Mary Rodgers
and Marshall Barer, Paul Klein and Fred Ebb,
Fred Ebb and Norma Martin, William Dyer and
Don Parks, Paul Klein and Lee Goldsmith and
Fred Ebb, Charles Zwar and Alan Melville
staging: Christopher Hewett
sets: Fred Voelpel
costumes: Fred Voelpel
choreography: Ray Harrison
Productions:
Opened April 20, 1960 for 22 performances
Reviews:
New York Theatre Critics' Reviews 1960:284+
New York Times page 23, Apr 21, 1960
New Yorker 36:84+, Apr 30, 1960

From Israel with Love
staging: Avi David
choreography: Yakov Kalusky
Productions:
Opened October 2, 1972 for 8 performances
Reviews:
New York Times page 41, Oct 3, 1972

From Nowhere
book: Bill Solly
music: Bill Solly
lyrics: Bill Solly
choreography: Brian MacDonald
Productions:
(Off-Off-Broadway) Opened December 4, 1973
No Reviews.

From the Second City
sketches: Howard Alk, Severn Darden, Barbara Harris,
Paul Sand, Alan Arkin, Andrew Duncan, Mina
Kolb, Eugene Troobnick
music: William Mathieu

staging: Paul Sills
sets: Frederick Fox
Productions:
   Opened September 26, 1961 for 87 performances
Reviews:
   Commonweal 75:94, Oct 20, 1961
   Nation 193:255, Oct 14, 1961
        194:127, Feb 10, 1962
   New York Theatre Critics' Reviews 1961:259+
   New York Times page 32, Sep 27, 1961
               II, page 1, Oct 8, 1961
               page 49, Dec 5, 1961
               page 47, Dec 15, 1961
               page 30, Jan 12, 1962
   New Yorker 37:129, Oct 7, 1961
   Reporter 25:44+, Nov 23, 1961
   Saturday Review 44:78, Oct 14, 1961

From Vienna

sketches: Lothar Metzl, Werner Michel, Hans Weigel, Jura
                  Soyfer, Peter Hammerschlag, David Gregory;
                  adaptations by John LaTouche, Eva Franklin,
                  Hugo Hauff
music: Werner Michel, Walter Drix, Otto Andreas, Jimmy
                  Berg
lyrics: Lothar Metzl, Werner Michel, Hans Weigel, Jura
                  Soyfer, Peter Hammerschlag, David Gregory;
                  adaptations by John LaTouche, Eva Franklin,
                  Hugo Hauff
staging: Herbert Berghof
sets: Donald Oenslager
costumes: Irene Sharaff
Productions:
   Opened June 20, 1939 for 79 performances
Reviews:
   Life 7:32-3, Jul 17, 1939
   Nation 149:109, Jul 22, 1939
   New York Times page 26, Jun 21, 1939
               IX, page 1, Jun 25, 1939
               IX, page 1, Jul 2, 1939
   Newsweek 14:24, Jul 19, 1939
   Time 34:43, Jul 3, 1939

Fun City

sketches: David Rogers
special
  material: Fred Silver, Nelson Garringer, Jay Jeffries,
                  Franklin Underwood, Norman Martin, David
                  Rogers and James Reed Lawlor
staging: David Rogers
sets: Sal Tinnerello and Richard Burnside
costumes: Frank Page

Productions:
   (Off-Broadway) Opened March 6, 1968 for 31 performances
Reviews:
  New York Times page 53, Mar 7, 1968
                page 37, Apr 3, 1968

Fun to Be Free
  book: Ben Hecht and Charles MacArthur
  music: Kurt Weill
  staging: Brett Warren
Productions:
  (Off-Broadway) Opened October 5, 1941
No Reviews.

Funny Face
  book: Fred Thompson and Paul Gerard Smith
  music: George Gershwin
  lyrics: Ira Gershwin
Productions:
  Opened November 22, 1927 for 244 performances
Reviews:
  New York Times page 28, Nov 23, 1927
                X, page 2, Dec 4, 1927
                page 22, Nov 9, 1928
  Theatre Magazine 47:58, Feb 1928
  Vogue 71:118, Jan 15, 1928

Funny Feet
  conceived: Bob Bowyer
  songs: Various authors and composers
  staging: Bob Bowyer
  sets: Lindsay W. Davis
  costumes: Lindsay W. Davis
  choreography: Bob Bowyer
Productions:
  (Off-Broadway) Opened April 21, 1987 for 103 performances
Reviews:
  Nation 244:775, Jun 6, 1987
  New York Times III, page 18, Apr 23, 1987

Funny Girl
  book: Isobel Lennart
  music: Jule Styne
  lyrics: Bob Merrill
  staging: Garson Kanin
  sets: Robert Randolph
  costumes: Irene Sharaff
  choreography: Carol Haney
Productions:
  Opened March 26, 1964 for 1,348 performances
Reviews:
  America 111:114, Aug 1, 1964

Commonweal 80:147, Apr 24, 1964
Life 56:10, Apr 17, 1964
Nation 198:384, Apr 13, 1964
New York Theatre Critics' Reviews 1964:314+
New York Times II, page 3, Mar 22, 1964
              page 15, Mar 27, 1964
              II, page 3, Apr 5, 1964
              page 24, Dec 11, 1965
              II, page 14, Apr 24, 1966
              page 47, Jun 22, 1967
New Yorker 40:76, Apr 4, 1964
Newsweek 63:76-7, Apr 6, 1964
Saturday Review 47:34, Apr 11, 1964
Time 83:54, Apr 3, 1964

A Funny Thing Happened on the Way to the Forum
book: Burt Shevelove and Larry Gelbart, based on
                      Plautus' plays
music: Stephen Sondheim
lyrics: Stephen Sondheim
staging: George Abbott
sets: Tony Walton
costumes: Tony Walton
choreography: Jack Cole
Productions:
Opened May 8, 1962 for 964 performances
Opened March 30, 1972 for 156 performances
Reviews:
America 107:360-1, Jun 2, 1962
        126:405-6, Apr 15, 1972
Commonweal 76:279, Jun 8, 1962
Dance Magazine 36:27, Jul 1962
Life 53:93-5, Jul 20, 1962
Nation 195:60, Aug 11, 1962
       214:509, Apr 17, 1972
New Republic 146:28-30, May 28, 1962
New York Theatre Critics' Reviews 1962:290+
                              1972:348
New York Times page 49, May 9, 1962
              II, page 1, May 20, 1962
              page 22, Jul 6, 1962
              page 83, Oct 14, 1962
              page 14, May 11, 1963
              page 20, Aug 6, 1964
              page 14, Aug 7, 1964
              page 13, Mar 31, 1972
              II, page 1, Apr 9, 1972
              II, page 11, Apr 16, 1972
New Yorker 38:103, May 19, 1962
       48:108, Apr 15, 1972
Newsweek 59:85, May 21, 1962
       79:50, Apr 24, 1972

Saturday Review 45:22, May 26, 1962
Theatre Arts 46:66-8, Jul 1962
Time 79:76, May 18, 1962
    99:73, Apr 17, 1972

Furs and Frills
    book: Edward Clark
    music: Silvio Hein
    lyrics: Edward Clark
    staging: Edward Clark and Arthur Hammerstein
Productions:
Opened October 9, 1917 for 32 performances
Reviews:
Dramatic Mirror 77:7, Oct 20, 1917
New York Dramatic News 64:6, Oct 13, 1917
New York Times page 9, Oct 10, 1917
Theatre Magazine 26:275, Nov 1917
                  26:349, Dec 1917

The Future
    book: Al Carmines
    music: Al Carmines
    lyrics: Al Carmines
    staging: Al Carmines
    choreography: Dan Wagoner
Productions:
(Off-Off-Broadway) Opened March 25, 1974
Reviews:
New York Times page 37, Mar 27, 1974
New Yorker 50:106, Apr 15, 1974

-G-

Gaby
    book: Harry B. and Robert B. Smith
    lyrics: Harry B. and Robert B. Smith
    staging: George Marion
Productions:
Opened April 27, 1911 for 92 performances
Reviews:
Green Book Album 6:231-6, Aug 1911
Theatre Magazine 13:183, Jun 1911

Gaieties 1919 (see Shubert Gaieties 1919)

The Game Is Up
    conceived: Rod Warren
    music: Rod Warren and others
    lyrics: Rod Warren and others
    staging: Jonathan Lucas

Productions:
     (Off-Broadway) Opened September 29, 1964 for 620 performances
No Reviews.

The Game Is Up (New Edition)
     book: Rod Warren
     music and
       lyrics: Rod Warren, Alan Friedman, Linda Ashton,
                     Michael Cohen, Michael McWhinney, Lesley David-
                     son, Kenny Solms, Gayle Parent
     staging: Sandra Devlin
Productions:
     (Off-Broadway) Opened June 15, 1965 for 228 performances
No Reviews.

The Gang's All Here
     book: Russel Crouse, Oscar Hammerstein II, Morrie
                     Ryskind
     music: Lewis E. Gensler
     lyrics: Owen Murphy and Robert A. Simon
     staging: Oscar Hammerstein II
     choreography: Dave Gould and Tilly Losch
Productions:
     Opened February 18, 1931 for 23 performances
Reviews:
     New York Times page 21, Feb 19, 1931
     Theatre Magazine 53:27, Mar 1931
                      53:36, Apr 1931

Gantry
     book: Peter Bellwood; based on the novel Elmer Gantry
                     by Sinclair Lewis
     music: Stanley Lebowsky
     lyrics: Fred Tobias
     staging: Onna White
     sets: Robin Wagner
     costumes: Ann Roth
     choreography: Onna White and Patrick Cummings
Productions:
     Opened February 14, 1970 for one performance
Reviews:
     New York Theatre Critics' Reviews 1970:370
     New York Times page 48, Jan 5, 1970
                     page 44, Feb 16, 1970
                     page 34, Feb 17, 1970
     New Yorker 46:62+, Feb 21, 1970
     Saturday Review 53:61, Feb 28, 1970

The Garden of Earthly Delights
     conceived: Martha Clarke, based on Hieronymus Bosch's
                     painting

written: Martha Clarke, in collaboration with Robert
                     Barnett, Felix Blaska, Robert Faust, Marie Four-
                     caut, Margie Gillis, and Polly Styron
music: Richard Peaslee, in collaboration with Eugene
                     Friesen, William Ruyle, and Stephen Silverstein
staging: Martha Clarke
costumes: Jane Greenwood
Productions:
(Off-Off-Broadway) Opened November 20, 1984
Reviews:
New York Times III, page 15, Apr 5, 1984
            III, page 3, Nov 23, 1984
New Yorker 60:158, Dec 10, 1984

Garland, Judy (see Judy Garland)

Garrick Gaieties (1925)
sketches: Benjamin Kaye, Louis Sorin, Sam Jaffe, Newman
                     Levy, Morrie Ryskind
music: Richard Rodgers
lyrics: Lorenz Hart
additional
  lyrics: Benjamin Kaye, Louis Sorin, Sam Jaffe, Newman
                     Levy, Morrie Ryskind
staging: Philip Loeb
choreography: Herbert Fields
Productions:
Opened June 8, 1925 for 211 performances
Reviews:
Nation 121:77, Jul 8, 1925
New York Times page 12, May 18, 1925
              page 16, Jun 9, 1925
Theatre Magazine 44:15, Aug 1926

Garrick Gaieties (1926)
sketches: Benjamin Kaye, Newman Levy, Herbert Fields,
                     Philip Loeb
music: Richard Rodgers
lyrics: Lorenz Hart
staging: Philip Loeb
choreography: Herbert Fields
Productions:
Opened May 10, 1926 for 174 performances
Reviews:
Bookman 63:588-9, Jul 1926
New York Times page 25, May 11, 1926
              VII, page 1, Jun 13, 1926
Theatre Magazine 44:15, Aug 1926

Garrick Gaieties (1930)
sketches: H. Alexander, Carroll Carroll, Ruth Chorpenning,

Leopoldine Damrosch, Gretchen Damrosch Finlet-
ter, Landon Herrick, Sterling Holloway, Benjamin
M. Kaye, Newman Levy, Dorian Otvos, Louis M.
Simon

music: Marc Blitzstein, Aaron Copland, Vernon Duke,
             Basil Fomeen, Harold Goldman, William Irwin,
             Ned Lehak, Everett Miller, Peter Nolan, Willard
             Robison, Charles M. Schwab, Kay Swift
lyrics: Allen Boretz, Ruth Chorpenning, Ira Gershwin,
             E. Y. Harburg, Sterling Holloway, Paul James,
             Ronald Jeans, Malcolm McComb, John Mercer,
             Henry Myers, Louis M. Simon, Josiah Titzell
staging: Philip Loeb and Olin Howard
Productions:
    Opened June 4, 1930 for 158 performances
Reviews:
    Life (New York) 95:16, Jun 27, 1930
    New Republic 63:127-8, Jun 18, 1930
    New York Times page 29, Jun 5, 1930
                    VIII, page 1, Jun 22, 1930
    Theatre Magazine 52:24, Aug 1930

Gay Company
    music: Fred Silver
    lyrics: Fred Silver
    staging: Sue Lawless
    design: Michael J. Hotopp and Paul de Pass
Productions:
    (Off-Broadway) Opened April 4, 1975 for 13 performances
Reviews:
    New York 8:57, Jan 20, 1975
    New York Times page 57, Nov 7, 1974

Gay Divorce
    book: Dwight Taylor, based on J. Hartley Manners'
                 unproduced play. Musical adaptation by Kenneth
                 Webb and Samuel Hoffenstein
    music: Cole Porter
    lyrics: Cole Porter
    staging: Howard Lindsay
    sets: Jo Mielziner
Productions:
    Opened November 29, 1932 for 248 performances
    (Off-Broadway) Season of 1959-60
    (Off-Off-Broadway) Opened March 9, 1978
Reviews:
    New Outlook 161:47, Jan 1933
    New Republic 73:89, Dec 28, 1932
    New York Times page 23, Nov 30, 1932
                    page 15, Apr 19, 1933
                    IX, page 3, Nov 19, 1933

page 37, Apr 4, 1960
page 13, Mar 11, 1978
New Yorker 36:136, Apr 16, 1960
54:98, Mar 27, 1978

The Gay Life
book: Fay and Michael Kanin, suggested by Arthur
                    Schnitzler's Anatol
music: Arthur Schwartz
lyrics: Howard Dietz
staging: Gerald Freedman
sets: Oliver Smith
costumes: Lucinda Ballard
choreography: Herbert Ross
Productions:
Opened November 18, 1961 for 113 performances
Reviews:
America 106:737, Mar 3, 1962
Dance Magazine 36:13-14, Jan 1962
Life 52:49-51, Jan 19, 1962
New York Theatre Critics' Reviews 1961:168+
New York Times II, page 1, Nov 12, 1961
page 38, Nov 18, 1961
New Yorker 37:118, Dec 2, 1961
Newsweek 58:79, Dec 4, 1961
Theatre Arts 46:11-12, Feb 1962
Time 78:64, Dec 1, 1961

Gay Paree
sketches: Harold Atteridge
music: Alfred Goodman, Maurie Rubens and J. Fred
                  Coots
lyrics: Clifford Grey
staging: J. J. Shubert
Productions:
Opened August 18, 1925 for 190 performances
Reviews:
New York Times page 14, Aug 19, 1925
Theatre Magazine 42:70, Oct 1925

The Geisha
libretto: Owen Hall
music: Sidney Jones
lyrics: Harry Greenbank
staging: Edwin T. Emery
Productions:
Opened March 27, 1913 for 52 performances
Opened October 5, 1931 for 16 performances
Reviews:
Dramatic Mirror 69:6, Apr 2, 1913
69:2, Apr 16, 1913
69:2, Apr 23, 1913
69:2, May 7, 1913

Harper's Weekly 57:20, Apr 19, 1913
Life (New York) 61:734, Apr 10, 1913
New York Times page 15, Mar 28, 1913
Theatre Magazine 17:xii, May 1913
                 17:129, May 1913
                 17:133, May 1913

Genesis: Music and Miracles for a New Age
     book: A. J. Antoon and Robert Montgomery, based on the medieval Mystery Plays
     music: Michael Ward
     lyrics: A. J. Antoon and Robert Montgomery
     staging: A. J. Antoon
     sets: John Conklin
     costumes: John Conklin
     choreography: Lynne Taylor-Corbett
Productions:
     (Off-Broadway) Opened January 17, 1989 for 8 performances
Reviews:
     New York Theatre Critics' Reviews 1989:325
     New York Times III, page 20, Jan 18, 1989

Gentlemen, Be Seated!
     book: Jerome Moross and Edward Eager
     music: Jerome Moross
     lyrics: Edward Eager
     staging: Robert Turoff
     sets: William Pitkin
     costumes: Henry Heymann
     choreography: Paul Draper
Productions:
     (Off-Broadway) Opened October 10, 1963 for 3 performances
No Reviews.

Gentlemen Prefer Blondes
     book: Joseph Fields and Anita Loos, based on a collection of stories by Anita Loos
     music: Jule Styne
     lyrics: Leo Robin
     staging: John C. Wilson
     sets: Oliver Smith
     costumes: Miles White
     choreography: Agnes De Mille
Productions:
     Opened December 8, 1949 for 740 performances
Reviews:
     Catholic World 170:387, Feb 1950
     Commonweal 51:342, Dec 30, 1949
     Life 27:68-71, Dec 26, 1949
     Nation 169:629, Dec 24, 1949
     New Republic 122:21, Jan 2, 1950

New York Theatre Critics' Reviews 1949:198+
New York Times II, page 5, Dec 4, 1949
            page 35, Dec 9, 1949
            II, page 3, Dec 18, 1949
            II, page 3, Jan 8, 1950
New Yorker 25:50+, Dec 17, 1949
Newsweek 34:72, Dec 19, 1949
Saturday Review 32:28-9, Dec 31, 1949
Theatre Arts 34:13, Feb 1950
Time 54:62, Dec 19, 1949
      55:50-2+, Jan 9, 1950

George M!
  book: Michael Stewart and John and Fran Pascal
  music: George M. Cohan; revised by Mary Cohan
  lyrics: George M. Cohan; revised by Mary Cohan
  staging: Joe Layton
  sets: Tom John
  costumes: Freddy Wittop
  choreography: Joe Layton
Productions:
  Opened April 10, 1968 for 427 performances
Reviews:
  America 118:651, May 11, 1968
  Dance Magazine 42:29+, Jun 1968
  Nation 206:581, Apr 29, 1968
  New York Theatre Critics' Reviews 1968:302
  New York Times page 48, Apr 11, 1968
              II, page 1, Apr 21, 1968
              XXII, page 20, Mar 27, 1977
  New Yorker 44:156, Apr 20, 1968
  Newsweek 71:105, Apr 22, 1968
  Saturday Review 51:26, Apr 27, 1968
  Time 91:64, Apr 19, 1968

George White's Music Hall Varieties
  book: William K. Wells and George White
  music and
    lyrics: Irving Caesar and others
  staging: George White and Russell Markert
Productions:
  Opened November 22, 1932 for 72 performances
Reviews:
  New Outlook 161:47, Jan 1933
  New York Times page 15, Nov 15, 1932
              page 19, Jan 3, 1933
  Vogue 81:73, Jan 15, 1933
        81:88, Mar 1, 1933

George White's Scandals (1919)
  book: Arthur Jackson and George White

songs: Richard Whiting, Herbert Spencer, Arthur Jackson
staging: George White
sets: Herbert Ward

Productions:
Opened June 2, 1919 for 128 performances
Reviews:
New York Times page 9, June 3, 1919
Theatre Magazine 30:11+, Jul 1919

George White's Scandals (1920)
book: Andy Rice and George White
music: George Gershwin
lyrics: Arthur Jackson
staging: George White
sets: Law Studios

Productions:
Opened June 7, 1920 for 318 performances
Reviews:
New York Clipper 68:25, Jun 2, 1920
               68:18, Jun 9, 1920
New York Times page 9, Jun 8, 1920
Theatre Magazine 32:19+, Jul-Aug 1920

George White's Scandals (1921)
book: "Bugs" Baer and George White
music: George Gershwin
lyrics: Arthur Jackson
staging: George White

Productions:
Opened July 11, 1921 for 97 performances
Reviews:
Life (New York) 78:18, Jul 28, 1921
New York Clipper 69:25, Jul 20, 1921
New York Times page 14, Jul 12, 1921

George White's Scandals (1922)
book: George White, W. C. Fields, Andy Rice
music: George Gershwin
lyrics: B. G. DeSylva and Ray Goetz
staging: George White

Productions:
Opened August 28, 1922 for 88 performances
Reviews:
New York Clipper 70:20, Sep 6, 1922
New York Times page 10, Aug 29, 1922

George White's Scandals (1923)
book: George White and W. K. Wells
music: George Gershwin
lyrics: B. G. DeSylva, Ray Goetz, Ballard McDonald
staging: George White

Productions:
Opened June 18, 1923 for 168 performances
Reviews:
Life (New York) 82:20, Jul 12, 1923
New York Clipper 71:14, Jun 27, 1923
New York Times page 22, Jun 19, 1923
Theatre Magazine 38:15, Aug 1923

George White's Scandals (1924)
book: William K. Wells and George White
music: George Gershwin
lyrics: B. G. DeSylva
staging: George White
Productions:
Opened June 30, 1924 for 171 performances
Reviews:
Life (New York) 84:18, Jul 31, 1924
New York Times page 16, Jul 1, 1924
Theatre Magazine 40:15, Sep 1924

George White's Scandals (1926)
sketches: George White and William K. Wells
music: Ray Henderson
lyrics: B. G. DeSylva and Lew Brown
staging: George White
Productions:
Opened June 14, 1926 for 424 performances
Reviews:
Life (New York) 88:21, Jul 8, 1926
New York Times page 23, Jun 15, 1926
                VII, page 1, Jul 3, 1927
Theatre Magazine 44:15, Aug 1926
Vogue 68:71+, Sep 1, 1926

George White's Scandals (1928)
sketches: William K. Wells and George White
music: Ray Henderson
lyrics: B. G. DeSylva and Lew Brown
staging: George White
Productions:
Opened July 2, 1928 for 230 performances
Reviews:
Life (New York) 92:16, Jul 19, 1928
New York Times page 19, Jul 3, 1928
Outlook 149:467, Jul 18, 1928
Theatre Magazine 48:36, Sep 1928
                48:41, Oct 1928
Vogue 72:74-5, Sep 1, 1928

George White's Scandals (1929)
book: W. K. Wells and George White

```
       music:              Cliff Friend, George White, Irving Caesar
       lyrics:             Cliff Friend, George White, Irving Caesar
       staging:            George White
       choreography:       Florence Wilson
Productions:
   Opened September 23, 1929 for 161 performances
Reviews:
   Life (New York) 94:26, Oct 18, 1929
   New York Times page 29, Sep 24, 1929
                   page 21, Dec 25, 1929
   Theatre Magazine 50:70, Nov 1929
```

George White's Scandals (1931)

```
       sketches:           George White, Lew Brown, Irving Caesar
       music:              Ray Henderson
       lyrics:             Lew Brown
       staging:            George White
Productions:
   Opened September 14, 1931 for 202 performances
Reviews:
   New York Times page 28, Aug 11, 1931
                   VIII, page 1, Aug 16, 1931
                   page 30, Sep 15, 1931
                   page 26, Feb 10, 1932
   Vogue 78:55+, Nov 15, 1931
```

George White's Scandals (1935)

```
       sketches:           George White, William K. Wells, Howard A.
                           Shiebler
       music:              Ray Henderson
       lyrics:             Jack Yellen
       staging:            George White
       sets:               Russell Patterson and Walter Jagemann
       costumes:           Charles LeMaire
       choreography:       Russell Markert
Productions:
   Opened December 25, 1935 for 110 performances
Reviews:
   Nation 142:56, Jan 8, 1936
   New York Times page 20, Dec 26, 1935
                   page 17, Mar 30, 1936
   Newsweek 7:25, Jan 4, 1936
   Time 27:24, Jan 6, 1936
```

George White's Scandals (1939)

```
       sketches:           Matt Brooks, Eddie Davis, George White
       music:              Sammy Fain
       lyrics:             Jack Yellen
       staging:            George White
       sets:               Albert Johnson
       costumes:           Charles LeMaire
```

Productions:
    Opened August 28, 1939 for 120 performances
Reviews:
    New York Times IX, page 2, Aug 20, 1939
                       page 17, Aug 29, 1939
                    IX, page 1, Sep 3, 1939
        Newsweek 14:40-1, Sep 11, 1939
        Time 34:55, Sep 11, 1939

Georgy
    book: Tom Mankiewicz; based on a novel by Margaret
                    Forster and a screenplay by Margaret Forster
                    and Peter Nichols
    music: George Fischoff
    lyrics: Carole Bayer
    staging: Peter Hunt
    sets: Jo Mielziner
    costumes: Patricia Zipprodt
    choreography: Howard Jeffrey
Productions:
    Opened February 26, 1970 for 4 performances
Reviews:
    New York Theatre Critics' Reviews 1970:354
    New York Times page 26, Feb 27, 1970
                   page 20, Feb 28, 1970
    New Yorker 46:83, Mar 7, 1970

Gertrude Stein's First Reader
    words: Gertrude Stein
    music: Ann Sternberg
    staging: Herbert Machiz
    sets: Kendall Shaw
Productions:
    (Off-Broadway) Opened December 15, 1969 for 40 performances
Reviews:
    New York Times II, page 33, Dec 14, 1969
                       page 56, Dec 16, 1969
    New Yorker 45:39, Dec 27, 1969

Gest, Morris (see Morris Gest)

Get Thee to Canterbury
    book: Jan Steen and David Secter; adapted from
                    Chaucer's The Canterbury Tales
    music: Paul Hoffert
    lyrics: David Secter
    staging: Jan Steen
    sets: James F. Gohl
    costumes: Jeanne Button
    choreography: Darwin Knight
Productions:
    (Off-Broadway) Opened January 25, 1969 for 20 performances

Reviews:
New York Times page 74, Jan 26, 1969

Getout
    book: Joseph Renard
    music: Joseph Blunt
    lyrics: Joseph Renard
    staging: Joseph Renard
    choreography: Joaquin La Habana
Productions:
    (Off-Off-Broadway) Opened February 24, 1974
No Reviews.

Gift of the Magi
    book: Ronnie Britton, based on the O. Henry short
                       story
    music: Ronnie Britton
    lyrics: Ronnie Britton
    staging: M. T. Knoblauh
    sets: Michael Dulin
    costumes: Neil Cooper
Productions:
    (Off-Broadway) Opened December 1, 1975 for 48 performances
Reviews:
New York Theatre Critics' Reviews 1975:95
New York Times page 47, Dec 2, 1975

Gigi
    book: Alan Jay Lerner, based on the novel by Colette
    music: Frederick Loewe
    lyrics: Alan Jay Lerner
    staging: Joseph Hardy
    sets: Oliver Smith
    costumes: Oliver Messel
    choreography: Onna White
Productions:
    Opened November 24, 1951 for 219 performances
    Opened November 13, 1973 for 103 performances
    (Off-Off-Broadway) Opened May 11, 1989
Reviews:
Catholic World 174:309-10, Jan 1952
Commonweal 55:254, Dec 14, 1951
Nation 173:530, Dec 15, 1951
        217:603, Dec 3, 1973
New York 6:105, Dec 3, 1973
New York Theatre Critics' Reviews 1951:159
                          1973:190
New York Times page 20, Nov 26, 1951
                 page 27, May 24, 1956
                 page 39, Nov 14, 1973
                 II, page 1, Nov 25, 1973
                 I, page 57, May 28, 1989

New Yorker 27:87, Dec 1, 1951
        49:80, Nov 26, 1973
Newsweek 38:60, Dec 3, 1951
        82:113, Nov 26, 1973
Playboy 21:40, Mar 1974
Saturday Review 34:32-3, Dec 15, 1951
School and Society 75:107-8, Feb 16, 1952
Theatre Arts 36:31, Feb 1952
        36:41-7+, Jul 1952
Time 58:49, Dec 3, 1951
        102:79, Nov 26, 1973

Gilbert Becaud on Broadway
    music: Gilbert Becaud
    lyrics: Pierre Delanoe, Louis Amade, Maurice Vidalin,
                          Charles Aznavour, Jean Broussolle, Mack David,
                          Gilbert Becaud
    staging: Raymond Bernard
    sets: Ralph Alswang
Productions:
    Opened October 31, 1966 for 19 performances
Reviews:
    New York Times page 35, Nov 1, 1966
                       page 46, Nov 8, 1966

Gilbert Becaud Sings Love
    music: Gilbert Becaud
    lyrics: Pierre Delanoe, Louis Amade, Maurice Vidalin,
                          Charles Aznavour, Jean Broussolle, Mack David,
                          Carl Sigman and Gilbert Becaud
    staging: Raymond Bernard
    sets: Ralph Alswang
Productions:
    Opened October 6, 1968 for 24 performances
No Reviews.

Gilda Radner: Live From New York
    written: Gilda Radner, Lorne Michaels, and Don Novello
    additional
      material: Anne Beatts, Marilyn Suzanne Miller, Michael
                          O'Donoghue, Paul Shaffer, Rosie Shuster, Alan
                          Zweibel
    staging: Lorne Michaels
    design: Eugene Lee and Akira Yoshimura
    costumes: Franne Lee and Karen Roston
Productions:
    Opened August 2, 1979 for 52 performances
Reviews:
    New York 12:54+, Aug 6, 1979
                12:91, Aug 27, 1979
    New York Theatre Critics' Reviews 1979:164

New York Times III, page 3, Aug 3, 1979
New Yorker 55:62, Aug 13, 1979
Newsweek 94:68, Aug 13, 1979

Ginger
    book: Harold Orlob and H. I. Phillips
Productions:
    Opened October 16, 1923 for 38 performances
Reviews:
    New York Times page 14, Oct 17, 1923

The Gingham Girl
    book: Daniel Kusell
    music: Albert Van Tilzer
    lyrics: Neville Fleeson
Productions:
    Opened August 28, 1922 for 422 performances
Reviews:
    New York Clipper 70:20, Sep 6, 1922
    New York Times page 15, Apr 29, 1922
    Theatre Magazine 36:377, Dec 1922
                       36:387, Dec 1922

The Girl and the Wizard
    book: J. Hartley Manners
    music: Julian Edwards
    lyrics: Robert B. Smith and Edward Madden
    staging: Ned Wayburn
Productions:
    Opened September 27, 1909 for 96 performances
Reviews:
    Cosmopolitan 48:202, Jan 1910
    Dramatic Mirror 62:6, Oct 9, 1909
    Hampton 23:823, Dec 1909
    Harper's Weekly 53:25, Oct 16, 1909
    Leslie's Weekly 109:370, Oct 14, 1909
                     109:391, Oct 21, 1909
    Life (New York) 54:517, Oct 14, 1909
    Metropolitan Magazine 31:390-1, Dec 1909
    Theatre Magazine 10:137, Nov 1909
                     10:141, Nov 1909

The Girl Behind the Counter (see Step This Way)

The Girl Behind the Gun
    book: Guy Bolton and P. G. Wodehouse
    music: Ivan Caryll
    lyrics: Guy Bolton and P. G. Wodehouse
    staging: Edgar MacGregor and Julian Mitchell
Productions:
    Opened September 16, 1918 for 160 performances

Reviews:
Dramatic Mirror 79:435, Sep 21, 1918
79:472-3, Sep 28, 1918
79:647, Nov 2, 1918
79:683, Nov 9, 1918
79:755, Nov 23, 1918
79:827, Dec 7, 1918
Green Book 20:949+, Dec 1918
New York Times page 11, Sep 1, 1918
IV, page 2, Sep 22, 1918
Theatre Magazine 28:271, Nov 1-18

Girl Crazy
   book: Guy Bolton and John McGowan
   music: George Gershwin
   lyrics: Ira Gershwin
   staging: Alexander Leftwich
   choreography: George Hale
Productions:
Opened October 14, 1930 for 272 performances
Reviews:
Life (New York) 96:16, Nov 7, 1930
Nation 131:479, Oct 29, 1930
New York Times IX, page 4, Oct 5, 1930
page 27, Oct 15, 1930
Theatre Magazine 52:64, Dec 1930
Vogue 76:136, Dec 8, 1930

The Girl Friend
   book: Herbert Fields
   music: Richard Rodgers
   lyrics: Lorenz Hart
   staging: Lew Fields
Productions:
Opened March 17, 1926 for 409 performances
Reviews:
New York Times page 26, Mar 18, 1926
page 8, Dec 14, 1927
Theatre Magazine 43:50, Jun 1926

The Girl from Brazil
   book: Edgar Smith; from the original of Julius Brammer and Alfred Grunwald
   music: Robert Winterberg and Sigmund Romberg
   staging: J. H. Benrimo
   choreography: Allen K. Foster
Productions:
Opened August 30, 1916 for 61 performances
Reviews:
Dramatic Mirror 76:8, Sep 9, 1916
Life (New York) 68:450, Sep 14, 1916

Munsey 59:278, Nov 1916
New York Times page 7, Aug 31, 1916
                page 8, Sep 5, 1916
                page 7, Sep 13, 1916
Theatre Magazine 24:204b, Oct 1916
                24:280, Nov 1916

The Girl from Brighton
    book: Jean C. Havez and Aaron Hoffman
    music: William Backer
    lyrics: Jean C. Havez and Aaron Hoffman
    staging: Jack Mason
Productions:
Opened August 31, 1912 for 49 performances
Reviews:
Dramatic Mirror 68:7, Sep 11, 1912
New York Dramatic News 56:12, Sep 14, 1912

The Girl from Home
    book: Frank Craven; based on the Richard Harding
                    Davis farce
    music: Silvio Hein
    lyrics: Frank Craven
    staging: R. H. Burnside
Productions:
Opened May 3, 1920 for 24 performances
Reviews:
Dramatic Mirror 82:889, May 8, 1920
New York Clipper 68:17, May 12, 1920
New York Times page 9, May 4, 1920
Theatre Magazine 32:505, Jun 1920

The Girl from Nantucket
    book: Paul Stamford and Harold M. Sherman from a
                    story by Fred Thompson and Berne Giler
    music: Jacques Belasco
    lyrics: Kay Twomey
    staging: Edward Clarke Lilley
    sets: Albert Johnson
    costumes: Lou Eisele
    choreography: Val Raset and Van Grona
Productions:
Opened November 8, 1945 for 12 performances
Reviews:
New York Theatre Critics' Reviews 1945:121+
New York Times page 17, Nov 9, 1945
Time 48:64, Nov 19, 1945

The Girl from Utah
    book: James T. Tanner
    music: Paul Rubens and Sydney Jones; additional num-
                    bers by Jerome D. Kern

staging: J. A. E. Malone
Productions:
  Opened August 24, 1914 for 120 performances
Reviews:
  Dramatic Mirror 72:8, Sep 2, 1914
  Everybody's 31:698-9, Nov 1914
  Green Book 12:893, Nov 1914
  New York Times page 9, Aug 25, 1914
  Theatre Magazine 20:157-8+, Oct 1914
              20:167, Oct 1914

The Girl in Pink Tights

book: Jerome Chodorov and Joseph Fields
music: Sigmund Romberg
lyrics: Leo Robin
staging: Shepard Traube
sets: Eldon Elder
costumes: Miles White
choreography: Agnes de Mille
Productions:
  Opened March 5, 1954 for 115 performances
Reviews:
  America 91:79, Apr 17, 1954
  Catholic World 179:149, May 1954
  Commonweal 60:95-6, Apr 30, 1954
  Life 36:67-8+, Mar 29, 1954
  Mademoiselle 38:124, Apr 1954
  Musical America 74:7, Jun 1954
  Nation 178:246, Mar 20, 1954
  New York Theatre Critics' Reviews 1954:354+
  New York Times II, page 1, Feb 21, 1954
            page 13, Mar 6, 1954
  New Yorker 30:71, Mar 13, 1954
  Newsweek 43:63, Mar 15, 1954
  Theatre Arts 38:24-5, Apr 1954
           38:16-17, May 1954
  Time 63:87, Mar 15, 1954

The Girl in the Spotlight

book: Richard Bruce (Robert B. Smith)
music: Victor Herbert
lyrics: Richard Bruce (Robert B. Smith)
staging: George W. Lederer
Productions:
  Opened July 12, 1920 for 56 performances
Reviews:
  Dramatic Mirror page 97, Jul 17, 1920
  Independent 103:97, Jul 24, 1920
  New York Clipper 68:23, Jul 21, 1920
  New York Times page 9, Jul 13, 1920
  Theatre Magazine 32:105, Sep 1920

The Girl in the Taxi
    book: Anthony Mars; adapted by Stanislaus Stange
    staging: Carter DeHaven
Productions:
    Opened October 24, 1910 for 48 performances
Reviews:
    Dramatic Mirror 64:7, Oct 26, 1910
                    64:8, Nov 2, 1910
    Life (New York) 56:762, Nov 3, 1910
    Metropolitan Magazine 32:676-7, Aug 1910

Girl o' Mine
    book: Philip Bartholomae
    music: Frank Tours
    lyrics: Philip Bartholomae
    staging: Clifford Brooke and E. P. Temple
Productions:
    Opened January 28, 1918 for 48 performances
Reviews:
    Dramatic Mirror 78:35, Jan 12, 1918
                   78:5, Feb 9, 1918
    Green Book 19:785-6, May 1918
    New York Dramatic News 65:6, Feb 2, 1918
    New York Times page 13, Jan 29, 1918
    Theatre Magazine 27:151, Mar 1918
                     27:231, Apr 1918

The Girl of Montmartre
    book: Georges Feydeau and Rudolph Schanzer; American version by Harry B. and Robert B. Smith
    music: Henry Bereny and Jerome D. Kern
Productions:
    Opened August 5, 1912 for 64 performances
No Reviews.

The Girl of My Dreams
    book: Wilbur Nesbit and Otto Hauerbach
    music: Karl Haschna
    staging: Frank Smithson
Productions:
    Opened August 7, 1911 for 40 performances
Reviews:
    Dramatic Mirror 66:4, Jul 26, 1911
                 66:4, Aug 2, 1911
                 66:12, Aug 9, 1911
                 66:2, Sep 20, 1911
    Green Book Album 6:984, Nov 1911
    Hampton 27:519, Oct 1911
    Leslie's Weekly 113:138, Aug 3, 1911
               113:278, Sep 7, 1911
    New York Times page 9, Aug 8, 1911

Red Book 17:1145-6+, Oct 1911
Theatre Magazine 14:79, Sep 1911
14:89, Sep 1911

The Girl on the Film
book: James T. Tanner; from the German of Rudolph
                   Schanzer
music: Walter Kollo, Willy Bredschneider and Albert
                   Sirmay
lyrics: Adrian Ross
Productions:
Opened December 29, 1913 for 64 performances
Reviews:
Blue Book 18:1054-6, Apr 1914
Dramatic Mirror 70:6, Dec 31, 1913
71:5, Jan 7, 1914
71:2, Jan 21, 1914
Munsey 49:596-7, Jul 1913
New York Times page 9, Dec 31, 1913
Theatre Magazine 19:59-60+, Feb 1914
19:69, Feb 1914

The Girl Who Came to Supper
book: Harry Kurnitz, based on Terence Rattigan's
                   play The Sleeping Prince
music: Noel Coward
lyrics: Noel Coward
staging: Joe Layton
sets: Oliver Smith
costumes: Irene Sharaff
Productions:
Opened December 8, 1963 for 112 performances
Reviews:
America 110:26, Jan 4, 1964
New York Theatre Critics' Reviews 1963:178+
New York Times VI, pages 64, 67, Nov 24, 1963
II, page 5, Dec 8, 1963
page 49, Dec 9, 1963
page 54, Dec 10, 1963
New Yorker 39:62, Dec 21, 1963
Saturday Review 47:52, Jan 11, 1964
Time 82:81, Dec 20, 1963
Vogue 143:62, Feb 1, 1964

The Girl Who Smiles
book: Paul Herve and Jean Briquet; English version by
                   Adolf Philipp and Edward A. Paulton
staging: Ben Teal
Productions:
Opened August 9, 1915 for 104 performances
Reviews:
Dramatic Mirror 74:8, Aug 11, 1915

74:4, Aug 25, 1915
74:2, Oct 6, 1915
New York Times VI, page 2, Sep 5, 1915
Opera Magazine 2:25-6, Oct 1915
Theatre Magazine 22:113, Sep 1915
22:170, Oct 1915

Girlies
  book: George V. Hobart
  music: Williams and Van Alsteyne
  lyrics: Williams and Van Alsteyne
Productions:
  Opened June 13, 1910 for 88 performances
Reviews:
  Cosmopolitan 49:613, Oct 1910
  Dramatic Mirror 63:6, Jun 25, 1910
  Leslie's Weekly 111:11, Jul 7, 1910
  Metropolitan Magazine 32:666-7, Aug 1910
  Theatre Magazine 12:x, Jul 1910
                  12:42, Aug 1910

The Girls Against the Boys
  sketches: Arnold B. Horwitt
  music: Richard Lewine (additional music by Albert
                  Hague)
  lyrics: Arnold B. Horwitt
  staging: Aaron Ruben
  sets: Ralph Alswang
  costumes: Sal Anthony
  choreography: Boris Runanin
Productions:
  Opened November 2, 1959 for 16 performances
Reviews:
  New York Theatre Critics' Reviews 1959:239+
  New York Times page 26, Nov 3, 1959
                  II, page 1, Nov 8, 1959
                  page 56, Nov 10, 1959
  New Yorker 35:121-2, Nov 14, 1959
  Newsweek 54:108, Nov 16, 1959
  Time 74:57, Nov 16, 1959

Girls, Girls, Girls
  book: Marilyn Suzanne Miller
  music: Cheryl Hardwick
  lyrics: Marilyn Suzanne Miller
  staging: Bob Balaban
  sets: Akira Yoshimura
  costumes: Karen Roston
  choreography: Graciela Daniele
Productions:
  (Off-Broadway) Opened September 30, 1980 for 6 performances

Reviews:
New York Times III, page 25, Oct 1, 1980

Glorianna
    book: Catherine Chisholm Cushing
    music: Rudolf Friml
    lyrics: Catherine Chisholm Cushing
    staging: Clifford Brooke
Productions:
Opened October 28, 1918 for 96 performances
Reviews:
Dramatic Mirror 79:688, Nov 9, 1918
New York Times page 9, Oct 29, 1918
Theatre Magazine 38:339, Dec 1918
                      38:378, Dec 1918

The Glorious Age
    book: Cy Young and Mark Gordon
    music: Cy Young
    lyrics: Cy Young
    staging: John Michael Tebelak
    sets: Stuart Wurtzel
    costumes: Jennifer von Mayrhauser
Productions:
   (Off-Broadway) Opened May 11, 1975 for 9 performances
Reviews:
New York Times page 39, May 12, 1975

Glory
    book: James Montgomery
    music: Maurice de Packh and Harry Tierney
    lyrics: James Dyrenforth and Joseph McCarthy
Productions:
Opened December 25, 1922 for 64 performances
Reviews:
New York Clipper 70:14, Jan 17, 1923
New York Times page 10, Dec 26, 1922

Go Easy, Mabel
    book: Charles George
    staging: Bertram Harrison and Julian Alfred
Productions:
Opened May 8, 1922 for 16 performances
Reviews:
New York Clipper 70:20, May 17, 1922
New York Times page 22, May 9, 1922
Theatre Magazine 36:32, Jul 1922

Go Fight City Hall
    book: Harry Kalmanowich
    music: Murray Rumshinsky

lyrics: Bella Mysell
staging: Menachem Rubin
Productions:
  (Off-Broadway) Opened November 2, 1961 for 77 performances
Reviews:
  New York Times page 28, Nov 3, 1961

Go-Go
    book: Harry L. Cort and George E. Stoddard
    music: C. Luckyeth Roberts
    lyrics: Alex Rogers
Productions:
  Opened March 12, 1923 for (102) performances
Reviews:
  Life (New York) 81:20, Apr 12, 1923
  New York Clipper 71:14, Mar 21, 1923
  New York Times page 19, Mar 13, 1923

Goblin Market
    words: Peggy Harmon and Polly Pen, adapted from the
               poem by Christina Rossetti
    music: Polly Pen
    staging: Andre Ernotte
    sets: William Barclay
    costumes: Muriel Stockdale and Kitty Leech
    choreography: Ara Fitzgerald
Productions:
  (Off-Off-Broadway) Season of 1985-86
  (Off-Broadway) Opened April 13, 1986 for 89 performances
Reviews:
  Dance Magazine 60:78-9, Feb 1986
  New York 19:107-8, Apr 28, 1986
  New York Times I, page 9, Apr 19, 1986
  New Yorker 62:105, Apr 28, 1986

God Bless Coney
    book: John Glines
    music: John Glines
    lyrics: John Glines
    staging: Bob Schwartz
    sets: Don Tirrell
    costumes: Margaretta Mazanini
Productions:
  (Off-Broadway) Opened May 3, 1972 for 3 performances
Reviews:
  New York Times page 55, May 4, 1972
                    page 31, May 5, 1972

God Bless You, Mr. Rosewater
    book: Howard Ashman, based on the novel by Kurt
               Vonnegut

music: Alan Menken
lyrics: Howard Ashman; additional lyrics by Dennis
                     Green
staging: Howard Ashman
sets: Edward T. Gianfrancesco
costumes: David Graden
choreography: Mary Kyte
Productions:
   (Off-Broadway) Opened October 14, 1979 for 49 performances
Reviews:
   New York 12:87, Nov 5, 1979
   New York Theatre Critics' Reviews 1979:104
   New York Times III, page 14, May 21, 1979
                   III, page 16, Oct 15, 1979
                   II, page 3, Nov 4, 1979
   New Yorker 55:82, Oct 29, 1979
   Newsweek 94:114, Oct 29, 1979
   People 12:36-9, Oct 15, 1979

God Is a (Guess What?)
   book: Ray McIver
   music: Coleridge-Taylor Perkinson
   staging: Michael A. Schultz
   sets: Edward Burbridge
   costumes: Bernard Johnson
   choreography: Louis Johnson
Productions:
   (Off-Broadway) Opened December 17, 1968 for 32 performances
Reviews:
   New York Theatre Critics' Reviews 1968:129
   New York Times page 56, Dec 18, 1968
                   page 63, Dec 19, 1968
                   II, page 3, Dec 29, 1968

The Goddess of Liberty
   book: Adams and Hough
   music: Joseph E. Howard
   staging: Ned Wayburn and Percy Leach
Productions:
   Opened December 22, 1909 for 29 performances
Reviews:
   Cosmopolitan 48:621, Apr 1910
   Leslie's Weekly 110:35, Jan 13, 1910
   Theatre Magazine 11:xvi, Feb 1910

Godspell
   book: John-Michael Tebelak; based on the Gospel ac-
                     cording to St. Matthew
   music: Stephen Schwartz
   lyrics: Stephen Schwartz
   staging: John-Michael Tebelak
   costumes: Susan Tzu

Productions:
    (Off-Broadway) Opened May 17, 1971 for 2,124 performances
    Opened June 22, 1976 for 527 performances
    (Off-Off-Broadway) Opened January 8, 1981
    (Off-Broadway) Opened June 12, 1988 for 225 performances
Reviews:
    America 125:516-17, Dec 11, 1971
           127:542-4, Dec 23, 1972
           159:40, Jul 9-16, 1988
    Christian Century 88:938, Aug 4, 1971
                  89:785-6, Jul 19, 1972
                  99:46, Jan 20, 1982
    Commonweal 95:447, Feb 11, 1972
    Christianity Today 15:36-7, Aug 27, 1971
    Life 73:20, Aug 4, 1972
    New York Theatre Critics' Reviews 1971:264
                                 1976:218
    New York Times page 45, May 18, 1971
                II, page 1, May 30, 1971
                page 81, Nov 21, 1971
                page 47, May 1, 1973
                page 34, May 14, 1973
                page 48, Jun 23, 1976
                III, page 20, Jan 12, 1981
                II, page 5, Jun 12, 1988
                III, page 16, Jun 13, 1988
    New Yorker 47:56, May 29, 1971
    People 14:101-2, Dec 15, 1980

Gogo Loves You
    book: Anita Loos; adapted from the French comedy
                       L'Ecole des Cocottes
    music: Claude Leveillee
    lyrics: Gladys Shelley
    staging: Fred Weintraub
    sets: Kert Lundell
    costumes: Alfred Lehman
    choreography: Marvin Gordon
Productions:
    (Off-Broadway) Opened October 9, 1964 for 2 performances
Reviews:
    New York Times page 10, Oct 10, 1964

Going Up
    book: Otto Hauerbach, based on James Montgomery's
                     The Aviator
    music: Louis A. Hirsch
    lyrics: Otto Hauerbach
    staging: Edward Royce and James Montgomery
Productions:
    Opened December 25, 1917 for 351 performances
    Opened September 19, 1976 for 49 performances

Reviews:
    Dramatic Mirror 78:4+, Jan 5, 1918
                    78:729, May 25, 1918
    Green Book 19:397+, Mar 1918
    New York 9:73, Oct 4, 1976
    New York Theatre Critics' Reviews 1976:190
    New York Times page 7, Dec 26, 1917
                    page 22, Jun 30, 1976
                    page 39, Sep 20, 1976
                    II, page 3, Sep 26, 1976
    New Yorker 52:75, Oct 4, 1976
    Theatre Magazine 27:88, Feb 1918
                      27:93, Feb 1918
    Time 108:100, Oct 4, 1976

The Golden Age
    devised: Richard Johnson; from words and music of the
                       Elizabethan Age
    staging: Douglas Campbell
Productions:
    Opened November 18, 1963 for 7 performances
Reviews:
    New York Theatre Critics' Reviews 1963:191
    New York Times page 17, Nov 16, 1963
                    page 49, Nov 19, 1963

The Golden Apple
    book: John Latouche
    music: Jerome Moross
    lyrics: John Latouche
    staging: Norman Lloyd
    sets: William and Jean Eckart
    costumes: Alvin Colt
    choreography: Hanya Holm
Productions:
    Opened March 11, 1954 for 125 performances
    (Off-Broadway) Season of 1960-61
    (Off-Broadway) Opened February 12, 1962 for 112 performances
Reviews:
    America 91:24-5+, Apr 3, 1954
    Catholic World 179:148, May 1954
    Commonweal 60:95, Apr 30, 1954
                    76:210, May 18, 1962
    Harper's 208:91-2, May 1954
    Life 36:163-4+, Apr 12, 1954
    Musical America 74:7, Jun 1954
    Nation 178:265-6, Mar 27, 1954
    New York Theatre Critics' Reviews 1954:346+
    New York Times page 15, Mar 12, 1954
                    II, page 1, Mar 21, 1954
                    page 38, Feb 13, 1962
                    page 47, May 9, 1962

New Yorker 30:60+, May 20, 1954
Saturday Review 37:23, Mar 27, 1954
Theatre Arts 38:80, May 1954
            38:23, Jun 1954
            38:22-5, Aug 1954
            46:59-61, Apr 1962
Time 63:96+, Mar 22, 1954

Golden Bat
book: Yutaka Higashi
music: Itsuro Shimoda
lyrics: Yutaka Higashi
staging: Yutaka Higashi and Kazuko Oshima
sets: Kenkichi Sato
costumes: Kiyoko Chiba

Productions:
  (Off-Broadway) Opened July 21, 1970 for 152 performances
Reviews:
  Commonweal 93:278, Dec 11, 1970
  Dance Magazine 44:81, Nov 1970
  Nation 211:285, Sep 28, 1970
  New York Times page 18, Jun 27, 1970
                 II, page 1, Aug 16, 1970
  New Yorker 46:59, Aug 1, 1970
  Newsweek 76:77, Aug 31, 1970
  Saturday Review 53:53, Sep 19, 1970
  Time 96:68-9, Aug 3, 1970

Golden Boy
book: Clifford Odets and William Gibson, based on
                Odets' play
music: Charles Strouse
lyrics: Lee Adams
staging: Arthur Penn
sets: Tony Walton
costumes: Tony Walton
choreography: Donald McKayle, Jaime Rogers

Productions:
  Opened October 20, 1964 for 568 performances
Reviews:
  America 111:639, Nov 14, 1964
  Commonweal 81:287-9, Nov 20, 1964
  Dance Magazine 38:16, Dec 1964
  Life 57:84A-85+, Nov 13, 1964
  Nation 199:340-1, Nov 9, 1964
  New York Theatre Critics' Reviews 1964:185+
  New York Times II, page 3, Oct 18, 1964
                 page 56, Oct 21, 1964
                 II, page 1, Nov 1, 1964
  Newsweek 64:94-5, Nov 2, 1964
  New Yorker 40:129, Oct 31, 1964

Golden Dawn / 233

Saturday Review 47:29, Nov 7, 1964
Time 84:79, Oct 30, 1964

Golden Dawn

book:	Otto Harbach and Oscar Hammerstein II
music:	Emmerich Kalman and Herbert Stothart
lyrics:	Otto Harbach and Oscar Hammerstein II
staging:	Dave Bennett and Reginald Hammerstein

Productions:
Opened November 30, 1927 for 184 performances
Reviews:
New York Times VIII, page 4, Oct 2, 1927
page 32, Dec 1, 1927

The Golden Land

created:	Zalmen Mlotek and Moishe Rosenfeld
staging:	Jacques Levy
sets:	Lindsey Decker
costumes:	Natasha Landau
choreography:	Donald Saddler

Productions:
(Off-Off-Broadway) Opened October 27, 1984
(Off-Broadway) Opened November 11, 1985 for 277 performances
Reviews:
New York Theatre Critics' Reviews 1985:113
New York Times III, page 14, Oct 30, 1984
XXI, page 19, Feb 10, 1985
III, page 25, Nov 12, 1985

Golden Rainbow

book:	Ernest Kinoy; based on a play by Arnold Schulman
music:	Walter Marks
lyrics:	Walter Marks
staging:	Arthur Storch
sets:	Robert Randolph
costumes:	Alvin Colt
choreography:	Tom Panko

Productions:
Opened February 4, 1968 for 383 performances
Reviews:
America 118:356-7, Mar 16, 1968
Dance Magazine 42:30-1, Apr 1968
New York Theatre Critics' Reviews 1968:350
1968:355
New York Times page 27, Feb 5, 1968
II, page 3, Mar 3, 1968
New Yorker 43:88, Feb 10, 1968

The Golden Screw

book:	Tom Sankey

music:	Tom Sankey
lyrics:	Tom Sankey
staging:	David Eliscu
sets:	C. Murawski

Productions:
  (Off-Broadway) Opened January 30, 1967 for 40 performances
Reviews:
  New York Times page 52, Jan 31, 1967
  New Yorker 42:116+, Feb 11, 1967

Goldilocks
book:	Walter and Jean Kerr
music:	Leroy Anderson
lyrics:	Joan Ford, Walter and Jean Kerr
staging:	Walter Kerr
sets:	Peter Larkin
costumes:	Castillo
choreography:	Agnes de Mille

Productions:
  Opened October 11, 1958 for 161 performances
Reviews:
  America 100:255, Nov 22, 1958
  Catholic World 188:333, Jan 1959
  Christian Century 75:1338, Nov 19, 1958
  Dance Magazine 32:16-17, Nov 1958
  New Republic 139:22, Oct 27, 1958
  New York Theatre Critics' Reviews 1958:273+
  New York Times page 33, Oct 13, 1958
                 II, page 1, Oct 19, 1958
                 page 25, Feb 21, 1959
  New Yorker 34:55, Oct 18, 1958
  Reporter 18:37-8, Nov 13, 1958
  Theatre Arts 42:12, Dec 1958
  Time 72:100, Oct 20, 1958
  Vogue 132:104, Nov 15, 1958

Good Boy
book:	Otto Harbach, Oscar Hammerstein II, Henry Myers
music:	Herbert Stothart and Harry Ruby
lyrics:	Bert Kalmar
staging:	Reginald Hammerstein
choreography:	Busby Berkeley

Productions:
  Opened September 5, 1928 for 235 performances
Reviews:
  Life (New York) 92:17, Sep 28, 1928
  New York Times page 23, Sep 6, 1928
  Theatre Magazine 48:78, Dec 1928

Good Evening
| written: | Peter Cook and Dudley Moore |

staging: Jerry Adler
sets: Robert Randolph
Productions:
   Opened November 14, 1973 for 438 performances
Reviews:
   Nation 217:603, Dec 3, 1973
   New Republic 169:34, Dec 15, 1973
   New York 6:92, Nov 26, 1973
   New York Theatre Critics' Reviews 1973:186
   New York Times page 58, Nov 15, 1973
                    II, page 1, Dec 2, 1973
                    page 30, Mar 19, 1974
   New Yorker 49:80, Nov 26, 1973
   Newsweek 82:113, Nov 26, 1973
   Playboy 21:40, Mar 1974
   Time 102:114, Dec 3, 1973

Good Luck
   book: Chaim Tauber and Louis Freiman
   music: Sholom Secunda
   lyrics: Jacob Jacobs
   staging: Max Perlman
   sets: Arthur Aronson
Productions:
   (Off-Broadway) Opened October 17, 1964 for 117 performances
Reviews:
   New York Times page 38, Oct 19, 1964

Good Morning Dearie
   book: Anne Caldwell
   music: Jerome Kern
   lyrics: Anne Caldwell
   staging: Edward Royce
Productions:
   Opened November 1, 1921 for 265 performances
Reviews:
   Dramatic Mirror 84:665, Nov 5, 1921
   Life (New York) 78:18, Nov 17, 1921
   New York Clipper 69:20, Nov 9, 1921
   New York Times page 20, Nov 2, 1921
                    VI, page 1, Nov 27, 1921
   Theatre Magazine 35:32, Jan 1922

Good Morning, Judge
   book: Fred Thompson; based on Sir Arthur Wing
                Pinero's The Magistrate
   music: Lionel Monckton and Howard Talbot
   staging: Wybert Stamford
Productions:
   Opened February 6, 1919 for 140 performances
Reviews:
   Dramatic Mirror 80:268, Feb 22, 1919

New York Dramatic News 65:8, Feb 8, 1919
New York Times page 15, Feb 7, 1919
                IV, page 2, Feb 16, 1919
Theatre Magazine 29:144, Mar 1919
                29:163, Mar 1919

Good News
book: Laurence Schwab and B. G. DeSylva
music: Ray Henderson
lyrics: B. G. DeSylva and Lew Brown
staging: Edgar MacGregor
Productions:
Opened September 6, 1927 for 551 performances
Opened December 23, 1974 for 16 performances
Reviews:
National Review 26:819, Jul 19, 1974
New York 8:55, Jan 13, 1975
New York Theatre Critics' Reviews 1974: 110, 118
New York Times VII, page 2, Aug 14, 1927
                page 35, Sep 7, 1927
                IX, page 4, Apr 1, 1928
                page 8, Dec 24, 1974
                II, page 5, Jan 5, 1975
New Yorker 50:50, Jan 6, 1975
Newsweek 85:64, Jan 6, 1975
Theatre Magazine 48:39, Aug 1928
Time 105:94, Jan 6, 1975
Vogue 70:124, Nov 1, 1927

Good Night, Paul
book: Roland Oliver and Charles Dickson
music: Harry B. Olsen
lyrics: Roland Oliver and Charles Dickson
Productions:
Opened September 3, 1917 for 40 performances
Reviews:
Dramatic Mirror 77: 7, Sep 15, 1917
New York Times page 9, Sep 4, 1917
Theatre Magazine 26:203, Oct 1917
                26:207, Oct 1917

Good Times
book: R. H. Burnside
music: Raymond Hubbell
Productions:
Opened August 9, 1920 for 456 performances
Reviews:
Dramatic Mirror page 1208, Dec 25, 1920
New York Times page 10, Aug 10, 1920
Theatre Magazine 32:242, Oct 1920

Goodbye Tomorrow
book: Sue Brock
music: Carl Friberg
lyrics: Sue Brock
staging: Anthony Stimac
Productions:
 (Off-Off-Broadway) Opened March 23, 1973
No Reviews.

Goodtime Charley
book: Sidney Michaels, based on the lives of Joan of
       Arc and the Dauphin, Charles
music: Larry Grossman
lyrics: Hal Hackady
staging: Peter H. Hunt
sets: Rouben Ter-Artunian
costumes: Willa Kim
choreography: Onna White
Productions:
Opened March 3, 1975 for 104 performances
Reviews:
 America 132:246, Mar 29, 1975
 Dance Magazine 49:28+, May 1975
 New York 8:78, Apr 7, 1975
 New York Theatre Critics' Reviews 1975:324
 New York Times page 40, Mar 4, 1975
 New Yorker 51:92, Mar 17, 1975
 Time 105:73, Mar 17, 1975

Gorky
book: Steve Tesich
music: Mel Marvin
lyrics: Steve Tesich
staging: Dennis Rosa
sets: David Jenkins
costumes: Shadow
Productions:
 (Off-Broadway) Opened October 24, 1975 for 44 performances
Reviews:
 America 133:448, Dec 20, 1975
 New York 8:90, Dec 1, 1975
 New York Theatre Critics' Reviews 1975:100
 New York Times page 47, Nov 17, 1975
 Time 106:67, Dec 1, 1975

The Gospel at Colonus
book: Lee Breuer, based on an adaptation of Sophocles'
       Oedipus at Colonus by Robert Fitzgerald, in-
       corporating passages from Sophocles' Oedipus Rex
       and Antigone in the versions by Dudley Fitts
       and Robert Fitzgerald

music:	Bob Telson
lyrics:	Lee Breuer
staging:	Lee Breuer
sets:	Alison Yerxa
costumes:	Ghrett Hynd

Productions:
  (Off-Off-Broadway) Opened November 1983
  Opened March 24, 1988 for 61 performances
Reviews:
  America 158:433, Apr 23, 1988
  Christianity Today 31:58-60, Jul 10, 1987
  High Fidelity (Musical America edition) 36:MA27-MA29, Apr 1986
  Los Angeles 31:52+, Feb 1986
  Nation 246:690, May 14, 1988
  New Leader 71:23, Apr 18, 1988
  New Republic 198:28, Apr 25, 1988
  New York 17:76-7, Feb 27, 1984
            21:96, Apr 18, 1988
  New York Theatre Critics' Reviews 1988:326
  New York Times I, page 12, Nov 12, 1983
                  II, page 5, Mar 25, 1988
                  II, page 5, Apr 3, 1988
  New Yorker 64:72-4, Apr 4, 1988
  Newsweek 102:105+, Nov 21, 1983
           111:75, Apr 4, 1988
  Saturday Review 10:114, Nov/Dec 1984
  Time 123:90, Jan 2, 1984
  Vogue 175:133, Nov 1985

Got Tu Go Disco

book:	John Zodrow, loosely based on "Cinderella"
music and lyrics:	Kenny Lehman, John Davis, Ray Chew, Nat Adderley Jr., Thomas Jones, Wayne Morrison, Steve Boston, Eugene Narmore, Betty Rowland, and Jerry Powell
staging:	Larry Forde
sets:	James Hamilton
costumes:	Joe Eula
choreography:	Jo Jo Smith and Troy Garza

Productions:
  Opened June 25, 1979 for 8 performances
Reviews:
  New York 12:54-8, Jun 25, 1979
  New York Theatre Critics' Reviews 1979:192
  New York Times III, page 7, Jun 26, 1979

Gotta Gettaway!

conceived:	Stephen Nisbet and James Lecesne
book:	James Lecesne

music and
lyrics: Glen Roven, Marc Elliot, Chip Orton, Gene Pa-
               lumbo, Marc Shaman, and Eric Watson
staging: Larry Fuller
sets: Eduardo Sicangco
costumes: Michael Casey
choreography: Larry Fuller and Marianne Selbert
Productions:
    Opened June 16, 1984 for 151 performances
Reviews:
    Dance Magazine 58:54-5, Jul 1984

The Grab Bag
    book: Ed Wynn
    music: Ed Wynn
    lyrics: Ed Wynn
    staging: Ed Wynn
Productions:
    Opened October 6, 1924 for 184 performances
Reviews:
    New York Times page 26, Oct 7, 1924
                   page 7, Feb 17, 1925
    Theatre Magazine 40:70, Dec 1924

Graham Crackers
    conceived: Ronny Graham
    devised: Ronny Graham
    choreography: Lee Becker
Productions:
    (Off-Broadway) Opened January 23, 1963 for 286 performances
No Reviews.

The Grand Music Hall of Israel
    conceived: Jonathon Karmon
    staging: Jonathon Karmon
    costumes: Hovav Kruvi
    choreography: Jonathon Karmon
Productions:
    Opened February 6, 1968 for 64 performances
    (Off-Broadway) Opened January 4, 1973 for 15 performances
Reviews:
    New York Times page 42, Feb 7, 1968
                   page 39, Feb 8, 1968

Grand Street Follies (1925)
    book: Agnes Morgan
    music: Lily Hyland
    lyrics: Agnes Morgan
Productions:
    Opened June 18, 1925 for 148 performances
Reviews:
    Nation 121:77, Jul 8, 1925

New York Times page 24, Jun 19, 1925
Theatre Magazine 42:15, Sep 1925
          42:21, Sep 1925

Grand Street Follies (1926)
    book: Agnes Morgan
    music: Lily Hyland, Arthur Schwartz, and Randall
                 Thompson
    lyrics: Agnes Morgan
    staging: Agnes Morgan
Productions:
    Opened June 15, 1926 for 53 performances
Reviews:
    Bookman 64:85-6, Sep 1926
    Independent 117:133, Jul 31, 1926
    Life (New York) 88:21, Jul 8, 1926
    New York Times page 23, Jun 16, 1926
    Theatre Magazine 44:15, Aug 1926
              44:19, Sep 1926

Grand Street Follies (1927)
    book: Agnes Morgan
    music: Max Ewing
    lyrics: Agnes Morgan
    staging: Agnes Morgan
Productions:
    Opened May 19, 1927 for 148 performances
Reviews:
    Nation 124:616-17, Jun 1, 1927
    New Republic 51:70, Jun 8, 1927
    New York Times page 22, May 20, 1927
              page 24, Jun 1, 1927
              VII, page 1, Jul 3, 1927
    Vogue 70:98, Jul 15, 1927

Grand Street Follies (1928)
    book: Agnes Morgan
    music: Max Ewing, Lily Hyland and Serge Walter
    lyrics: Agnes Morgan
    staging: Agnes Morgan
Productions:
    Opened May 28, 1928 for 144 performances
Reviews:
    Life (New York) 92:12, Jul 12, 1928
    Nation 126:675, Jun 13, 1928
    New Republic 55:95, Jun 15, 1928
    New York Times page 16, May 29, 1928
              VIII, page 1, Jun 3, 1928
              page 7, Jun 23, 1928
    Outlook 149:345, Jun 27, 1928
    Theatre Arts 12:537-8, Aug 1928
    Vogue 72:56+, Aug 1, 1928

Grand Street Follies (1929)
    book: Agnes Morgan
    music: Arthur Schwartz and Max Ewing, additional num-
                       bers by William Irwin and Serge Walter
    lyrics: Agnes Morgan
    staging: Agnes Morgan
    choreography: Dave Gould
Productions:
    Opened May 1, 1929 for 93 performances
Reviews:
    Bookman 64:85-6, Sep 1926
    Independent 117:133, Jul 31, 1926
    Life (New York) 88:21, Jul 8, 1926
                     93:20, May 31, 1929
    Nation 121:77, Jul 8, 1925
           124:616-17, Jun 1, 1927
           128:594-5, May 15, 1929
    New Republic 51:70, Jun 8, 1927
                 59:24-5, May 22, 1929
    New York Times IX, page 2, Apr 18, 1929
                   page 20, May 2, 1929
                   IX, page 1, May 12, 1929
                   page 34, Jun 19, 1929
    Outlook 152:191, May 29, 1929
    Theatre Magazine 42:15+, Sep 1925
                     50:42, Jul 1929
    Vogue 70:98, Jul 15, 1927
          74:92+, Jul 6, 1929

The Grand Tour
    book: Michael Stewart and Mark Bramble, based on the
                       play Jacobowsky and the Colonel by Franz Werfel
                       and its American version by S. N. Behrman
    music: Jerry Herman
    lyrics: Jerry Herman
    staging: Gerald Freedman
    sets: Ming Cho Lee
    costumes: Theoni V. Aldredge
    choreography: Donald Saddler
Productions:
    Opened January 11, 1979 for 61 performances
Reviews:
    Nation 228:156, Feb 10, 1979
    New Leader 62:21-2, Jan 29, 1979
    New York 12:119, Jan 29, 1979
    New York Theatre Critics' Reviews 1979:390
    New York Times III, page 3, Jan 12, 1979
                   II, page 3, Jan 21, 1979
    New Yorker 54:88, Jan 22, 1979
    Newsweek 93:86, Jan 22, 1979
    Time 113:84, Jan 22, 1979

Grande de Coca-Cola, El   (see El Grande de Coca-Cola)

The Grass Harp
    book: Kenward Elmslie; based on the novel by Truman
                       Capote
    music: Claibe Richardson
    lyrics: Kenward Elmslie
    staging: Ellis Rabb
    sets: James Tilton
    costumes: Nancy Potts
    choreography: Rhoda Levine
Productions:
    Opened November 2, 1971 for 7 performances
    (Off-Off-Braodway) Opened Aug 11, 1977
Reviews:
    America 125:427, Nov 20, 1971
    New York Theatre Critics' Reviews 1971:196
    New York Times page 56, Oct 7, 1971
                    page 41, Nov 3, 1971
    New Yorker 47:66, Nov 13, 1971

The Grass Widow
    book: Channing Pollock and Rennold Wolf; adapted from
                       Le Peril Jaune by Bisson and St. Albin
    music: Louis A. Hirsch
    lyrics: Channing Pollock and Rennold Wolf
    staging: George Marion
Productions:
    Opened December 3, 1917 for 48 performances
Reviews:
    Dramatic Mirror 77:31, Oct 20, 1917
                    77:5, Dec 15, 1917
    Green Book 19:196+, Feb 1918
    New York Times page 11, Dec 4, 1917

Grease
    book: Jim Jacobs and Warren Casey
    music: Jim Jacobs and Warren Casey
    lyrics: Jim Jacobs and Warren Casey
    staging: Tom Moore
    sets: Douglas W. Schmidt
    costumes: Carrie F. Robbins
    choreography: Patricia Birch
Productions:
    Opened February 14, 1972 for 3,388 performances
    (Off-Off-Broadway) Opened July 13, 1982
    (Off-Off-Broadway) Opened August 3, 1982
Reviews:
    Dance Magazine 49:90, Apr 1975
    Glamour 84:86+, Nov 1986
    New West 2:SC-19, Aug 1, 1977

New York 10:114, Jun 27, 1977
New York Theatre Critics' Reviews 1972:336
New York Times page 27, Feb 15, 1972
            page 11, Feb 27, 1972
            II, page 1, Jun 4, 1972
            page 13, Jul 17, 1982
            XXI, page 15, Jul 25, 1982
New Yorker 48:68, Feb 26, 1972
Newsweek 79:95, Feb 28, 1972
Saturday Review 55:64, Jul 15, 1972
Theatre Crafts 20:34-5+, May 1986
Time 99:56, May 29, 1972

Great Day
    book: William Cary Duncan and John Wells
    music: Vincent Youmans
    lyrics: William Rose
    staging: R. H. Burnside and Frank M. Gillespie
    choreography: LeRoy Prinz
Productions:
    Opened October 17, 1929 for 36 performances
Reviews:
    New York Times VIII, page 1, Jun 9, 1929
            page 24, Oct 18, 1929
            IX, page 1, Nov 3, 1929
    Theatre Magazine 50:16, Oct 1929

Great Lady
    book: Earle Crooker and Lowell Brentano
    music: Frederick Loewe
    lyrics: Earle Crooker and Lowell Brentano
    staging: Bretaigne Windust
    sets: Albert R. Johnson
    costumes: Lucinda Ballard and Scott Wilson
    choreography: William Dollar
Productions:
    Opened December 1, 1938 for 20 performances
Reviews:
    Catholic World 148:477-8, Jan 1939
    New York Times page 26, Dec 2, 1938
    Time 32:32, Dec 12, 1938

Great Macdaddy
    book: Paul Carter Harrison
    music: Coleridge-Taylor Perkinson
    staging: Douglas Turner Ward
    sets: Gary James Wheeler
    costumes: Mary Mease Warren
    choreography: Dianne McIntyre
Productions:
    (Off-Broadway)   Opened February 12, 1974 for 72 performances
    (Off-Broadway)   Opened April 5, 1977 for 56 performances

Reviews:
New York 10:69, May 2, 1977
New York Theatre Critics' Reviews 1974:364
New York Times page 51, Feb 13, 1974
              II, page 3, Mar 3, 1974
              III, page 20, Apr 14, 1977
New Yorker 50:84, Feb 25, 1974
Time 103:69, Feb 25, 1974

The Great Magician
book: Lawrence Carra
music: Wenner Laise
staging: Edward Padula
Productions:
(Off-Broadway) Opened April 1939
No Reviews.

Great Scot!
book: Mark Conradt and Gregory Dawson
music: Dan McAfee
lyrics: Nancy Leeds
staging: Charles Tate
sets: Herbert Senn and Helen Pond
costumes: Patton Campbell
Productions:
(Off-Broadway) Opened November 10, 1965 for 38 performances
Reviews:
New York Times page 50, Nov 9, 1965
                        page 56, Nov 12, 1965

Great Temptations
book: Harold Atteridge
music: Maurice Rubens
lyrics: Clifford Grey
staging: J. J. Shubert
Productions:
Opened May 18, 1926 for 197 performances
Reviews:
Bookman 63:691-3, Aug 1926
Nation 122:616, Jun 2, 1926
New York Times page 29, May 19, 1926
                        VIII, page 1, May 23, 1926
                        VIII, page 1, May 30, 1926
                        page 13, Jun 26, 1926
Theatre Magazine 44:15, Aug 1926
                        44:19, Aug 1926

Great to Be Alive
book: Walter Bullock and Sylvia Regan
music: Abraham Ellstein
lyrics: Walter Bullock

staging: Mary Hunter
sets: Stewart Chaney
costumes: Stewart Chaney
choreography: Helen Tamiris

Productions:
   Opened March 23, 1950 for 52 performances
Reviews:
   Catholic World 171:149, May 1950
   New York Theatre Critics' Reviews 1950:324+
   New York Times page 28, Mar 24, 1950
   New Yorker 26:46+, Apr 1, 1950
   Newsweek 35:73, Apr 3, 1950
   Theatre Arts 34:18, May 1950
   Time 55:51, Apr 3, 1950

The Great Waltz

book: Moss Hart, based on libretti by Dr. A. M. Will-
                ner, Heinz Reichert, Ernst Marischka, Caswell
                Garth
music: Johann Strauss, father and son
lyrics: Desmond Carter
staging: Hassard Short
sets: Albert Johnson
choreography: Albertina Rasch

Productions:
   Opened September 22, 1934 for 298 performances
   Opened August 5, 1935 for 49 performances
Reviews:
   Catholic World 140:213, Nov 1934
   Golden Book Magazine 20:508+, Nov 1934
   Literary Digest 118:19, Oct 6, 1934
   New Republic 81:131, Dec 12, 1934
   New York Times page 14, Sep 23, 1934
                   IX, page 1, Sep 30, 1934
                   IX, page 1, Aug 4, 1935
                   page 20, Aug 6, 1935
                   IX, page 2, Sep 8, 1935
   Newsweek 4:27, Sep 29, 1934
              4:23, Dec 1, 1934
   Stage 12:3+, Nov 1934
   Theatre Arts 18:819-20, Nov 1934
                19:19, Jan 1935
   Time 24:34, Oct 1, 1934

Green, Adolph (see A Party with Betty Comden and Adolph Green)

Green Fruit (see The Madcap)

Green Pond

book: Robert Montgomery
music: Mel Marvin

```
lyrics:            Robert Montgomery
staging:           David Chambers
sets:              Marjorie Kellogg
costumes:          Marjorie Kellogg
```
Productions:
(Off-Broadway) Opened November 22, 1977 for 32 performances
Reviews:
New York Times III, page 19, Dec 15, 1977

Greenwich Village Follies (1919)
```
book:              Philip Bartholomae and John Murray Anderson
music:             A. Baldwin Sloane
lyrics:            Philip Bartholomae and John Murray Anderson
staging:           John Murray Anderson
sets:              Pieter Myer and Charles Ellis
costumes:          Pieter Myer and Charles Ellis
```
Productions:
Opened July 15, 1919 for 232 performances
Reviews:
Dramatic Mirror 80:1165, Jul 29, 1919
New York Times page 14, Jul 16, 1919
Theatre Magazine 30:152-3, Sep 1919

The Greenwich Village Follies (1920)
```
dialogue:          Thomas J. Gray
music:             A. Baldwin Sloane
lyrics:            John Murray Anderson and Arthur Swanstrom
sets:              Robert Locher and James Reynolds
costumes:          Robert Locher and James Reynolds
```
Productions:
Opened August 30, 1920 for 192 performances
Reviews:
Dramatic Mirror page 415, Sep 4, 1920
Forum 64:234, Sep-Oct 1920
New York Clipper 68:28-9, Sep 8, 1920
New York Times page 7, Aug 31, 1920
Theatre Magazine 32:259, Nov 1920
               32:279, Nov 1920
               32:375, Dec 1920

Greenwich Village Follies (1921)
```
music:             Carey Morgan
lyrics:            Arthur Swanstrom and J. M. Anderson
staging:           John Murray Anderson
sets:              Robert Locher and James Reynolds
costumes:          Robert Locher and James Reynolds
```
Productions:
Opened August 31, 1921 for 167 performances
Reviews:
New York Clipper 69:22, Sep 7, 1921
New York Times page 18, Sep 1, 1921
Theatre Magazine 34:314, Nov 1921

Greenwich Village Follies (1922)
    book: George V. Hobart
    music: Louis A. Hirsch
    lyrics: John Murray Anderson and Irving Caesar
    sets and
    costumes: Howard Greer, Erté of Paris, Ingeborg Hansell,
                    Cleon Throckmorten, Earl Payne Franke, Blanding
                    Sloan, Georgianna Brown, Alice O'Neill, Reginald
                    Marsh, Dorothy Armstrong, Pieter Myer, James
                    Reynolds
    choreography: Carl Randall
Productions:
    Opened September 21, 1922 for 216 performances
Reviews:
    Forum 68:1034-7, Dec 1922
    New Republic 32:175-6, Oct 11, 1922
                 33:21-4, Nov 29, 1922
    New York Times page 18, Sep 13, 1922
    Theatre Magazine 36:299, Nov 1922

Greenwich Village Follies (1923)
    music: Louis A. Hirsch and Con Conrad
    lyrics: Irving Caesar and John M. Anderson
    sketches: Lew Fields
    staging: John Murray Anderson
    sets: Howard Greer, Ingeborg Hansell, James Reynolds
    costumes: Howard Greer, Ingeborg Hansell, James Reynolds
    choreography: Larry Ceballos and Michio Itow
Productions:
    Opened September 20, 1923 for 140 performances
Reviews:
    Life 82:18, Oct 18, 1923
    New York Times page 4, Sep 21, 1923
                 page 21, Oct 16, 1923
    Theatre Magazine 38:54, Nov 1923

Greenwich Village Follies (1924)
    music: Cole Porter
    lyrics: Cole Porter, Irving Caesar, John Murray Ander-
                    son
    staging: John Murray Anderson
Productions:
    Opened September 16, 1924 for 180 performances
Reviews:
    Life (New York) 84:18, Oct 9, 1924
    New York Times page 19, Feb 11, 1924
                 page 16, Sep 17, 1924
                 VII, page 1, Sep 21, 1924
                 VIII, page 1, Sep 28, 1924
    Theatre Magazine 40:64, Nov 1924

Greenwich Village Follies (1925)
    music: Harold Levey and Owen Murphy
    lyrics: Harold Levey and Owen Murphy
    staging: Hassard Short
    sets: Clark Robinson
    costumes: Mark Mooring, Charles LeMaire, Gilbert Adrian
    choreography: Larry Ceballos and Alexander Gabrilov
Productions:
    Opened December 24, 1925 for 180 performances
Reviews:
    Life (New York) 87:18, Jan 28, 1926
    New York Times page 23, Dec 25, 1925
                   VII, page 1, Jan 10, 1926
                   page 22, Mar 16, 1926
    Theatre Magazine 43:18, Mar 1926
                  44:25, Jul 1926

Greenwich Village Follies (1928)
    sketches: Harold Atteridge
    music: Ray Perkins and Maurie Rubens
    lyrics: Max and Nathaniel Lief
    staging: J. C. Huffman, Chester Hale and Ralph Reader
    sets: Watson Barratt
    costumes: Ernest Schraps
Productions:
    Opened April 9, 1928 for 158 performances
Reviews:
    New York Times page 32, Apr 10, 1928
    Outlook 149:185, May 30, 1928
    Vogue 71:79, Jun 1, 1928

Greenwich Village USA
    sketches: Frank Gehrecke
    music: Jeanne Bargy
    lyrics: Jeanne Bargy
Productions:
    (Off-Broadway) Opened Season of 1960-61
Reviews:
    New York Times page 30, Sep 29, 1960
                   page 56, Dec 7, 1960
    New Yorker 36:97-8, Oct 8, 1960

Greenwillow
    book: Lesser Samuels and Frank Loesser, based on the
                     novel by B. J. Chute
    music: Frank Loesser
    lyrics: Frank Loesser
    staging: George Roy Hill
    sets: Peter Larkin
    costumes: Alvin Colt
    choreography: Joe Layton

Productions:
Opened March 8, 1960 for 97 performances
(Off-Broadway)   Season of 1970-71
Reviews:
Commonweal 72:16, Apr 1, 1960
New York Theatre Critics' Reviews 1960:325+
New York Times II, page 3, Feb 28, 1960
                page 38, Mar 9, 1960
                II, page 1, Mar 20, 1960
                page 26, May 13, 1960
                page 60, Dec 8, 1970
New Yorker 36:117, Mar 19, 1960
Newsweek 55:116, Mar 21, 1960
Time 75:75, Mar 21, 1960

Grenfell, Joyce   (see Joyce Grenfell)

Grind
    book: Fay Kanin
    music: Larry Grossman
    lyrics: Ellen Fitzhugh
    staging: Harold Prince
    sets: Clarke Dunham
    costumes: Florence Klotz
    choreography: Lester Wilson
Productions:
Opened April 16, 1985 for 79 performances
Reviews:
America 152:434, May 25, 1985
Black Enterprise 16:124, Aug 1985
Dance Magazine 59:62+, Jun 1985
Harper's Bazaar 118:186-7, May 1985
Jet 68:55, Jun 3, 1985
New York 18:93, Apr 29, 1985
New York Theatre Critics' Reviews 1985:307
New York Times III, page 20, Apr 17, 1985
New Yorker 61:129, Apr 22, 1985
Newsweek 105:65, Apr 29, 1985
Theatre Crafts 19:42-3+, Aug/Sep 1985
Time 125:87, Apr 29, 1985

La Grosse Valise
    book: Robert Dhery
    music: Gerard Calvi
    lyrics: Harold Rome
    staging: Robert Dhery
    sets: Jacques Dupont and Frederick Fox
    costumes: Jacques Dupont and Frederick Fox
    choreography: Colette Brosset and Tom Panko
Productions:
Opened December 14, 1965 for 7 performances

Reviews:
Dance Magazine 40:14-15+, Feb 1966
New York Theatre Critics' Reviews 1965: 218
New York Times page 52, Dec 15, 1965
                page 64, Dec 16, 1965
New Yorker 41:50, Dec 25, 1965

Guys and Dolls
    book: Jo Swerling and Abe Burrows, based on a story
                    and characters of Damon Runyon
    music: Frank Loesser
    lyrics: Frank Loesser
    staging: George S. Kaufman
    sets: Jo Mielziner
    costumes: Alvin Colt
    choreography: Michael Kidd
Productions:
Opened November 24, 1950 for 1,200 performances
Opened April 20, 1955 for 31 performances
Opened April 28, 1965 for 15 performances
Opened June 8, 1966 for 23 performances
Opened July 21, 1976 for 239 performances
Reviews:
America 93:192, May 14, 1955
Atlantic 245:40-7+, Jan 1980
Catholic World 172:309, Jan 1951
                181:228, Jun 1955
Christian Science Monitor Magazine page 13, Dec 2, 1950
Commonweal 53:252, Dec 15, 1950
Dance Magazine 40:59, Jul 1966
Essence 7:39, Nov 1976
Holiday 20:75+, Oct 1956
Horizon 28:55, Nov 1985
Life 29:64-5, Dec 25, 1950
     60:18, Jun 17, 1966
Los Angeles 25:226+, Jun 1980
Nation 171:515, Dec 2, 1950
New Republic 123:22, Dec 25, 1950
              132:22, May 2, 1955
New West 5:SC-25, Jun 2, 1980
New York 9:58, Aug 9, 1976
New York Theatre Critics' Reviews 1950:185+
                                   1976:208
New York Times page 32, Oct 24, 1950
               II, page 1, Nov 12, 1950
               page 11, Nov 25, 1950
               II, page 1, Dec 3, 1950
               VI, page 63, Dec 10, 1950
               II, page 1, Dec 17, 1950
               page 20, Mar 26, 1951
               page 34, Apr 4, 1951

II, page 1, Oct 7, 1951
page 17, May 29, 1953
II, page 1, Jun 7, 1953
page 32, Apr 21, 1955
page 22, Jul 22, 1959
page 39, Apr 29, 1965
page 55, Jun 9, 1966
page 26, Jul 22, 1976
II, page 5, Aug 1, 1976
III, page 5, Sep 10, 1976
III, page 3, Sep 17, 1976
New Yorker 26:77, Dec 2, 1950
52:53, Aug 2, 1976
Newsweek 36:75, Dec 4, 1950
88:70, Aug 2, 1976
Saturday Review 33:27-8, Dec 23, 1950
33:38+, Dec 30, 1950
Theatre Arts 35:13+, Feb 1951
35:32+, Jul 1951
39:88, Jul 1955
Theatre Crafts 20:18-19+, May 1986
Time 56:63, Dec 4, 1950

Gypsy

book: Arthur Laurents, suggested by the memoirs of
               Gypsy Rose Lee
music: Jule Styne
lyrics: Stephen Sondheim
staging: Jerome Robbins
sets: Jo Mielziner
costumes: Raoul Pene du Bois
choreography: Jerome Robbins
Productions:
Opened May 21, 1959 for 702 performances
Opened September 23, 1974 for 120 performances
Reviews:
America 101:438, Jun 13, 1959
Coronet 46:12, Oct 1959
Dance Magazine 33:12-13, Jul 1959
Life 47:63-4, Jul 27, 1959
Nation 188:521, Jun 6, 1959
219:348-9, Oct 12, 1974
New York 7:97, Oct 7, 1974
New York Theatre Critics' Reviews 1959:300+
1974:247
New York Times II, page 1, May 17, 1959
page 31, May 22, 1959
II, page 1, May 31, 1959
VI, pages 12-13, May 31, 1959
II, page 1, Jun 7, 1959
page 47, Sep 24, 1974
II, page 1, Sep 29, 1974

New Yorker 35:65-7, May 30, 1959
           50:74, Oct 7, 1974
           65:142-3, Dec 4, 1989
Newsweek 53:58, Jun 1, 1959
          84:72-3, Oct 7, 1974
People 32:88-9, Jul 3, 1989
Playboy 22:78, Jan 1975
Saturday Review 42:29, Jun 6, 1959
Theatre Arts 43:18-20, May 1959
           43:9+, Aug 1959
Theatre Crafts 20:32-3+, May 1986
Time 73:84+, Jun 1, 1959
      104:107, Oct 7, 1974
Vogue 134:60-1, Jul 1959

Gypsy Blonde
   book: Kenneth Johns, based on Michael Balfe's opera
                    Bohemian Girl
   music: Michael Balfe
   lyrics: Frank Gabrielson
   staging: Dmitri Ostrov
   sets: Karl Amend
   choreography: Vaughn Godfrey
Productions:
   Opened June 25, 1934 for 24 performances
Reviews:
   New York Times page 22, Jun 26, 1934

- H -

Haarlem Nocturne
   conceived: Andre De Shields
   written: Andre De Shields and Murray Horwitz
   songs: Various authors and composers
   staging: Andre De Shields and Murray Horwitz
   sets: David Chapman
   costumes: Jean-Claude Robin
Productions:
   Opened November 18, 1984 for 49 performances
Reviews:
   Dance Magazine 59:70, Feb 1985
   New York 17:140, Dec 3, 1984
   New York Theatre Critics' Reviews 1984:144
   New York Times III, page 17, Nov 19, 1984
   New Yorker 60:182-3, Dec 3, 1984

Hackett, Buddy (see Buddy Hackett)

The Haggadah, a Passover Cantata
   book: Elizabeth Swados, adapted from Elie Wiesel's

Moses: Portrait of a Leader and portions of the
Haggadah and the Old Testament
music: Elizabeth Swados
lyrics: Elizabeth Swados
staging: Elizabeth Swados
sets: Julie Taymor
costumes: Julie Taymor
Productions:
(Off-Broadway) Opened March 31, 1980 for 64 performances
(Off-Broadway) Opened April 14, 1981 for 72 performances
Reviews:
New York 13: 79, Apr 21, 1980
New York Times III, page 22, Apr 2, 1980
Saturday Review 7:56, May 1980

Hair
book: Gerome Ragni and James Rado
music: Galt MacDermot
lyrics: Gerome Ragni and James Rado
staging: Tom O'Horgan
sets: Robin Wagner
costumes: Nancy Potts
Productions:
(Off-Broadway) Opened October 29, 1967 for 94 performances
Opened April 29, 1968 for 1,750 performances
Opened October 5, 1977 for 43 performances
Reviews:
America 118:759-60, Jun 8, 1968
Commonweal 88:268, May 17, 1968
Dance Magazine 41:28-9, Dec 1967
                42:24-5+, Jul 1968
Ebony 25:120-2+, May 1970
English Journal 60:626-8, May 1971
High Fidelity 19:108, Jul 1969
Harper's 237:107-9, Sep 1968
Life 68:83-6, Apr 17, 1970
Los Angeles 33:164, Jul 1988
National Review 20:519, May 21, 1968
                22:319, Mar 24, 1970
New Republic 157 38-9, Nov 18, 1967
New York 10:85, Oct 24, 1977
            12:11, Mar 19, 1979
New York Theatre Critics' Reviews 1968:280
                                  1968:288
                                  1977:183
New York Times page 55, Oct 30, 1967
               page 50, Nov 14, 1967
               II, page 1, Nov 19, 1967
               page 25, Jan 23, 1968
               II, page 1, Apr 28, 1968
               page 40, Apr 30, 1968

page 41, May 1, 1968
II, page 1, May 19, 1968
II, page 3, May 19, 1968
page 76, Sep 29, 1968
page 36, Feb 5, 1969
II, page 1, May 11, 1969
page 53, Jun 2, 1969
page 26, Jun 7, 1969
page 13, Jun 8, 1969
page 52, Jun 10, 1969
page 30, Sep 13, 1969
II, page 3, Sep 14, 1969
page 62, Nov 3, 1969
page 64, Dec 10, 1969
page 39, Jan 13, 1970
page 44, Jun 29, 1970
page 10, Sep 5, 1970
II, page 1, Sep 27, 1970
page 17, Mar 13, 1971
page 26, May 10, 1971
VI, page 14, Jan 2, 1972
page 41, May 8, 1972
page 42, May 17, 1972
III, page 22, Oct 6, 1977
New Yorker 43:128+, Nov 11, 1967
44:84-5, May 11, 1968
45:102, Jun 14, 1969
Newsweek 70:124, Nov 13, 1967
71:110, May 13, 1968
74:94, Jul 7, 1969
90:117, Oct 17, 1977
112:83, Dec 5, 1988
Opera News 34:8-13, Dec 20, 1969
Reporter 33:36+, Apr 4, 1968
Saturday Evening Post 241:66-9, Aug 10, 1968
Saturday Review 51:95, Jan 13, 1968
51:26, May 11, 1968
Time 91:72, May 10, 1968
94:76, Dec 12, 1969
110:94+, Oct 17, 1977

Hairpin Harmony

book:	Harold Orlob
music:	Harold Orlob
lyrics:	Harold Orlob
staging:	Dora Maugham
sets:	Donald Oenslager
costumes:	Mahieu

Productions:
Opened October 1, 1943 for 3 performances

Reviews:
    New York Theatre Critics' Reviews 1943:269
    New York Times page 18, Oct 2, 1943

Halala! (a Zulu musical performed in English)
    written: Welcome Msomi
    music: Zulu composers
    staging: Welcome Msomi
    choreography: Thuli Dumakude
Productions:
    (Off-Broadway) Opened February 12, 1986 for 31 performances
Reviews:
    New York Times III, page 25, Feb 13, 1986

Half a Sixpence
    book: Beverly Cross, based on H. G. Wells's Kipps
    music: David Heneker
    lyrics: David Heneker
    staging: Gene Saks
    sets: Loudon Sainthill
    costumes: Loudon Sainthill
    choreography: Onna White and Tom Panko
Productions:
    Opened April 25, 1965 for 511 performances
Reviews:
    America 113:63, Jul 10, 1965
    Commonweal 82:383-4, Jun 11, 1965
    Dance Magazine 39:22-3, Jul 1965
    New York Theatre Critics' Reviews 1965:346+
    New York Times page 38, Apr 26, 1965
                    II, page 12, Aug 29, 1965
    New Yorker 41:120, May 8, 1965
    Newsweek 65:100, May 10, 1965
    Saturday Review 48:24, May 15, 1965
    Time 85:88, May 7, 1965

Half a Widow
    book: Harry B. Smith and Frank Dupree
    music: Shep Camp
    lyrics: Harry B. Smith and Frank Dupree
    staging: Lawrence Marston and Edwin T. Emery
Productions:
    Opened September 12, 1927 for 8 performances
Reviews:
    New York Times page 37, Sep 13, 1927
    Theatre Magazine 46:24+, Nov 1927

The Half Moon
    book: William Le Baron
    music: Victor Jacobi
    lyrics: William Le Baron
    staging: Fred G. Latham

Productions:
  Opened November 1, 1920 for 48 performances
Reviews:
  Dramatic Mirror page 847, Nov 6, 1920
  Life (New York) 76:960-1, Nov 25, 1920
  New York Clipper 68:31, Nov 17, 1920
  New York Times page 15, Nov 2, 1920
  Theatre Magazine 33:30-31, Jan 1921

Half-Past Wednesday
  book: Anna Marie Barlow
  music: Robert Colby
  lyrics: Robert Colby and Nita Jonas
  staging: Hal Raywin
  sets: Lloyd Burlingame
  costumes: Robert Fletcher
  choreography: Gene Bayliss
Productions:
  (Off-Broadway) Opened April 6, 1962 for 2 performances
Reviews:
  New York Times page 16, Apr 7, 1962
                  page 34, Apr 9, 1962

Hallelujah, Baby!
  book: Arthur Laurents
  music: Jule Styne
  lyrics: Betty Comden and Adolph Green
  staging: Burt Shevelove
  sets: William and Jean Eckart
  costumes: Irene Sharaff
  choreography: Kevin Carlisle, William Guske, and Marie Lake
Productions:
  Opened April 26, 1967 for 293 performances
Reviews:
  America 116:879, Jun 24, 1967
  Christian Century 84:1106, Aug 30, 1967
  Commonweal 86:342-5, Jun 9, 1967
  Dance Magazine 41:78-9, Jun 1967
  National Review 19:976-7, Sep 5, 1967
  New York Theatre Critics' Reviews 1967:312
  New York Times page 51, Apr 27, 1967
                  II, page 1, May 7, 1967
                  page 41, Jan 5, 1968
  New Yorker 43:150, May 6, 1967
  Newsweek 69:116, May 8, 1967
  Saturday Review 50:66, May 13, 1967
  Time 89:58, May 5, 1967

Hamelin: A Musical Tale From Rats to Riches
  book: Richard Jarboe, Harvey Shield and Matthew Wells
  music: Richard Jarboe and Harvey Shield

staging: Ron Nash
sets: Steven Rubin
costumes: Mark Bridges
choreography: Jerry Yoder
Productions:
    (Off-Broadway) Opened November 10, 1985 for 33 performances
Reviews:
    New York 18:105-6, Nov 25, 1985
    New York Times III, page 15, Nov 11, 1985

Hammerstein's 9 O'Clock Revue
    book: Harold Simpson and Morris Harvey
Productions:
    Opened October 4, 1923 for 12 performances
Reviews:
    New York Times page 22, Oct 5, 1923
                   VIII, page 1, Oct 14, 1923

A Hand Is on the Gate
    arranged: Roscoe Lee Browne
    staging: Ivor David Balding, Peter Cook and Joseph E.
                 Levine
Productions:
    Opened September 21, 1966 for 21 performances
Reviews:
    New York Theatre Critics' Reviews 1966:298
    New York Times page 54, Sep 22, 1966
                   page 58, Sep 29, 1966

Hands Up
    book: Edgar Smith
    music: E. Ray Goetz and Sigmund Romberg
    lyrics: E. Ray Goetz
    staging: J. H. Benrimo
    choreography: Jack Mason
Productions:
    Opened July 22, 1915 for 52 performances
Reviews:
    Dramatic Mirror 74:8, Jul 28, 1915
    Green Book 14:615, Oct 1915
    Theatre Magazine 22:139, Sep 1915

Hang Down Your Head and Die
    book: David Wright
    staging: Braham Murray
    sets: Fred Voelpel
    choreography: Braham Murray
Productions:
    (Off-Broadway) Opened October 18, 1964 for 1 performance
Reviews:
    New York Times page 38, Oct 19, 1964
                   page 42, Oct 20, 1964

Hang on to the Good Times
    conceived: Richard Maltby Jr., Gretchen Cryer and Nancy
                      Ford
    songs: Gretchen Cryer and Nancy Ford
    staging: Richard Maltby Jr.
    sets: James Morgan
    costumes: Karen Gerson
    choreography: Kay Cole
Productions:
    (Off-Broadway) Opened January 22, 1985 for 40 performances
Reviews:
    New York 18:111, Mar 4, 1985
    New York Times III, page 18, Feb 19, 1985
                    II, page 5, Feb 24, 1985

Hanky Panky
    book: Edgar Smith
    music: A. Baldwin Sloane
    lyrics: E. Ray Goetz
    staging: Gus Sohlke
Productions:
    Opened August 5, 1912 for 104 performances
Reviews:
    Blue Book 16:29-32, Nov 1912
    Dramatic Mirror 68:11, Aug 7, 1912
    Green Book 8:568-70, Oct 1912
    Theatre Magazine 16:xi, Sep 1912

Hannah Senesh
    conceived: Dafna Soltes
    written: David Schechter, developed in collaboration with
                      Lori Wilner, based on diaries and poems of Hannah
                      Senesh, English translation by Marta Cohn and
                      Peter Hay
    music: Steven Lutvak
    additional
      music: Elizabeth Swados and David Schechter
    staging: David Schechter
    sets: Jennifer Gallagher
    costumes: David Woolard
Productions:
    (Off-Broadway) Opened April 10, 1985 for 161 performances
Reviews:
    New York Theatre Critics' Reviews 1985:229
    New York Times I, page 60, Apr 14, 1985

The Happiest Girl in the World
    book: Fred Saidy and Henry Myers, based on Aris-
                      tophanes' Lysistrata and Bulfinch's stories of
                      Greek mythology
    music: Jacques Offenbach

lyrics: E. Y. Harburg
staging: Cyril Ritchard
sets: William and Jean Eckart
costumes: Robert Fletcher
choreography: Dania Krupska
Productions:
Opened April 3, 1961 for 96 performances
Reviews:
America 105:410, Jun 3, 1961
Dance Magazine 35:13-14, May 1961
Nation 192:358, Apr 22, 1961
New York Theatre Critics' Reviews 1961:314+
New York Times II, page 1, Apr 2, 1961
             page 42, Apr 4, 1961
Newsweek 57:69, Apr 17, 1961
New Yorker 37:76, Apr 15, 1961
Theatre Arts 45:32, Jun 1961
Time 77:106+, Apr 14, 1961

Happy
  book: Vincent Lawrence and McElbert Moore
  music: Frank Grey
  lyrics: Earle Crooker and McElbert Moore
  staging: Walter Brooks
Productions:
Opened December 5, 1927 for 80 performances
Reviews:
New York Times page 26, Dec 6, 1927
             page 30, Feb 7, 1928
Theatre Magazine 47:40, Feb 1928

Happy as Larry
  book: Donagh MacDonagh
  music: Mescha and Wesley Portnoff
  lyrics: Donagh MacDonagh
  staging: Burgess Meredith
  sets: Motley
  costumes: Motley
  choreography: Anna Sokolow
Productions:
Opened January 6, 1950 for 3 performances
Reviews:
New York Theatre Critics' Reviews 1950:394+
New York Times page 11, Jan 7, 1950
New Yorker 25:48, Jan 14, 1950
Newsweek 35:74, Jan 16, 1950
Theatre Arts 34:14, Mar 1950
Time 55:45, Jan 16, 1950

Happy Birthday
  book: Anita Loos

songs: Richard Rodgers, Oscar Hammerstein II, James Livingston

incidental
  music: Robert Russell Bennett
staging: Joshua Logan
sets: Jo Mielziner
costumes: Lucinda Ballard

Productions:
  Opened October 31, 1946 for 564 performances

Reviews:
  Catholic World 164:261, Dec 1946
  Commonweal 45:116, Nov 15, 1946
  Life 21:79-82, Nov 18, 1946
  Nation 163:565, Nov 16, 1946
  New Republic 115:662, Nov 18, 1946
  New York Theatre Critics' Reviews 1946:280
  New York Times VI, page 27, Sep 22, 1946
               VI, page 30, Oct 27, 1946
               page 31, Nov 1, 1946
               II, page 1, Nov 10, 1946
               II, page 1, Jan 26, 1947
               II, page 1, Apr 20, 1947
               II, page 1, Oct 26, 1947
  New Yorker 22:55, Nov 9, 1946
  Newsweek 28:92, Nov 11, 1946
  Saturday Review 29:23, Dec 21, 1946
  School and Society 66:327-8, Oct 25, 1947
  Theatre Arts 31:18-19+, Jan 1947
  Time 48:56, Nov 11, 1946

Happy Days

words: R. H. Burnside and Raymond Hubbell
music: R. H. Burnside and Raymond Hubbell
staging: R. H. Burnside

Productions:
  Opened August 23, 1919 for 452 performances

Reviews:
  New York Times page 8, Aug 25, 1919
  Theatre Magazine 34:217, Jul 1921

Happy End

book: Michael Feingold, based on a German play Dorothy Lane by Elisabeth Hauptmann
music: Kurt Weill
lyrics: Bertolt Brecht, adapted by Michael Feingold
staging: Michael Posnick
sets: Robert U. Taylor
costumes: Carrie F. Robbins
choreography: Patricia Birch

Productions:
  (Off-Broadway) Opened March 8, 1977 for 56 performances
  Opened May 7, 1977 for 75 performances

Reviews:
  Nation 224:603, May 14, 1977
  New York 10:63, May 9, 1977
  New York Theatre Critics' Reviews 1977:239
  New York Times III, page 17, Apr 27, 1977
                III, page 15, Jun 1, 1977
  New Yorker 53:59, May 9, 1977
  Saturday Review 4:49, Jun 11, 1977
  Texas Monthly 7:136, Feb 1979
  Time 109:89, Jun 13, 1977

Happy Go Lucky
  book: Helena Phillips Evans
  music: Lucien Denni
  lyrics: Helena Phillips Evans
  staging: Fred G. Latham
Productions:
  Opened September 30, 1926 for 52 performances
Reviews:
  New York Times page 13, Aug 6, 1926
  Theatre Magazine 44:18, Dec 1926

Happy Hunting
  book: Howard Lindsay and Russel Crouse
  music: Harold Karr
  lyrics: Matt Dubey
  staging: Abe Burrows
  sets: Jo Mielziner
  costumes: Irene Sharaff
  choreography: Alex Romero and Bob Herget
Productions:
  Opened December 6, 1956 for 412 performances
Reviews:
  America 96:743, Mar 30, 1957
  Catholic World 184:386, Feb 1957
  New York Theatre Critics' Reviews 1956:166+
  New York Times VI, page 29, Sep 16, 1956
                VI, page 29, Nov 4, 1956
                page 30, Dec 7, 1956
                II, page 3, Dec 16, 1956
  New Yorker 32:54+, Dec 22, 1956
  Newsweek 48:66, Dec 17, 1956
  Reporter 16:35, Jan 24, 1957
  Saturday Review 39:25, Dec 29, 1956
  Theatre Arts 41:20-1, Feb 1957
  Time 68:62+, Dec 17, 1956
  Vogue 128:11, Dec 1956

The Happy Hypocrite
  book: Edward Eager; based on the short story by Max
                   Beerbohm

music: James Bredt; additional material by Tony Tanner
lyrics: Edward Eager
staging: Tony Tanner
sets: Michael Horen
costumes: Deidre Cartier
Productions:
(Off-Broadway)   Opened September 5, 1968 for 17 performances
Reviews:
New York Times page 38, Sep 6, 1968
New Yorker 44:129-30, Sep 14, 1969

Happy New Year
book: Burt Shevelove, based on Philip Barry's play
                  Holiday
music: Cole Porter
lyrics: Cole Porter, edited by Buster Davis
staging: Burt Shevelove
sets: Michael Eagan
costumes: Pierre Balmain
choreography: Donald Saddler
Productions:
Opened April 27, 1980 for 25 performances
Reviews:
Dance Magazine 54:94, Jul 1980
New York 13:59-61, May 12, 1980
New York Theatre Critics' Reviews 1980:272
New York Times II, page 1, Apr 27, 1980
                III, page 13, Apr 28, 1980
                II, page 7, May 11, 1980
Time 115:83, May 12, 1980

The Happy Time
book: N. Richard Nash; based on the play by Samuel
                  Taylor and the book by Robert L. Fontaine
music: John Kander
lyrics: Fred Ebb
staging: Gower Champion
sets: Peter Wexler
costumes: Freddy Wittop
choreography: Gower Champion
Productions:
Opened January 18, 1968 for 285 performances
Reviews:
America 118:356, Mar 16, 1968
Dance Magazine 42:27, Apr 1968
Nation 206:186+, Feb 5, 1968
New York Theatre Critics' Reviews 1968:375
                                   1968:378
New York Times page 32, Jan 19, 1968
                II, page 3, Jan 28, 1968
                page 36, Sep 14, 1968

New Yorker 43:84+, Jan 27, 1968
Newsweek 71:76, Jan 29, 1968
Saturday Review 51:45, Feb 3, 1968

Happy Town

book:	Max Hampton
music:	Gordon Duffy (additional music by Paul Nassau)
lyrics:	Harry M. Haldane (additional lyrics by Paul Nassau)
staging:	Allan A. Buckhantz
sets:	Curt Nations
costumes:	J. Michael Travis
choreography:	Lee Scott

Productions:
Opened October 7, 1959 for 5 performances
Reviews:
New York Theatre Critics' Reviews 1959:279+
New York Times page 49, Oct 8, 1959
page 22, Oct 9, 1959
New Yorker 35:134, Oct 17, 1959

Hard Job Being God

book:	Based on the Old Testament
music:	Tom Martel
lyrics:	Tom Martel
staging:	Bob Yde
sets:	Ray Wilke
costumes:	Mary Whitehead
choreography:	Lee Theodore

Productions:
Opened May 15, 1972 for 6 performances
Reviews:
New York Times page 49, May 16, 1972
New Yorker 48:82+, May 27, 1972

Harlem Cavalcade

assembled:	Ed Sullivan
staging:	Ed Sullivan and Noble Sissle
costumes:	Veronica
choreography:	Leonard Harper

Productions:
Opened May 1, 1942 for 49 performances
Reviews:
New York Theatre Critics' Reviews 1942:296
New York Times page 11, May 2, 1942
VIII, page 1, May 17, 1942

The Harold Arlen Songbook

conceived:	Robert Elston
music:	Harold Arlen
lyrics:	Truman Capote, Harold Arlen, Dorothy Fields,

Ira Gershwin, E. Y. Harburg, Ted Koehler,
Dory Langdon, Johnny Mercer, Leo Robin and
Billy Rose
staging: Robert Elston
Productions:
(Off-Broadway) Opened February 28, 1967 for 41 performances
Reviews:
New York Times page 48, Mar 1, 1967
page 37, Mar 29, 1967

Harrigan 'n Hart
book: Michael Stewart, based on material compiled by
Nedda Harrigan Logan and The Merry Partners
by E. J. Kahn Jr.
music: Max Showalter
lyrics: Peter Walker
additional
songs: Edward Harrigan and David Braham
staging: Joe Layton
sets: David Mitchell
costumes: Ann Hould-Ward
choreography: D. J. Giagni
Productions:
Opened January 31, 1985 for 5 performances
Reviews:
New York 18:56-8, Feb 11, 1985
New York Theatre Critics' Reviews 1985:382
New York Times III, page 3, Feb 1, 1985
New Yorker 60:118, Feb 11, 1985
Newsweek 105:63, Feb 11, 1985
Theatre Crafts 19:24-6+, Apr 1985
Vogue 175:115, Mar 1985

Harry Stoones (see Another Evening with Harry Stoones)

Hassard Short's Ritz Revue
staging: Hassard Short
Productions:
Opened September 17, 1924 for 109 performances
Reviews:
New York Times page 19, Sep 18, 1924
Theatre Magazine 40:70, Nov 1924

Hats Off to Ice
assembled: Sonja Henie and Arthur M. Wirtz
music: James Littlefield and John Fortis
lyrics: James Littlefield and John Fortis
staging: William H. Burke and Catherine Littlefield
sets: Bruno Maine
costumes: Grace Houston
choreography: Catherine Littlefield and Dorothie Littlefield

Productions:
  Opened June 22, 1944 for 889 performances
Reviews:
  Catholic World 159:459, Aug 1944
  Commonweal 40:279, Jul 7, 1944
  New York Times page 15, Jun 23, 1944
  Time 44:70, Jul 3, 1944

Have a Heart
  book: Guy Bolton and P. G. Wodehouse
  music: Jerome Kern
  lyrics: Guy Bolton and P. G. Wodehouse
  staging: Edward Royce
Productions:
  Opened January 11, 1917 for 76 performances
Reviews:
  Dramatic Mirror 77:7, Jan 13, 1917
                  77:10, Jan 20, 1917
                  77:8, Feb 17, 1917
                  77:9, Mar 10, 1917
  Green Book 17:590+, Apr 1917
  Leslie's Weekly 124:327, Mar 22, 1917
  National Magazine 46:121-4, Oct-Nov 1917
  New York Dramatic News 63:22, Jan 13, 1917
                          63:22, Jan 20, 1917
  New York Times page 11, Jan 12, 1917
  Theatre Magazine 25:84, Feb 1917
                   25:128, Feb 1917

Have I Got a Girl For You!
  book: Joel Greenhouse and Penny Rockwell
  music: Dick Gallagher
  lyrics: Dick Gallagher
  staging: Bruce Hopkins
  sets: Harry Darrow
  costumes: Kenneth M. Yount
  choreography: Felton Smith
Productions:
  (Off-Broadway) Opened October 29, 1986 for 78 performances
Reviews:
  Dance Magazine 61:89, Jan 1987
  New York 19:120, Nov 17, 1986
  New York Times page 73, Nov 21, 1986

Have I Got One for You
  book: Jerry Blatt and Lonnie Burstein
  music: Jerry Blatt
  lyrics: Jerry Blatt and Lonnie Burstein
  staging: Roberta Sklar
  sets: John Conklin
  costumes: John Conklin

Productions:
    (Off-Broadway) Opened January 7, 1968 for one performance
Reviews:
    New York Times page 32, Jan 8, 1968
                  page 36, Jan 9, 1968

Hayride
    book: Based on folk material
    music: Based on folk music
    sets: Art Guild, Jack Woodson and Jack Derrenberger
Productions:
    Opened September 13, 1954 for 24 performances
Reviews:
    America 92:25, Oct 2, 1954
    New York Theatre Critics' Reviews 1954:319
    New York Times page 24, Sep 14, 1954
    Theatre Arts 38:13+, Nov 1954

Hazel Flagg
    book: Ben Hecht, based on a story by James Street
                       and the film Nothing Sacred
    music: Jule Styne
    lyrics: Bob Hilliard
    staging: David Alexander
    sets: Harry Horner
    costumes: Miles White
    choreography: Robert Alton
Productions:
    Opened February 11, 1953 for 190 performances
Reviews:
    America 88:661, Mar 14, 1953
    Catholic World 177:70, Apr 1953
    Commonweal 57:552, Mar 6, 1953
    Dance Magazine 27:12-15+, Mar 1953
    Life 34:102-4+, Mar 9, 1953
    Look 17:20, Mar 24, 1953
    Nation 176:193, Feb 28, 1953
    New York Theatre Critics' Reviews 1953:362+
    New York Times page 22, Feb 12, 1953
                      II, page 3, Sep 13, 1953
    New Yorker 29:58, Feb 21, 1953
    Newsweek 41:62, Feb 23, 1953
    Saturday Review 36:38, Feb 18, 1953
    Theatre Arts 37:14-15, Feb 1953
                   37:15, May 1953
    Time 61:86, Feb 23, 1953

He Came from Milwaukee
    book: Mark Swan
    music: Ben M. Jerome and Louis A. Hirsch
    lyrics: Edward Madden
    staging: Sidney Ellison

Productions:
Opened September 21, 1910 for 117 performances
Reviews:
Blue Book 12:644-7, Feb 1911
Dramatic Mirror 64:7, Sep 28, 1910
Green Book Album 5:254-5+, Feb 1911
Hampton 25:680, Nov 1910
Leslie's Weekly 111:403, Oct 20, 1910
Metropolitan Magazine 33:400-1, Dec 1910
Theatre Magazine 12:xiv, Nov 1910
  12:153, Nov 1910
Woman's Home Companion 38:43, Feb 1911

He Didn't Want to Do It
    book: George Broadhurst
    music: Silvio Hein
    lyrics: George Broadhurst
    staging: Clifford Brooke
Productions:
Opened August 20, 1918 for 23 performances
Reviews:
Dramatic Mirror 79:360, Sep 7, 1918
  79:399, Sep 14, 1918
Life (New York) 72:344, Sep 5, 1918
New York Times page 7, Aug 21, 1918
Theatre Magazine 28:242, Oct 1918

Head over Heels (1918)
    book: Edgar Allan Woolf; suggested by Lee Arthur's
                    dramatization of Nalbro Bartley's Shadows
    music: Jerome Kern
    lyrics: Edgar Allan Woolf
    staging: George Marion
Productions:
Opened August 29, 1918 for 100 performances
Reviews:
Dramatic Mirror 78:802, Jun 8, 1918
  79:434, Sep 21, 1918
National Magazine 47:461-2, Sep 1918
New York Times page 9, Aug 30, 1918
Theatre Magazine 28:11, Jul 1918
  28:212, Oct 1918

Head Over Heels (1981)
    book: William S. Kilborne Jr. and Albert T. Viola,
                    based on the play The Wonder Hat by Kenneth
                    Sawyer Goodman and Ben Hecht
    music: Albert T. Viola
    lyrics: William S. Kilborne Jr.
    staging: Jay Binder
    sets: John Falabella

costumes: John Falabella
choreography: Terry Rieser
Productions:
  (Off-Broadway)   Opened December 15, 1981 for 22 performances
Reviews:
  New York Times page 17, Dec 19, 1981

Heads Up
  book: John McGowan and Paul Gerard Smith
  music: Richard Rodgers
  lyrics: Lorenz Hart
  staging: George Hale
Productions:
  Opened November 11, 1929 for 114 performances
Reviews:
  New York Times page 34, Nov 12, 1929
               IX, page 14, Nov 17, 1929
  Outlook 153:513, Nov 27, 1929
  Theatre Magazine 51:49, Jan 1930
  Vogue 75:60+, Jan 18, 1930

Heathen!
  book: Robert Helpman and Eaton Magoon Jr.
  music: Eaton Magoon Jr.
  lyrics: Eaton Magoon Jr.
  staging: Lucia Victor
  sets: Jack Brown
  costumes: Bruce Harrow
  choreography: Sammy Bayes and Dan Siretta
Productions:
  Opened May 21, 1972 for one performance
Reviews:
  New York Theatre Critics' Reviews 1972:276
  New York Times page 43, May 22, 1972
  New Yorker 48:84, May 27, 1972

Heaven On Earth
  book: Barry Trivers
  music: Jay Gorney
  lyrics: Barry Trivers
  staging: John Murray Anderson
  sets: Raoul Pene du Bois
  costumes: Raoul Pene du Bois
  choreography: Nick Castle
Productions:
  Opened September 16, 1948 for 12 performances
Reviews:
  New York Theatre Critics' Reviews 1948:240+
  New York Times page 29, Sep 17, 1948
               II, page 1, Sep 26, 1948
  New Yorker 24:53, Sep 25, 1948

Newsweek 32:79, Sep 27, 1948
Time 52:63, Sep 27, 1948

The Heebie Jeebies
    conceived: Mark Hampton
    by: Mark Hampton and Stuart Ross
    songs: Various authors and composers
    staging: Stuart Ross
    sets: Michael Sharp
    costumes: Carol Oditz
    choreography: Stuart Ross and Terry Reiser
Productions:
    (Off-Broadway) Opened June 18, 1981 for 37 performances
Reviews:
    New York Times III, page 4, Jun 19, 1981

Helen of Troy, New York
    book: George Kaufman and Marc Connelly
    music: Bert Kalmar and Harry Ruby
    lyrics: Bert Kalmar and Harry Ruby
    staging: Bertram Harrison and Bert French
Productions:
    Opened June 19, 1923 for 191 performances
Reviews:
    Life (New York) 82:20, Jul 12, 1923
    New York Clipper 71:14, Jun 27, 1923
    New York Times page 22, Jun 20, 1923
    Stage 15:28, Aug 1938
    Theatre Arts 32:44, Fall 1948
    Theatre Magazine 38:15, Aug 1923

Hell
    book: Rennold Wolf
    lyrics: Rennold Wolf
Productions:
    Opened April 27, 1911 for 92 performances
Reviews:
    Theatre Magazine 13:183, Jun 1911

Hello Alexander
    book: Edgar Smith and Emily Young
    music: Jean Schwartz
    lyrics: Alfred Bryan
Productions:
    Opened October 7, 1919 for 56 performances
Reviews:
    Dramatic Mirror 80:1612, Oct 16, 1919
    New York Times page 22, Oct 8, 1919
    Theatre Magazine 30:354, Nov 1919

Hello Broadway
    words: George M. Cohan

music: George M. Cohan
Productions:
    Opened December 25, 1914 for 123 performances
Reviews:
    American Mercury 79:42, May 1915
    Current Opinion 58:98, Feb 1915
    Dramatic Mirror 72:8, Dec 30, 1914
                    73:2, Jan 27, 1915
                    73:2, Mar 31, 1915
    Green Book 13:476-7, Mar 1915
               13:576, Mar 1915
    Life (New York) 65:24, Jan 7, 1915
    Munsey 54:330, Mar 1915
           54:537, Apr 1915
    New York Times page 7, Dec 26, 1914
    Smart Set 45:287-8, Mar 1915
    Theatre Magazine 21:52+, Feb 1915
                     21:101, Feb 1915
                     25:272, May 1917

Hello Charlie
    book: Harry Kalmanowich
    music: Maurice Rauch
    lyrics: Jacob Jacobs
    staging: Max Perlman
    sets: Arthur Aaronson
    choreography: Michael Aubrey
Productions:
    (Off-Broadway) Opened October 23, 1965 for 129 performances
Reviews:
    New York Times page 47, Oct 25, 1965

Hello Daddy
    book: Herbert Fields
    music: Jimmy McHugh
    lyrics: Dorothy Fields
    staging: John Murray Anderson
Productions:
    Opened December 26, 1928 for 198 performances
Reviews:
    Life (New York) 93:21, Jan 25, 1929
    New York Times page 26, Dec 27, 1928

Hello Dolly!
    book: Michael Stewart, suggested by Thornton Wilder's
                     The Matchmaker
    music: Jerry Herman
    lyrics: Jerry Herman
    staging: Gower Champion
    sets: Oliver Smith
    costumes: Freddy Wittop
    choreography: Gower Champion

Productions:
   Opened January 16, 1964 for 2,844 performances
   Opened November 6, 1975 for 51 performances
   Opened March 5, 1978 for 145 performances
Reviews:
   America 110:552, Apr 18, 1964
           118:20, Jan 6, 1968
   Christian Century 85:118, Jan 24, 1968
   Ebony 23:83-9, Jan 1968
   Essence 6:31, Feb 1976
   Harper's 236:112, Apr 1968
   Life 56:107-9, Apr 3, 1964
        63:128-30+, Dec 8, 1967
   Los Angeles 20:105, Oct 1975
   Mademoiselle 59:56, May 1964
   New York 8:91+, Nov 24, 1975
           11:89-90, Mar 20, 1978
   New York Theatre Critics' Reviews 1964:384+
                                     1975:153
                                     1978:362
   New York Times II, page 1, Jan 12, 1964
                  page 22, Jan 17, 1964
                  II, page 1, Jan 26, 1964
                  page 28, Feb 5, 1964
                  II, page 1, Jan 10, 1965
                  II, page 8, Aug 8, 1965
                  page 17, Aug 10, 1965
                  page 43, Dec 3, 1965
                  II, page 7, Dec 12, 1965
                  page 79, Feb 8, 1966
                  page 47, Mar 9, 1966
                  II, page 1, Jun 26, 1966
                  page 40, Jan 19, 1967
                  page 34, Feb 16, 1967
                  page 19, Feb 18, 1967
                  page 56, Feb 21, 1967
                  page 30, Mar 2, 1967
                  page 55, Jun 6, 1967
                  page 56, Jun 12, 1967
                  page 38, Jun 14, 1967
                  page 12, Jul 29, 1967
                  page 40, Oct 25, 1967
                  page 56, Nov 5, 1967
                  page 61, Nov 13, 1967
                  II, page 3, Nov 26, 1967
                  page 21, May 31, 1968
                  page 36, Nov 13, 1968
                  page 43, Nov 16, 1968
                  page 42, Jun 3, 1969
                  page 32, Oct 31, 1969
                  page 70, Jan 25, 1970

                    page 52, Mar 30, 1970
                    II, page 1, Apr 12, 1970
                    II, page 1, Sep 6, 1970
                    page 44, Sep 8, 1970
                    pages 51-53, Sep 9, 1970
                    page 61, Sep 10, 1970
                    II, page 38, Nov 29, 1970
                    II, page 40, Dec 27, 1970
                    page 38, Dec 28, 1970
                    page 24, Nov 7, 1975
                    III, page 15, Mar 6, 1978
                    II, page 3, Apr 2, 1978
        New Yorker 39:72, Jan 25, 1964
        Newsweek 63:59, Jan 27, 1964
                  70:105, Nov 27, 1967
        Saturday Review 47:22, Feb 8, 1964
                        50:24, Dec 2, 1967
        Time 83:44, Jan 24, 1964
             90:56, Nov 24, 1967

Hello, Lola!
    book: Dorothy Donnelly
    music: William B. Kernell
    lyrics: Dorothy Donnelly
    staging: Seymour Felix
Productions:
    Opened January 12, 1926 for 47 performances
Reviews:
    New York Times page 30, Jan 13, 1926

Hello, Paris (1911)
    dialogue: William Le Baron
    music: J. Rosamond Johnson
    lyrics: J. L. Hill
    staging: Ned Wayburn
Productions:
    Opened September 22, 1911 for 8 performances
No Reviews.

Hello, Paris (1930)
    book: Edgar Smith, adapted from Homer Croy's novel
    music: Russell Tarbox and Michael Cleary
    lyrics: Edgar Smith
    staging: Ben Holmes
Productions:
    Opened November 15, 1930 for 33 performances
Reviews:
    Life (New York) 96:35, Dec 5, 1930
    New York Times page 29, Nov 19, 1930

Hello, Solly!
    staging: Al Hausman

Productions:
Opened April 4, 1967 for 68 performances
Reviews:
New York Times page 44, Apr 6, 1967
page 54, May 26, 1967

Hello Yourself
book: Walter De Leon
music: Richard Myers
lyrics: Leo Robin
staging: Clarke Silvernail
Productions:
Opened October 30, 1928 for 87 performances
Reviews:
New York Times page 28, Oct 31, 1928
Theatre Magazine 49:60, Jan 1929

Hellzapoppin
assembled by: Ole Olson and Chic Johnson
music: Sammy Fain
lyrics: Charles Tobias
staging: Edward Duryea Dowling
Productions:
Opened September 22, 1938 for 1,404 performances
Reviews:
Catholic World 148:215, Nov 1938
Collier's 102:16-17+, Dec 10, 1938
Commonweal 31:227, Dec 29, 1939
Life 5:30-3, Oct 24, 1938
New York Theatre Critics' Reviews 1940:493+
1941:495+
New York Times page 34, Sep 23, 1938
IX, page 1, Oct 2, 1938
X, page 1, Sep 17, 1939
page 36, Dec 12, 1939
page 14, Sep 20, 1940
page 39, Jan 19, 1941
IX, page 2, Mar 2, 1941
IX, page 1, Aug 3, 1941
VIII, page 2, Feb 15, 1942
Newsweek 12:28, Oct 10, 1938
14:28, Dec 25, 1939
Stage 16:20-2, Jan 1939
Theatre Arts 22:783, Nov 1938
24:93-4, Feb 1940
Time 32:30, Oct 3, 1938
34:24, Dec 25, 1939

The Hen-Pecks
words: Glen MacDonough
notes: A. Baldwin Sloane

```
rhymes:          E. Ray Goetz
staging:         Ned Wayburn
```
Productions:
Opened February 4, 1911 for 137 performances
Reviews:
Blue Book 13:12-15, May 1911
Dramatic Mirror 65:7, Feb 8, 1911
                65:9, Feb 22, 1911
                65:2, Jun 7, 1911
                67:26, Jan 31, 1912
Green Book Album 5:682-3, Apr 1911
Munsey 45:134, Apr 1911
New York Dramatic News 56:31, Sep 21, 1912
Red Book 16:1149+, Apr 1911
Stage 13:59, Aug 1936
Theatre Magazine 13:xi, Mar 1911
                 13:71, Mar 1911

Henry, Sweet Henry
```
book:            Nunnally Johnson; based on the novel The World
                 of Henry Orient by Nora Johnson
music:           Bob Merrill
lyrics:          Bob Merrill
staging:         George Roy Hill
sets:            Robert Randolph
costumes:        Alvin Colt
choreography:    Michael Bennett
```
Productions:
Opened October 23, 1967 for 80 performances
Reviews:
America 117:624, Nov 18, 1967
New York Theatre Critics' Reviews 1967:241
                                  1967:244
New York Times page 51, Oct 24, 1967
                 page 39, Oct 25, 1967
                 II, page 3, Nov 5, 1967
                 page 25, Dec 28, 1967
Newsweek 70:89A, Nov 6, 1967
Saturday Review 50:26, Nov 11, 1967

Her Family Tree
```
book:            Al Weeks and "Bugs" Baer
staging:         Hassard Short
```
Productions:
Opened December 27, 1920 for 98 performances
Reviews:
Dramatic Mirror 83:11+, Jan 1, 1921
Life (New York) 77:100, Jan 20, 1921
New York Clipper 69:30, Jan 5, 1921
New York Times page 9, Dec 28, 1920
Theatre Magazine 33:159, Mar 1921
                 33:180, Mar 1921

Her First Roman
    book: Ervin Drake; based on George Bernard Shaw's
                         Caesar and Cleopatra
    music: Ervin Drake
    lyrics: Ervin Drake
    staging: Derek Goldby
    sets: Michael Annals
    costumes: Michael Annals
    choreography: Dania Krupska
Productions:
    Opened October 20, 1968 for 17 performances
Reviews:
    New York Theatre Critics' Reviews 1968:183
                                      1968:200
    New York Times page 53, Oct 21, 1968
                    page 53, Oct 29, 1968
                    II, page 1, Nov 3, 1968
    New Yorker 44:139-40, Oct 26, 1968
    Newsweek 72:118, Nov 4, 1968

Her Little Highness
    book: Channing Pollock and Rennold Wolf; based on
                         Such a Little Queen by Channing Pollock
    music: Reginald De Koven
    staging: George Marion
Productions:
    Opened October 13, 1913 for 16 performances
Reviews:
    Dramatic Mirror 70:6-7, Oct 15, 1913
    Green Book 11:161, Jan 1914
    New York Dramatic News 58:14, Oct 18, 1913
    New York Times page 13, Oct 14, 1913
    Theatre Magazine 18:xxii+, Nov 1913

Her Soldier Boy
    book: Victor Leon; adapted by Rida Johnson Young
    music: Emmerich Kalman and Sigmund Romberg
    staging: J. J. Shubert
Productions:
    Opened December 6, 1916 for 198 performances
Reviews:
    Dramatic Mirror 76:4, Dec 9, 1916
                    76:4+, Dec 16, 1916
    Munsey 59:501, Dec 1916
    New York Dramatic News 63:6, Dec 16, 1916
    New York Times page 11, Dec 7, 1916
    Theatre Magazine 25:24, Jan 1917

Here Goes the Bride
    book: Peter Arno
    music: John W. Green and Richard Myers

```
    lyrics:          Peter Arno
    staging:         Edward Clarke Lilley
    choreography:    Russell Markert
Productions:
    Opened November 3, 1931 for 7 performances
Reviews:
    New York Times page 31, Nov 4, 1931
                    page 22, Nov 9, 1931
```

Here's Howe
```
    book:            Fred Thompson and Paul Gerard Smith
    music:           Roger Wolfe Kahn and Joseph Meyer
    lyrics:          Irving Caesar
Productions:
    Opened May 1, 1928 for 71 performances
Reviews:
    New York Times page 19, May 2, 1928
    Outlook 149:305, Jun 30, 1928
    Theatre Magazine 48:39, Jul 1928
    Vogue 72:92, Jul 1, 1928
```

Here's Love
```
    book:            Meredith Willson, based on Valentine Davies and
                     George Seaton's screenplay Miracle on 34th
                     Street
    music:           Meredith Willson
    lyrics:          Meredith Willson
    staging:         Stuart Ostrow
    sets:            William and Jean Eckart
    costumes:        Alvin Colt
    choreography:    Michael Kidd
Productions:
    Opened October 3, 1963 for 334 performances
Reviews:
    America 109:642-3, Nov 16, 1963
    New York Theatre Critics' Reviews 1963:258+
    New York Times page 24, Aug 6, 1963
                    page 28, Sep 20, 1963
                    VI, page 51, Sep 22, 1963
                    II, page 3, Sep 29, 1963
                    page 28, Oct 4, 1963
                    page 28, Jul 2, 1964
    Newsweek 62:72, Oct 14, 1963
    Saturday Review 46:18, Nov 2, 1963
    Theatre Arts 48:11, Jan 1964
    Time 82:72, Oct 11, 1963
```

Here's Where I Belong
```
    book:            Alex Gordon; based on the novel East of Eden
                     by John Steinbeck
    music:           Robert Waldman
```

lyrics:	Alfred Uhry
staging:	Michael Kahn
sets:	Ming Cho Lee
costumes:	Ruth Morley
choreography:	Tony Mordente

Productions:
Opened March 3, 1968 for one performance
Reviews:
New York Theatre Critics' Reviews 1968:331
New York Times page 32, Mar 4, 1968
page 35, Mar 5, 1968
New Yorker 44:132, Mar 9, 1968

Herman van Veen: All of Him
conceived:	Herman van Veen and Michel LaFaille; English adaptation by Christopher Adler, with Herman van Veen
music:	Herman van Veen and various composers
lyrics:	Christopher Adler, with Herman van Veen, and various authors
staging:	Michel LaFaille
sets:	Gerard Jongerius and Ed de Boer
costumes:	Ellen van der Horst

Productions:
Opened December 8, 1982 for 6 performances
Reviews:
New York Theatre Critics' Reviews 1982:134
New York Times III, page 28, Dec 9, 1982

A Hero Is Born
book:	Theresa Helburn, based on a fairy tale by Andrew Lang
music:	A. Lehman Engel
lyrics:	Agnes Morgan
staging:	Agnes Morgan
sets:	Tom Adrian Cracraft
costumes:	Alexander Saron

Productions:
Opened October 1, 1937 for 50 performances
Reviews:
Catholic World 146:218, Nov 1937
New York Times page 18, Oct 2, 1937
Time 30:54, Oct 11, 1937

Herringbone
book:	Tom Cone, based on an original play by Tom Cone
music:	Skip Kennon
lyrics:	Ellen Fitzhugh
staging:	Ben Levit
sets:	Christopher Nowak

costumes: Karen Matthews
choreography: Theodore Pappas
Productions:
  (Off-Broadway) Opened June 30, 1982 for 46 performances
Reviews:
  New York 15:62, Aug 2, 1982
  New York Theatre Critics' Reviews 1982:228
  Newsweek 100:45, Jul 26, 1982

Hey, Ma ... Kaye Ballard

conceived: David Levy and Leslie Eberhard
words: Kaye Ballard
songs: Various authors and composers, with original
                   songs by David Levy and Leslie Eberhard
staging: Susan H. Schulman
sets: Linda Hacker
costumes: William Ivey Long
Productions:
  (Off-Broadway) Opened February 27, 1984 for 62 performances
Reviews:
  New York Theatre Critics' Reviews 1984:264
  New York Times III, page 11, Feb 28, 1984

Hey Nonny Nonny!

book: Max and Nathaniel Lief
music: Michael H. Cleary
lyrics: Max and Nathaniel Lief
staging: Alexander Leftwich
Productions:
  Opened June 6, 1932 for 32 performances
Reviews:
  Nation 134:708, Jun 22, 1932
  New York Times page 22, Jun 7, 1932

Hey, You

music: Norman Meranus
lyrics: June Carroll
Productions:
  (Off-Broadway) Opened Season of 1952-53
No Reviews.

Hi, Paisano!

book: Ernest Chambers
music: Robert Holton
lyrics: June Carroll
staging: Vassili Lambrinos
Productions:
  (Off-Broadway) Opened September 30, 1961 for 3 performances
Reviews:
  New York Times page 36, Oct 2, 1961
  New Yorker 37:131-2, Oct 7, 1961

High Button Shoes
  book: Stephen Longstreet, adapted from his novel The
                     Sisters Liked Them Handsome
  music: Jule Styne
  lyrics: Sammy Cahn
  staging: George Abbott
  sets: Oliver Smith
  costumes: Miles White
  choreography: Jerome Robbins
Productions:
  Opened October 9, 1947 for 727 performances
Reviews:
  Catholic World 166:172, Nov 1947
  Commonweal 47:71, Oct 31, 1947
  Life 23:102-4, Nov 10, 1947
  New Republic 117:35, Oct 27, 1947
  New York 15:42-3, Aug 9, 1982
  New York Theatre Critics' Reviews 1947:304+
  New York Times II, page 3, Oct 5, 1947
                    page 32, Oct 10, 1947
                    II, page 6, Nov 9, 1947
                    II, page 1, Nov 23, 1947
                    II, page 3, Nov 30, 1947
                    page 23, Dec 23, 1948
                    page 10, Mar 12, 1955
  New Yorker 23:56+, Oct 18, 1947
  Newsweek 30:86+, Oct 20, 1947
  Theatre Arts 31:15-16, Nov 1947
  Time 50:73, Oct 20, 1947
  Vogue 110:190, Nov 15, 1947

High Jinks
  book: Leo Ditrichstein and Otto Hauerbach
  music: Rudolf Friml
  lyrics: Leo Ditrichstein and Otto Hauerbach
  staging: Frank Smithson
Productions:
  Opened December 10, 1913 for 213 performances
Reviews:
  Dramatic Mirror 70:6, Dec 17, 1913
  Life (New York) 61:1155, Dec 25, 1913
  New York Times page 11, Dec 11, 1913
  Theatre Magazine 19:46, Jan 1914

High Kickers
  book: George Jessel, from a suggestion by Sid Silvers
  music: Harry Ruby
  lyrics: Bert Kalmar
  staging: Edward Sobel
  sets: Nat Karson
  choreography: Carl Randall

Productions:
    Opened October 31, 1941 for 171 performances
Reviews:
    New York Theatre Critics' Reviews 1941: 246+
    New York Times page 54, Oct 12, 1941
                    page 21, Nov 1, 1941
    Theatre Arts 26-8, Jan 1942
    Time 38:55, Nov 10, 1941

High Spirits
    book: Hugh Martin and Timothy Gray, based on Noel
                     Coward's play Blithe Spirit
    music: Hugh Martin
    lyrics: Timothy Gray
    staging: Noel Coward
    sets: Robert Fletcher
    costumes: Robert Fletcher and Valentina Rasch
    choreography: Danny Daniels
Productions:
    Opened April 7, 1964 for 375 performances
Reviews:
    America 111:114, Aug 1, 1964
    Life 56:9, May 1, 1964
         56:125-7, May 15, 1964
    Look 28:87-91, Mar 10, 1964
    National Review 16:546-7, Jun 30, 1964
    New York Theatre Critics' Reviews 1964: 292+
    New York Times page 34, Apr 8, 1964
                    page 46, Nov 4, 1964
    New Yorker 40:108, Apr 18, 1964
    Time 83:65, Apr 17, 1964

Higher and Higher
    book: Gladys Hurlbut and Joshua Logan, based on an
                     idea by Irvin Pincus
    music: Richard Rodgers
    lyrics: Lorenz Hart
    staging: Joshua Logan
    sets: Jo Mielziner
    costumes: Lucinda Ballard
    choreography: Robert Alton
Productions:
    Opened April 4, 1940 for 84 performances
    Opened August 5, 1940 for 24 performances
Reviews:
    Life 8:42+, Apr 15, 1940
    New York Theatre Critics' Reviews 1940: 337+
    New York Times X, page 2, Mar 17, 1940
                    page 24, Apr 5, 1940
                    page 15, Aug 6, 1940
                    IX, page 1, Aug 11, 1940
    Time 35:76, Apr 15, 1940

The Highway of Life   (see Dude)

Hijinks!
    book: Robert Kalfin, Steve Brown and John McKinney,
                         adapted from Captain Jinks of the Horse Marines
                         by Clyde Fitch
    music: Various composers
    lyrics: Various authors
    staging: Robert Kalfin
    sets: Sandro La Ferla
    costumes: Elizabeth P. Palmer
    choreography: Larry Hayden
Productions:
    (Off-Broadway) Opened December 17, 1980 for 39 performances
Reviews:
    New York Times III, page 6, Dec 19, 1980
    New Yorker 56:62, Jan 5, 1981

Hilarities
    sketches: Sidney Zelinka, Howard Harris, Morey Amsterdam
    music: Buddy Kaye, Carl Lampl
    lyrics: Stanley Arnold
Productions:
    Opened September 9, 1948 for 14 performances
Reviews:
    New Republic 119:38, Sep 27, 1948
    New York Theatre Critics' Reviews 1948:250+
    New York Times page 20, Sep 10, 1948

Hip-Hip-Hooray
    book: R. H. Burnside
    music: Raymond Hubbell
    lyrics: John L. Golden
    staging: R. H. Burnside
Productions:
    Opened September 30, 1915 for 425 performances
Reviews:
    Current Opinion 59:326-7, Nov 1915
    Dramatic Mirror 74:8, Oct 6, 1915
    Green Book 14:986-7, Dec 1915
    New York Times page 11, Oct 1, 1915
                     VI, page 6, Oct 3, 1915
                     page 11, May 2, 1916
    Opera Magazine 3:29-31, Jan 1916
    Theatre Magazine 22:221, Nov 1915
                     23:15, Jan 1916
                     23:84, Feb 1916

The Hired Man
    book: Melvyn Bragg, adapted from his novel
    music: Howard Goodall

staging: Brian Aschinger
sets: Tamara Kinkman
costumes: Patricia Adshead
choreography: Rodney Griffin
Productions:
  (Off-Broadway) Opened November 10, 1988 for 33 performances
Reviews:
  New York Times III, page 18, Nov 9, 1988

His Honor, the Barber
    book: Edwin Hanaford
    music: James Brymm
    staging: S. H. Dudley
Productions:
  Opened May 8, 1911 for 16 performances
Reviews:
  Dramatic Mirror 65:7, May 10, 1911
  New York Times page 11, May 9, 1911

His Little Widows
    book: Rida Johnson Young and William Cary Duncan
    music: William Schroeder
    lyrics: Rida Johnson Young and William Cary Duncan
    staging: Frank Stammers
    choreography: David Bennett
Productions:
  Opened April 30, 1917 for 72 performances
Reviews:
  Dramatic Mirror 77:7, May 12, 1917
  Green Book 18:4-5+, Jul 1917
  New York Dramatic News 64:18, May 12, 1917
  New York Times page 11, May 1, 1917
  Public 69:816-17, May 10, 1917
  Theatre Magazine 25:340+, Jun 1917

A History of the American Film
    by: Christopher Durang
    music: Mel Marvin
    staging: David Chambers
    sets: Tony Straiges
    costumes: Marjorie Slaiman
    choreography: Graciela Daniele
Productions:
  Opened March 30, 1978 for 21 performances
Reviews:
  New York Theatre Critics' Reviews 1978:310
  New York Times III, page 3, Mar 31, 1978

Hit the Deck
    book: Herbert Fields, adapted from the play Shore
                 Leave

```
music:              Vincent Youmans
lyrics:             Leo Robin and Clifford Grey
staging:            Lew Fields, Seymour Felix, Alexander Leftwich
Productions:
```
Opened April 25, 1927 for 352 performances
Reviews:
Life (New York) 89:23, May 19, 1927
New York Times page 32, Apr 26, 1927
                 page 8, Dec 14, 1927
                 IX, page 4, Apr 1, 1928
                 IX, page 2, Apr 29, 1928
Theatre Magazine 46:18, Jul 1927
Vogue 69:75+, Jun 15, 1927

Hit the Trail

```
book:               Frank O'Neill
music:              Frederico Valerio
lyrics:             Elizabeth Miele
staging:            Charles W. Christenberry Jr. and Byrle Cass
sets:               Leo Kerz
costumes:           Michi
choreography:       Gene Bayliss
Productions:
```
Opened December 2, 1954 for 4 performances
Reviews:
New York Theatre Critics' Reviews 1954:228+
New York Times page 31, Dec 3, 1954
New Yorker 30:98, Dec 11, 1954
Theatre Arts 39:16, 92, Feb 1955

Hitchy-Koo (1917)

```
book:               Harry Grattan, Glen MacDonough and E. Ray
                    Goetz
music:              E. Ray Goetz
lyrics:             Harry Grattan, Glen MacDonough and E. Ray
                    Goetz
staging:            Julian Mitchell and Leon Errol
Productions:
```
Opened June 7, 1917 for 220 performances
Reviews:
Dramatic Mirror 77:7, Jun 16, 1917
                77:7, Jun 30, 1917
                77:4, Jul 7, 1917
New York Times page 9, Jun 8, 1917
                VIII, page 5, Jun 10, 1917
                VIII, page 5, Jun 17, 1917
Theatre Magazine 26:22, Jul 1917
                 26:83, Jul 1917

Hitchy-Koo (1918)

```
book:               Glen MacDonough and Raymond Hubbell
staging:            Leon Errol
```

Productions:
 Opened June 6, 1918 for 68 performances
Reviews:
 Dramatic Mirror 78:847, Jun 15, 1918
 Green Book 20:204-5+, Aug 1918
 New York Times page 11, Jun 7, 1918
 Theatre Magazine 28:23, Jul 1918

Hitchy-Koo (1919)
 book: George V. Hobart
 music: Cole Porter
 lyrics: Cole Porter
Productions:
 Opened October 6, 1919 for 56 performances
Reviews:
 Dramatic Mirror 80:1612, Oct 16, 1919
 New York Times page 22, Oct 7, 1919

Hitchy-Koo (1920)
 book: Glen MacDonough and Anne Caldwell
 music: Jerome Kern
 lyrics: Glen MacDonough and Anne Caldwell
 staging: Ned Wayburn
Productions:
 Opened October 19, 1920 for 71 performances
Reviews:
 Dramatic Mirror page 777, Oct 23, 1920
 New York Clipper 68:28, Oct 27, 1920
 New York Times page 11, Oct 20, 1920
 Theatre Magazine 33:29, Jan 1921

Hobo
 book: John Dooley
 music: John Dooley
 lyrics: John Dooley
Productions:
 (Off-Broadway) Opened Season of 1960-61
Reviews:
 New York Times page 41, Apr 11, 1961
                 page 33, Apr 19, 1961
 New Yorker 37:118-19, Apr 22, 1961

Hokey-Pokey and Bunty, Bulls and Strings
 music: John Stromberg, A. Baldwin Sloane and W. T.
                 Francis
 lyrics: Edgar Smith and E. Ray Goetz
 staging: Gus Sohlke
Productions:
 Opened February 8, 1912 for 108 performances
Reviews:
 Blue Book 15:8-11, May 1912

Dramatic Mirror 67:4, Mar 6, 1912
              67:2, Apr 3, 1912
              67:7, May 1912
Everybody's 26:689, May 1912
Theatre Magazine 15:xii, Mar 1912

Hold Everything
  book: B. G. DeSylva and John McGowan
  music: Ray Henderson
  lyrics: B. G. DeSylva, Lew Brown
  choreography: Jack Haskell and Sam Rose
Productions:
  Opened October 10, 1928 for 413 performances
Reviews:
  Life (New York) 92:21, Nov 2, 1928
  New York Times page 24, Oct 11, 1928
  Theatre Magazine 49:60, Jan 1929

Hold It!
  book: Matt Brooks and Art Arthur
  music: Gerald Marks
  lyrics: Sam Lerner
  staging: Robert E. Perry
  sets: Edward Gilbert
  costumes: Julia Sze
  choreography: Irma Jurist
Productions:
  Opened May 5, 1948 for 46 performances
Reviews:
  New York Theatre Critics' Reviews 1948:274+
  New York Times page 31, May 6, 1948
  New Yorker 24:48, May 15, 1948
  Newsweek 31:89, May 17, 1948
  Theatre Arts 32:14+, Jun 1948

Hold on to Your Hats
  book: Guy Bolton, Matt Brooks, Eddie Davis
  music: Burton Lane
  lyrics: E. Y. Harburg
  staging: Edgar MacGregor
  sets: Raoul Pene du Bois
  choreography: Catherine Littlefield
Productions:
  Opened September 11, 1940 for 158 performances
Reviews:
  Catholic World 152:218-19, Nov 1940
  Life 9:60-2, Jul 29, 1940
  Nation 151:281, Sep 28, 1940
  New York Theatre Critics' Reviews 1940:278+
                          1941:481+
  New York Times page 25, Jul 17, 1940

IX, page 1, Jul 21, 1940
page 30, Sep 12, 1940
IX, page 3, Oct 20, 1940
Stage 1:12, Nov 1940
1:12, Dec 1940
Theatre Arfs 24:770-1+, Nov 1940
Time 36:41, Sep 23, 1940

Hold Your Horses
    book: Russel Crouse and Corey Ford, based on a play
                     by Crouse, Ford, and Charles Beahan
    music and
        lyrics: Russell Bennett, Robert A. Simon, Louis Alter,
                     Arthur Swanstrom, Ben Oakland, Owen Murphy
    staging: Russell Patterson
    choreography: Robert Alton and Harriet Hoctor
Productions:
    Opened September 25, 1933 for 88 performances
Reviews:
    Catholic World 138:218, Nov 1933
    Commonweal 18:592, Oct 20, 1933
    New Outlook 162:43, Nov 1933
    New York Times page 20, Aug 31, 1933
                     X, page 1, Sep 10, 1933
                     page 26, Sep 26, 1933
                     IX, page 2, Oct 29, 1933
    Stage 11:9-11, Oct 1933

Holka Polka
    book: Bert Kalmar and Harry Ruby, adapted from the
                     European success by W. Walzer
    music: Will Ortman
    lyrics: Gus Kahn and Raymond B. Eagan
    staging: Oscar Eagle
Productions:
    Opened October 14, 1925 for 21 performances
Reviews:
    New York Times page 27, Oct 15, 1925

Hollywood Ice Revue
    assembled: Sonja Henie
    staging: Catherine Littlefield
    sets: Bruno Maine
    costumes: Billy Livingston
    choreography: Catherine Littlefield
Productions:
    (Off-Broadway)   Opened January 18, 1943
    (Off-Broadway)   Opened January 18, 1944
    (Off-Broadway)   Opened January 17, 1945 for 18 performances
    (Off-Broadway)   Opened January 23, 1947
    (Off-Broadway)   Opened February 3, 1947

(Off-Broadway) Opened January 22, 1948
Reviews:
  Collier's 119:76-7, Jan 25, 1947
           122:20-21, Dec 4, 1948
  Life 20:50-55, May 20, 1946
  Time 48:50, Jul 1, 1946

Hollywood Pinafore
  book: George S. Kaufman, based on Gilbert and Sul-
                   livan's H. M. S. Pinafore
  music: Original Sullivan score
  lyrics: George S. Kaufman
  staging: George S. Kaufman
  sets: Jo Mielziner
  costumes: Kathryn Kuhn and Mary Percy Schenck
  choreography: Antony Tudor and Douglas Coudy
Productions:
  Opened May 31, 1945 for 53 performances
Reviews:
  Catholic World 161:351, Jul 1945
  Commonweal 42:213, Jun 15, 1945
  Nation 160:705, Jun 23, 1945
  New York Theatre Critics' Reviews 1945:203+
  New York Times page 20, Jun 1, 1945
                  II, page 1, Jun 10, 1945
                  II, page 4, Jun 17, 1945
                  page 14, Jul 9, 1945
  New Yorker 21:38, Jun 9, 1945
  Newsweek 25:93, Jun 11, 1945
  Saturday Review 28:24-5, Jun 16, 1945
  Theatre Arts 29:389, Jul 1945
  Time 45:58, Jun 11, 1945

Holman, Libby (see Libby Holman)

Home Movies (Presented with Softly, and Consider the Nearness)
  book: Rosalyn Drexler
  music: Al Carmines
  lyrics: Rosalyn Drexler
  staging: Lawrence Kornfeld
  sets: Larry Siegel
  costumes: Judith Berkowitz
Productions:
  (Off-Broadway) Opened May 11, 1964 for 72 performances
Reviews:
  New York Times page 32, May 12, 1964
  New Yorker 40:134, May 23, 1964

Home Sweet Homer
  book: Roland Kibbee and Albert Marre, based on Homer's
                   Odyssey

music:	Mitch Lee
lyrics:	Charles Burr and Forman Brown
staging:	Albert Marre
sets:	Howard Bay
costumes:	Howard Bay
choreography:	Michael Mann

Productions:
Opened January 4, 1976 for one performance
Reviews:
Los Angeles 20:111+, Jul 1975
New York 9:67, Jan 19, 1976
New York Theatre Critics' Reviews 1976:398
New York Times page 36, Jan 5, 1976
New Yorker 51:55, Jan 12, 1976
Time 104:54, Dec 30, 1974

Honey Girl
book:	Edward Clark; based on Henry Blossom's Checkers
music:	Albert von Tilzer
lyrics:	Neville Fleeson
staging:	Bert French and Sam Forrest

Productions:
Opened May 3, 1920 for 32 performances
Reviews:
Dramatic Mirror 82:889, May 8, 1920
Life (New York) 75:946, May 20, 1920
New York Clipper 68:17, May 12, 1920
New York Times page 9, May 4, 1920
Theatre Magazine 31:505, Jun 1920
31:521, Jun 1920
31:527, Jun 1920

Honeydew
book:	Joseph Herbert
music:	Efrem Zimbalist
lyrics:	Joseph Herbert
staging:	Hassard Short

Productions:
Opened September 6, 1920 for (231) performances
Reviews:
Dramatic Mirror page 459, Sep 11, 1920
Life (New York) 76:542-3, Sep 23, 1920
Musical Courier 81:12, Sep 9, 1920
New York Clipper 68:19, Sep 15, 1920
New York Times page 20, Sep 7, 1920
Theatre Magazine 32:281, Nov 1920
32:332, Nov 1920

The Honeymoon Express
book:	Joseph W. Herbert and Harold Atteridge

music: Jean Schwartz
lyrics: Joseph W. Herbert and Harold Atteridge
staging: Ned Wayburn
Productions:
  Opened February 6, 1913 for 156 performances
Reviews:
  Blue Book 17:656-8, Aug 1913
  Dramatic Mirror 69:6, Feb 12, 1913
                 69:2, Apr 2, 1913
  Life (New York) 61:375, Feb 20, 1913
  Munsey 49:148-9, Apr 1913
  New York Dramatic News 57:20, Feb 15, 1913
  New York Times page 11, Feb 17, 1913
  Theatre Magazine 17:66-7, Mar 1913
                 17:147, Mar 1913

Honeymoon Lane
  book: Eddie Dowling and James Hanley
  music: Eddie Dowling and James Hanley
  lyrics: Eddie Dowling and James Hanley
  staging: Edgar MacGregor
Productions:
  Opened September 20, 1926 for 364 performances
Reviews:
  New York Times page 32, Sep 21, 1926
  Theatre Magazine 44:15, Nov 1926

Honky Tonk Nights
  book: Ralph Allen and David Campbell
  music: Michael Valenti
  lyrics: Ralph Allen and David Campbell
  staging: Ernest O. Flatt
  sets: Robert Cothran
  costumes: Mardi Philips
  choreography: Ernest O. Flatt
Productions:
  Opened August 7, 1986 for 4 performances
Reviews:
  New York Theatre Critics' Reviews 1986:254
  New York Times III, page 3, Aug 8, 1986
  New Yorker 62:58, Aug 18, 1986

Honor Challenged (see Frank Merriwell, or Honor Challenged)

Hooray for What!
  book: Howard Lindsay and Russel Crouse (conceived
                    by E. Y. Harburg)
  music: Harold Arlen
  lyrics: E. Y. Harburg
  staging: Howard Lindsay
  sets: Vincente Minnelli

costumes: Raoul Pene du Bois
choreography: Robert Alton
Productions:
Opened December 1, 1937 for 200 performances
Reviews:
Catholic World 146:470, Jan 1938
Commonweal 27:220, Dec 17, 1937
Life 3:44-6, Dec 20, 1937
Literary Digest 124:34-5, Dec 25, 1937
Nation 145:698, Dec 18, 1937
New Republic 93:198, Dec 22, 1937
New York Times XI, page 2, Nov 7, 1937
                page 32, Dec 2, 1937
                X, page 3, Jan 9, 1938
Stage 15:51-3, Dec 1937
Time 30:57, Dec 13, 1937

Hooray! It's a Glorious Day ... and All That
book: Maurice Teitelbaum and Charles Grodin
music: Arthur Gordon
lyrics: Ethel Bieber, Messrs. Teitelbaum and Charles
              Grodin
staging: Charles Grodin
sets: Peter Harvey
costumes: Peter Harvey
choreography: Sandra Devlin
Productions:
(Off-Broadway) Opened March 9, 1966 for 15 performances
Reviews:
New York Times page 28, Mar 10, 1966
New Yorker 42:163-4, Mar 19, 1966

Hop o' My Thumb
book: George R. Sims, Frank Dix and Arthur Collins;
              American version by Sydney Rosenfeld
music: Manuel Klein
lyrics: Ernest D'Auban
Productions:
Opened November 26, 1913 for 46 performances
Reviews:
Blue Book 18:838-40, Mar 1914
Collier's 52:30, Jan 10, 1914
Dramatic Mirror 70:6, Dec 3, 1913
New York Times page 13, Nov 27, 1913
Theatre Magazine 19:9, Jan 1914
                 19:46, Jan 1914

Horseman, Pass By
book: Rocco Bufano and John Duffy; based on writings
              of W. B. Yeats
music: John Duffy

```
staging:          Rocco Bufano
sets:             Dennis Dougherty
costumes:         Nancy Potts
choreography:     Rhoda Levine
```
Productions:
 (Off-Broadway) Opened January 15, 1969 for 37 performances
Reviews:
 New York Times page 46, Jan 16, 1969
 New Yorker 44: 77-8, Jan 25, 1969

Hot and Cold Heros
```
conceived:        Joe Jakubowitz
staging:          Joe Jakubowitz
sets:             R. Thomas Finch
costumes:         Fran Caruso
choreography:     Ivan Todd
```
Productions:
 (Off-Broadway) Opened May 9, 1973 for 16 performances
Reviews:
 New York Times page 27, May 11, 1973

Hot-Cha!
```
book:             Lew Brown, Ray Henderson, Mark Hellinger,
                  H. S. Kraft
music:            Ray Henderson
lyrics:           Lew Brown
staging:          Edgar McGregor
choreography:     Bobby Connelly
```
Productions:
 Opened March 8, 1932 for 119 performances
Reviews:
 Bookman 75: 77, Apr 1932
 New York Times VIII, page 2, Feb 21, 1932
        page 17, Mar 9, 1932
        VIII, page 1, Mar 20, 1932
 Outlook 160: 229, Apr 1932
 Vogue 79: 60+, May 1, 1932

Hot Chocolates
```
book:             Andy Razaf
music:            Thomas Waller and Harry Brooks
staging:          Leonard Harper
```
Productions:
 Opened June 20, 1929 for 219 performances
Reviews:
 New York Times page 17, Jun 21, 1929
 Outlook 152: 553, Jul 31, 1929
 Theatre Magazine 50: 43, Aug 1929

Hot Grog
```
book:             Jim Wann
```

music: Bland Simpson and Jim Wann
lyrics: Bland Simpson and Jim Wann
staging: Edward Berkeley
sets: James Tilton
costumes: Hilary Rosenfeld
choreography: Patricia Birch
Productions:
    (Off-Broadway)   Opened October 6, 1977 for 22 performances
Reviews:
    New York Times page 32, Oct 18, 1977

Hot Rhythm
sketches: Ballard McDonald, Will Morrissey, Edward Hurley
music: Porter Grainger and Donald Heywood
lyrics: Porter Grainger and Donald Heywood
staging: Will Morrissey and Nat Cash
Productions:
    Opened August 21, 1930 for 68 performances
Reviews:
    Life (New York) 96:16, Sep 12, 1930
    New York Times page 18, Aug 22, 1930

Hot Spot
book: Jack Weinstock and Willie Gilbert
music: Mary Rodgers
lyrics: Martin Charnin
sets: Rouben Ter-Arutunian
costumes: Rouben Ter-Arutunian
Productions:
    Opened April 19, 1963 for 43 performances
Reviews:
    Commonweal 78:225, May 17, 1963
    New York Theatre Critics' Reviews 1963:336+
    New York Times II, page 1, Apr 14, 1963
                    page 17, Apr 20, 1963
                    page 26, May 21, 1963
    New Yorker 39:82, Apr 27, 1963
    Newsweek 61:54, Apr 29, 1963
    Theatre Arts 47:66, Jun 1963
    Time 81:58, Apr 26, 1963

Hotel for Criminals
conceived: Richard Foreman
music: Stanley Silverman
staging: Richard Foreman
sets: Richard Foreman
costumes: Whitney Blausen
Productions:
    (Off-Broadway)   Opened December 30, 1974 for 15 performances
Reviews:
    New Republic 172:22+, Feb 8, 1975

New York Times page 39, Aug 26, 1974
                page 13, Dec 31, 1974
                II, page 21, Jan 26, 1975
New Yorker 50:65, Jan 13, 1975

The Hotel Mouse
book: Adapted from a French source by Guy Bolton
music: Armand Vecsey and Ivan Caryll
lyrics: Clifford Grey
Productions:
Opened March 13, 1922 for 88 performances
Reviews:
New York Clipper 70:20, Mar 22, 1922
New York Times page 11, Mar 14, 1922
Theatre Magazine 35:283, May 1922
                      35:334, May 1922

Hotel Passionato
book: Jerome J. Schwartz
music: Philip Springer
lyrics: Joan Javits
staging: Michael Ross
sets: Paul Barnes
costumes: Robert Mackintosh
Productions:
(Off-Broadway) Opened October 22, 1965 for 11 performances
Reviews:
New York Times page 16, Oct 23, 1965
New Yorker 41:116, Nov 6, 1965

House of Flowers
book: Truman Capote
music: Harold Arlen
lyrics: Truman Capote and Harold Arlen
staging: Peter Brook
sets: Oliver Messel
costumes: Oliver Messel
choreography: Herbert Ross
Productions:
Opened December 30, 1954 for 165 performances
(Off-Broadway) Opened January 28, 1968 for 57 performances
Reviews:
Catholic World 180:469, Mar 1955
Commonweal 61:454-5, Jan 28, 1955
Dance Magazine 42:28+, Apr 1968
Mademoiselle 40:142, Nov 1954
Nation 180:106, Jan 29, 1955
New York Theatre Critics' Reviews 1954:189+
New York Times page 75, Dec 19, 1954
                page 11, Dec 31, 1954
                page 39, Jan 24, 1968

                  page 26, Jan 29, 1968
                  page 50, Mar 14, 1968
New Yorker 30:62, Jan 8, 1955
Newsweek 45:62, Jan 10, 1955
Saturday Review 38:31, Jan 15, 1955
Theatre Arts 39:30-1+, Jan 1955
               39:20-1+, Mar 1955
Time 65:34, Jan 10, 1955
      91:75, Feb 9, 1968
Vogue 125:125, Jan 1955

The House of Leather

    book: Frederick Gaines
    music: Dale F. Menten
    lyrics: Dale F. Menten and Frederick Gaines
    staging: H. Wesley Balk
    sets: David F. Segal
    costumes: Judith Cooper and James K. Shearon
Productions:
    (Off-Broadway) Opened March 18, 1970 for one performance
Reviews:
    New York Times page 56, Mar 19, 1970
    New Yorker 46:86+, Mar 28, 1970

The Housewives' Cantata

    book: William Holtzman
    music: Mira J. Spektor
    lyrics: June Siegel
    staging: Rina Elisha
    sets: Raymond C. Recht
    costumes: Judy Dearing
    choreography: Rina Elisha
Productions:
    (Off-Broadway) Opened February 18, 1980 for 24 performances
Reviews:
    New York Times III, page 5, Feb 19, 1980

How Come?

    book: Eddie Hunter
    staging: Sam H. Grisman
Productions:
    Opened April 16, 1923 for 32 performances
Reviews:
    New York Clipper 71:14, Apr 25, 1923
    New York Times page 26, Apr 17, 1923

How Now, Dow Jones

    book: Max Shulman; based on an original idea by
                        Carolyn Leigh
    music: Elmer Bernstein
    lyrics: Carolyn Leigh

staging: George Abbott
sets: Oliver Smith
costumes: Robert Mackintosh
choreography: Gillian Lynne
Productions:
  Opened December 7, 1967 for 220 performances
Reviews:
  America 118: 330, Mar 9, 1968
  Christian Century 85: 269, Feb 28, 1968
  Dance Magazine 42: 29+, Feb 1968
  Nation 206: 28, Jan 1, 1968
  New York Theatre Critics' Reviews 1967: 190
                                     1967: 198
  New York Times page 60, Nov 10, 1967
                  page 53, Dec 8, 1967
                  page 38, Jun 18, 1968
  New Yorker 43: 97, Dec 16, 1967
  Newsweek 70: 94+, Dec 18, 1967

How to Be a Jewish Mother
  book: Seymour Vall; based on the book by Dan Green-
                     burg
  music: Michael Leonard
  lyrics: Herbert Martin
  staging: Avery Schreiber
  sets: Robert Randolph
  costumes: Michael Travis
Productions:
  Opened December 28, 1967 for 21 performances
Reviews:
  New York Theatre Critics' Reviews 1967: 187
  New York Times page 18, Dec 29, 1967
                  page 32, Jan 15, 1968

How to Get Rid of It
  book: Eric Blau, based on Eugene Ionesco's Amedee
  music: Mort Shuman
  lyrics: Eric Blau
  staging: Eric Blau
  sets: Don Jensen
  costumes: Don Jensen
Productions:
  (Off-Broadway) Opened November 17, 1974 for 9 performances
Reviews:
  New York Times page 51, Nov 18, 1974

How to Steal an Election
  book: William F. Brown
  music: Oscar Brand
  lyrics: Oscar Brand
  staging: Robert H. Livingston

```
    sets:            Clarke Dunham
    costumes:        Mopsy
Productions:
    (Off-Broadway)  Opened October 13, 1968 for 89 performances
Reviews:
    New York Times page 56, Oct 14, 1968
                   page 39, Dec 19, 1968
    New Yorker 44:142, Oct 26, 1968
    Newsweek 72:121, Nov 11, 1968
```

How to Succeed in Business without Really Trying

```
    book:            Abe Burrows, Jack Weinstock, Willie Gilbert,
                     based on Shepherd Mead's novel
    music:           Frank Loesser
    lyrics:          Frank Loesser
    staging:         Abe Burrows
    sets:            Robert Randolph
    costumes:        Robert Fletcher
    choreography:    Hugh Lambert
Productions:
    Opened October 14, 1961 for 1,417 performances
    Opened April 20, 1966 for 23 performances
    (Off-Off-Broadway)  Opened November 9, 1972
Reviews:
    America 106:632, Feb 10, 1962
    Business Week pages 30-1, Oct 21, 1961
    Christian Century 79:234, Feb 21, 1962
    Commonweal 75:154, Nov 3, 1961
    Dance Magazine 35:23, Dec 1961
                   36:12-13, Jan 1962
                   40:22, Jun 1966
    Life 51:192-4, Nov 17, 1961
         60:18, Jun 17, 1966
    National Review 12:31-3, Jan 16, 1962
    Nation 193:361-2, Nov 4, 1961
    New Republic 145:23, Nov 6, 1961
    New York Theatre Critics' Reviews 1961:224+
    New York Times II, page 1, Oct 8, 1961
                       page 34, Oct 16, 1961
                       II, page 3, Sep 2, 1962
                       page 5, Mar 30, 1963
                       page 43, Oct 11, 1963
                       page 30, Feb 12, 1964
                       II, page 7, Mar 8, 1964
                       page 10, Jul 18, 1964
                       page 45, Apr 21, 1966
                       page 45, Nov 12, 1972
    New Yorker 37:129, Oct 21, 1961
    Newsweek 58:62, Oct 23, 1961
             58:50-3, Nov 27, 1961
    Reporter 25:58, Nov 9, 1961
```

Saturday Evening Post 235:24-7, Jun 23, 1962
Saturday Review 44:33, Oct 28, 1961
Theatre Arts 45:8-9, Dec 1961
Time 78:79, Oct 27, 1961
     80:38, Dec 14, 1962

Howdy, Mr. Ice!
    assembled: Sonja Henie and Arthur M. Wirtz
    music: Al Stillman and Alan Moran
    lyrics: Al Stillman and Alan Moran
    staging: Catherine Littlefield
    sets: Bruno Maine
    costumes: Billy Livingston and Katherine Kuhn
Productions:
    Opened June 24, 1948 for 406 performances
Reviews:
    Catholic World 167:459, Aug 1948
    Commonweal 48:308, Jul 9, 1948
    New Republic 119:27, Jul 12, 1948
    New York Times page 28, Jun 25, 1948
    Theatre Arts 32:40, Oct 1948
    Time 52:42, Jul 5, 1948

Howdy, Mr. Ice of 1950!
    assembled: Sonja Henie and Arthur M. Wirtz
    music: Al Stillman and Alan Moran
    lyrics: Al Stillman and Alan Moran
    staging: Catherine Littlefield
    sets: Bruno Maine
    costumes: Grace Huston, Billy Livingston and Katherine
                    Kuhn
Productions:
    Opened May 26, 1949 for 430 performances
Reviews:
    New York Times page 24, May 27, 1949

The Human Comedy
    book: William Dumaresq, based on the novel by William
                    Saroyan
    music: Galt MacDermot
    lyrics: William Dumaresq
    staging: Wilford Leach
    sets: Bob Shaw
    costumes: Rita Ryack
Productions:
    (Off-Broadway) Opened December 28, 1983 for 79 performances
    Opened April 5, 1984 for 13 performances
Reviews:
    New York 17:57-8, Jan 9, 1984
    New York Theatre Critics' Reviews 1984:320
    New York Times III, page 15, Dec 29, 1983

II, page 6, Apr 1, 1984
III, page 17, Apr 5, 1984
II, page 9, Apr 15, 1984
New Yorker 59:105, Jan 9, 1984
Newsweek 103:78, Apr 16, 1984
Playboy 22:78, Jan 1975
Time 123:75, Feb 6, 1984

Humming Sam
    book: Eileen Nutter
    music: Alexander Hill
    staging: Carey and Davis
Productions:
    Opened April 8, 1933 for one performance
Reviews:
    New York Times page 8, Apr 10, 1933

Hurry, Harry
    book: Jeremiah Morris, Lee Kalcheim and Susan Perkins
    music: Bill Weeden
    lyrics: David Finkle
    staging: Jeremiah Morris
    sets: Fred Voelpel
    costumes: Sara Brook
    choreography: Gerald Teijelo
Productions:
    Opened October 12, 1972 for 2 performances
Reviews:
    New York Theatre Critics' Reviews 1972:220

-I-

I Can Get It for You Wholesale
    book: Jerome Weidman, based on his novel
    music: Harold Rome
    lyrics: Harold Rome
    staging: Arthur Laurents
    sets: Will Steven Armstrong
    costumes: Theoni V. Aldredge
    choreography: Herbert Ross
Productions:
    Opened March 22, 1962 for 300 performances
Reviews:
    Dance Magazine 36:18, May 1962
    Life 52:103-4, May 18, 1962
    Nation 194:338, Apr 14, 1962
    New York Theatre Critics' Reviews 1962:314+
    New York Times page 29, Mar 23, 1962

Newsweek 59:58, Apr 2, 1962
Saturday Review 45:28, Apr 14, 1962
Theatre Arts 46:58+, May 1962
Time 79:46, Mar 30, 1962

I Can't Keep Running in Place

book:	Barbara Schottenfeld
music:	Barbara Schottenfeld
lyrics:	Barbara Schottenfeld
staging:	Susan Einhorn
sets:	Ursula Belden
costumes:	Christina Weppner
choreography:	Baayork Lee

Productions:
  (Off-Off-Broadway) Opened February 21, 1980
  (Off-Broadway) Opened May 14, 1981 for 45 performances
Reviews:
  New York 14:97-8, May 25, 1981
  New York Times page 13, Mar 1, 1980
              III, page 4, May 15, 1981

I Do! I Do!

book:	Tom Jones; based on Jan de Hartog's play The Fourposter
music:	Harvey Schmidt
lyrics:	Tom Jones
staging:	Gower Champion
sets:	Oliver Smith
costumes:	Freddy Wittop

Productions:
  Opened December 5, 1966 for 560 performances
  (Off-Off-Broadway) Opened May 19, 1977
Reviews:
  America 116:263, Feb 18, 1967
  Christian Century 84:144, Feb 1, 1967
  Commonweal 85:402-3, Jan 13, 1967
  Life 62:16, Jan 13, 1967
      62:82-5, Jan 13, 1967
  Los Angeles 25:248, Jul 1980
  Nation 204:29-30, Jan 2, 1967
  New West 5:SC-26, Jul 14, 1980
  New York Theatre Critics' Reviews 1966:217
  New York Times page 58, Dec 6, 1966
              II, page 3, Dec 18, 1966
              page 54, Nov 28, 1967
              page 38, Jun 18, 1968
  New Yorker 42:117, Dec 17, 1966
  Newsweek 68:106, Dec 19, 1966
  People 31:89-90, May 1, 1989
  Saturday Review 49:61+, Dec 24, 1966
  Time 88:87, Dec 16, 1966

I Dreamt I Dwelt in Bloomingdale's
    book: Jack Ramer
    music: Ernest McCarty
    lyrics: Jack Ramer and Ernest McCarty
    staging: David Dunham
    sets: Ed Wittstein
    choreography: Bick Goss
Productions:
    (Off-Broadway)   Opened February 12, 1970 for 6 performances
Reviews:
    New York Times page 26, Feb 13, 1970
    New Yorker 46:67, Feb 21, 1970

I Feel Wonderful
    sketches: Barry Alan Grael
    music: Jerry Herman
    lyrics: Jerry Herman
Productions:
    (Off-Broadway) Opened Season of 1954-1955
Reviews:
    Catholic World 180:228, Dec 1954
    New York Times page 22, Oct 19, 1954
    Saturday Review 37:38, Nov 6, 1954

I Had a Ball
    book: Jerome Chodorov
    music: Jack Lawrence and Stan Freeman
    lyrics: Jack Lawrence and Stan Freeman
    staging: Lloyd Richards
    sets: Will Steven Armstrong
    costumes: Ann Roth
    choreography: Onna White and Tom Panko
Productions:
    Opened December 15, 1964 for 199 performances
Reviews:
    America 112:335-6, Mar 6, 1965
    New York Theatre Critics' Reviews 1964:107+
    New York Times page 50, Dec 16, 1964
    New Yorker 40:50, Dec 26, 1964
    Newsweek 64:57, Dec 28, 1964
    Saturday Review 48:32, Jan 2, 1965
    Time 84:62, Dec 25, 1964

I Have a Dream
    conceived: Robert Greenwald
    book: Josh Greenfeld, based on the words of Dr.
                    Martin Luther King
    songs: Various authors and composers
    staging: Robert Greenwald
    sets: Donald Harris
    costumes: Terence Tam Soon

Productions:
  Opened September 20, 1976 for 80 performances
  (Off-Off-Broadway) Opened December 19, 1985 for 24 performances
Reviews:
  New York 9:73, Oct 4, 1976
  New York Theatre Critics' Reviews 1976:86
  New York Times II, page 7, April 11, 1976
                 page 32, September 21, 1976
                 III, page 12, Dec 31, 1985

I Hear Music ... of Frank Loesser and Friends
  assembled: Jo Sullivan (Mrs. Frank Loesser)
  songs: Frank Loesser, George Gershwin, Richard Rodgers,
                   Kurt Weill, Stephen Sondheim, Giacomo Puccini,
                   Jule Styne, and others
  staging: Donald Saddler
  costumes: Robert Mackintosh
Productions:
  (Off-Broadway) Opened October 29, 1984 for 32 performances
No Reviews.

I Love My Wife
  book: Michael Stewart, based on Luis Rego's Viens
                   Chez Moi, J'Habite Chez une Copine
  music: Cy Coleman
  lyrics: Michael Stewart
  staging: Gene Saks
  sets: David Mitchell
  costumes: Ron Talsky
  choreography: Onna White
Productions:
  Opened April 17, 1977 for 872 performances
Reviews:
  Dance Magazine 51:20-2, Aug 1977
  Los Angeles 25:278+, May 1980
  New York 10:69, May 2, 1977
  New York Theatre Critics' Reviews 1977:274
  New York Times page 47, April 18, 1977
                 II, page 5, May 1, 1977
                 III, page 24, May 16, 1979
  New Yorker 53:92, Apr 25, 1977
  Time 109:87, May 2, 1977

I Married an Angel
  book: Richard Rodgers and Lorenz Hart, adapted from
                   John Veszary's Hungarian play
  music: Richard Rodgers
  lyrics: Lorenz Hart
  staging: Joshua Logan
  sets: Jo Mielziner
  costumes: John Hambleton
  choreography: George Balanchine

Productions:
    Opened May 11, 1938 for 338 performances
    (Off-Off-Broadway) Opened May 17, 1986
Reviews:
    Catholic World 147:474-5, Jul 1938
    Commonweal 28:133, May 27, 1938
    Life 4:48-9, May 30, 1938
    New York Times page 26, May 12, 1938
                    XI, page 1, May 22, 1938
                    IX, page 8, Jul 17, 1938
                    page 28, Aug 9, 1977
                    III, page 23, May 21, 1986
    Newsweek 11:20, May 23, 1938
    Stage 15:13-15, Jun 1938
    Theatre Arts 22:464, Jul 1938
    Time 31:20, May 23, 1938

I Remember Mama
    book: Thomas Meehan, based on the play I Remember
                     Mama by John Van Druten and stories by Kath-
                     ryn Forbes
    music: Richard Rodgers
    lyrics: Martin Charnin
    staging: Cy Feuer
    sets: David Mitchell
    costumes: Theoni V. Aldredge
    choreography: Danny Daniels
Productions:
    Opened May 31, 1979 for 108 performances
Reviews:
    New Leader 62:23-4, Jun 18, 1979
    New York 12:60-1, May 14, 1979
    New York Theatre Critics' Reviews 1979:227
    New York Times III, page 3, Jun 1, 1979
                    II, page 5, Jun 10, 1979
    New Yorker 55:79, Jun 11, 1979
    Newsweek 93:75, Jun 11, 1979
    Time 113:62, Jun 11, 1979

I Want You
    book: Stefan Kanfer and Jess J. Korman
    music: Stefan Kanfer, Jess J. Korman and Joseph Gray-
                     hon
    lyrics: Stefan Kanfer, Jess J. Korman and Joseph Gray-
                     hon
    staging: Theodore J. Flicker
Productions:
    (Off-Broadway) Opened September 14, 1961 for 4 performances
Reviews:
    New York Times page 29, Sep 15, 1961
                    page 10, Sep 16, 1961

Ice Follies of 1942
    Productions:
    (Off-Broadway)   Opened December 1941
No Reviews.

Icetime of 1948
    assembled: Sonja Henie and Arthur M. Wirtz
    music: James Littlefield and John Fortis
    lyrics: James Littlefield and John Fortis
    songs: Al Stillman and Paul McGrane
    staging: Catherine Littlefield
    sets: Bruno Maine and Edward Gilbert
    costumes: Lou Eisele, Billy Livingston, Katherine Kuhn
    choreography: Catherine Littlefield and Dorothie Littlefield
Productions:
Opened May 28, 1947 for 422 performances
Reviews:
    Life 24:120-21, Mar 8, 1948
    New York Times page 28, May 29, 1947
                    II, page 3, Nov 9, 1947
    Newsweek 32:86, Oct 25, 1948
    Time 49:54, Jun 9, 1947

I'd Rather Be Right
    book: George S. Kaufman and Moss Hart
    music: Richard Rodgers
    lyrics: Lorenz Hart
    staging: George S. Kaufman
    sets: Donald Oenslager
    costumes: Irene Sharaff
    choreography: Charles Weidman
Productions:
Opened November 2, 1937 for 290 performances
Reviews:
    Catholic World 146:339-40, Dec 1937
    Commonweal 27:106, Nov 19, 1937
    Independent Woman 16:351, Nov 1937
    Life 3:27-9, Oct 25, 1937
    Literary Digest 1:35, Nov 20, 1937
    New Republic 93:44, Nov 17, 1937
    New York Times page 27, Oct 12, 1937
                    IX, page 2, Oct 17, 1937
                    page 18, Oct 26, 1937
                    page 28, Nov 3, 1937
                    XI, page 2, Nov 7, 1937
    Newsweek 10:24-6, Oct 25, 1937
            10:29, Nov 15, 1937
    Scholastic 31:2, Oct 30, 1937
    Scribner's Magazine 103:70, Jan 1938
    Stage 15:52-4, Nov 1937
        15:94, Nov 1937
        15:56-9, Dec 1937

Theatre Arts 21:924+, Dec 1937
Time 30:45, Oct 25, 1937
      30:25, Nov 15, 1937
Vogue 90:108+, Dec 1, 1937

If the Shoe Fits
  book: June Carroll and Robert Duke
  music: David Raksin
  lyrics: June Carroll and Robert Duke
  staging: Eugene Bryden
  sets: Edward Gilbert
  costumes: Kathryn Kuhn
  choreography: Charles Weidman
Productions:
  Opened December 5, 1946 for 21 performances
Reviews:
  New York Theatre Critics' Reviews 1946:226+
  New York Times II, page 1, Dec 1, 1946
                  page 29, Dec 6, 1946
  New Yorker 22:64, Dec 14, 1946

I'll Die If I Can't Live Forever
  book: Karen Johnson, additional material by William
                    Brooke
  music: Joyce Stoner
  lyrics: Joyce Stoner
  staging: Joyce Stoner
  sets: Irving Milton Duke
Productions:
  (Off-Broadway) Opened October 31, 1974 for 81 performances
Reviews:
  Saturday Review 2:39-40, Mar 22, 1975

I'll Say She Is
  book: Will B. Johnstone
  music: Tom Johnstone
  lyrics: Will B. Johnstone
  staging: Eugene Sanger and Vaughan Godfrey
Productions:
  Opened May 19, 1924 for (32) performances
Reviews:
  New York Times page 15, May 20, 1924
  Theatre Magazine 40:16, Aug 1924

The Illustrator's Show
  assembled by: The Society of Illustrators, edited by Tom
                    Weatherly
  music: Frank Loesser and Irving Actman
  lyrics: Frank Loesser and Irving Actman
  staging: Tom Weatherly
  sets: Arne Lundborg

```
costumes:          Carl Sidney
choreography:      Carl Randall
Productions:
   Opened January 22, 1936 for 5 performances
Reviews:
   New York Times page 25, Jan 23, 1936
```

Illya Darling

```
   book:              Jules Dassin; based on the movie Never on Sun-
                      day
   music:             Manos Hadjidakis
   lyrics:            Joe Darion
   staging:           Jules Dassin
   sets:              Oliver Smith
   costumes:          Theoni V. Aldredge
   choreography:      Onna White and Tommy Panko
Productions:
   Opened April 11, 1967 for 318 performances
Reviews:
   America 116:737-8, May 13, 1967
   Commonweal 86:342-5, Jun 9, 1967
   Dance Magazine 41:38, Jun 1967
   New York Theatre Critics' Reviews 1967:328
   New York Times page 37, Apr 12, 1967
                    II, page 1, Apr 30, 1967
                    page 58, Nov 2, 1967
                    page 50, Jan 3, 1968
   Newsweek 69:107, Apr 24, 1967
   Saturday Review 50:47, Apr 29, 1967
   Time 89:83, Apr 21, 1967
```

I'm Getting My Act Together and Taking It On the Road

```
   book:              Gretchen Cryer
   music:             Nancy Ford
   lyrics:            Gretchen Cryer
   staging:           Word Baker
   costumes:          Pearl Somner
Productions:
   (Off-Broadway) Opened May 16, 1978 for 1,165 performances
Reviews:
   Horizon 22:60-4, Jan 1979
   Los Angeles 26:217, Jan 1981
   Ms. 7:49, Dec 1978
   Nation 228:155, Feb 10, 1979
   New York 11:74-5, Jul 3, 1978
   New York Times III, page 17, Jun 15, 1978
                   II, page 2, July 9, 1978
   New Yorker 54:51+, Jun 26, 1978
```

I'm Solomon

```
   book:              Anne Croswell and Dan Almagor; based on the
```

play <u>King Solomon and the Cobbler</u> by Sammy
Gronemann
music: Ernest Gold
lyrics: Anne Croswell
staging: Michael Benthall
sets: Rouben Ter-Arutunian
choreography: Dorothea Freitag
Productions:
Opened April 23, 1968 for 7 performances
Reviews:
New York Theatre Critics' Reviews 1968:297
New York Times page 51, Apr 24, 1968
               page 42, Apr 30, 1968
New Yorker 44:129, May 4, 1968

<u>In a Pig's Valise</u>
book: Eric Overmyer
music: August Darnell
lyrics: Eric Overmyer
staging: Graciela Daniele
Productions:
(Off-Off-Broadway) Opened January 11, 1989 for 57 performances
Reviews:
New York 22:138, Feb 27, 1989
New York Theatre Critics' Reviews 1989:314
New York Times III, page 15, Feb 15, 1989
New Yorker 65:66-7, Feb 27, 1989

<u>In Gay Company</u> (see <u>Gay Company</u>)

<u>In Hayti</u>
book: John J. McNally
music: Jerome and Schwartz
lyrics: Jerome and Schwartz
staging: Julian Alfred
Productions:
Opened August 30, 1909 for 56 performances
Reviews:
Dramatic Mirror 62:5, Sep 11, 1909
Theatre Magazine 10:xv, Oct 1909

<u>In the House of Blues</u>
by: David Charles
staging: Buddy Butler
sets: Llewellyn Harrison
costumes: Judy Dearing
choreography: Hope Clarke
Productions:
(Off-Off-Broadway) Opened December 5, 1985
Reviews:
New York Times III, page 23, Dec 18, 1985
New Yorker 61:60, Dec 30, 1985

In the Nick of Time
    contributors: Barbara Fried, Charles Appel, Herb Suffrin,
                       Leni Stern, Sue Lawless and Ted Pugh
    staging: Earl Durham
Productions:
    (Off-Broadway) Opened June 1, 1967 for 22 performances
Reviews:
    Commonweal 86:394, Jun 23, 1967
    New York Times page 36, Jun 2, 1967

In Trousers
    book: William Finn
    music: William Finn
    lyrics: William Finn
    staging: Matt Casella
    sets: Santo Loquasto
    costumes: Madeline Ann Graneto
Productions:
    (Off-Off-Broadway) Opened February 21, 1979 for 28 performances
    (Off-Off-Broadway) Opened March 22, 1981
    (Off-Broadway) Opened March 26, 1985 for 16 performances
Reviews:
    New York 18:96, Apr 15, 1985
    New York Times page 12, Mar 17, 1979
                    III, page 20, Mar 4, 1981
                    III, page 19, Mar 27, 1985

Inacent Black
    by: A. Marcus Hemphill
    original music: McFadden & Whitehead & Moore
    original lyrics: McFadden & Whitehead & Moore
    staging: Mikell Pinkney
    sets: Felix E. Cochren
    costumes: Marty Pakledinaz
Productions:
    Opened May 6, 1981 for 14 performances
Reviews:
    New York Theatre Critics' Reviews 1981:242
    New York Times III, page 19, May 7, 1981

Inner City
    conceived: Tom O'Horgan; based on the book The Inner
                       City Mother Goose, by Eve Merriam
    music: Helen Miller
    lyrics: Eve Merriam
    staging: Tom O'Horgan
    sets: Robin Wagner
    costumes: Joseph G. Aulisi
Productions:
    Opened December 19, 1971 for 97 performances
Reviews:
    Nation 214:81, Jan 10, 1972

New York Theatre Critics' Reviews 1971:147
New York Times page 40, Sep 15, 1971
                 page 48, Dec 20, 1971
                 II, page 1, Dec 26, 1971
                 II, page 18, Feb 13, 1972

Innocent Eyes
    book: Harold Atteridge
    music: Sigmund Romberg and Jean Schwartz
    lyrics: Harold Atteridge and Tot Seymour
Productions:
Opened May 20, 1924 for 126 performances
Reviews:
    New York Times page 22, May 21, 1924
                   page 8, Aug 22, 1924
    Theatre Magazine 40:15, Aug 1924

Inside U.S.A.
    sketches: Arnold Auerbach, Moss Hart, Arnold B. Horwitt,
                    suggested by John Gunther's book
    music: Arthur Schwartz
    lyrics: Howard Dietz
    staging: Victor Samrock
    sets: Lemuel Ayers
    costumes: Eleanor Goldsmith and Castillo
    choreography: Helen Tamiris
Productions:
Opened April 30, 1948 for 399 performances
Reviews:
    Catholic World 167:265, Jun 1948
    Collier's 121:24-5+, May 15, 1948
    Commonweal 48:100, May 14, 1948
    Harper 196:478-80, May 1948
    Life 24:135-6+, May 17, 1948
    New Republic 118:35-6, May 17, 1948
    New York Theatre Critics' Reviews 1948:279+
    New York Times page 27, Mar 30, 1948
                   page 19, May 1, 1948
                   II, page 1, May 23, 1948
                   II, page 6, Jun 13, 1948
                   II, page 1, Aug 29, 1948
                   page 34, Jun 9, 1949
    New Yorker 24:52+, May 8, 1948
    Newsweek 31:76, May 10, 1948
    Saturday Review 31:25, May 22, 1948
    Theatre Arts 32:14-15+, Jun 1948
    Time 51:80, May 10, 1948
    Vogue 111:137, May 1, 1948

The International
    book: John Howard Lawson

music: Edward A. Ziman
staging: John Howard Lawson
Productions:
Opened January 12, 1928 for 27 performances
Reviews:
Life (New York) 92:21, Feb 2, 1928
Nation 126:130, Feb 1, 1928

The International Cup, the Ballet of Niagra and the Earthquake
written: R. H. Burnside
music: Manuel Klein
lyrics: Manuel Klein
staging: R. H. Burnside
Productions:
Opened September 3, 1910 for 333 performances
Reviews:
Theatre Magazine 12:110, Oct 1910

The International Revue
book: Nat N. Dorfman and Lew Leslie
music: Jimmy McHugh
lyrics: Dorothy Fields
staging: Lew Leslie and E. C. Lilley
choreography: Busby Berkeley and Harry Crosley
Productions:
Opened February 25, 1930 for 95 performances
Reviews:
Life (New York) 95:18, Mar 28, 1930
New York Times VIII, page 4, Feb 9, 1930
                page 22, Feb 26, 1930
Outlook 155:109, May 21, 1930

Into the Light
book: Jeff Tambornino
music: Lee Holdridge
lyrics: John Forster
staging: Michael Maurer
sets: Neil Peter Jampolis and Hervig Libowitsky
costumes: Karen Roston
choreography: Mary Jane Houdina
Productions:
Opened October 22, 1986 for 6 performances
Reviews:
America 156:283, Apr 4, 1987
New York 19:111-12, Nov 3, 1986
New York Theatre Critics' Reviews 1986:175
New York Times III, page 19, Oct 23, 1986
New Yorker 62:145-6, Nov 3, 1986

Into the Woods
book: James Lapine

music: Stephen Sondheim
lyrics: Stephen Sondheim
staging: James Lapine
sets: Tony Straiges
costumes: Ann Hould-Ward, based on original concepts of
                    Patricia Zipprodt and Ann Hould-Ward
choreography: Lar Lubovitch
Productions:
Opened November 5, 1987 for *655 performances (still running
6/1/89)
Reviews:
America 157:458, Dec 12, 1987
Commonweal 115:18-19, Jan 15, 1988
Dance Magazine 62:64, Jan 1988
Horizon 31:27-8, Jan/Feb 1988
Jet 74:56-7, Jun 13, 1988
Nation 245:726-7, Dec 12, 1987
New Leader 70:18-19, Dec 28, 1987
New Republic 197:29-30, Dec 21, 1987
New York 20:50-1, Sep 21, 1987
          20:74-6+, Sep 28, 1987
          20:109-10, Nov 16, 1987
New York Theatre Critics' Reviews 1987:132
New York Times III, page 5, Nov 6, 1987
            II, page 1, Nov 29, 1987
New Yorker 63:147-8, Nov 16, 1987
Newsweek 110:106-7, Nov 16, 1987
Theatre Crafts 22:28-32+, Jan 1988
Time 130:96-7, Nov 16, 1987
Vogue 178:118, Feb 1988

Iole
book: Robert W. Chambers and Ben Teal
music: William Frederick
lyrics: Robert W. Chambers and Ben Teal
staging: Ben Teal
Productions:
Opened December 29, 1913 for 24 performances
Reviews:
Blue Book 18:1046-7, Apr 1914
Dramatic Mirror 70:6-7, Dec 31, 1913
                71:2, Jan 7, 1914
Green Book 11:521, Mar 1914
Leslie's Weekly 118:107, Jan 29, 1914
New York Life 63:110, Jan 15, 1914
New York Dramatic News 58:20, Jan 3, 1914
New York Times page 11, Dec 9, 1913
              VII, page 6, Dec 28, 1913
Theatre Magazine 19:55+, Feb 1914
                 19:106, Feb 1914

Ionescopade
  conceived: Robert Allan Ackerman, adapted from the works
                     of Eugene Ionesco
  music: Mildred Kayden
  lyrics: Mildred Kayden
  staging: Robert Allan Ackerman
  sets: David Sackeroff
  costumes: Patricia Adshead
  choreography: Merry Lynn Katis
Productions:
  (Off-Off-Broadway) Opened July 26, 1973
  (Off-Broadway) Opened April 25, 1974 for 14 performances
Reviews:
  New York Times page 16, Jul 28, 1973
               page 29, Apr 26, 1974
  New Yorker 50:76-7, May 6, 1974

Ipi-Tombi
  conceived: Bertha Egnos, based on South African black
                     tribal languages
  original music: Bertha Egnos
  lyrics: Gail Lakier
  staging: Bertha Egnos
  sets: Eliz. MacLeish
  costumes: David Toser
  choreography: Sheila Wartski, with Neil McKay and members of
                     the cast
Productions:
  Opened January 12, 1977 for 39 performances
Reviews:
  New York 10:68, Jan 31, 1977
  New York Theatre Critics' Reviews 1977:384
  New York Times page 47, Jan 13, 1977
  New Yorker 52:63, Jan 24, 1977
  Time 109:55-6, Jan 24, 1977

Irene (1919)
  book: James Montgomery
  music: Harry Tierney
  lyrics: Joe McCarthy
Productions:
  Opened November 18, 1919 for 228 performances
Reviews:
  Dramatic Mirror 80:1861, Dec 4, 1919
  New York Times page 11, Nov 19, 1919

Irene (1973)
  book: Hugh Wheeler and Joseph Stein; from an adaption
                     by Harry Rigby of the original 1919 musical
  music: Harry Tierney (original)
  lyrics: Joe McCarthy (original)

additional music:	Charles Gaynor and Otis Clements
additional lyrics:	Charles Gaynor and Otis Clements
staging:	Gower Champion
sets:	Raoul Pene du Bois
costumes:	Raoul Pene du Bois
choreography:	Peter Gennaro

Productions:
Opened March 13, 1973 for 604 performances
Reviews:
America 128:336, Apr 14, 1973
Dance Magazine 47:58D-59+, Jun 1973
Nation 216:444-5, Apr 2, 1973
National Review 25:473-4, Apr 27, 1973
New York 6:62+, Mar 12, 1973
New York Theatre Critics' Reviews 1973:328
New York Times II, page 1, Feb 25, 1973
        page 28, Mar 14, 1973
        page 16, Feb 8, 1974
New Yorker 49:74, Mar 24, 1973
Newsweek 81:56, Mar 26, 1973
Playboy 20:49, Jun 1973
Saturday Evening Post 246:52-3, Apr 1974
Time 101:101, Mar 26, 1973

Irma La Douce
book:	Julian More, David Heneker and Monty Norman, English version of the original book by Alexandre Breffort
music:	Marguerite Monnot
lyrics:	Julian More, David Heneker and Monty Norman, English version of the original lyrics by Alex- andre Breffort
staging:	Peter Brook
sets:	Rolf Gerard
costumes:	Rolf Gerard
choreography:	Onna White

Productions:
Opened September 29, 1960 for 524 performances
Reviews:
America 104:130+, Oct 22, 1960
Commonweal 73:152, Nov 4, 1960
Coronet 49:14, Jan 1961
Dance Magazine 34:32, Dec 1960
Life 49:53+, Nov 14, 1960
Nation 188:462, May 16, 1959
    191:253, Oct 15, 1960
New Republic 143:21-2, Oct 17, 1960
New York Theatre Critics' Reviews 1960:230+
New York Times II, page 3, Sep 25, 1960

page 31, Sep 30, 1960
II, page 1, Oct 16, 1960
II, page 1, Oct 30, 1960
New Yorker 36:95, Oct 8, 1960
Newsweek 56:65, Oct 10, 1960
Saturday Review 43:36, Oct 15, 1960
Time 76:84, Oct 10, 1960

Is There Life After High School?

book: Jeffrey Kindley, suggested by the book by Ralph Keyes
music: Craig Carnelia
lyrics: Carig Carnelia
staging: Robert Nigro
sets: John Lee Beatty
costumes: Carol Oditz
Productions:
Opened May 7, 1982 for 12 performances
Reviews:
Los Angeles 29:44+, Apr 1984
New York Theatre Critics' Reviews 1982:295
New York Times page 17, May 8, 1982
New Yorker 58:114-15, May 17, 1982

Isn't It Romantic (see Michael Feinstein in Concert)

It Happens on Ice

assembled: Sonja Henie and Arthur Wirtz
lyrics: Al Stillman
songs: Vernon Duke, Fred E. Ahlert and Peter de Rose
staging: Leon Leonidoff
sets: Norman Bel Geddes
costumes: Norman Bel Geddes
choreography: Catherine Littlefield and Robert Linden
Productions:
Opened October 10, 1940 for 180 performances
Opened April 4, 1941 for 96 performances
Opened July 15, 1941 for 386 performances
Reviews:
New York Theatre Critics' Reviews 1940:259
                                   1941:340
                                   1941:472
New York Times page 24, Oct 11, 1940
II, page 1, Nov 3, 1940
page 13, Apr 5, 1941
IX, page 1, Aug 31, 1941
page 25, Feb 17, 1942
page 18, Apr 6, 1942
Scholastic 37:36, Jan 13, 1941
Stage 1:12, Nov 1940
Theatre Arts 24:847-8+, Dec 1940
Time 36:71, Oct 21, 1940

It's a Bird It's a Plane It's SUPERMAN
    book: David Newman and Robert Benton; based on the
                    comic strip "Superman"
    music: Charles Strouse
    lyrics: Lee Adams
    staging: Harold Prince
    sets: Robert Randolph
    costumes: Florence Klotz
    choreography: Betty Walberg
Productions:
    Opened March 29, 1966 for 129 performances
Reviews:
    America 114:704, May 14, 1966
    Commonweal 84:156, Apr 22, 1966
    Dance Magazine 40:25, May 1966
    Life 60:25, Mar 11, 1966
    New York Theatre Critics' Reviews 1966:310
    New York Times II, page 1, Mar 27, 1966
                  page 34, Mar 30, 1966
                  page 15, Jul 16, 1966
    New Yorker 42:81, Apr 9, 1966
    Newsweek 67:94, Apr 11, 1966
    Saturday Review 49:62, Apr 16, 1966
    Time 78:81, Apr 8, 1966

It's About Time
    sketches: Peter Barry, Arnold Horwitt, Arthur Elmer,
                    Sam Locke, David Gregory, and Reuben Shipp
    music: Will Lorin, Al Moss and Genevieve Pitot
    lyrics: David Gregory
    sets: William Martin and Walter Ketchum
Productions:
    (Off-Broadway) Opened March 28, 1942
Reviews:
    New York Times page 28, Mar 31, 1942

It's Better With a Band
    words and
    music: Wally Harper, Doug Datsaros, Rob LaRocco, Alan
                    Menken, Jimmy Roberts, Jonathon Sheffer, Bryon
                    Sommers and Pamala Stanley
    lyrics: David Zippel
    staging: Joseph Leonardo
    sets: Michael J. Hotopp and Paul de Pass
    costumes: Cinthia Waas
Productions:
    (Off-Broadway) Opened March 28, 1983 for 47 performances
Reviews:
    New York Times III, page 16, February 14, 1983

It's Me, Sylvia
    book: Sylvia Miles, based on her life

music: Galt MacDermot
lyrics: Sylvia Miles
staging: Arthur Sherman
sets: Eugene Lee
costumes: Clifford Capone
Productions:
  (Off-Broadway)   Opened April 13, 1981 for 9 performances
Reviews:
  New York Times III, page 28, Apr 15, 1981

It's So Nice To Be Civilized
  book: Micki Grant
  music: Micki Grant
  lyrics: Micki Grant
  staging: Frank Corsaro
  sets: Charles E. Hoefler
  costumes: Ruth Morley
  choreography: Mabel Robinson
Productions:
  Opened June 3, 1980 for 8 performances
Reviews:
  New York Theatre Critics' Reviews 1980:220
  New York Times III, page 22, June 4, 1980

It's Up to You
  book: Augustin MacHugh, Douglas Leavitt, Edward
                    Paulton and Harry Clarke
  lyrics: Augustin MacHugh, Douglas Leavitt, Edward
                    Paulton and Harry Clarke
  staging: Frank Stammers
Productions:
  Opened March 24, 1921 for 24 performances
Reviews:
  Dramatic Mirror 83:601, Apr 2, 1921
  New York Life 77:536, Apr 14, 1921
  New York Clipper 69:19, Apr 6, 1921
  New York Times page 20, Mar 29, 1921
  Theatre Magazine 33:460, Jun 1921

It's Wilde!
  book: Burton Wolfe
  music: Randy Klein
  lyrics: Burton Wolfe
  staging: Burton Wolfe
  sets: John Falabella
  costumes: James Corry
  choreography: Buck Heller
Productions:
  (Off-Broadway)   Opened May 21, 1980 for 7 performances
Reviews:
  New York Times III, page 7, May 23, 1980

I've Got the Tune
    book: Mark Blitzstein
    music: Mark Blitzstein
    lyrics: Mark Blitzstein
Productions:
    (Off-Broadway) Opened April 1939
    (Off-Broadway) Opened June 24, 1939
No Reviews.

-J-

Jack and Jill
    book: Frederick Isham and Otto Harbach
    music: John Murray Anderson and A. Barratt
    lyrics: John Murray Anderson and A. Barratt
Productions:
    Opened March 22, 1923 for 92 performances
Reviews:
    Life (New York) 81:20, Apr 12, 1923
    New York Clipper 71:14, Mar 28, 1923
    New York Times page 17, Mar 23, 1923
    Theatre Magazine 37:16, May 1923
                      38:18, Sep 1923

Jack O'Lantern
    book: Anne Caldwell and R. H. Burnside
    music: Ivan Caryll
    staging: R. H. Burnside
Productions:
    Opened October 16, 1917 for 265 performances
Reviews:
    Dramatic Mirror 77:7, Oct 27, 1917
    Green Book 19:8+, Jan 1918
    Life (New York) 70:714, Nov 1, 1917
    Munsey 64:430, Jul 1918
    New York Dramatic Mirror 64:6, Oct 27, 1917
    New York Times page 13, Oct 17, 1917
    Theatre Magazine 26:392, Dec 1917

Jackpot
    book: Guy Bolton, Sidney Sheldon, Ben Roberts
    music: Vernon Duke
    lyrics: Howard Dietz
    staging: Roy Hargrave
    sets: Raymond Sovey and Robert Edmund Jones
    costumes: Kiviette
    choreography: Lauretta Jefferson and Charles Weidman
Productions:
    Opened January 13, 1944 for 69 performances
Reviews:
    New York Theatre Critics' Reviews 1944:284+

New York Times page 15, Jan 14, 1944
            II, page 1, Jan 30, 1944
New Yorker 19:34+, Jan 22, 1944
Theatre Arts 28:142, Mar 1944

Jacques Brel Is Alive and Well and Living in Paris
   music: Jacques Brel
   lyrics: Eric Blau and Mort Shuman; based on lyrics and
                   commentary by Jacques Brel
   staging: Moni Yakim
   sets: Henry E. Scott III
   costumes: Ilka Suarez
Productions:
   (Off-Broadway) Opened January 22, 1968 for 1,847 performances
   Opened September 15, 1972 for 51 performances
   (Off-Broadway) Opened May 17, 1974 for 125 performances
   Opened February 19, 1981 for 21 performances
   (Off-Broadway) Opened May 15, 1983 for 48 performances
   (Off-Off-Broadway) Opened January 3, 1985
Reviews:
   Nation 206:318, Mar 4, 1968
   New York Theatre Critics' Reviews 1972:248
   New York Times page 25, Jan 23, 1968
                  page 43, Jan 27, 1972
                  page 39, Feb 28, 1972
                  page 39, May 20, 1974
                  XXII, page 24, Dec 11, 1977
                  page 26, Jan 21, 1978
                  III, page 6, Feb 20, 1981
                  III, page 13, May 24, 1983
                  XXIII, page 11, Jul 3, 1983
                  III, page 16, Jan 8, 1985
   Newsweek 80:98, Oct 30, 1972
   Saturday Review 51:26, Apr 27, 1968

Jamaica
   book: E. Y. Harburg and Fred Saidy
   music: Harold Arlen
   lyrics: E. Y. Harburg
   staging: Robert Lewis
   sets: Oliver Smith
   costumes: Miles White
   choreography: Jack Cole
Productions:
   Opened October 31, 1957 for 555 performances
Reviews:
   America 98:436, Jan 11, 1958
   Catholic World 186:304-5, Jan 1958
   Dance Magazine 31:13, Dec 1957
   Life 43:112+, Nov 18, 1957
   Nation 185:394, Nov 23, 1957

New York Theatre Critics' Reviews 1957:196+
New York Times VI, page 28, Aug 25, 1957
              page 32, Nov 1, 1957
              II, page 1, Nov 10, 1957
New York Times Magazine pages 72-3, Oct 13, 1957
New Yorker 33:103, Nov 9, 1957
Newsweek 50:83, Nov 11, 1957
Saturday Review 40:48, Nov 16, 1957
Theatre Arts 41:73-4+, Oct 1957
              42:17, Jan 1958
Time 70:93, Nov 11, 1957

The James Joyce Memorial Liquid Theatre
  conceived: Steven Kent
  music: Jack Rowe, Robert Walker and Lance Larsen
  staging: Steven Kent
  sets: Donald Harris
Productions:
  (Off-Broadway) Opened October 11, 1971 for 189 performances
Reviews:
  New York Theatre Critics' Reviews 1971:210
  New York Times page 44, Aug 26, 1971
                 page 51, Oct 12, 1971
                 II, page 1, Oct 17, 1971

James Joyce's Dubliners
  book: J. W. Riordan, based on My Brother's Keeper
                   by Stanislaus Joyce
  music: Philip Campanella
  lyrics: Philip Campanella
  staging: Gene Feist
  sets: Holmes Easley
  costumes: Christina Giannini
Productions:
  (Off-Broadway) Opened February 25, 1975 for 80 performances
Reviews:
  New York 8:72, Apr 14, 1975
  New York Theatre Critics' Reviews 1975:253
  New York Times page 24, Mar 25, 1975

Jane White, Who?...
  by: Jane White and Joe Masteroff
  songs: Various authors and composers
Productions:
  (Off-Broadway) Opened January 29, 1980 for 51 performances
No Reviews.

Janis, Elsie (see Elsie Janis)

Jennie
  book: Arnold Schulman, suggested by Marguerite Court-
                   ney's biography Laurette

music: Arthur Schwartz
lyrics: Howard Dietz
staging: Vincent J. Donehue
sets: George Jenkins
costumes: Irene Sharaff
choreography: Matt Mattox
Productions:
    Opened October 17, 1963 for 82 performances
Reviews:
    America 109: 644, Nov 16, 1963
    New York Theatre Critics' Reviews 1963: 234+
    New York Times II, page 1, Oct 13, 1963
                    page 35, Oct 18, 1963
                    page 21, Dec 20, 1963
    New Yorker 39: 113, Oct 26, 1963
    Newsweek 62: 91, Oct 28, 1963
    Saturday Review 46: 18, Nov 2, 1963
    Theatre Arts 48: 67, Jan 1964
    Time 82: 75, Oct 25, 1963

Jerome Kern Goes to Hollywood
    conceived: David Kernan
    written: Dick Vosburgh
    music: Jerome Kern
    lyrics: Oscar Hammerstein II, Otto Harbach, Dorothy
                    Fields, E. Y. Harburg, Ira Gershwin, Jimmy
                    McHugh, Johnny Mercer, Gus Kahn, and others
    staging: David Kernan
    sets: Colin Pigott
    costumes: Christine Robinson
Productions:
    Opened January 23, 1986 for 13 performances
Reviews:
    New York 19: 56-7, Feb 10, 1986
    New York Theatre Critics' Reviews 1986: 387
    New York Times III, page 3, Jan 24, 1986
    New Yorker 61: 85, Feb 3, 1986

Jerome Robbins' Broadway
    conceived: Jerome Robbins
    music: Various composers
    lyrics: Various authors
    staging: Jerome Robbins
    sets: Various set designers
    costumes: Various costume designers
    choreography: Jerome Robbins
Productions:
    Opened February 26, 1989 for *109 performances (still running
    6/1/89)
Reviews:
    America 160: 330, Apr 8, 1989

Dance Magazine 63:44-51, Apr 1989
                63:73-5, Jun 1989
Life 12:122-4+, Mar 1989
Nation 248:713-15, May 22, 1989
New Leader 72:22, Apr 3-17, 1989
New Republic 200:28-9, Apr 3, 1989
New York 22:72+, Mar 13, 1989
New York Theatre Critics' Reviews 1989:358
New York Times III, page 13, Feb 27, 1989
             IV, page 25, Mar 12, 1989
             II, page 9, Apr 2, 1989
New Yorker 65:76-7, Mar 13, 1989
Newsweek 113:52-4, Mar 6, 1989
Time 133:78-9+, Mar 6, 1989
Theatre Crafts 23:56-63, Aug/Sep 1989
Vogue 179:262-3, Mar 1989

Jerry's Girls
     conceived: Larry Alford, Wayne Cilento and Jerry Herman
     songs: Jerry Herman
     staging: Larry Alford
     sets: Hal Tine
     costumes: Florence Klotz
     choreography: Wayne Cilento
Productions:
     Opened December 18, 1985 for 139 performances
Reviews:
     Dance Magazine 60:102-3, Mar 1986
     New York 19:50, Jan 13, 1986
     New York Theatre Critics' Reviews 1985:123
     New York Times III, page 14, Dec 19, 1985
     Vogue 176:211, Jan 1986

Jesus Christ Superstar
     conceived: Tom O'Horgan, for the stage; based on the last
                     seven days in the life of Jesus of Nazareth
     music: Andrew Lloyd Webber
     lyrics: Tim Rice
     staging: Tom O'Horgan
     sets: Robin Wagner
     costumes: Randy Barcelo
Productions:
     Opened October 12, 1971 for 720 performances
     Opened November 23, 1977 for 96 performances
Reviews:
     America 125:352-3, Oct 30, 1971
     Business Week pages 46-7, Sep 11, 1971
     Catholic World 213:217-21, Aug 1971
     Christian Century 88:1333-4, Nov 10, 1971
                       89:785-6, Jul 19, 1972
     Christianity Today 16:42-3, Dec 3, 1971

Commentary 52:36, Dec 1971
Commonweal 95:447-9, Feb 11, 1972
Life 70:20 B-26, May 28, 1971
Mademoiselle 74:102-5, Dec 1971
Nation 213:444, Nov 1, 1971
New Republic 165:24, Nov 6, 1971
New York Theatre Critics' Reviews 1971:239
New York Times II, page 1, May 30, 1971
                page 46, Sep 1, 1971
                page 48, Oct 12, 1971
                page 40, Oct 13, 1971
                II, page 1, Oct 24, 1971
                II, page 1, Oct 31, 1971
                VI, page 14, Jan 2, 1972
                II, page 18, Mar 26, 1972
New Yorker 47:109, Oct 23, 1971
Newsweek 78:84-5, Oct 25, 1971
Saturday Review 54:38, Oct 30, 1971
            54:65-7+, Oct 30, 1971
Senior Scholastic 99:10-11, Dec 13, 1971
Seventeen 30:156-7+, Mar 1971
Time 98:64-8+, Oct 25, 1971
Vogue 158:102-3, Dec 1971

Jim Jam Jems
    book: Harry L. Cort and George E. Stoddard
    music: James Hanley
    staging: Edward J. McGregor
Productions:
   Opened October 4, 1920 for 105 performances
Reviews:
   Dramatic Mirror page 664, Oct 9, 1920
   New York Clipper 68:29, Oct 13, 1920
   New York Times page 12, Oct 5, 1920
   Theatre Magazine 33:76, Jan 1921

Jimmie
    book: Otto Harbach, Oscar Hammerstein II and Frank
                   Mandel
    music: Herbert Stothart
Productions:
   Opened November 17, 1920 for 71 performances
Reviews:
   New York Times page 15, Nov 18, 1920
   Theatre Magazine 33:74, Jan 1921

Jimmy
    book: Melville Shavelson; based on Gene Fowler's novel
                   Beau James
    music: Bill and Patti Jacob
    lyrics: Bill and Patti Jacob

staging: Joseph Anthony
sets: Oliver Smith
costumes: W. Robert Lavine
choreography: Peter Gennaro
Productions:
Opened October 23, 1969 for 84 performances
Reviews:
America 121:544-5, Nov 29, 1969
Commonweal 91:382-3, Dec 26, 1969
New York Theatre Critics' Reviews 1969:192
                                  1969:218
New York Times page 38, Oct 24, 1969
               II, page 3, Nov 9, 1969
               page 20, Jan 3, 1970
New Yorker 45:128, Nov 1, 1969
Newsweek 74:94, Nov 3, 1969

Jimmy & Billy

book: David I. Levine
music: David I. Levine and Pat Curtis
lyrics: David I. Levine
staging: Robert Pagent
sets: James Steere
costumes: Terry Leong
choreography: Robert Pagent
Productions:
(Off-Broadway) Opened December 10, 1978 for one performance
No Reviews.

Jo

book: Don Parks and William Dyer; based on Little
                  Women by Louisa May Alcott
music: William Dyer
lyrics: Don Parks and William Dyer
staging: John Bishop
sets: Gordon Micunis
costumes: Evelyn Norton Anderson
choreography: Chele Abel and Gerald Teijelo
Productions:
(Off-Broadway) Opened February 12, 1964 for 63 performances
Reviews:
America 110:322, Mar 7, 1964
New York Times page 25, Feb 13, 1964
New Yorker 40:92+, Feb 22, 1964

Joan

book: Al Carmines
music: Al Carmines
lyrics: Al Carmines
staging: Al Carmines
sets: Earl Eidman

costumes:	Ira Siff and Joan Kilpatrick
choreography:	Gus Solomons, Jr. and David Vaughan

Productions:
   (Off-Broadway) Opened Season of 1971-1972
   (Off-Broadway) Opened June 19, 1972 for 64 performances
Reviews:
America 127:292-3, Oct 4, 1972
New York Theatre Critics' Reviews 1972:235
New York Times page 33, Jun 20, 1972
           II, page 1, Jun 25, 1972
New Yorker 47:101, Dec 11, 1971
Saturday Review 55:72, Jul 8, 1972
Time 100:72, Jul 10, 1972

Joan Crawford (see Evening With Joan Crawford)

Jockeys

by:	Frank Spiering and Milton Katselas
script super-vision:	Michael Shurtleff
music:	Bernardo Segall
staging:	Milton Katselas
sets:	Peter Wexler
choreography:	Gerald Arpino

Productions:
   (Off-Broadway) Opened April 11, 1977 for 8 performances
Reviews:
Dance Magazine 51:92, Jul 1977
New York Times page 38, Apr 12, 1977

Joe Masiell Not at the Palace

special material:	Jerry Herman, Will Holt, Fred Ebb and John Kander
songs:	Various authors and composers
staging:	James Coco
sets:	C. Tod Jackson
costumes:	C. Tod Jackson
choreography:	C. Tod Jackson

Productions:
   (Off-Broadway) Opened December 11, 1977 for 23 performances
No Reviews.

John Henry

book:	Roark Bradford
music:	Jaques Wolfe
lyrics:	Roark Bradford
staging:	Anthony Brown and Charles Friedman
sets:	Albert Johnson
costumes:	John Hambleton

Productions:
Opened January 10, 1940 for 7 performances

Reviews:
    Catholic World 150:598-9, Feb 1940
    Collier's 105:15+, Jan 13, 1940
    New York Theatre Critics' Reviews 1940:421+
    New York Times IX, page 1, Jan 7, 1940
                       page 18, Jan 11, 1940
    Newsweek 15:33, Jan 22, 1940
    Theatre Arts 24:166-7, Mar 1940
    Time 35:49, Jan 22, 1940

John Murray Anderson's Almanac
    sketches: Jean Kerr, Summer Locke-Elliot, Arthur Macrae,
                        Herbert Farjeon, Lauri Wylie, Billy K. Wells
    music and
      lyrics: Richard Adler, Jerry Ross, Cy Coleman, Michael
                        Grace, Joseph McCarthy, Jr., Henry Sullivan,
                        John Rox, Bart Howard
    staging: John Murray Anderson
    sets: Raoul Pene du Bois
    costumes: Thomas Becher
    choreography: Donald Saddler
Productions:
    Opened December 10, 1953 for 229 performances
Reviews:
    America 90:366, Jan 2, 1954
    Catholic World 178:390, Feb 1954
    Commonweal 59:353, Jan 8, 1954
    Life 35:72-3, Dec 28, 1953
    Nation 177:574, Dec 26, 1953
    New Republic 130:21, Jan 4, 1954
    New York Theatre Critics' Reviews 1953:191+
    New York Times page 42, Dec 11, 1953
                    page 51, Dec 14, 1953
                    II, page 1, Jan 3, 1954
    New Yorker 29:75, Dec 19, 1953
    Newsweek 42:60, Dec 21, 1953
    Saturday Review 37:30, Jan 9, 1954
    Theatre Arts 38:76-8, Jan 1954
                 38:22-3, Feb 1954
    Time 62:57, Dec 21, 1953

Johnny Doodle
    by: Jane McLeod and Alfred Saxe
    staging: Lan Adomian
Productions:
    (Off-Broadway) Opened March 18, 1942
Reviews:
    New York Times page 28, Mar 19, 1942

The Jolly Bachelors
    words: Glen MacDonough

music: Raymond Hubbell
staging: Ned Wayburn
Productions:
  Opened January 6, 1910 for 84 performances
Reviews:
  Dramatic Mirror 63:5, Jan 15, 1910
  Hampton 204:409, Mar 1910
  Harper's Weekly 54:24, Feb 5, 1910
  Life (New York) 55:20, Jan 20, 1910
  Metropolitan Magazine 32:123-4+, Apr 1910
  Theatre Magazine 11:xiv, Feb 1910

Jonica
  book: Dorothy Heyward and Moss Hart
  music: Joseph Meyer
  lyrics: William Moll
  staging: William B. Friedlander
  choreography: Pal'mere Brandeaux
Productions:
  Opened April 7, 1930 for 40 performances
Reviews:
  New York Times VIII, page 2, Mar 30, 1930
                  page 27, Apr 8, 1930
  Outlook 154:671, Apr 23, 1930

Joseph and the Amazing Technicolor Dreamcoat
  book: Tim Rice and Andrew Lloyd Webber, based on the
                      Old Testament story
  music: Tim Rice and Andrew Lloyd Webber
  lyrics: Tim Rice and Andrew Lloyd Webber
  staging: Frank Dunlop
  sets: John Pitts
  costumes: Dona Granata
  choreography: Grace Daniele
Productions:
  (Off-Broadway) Opened December 30, 1976 for 23 performances
  (Off-Broadway) Opened December 13, 1977 for 16 performances
  (Off-Broadway) Opened November 18, 1981 for 77 performances
  Opened January 27, 1982 for 747 performances
Reviews:
  Los Angeles 27:257, Oct 1982
  New York 14:89, Nov 30, 1981
  New York Theatre Critics' Reviews 1981:84
  New York Times III, page 3, Dec 31, 1976
                  III, page 32, Dec 16, 1977
                  XXIII, page 22, Jan 11, 1981
                  III, page 21, Nov 19, 1981
  People 19:20-1, Jan 31, 1983
  Time 118:91, Dec 7, 1981

Josephine Baker
  songs: Josephine Baker

```
staging:            Felix G. Gerstman
costumes:           Christian Dior, Pierre Balmain, House of Lanvin,
                    Balenciaga
choreography:       Geoffrey Holder
```
Productions:
    Opened February 4, 1964 for 16 performances
    Opened March 31, 1964 for 24 performances
Reviews:
    New York Times page 37, Feb 7, 1964
    Newsweek 63:90, Feb 17, 1964
    (also see Evening With Josephine Baker)

The Journey of Snow White
```
music:              Al Carmines
staging:            Gus Solomons Jr.
```
Productions:
    (Off-Broadway) Season of 1970-1971
Reviews:
    New York Times page 39, Mar 22, 1971

Joy
```
sketches:           Oscar Brown, Jr.
songs:              Oscar Brown, Jr. and others
```
Productions:
    (Off-Broadway) Opened January 27, 1970 for 208 performances
Reviews:
    New York Times page 50, Jan 28, 1970
    Newsweek 75:95, Feb 9, 1970
    Time 95:63, Mar 30, 1970

Joyce Grenfell
```
monologues:         Joyce Grenfell
songs:              Joyce Grenfell
music:              Richard Addinsell
costumes:           Victor Stiebel
```
Productions:
    Opened April 7, 1958 for 24 performances
Reviews:
    Christian Century 75:533, Apr 30, 1958
    New York Times page 32, Apr 8, 1958
    Time 71:76, Apr 21, 1958

Joyce Grenfell Requests the Pleasure...
```
book:               Joyce Grenfell
music:              Richard Addinsell
lyrics:             Joyce Grenfell
staging:            Laurier Lister
sets:               Paul Morrison
choreography:       Wendy Toye, John Heathwood, and others
```
Productions:
    Opened October 10, 1955 for 65 performances

Reviews:
America 94:138, Oct 29, 1955
Catholic World 182:224, Dec 1955
Commonweal 63:116-7, Nov 18, 1955
New York Times page 48, Oct 11, 1955
New Yorker 31:90-92, Oct 22, 1955
       31:41-2, Nov 19, 1955
Newsweek 46:54, Oct 24, 1955
Saturday Review 38:20, Oct 29, 1955
Theatre Arts 39:20, Dec 1955
Time 66:86, Oct 24, 1955

Joyce, James   (see James Joyce Memorial Liquid Theatre)

A Joyful Noise
  book: Edward Padula; based on Borden Deal's novel
                 The Insolent Breed
  music: Oscar Brand and Paul Nassau
  lyrics: Oscar Brand and Paul Nassau
  staging: Edward Padula
  sets: Peter Wexler
  costumes: Peter Joseph
  choreography: Michael Bennett, Leland Palmer, Jo Jo Smith
Productions:
Opened December 15, 1966 for 12 performances
Reviews:
Dance Magazine 41:23, Feb 1967
New York Theatre Critics' Reviews 1966:202
New York Times page 41, Jul 5, 1966
            II, page 4, Nov 27, 1966
            page 57, Dec 16, 1966
            page 10, Dec 24, 1966
New Yorker 42:45, Dec 24, 1966
Newsweek 68:45, Dec 26, 1966

Jubilee
  book: Moss Hart
  music: Cole Porter
  lyrics: Cole Porter
  staging: Hassard Short
  sets: Jo Mielziner
  costumes: Irene Sharaff and Connie de Pinna
  choreography: Albertina Rasch
Productions:
Opened October 12, 1935 for 169 performances
(Off-Off-Broadway) Opened March 2, 1986
Reviews:
Catholic World 142:340, Dec 1935
Commonweal 22:642, Oct 1935
Dance Magazine 55:106, Nov 1981
               58:86-7, Apr 1984

Nation 141:548, Nov 6, 1935
New York Times IX, page 2, Sep 15, 1935
　　　　　　　　page 20, Sep 23, 1935
　　　　　　　　X, page 1, Sep 29, 1935
　　　　　　　　page 20, Oct 14, 1935
　　　　　　　　X, page 3, Oct 20, 1935
　　　　　　　　IX, page 1, Oct 27, 1935
　　　　　　　　IX, page 8, Nov 24, 1935
　　　　　　　　III, page 17, Mar 4, 1986
Newsweek 6:26-7, Oct 19, 1935
Stage 13:30-1, Oct 1935
　　　　13:33-4, Dec 1935
Theatre Arts 19:901-2, Dec 1935
Time 26:51, Oct 21, 1935
Vanity Fair 45:68, Dec 1935

Judy
book:　　　　　　Mark Swan
staging:　　　　Bobby Connolly
Productions:
Opened February 7, 1927 for 96 performances
Reviews:
New York Times page 20, Feb 8, 1927
Theatre Magazine 45:19, Apr 1927

Judy Forgot
book:　　　　　　Avery Hopwood; based on The Winking Princess
music:　　　　　Silvio Hein
lyrics:　　　　Avery Hopwood
staging:　　　　Daniel V. Arthur
Productions:
Opened October 6, 1910 for 44 performances
Reviews:
Blue Book 12:427-30, Jan 1911
Dramatic Mirror 64:9, Oct 19, 1910
Green Book Album 5:476-7, Mar 1911
Hampton 25:830, Dec 1910
Leslie's Weekly 111:461, Nov 3, 1910
Life (New York) 56:660, Oct 20, 1910
Metropolitan Magazine 33:522-3, Jan 1911
Munsey 44:413, Dec 1910
Theatre Magazine 12:130, Nov 1910
　　　　　　　　　　12:133, Nov 1910

Judy Garland at Home at the Palace
staging:　　　　Richard Barstow
costumes:　　　Bill Smith Travilla
Productions:
Opened July 31, 1967 for 24 performances
Reviews:
America 117:208, Aug 26, 1967

Ladies Home Journal 84:64-5+, Aug 1967
New York Times page 23, Aug 1, 1967
                 page 45, Dec 26, 1967
Saturday Review 50:66, Sep 30, 1967
Time 90:40, Aug 18, 1967

Jumbo

book:	Ben Hecht and Charles MacArthur
music:	Richard Rodgers
lyrics:	Lorenz Hart
staging:	John Murray Anderson
sets:	Albert Johnson
costumes:	Raoul Pene du Bois and James Reynolds
choreography:	Allen K. Foster and Marjorie Fielding

Productions:
   Opened November 16, 1935 for 233 performances
Reviews:
   Literary Digest 120:18-19, Nov 30, 1935
   Nation 141:660, Dec 4, 1935
   New Republic 85:134, Dec 11, 1935
   New York Times page 12, Aug 8, 1935
                    IX, page 1, Aug 11, 1935
                    page 20, Nov 18, 1935
                    IX, page 1, Nov 24, 1935
                    IX, page 4, Dec 22, 1935
   Newsweek 6:30-2, Nov 23, 1935
   Stage 13:49-51, Jan 1936
   Theatre Arts 20:12+, Jan 1936
   Time 26:47, Nov 25, 1935
   Vanity Fair 45:57, Jan 1936

Jumping Jupiter

book:	Richard Carle and Sydney Rosenfeld
music:	Karl Hoschna
staging:	Richard Carle

Productions:
   Opened March 6, 1911 for 24 performances
Reviews:
   Dramatic Mirror 65:7, Mar 8, 1911
   Life (New York) 57:581, Mar 23, 1911
   Pearson 25:671, May 1911
   Theatre Magazine 13:xiii, Apr 1911

June Days

book:	Cyrus Wood; based on a play by Alice Duer Miller and Robert Milton
music:	J. Fred Coots
lyrics:	Clifford Grey
staging:	J. J. Shubert

Productions:
   Opened August 6, 1925 for 84 performances

Reviews:
    New York Times page 12, Aug 7, 1925
                    VII, page 4, Aug 7, 1925
                    VII, page 1, Aug 23, 1925

June Love
    book: Otto Harbach and W. H. Post, adapted from a
                    story by Charlotte Thompson
    music: Rudolf Friml
    lyrics: Brian Hooker
    staging: George Vivian
Productions:
    Opened April 25, 1921 for 50 performances
Reviews:
    Dramatic Mirror 83:733, Apr 30, 1921
    Life (New York) 77:688, May 12, 1921
    New York Clipper 69:19, Apr 27, 1921
    New York Times page 20, Apr 26, 1921
    Theatre Magazine 34:30, Jul 1921

Juno
    book: Joseph Stein, based on Sean O'Casey's play
                    Juno and the Paycock
    music: Marc Blitzstein
    lyrics: Marc Blitzstein
    staging: Jose Ferrer
    sets: Oliver Smith
    costumes: Irene Sharaff
    choreography: Agnes de Mille
Productions:
    Opened March 9, 1959 for 16 performances
Reviews:
    Dance Magazine 33:22, Apr 1959
    New Republic 140:20, Mar 30, 1959
    New York Theatre Critics' Reviews 1959:351+
    New York Times II, page 1, Mar 1, 1959
                    page 41, Mar 10, 1959
                    II, page 1, Mar 15, 1959
                    page 42, Mar 17, 1959
    New Yorker 35:97, Mar 21, 1959
    Newsweek 53:76, Mar 23, 1959
    Theatre Arts 43:65-6, May 1959
    Time 73:60, Mar 23, 1959

Just a Minute (1919)
    by: Harry L. Cort, George E. Stoddard, Harold
                    Orlob
Productions:
    Opened October 27, 1919 for 40 performances
Reviews:
    New York Times page 11, Oct 29, 1919

Theatre Magazine 30:391, Dec 1919
30:426, Dec 1919

Just a Minute (1928)
- book: H. C. Greene
- music: Harry Archer
- lyrics: Walter O'Keefe
- staging: H. C. Greene

Productions:
Opened October 8, 1928 for 80 performances
Reviews:
New York Times page 34, Oct 9, 1928

Just Because
- book: Anne Wynne O'Ryan and Helen S. Woodruff
- music: Madelyn Sheppard
- lyrics: Anne Wynne O'Ryan and Helen S. Woodruff
- staging: Oscar Eagle

Productions:
Opened March 22, 1922 for 46 performances
Reviews:
New York Clipper 70:20, Mar 29, 1922
New York Times page 11, Mar 23, 1922
Theatre Magazine 35:379, Jun 1922

Just Fancy
- book: Joseph Santley and Gertrude Purcell; based on a play by A. E. Thomas
- music: Joseph Meyer and Philip Charig
- lyrics: Leo Robin
- staging: Joseph Santley

Productions:
Opened October 11, 1927 for 79 performances
Reviews:
Life (New York) 90:23, Nov 3, 1927
New York Times page 30, Oct 12, 1927
Theatre Magazine 47:38, Jan 1928

Just for Love
- book: Jill Showell and Henry Comor
- music: Michael Valenti
- lyrics: Jill Showell and Henry Comor
- staging: Henry Comor
- sets: Jack Blackmon
- costumes: Sara Brook

Productions:
(Off-Broadway) Opened October 17, 1968 for 6 performances
Reviews:
New York Times page 40, Oct 18, 1968

Just for Openers
- conceived: Rod Warren

```
    sketches:       Rod Warren and others
    songs:          Rod Warren and others
    staging:        Sandra Devlin
Productions:
    (Off-Broadway)  Opened November 3, 1965 for 395 performances
No Reviews.
```

Just So
```
    conceived:      Julianne Boyd
    book:           Mark St. Germain, based on Rudyard Kipling's
                    Just So Stories
    music:          Doug Katsaros
    lyrics:         David Zippel
    staging:        Julianne Boyd
    sets:           Atkin Pace
    costumes:       Ann Hould-Ward
    choreography:   David Storey
Productions:
    (Off-Broadway)  Opened December 3, 1985 for 6 performances
Reviews:
    New York Times III, page 30, Dec 4, 1985
```

-K-

Kaboom! (1974)
```
    book:           Ira Wallach
    music:          Doris Schwerin
    lyrics:         Ira Wallach
    staging:        Don Price
    sets:           Peter Harvey
    costumes:       Lohr Wilson
Productions:
    (Off-Broadway)  Opened May 1, 1974 for 1 performance
Reviews:
    New York Times page 64, May 2, 1974
```

Ka-Boom! (1980)
```
    book:           Bruce Kluger
    music:          Joe Ercole
    lyrics:         Bruce Kluger
    staging:        John-Michael Tebelak
    sets:           Ken Holamon
    costumes:       Erica Hollmann
    choreography:   Lynne Gannaway
Productions:
    (Off-Broadway)  Opened November 20, 1980 for 71 performances
Reviews:
    New York Times III, page 21, Nov 21, 1980
```

Katinka
```
    book:           Otto Hauerbach
```

music: Rudolf Friml
lyrics: Otto Hauerbach
staging: Frank Smithson
Productions:
    Opened December 23, 1915 for 220 performances
Reviews:
    Dramatic Mirror 75: 8, Jan 1, 1916
                    75: 2, Feb 5, 1916
    Green Book 15: 447, Mar 1916
    Munsey 57: 512, Apr 1916
    New York Dramatic News 62: 18, Jan 1, 1916
    Opera Magazine 3: 31-2, Feb 1916
    Theatre Magazine 23: 65-6, Feb 1916

Kaye Ballard: Working 42nd Street at Last! (one-woman show)
    creative
        consultant: Ben Bagley
    songs: Various authors and composers
    sets: Jeffrey Schissler
    costumes: Clovis Ruffin, Grace Costumes, Reuben Panis
Productions:
    (Off-Broadway) Opened May 16, 1988 for 29 performances
Reviews:
    New York Times III, page 28, May 19, 1988
    (also see Hey, Ma ... Kaye Ballard)

Kean
    book: Peter Stone, based on Jean Paul Sartre's play
                    and Alexandre Dumas' play
    music: Robert Wright and George Forrest
    lyrics: Robert Wright and George Forrest
    staging: Jack Cole
    sets: Ed Wittstein
    costumes: Ed Wittstein
    choreography: Jack Cole
Productions:
    Opened November 2, 1961 for 92 performances
Reviews:
    Commonweal 75: 389, Jan 5, 1962
    Dance Magazine 35: 23, Dec 1961
    Nation 193: 438, Nov 25, 1961
    New York Theatre Critics' Reviews 1961: 180+
    New York Times page 28, Nov 3, 1961
                    II, page 1, Nov 12, 1961
    New Yorker 37: 117, Nov 11, 1961
    Newsweek 58: 94, Nov 13, 1961
    Theatre Arts 45: 17-24, Dec 1961
                  46: 11-12, Jan 1962
    Time 78: 66, Nov 10, 1961

Keep 'em Laughing
    assembled: Clifford C. Fischer

sketches:	Arthur Pierson and Eddie Davis
staging:	Clifford Fischer
sets:	Frank W. Stevens

Productions:
Opened April 24, 1942 for 77 performances
Reviews:
New York Theatre Critics' Reviews 1942: 306
New York Times page 9, Apr 25, 1942
page 24, May 20, 1942
Time 39: 70, May 4, 1942
(Also see Top-Notchers)

Keep It Clean
book:	Jimmy Duffy and Will Morrissey
music:	Lester Lee, Jimmy Duffy, Harry Archer, Benny Ryan, James Hanley, Clarence Gaskill, Violinsky, Charles Tobias, Harry Converse
staging:	Will Morrissey and Russell Markert

Productions:
Opened June 24, 1929 for 16 performances
Reviews:
New York Times page 35, Jun 25, 1929

Keep Kool
book:	Paul Gerard Smith
music:	Jack Frost
lyrics:	Paul Gerard Smith
staging:	Earl Lindsay

Productions:
Opened May 22, 1924 for (28) performances
Reviews:
New York Times page 16, May 23, 1924
Theatre Magazine 40: 15, Aug 1924

Keep Moving
sketches:	Newman Levy and Jack School
music:	Max Rich
lyrics:	Newman Levy and Jack School
staging:	George Rosener and Harry Losee
sets:	Clark Robinson

Productions:
Opened August 23, 1934 for 20 performances
Reviews:
New York Times page 10, Aug 24, 1934

Keep off the Grass
book:	Mort Lewis, Parke Levy, Alan Lipscott, S. J. Kaufman, Reginald Beckwith, Panama and Frank
music:	James McHugh
lyrics:	Al Dubin and Howard Dietz
staging:	Fred deCordova

```
      sets:          Nat Carson
      costumes:      Nat Carson
      choreography:  George Balanchine
```
Productions:
    Opened May 23, 1940 for 44 performances
Reviews:
    Catholic World 151: 471-2, Jul 1940
    Commonweal 32: 212, Jun 18, 1940
    Life 9: 52-4, Jul 8, 1940
    Nation 150: 716, Jun 8, 1940
    New York Theatre Critics' Reviews 1940: 302+
    New York Times X, page 1, May 5, 1940
                    page 22, May 24, 1940
                    IX, page 1, Jun 16, 1940
    Newsweek 15: 44, Jun 3, 1940
    Time 35: 52, Jun 3, 1940

Keep Shufflin'
```
      book:     Flourney Miller and Aubrey Lyles
      music:    Jimmy Johnson, "Fats" Waller and Clarence Todd
      lyrics:   Henry Creamer and Andy Razaf
      staging:  Con Conrad
```
Productions:
    Opened February 27, 1928 for 104 performances
Reviews:
    New York Times page 18, Feb 28, 1928
    Theatre Magazine 47: 41+, May 1927
    Vogue 71: 136, May 1, 1928

Kelly
```
      book:          Eddie Lawrence
      music:         Moose Charlap
      lyrics:        Eddie Lawrence
      staging:       Herbert Ross
      sets:          Oliver Smith
      costumes:      Freddy Wittop
      choreography:  Herbert Ross
```
Productions:
    Opened February 6, 1965 for one performance
Reviews:
    New York Theatre Critics' Reviews 1965: 382+
    New York Times page 28, Feb 8, 1965
                    page 42, Feb 9, 1965
    New Yorker 40: 76, Feb 13, 1965
    Saturday Evening Post 238: 32-4+, Apr 24, 1965
    Time 85: 64, Feb 19, 1965

Ken Murray's Blackouts of 1949
```
      music:    Charles Henderson and Ray Foster
      lyrics:   Charles Henderson and Ray Foster
      sets:     Ben Tipton
```

Productions:
  Opened September 6, 1949 for 51 performances
Reviews:
  Life 27:12-13, Oct 3, 1949
  New Republic 121:29, Sep 26, 1949
  New York Theatre Critics' Reviews 1949:273+
  New York Times page 39, Sep 7, 1949
  New Yorker 25:56, Sep 17, 1949
  Newsweek 34:79, Sep 19, 1949
  Saturday Evening Post 222:38-9+, Sep 10, 1949
  Theatre Arts 33:8, Oct 1949
  Time 54:70, Sep 19, 1949

Kenny Loggins on Broadway
  by: Kenny Loggins
  songs: Kenny Loggins
  sets: Michael Ledesma
Productions:
  Opened November 1, 1988 for 8 performances
Reviews:
  New York Theatre Critics' Reviews 1988:170

Kid Boats
  book: William Anthony McGuire and Otto Harbach
  music: Harry Tierney
  lyrics: Joseph McCarthy
Productions:
  Opened December 31, 1923 for (192) performances
Reviews:
  New York Times IX, page 2, Dec 16, 1923
                  page 21, Jan 1, 1924
  Theatre Magazine 39:70, Mar 1924
                  39:17, Apr 1924

The King and I
  book: Oscar Hammerstein II, based on Margaret Landon's
                  novel Anna and the King of Siam
  music: Richard Rodgers
  lyrics: Oscar Hammerstein II
  staging: John Van Druten
  sets: Jo Mielziner
  costumes: Irene Sharaff
  choreography: Jerome Robbins
Productions:
  Opened March 29, 1951 for 1,246 performances
  Opened April 18, 1956 for 23 performances
  (Off-Broadway) Season of 1959-60
  Opened May 11, 1960 for 24 performances
  Opened June 12, 1963 for 15 performances
  Opened July 6, 1964 for 40 performances
  Opened May 23, 1968 for 22 performances

(Off-Off-Broadway) Opened June 28, 1972
Opened May 2, 1977 for 696 performances
Opened January 7, 1985 for 191 performances
Reviews:
America 95:147, May 5, 1956
            111:143-4, Aug 8, 1964
    Catholic World 173:145-6, May 1951
                183:229, Jun 1956
                183:311, Jul 1956
    Collier's 127:24-5+, Apr 7, 1951
    Commonweal 54:12, Apr 13, 1951
            64:299, Jun 22, 1956
    Dance Magazine 42:19, Aug 1968
                51:20, Aug 1977
                59:78-9, Mar 1985
                59:112, May 1985
    Harper's 203:99-100, Sep 1951
    Life 30:79-80+, Apr 23, 1951
    Los Angeles 24:278+, Apr 1979
    Nation 172:353, Apr 14, 1951
    New Republic 124:29, Apr 16, 1951
    New York 10:73, May 16, 1977
            18:61, Jan 21, 1985
    New York Theatre Critics' Reviews 1951:304+
                        1960:267+
                        1977:247
                        1985:388
    New York Times II, page 1, Mar 25, 1951
                page 26, Mar 30, 1951
                II, page 1, Apr 8, 1951
                II, page 1, Oct 5, 1952
                page 33, Oct 9, 1953
                II, page 3, Oct 18, 1953
                page 33, May 17, 1955
                page 35, Apr 19, 1956
                page 40, May 12, 1960
                II, page 1, May 22, 1960
                I, page 22, Mar 19, 1961
                page 30, Jun 13, 1963
                page 20, Jul 6, 1964
                page 26, Jul 7, 1964
                page 39, Jul 8, 1964
                page 27, Jul 9, 1964
                page 39, May 24, 1968
                page 24, Jun 30, 1972
                page 50, May 3, 1977
                III, page 18, Apr 13, 1978
                III, page 13, Jan 8, 1985
                II, page 5, Feb 3, 1985
    New Yorker 27:70+, Apr 7, 1951
            53:83, May 23, 1977

Newsweek 37:78, Apr 9, 1951
             89:101+, May 16, 1977
Saturday Review 34:32, Mar 31, 1951
             34:44-6, Apr 14, 1951
             47:18, Jul 25, 1964
             11:74, Mar/Apr 1985
Theatre Arts 35:30-1, Jul 1951
             40:19, Jun 1956
Time 57:78, Apr 9, 1951
     125:74, Jan 21, 1985

The King of Cadonia
    book: Frederick Lonsdale
    music: Sidney Jones and Jerome D. Kern
    lyrics: Adrian Ross and M. E. Rourke
    staging: Joseph Herbert
Productions:
    Opened January 10, 1910 for 16 performances
Reviews:
    American Mercury 70:109, May 1910
    Cosmopolitan 48:619, Apr 1910
    Dramatic Mirror 63:5, Jan 22, 1910
    Munsey 41:902-3, Sep 1909
    Theatre Magazine 11:iii, Feb 1910
                     11:38, Feb 1910

King of Hearts
    book: Joseph Stein, based on an original screenplay by
                   Philippe de Broca, Maurice Bessy and Daniel
                   Boulanger
    music: Peter Link
    lyrics: Jacob Brackman
    staging: Ron Field
    sets: Santo Loquasto
    costumes: Patricia Zipprodt
    choreography: Ron Field
Productions:
    Opened October 22, 1978 for 48 performances
Reviews:
    New York 11:134, Nov 6, 1978
    New York Theatre Critics' Reviews 1978:200
    New York Times III, page 15, Feb 13, 1978
    New Yorker 54:131, Oct 30, 1978
    Newsweek 92:92, Nov 6, 1978

King of Schnorrers
    book: Judd Woldin, based on Israel Zangwill's The
                   King of Schnorrers
    music: Judd Woldin
    lyrics: Judd Woldin
    staging: Grover Dale

sets: Adrianne Lobel
costumes: Patricia Adshead
choreography: Grover Dale
Productions:
  (Off-Broadway) Opened October 9, 1979 for 30 performances
  Opened November 28, 1979 for 63 performances
  (Off-Broadway) Opened October 27, 1985 for 25 performances
Reviews:
  New York Theatre Critics' Reviews 1979: 80
  New York Times III, page 5, Oct 12, 1979
              III, page 17, Nov 29, 1979
              III, page 22, Oct 31, 1985

King of the Whole Damn World
  book: George Panetta
  music: Robert Larimer
  lyrics: Robert Larimer
  staging: Jack Ragotzy
  sets: Jack Cornwell
  costumes: Rachel Mehr
  choreography: Zachary Solov
Productions:
  (Off-Broadway) Opened April 14, 1962 for 43 performances
Reviews:
  New York Times page 32, Apr 16, 1962
              page 30, May 22, 1962
  New Yorker 38:97, Apr 28, 1962
  Saturday Review 45:29, May 5, 1962

Kismet
  book: Charles Lederer and Luther Davis, based on
                    the play by Edward Knoblock
  music: Alexander Borodin, adapted by Robert Wright
                    and George Forrest
  lyrics: Robert Wright and George Forrest
  staging: Albert Marre
  sets: Lemuel Ayers
  costumes: Lemuel Ayers
  choreography: Jack Cole
Productions:
  Opened December 3, 1953 for 583 performances
  (Off-Off-Broadway) Opened November 16, 1963 for 8 performances
  Opened June 22, 1965 for 48 performances
  (Off-Off-Broadway) Opened October 29, 1987
Reviews:
  America 90:366, Jan 2, 1954
          113:122, Jul 31, 1965
  Catholic World 178:388, Feb 1954
  Collier's 133:78-9, Jan 8, 1954
  Commonweal 59:353, Jan 8, 1954
  Dance Magazine 39:24, Aug 1965

Life 35:25-8, Dec 21, 1953
Los Angeles 21:193+, Aug 1976
Maclean's 99:54-5, Jul 7, 1986
Nation 177:555, Dec 19, 1953
New York 18:66+, Oct 21, 1985
New York Theatre Critics' Reviews 1953:198+
New York Times page 2, Dec 4, 1953
                page 51, Dec 14, 1953
                II, page 1, Jun 20, 1965
                page 45, Jun 23, 1965
                page 16, Aug 28, 1974
                III, page 26, Nov 4, 1987
New Yorker 29:85-7, Dec 12, 1953
Newsweek 42:61, Dec 14, 1953
         42:60, Dec 21, 1953
Saturday Review 36:28-9, Dec 26, 1953
Theatre Arts 38:18-19, Feb 1954
Time 62:94, Dec 14, 1953
Vogue 175:106+, Oct 1985

The Kiss Burglar
    book: Glen MacDonough
    music: Raymond Hubbell
    lyrics: Glen MacDonough
    staging: Julian Mitchell and Edgar MacGregor
Productions:
    Opened May 9, 1918 for 100 performances
    Opened March 17, 1919 for 24 performances
Reviews:
    Dramatic Mirror 78:730, May 25, 1918
                    78:801, Jun 8, 1918
    Green Book 20:10, Jul 1918
    Life (New York) 71:842, May 23, 1918
    New York Times page 9, May 10, 1918
                   page 9, Mar 18, 1919
    Theatre Magazine 27:356-8, Jun 1918

Kiss Me
    book: Adapted by Derick Wulff and Max Simon
    music: Winthrop Cortelyou
    lyrics: Derick Wulff
Productions:
    Opened July 18, 1927 for 32 performances
Reviews:
    New York Times page 17, Jul 22, 1927

Kiss Me, Kate
    book: Bella Spewack and Samuel Spewack, based on
                 Shakespeare's The Taming of the Shrew
    music: Cole Porter
    lyrics: Cole Porter

staging: John C. Wilson
sets: Lemuel Ayers
costumes: Lemuel Ayers
choreography: Hanya Holm
Productions:
  Opened December 30, 1948 for 1,070 performances
  Opened January 8, 1952 for 8 performances
  (Off-Broadway) Season of 1953-54
  Opened May 9, 1956 for 23 performances
  Opened May 12, 1965 for 23 performances
Reviews:
  America 95:252, Jun 2, 1956
  Catholic World 168:402-3, Feb 1949
                 193:311, Jul 1956
  Commonweal 49:376, Jan 21, 1949
  Good Housekeeping 139:4+, Dec 1949
  Life 26:99-100+, Feb 7, 1949
  New Republic 120:25, Jan 24, 1949
  New York Theatre Critics' Reviews 1948:91+
  New York Times page 10, Dec 31, 1948
                  II, page 1, Jan 9, 1949
                  II, page 1, Jan 16, 1949
                  VI, page 20, Jan 16, 1949
                  II, page 6, Jan 30, 1949
                  page 30, Mar 9, 1951
                  II, page 3, Apr 15, 1951
                  page 31, Jul 17, 1951
                  page 24, Jan 9, 1952
                  page 23, Jan 31, 1952
                  page 13, Mar 27, 1954
                  page 19, Dec 17, 1955
                  page 27, Feb 15, 1956
                  page 94, Feb 19, 1956
                  page 27, May 10, 1956
                  page 24, Aug 10, 1959
                  page 184, Dec 1, 1963
                  page 31, May 13, 1965
  New Yorker 24:50-2, Jan 8, 1949
             41:130+, Jun 12, 1965
  Newsweek 33:72, Jan 10, 1949
  Saturday Review 32:34-5, Jan 22, 1949
                  39:24, May 26, 1956
  Theatre Arts 33:17+, Mar 1949
               39:32, Jan 1955
               40:78-80+, Jun 1956
               40:21, Jul 1956
  Time 53:36+, Jan 10, 1949
       53:40-4, Jan 31, 1949
       67:47, Mar 5, 1956

Kiss Now
  book: Maxine Klein

```
music:          William S. Fischer
lyrics:         Maxine Klein
staging:        Maxine Klein
sets:           Richard Devin
costumes:       Nancy Adzima
choreography:   Sandra Caprin
Productions:
(Off-Broadway)  Opened April 20, 1971 for 4 performances
No Reviews.
```

Kissing Time
```
    book:       George V. Hobart; based on the French of A.
                Philipp and E. Paulton
    music:      Ivan Caryll
    lyrics:     Philander Johnson
    staging:    Edward Royce
Productions:
Opened October 11, 1920 for 72 performances
Reviews:
Dramatic Mirror page 693, Oct 16, 1920
New York Clipper 68:21, Aug 18, 1920
                 68:20, Oct 20, 1920
New York Times page 18, Oct 12, 1920
Theatre Magazine 32:414, Dec 1920
```

Kittiwake Island
```
    book:           Arnold Sundgaard
    music:          Alec Wilder
    lyrics:         Arnold Sundgaard
    staging:        Lawrence Carra
    sets:           Romaine Johnston
    costumes:       Al Lehman
    choreography:   Peter Hamilton
Productions:
(Off-Broadway)  Opened October 12, 1960 for 7 performances
Reviews:
New York Times page 43, Oct 13, 1960
               page 46, Oct 18, 1960
New Yorker 36:93, Oct 22, 1960
```

Kitty Darlin'
```
    book:       Otto Hauerbach
    music:      Rudolf Friml
    lyrics:     Otto Hauerbach
    staging:    Edward Royce
Productions:
Opened November 7, 1917 for 14 performances
Reviews:
Dramatic Mirror 77:31, Sep 22, 1917
                77:5, Nov 17, 1917
New York Times page 13, Nov 8, 1917
```

Kitty's Kisses
  book: Philip Bartholomae and Otto Harbach; based on
                   Little Miss Brown
  music: Con Conrad
  lyrics: Gus Kahn
  staging: John Cronwell and Bobby Connolly
Productions:
  Opened May 6, 1926 for 170 performances
Reviews:
  New York Times page 12, May 7, 1926
  Theatre Magazine 44:16, Jul 1926

The Knee Plays
  scenario: Robert Wilson
  words: David Byrne
  music: David Byrne
  staging: Robert Wilson
  choreography: Suzushi Hanayagi
Productions:
  Opened December 2, 1986 for 4 performances
Reviews:
  New York Times III, page 25, Dec 4, 1986

Knickerbocker Holiday
  book: Maxwell Anderson
  music: Kurt Weill
  lyrics: Maxwell Anderson
  staging: Joshua Logan
  sets: Jo Mielziner
  costumes: Frank Bevan
  choreography: Carl Randall and Edwin Denby
Productions:
  Opened October 19, 1938 for 168 performances
Reviews:
  Catholic World 148:343-4, Dec 1938
  Commonweal 29:48, Nov 4, 1938
  Life 5:27, Nov 21, 1938
  Modern Music 16:54-6, Nov 1938
  Nation 147:488-9, Nov 5, 1938
         147:673, Dec 17, 1938
  New Republic 97:18, Nov 9, 1938
  New York 10:63, May 9, 1977
  New York Theatre Critics' Reviews 1977:266
  New York Times IX, page 1, Sep 25, 1938
                  IX, page 3, Oct 2, 1938
                  page 26, Oct 20, 1938
                  IX, page 1, Nov 20, 1938
                  III, page 19, Apr 20, 1977
  Newsweek 12:29, Oct 31, 1938
  North American Review 246 no2:374-6, Dec 1938
  Theatre Arts 22:862, Dec 1938
  Time 32:55, Oct 31, 1938

The Knife

book:	David Hare
music:	Nick Bicat
lyrics:	Tim Rose Price
staging:	David Hare
sets:	Hayden Griffin
costumes:	Joan Greenwood
choreography:	Graciela Daniele

Productions:
(Off-Broadway) Opened March 10, 1987 for 32 performances

Reviews:
Harper's Bazaar 120:206-7+, Apr 1987
Nation 244:480, Apr 11, 1987
New York 20:89-90, Mar 23, 1987
New York Theatre Critics' Reviews 1987:232
New York Times III, page 22, Mar 11, 1987
            II, page 5, Mar 15, 1987
New Yorker 63:77, Mar 23, 1987

Knights of Song

book:	Glendon Allvine, based on a story by Glendon Allvine and Adele Gutman Nathan
music:	excerpts from Gilbert and Sullivan operettas
lyrics:	excerpts from Gilbert and Sullivan operettas
staging:	Oscar Hammerstein and Avalon Collard
sets:	Raymond Sovey
costumes:	Kate Lawson

Productions:
Opened October 17, 1938 for 16 performances

Reviews:
Commonweal 29:48, Nov 4, 1938
Musical Courier 118:11, Aug 15, 1938
New York Times page 29, Oct 18, 1938
Time 32:54, Oct 31, 1938

Kosher Kitty Kelly

book:	Leon DeCosta
staging:	A. H. Van Buren

Productions:
Opened June 15, 1925 for one performance

Reviews:
New York Times page 24, Jun 16, 1925

The Kumquat in the Persimmon Tree

sketches:	William C. Curtis
music:	Bruce Haack and Ted Pandel
staging:	George Lanin
sets:	Charles Copenhaver
choreography:	Mamie Jones

Productions:
(Off-Broadway) Opened June 18, 1962 for 11 performances

Reviews:
New York Times page 27, Jun 19, 1962

Kuni-Leml
 book: Nahma Sandrow
 music: Raphael Crystal
 lyrics: Richard Engquist
 staging: Ran Avni
 sets: Joel Fontaine
 costumes: Karen Hummel
 choreography: Haila Strauss
Productions:
 (Off-Broadway) Opened October 9, 1984 for 298 performances
Reviews:
 New York Theatre Critics' Reviews 1984:168
 New York Times page 13, Jun 16, 1984

A Kurt Weill Cabaret
 music: Kurt Weill
 lyrics: Bertolt Brecht, Marc Blitzstein, George Tabori,
                  Arnold Weinstein, Ogden Nash, Maxwell Anderson,
                  Ira Gershwin and Will Holt
 staging: Herb Vogler and Billie McBride
Productions:
 Opened November 5, 1979 for 72 performances
 (Off-Broadway) Opened December 20, 1985 for 130 performances
Reviews:
 New York Times III, page 9, Nov 6, 1979
 Time 115:97, Jan 7, 1980
(Also see Berlin to Broadway with Kurt Weill and World of Kurt Weill
in Song)

Kwamina
 book: Robert Alan Aurthur
 music: Richard Adler
 lyrics: Richard Adler
 staging: Robert Lewis
 sets: Will Steven Armstrong
 costumes: Motley
 choreography: Agnes de Mille
Productions:
 Opened October 23, 1961 for 32 performances
Reviews:
 America 106:257, Nov 18, 1961
 Dance Magazine 35:23, Dec 1961
 New Republic 145:23, Nov 6, 1961
 New York Theatre Critics' Reviews 1961:206+
 New York Times II, page 3, Oct 22, 1961
                 page 42, Oct 24, 1961
                 II, page 1, Nov 12, 1961
 New Yorker 37:126, Nov 4, 1961

Newsweek 58:69, Nov 6, 1961
Saturday Review 44:39, Nov 18, 1961
Theatre Arts 46:13-14, Jan 1962
Time 78:44, Nov 3, 1961

-L-

La Belle Paree
    book: Edgar Smith
    music: Jerome Kern and Frank Tours
    lyrics: Edward Madden
Productions:
Opened March 1910 for 104 performances
Reviews:
    Blue Book 13:700-2+, Aug 1911
    Dramatic Mirror 65:2, May 31, 1911

La Cage aux Folles
    book: Harvey Fierstein, based on the play La Cage aux
                     Folles by Jean Poiret
    music: Jerry Herman
    lyrics: Jerry Herman
    staging: Arthur Laurents
    sets: David Mitchell
    costumes: Theoni V. Aldredge
    choreography: Scott Salmon
Productions:
Opened August 21, 1983 for 1,761 performances
Reviews:
    America 149:155, Sep 24, 1983
    California 9:46+, Aug 1984
    Dance Magazine 57:66-7, Nov 1983
                   61:70-1, Dec 1987
    Horizon 26:48-54, Oct 1983
    Los Angeles 29:50, Nov 1984
    Nation 237:219-20, Sep 17, 1983
    New Leader 66:21-2, Sep 5, 1983
    New Republic 189:26-7, Sep 19-26, 1983
    New York 16:30-7, Aug 22, 1983
                  16:61-2, Sep 5, 1983
    New York Theatre Critics' Reviews 1983:188
    New York Times III, page 13, Aug 22, 1983
                  II, page 1, Aug 28, 1983
    New Yorker 59:102+, Sep 5, 1983
    Newsweek 102:70-1, Aug 29, 1983
    People 20:71-2+, Dec 5, 1983
          20:47-8+, Sep 5, 1983
    Saturday Review 9:49-50, Nov/Dec 1983
    Theatre Crafts 17:4, 16-19+, Nov/Dec 1983
    Time 122:64-5, Aug 29, 1983
    Vogue 173:640-1, Sep 1983

La, La, Lucille
   book: Fred Jackson
   music: George Gershwin
   lyrics: Arthur J. Jackson and B. G. DeSylva
   staging: Herbert Gresham and Julian Alfred
Productions:
   Opened May 26, 1919 for 104 performances
Reviews:
   New York Times page 15, May 27, 1919
   Theatre Magazine 30:7+, Jul 1919

La Mama   (see Everyman at La Mama)

La Plume de Ma Tante
   book: Robert Dhery
   music: Gerard Calvi
   lyrics: Ross Parker
   staging: Alec Shanks
   sets: Charles Elson
   choreography: Colette Brosset
Productions:
   Opened November 11, 1958 for 835 performances
Reviews:
   America 100:381, Dec 20, 1958
   Christian Century 75:1435, Dec 10, 1958
   Dance Magazine 33:16, Jan 1959
   Life 45:67-8+, Dec 8, 1958
   New York Theatre Critics' Reviews 1958:206+
   New York Times page 42, Nov 12, 1958
                   page 39, Nov 13, 1958
                   II, page 1, Nov 16, 1958
                   II, page 1, Sep 13, 1959
                   II, page 3, Dec 18, 1960
   New Yorker 34:99-100, Nov 22, 1958
   Newsweek 52:78-9, Nov 24, 1958
   Saturday Review 41:24, Nov 29, 1958
   Theatre Arts 43:11+, Jan 1959
   Time 72:80+, Nov 24, 1958
   Vogue 133:94-5, Jan 1, 1959

La Strada
   book: Charles K. Peck, Jr.; based on the Federico
                    Fellini film
   music: Lionel Bart
   lyrics: Lionel Bart
   staging: Alan Schneider
   sets: Ming Cho Lee
   costumes: Nancy Potts
   choreography: Alvin Ailey
Productions:
   Opened December 14, 1969 for one performance

Reviews:
    New York Times page 40, Sep 23, 1969
                    page 63, Dec 15, 1969
                    page 56, Dec 16, 1969
    New Yorker 45:57, Dec 20, 1969

La Tierra de la Alegria (see Land of Joy)

La Tragedie de Carmen
    book: Jean-Claude Carriere and Peter Brook, adapted
                   from Georges Bizet's opera Carmen
    music: Marius Constant
    lyrics: Jean-Claude Carriere and Peter Brook
    staging: Peter Brook
    sets: Jean-Guy Lecat
    costumes: Chloe Obolensky
Productions:
    Opened November 17, 1983 for 187 performances
Reviews:
    New York Theatre Critics' Reviews 1983:124
    New York Times II, page 1, Nov 13, 1983
                   III, page 3, Nov 18, 1983
                   II, page 1, Nov 27, 1983

Labor Sings
    script: Alfred Hayes
    music: George Kleinsinger
    sets: Sointu Syrjala
    choreography: Lily Mehlmann
Productions:
    (Off-Broadway) Opened October 5, 1940 for 2 performances
No Reviews.

Lace Petticoat
    book: Stewart St. Clair
    music: Emil Gerstenberger and Carl Carlton
    lyrics: Howard Johnson
    staging: Carl Carlton
Productions:
    Opened January 4, 1927 for 15 performances
Reviews:
    New York Times page 18, Jan 5, 1927
    Theatre Magazine 45:21, Mar 1927

Ladies and Gentlemen, Jerome Kern (Kern songs, 1905-1946)
    conceived: William E. Hunt
    music: Jerome Kern
    lyrics: Various collaborators
    staging: William E. Hunt
    sets: James Wolk
    costumes: David P. Pearson
    choreography: Valarie Pettiford

Productions:
 (Off-Broadway) Opened June 10, 1985 for 22 performances
Reviews:
 New York Times III, page 25, Jun 12, 1985

Ladies First
 book: Harry B. Smith; based on A Contented Woman
 music: A. Baldwin Sloane
 lyrics: Harry B. Smith
 staging: Frank Smithson
Productions:
 Opened October 24, 1918 for 164 performances
Reviews:
 Dramatic Mirror 79:688, Nov 9, 1918
 New York Times page 11, Oct 25, 1918
 Theatre Magazine 28:378, Dec 1918

Lady and Her Music (see Lena Horne: The Lady and Her Music)

Lady Audley's Secret
 book: Douglas Seale, adapted from the novel by Mary
                  Elizabeth Braddon
 music: George Goehring
 lyrics: John Kuntz
 staging: Douglas Seale
 sets: Alicia Finkel
 costumes: Alicia Finkel
 choreography: George Bunt
Productions:
 (Off-Broadway) Opened October 3, 1972 for 7 performances
Reviews:
 New York Times page 40, Oct 4, 1972
 Saturday Review 54:33, Aug 7, 1971

Lady Be Good
 book: Guy Bolton and Fred Thompson
 music: George Gershwin
 lyrics: Ira Gershwin
Productions:
 Opened December 1, 1924 for 330 performances
Reviews:
 Canadian Magazine 64:164-6, Jul 1925
 Nation 245:173-4, Aug 29, 1987
 New York Times page 23, Dec 2, 1924
              VII, page 1, Dec 28, 1924
 Theatre Magazine 41:16, Feb 1925

Lady Billy
 book: Zelda Sears
 music: Harold A. Levey
 lyrics: Zelda Sears
 staging: John McKee

Productions:
    Opened December 14, 1920 for 188 performances
Reviews:
    Dramatic Mirror page 1155, Dec 18, 1920
                    83:249, Feb 5, 1921
    New York Clipper 68:18, Dec 29, 1920
    New York Times page 18, Dec 15, 1920
    Theatre Magazine 33:107, Feb 1921

Lady Butterfly
    book: Clifford Grey; adapted from a farce by Mark
                    Swan and James T. Powers
    music: Werner Janssen
    staging: Walter Wilson
Productions:
    Opened January 22, 1923 for 128 performances
Reviews:
    Life (New York) 81:18, Feb 15, 1923
    New York Clipper 70:14, Jan 31, 1923

The Lady Comes Across
    book: Fred Thompson and Dawn Powell
    music: Vernon Duke
    lyrics: John Latouche
    staging: Romney Brent
    sets: Stewart Chaney
    costumes: Stewart Chaney
    choreography: George Balanchine
Productions:
    Opened January 9, 1942 for 3 performances
Reviews:
    New York Theatre Critics' Reviews 1942:388+
    New York Times page 10, Jan 10, 1942
                    IX, page 3, Jan 11, 1942

Lady Day: A Musical Tragedy
    book: Aishah Rahman; based on the career of Billie
                    Holiday
    music: Archie Shepp; additional music by Stanley
                    Cowell and Cal Massey
    staging: Paul Carter Harrison
    sets: Robert U. Taylor
    costumes: Randy Barcelo
Productions:
    (Off-Broadway) Opened October 17, 1972 for 24 performances
Reviews:
    New York Theatre Critics' Reviews 1972:165
    New York Times page 39, Oct 26, 1972
                    II, page 5, Nov 5, 1972
    New Yorker 48:105-6+, Nov 4, 1972
    Newsweek 80:133-4, Nov 6, 1972

Lady Do
- book: Jack McClellan and Albert Cowles
- music: Abel Baer
- lyrics: Sam M. Lewis and Joe Young
- staging: Edgar J. Macgregor

Productions:
Opened April 18, 1927 for 56 performances
Reviews:
New York Times page 24, Apr 19, 1927

Lady Fingers
- book: Eddie Buzzell, based on Owen Davis's Easy Come, Easy Go
- music: Joseph Meyer
- lyrics: Edward Eliscu
- staging: Lew Levenson

Productions:
Opened January 31, 1929 for 132 performances
Reviews:
New York Times VIII, page 2, Jan 13, 1929
page 22, Feb 1, 1929

The Lady in Ermine
- book: Frederick Lonsdale and Cyrus Wood; adapted from the book by Rudolph Schanzer and Ernest Welisch
- music: Jean Gilbert and Alfred Goodman
- lyrics: Harry Graham and Cyrus Wood
- staging: Charles Sinclair and Allen K. Foster

Productions:
Opened October 2, 1922 for 232 performances
Reviews:
New York Clipper 70:20, Oct 11, 1922
New York Times page 22, Oct 3, 1922

The Lady in Red
- book: Anne Caldwell
- music: Robert Winterberg
- lyrics: Anne Caldwell
- staging: Frank Smithson

Productions:
Opened May 12, 1919 for 48 performances
Reviews:
Forum 61:755-6, Jun 1919
Life (New York) 73:904-5, May 22, 1919
New York Dramatic News 65:6, May 17, 1919
New York Times page 18, May 13, 1919

Lady in the Dark
- book: Moss Hart
- music: Kurt Weill

lyrics: Ira Gershwin
staging: Hassard Short and Moss Hart
sets: Harry Horner
costumes: Irene Sharaff and Hattie Carnegie
choreography: Albertina Rasch
Productions:
 Opened January 23, 1941 for 162 performances
 Opened September 2, 1941 for 305 performances
 Opened February 27, 1943 for 83 performances
Reviews:
 Catholic World 152:726-7, Mar 1941
 Commonweal 33:401, Feb 7, 1941
       37:542, Mar 19, 1943
 Life 10:43, Feb 17, 1941
 Nation 152:164, Feb 8, 1941
 New Republic 104:179, Feb 10, 1941
 New York Theatre Critics' Reviews 1941:400+
 New York Times page 18, Dec 31, 1940
        IX, page 1, Jan 5, 1941
        page 14, Jan 24, 1941
        IX, page 1, Feb 2, 1941
        IX, page 3, Apr 6, 1941
        page 26, Sep 3, 1941
        IX, page 1, Sep 7, 1941
        page 14, Mar 1, 1943
        II, page 1, Mar 7, 1943
 New Yorker 16:27, Feb 1, 1941
 Newsweek 17:59, Feb 3, 1941
 Stage 1:26-7, Feb 1941
 Theatre Arts 25:177-8+, Mar 1941
       25:265-75, Apr 1941
 Time 37:53-4, Feb 3, 1941
 Vogue 97:72-3, May 15, 1941

Lady Luxury
 book: Rida Johnson Young
 music: William Schroeder
 lyrics: Rida Johnson Young
 staging: J. H. Benrimo
Productions:
 Opened December 25, 1914 for 35 performances
Reviews:
 Dramatic Mirror 72:8, Dec 30, 1914
        73:2, Jan 20, 1915
 Green Book 13:574-5, Mar 1915
 Nation 99:783-4, Dec 31, 1914
 New York Times page 7, Dec 26, 1914
 Theatre Magazine 21:60, Feb 1915

The Lady of the Slipper
 book: Anne Caldwell and Lawrence McCarty; based on
        the Cinderella story

music: Victor Herbert
lyrics: James O'Dea
staging: R. H. Burnside
Productions:
    Opened October 28, 1912 for 232 performances
Reviews:
    Collier's 50:15, Jan 25, 1913
    Dramatic Mirror 68:6, Oct 30, 1912
    Green Book 9:4-6+, Jan 1913
                 9:182, Jan 1913
    Harper's Weekly 56:20, Nov 9, 1912
    Munsey 48:530, Dec 1912
    New York Dramatic News 56:11, Oct 26, 1912
                            56:21-2, Nov 2, 1912
    Red Book 20:702-4, Feb 1913
    Theatre Magazine 16:193, Dec 1912
                     17:3, Mar 1913
                     17:79, Mar 1913

A Lady Says Yes
    book: Clayton Ashley (Dr. Maxwell Maltz) and Stanley
                   Adams
    music: Fred Spielman and Arthur Gershwin
    lyrics: Clayton Ashley and Stanley Adams
    sets: Watson Barratt
    costumes: Lou Eisele
    choreography: Boots McKenna and Natalie Kamarova
Productions:
    Opened January 10, 1945 for 87 performances
Reviews:
    Nation 160:136, Feb 3, 1945
    New York Theatre Critics' Reviews 1945:294+
    New York Times page 18, Jan 11, 1945
    Time 45:63, Jan 22, 1945

Laffing Room Only
    book: Ole Olsen, Chic Johnson, Eugene Conrad
    music: Burton Lane
    lyrics: Burton Lane
    staging: John Murray Anderson
    sets: Stewart Chaney
    costumes: Billy Livingston
    choreography: Robert Alton
Productions:
    Opened December 23, 1944 for 233 performances
Reviews:
    Life 18:76, Apr 9, 1945
    New York Theatre Critics' Reviews 1944:52+
    New York Times page 15, Dec 25, 1944
                     page 31, Sep 20, 1945
    Theatre Arts 29:142+, Mar 1945
    Time 45:67, Jan 8, 1945

The Land of Joy (La Tierra de la Alegria)
    book: J. F. Elizondo and E. Velasco
    adapted: Ruth Boyd Ober
    music: J. Valverde
    lyrics: Ruth Boyd Ober
Productions:
Opened October 31, 1917 for 86 performances
Reviews:
    Dramatic Mirror 77:7, Nov 10, 1917
    Green Book 19:218-20, Feb 1918
    Life (New York) 70:795, Nov 15, 1917
    New York Dramatic News 64:10, Nov 10, 1917
    New York Times page 13, Nov 2, 1917
                    VIII, page 6, Nov 11, 1917
    Theatre Magazine 27:9, Jan 1918
                    27:23, Jan 1918
                    27:78, Feb 1918

Lassie
    book: Catherine Chisholm Cushing; based on Kitty
                    MacKaye
    music: Hugo Felix
    lyrics: Catherine Chisolm Cushing
    staging: Edward Royce
Productions:
Opened April 6, 1920 for 63 performances
Reviews:
    Dramatic Mirror 82:680, Apr 10, 1920
    New York Clipper 68:14, Mar 17, 1920
    New York Times page 9, Apr 7, 1920
    Theatre Magazine 31:401-2, May 1920
                    31:407, May 1920

The Last Savage
    book: Gian Carlo Menotti; translated by George Meade
    music: Gian Carlo Menotti
    lyrics: Gian Carlo Menotti
    staging: Gian Carlo Menotti
    sets: Beni Montresor
    costumes: Beni Montresor
Productions:
Opened January 23, 1964 for 7 performances
Reviews:
    Life 56:66A-66B, Feb 14, 1964
    New Yorker 39:198-200, Nov 2, 1963
                    39:60+, Feb 1, 1964
    Newsweek 63:77, Feb 3, 1964
    Opera News 28:28-30, Dec 7, 1963
                    28:13-15, Feb 8, 1964
                    28:24-5, Feb 8, 1964
                    28:27-8, Feb 8, 1964

Saturday Review 47:27-7, Feb 8, 1964
48:22, Jan 16, 1965
Time 82:63, Nov 1, 1963
83:33, Jan 31, 1964

The Last Sweet Days of Isaac
book: Gretchen Cryer
music: Nancy Ford
lyrics: Gretchen Cryer
staging: Word Baker
sets: Ed Wittstein
costumes: Caley Summers

Productions:
(Off-Broadway) Opened January 26, 1970 for 485 performances
Reviews:
Nation 210:284, Mar 9, 1970
New York Theatre Critics' Reviews 1970:292
New York Times page 49, Jan 27, 1970
II, page 1, Feb 8, 1970
II, page 1, Feb 15, 1970
page 34, Mar 3, 1970
II, page 17, Jun 28, 1970
page 17, Jan 9, 1971
II, page 24, May 2, 1971
New Yorker 45:73-4+, Feb 7, 1970
Newsweek 75:95, Feb 9, 1970

The Last Waltz
book: Julius Brammer and Alfred Grunwald; adapted by
Harold Atteridge and Edward Delaney Dunn
music: Oscar Straus
staging: J. C. Huffman and Frank Smithson

Productions:
Opened May 10, 1921 for (43) performances
Reviews:
Dramatic Mirror 83:817, May 14, 1921
Life (New York) 77:760, May 26, 1921
New York Clipper 69:23, May 18, 1921
New York Times page 20, May 11, 1921
Theatre Magazine 34:64, Jul 1921
34:101, Aug 1921
Woman's Home Companion 48:61, Sep 1921

Late Nite Comic
book: Allan Knee
music: Brian Gari
lyrics: Brian Gari
sets: Clarke Dunham
costumes: Gail Cooper-Hecht
choreography: Dennis Dennehy

Productions:
Opened October 15, 1987 for 4 performances

Reviews:
New York Theatre Critics' Reviews 1987:167
New York Times III, page 3, Oct 16, 1987
New Yorker 63:130+, Oct 26, 1987

The Laugh Parade
book: Ed Wynn and Ed Preble
music: Harry Warren
lyrics: Mort Dixon and Joe Young
staging: Ed Wynn
choreography: Albertina Rasch
Productions:
Opened November 2, 1931 for 231 performances
Reviews:
Catholic World 134:471, Jan 1932
Nation 133:582, Nov 25, 1931
New York Times VIII, page 3, Sep 20, 1931
                 page 31, Nov 3, 1931
                 VIII, page 1, Dec 6, 1931

The Laughing Husband
book: Julius Brammer and Alfred Grunwald; adapted
                  by Arthur Wimperis
music: Edmund Eysler
staging: Edward Royce
Productions:
Opened February 2, 1914 for 48 performances
Reviews:
Dramatic Mirror 71:7, Feb 4, 1914
                71:4, Feb 11, 1914
                71:2, Mar 18, 1914
Green Book 11:605-6, Apr 1914
           11:702, Apr 1914
Life (New York) 63:277, Feb 12, 1914
New York Dramatic News 59:20, Feb 7, 1914
New York Times page 9, Jan 13, 1914
               page 11, Feb 3, 1914
Theatre Magazine 19:113, Mar 1914
                 19:156, Mar 1914

Laughing Matters
written: Linda Wallem and Peter Tolan
music: Peter Tolan
lyrics: Peter Tolan
staging: Martin Charnin
sets: Ray Recht
costumes: Jade Jobson, Isaac Mizrahi, and Giorgio Armani
Productions:
(Off-Broadway) Opened May 18, 1989
Reviews:
New York Theatre Critics' Reviews 1989:223
New York Times I, page 68, May 21, 1989

Laughs and Other Events
  songs and
    monologues: Stanley Holloway
    staging: Tony Charmoli
    sets: John Robert Lloyd
Productions:
  Opened October 10, 1960 for 8 performances
Reviews:
  New York Theatre Critics' Reviews 1960:213
  New York Times page 57, Oct 11, 1960
              page 41, Oct 13, 1960

The Laundry Hour
  words: Mark Linn-Baker and Lewis Black
  music: Paul Schierhorn
  staging: William Peters
  choreography: Rick Elice
Productions:
  (Off-Broadway) Opened August 4, 1981 for 8 performances
No Reviews.

Lawless, Sue (see An Evening with Sue and Pugh)

L'Chaim to Life
  sketches: Various authors, in the Yiddish and English languages, including Martin Buber
  songs: Various authors and composers, including Ben Zion Witler
  staging: Neil Steinberg
  sets: Ari Roussimoff
  costumes: Eber Lobato
  choreography: Eber Lobato
Productions:
  Opened November 5, 1986 for 42 performances
Reviews:
  New York Times I, page 13, Nov 8, 1986

Leader of the Pack
  by: Ellie Greenwich, based on an original concept by Melanie Mintz ("The life and songs of Ellie Greenwich.")
  songs: Ellie Greenwich, Jeff Barry, Phil Spector, Tony Powers, George "Shadow" Morton, Jeff Kent, and Ellen Foley
  additional
    material: Jack Heifner and Anne Beatts
  staging: Michael Peters
  sets: Tony Walton
  costumes: Robert de Mora
  choreography: Michael Peters
Productions:
  Opened April 8, 1985 for 120 performances

Reviews:
    Dance Magazine 59:62, Jun 1985
    Ms. 14:107+, Sep 1985
    New York 17:27, May 28, 1984
            18:97-8, Apr 22, 1985
    New York Theatre Critics' Reviews 1985:316
    New York Times III, page 11, Apr 9, 1985
    New Yorker 61:126, Apr 22, 1985
    Newsweek 105:83, Apr 22, 1985
    People 23:121, Mar 4, 1985
    Time 125:87, Apr 29, 1985

Leave It to Jane

book:	Guy Bolton and P. G. Wodehouse; based on George Ade's The College Widow
music:	Jerome Kern
lyrics:	Guy Bolton and P. G. Wodehouse
staging:	Edward Royce

Productions:
    Opened August 28, 1917 for 167 performances
    (Off-Broadway) Season of 1959-60 for 928 performances
    (Off-Off-Broadway) Opened March 9, 1989
Reviews:
    Dance Magazine 33:12, Sep 1959
    Dramatic Mirror 77:31, Aug 11, 1917
              77:32, Sep 1, 1917
              77:8, Sep 8, 1917
              77:7, Dec 22, 1917
    Independent 92:602, Dec 29, 1917
    New York Dramatic News 64:2, Sep 1, 1917
    New York Times page 7, Aug 29, 1917
              page 30, May 26, 1959
              II, page 7, Oct 25, 1959
              III, page 33, Nov 7, 1985
              III, page 17, Mar 23, 1989
    New Yorker 35:120, Jun 6, 1959
    Saturday Review 42:29, Jun 13, 1959
    Theatre Magazine 26:203, Oct 1917
              26:242, Oct 1917

Leave It to Me

book:	Bella and Samuel Spewack
music:	Cole Porter
lyrics:	Cole Porter
staging:	Samuel Spewack
sets:	Albert Johnson
costumes:	Raoul Pene du Bois
choreography:	Robert Alton

Productions:
    Opened November 9, 1938 for 307 performances
    Opened September 4, 1939 for 16 performances

Reviews:
  Catholic World 148:477, Jan 1939
  Commonweal 29:132, Nov 25, 1938
  Life 5:53-5, Nov 7, 1938
  Nation 147:572-3, Nov 26, 1938
  New Republic 97:100, Nov 30, 1938
  New York Times IX, page 3, Oct 23, 1938
                  page 32, Nov 10, 1938
                  IX, page 1, Nov 20, 1938
                  IX, page 3, Nov 20, 1938
                  page 25, Sep 5, 1939
                  IX, page 1, Sep 10, 1939
                  page 20, Sep 16, 1939
                  page 27, Jan 18, 1940
  Newsweek 12:24, Nov 21, 1938
  North American Review 247 no2:369, (Jun) 1939
  Stage 16:10-11, Nov 1938
        16:12-15, Dec 1938
  Theatre Arts 23:6+, Jan 1939
  Time 32:39, Nov 7, 1938
       32:66, Nov 21, 1938

Leaves of Grass

  book: adapted by Stan Harte, Jr.; based on the writ-
                   ings of Walt Whitman
  music: Stan Harte, Jr.
  staging: Stan Harte, Jr. and Bert Michaels
  sets: David Chapman
  choreography: Bert Michaels
Productions:
  (Off-Broadway) Opened September 12, 1971 for 49 performances
Reviews:
  New York Theatre Critics' Reviews 1971:217
  New York Times page 47, Sep 13, 1971

Legends in Concert

  created: John Stuart
  songs: Various authors and composers
  staging: John Stuart
  multimedia
    design: Media Innovations/Joseph Jarred
  choreography: Inez Mourning
Productions:
  (Off-Broadway) Opened May 10, 1989 for 22 performances
Reviews:
  New York Times I, page 49, May 14, 1989

Legs Diamond

  book: Harvey Fierstein and Charles Suppon, based on
                   the motion picture The Rise and Fall of Legs
                   Diamond

music:	Peter Allen
lyrics:	Peter Allen
staging:	Robert Allan Ackerman
sets:	David Mitchell
costumes:	Willa Kim
choreography:	Alan Johnson

Productions:
Opened December 26, 1988 for 64 performances
Reviews:
Dance Magazine 63:40-4, Jan 1989
New York 21:48-9, Sep 12, 1988
          22:56-7, Jan 9, 1989
New York Theatre Critics' Reviews 1988:89
New York Times III, page 13, Dec 27, 1988
New Yorker 64:26-8, Oct 31, 1988
         64:82-3, Jan 9, 1989
Time 133:67, Jan 9, 1989

Lemmings (see National Lampoon's Lemmings)

Lena Horne: The Lady and Her Music

by:	Lena Horne
songs:	Various authors and composers
staging:	Arthur Faria
sets:	David Gropman
costumes:	Stanley Simmons and Giorgio Sant'Angelo

Productions:
Opened May 12, 1981 for 333 performances
Reviews:
Ebony 38:46+, Dec 1982
Los Angeles 28:126+, Jan 1983
New York 14:95-6, May 25, 1981
New York Theatre Critics' Reviews 1981:222
New York Times III, page 27, May 13, 1981
         II, page 3, May 24, 1981
New Yorker 57:115, May 25, 1981
Newsweek 97:94+, May 25, 1981
Time 117:96, May 25, 1981

Lend An Ear

sketches:	Charles Gaynor, additional sketches by Joseph Stein and Will Glickman
music:	Charles Gaynor
lyrics:	Charles Gaynor
staging:	Gower Champion
sets:	Raoul Pene du Bois
costumes:	Raoul Pene du Bois
choreography:	Gower Champion

Productions:
Opened December 16, 1948 for 460 performances
(Off-Broadway) Season of 1959-60
(Off-Broadway) Opened October 16, 1969 for 19 performances

Reviews:
    Catholic World 168: 403, Feb 1949
    Commonweal 49: 306, Dec 31, 1948
    Life 26: 79-80+, Feb 28, 1949
    Nation 168: 25, Jan 1, 1949
    New Republic 120: 29-31, Jan 3, 1949
    New York Theatre Critics' Reviews 1948: 122+
    New York Times page 38, Dec 17, 1948
                    II, page 3, Sep 20, 1959
                    page 20, Sep 25, 1959
                    page 48, Dec 1, 1959
                    page 32, Oct 29, 1969
    New Yorker 24: 32, Dec 25, 1948
    Newsweek 32: 65, Dec 27, 1948
    Theatre Arts 32: 22, Aug 1948
                  33: 56, Mar 1949
    Time 52: 46, Dec 27, 1948
    Vogue 113: 214, Feb 1, 1949
          113: 90, Feb 15, 1949

Lennon
    by: Bob Eaton
    music and
      lyrics: Lennon/McCartney songs written by John Lennon
    staging: Bob Eaton
    sets: Peter David Gould
    costumes: Deborah Shaw
Productions:
    (Off-Broadway) Opened October 5, 1982 for 25 performances
Reviews:
    New York 15: 88, Oct 18, 1982
    New York Theatre Critics' Reviews 1982: 164
    New York Times III, page 23, Oct 6, 1982

Lenny and the Heartbreakers
    book: Kenneth Robins
    music: Scott Killian and Kim D. Sherman
    lyrics: Kenneth Robins, Scott Killian, and Kim D.
                    Sherman
    staging: Murray Louis and Alwin Nikolais
    sets: Alwin Nikolais with Nancy Winters
    costumes: Linsay W. Davis
    choreography: Murray Louis and Alwin Nikolais
Productions:
    (Off-Broadway) Opened December 22, 1983 for 20 performances
Reviews:
    New York Times III, page 10, Dec 23, 1983

Leonard Bernstein's Theater Songs
    music: Leonard Bernstein
    lyrics: Stephen Sondheim, Betty Comden, Adolph Green,

staging: Richard Wilbur, Lillian Hellman, Leonard Bernstein
staging: Will Holt

Productions:
Opened June 28, 1965 for 88 performances
Reviews:
America 113:122, Jul 31, 1965
Life 59:12, Jul 30, 1965
New York Times page 49, Jun 16, 1965
               page 27, Jun 29, 1965
               page 29, Sep 1, 1965

Leonard Sillman's New Faces of 1968

conceived: Leonard Sillman
staging: Frank Wagner
sets: Winn Morton
costumes: Winn Morton
choreography: Frank Wagner
Productions:
Opened May 2, 1968 for 52 performances
Reviews:
New York Theatre Critics' Reviews 1968:279
                                  1968:282
New York Times page 43, May 3, 1968
               II, page 3, May 12, 1968
               page 54, Jun 6, 1968

Les Miserables

book: Alain Boublil and Claude-Michel Schonberg, based on the novel by Victor Hugo. From the original French text of Alain Boublil and Jean-Marc Natel
music: Claude-Michel Schonberg
lyrics: Herbert Kretzmer
additional
  material: James Fenton
staging: Trevor Nunn and John Caird
sets: John Napier
costumes: Andreane Neofitou
Productions:
Opened March 12, 1987 for *868 performances (still running 6/1/89)
Reviews:
America 156:427+, May 23, 1987
Chicago 38:107+, Jun 1989
Commonweal 114:245-7, Apr 24, 1987
Harper's Bazaar 119:304-5, Mar 1986
Horizon 30:37-9, Mar 1987
Los Angeles 33:162+, Jul 1988
Maclean's 102:40-6+, Mar 27, 1989
Nation 243:26, Jul 5-12, 1986

New Leader 70:17-18, Mar 23, 1987
New York 20:88-9, Mar 23, 1987
New York Review Books 34:14-16, May 7, 1987
New York Theatre Critics' Reviews 1987:362
New York Times II, page 8, Mar 8, 1987
　　　　　　　　III, page 1, Mar 13, 1987
　　　　　　　　III, page 19, Mar 16, 1988
New Yorker 63:77, Mar 23, 1987
Newsweek 109:44, Mar 23, 1987
　　　　　109:62-6+, Mar 30, 1987
Opera News 52:41, Jul 1987
Theatre Crafts 20:32-5+, Nov 1986
Time 126:83, Oct 21, 1985
　　　129:90-1, Mar 23, 1987
U S News and World Report 102:72-3, Mar 16, 1987
Vogue 177:92, Feb 1987

Leslie, Lew　(see Lew Leslie)

Let 'em Eat Cake
　　book:　　　　　George S. Kaufman and Morrie Ryskind
　　music:　　　　　George Gershwin
　　lyrics:　　　　Ira Gershwin
　　staging:　　　George S. Kaufman
　　sets:　　　　　Albert R. Johnson
　　choreography:　Van Grona and Ned McGurn
Productions:
　Opened October 21, 1933 for 90 performances
Reviews:
　Catholic World 138:338, Dec 1933
　Commonweal 19:47, Nov 10, 1933
　Nation 137:550, Nov 8, 1933
　New Outlook 162:47, Dec 1933
　New York Times page 16, Apr 17, 1933
　　　　　　　　　page 26, Oct 3, 1933
　　　　　　　　　X, page 2, Oct 8, 1933
　　　　　　　　　page 18, Oct 23, 1933
　　　　　　　　　IX, page 1, Nov 12, 1933
　　　　　　　　　III, page 14, Jul 5, 1978
　Saturday Review 5:35, Sep 16, 1978
　Stage 11:9-10, Dec 1933
　Time 22:29-30, Oct 30, 1933

Let Freedom Sing
　　book:　　　　　Sam Locke
　　music and
　　　lyrics:　　　Harold Rome, Earl Robinson, Marc Blitzstein,
　　　　　　　　　　Lou Cooper, Roslyn Harvey, Walter Kent, John
　　　　　　　　　　Latouche, Hy Zaret, Lewis Allan
　　staging:　　　Joseph Pevney and Robert H. Gordon
　　sets:　　　　　Herbert Andrews

costumes:	Paul DuPont
choreography:	Dan Eckley

Productions:

Opened October 5, 1942 for 8 performances

Reviews:

New York Theatre Critics' Reviews 1942: 216+

New York Times page 18, Oct 6, 1942

Let It Ride

book:	Abram S. Grimes, based on John Cecil Holm and George Abbott's Three Men on a Horse
music:	Jay Livingston and Ray Evans
lyrics:	Jay Livingston and Ray Evans
staging:	Stanley Prager
sets:	William and Jean Eckart
costumes:	Guy Kent
choreography:	Onna White

Productions:

Opened October 12, 1961 for 68 performances

Reviews:

Commonweal 75:154, Nov 3, 1961

Dance Magazine 35:22, Dec 1961

New York Theatre Critics' Reviews 1961: 230+

New York Times page 27, Oct 13, 1961

page 49, Dec 4, 1961

New Yorker 37:129, Oct 21, 1961

Theatre Arts 45:13, Dec 1961

Time 78:64, Oct 20, 1961

Let My People Come

music:	Earl Wilson, Jr.
lyrics:	Earl Wilson, Jr.
staging:	Phil Oesterman
choreography:	Ian Naylor

Productions:

(Off-Broadway) Opened January 8, 1974 for 1,327 performances

Opened July 7, 1976 for 108 performances

Reviews:

Essence 6:9, Oct 1975

Los Angeles 21:115+, Jan 1976

New York Times page 52, May 7, 1974

II, page 3, Sep 15, 1974

Playboy 21:144+, Jul 1974

Let's Face It

book:	Herbert and Dorothy Fields, based on Russell Medcraft and Norma Mitchell's play The Cradle Snatchers
music:	Cole Porter
lyrics:	Cole Porter
staging:	Edgar MacGregor

sets:	Harry Horner
costumes:	John Harkrider
choreography:	Charles Walters

Productions:

    Opened October 29, 1941

    Reopened August 17, 1942 for a total of 547 performances

Reviews:

    Catholic World 154: 601-2, Feb 1942

    Cosmopolitan 115: 98, Nov 1943

    Harper's Bazaar 75: 77, Nov 1941

    Life 11: 114-16+, Nov 10, 1941

    New York Theatre Critics' Reviews 1941: 249+

    New York Times page 27, Oct 10, 1941

                   page 26, Oct 30, 1941

                     IX, page 1, Nov 16, 1941

                     page 11, Feb 15, 1943

                     page 23, Mar 2, 1943

    New Yorker 17: 36, Nov 8, 1941

    Theatre Arts 26: 6-8, Jan 1942

    Time 38: 54, Nov 10, 1941

    Vogue 98: 90, Dec 1, 1941

Let's Make an Opera

book:	Eric Crozier
music:	Benjamin Britten
lyrics:	Eric Crozier
staging:	Marc Blitzstein
sets:	Ralph Alswang
costumes:	Aline Bernstein

Productions:

    Opened December 13, 1950 for 5 performances

Reviews:

    Commonweal 53: 328, Jan 5, 1951

    Home and Garden 98: 122-3, Dec 1950

    Musical America 69: 34, Dec 1, 1949

                   70: 16+, Apr 1950

    Nation 171: 682, Dec 23, 1950

    New York Theatre Critics' Reviews 1950: 173

    New York Times II, page 7, Dec 10, 1950

                   page 50, Dec 14, 1950

    New Yorker 26: 40+, Dec 23, 1950

    Newsweek 36: 58, Dec 25, 1950

    Theatre Arts 35: 17, Feb 1951

    Time 53: 39, Jun 27, 1949

        56: 47, Dec 25, 1950

Let's Sing Yiddish

music:	Renee Solomon
lyrics:	Itsik Manger, Mordecai Geloirtig, Morris Rosenfield, M. Nudelman and Wolf Younin
staging:	Mina Bern and Felix Fibich
choreography:	Felix Fibich and Judith Fibich

Productions:
  Opened November 9, 1966 for 107 performances
Reviews:
  Dance Magazine 41:25, Jan 1967
  New York Times page 63, Nov 10, 1966

A Letter for Queen Victoria
  book: Robert Wilson
  music: Alan Lloyd in collaboration with Michael Galasso
  staging: Robert Wilson
  sets: Peter Harvey
  costumes: Peter Harvey
  choreography: Andrew De Groat
Productions:
  Opened March 22, 1975 for 16 performances
Reviews:
  New York 8:80, Apr 7, 1975
  New York Theatre Critics' Reviews 1975:284
  New York Times page 46, Jul 10, 1974
                 page 40, Mar 24, 1975
                 II, page 5, Mar 30, 1975

Letty Pepper
  book: Oliver Morosco and George V. Hobart; based on
                   a comedy Maggie Pepper by Charles Klein
  music: Werner Janssen
  staging: George V. Hobart
Productions:
  Opened April 10, 1922 for 32 performances
Reviews:
  New York Clipper 70:20, Apr 12, 1922
  New York Times page 22, Apr 11, 1922

Lew Leslie's Blackbirds of 1928
  music: Jimmy McHugh
  lyrics: Dorothy Fields
  staging: Lew Leslie
Productions:
  Opened May 9, 1928 for 518 performances
Reviews:
  Life (New York) 92:12, Jul 12, 1928
  New York Times page 31, May 10, 1928
                 IX, page 4, Oct 28, 1928
                 page 22, Mar 1, 1929
  Theatre Magazine 48:39, Jul 1928
  Vogue 72:92, Jul 1, 1928

Lew Leslie's Blackbirds (1930)
  book: Flourney Miller
  music: Eubie Blake
  lyrics: Andy Razaf
  staging: Lew Leslie

Productions:
   Opened October 22, 1930 for 57 performances
Reviews:
   Bookman 72:409-10, Dec 1930
   Life (New York) 96:17, Nov 14, 1930
   New York Times page 34, Oct 23, 1930

Lew Leslie's Blackbirds of 1933
   book: Nat N. Dorfman, Mann Holiner, Lew Leslie
   music and
     lyrics: Mann Holiner, Alberta Nichols, Joseph Young,
                  Ned Washington, Victor Young
   staging: Lew Leslie
   sets: Mabel A. Buell
Productions:
   Opened December 2, 1933 for 25 performances
Reviews:
   New York Times page 32, Dec 4, 1933
                  II, page 6, Aug 26, 1934

Les Leslie's Blackbirds of 1939
   assembled by: Lew Leslie
   music: Rube Bloom and others
   lyrics: Johnny Mercer and others
   staging: Lew Leslie
   sets: Mabel A. Buell
   costumes: Frances Feist
Productions:
   Opened February 11, 1939 for 9 performances
Reviews:
   New York Times IX, page 2, Nov 13, 1938
                  page 12, Feb 13, 1939

The Liar
   book: Edward Eager and Alfred Drake, based on the
                  Carlo Goldoni play
   music: John Mundy
   lyrics: Edward Eager
   staging: Alfred Drake
   sets: Donald Oenslager
   costumes: Motley
   choreography: Hanya Holm
Productions:
   Opened May 18, 1950 for 12 performances
Reviews:
   Christian Science Monitor Magazine page 6, May 27, 1950
   New York Theatre Critics' Reviews 1950:296+
   New York Times page 30, May 19, 1950
   New Yorker 26:49, May 27, 1950
   Newsweek 35:69, May 29, 1950
   Theatre Arts 34:17, Jul 1950

Libby Holman's Blues, Ballads, and Sin-Songs
```
    songs:          Libby Holman
    sets:           Gerald Cook
    costumes:       Mainbocher, and Frank Stanley
```
Productions:
    Opened October 4, 1954 for 12 performances
Reviews:
    New York Times II, page 1, Oct 3, 1954
                   page 23, Oct 5, 1954
    Time 64:76, Oct 18, 1954

Lies & Legends: The Musical Stories of Harry Chapin
```
    conceived:      Joseph Sternby
    written:        Harry Chapin
    songs:          Harry Chapin
    staging:        Sam Weisman
    sets:           Gerry Hariton and Vicki Baral
    costumes:       Marsha Kowal
    choreography:   Tracy Friedman
```
Productions:
    (Off-Broadway) Opened April 24, 1985 for 79 performances
Reviews:
    Los Angeles 33:260, Nov 1988
    New York Times XXI, page 17, Apr 21, 1985
                    III, page 16, Apr 30, 1985

The Lieutenant
```
    book:           Gene Curty, Nitra Scharfman, and Chuck Strand
    music and
      lyrics:       Gene Curty, Nitra Scharfman, and Chuck Strand
    staging:        William Martin
    sets:           Frank J. Boros
    costumes:       Frank J. Boros
    choreography:   Dennis Dennehy
```
Productions:
    Opened March 9, 1975 for 9 performances
Reviews:
    America 132:247, Mar 29, 1975
    New York Theatre Critics' Reviews 1975:314
    New York Times page 35, Sep 20, 1974

Life Begins at 8:40
```
    book:           David Freedman
    music:          Harold Arlen
    lyrics:         Ira Gershwin and E. Y. Harburg
    staging:        John Murray Anderson and Philip Loeb
    sets:           Albert Johnson
    choreography:   Robert Alton and Charles Weidman
```
Productions:
    Opened August 27, 1934 for 237 performances
Reviews:
    Catholic World 140:88, Oct 1934

Literary Digest 118:20, Sep 8, 1934
New York Times page 20, Aug 7, 1934
       IX, page 1, Aug 12, 1934
       page 24, Aug 28, 1934
       IX, page 1, Sep 2, 1934
Stage 12:8-9, Oct 1934
Time 24:30, Sep 10, 1934

A Life in the Day of a Secretary
 book: Alfred Hayes and Jay Williams
 music: George Kleinsinger
 lyrics: Alfred Hayes and Jay Williams
 staging: Peter Frye
Productions:
 (Off-Broadway) Season of 1938-1939
 (Off-Broadway) Opened June 24, 1939
No Reviews.

Life Is Not a Doris Day Movie
 book: Boyd Graham
 music: Stephen Graziano
 lyrics: Boyd Graham
 staging: Norman Rene
 sets: Mike Boak
 costumes: Walter Hicklin
 choreography: Marcia Milgrom Dodge
Productions:
 (Off-Broadway) Opened June 25, 1982 for 37 performances
Reviews:
 New York Times page 46, Jun 27, 1982

The Life of Man
 book: Al Carmines
 music: Al Carmines
 lyrics: Al Carmines
 staging: Al Carmines
Productions:
 (Off-Off-Broadway) Opened September 29, 1972
Reviews:
 Craft Horizon 32:10+, Dec 1972
 New York Times page 40, Oct 4, 1972
 New Yorker 48:125, Oct 14, 1972
 Saturday Review 55:85, Oct 21, 1972

Light, Lively and Yiddish
 book: A. Shulman, Wolf, Sylvia Younin
 music: Eli Rubinstein
 lyrics: A. Shulman, Wolf, Sylvia Younin
 staging: Mina Bern
 sets: Josef Ijaky
 costumes: Sylvia Friedlander
 choreography: Felix Fibich

Productions:
Opened October 27, 1970 for 88 performances
Reviews:
New York Times page 58, Oct 28, 1970
page 17, Jun 9, 1971

Li'l Abner
book: Norman Panama and Melvin Frank, based on
                   characters created by Al Capp
music: Gene de Paul
lyrics: Johnny Mercer
staging: Michael Kidd
sets: William and Jean Eckart
costumes: Alvin Colt
choreography: Michael Kidd
Productions:
Opened November 15, 1956 for 693 performances
Reviews:
America 96:398, Jan 5, 1957
Catholic World 184:307, Jan 1957
Commonweal 65:408, Jan 18, 1957
Life 42:81-3, Jan 14, 1957
Nation 183:485, Dec 1, 1956
New York Theatre Critics' Reviews 1956:202+
New York Times VI, page 29, Sep 16, 1956
             VI, page 28, Nov 4, 1956
             II, page 1, Nov 11, 1956
             page 24, Nov 16, 1956
             II, page 1, Nov 25, 1956
             II, page 3, Dec 16, 1956
New Yorker 32:114+, Dec 1, 1956
Newsweek 48:73, Nov 26, 1956
Saturday Review 39:50, Dec 1, 1956
Theatre Arts 41:28-9, Jan 1957
Time 68:58, Nov 26, 1956

The Lilac Domino
book: Emerich Von Gatti and Bela Jenbach; English
                   adaption by Harry B. Smith
lyrics: English lyrics by Robert B. Smith
staging: Sydney Ellison
Productions:
Opened October 28, 1914 for 109 performances
Reviews:
Dramatic Mirror 72:8, Nov 4, 1914
             72:2, Nov 25, 1914
Green Book 13:376-7, Feb 1915
Harper's Weekly 59:518, Nov 28, 1914
Nation 99:562, Nov 15, 1914
New York Dramatic News 60:17, Nov 7, 1914
             63:25, Aug 19, 1916

New York Times page 11, Oct 7, 1914
                        VII, page 8, Nov 8, 1914
    Theatre Magazine 20:267, Dec 1914
                        21:7, Jan 1915

Liliane Montevecchi on the Boulevard (one-woman performance)
    by: Liliane Montevecchi
    songs: Various authors and composers
    sets: Dain Marcus
    costumes: Michael Katz
Productions:
    (Off-Broadway) Opened April 17, 1988 for 64 performances
No Reviews.

Linger Longer Letty
    music: Alfred Goodman
    lyrics: Bernard Grosman
Productions:
    Opened November 20, 1919 for 69 performances
Reviews:
    Dramatic Mirror 80:1861, Dec 4, 1919
    New York Times page 14, Nov 21, 1919
    Theatre Magazine 31:20, Jan 1920

Listen Lester
    book: Harry L. Cort and George E. Stoddard
    music: Harold Orlob
    staging: Robert Marks
Productions:
    Opened December 23, 1918 for 272 performances
Reviews:
    Dramatic Mirror 79:831, Dec 17, 1918
                    80:9, Jan 4, 1919
    New York Times page 7, Dec 24, 1918
    Theatre Magazine 29:80, Feb 1919
                    29:87, Feb 1919

The Little Blue Devil
    book: Harold Atteridge, based on Clyde Fitch's The
                        Blue Mouse
    music: Harry Carroll
    lyrics: Harold Atteridge
Productions:
    Opened November 3, 1919 for 75 performances
Reviews:
    Dramatic Mirror 80:1756, Nov 13, 1919
    New York Times page 18, Nov 4, 1919
    Theatre Magazine 30:424+, Dec 1919

The Little Cafe
    book: C. M. S. McLellan; based on Tristan Bernard's
                        La Petit Café

music: Ivan Caryll
lyrics: C. M. S. McLellan
Productions:
  Opened November 10, 1913 for 144 performances
Reviews:
  Blue Book 18:628-30, Feb 1914
  Dramatic Mirror 70:6, Nov 12, 1913
                  70:2, Nov 19, 1913
                  70:2, Dec 17, 1913
                  70:1, Dec 31, 1913
  Everybody's 30:254-5, Feb 1914
  Green Book 11:188-90, Feb 1914
             11:345-6, Feb 1914
  Leslie's Weekly 118:59, Jan 15, 1914
  Munsey 50:725, Jan 1914
  New York Dramatic News 58:18, Nov 15, 1913
                       58:1, Dec 20, 1913
  New York Times page 13, Nov 11, 1913
  Theatre Magazine 18:xii+, Dec 1913

The Little Comedy (see Romance Romance)

Little Jessie James
  book: Harlan Thompson
  music: Harry Archer
  staging: Ernest Cutting
Productions:
  Opened August 15, 1923 for (453) performances
Reviews:
  New York Times page 10, Aug 16, 1923
  Theatre Magazine 38:52, Oct 1923

Little Johnny Jones
  book: George M. Cohan, adapted by Alfred Uhry
  music: George M. Cohan
  lyrics: George M. Cohan
  staging: Gerald Guitierrez
  sets: Robert Randolph
  costumes: David Toser
  choreography: Dan Siretta
Productions:
  Opened March 21, 1982 for one performance
Reviews:
  New York Theatre Critics' Reviews 1982:330
  New York Times III, page 12, Mar 22, 1982

Little Mary Sunshine
  book: Rick Besoyan
  music: Rick Besoyan
  lyrics: Rick Besoyan
  staging: Ray Harrison

```
sets:              Howard Barker
costumes:          Howard Barker
choreography:      Ray Harrison
```
Productions:
  (Off-Broadway) Opened November 18, 1959 for 1,143 performances
  (Off-Broadway) Opened February 12, 1970 for 19 performances
Reviews:
  Dance Magazine 34:20-1, Feb 1960
  New York Times page 49, Nov 19, 1959
                 page 27, Nov 21, 1959
                 II, page 1, Nov 29, 1959
                 II, page 3, Dec 20, 1959
                 page 35, May 18, 1962
                 page 18, Jul 31, 1962
  New Yorker 35:110-12, Nov 28, 1959
  Newsweek 55:95, Feb 22, 1960
  Saturday Review 42:29, Dec 5, 1959
  Time 75:70, Jun 6, 1960

Little Me
```
  book:            Neil Simon, based on the novel by Patrick Dennis
  music:           Cy Coleman
  lyrics:          Carolyn Leigh
  staging:         Cy Feuer and Bob Fosse
  sets:            Robert Randolph
  costumes:        Robert Fletcher
  choreography:    Bob Fosse
```
Productions:
  Opened November 17, 1962 for 257 performances
  Opened January 21, 1982 for 36 performances
Reviews:
  America 107:1258, Dec 15, 1962
  Commonweal 77:280, Dec 7, 1962
  Dance Magazine 37:24+, Jan 1963
  Life 53:113-15, Nov 30, 1962
  Nation 195:411, Dec 8, 1962
  New Leader 65:22, Feb 8, 1982
  New York 15:57, Feb 1, 1982
  New York Theatre Critics' Reviews 1962:196+
                                    1982:393
  New York Times page 58, Oct 10, 1962
                 page 41, Nov 19, 1962
                 II, page 1, Dec 2, 1962
                 III, page 3, Jan 22, 1982
                 II, page 5, Jan 31, 1982
  New York Times Magazine pages 75-6, Nov 4, 1962
  New Yorker 38:118+, Dec 1, 1962
             57:114, Feb 1, 1982
  Newsweek 60:51-4, Nov 26, 1962
           99:77, Feb 1, 1982
  Reporter 27:43-4, Dec 20, 1962

Saturday Review 45:51, Dec 8, 1962
Theatre Arts 46:17-19+, Nov 1962
   47:12, Jan 1963
Time 80:53, Nov 30, 1962
  119:65, Feb 1, 1982

The Little Millionaire
  book: George M. Cohan
  staging: George M. Cohan
Productions:
Opened September 25, 1911 for 192 performances
Reviews:
  Blue Book 14:463-5, Jan 1912
  Dramatic Mirror 66:11, Sep 27, 1911
        66:4, Oct 4, 1911
        66:2, Oct 18, 1911
        66:2, Dec 13, 1911
        67:2, Jan 3, 1912
        67:1, Jan 31, 1912
  Green Book Album 6:1146-8, Dec 1911
          6:1195-6, Dec 1911
  Harper's Weekly 55:18, Oct 21, 1911
  Leslie's Weekly 113:409, Oct 12, 1911
        113:467, Oct 26, 1911
  Life (New York) 58:618, Oct 12, 1911
  Munsey 46:426, Dec 1911
  New York Times page 9, Sep 26, 1911
  Theatre Magazine 14:xvi, Nov 1911
        14:174, Nov 1911

Little Miss Charity
  book: Edward Clark
  music: S. R. Henry and M. Savin
  staging: Alfred Hickman and C. A. de Lima
Productions:
Opened September 2, 1920 for 77 performances
Reviews:
  Dramatic Mirror page 459, Sep 11, 1920
  New York Clipper 68:14, Mar 24, 1920
        68:19, Sep 8, 1920
  New York Times page 6, Sep 3, 1920

Little Miss Fix-It
  book: William J. Hurlbut and Harry B. Smith
  staging: Gustav Von Seyffertitz
Productions:
Opened April 3, 1911 for 56 performances
Reviews:
  Blue Book 13:227+, Jun 1911
  Dramatic Mirror 65:2, Apr 5, 1911
        65:7, Aug 5, 1911

Green Book Album 5:1133-5, Jun 1911
Leslie's Weekly 112:451+, Apr 20, 1911
Pearson 25:782-3, Jun 1911
Red Book 17:369+, Jun 1911
Stage 13:57, Aug 1936
Theatre Magazine 13:ix, May 1911
                 13:145, May 1911

Little Nellie Kelly
    book: George M. Cohan
    staging: George M. Cohan and Julian Mitchell
Productions:
    Opened November 13, 1922 for (248) performances
Reviews:
    National Magazine 52:37+, Jun 1923
    New York Clipper 70:20, Nov 29, 1922
    New York Times page 16, Nov 14, 1922

A Little Night Music
    book: Hugh Wheeler; suggested by Ingmar Bergman's
                      film Smiles of a Summer Night
    music: Stephen Sondheim
    lyrics: Stephen Sondheim
    staging: Harold Prince
    sets: Boris Aronson
    costumes: Florence Klotz
    choreography: Patricia Birch
Productions:
    Opened February 25, 1973 for 600 performances
    (Off-Off-Broadway) Opened September 18, 1975
    (Off-Off-Broadway) Opened March 20, 1981
    (Off-Off-Broadway) Opened May 9, 1985
Reviews:
    America 128:243, Mar 17, 1973
    Dance Magazine 47:60-1, Jun 1973
    Harper's 106:153, Mar 1973
    High Fidelity 23:70-1+, Jul 1973
    Los Angeles 27:266+, Sep 1982
    Nation 216:379, Mar 19, 1973
    New York 6:80, Mar 12, 1973
    New York Theatre Critics' Reviews 1973:348
    New York Times page 26, Feb 26, 1973
                    II, page 1, Mar 4, 1973
                    page 14, Sep 17, 1975
                    III, page 4, May 24, 1985
    New Yorker 49:78+, Mar 3, 1973
    Newsweek 81:88, Mar 12, 1973
    Playboy 20:36, Mar 1973
    Saturday Review (Arts) 1:77, Apr 1973
    Time 101:86+, Mar 12, 1973
    Vogue 161:180-1, Apr 1973

A Little Racketeer
    book: Harry Clarke, adapted from the German of F.
                     Kalbfuss and R. Wilde
    music: Haskell Brown
    lyrics: Edward Eliscu
    staging: William Caryl
    choreography: Albertina Rasch
Productions:
    Opened January 18, 1932 for 48 performances
Reviews:
    New York Times VIII, page 4, Oct 18, 1931
                       page 24, Jan 19, 1932
                       page 13, Feb 15, 1932

Little Shop of Horrors
    book: Howard Ashman, based on the film by Roger
                     Corman
    music: Alan Menken
    lyrics: Howard Ashman
    staging: Howard Ashman
    sets: Edward T. Gianfrancesco
    costumes: Sally Lesser
    choreography: Edie Cowan
Productions:
    (Off-Off-Broadway) Opened May 6, 1982 for 24 performances
    (Off-Broadway) Opened July 27, 1982 for 2,209 performances
Reviews:
    Los Angeles 28:58, Apr 1983
                  28:56, Jun 1983
    New York 15:82, Aug 23, 1982
    New York Theatre Critics' Reviews 1982:219
    New York Times page 47, May 30, 1982
                     II, page 3, Aug 22, 1982
    New Yorker 58:118, Sep 27, 1982
    Time 120:59, Aug 23, 1982

The Little Show (1929)
    book: Howard Dietz
    music: Arthur Schwartz; additional songs by Kay Swift
                     and Ralph Rainger
    lyrics: Howard Dietz
    staging: Dwight Deere Wiman
    choreography: Danny Dare
Productions:
    Opened April 30, 1929 for 321 performances
Reviews:
    Life (New York) 92:22, May 24, 1929
    Nation 131:331, Sep 24, 1930
    New Republic 59:25, May 22, 1929
    New York Times page 28, May 1, 1929
                     IX, page 1, May 12, 1929

IX, page 2, May 12, 1929
IX, page 7, Jul 14, 1929
Theatre Magazine 50:42, Jul 1929
Vogue 74:57+, Jul 6, 1929

Little Show (1953)   (see Anna Russell's Little Show)

Little Simplicity
    book: Rida Johnson Young
    music: Augustus Barratt
    lyrics: Rida Johnson Young
    staging: Edward P. Temple
Productions:
    Opened November 4, 1918 for 112 performances
Reviews:
    Dramatic Mirror 79:723, Nov 16, 1918
    New York Dramatic News 65:11, Nov 9, 1918
    New York Times page 11, Nov 5, 1918
    Theatre Magazine 28:347, Dec 1918
                    29:15, Jan 1919

The Little Whopper
    book: Otto A. Harbach; adapted from the movie Miss
                         Geo. Washington, Jr.
    music: Rudolf Friml
    lyrics: Bide Dudley and Otto A. Harbach
Productions:
    Opened October 13, 1919 for 224 performances
Reviews:
    Dramatic Mirror 80:1654, Oct 23, 1919
    New York Times page 20, Oct 16, 1919
    Theatre Magazine 30:391, Dec 1919

Little Wine with Lunch
    book: John von Hartz
    music: William Schimmel
    lyrics: John von Hartz
    staging: Norman Thomas Marshall
Productions:
    (Off-Off-Broadway) Opened March 16, 1977
Reviews:
    New York Times III, page 2, Mar 18, 1977

The Littlest Revue
    conceived by: Ben Bagley
    sketches: Nat Hiken, Billy Friedberg, Eudora Welty, Mike
                  Stewart, George Baxt, Bud McCreery, Allan
                  Manings, Bob Van Scoyk
    music and
    lyrics: Ogden Nash, Vernon Duke, John Latouche,
                  Sheldon Harnick, Lee Adams, Charles Strouse,
                  Sidney Shaw, Sammy Cahn, Michael Brown

staging: Paul Lammers
sets: Klaus Holm
costumes: Alvin Colt
choreography: Charles Weidman
Productions:
    Opened May 22, 1956 for 32 performances
Reviews:
    America 95:290-2, Jun 16, 1956
    Catholic World 183:311, Jul 1956
    Commonweal 64:299, Jun 22, 1956
    Nation 182:497, Jun 9, 1956
    New York Theatre Critics' Reviews 1956:297+
    New York Times page 37, May 23, 1956
    New Yorker 32:58, Jun 2, 1956
    Saturday Review 39:27, Jun 9, 1956
    Theatre Arts 40:73, Aug 1956
    Time 67:95, Jun 4, 1956

Live from New York (see Gilda Radner: Live from New York)

Livin' the Life
    book: Dale Wasserman and Bruce Geller, based on
                    Mark Twain's Mississippi River stories
    music: Jack Urbont
    lyrics: Bruce Geller
    staging: David Alexander
    sets: William and Jean Eckart
    costumes: Alvin Colt
    choreography: John Butler
Productions:
    Opened April 27, 1957 for 25 performances
Reviews:
    America 97:270, May 25, 1957
    Nation 184:427, May 11, 1957
    New York Theatre Critics' Reviews 1957:281+
    New York Times II, page 1, Apr 21, 1957
                    page 20, Apr 29, 1957
    New Yorker 33:142, May 4, 1957
    Theatre Arts 41:18, Jul 1957

Liza (1922)
    book: Irvin C. Miller
    music: Maceo Pinkard
    lyrics: Maceo Pinkard; special lyrics by Nat Vincent
    staging: Walter Brooks
Productions:
    Opened November 27, 1922 for 169 performances
Reviews:
    New York Clipper 70:20, Dec 6, 1922
    New York Times page 24, Nov 28, 1922

Liza (1974)
    written: Fred Ebb; original musical material by Fred Ebb
                    and John Kander
    staging: Bob Fosse
    choreography: Bob Fosse
Productions:
    Opened January 6, 1974 for 23 performances
No Reviews.

Loggins, Kenny   (see Kenny Loggins on Broadway)

Lollipop
    book: Zelda Sears
    music: Vincent Youmans
    lyrics: Zelda Sears and Walter DeLeon
Productions:
    Opened January 21, 1924 for 152 performances
Reviews:
    New York Times page 15, Jan 22, 1924
                  VIII, page 2, Apr 27, 1924
    Theatre Magazine 39:68, Mar 1924

The Long Christmas Dinner
    music: Paul Hindemith
    words: Thornton Wilder
    staging: Christopher West
    sets: Thea Neu
    costumes: Thea Neu
Productions:
    (Off-Broadway) Opened March 13, 1963 for 5 performances
No Reviews.

Long Time Coming and a Long Time Gone (see Richard Farina:
    Long Time Coming and a Long Time Gone)

A Look at the Fifties
    book: Al Carmines
    staging: Al Carmines
Productions:
    (Off-Broadway) Opened Season of 1971-72
Reviews:
    New York Times page 53, Apr 20, 1972
    New Yorker 48:105, Apr 29, 1972

Look at Us
    book: Arnold Sundgaard
    music: Lorenzo Fuller
    lyrics: Lorenzo Fuller
    staging: Michael Wright
Productions:
    (Off-Broadway) Opened June 5, 1962 for 16 performances
No Reviews.

Look, Ma, I'm Dancin'
book: Jerome Lawrence and Robert E. Lee
music: Hugh Martin
lyrics: Hugh Martin
staging: George Abbott and Jerome Robbins
sets: Oliver Smith
costumes: John Pratt
choreography: Trude Rittman

Productions:
Opened January 29, 1948 for 188 performances

Reviews:
Catholic World 166:553, Mar 1948
Commonweal 47:447, Feb 13, 1948
Forum 109:155, Mar 1948
New Republic 118:32, Feb 16, 1948
New York Theatre Critics' Reviews 1948:364+
New York Times page 20, Jan 30, 1948
II, page 1, Feb 8, 1948
II, page 2, Feb 8, 1948
New Yorker 23:40, Feb 7, 1948
Newsweek 31:70, Feb 9, 1948
Saturday Review 31:26-7, Feb 21, 1948
Time 51:55, Feb 9, 1948

Look to the Lilies
book: Leonard Spigelgass; based on William E. Barrett's
                   novel Lilies of the Field
music: Jule Styne
lyrics: Sammy Cahn
staging: Joshua Logan
sets: Jo Mielziner
costumes: Carrie F. Robbins
choreography: Joyce Trisler

Productions:
Opened March 29, 1970 for 25 performances

Reviews:
New York Theatre Critics' Reviews 1970:322
New York Times page 59, Mar 30, 1970
II, page 3, Apr 12, 1970
New Yorker 46:61-2, Apr 4, 1970
Time 95:98, Apr 13, 1970

Look Where I'm At
book: James Leasor and Gib Dennigan; based on Thorne
                   Smith's Rain in the Doorway
lyrics: Frank Stanton and Murray Semos
staging: Wakefield Poole
sets: Robert Guerra
costumes: Rosemary Heyer
choreography: Wakefield Poole

Productions:
(Off-Broadway) Opened March 5, 1971 for 5 performances

Reviews:
   New York Times page 20, Mar 6, 1971

Look Who's Here
   book: Frank Mandel
   music: Silvio Hein
   lyrics: Edward Paulton and Cecil Lean
Productions:
   Opened March 2, 1920 for 87 performances
Reviews:
   Dramatic Mirror 82:419, Mar 6, 1920
   New York Times page 12, Mar 3, 1920
   Theatre Magazine 31:309, Apr 1920
                     31:312, Apr 1920

Lorelei
   book: Kenny Solms and Gail Parent; based on the
                      musical Gentlemen Prefer Blondes
   music: Jule Styne
   lyrics: Betty Comden and Adolph Green
   staging: Robert Moore
   sets: John Conklin
   costumes: Alvin Colt
   choreography: Ernest O. Flatt
Productions:
   Opened January 27, 1974 for 321 performances
Reviews:
   Harper's 106:98+, Apr 1973
   Nation 218:222, Feb 16, 1974
   New York 7:76, Feb 11, 1974
   New York Theatre Critics' Reviews 1974:394
   New York Times page 35, Jan 28, 1974
                   II, page 1, Feb 3, 1974
   New Yorker 49:46, Feb 4, 1974
   Newsweek 83:96, Feb 11, 1974
   Playboy 21:51, May 1974
   Time 103:67, Feb 11, 1974

Lost in the Stars
   book: Maxwell Anderson, based on Alan Paton's Cry,
                      the Beloved Country
   music: Kurt Weill
   lyrics: Maxwell Anderson
   staging: Rouben Mamoulian
   sets: George Jenkins
   costumes: Anna Hill Johnstone
Productions:
   Opened October 30, 1949 for 273 performances
   (Off-Broadway) Opened March 22, 1968 for 15 performances
   Opened April 18, 1972 for 39 performances
Reviews:
   America 126:515, May 13, 1972

American Mercury 70:170-2, Feb 1950
Catholic World 170:226, Dec 1949
Commonweal 51:212, Nov 25, 1949
Forum 112:340, Dec 1949
Life 27:143-6+, Nov 14, 1949
Musical America 69:9, Nov 15, 1949
Nation 169:478, Nov 12, 1949
      186:398-9, May 3, 1958
      214:603-4, May 8, 1972
New Republic 121:19, Nov 21, 1949
New York Theatre Critics' Reviews 1949:241
                                1972:308
New York Times II, page 3, Oct 30, 1949
           page 21, Oct 31, 1949
           II, page 1, Nov 6, 1949
           VI, page 14, Dec 11, 1949
           page 21, Apr 11, 1958
           page 26, May 5, 1958
           page 20, Feb 18, 1972
           page 38, Apr 19, 1972
           II, page 3, Apr 30, 1972
New Yorker 25:64, Nov 5, 1949
         25:58, Nov 12, 1949
         34:138, Apr 19, 1958
         48:103, Apr 29, 1972
Newsweek 34:80, Nov 7, 1949
       51:84, Apr 21, 1958
Opera News 52:41, Jun 1988
Saturday Review 32:31-2, Nov 26, 1949
              32:43, Dec 31, 1949
              55:64, May 6, 1972
Theatre Arts 34:11, Jan 1950
Time 54:80, Nov 7, 1949

Lotta
    book: Robert Montgomery
    songs: Robert Montgomery
    staging: David Chambers
    sets: Tom H. John
    costumes: Nancy Adzima
    choreography: Dennis Nahat
Productions:
    (Off-Broadway) Opened October 18, 1973 for 54 performances
Reviews:
    America 129:485, Dec 22, 1973
    New York Theatre Critics' Reviews 1973:168
    New York Times page 42, Nov 23, 1973
                  II, page 3, Dec 2, 1973
    New Yorker 49:147, Dec 3, 1973
    Newsweek 82:73, Dec 3, 1973

Louie the 14th
book: Arthur Wimperis, adapted from the German
music: Sigmund Romberg
lyrics: Arthur Wimperis
staging: Edward Royce
Productions:
  Opened March 3, 1925 for 319 performances
Reviews:
  Life (New York) 85:22, Apr 2, 1925
  New York Times page 17, Mar 4, 1925
  Theatre Magazine 41:32, May 1925

Louis
book: Don Evans
music: Michael Renzi
lyrics: Don Evans
staging: Gilbert Moses
sets: Robert Edmonds
costumes: Judy Dearing
choreography: Billy Wilson
Productions:
  (Off-Off-Broadway) Opened September 18, 1981 for 12 performances
Reviews:
  New York 14:72, Oct 5, 1981
  New York Times III, page 21, Sep 24, 1981

Louisiana Lady
book: Isaac Green, Jr. and Eugene Berton
music: Monte Carlo and Alma Sanders
lyrics: Monte Carlo and Alma Sanders
staging: Edgar MacGregor
sets: Watson Barratt
choreography: Felicia Sorel
Productions:
  Opened June 2, 1947 for 4 performances
Reviews:
  New York Theatre Critics' Reviews 1947:362+
  New York Times II, page 1, Jun 1, 1947
                  page 35, Jun 3, 1947

Louisiana Purchase
book: Morrie Ryskind, based on a story by B. G.
                  DeSylva
music: Irving Berlin
lyrics: Irving Berlin
staging: Edgar MacGregor
sets: Tom Lee
costumes: Tom Lee
choreography: George Balanchine and Carl Randall
Productions:
  Opened May 28, 1940 for 444 performances

Reviews:
    Catholic World 151:471, Jul 1940
    Commonweal 32:191-2, Jun 21, 1940
    Life 8:100-3, Jun 10, 1940
    Nation 150:716, Jun 8, 1940
    New York Theatre Critics' Reviews 1940:296+
                                      1941:484+
    New York Times page 19, May 29, 1940
                    IX, page 1, Jun 16, 1940
    New Yorker 16:38, Jun 8, 1940
    Newsweek 15:43, Jun 10, 1940
    Theatre Arts 24:774+, Nov 1940
    Time 35:63, Jun 10, 1940

Love
    book: Jeffrey Sweet, based on the play Luv by Murray
                    Schisgal
    music: Howard Marren
    lyrics: Susan Birkenhead
    staging: Walton Jones
    sets: Kevin Rupnik
    costumes: Kevin Rupnik
    choreography: Ed Nolfi
Productions:
    (Off-Broadway) Opened April 15, 1984 for 17 performances
Reviews:
    New York 17:91-2, Apr 30, 1984
    New York Times III, page 19, Apr 16, 1984

Love and Let Love
    book: Based on Twelfth Night by William Shakespeare;
                    adapted by John Lollos
    music: Stanley Jay Gelber
    lyrics: John Lollos and Don Christopher
    staging: John Lollos
    sets: Barbara Miller
Productions:
    (Off-Broadway) Opened January 3, 1968 for 14 performances
Reviews:
    New York Times page 30, Jan 4, 1968
    New Yorker 43:58-9, Jan 13, 1968

Love and Maple Syrup
    devised: Louis Negin
    songs: Gordon Lightfoot and others
    sets: Charles L. Dunlop
Productions:
    (Off-Broadway) Opened January 7, 1970 for 15 performances
Reviews:
    New York Times page 47, Jan 8, 1970
    New Yorker 45:52, Jan 17, 1970

Love Birds
- book: Edgar Allen Woolf
- music: Sigmund Romberg
- lyrics: Ballard McDonald
- staging: Edgar MacGregor and Julian Alfred

Productions:
Opened March 15, 1921 for 105 performances
Reviews:
Dramatic Mirror 83:505+, Mar 19, 1921
Life (New York) 77:464, Mar 31, 1921
New York Clipper 69:19, Mar 23, 1921
New York Times page 12, Mar 16, 1921
Theatre Magazine 33:342, May 1921

The Love Call
- book: Harry B. Smith and Edward Locke
- music: Sigmund Romberg
- lyrics: Harry B. Smith
- staging: J. C. Huffman

Productions:
Opened October 24, 1927 for 88 performances
Reviews:
New York Times page 33, Oct 25, 1927
            IX, page 5, Nov 13, 1927

The Love Cure
- book: Oliver Herford; from the German of Leo Stein and Karl Lindau
- music: Edmund Eysler

Productions:
Opened September 1, 1909 for 35 performances
Reviews:
Dramatic Mirror 62:5-6, Sep 11, 1909
Hampton 23:695-6, Nov 1909
Leslie's Weekly 109:299, Sep 23, 1909
            109:318, Sep 30, 1909
Metropolitan Magazine 31:256-7, Nov 1909
Theatre Magazine 10:102, Oct 1909
            10:111, Oct 1909
Vanity Fair 6:199, Nov 1909

Love Dreams
- book: Ann Nichols
- music: Werner Janssen
- lyrics: Oliver Morosco
- staging: Oliver Morosco and John McKee

Productions:
Opened October 10, 1921 for 40 performances
Reviews:
Dramatic Mirror 84:484, Oct 1, 1921
New York Clipper 69:20, Oct 19, 1921

386 / Love in a Garden

New York Times page 22, Oct 11, 1921
Theatre Magazine 34:416+, Dec 1921

Love in a Garden   (see Prunella, or Love in a Garden)

The Love Letter
    book: William Le Baron; adapted from Ferenc Molnar's
                     The Phantom Rival
    music: Victor Jacobi
    staging: Edward Royce
Productions:
    Opened October 4, 1921 for 31 performances
Reviews:
    Dramatic Mirror 84:448, Sep 24, 1921
    New York Clipper 69:20, Oct 12, 1921
    New York Times page 20, Oct 5, 1921
    Theatre Magazine 34:388, Dec 1921

Love Life
    book: Alan Jay Lerner
    music: Kurt Weill
    lyrics: Alan Jay Lerner
    staging: Elia Kazan
    sets: Boris Aronson
    costumes: Lucinda Ballard
    choreography: Michael Kidd
Productions:
    Opened October 7, 1948 for 252 performances
Reviews:
    Catholic World 168:161, Nov 1948
    Commonweal 49:94, Nov 5, 1948
    Forum 111:32-3, Jan 1949
    Harper 198:110, Jan 1949
    Musical Courier 138:4, Nov 15, 1948
    New Republic 119:28, Nov 1, 1948
    New York Theatre Critics' Reviews 1948:201+
    New York Times II, page 3, Oct 3, 1948
                    page 31, Oct 8, 1948
    New Yorker 24:52, Oct 16, 1948
    Newsweek 32:89, Oct 18, 1948
    School and Society 68:385-6, Dec 4, 1948
    Theatre Arts 33:18, Jan 1949
    Time 52:82, Oct 18, 1948

Love Me, Love My Children
    book: Robert Swerdlow
    music: Robert Swerdlow
    lyrics: Robert Swerdlow
    staging: Paul Aaron
    sets: Jo Mielziner
    costumes: Patricia Quinn Stuart
    choreography: Elizabeth Swerdlow

Productions:

(Off-Broadway) Opened November 3, 1971 for 187 performances
Reviews:
New York Theatre Critics' Reviews 1971:166
New York Times page 53, Nov 4, 1971
New Yorker 47:66+, Nov 13, 1971

The Love Mill
book: Earl Carroll
music: Alfred Francis
lyrics: Earl Carroll
staging: George Marion
Productions:
Opened February 7, 1918 for 52 performances
Reviews:
Dramatic Mirror 78:5, Feb 23, 1918
Life (New York) 71:302, Feb 21, 1918
New York Times page 13, Feb 9, 1918

Love o' Mike
book: Thomas Sydney
music: Jerome Kern
lyrics: Harry B. Smith
staging: J. H. Benrimo
Productions:
Opened January 15, 1917 for 192 performances
Reviews:
Dramatic Mirror 77:5, Jan 20, 1917
             77:16, Jan 27, 1917
New York Dramatic Mirror 63:2, Jan 6, 1917
             63:22, Jan 20, 1917
New York Times page 10, Jan 16, 1917
Theatre Magazine 25:84, Feb 1917
             25:149, Mar 1917

Lovely Ladies, Kind Gentlemen
book: John Patrick; based on Vern J. Sneider's book
              The Teahouse of the August Moon and the play
              by John Patrick
music: Stan Freeman and Franklin Underwood
lyrics: Stan Freeman and Franklin Underwood
staging: Lawrence Kasha
sets: Oliver Smith
costumes: Freddy Wittop
choreography: Marc Breaux
Productions:
Opened December 28, 1970 for 16 performances
Reviews:
Dance Magazine 45:82, Mar 1971
New York Theatre Critics' Reviews 1970:114
New York Times page 26, Aug 11, 1970

page 38, Dec 29, 1970
page 15, Jan 1, 1971
page 17, Jan 9, 1971
II, page 1, Jan 10, 1971
New Yorker 46:51, Jan 9, 1971

Lovely Lady
    book: Gladys Unger and Cyrus Wood; based on the
                   French Déjeuner de Soleil
    music: Dave Stamper and Harold Levey
    lyrics: Cyrus Wood
Productions:
Opened December 29, 1927 for 164 performances
Reviews:
    New York Times page 22, Dec 30, 1927
    Theatre Magazine 47:56, Mar 1928
                     47:62, Mar 1928

Lovers
    book: Peter del Valle
    music: Steve Sterner
    lyrics: Peter del Valle
    staging: Peter del Valle
    costumes: Reve Richards
Productions:
    (Off-Broadway) Opened January 27, 1975 for 118 performances
Reviews:
    New York 8:75, Feb 17, 1975
    New York Times page 26, Jan 28, 1975

The Loves of Alonzo Fitz Clarence and Rosannah Ethelton
    book: Paul Zakrzewski; based on the short story by
                   Mark Twain
    music: Wally Harper
    lyrics: Paul Zakrzewski
    staging: Paul Zakrzewski
Productions:
    (Off-Off-Broadway) Opened February 6, 1974
Reviews:
    New York Times page 44, Feb 7, 1974

Lovesong
    conceived: Henry Comor
    book: Michael Valenti, based on words of James Agee,
                   Lord Byron, A. E. Houseman, John Lewin, Dorothy
                   Parker, Sir Walter Raleigh, Christina Rosetti,
                   and Richard Brinsley Sheridan
    music: Michael Valenti
    staging: John Montgomery
    sets: Jack Logan
    costumes: Joan Mayno
    choreography: John Montgomery and Michael Perrier

Productions:
    (Off-Off-Broadway)   Opened July 8, 1976
    (Off-Broadway)   Opened October 5, 1976 for 24 performances
Reviews:
    New York Times page 39, Oct 6, 1976

Luana
    book: Howard Emmett Rogers, based on Richard Walton
                             Tully's The Bird of Paradise
    music: Rudolf Friml
    lyrics: J. Kiern Brennan
    staging: Arthur Hammerstein, Howard Rogers, Earl Lind-
                             sey
Productions:
    Opened September 17, 1930 for 21 performances
Reviews:
    Life (New York) 96:18, Oct 10, 1930
    New York Times page 28, Sep 18, 1930
    Theatre Magazine 52:26, Nov 1930

Luckee Girl
    book: Gertrude Purcell; adapted from the French Un
                             Bon Garcon
    music: Maurice Yvain and Maurie Rubens
    lyrics: Max Lief and Nathaniel Lief
    staging: Lew Morton and Harry Puck
Productions:
    Opened September 15, 1928 for 81 performances
Reviews:
    New York Times page 28, Sep 17, 1928

Lucky
    book: Harry Ruby, Bert Kalmar, Otto Harbach
    music: Harry Ruby and Jerome Kern
    lyrics: Harry Ruby, Bert Kalmar, Otto Harbach
    staging: Hassard Short
Productions:
    Opened March 22, 1927 for 71 performances
Reviews:
    Life (New York) 89:31, Apr 7, 1927
    New Republic 50:196, Apr 6, 1927
    New York Times page 24, Mar 25, 1927
    Theatre Magazine 45:26, Jun 1927
    Vogue 69:118+, May 15, 1927

Lucky Sambo
    book: Porter Grainger and Freddie Johnson
    music: Porter Grainger and Freddie Johnson
    lyrics: Porter Grainger and Freddie Johnson
    staging: Leigh Whipper and Freddie Johnson
Productions:

Opened June 6, 1925 for 9 performances
Reviews:
New York Times page 19, Jun 8, 1925

Lucky Stiff
   book: Lynn Ahrens, based on The Man Who Broke the
                  Bank at Monte Carlo by Michael Butterworth
   music: Stephen Flaherty
   lyrics: Lynn Ahrens
   staging: Thommie Walsh
   sets: Bob Shaw
   costumes: Michael Krass
Productions:
   (Off-Broadway) Opened April 25, 1988 for 15 performances
Reviews:
   New York 21:88, May 9, 1988
   New York Times III, page 22, Apr 27, 1988
   New Yorker 64:100, May 9, 1988

Lullaby and Goodnight
   words: Elizabeth Swados
   music: Elizabeth Swados
   staging: Elizabeth Swados
   sets: David Jenkins
   costumes: Hilary Rosenfeld
   choreography: Ara Fitzgerald
Productions:
   (Off-Broadway) Opened February 9, 1982 for 30 performances
Reviews:
   New York 15:52-4, Feb 22, 1982
   New York Times III, page 24, Feb 10, 1982
   New Yorker 58:54, Feb 22, 1982

Lute Song
   book: Sidney Howard and Will Irwin from Chinese classic
   music: Raymond Scott
   lyrics: Bernard Hanighen
   staging: John Houseman
   sets: Robert Edmund Jones
   costumes: Robert Edmund Jones
   choreography: Yeichi Nimura
Productions:
   Opened February 6, 1946 for 142 performances
   (Off-Broadway) Season of 1958-59
   Opened March 12, 1959 for 14 performances
Reviews:
   American Mercury 62:587-90, May 1946
   Catholic World 162:553, Mar 1946
              189:159, May 1959
   Commonweal 43:479, Feb 22, 1946
   Dance Magazine 33:23, Apr 1959

Life 20:53-6, Mar 4, 1946
Modern Music 23no.2:145, Apr 1946
Nation 162:240, Feb 23, 1946
New Republic 114:254, Feb 18, 1946
New York Theatre Critics' Reviews 1946:459+
New York Times page 29, Feb 7, 1946
            II, page 1, Feb 17, 1946
            page 32, Oct 12, 1948
            page 24, Mar 13, 1959
New Yorker 22:48+, Feb 16, 1946
Newsweek 27:92, Feb 18, 1946
Saturday Review 29:28-9, May 2, 1946
Theatre Arts 30:199-200, Apr 1946
            32:67, Feb 1948
            43:67-8, May 1959
Time 47:49, Feb 18, 1946

-M-

Mack & Mabel

book: Michael Stewart, based on an idea by Leonard
                Spigelgass
music: Jerry Herman
lyrics: Jerry Herman
staging: Gower Champion
sets: Robin Wagner
costumes: Patricia Zipprodt
choreography: Gower Champion
Productions:
Opened October 6, 1974 for 65 performances
Reviews:
America 131:284+, Nov 9, 1974
Nation 219:414, Oct 26, 1974
New Republic 171:41+, Nov 2, 1974
New York 7:49+, Oct 7, 1974
        7:88, Oct 21, 1974
New York Theatre Critics' Reviews 1974:234
New York Times page 46, Sep 5, 1974
            page 54, Oct 7, 1974
            II, page 1, Oct 13, 1974
New Yorker 50:141, Oct 14, 1974
Newsweek 84:56, Oct 21, 1974
Playboy 21:24, Sep 1974
        22:26+, Jan 1975
Time 104:93, Oct 21, 1974

Mackey of Appalachia

book: Walter Cool
music: Walter Cool
lyrics: Walter Cool

staging: Walter Cool
sets: Allen Edward Klein
costumes: Alice Merrigal
Productions:
    (Off-Broadway)   Opened October 6, 1965 for 54 performances
Reviews:
    America 113:384-5, Oct 2, 1965

The Mad Show
    book: Larry Siegel and Stan Hart; based on Mad Maga-
                  zine
    music: Mary Rodgers
    lyrics: Marshall Barer, Larry Siegel and Steven Vinaver
    staging: Steven Vinaver
    sets: Peter Harvey
    costumes: Peter Harvey
Productions:
    (Off-Broadway)   Opened January 10, 1966 for 871 performances
Reviews:
    Commonweal 84:228, May 13, 1966
    Harper's 232:114-5, May 1966
    Life 60:24-5, Mar 11, 1966
    New Republic 154:36-7, Jan 29, 1966
    New York Times page 16, Jan 10, 1966
                    page 36, Jun 26, 1967
                    page 19, Jul 7, 1967
    Newsweek 67:82, Jan 24, 1966
    Time 37:65+, Feb 18, 1966
    Vogue 147:94, Mar 1, 1966

Madam Moselle
    adapted: Edward A. Paulton
    music: Ludwig Englander and William P. Chase
    staging: George W. Lederer
Productions:
    Opened May 23, 1914 for 9 performances
Reviews:
    Dramatic Mirror 71:8, May 27, 1914
                    71:4, Jun 3, 1914
    Green Book 12:94, Jul 1914
    New York Times III, page 7, May 24, 1914
    Theatre Magazine 20:37, Jul 1914

Madame Aphrodite
    book: Tad Mosel
    music: Jerry Herman
    lyrics: Jerry Herman
    staging: Robert Turoff
    sets: David Ballou
    costumes: Patricia Zipprodt
Productions:
    (Off-Broadway)   Opened December 29, 1961 for 13 performances

Reviews:
New York Times page 13, Dec 30, 1961
New Yorker 37:66, Jan 11, 1962

Madame Pompadour
    book: Rudolph Schanzer and Ernst Welisch; adapted by
                        Clare Kummer
    music: Leo Fall
    lyrics: Rudolph Schanzer and Ernst Welisch
Productions:
    Opened November 11, 1924 for 80 performances
Reviews:
    New York Times page 20, Nov 12, 1924
    Theatre Magazine 41:19, Jan 1925
                     41:21, Apr 1925

Madame Sherry
    book: Otto Hauerbach; adapted from George Edwarde's
                        English version
    music: Karl Hoschna
    staging: George W. Lederer
Productions:
    Opened August 30, 1910 for 231 performances
Reviews:
    Dramatic Mirror 64:6, Sep 10, 1910
    Leslie's Weekly 111:317, Sep 29, 1910
    Metropolitan Magazine 32:670-1, Aug 1910
    Theatre Magazine 11:179-80, Jun 1910
                     12:74, Sep 1910
                     12:xiv, Oct 1910

The Madcap (Green Fruit)
    book: Gertrude Purcell and Gladys Unger; adapted from
                        the French of Regis Gignoux and Jacques Thery
    music: Maurice Rubens
    staging: Duane Nelson
Productions:
    Opened January 31, 1928 for 103 performances
Reviews:
    New York Times page 31, Feb 1, 1928
    Theatre Magazine 47:41, May 1927

Mademoiselle Colombe (see Mlle. Colombe)

Mademoiselle Modiste (see Mlle. Modiste)

The Madwoman of Central Park West
    book: Phyllis Newman and Arthur Laurents
    music: Various composers
    lyrics: Various authors
    staging: Arthur Laurents

sets: Philipp Jung
costumes: Theoni V. Aldredge
Productions:
Opened June 13, 1979 for 85 performances
Reviews:
New York 12: 95, Jul 9, 1979
New York Theatre Critics' Reviews 1979: 212
New York Times III, page 15, Jun 14, 1979
New Yorker 55: 57+, Jun 25, 1979

Magdalena
    book: Frederick Hazlitt Brennan and Homer Curran
    music: Heitor Villa-Lobos
    lyrics: Robert Wright and George Forrest
    staging: Jules Dassin
    sets: Howard Bay
    costumes: Irene Sharaff
    choreography: Jack Cole
Productions:
Opened September 20, 1948 for 88 performances
Reviews:
Catholic World 168: 158-9, Nov 1948
Collier's 122: 24-5, Nov 20, 1948
Commonweal 48: 618, Oct 8, 1948
Life 25: 106-7, Oct 25, 1948
New Republic 119: 29, Oct 11, 1948
New York Theatre Critics' Reviews 1948: 235+
New York Times page 27, Jul 28, 1948
                 page 31, Sep 20, 1948
                 II, page 1, Sep 26, 1948
                 II, page 7, Sep 26, 1948
                 II, page 6, Nov 7, 1948
New Yorker 24: 50, Oct 2, 1948
             63: 163-4, Dec 7, 1987
Newsweek 32: 76, Oct 4, 1948
School and Society 68: 301-2, Oct 30, 1948
Theatre Arts 33: 18, Jan 1949
Time 52: 59, Oct 4, 1948
Vogue 112: 183, Dec 1948

Maggie
    book: Hugh Thomas, based on Sir James M. Barrie's
                    play What Every Woman Knows
    music: Hugh Thomas
    lyrics: Hugh Thomas
    staging: Michael Gordon
    sets: Raoul Pene du Bois
    costumes: Raoul Pene du Bois
    choreography: June Graham
Productions:
Opened February 18, 1953 for 5 performances

Reviews:

Commonweal 57:577, Mar 13, 1953
New York Theatre Critics' Reviews 1953:351+
New York Times page 20, Feb 19, 1953
New Yorker 29:65, Feb 28, 1953
Newsweek 41:84, Mar 2, 1953
Saturday Review 36:35, Mar 7, 1953
Theatre Arts 37:14, Jan 1953
         37:15, May 1953
 Time 61:77, Mar 2, 1953

Maggie Flynn

book, music,
and lyrics: Hugo Peretti, Luigi Creatore and George David
    Weiss: book in collaboration with Morton Da
    Costa; based on an idea by John Flaxman
staging: Morton Da Costa
sets: William and Jean Eckart
costumes: W. Robert Lavine
choreography: Brian Macdonald

Productions:

Opened October 23, 1968 for 81 performances
(Off-Off-Broadway) Opened March 4, 1976

Reviews:

America 119:530, Nov 23, 1969
Dance Magazine 42:106, Dec 1968
New York Theatre Critics' Reviews 1968:183
                1968:196
New York Times page 52, Oct 24, 1968
    II, page 1, Nov 3, 1968
    page 38, Jan 6, 1969
    page 22, Mar 6, 1976
New Yorker 44:125, Nov 2, 1968
Newsweek 72:118, Nov 4, 1968

The Magic Melody

book: Frederic Arnold Kummer
music: Sigmund Romberg
lyrics: Frederic Arnold Kummer

Productions:

Opened November 11, 1919 for 143 performances

Reviews:

Dramatic Mirror 80:1792, Nov 20, 1919
New York Times page 25, Nov 12, 1919
Theatre Magazine 30:368, Dec 1919
    31:23, Jan 1920

The Magic of Jolson!

book: Pearl Sieben, based on Al Jolson's famous song
    numbers
music: Additional music by Richard DeMone

lyrics: Additional lyrics by Pearl Sieben
staging: Isaac Dostis
sets: Chuck Hoefler
Productions:
   (Off-Broadway) Opened April 9, 1975 for 5 performances
No Reviews.

The Magic Ring
book: Zelda Sears
music: Harold Levey
Productions:
   Opened October 1, 1923 for 96 performances
Reviews:
   New York Times page 10, Oct 2, 1923
   Theatre Magazine 38:75, Nov 1923

The Magic Show
book: Bob Randall
music: Stephen Schwartz
lyrics: Stephen Schwartz
staging: Grover Dale

sets: David Chapman
costumes: Randy Barcelo
choreography: Grover Dale
Productions:
   Opened May 28, 1974 for 1,920 performances
Reviews:
   Commentary 58:75-6, Nov 1974
   Los Angeles 20:110+, Jul 1975
   New York 7:76, Jun 17, 1974
   New York Theatre Critics' Reviews 1974:254
   New York Times page 31, Mar 20, 1973
                page 49, May 29, 1974
   New Yorker 50:64, Jun 10, 1974
   Newsweek 83:84, Jun 10, 1974
   Playboy 21:24+, Sep 1974
   Senior Scholastic 106:33-4, Mar 27, 1975
   Time 103:106, Jun 10, 1974

The Magic Show of Dr. Magico
book: Jen Bernard and John Vaccaro
music: Richard Weinstock
staging: Jen Bernard and John Vaccaro
Productions:
   (Off-Off-Broadway) Opened March 15, 1973
No Reviews.

Magic Theater (see Doctor Selavy's Magic Theater)

The Magnificent Christmas Spectacular
conceived: Robert F. Jani

songs:	Various authors and composers
staging:	Dru Davis and Howard Parker
sets:	Charles Lisanby
costumes:	Frank Spencer
choreography:	Dru Davis, Howard Parker, and Violet Holmes

Productions:
Opened November 25, 1979 for 91 performances
Opened November 21, 1980 for 86 performances
Opened November 19, 1982 for 92 performances
Opened November 18, 1983 for 92 performances
Opened November 16, 1984 for 110 performances
Opened November 15, 1985 for 120 performances
Opened November 14, 1986 for 140 performances
Opened November 13, 1987 for 152 performances
Opened November 11, 1988 for 166 performances

Reviews:
New York Theatre Critics' Reviews 1979:88
New York Times III, page 15, Nov 24, 1980
III, page 12, Nov 23, 1982

The Magnolia Lady

book:	Anne Caldwell
music:	Harold Levey
lyrics:	Anne Caldwell

Productions:
Opened November 25, 1924 for 47 performances
Reviews:
New York Times page 17, Nov 26, 1924

Mahagonny

book:	Arnold Weinstein; adapted from Brecht and Weill's opera The Rise and Fall of the City of Mahagonny
music:	Kurt Weill
lyrics:	Bertolt Brecht
staging:	Carmen Capalbo
sets:	Robin Wagner
costumes:	Ruth Morley

Productions:
(Off-Broadway) Opened April 28, 1970 for 8 performances
Reviews:
High Fidelity 15:158-9, Sep 1965
22:MA 24+, May 1972
22:MA 29, Oct 1972
Nation 201:107, Aug 30, 1965
New York Theatre Critics' Reviews 1970:235
New York Times page 38, Jan 14, 1970
page 51, Apr 29, 1970
page 21, May 21, 1970
II, page 3, May 10, 1970
II, page 15, May 10, 1970
page 42, Dec 24, 1972

New Yorker 46:97, May 9, 1970
           48:59-62, Jan 6, 1973
           49:138+, Apr 28, 1973
Newsweek 66:82, Jul 19, 1965
Opera News 30:26, Nov 6, 1965
           34:8-12, Mar 14, 1970
Saturday Review (Education) 1:72, Feb 1973
Time 83:59, Mar 13, 1964

Maid in America
    words: Harold Atteridge and others
    music: Rewritten by Sigmund Romberg and Harry Carroll
    staging: J. C. Huffman
Productions:
    Opened February 18, 1915 for 108 performances
Reviews:
    Dramatic Mirror 73:8, Feb 24, 1915
                   73:2, Mar 10, 1915
    Life (New York) 65:374, Mar 4, 1915
    New York Times page 9, Feb 19, 1915

The Maid of the Mountains
    book: Frederick Lonsdale
    music: Harold Fraser-Simson, James W. Tate and Lieut.
                    Gitz Rice
    lyrics: Harry Graham, Clifford Harris and Valentine
    staging: Capt. J. A. E. Malone
Productions:
    Opened September 11, 1918 for 37 performances
Reviews:
    Dramatic Mirror 79:470, Sep 28, 1918
    Theatre Magazine 28:271, Nov 1918
                      28:280, Nov 1918

Mail
    book: Jerry Colker
    music: Michael Rupert
    lyrics: Jerry Colker
    staging: Andrew Cadiff
    sets: Gerry Hariton and Vicki Baral
    costumes: William Ivey Long
    choreography: Grover Dale
Productions:
    Opened April 14, 1988 for 36 performances
Reviews:
    Los Angeles 32:304+, Dec 1987
    New York Theatre Critics' Reviews 1988:308
    New York Times III, page 3, Apr 15, 1988
    New Yorker 64:102-3, Apr 25, 1988

Make a Wish
  book: Preston Sturges, based on Ferenc Molnar's The
                     Good Fairy
  music: Hugh Martin
  lyrics: Hugh Martin
  staging: John C. Wilson
  sets: Raoul Pene du Bois
  costumes: Raoul Pene du Bois
  choreography: Gower Champion
Productions:
  Opened April 18, 1951 for 103 performances
Reviews:
  Catholic World 173:228, Jun 1951
  Commonweal 54:88, May 4, 1951
  Life 30:137-8, May 14, 1951
  Musical America 71:7+, Jul 1951
  Nation 172:403, Apr 28, 1951
  New York Theatre Critics' Reviews 1951:294+
  New York Times page 38, Apr 19, 1951
  New Yorker 27:58, Apr 28, 1951
  Newsweek 37:53, Apr 30, 1951
  Theatre Arts 35:14, Jun 1951
  Time 57:89, Apr 30, 1951

Make It Snappy
  book: Harold Atteridge
  music: Jean Schwartz
  lyrics: Harold Atteridge
  staging: J. C. Huffman and Allen K. Foster
Productions:
  Opened April 13, 1922 for (77) performances
Reviews:
  New York Clipper 70:20, Apr 19, 1922
  New York Times page 20, Apr 14, 1922

Make Mine Manhattan
  book: Arnold B. Horwitt
  music: Richard Lewine
  lyrics: Arnold B. Horwitt
  staging: Hassard Short
  sets: Frederick Fox
  costumes: Morton Haack
  choreography: Lee Sherman
Productions:
  Opened January 15, 1948 for 429 performances
Reviews:
  Catholic World 166:553-4, Mar 1948
  Commonweal 47:399, Jan 30, 1948
  Forum 109:155, Mar 1948
  Life 24:121-1+, Feb 9, 1948
  Look 12:50-51, Mar 30, 1948

New Republic 118:34, Feb 9, 1948
New York Theatre Critics' Reviews 1948:382+
New York Times page 26, Jan 16, 1948
            II, page 2, Feb 8, 1948
New Yorker 23:40, Jan 24, 1948
Newsweek 31:81, Jan 26, 1948
Time 51:62, Jan 26, 1948

The Making of Americans
    libretto: Leon Katz; adapted from Gertrude Stein's novel
    music: Al Carmines
    staging: Lawrence Kornfeld
Productions:
    (Off-Off-Broadway) Opened November 10, 1972
Reviews:
    New York Times page 34, Nov 29, 1972

La Mama (see Everyman at La Mama)

Mama, I Want to Sing
    book: Vy Higginsen; additional story consultation with
                    Ken Wydro
    music: Richard Tee
    lyrics: Vy Higginsen and Ken Wydro
    staging: Duane L. Jones
    sets: Felix E. Cochren
    costumes: Georgia Collins-Langhorne
    choreography: Joseph Cohen
Productions:
    (Off-Off-Broadway) Opened December 3, 1980 for 13 performances
Reviews:
    Black Enterprise 20:66-8+, Aug 1989
    Essence 16:48, Sep 1985
    Jet 72:53, Jul 13, 1987
        73:34-5, Feb 1, 1988
    Ms. 15:17, Nov 1986
    New York Times III, page 34, Dec 17, 1980
    Time 125:90, Jan 7, 1985

Mama's Baby Boy
    book: Adapted by Junie McCree
    music: Hans S. Linne; additional numbers by Will H.
                    Becker
    lyrics: Junie McCree
Productions:
    Opened May 25, 1912 for 9 performances
Reviews:
    Dramatic Mirror 67:6, May 29, 1912
    Green Book 8:351, Aug 1912
    New York Dramatic News 55:25, Jun 1, 1912
    Theatre Magazine 16:2, Jul 1912

Mame
   book: Jerome Lawrence and Robert E. Lee; based on
                            Auntie Mame, the novel by Patrick Dennis and
                            the play by Jerome Lawrence and Robert E. Lee
   music: Jerry Herman
   lyrics: Jerry Herman
   staging: Gene Saks
   sets: William and Jean Eckart
   costumes: Robert Mackintosh
   choreography: Onna White and Tom Panko
Productions:
   Opened May 24, 1966 for 1,508 performances
   Opened July 24, 1983 for 41 performances
Reviews:
   America 115:79-80, Jul 16, 1966
   Commonweal 84:369-70, Jun 17, 1966
   Dance Magazine 40:25-7, Jul 1966
   Life 60:88-92+, Jun 17, 1966
   New York 16:70+, Aug 8, 1983
   New York Theatre Critics' Reviews 1966:302
                                            1983:196
   New York Times page 16, May 14, 1966
                     page 41, May 25, 1966
                     page 56, May 26, 1966
                     page 55, May 24, 1967
                     page 31, Aug 15, 1967
                     page 25, Apr 20, 1968
                     page 42, May 24, 1968
                     page 19, Jun 29, 1968
                     page 79, Jan 5, 1969
                     page 35, Feb 22, 1969
                     page 36, Jun 20, 1969
                     page 20, Jan 3, 1970
                     XXI, page 19, Apr 10, 1983
                     III, page 11, Jul 25, 1983
   New Yorker 42:75, Jun 4, 1966
   Newsweek 67:89, Jun 6, 1966
   Saturday Review 49:34, Jun 11, 1966
   Time 87:71, Jun 3, 1966
   Vogue 148:28, Jul 1966

Man Better Man
   book: Errol Hill
   music: Coleridge-Taylor Perkinson
   staging: Douglas Turner Ward
   sets: Edward Burbridge
   costumes: Bernard Johnson
   choreography: Percival Borde
Productions:
   (Off-Broadway) Opened July 2, 1969 for 23 performances
Reviews:
   New York Times page 22, Jul 3, 1969

                    II, page 1, Jul 13, 1969
                    II, page 3, Jul 13, 1969
        New Yorker 45:58, Jul 12, 1969

The Man from Cook's
    book: Henry Blossom; from the French of M. Ordon-
                    neau
    music: Raymond Hubbell
    staging: Ben Teal
Productions:
    Opened March 25, 1912 for 32 performances
Reviews:
    Blue Book 15:249-51, Jun 1912
    Dramatic Mirror 67:2, Mar 13, 1912
                    67:11, Mar 27, 1912
    Green Book 7:1091-3+, Jun 1912
    Munsey 47:285, May 1912
    New York Dramatic News 55:26, Mar 30, 1912
    Theatre Magazine 15:xiv+, May 1912

The Man from the East
    music: Stomu Yamash'ta
    words: Stomu Yamash'ta
    staging: Stomu Yamash'ta
    sets: Takeo Adachi and Chuck Murawski
Productions:
    (Off-Broadway) Opened October 23, 1973 for 8 performances
Reviews:
    New York Times page 18, Sep 22, 1973
                    II, page 3, Oct 14, 1973
                    page 38, Oct 24, 1973

Man of La Mancha
    book: Dale Wasserman; suggested by the works of
                    Cervantes
    music: Mitch Leigh
    lyrics: Joe Darion
    staging: Albert Marre
    sets: Howard Bay
    costumes: Howard Bay and Patton Campbell
    choreography: Jack Cole
Productions:
    Opened November 22, 1965 for 2,328 performances
    Opened June 22, 1972 for 140 performances
    Opened September 15, 1977 for 124 performances
Reviews:
    America 114:53, Jan 8, 1966
    Dance Magazine 40:16, Jan 1966
    Life 60:47-8+, Apr 8, 1966
    Los Angeles 23:246, Apr 1978
    Nation 201:484, Dec 13, 1965

National Review 18:1062-3, Oct 18, 1966
New West 3:SC-29, Apr 10, 1978
New York 10:78, Oct 3, 1977
New York Theatre Critics' Reviews 1965:251
                                  1972:253
                                  1977:295
New York Times page 52, Nov 23, 1965
               page 42, Oct 5, 1966
               page 61, Nov 24, 1967
               page 44, Jan 5, 1968
               page 57, Mar 18, 1968
               III, page 27, Nov 17, 1968
               page 61, Dec 12, 1968
               page 40, Apr 2, 1969
               page 38, May 3, 1969
               page 70, Jan 25, 1970
               page 38, Feb 18, 1970
               page 31, Feb 2, 1971
               page 51, May 13, 1971
               page 38, Jun 16, 1971
               page 21, Jun 23, 1972
               page 55, Sep 13, 1972
               III, page 3, Sep 16, 1977
               II, page 3, Sep 25, 1977
New Yorker 41:106+, Dec 4, 1965
          53:100, Sep 26, 1977
Saturday Reveiw 48:51, Dec 11, 1965
Time 86:54, Dec 3, 1965
Vogue 147:34, Jan 15, 1966

Man on the Moon
    book: John Phillips
    music: John Phillips
    lyrics: John Phillips
    staging: Paul Morrissey
    sets: John J. Moore
    costumes: Marsia Trinder
Productions:
    Opened January 29, 1975 for 5 performances
Reviews:
    New York 8:75, Feb 17, 1975
    New York Theatre Critics' Reviews 1975:364
    New York Times page 28, Jan 30, 1975
    New Yorker 50:74, Feb 10, 1975

The Man That Corrupted Hadleyburg
    book: Lewis Gardner; based on the story by Mark Twain
    music: Daniel Paget
    lyrics: Lewis Gardner; based on the story by Mark Twain
    staging: Bert Stimmel
    choreography: Bert Stimmel

Productions:
    (Off-Off-Broadway)   Opened August 6, 1963 for 7 performances
No Reviews.

The Man Who Owns Broadway
    book: George M. Cohan
    staging: George M. Cohan
Productions:
    Opened October 11, 1909 for 128 performances
Reviews:
    Cosmopolitan 48:206, Jan 1910
    Dramatic Mirror 62:5, Oct 23, 1909
    Metropolitan Magazine 31:540-1, Jan 1910
    Theatre Magazine 10:xiv, Nov 1909
                    10:134, Nov 1909

Man with a Load of Mischief
    book: Ben Tarver; adapted from the play by Ashley
                    Dukes
    music: John Clifton
    lyrics: John Clifton and Ben Tarver
    staging: Tom Gruenewald
    sets: Joan Larkey
    costumes: Volavkova
    choreography: Noel Schwartz
Productions:
    (Off-Broadway)   Opened November 6, 1966 for 241 performances
Reviews:
    New York Times page 65, Nov 7, 1966
    New Yorker 42:178+, Nov 19, 1966

Manhattan Mary
    book: B. G. DeSylva, Lew Brown, Ray Henderson,
                    William K. Wells and George White
    music,
      lyrics: B. G. DeSylva, Lew Brown, Ray Henderson,
                    William K. Wells and George White
    staging: George White
Productions:
    Opened September 26, 1927 for 264 performances
Reviews:
    Life (New York) 90:19, Oct 27, 1927
    New York Times VII, page 2, Sep 4, 1927
                   page 35, Sep 6, 1927
                   page 30, Sep 27, 1927
                   page 3, Sep 28, 1927
                   page 26, Sep 29, 1927
                   IX, page 1, Oct 30, 1927
    Theatre Magazine 46:44, Dec 1927

Manhattan Showboat
    conceived: Robert F. Jani

dialogue:	Stan Hart
special material:	Nan Mason
original music and lyrics:	Don Pippin, Sammy Cahn and Nan Mason
staging:	Frank Wagner
sets:	Robert Guerra
costumes:	Frank Spencer and Michael Casey
choreography:	Linda Lemac, Howard Parker, Debra Pigliavento, Frank Wagner, and Violet Holmes

Productions:
Opened June 30, 1980 for 191 performances
Reviews:
New York Times III, page 16, Jul 2, 1980

Manhattan Vanities (see Belmont Varieties)

The Manhatters
sketches:	Aline Erlanger and George S. Oppenheimer
music:	Alfred Nathan
lyrics:	George S. Oppenheimer
staging:	Dave Bennett

Productions:
Opened August 3, 1927 for 68 performances
Reviews:
New York Times page 27, Jul 19, 1927
                page 25, Aug 4, 1927
Vogue 70:85+, Oct 1, 1927

March of the Falsettos
book:	William Finn
music:	William Finn
lyrics:	William Finn
staging:	James Lapine
sets:	Douglas Stein
costumes:	Maureen Connor

Productions:
(Off-Broadway) Opened May 20, 1981 for 268 performances
Reviews:
New York 14:59-60, Apr 27, 1981
         14:31-3, Jun 8, 1981
New York Times III, page 3, Apr 10, 1981
                II, page 3, Apr 26, 1981
New Yorker 57:144-5, May 18, 1981
Time 118:72, Aug 3, 1981

Marching By
book:	Ernst Neubach, adapted by Harry Clarke and Harry B. Smith
music:	Jean Gilbert, Mack Gordon and Harry Revel
lyrics:	Ernst Neubach
staging:	J. C. Huffman

Productions:
    Opened March 3, 1932 for 12 performances
Reviews:
    New York Times page 17, Mar 4, 1932

Mardi Gras!
book:	Sig Herzig
music:	Carmen Lombardo and John Jacob Loeb
lyrics:	Carmen Lombardo and John Jacob Loeb
staging:	June Taylor
sets:	George Jenkins
costumes:	Winn Morton
choreography:	June Taylor

Productions:
    (Off-Broadway) Opened June 26, 1965 for 68 performances
    (Off-Broadway) Opened July 8, 1966 for 54 performances
Reviews:
    America 113:190, Aug 21, 1965
            115:140, Aug 6, 1966
    New York Times page 22, Jan 21, 1965
                   page 33, Jun 28, 1965
                   page 32, Jul 11, 1966
    Saturday Review 49:48, Jul 30, 1966

Maria Golovin
book:	Gian Carlo Menotti
music:	Gian Carlo Menotti
lyrics:	Gian Carlo Menotti
staging:	Gian Carlo Menotti
sets:	Rouben Ter-Arutunian
costumes:	Helene Pons

Productions:
    Opened November 5, 1958 for 5 performances
Reviews:
    Musical America 78:17, Oct 1958
                    78:18, Nov 15, 1958
    Nation 187:395-6, Nov 22, 1958
    New Republic 139:22-3, Nov 17, 1958
    New York Theatre Critics' Reviews 1958:215
    New York Times II, page 1, Nov 2, 1958
                   page 43, Nov 6, 1958
                   II, page 11, Nov 30, 1958
    New Yorker 34:200-1, Nov 15, 1958
    Newsweek 52:54, Sep 1, 1958
             52:75, Nov 17, 1958
    Saturday Review 41:43, Nov 22, 1958
    Theatre Arts 43:68, Jan 1959
    Time 72:40, Sep 1, 1958
         72:54+, Nov 17, 1958

Marie Dressler's All Star Gambol
arranged:	Marie Dressler

```
compiled:          Marie Dressler
music:             A. Baldwin Sloane
```
Productions:
Opened March 10, 1913 for 8 performances
No Reviews.

Marilyn: An American Fable
```
book:              Patricia Michaels
music and
  lyrics:          Jeanne Napoli, Doug Frank, Gary Portnoy, and
                   Beth Lawrence and Norman Thalheimer
staging:           Kenny Ortega
sets:              Tom H. John
costumes:          Joseph G. Aulisi
choreography:      Kenny Ortega
```
Productions:
Opened November 20, 1983 for 16 performances
Reviews:
Dance Magazine 58:90, Feb 1984
New York 16:151-2, Dec 5, 1983
New York Theatre Critics' Reviews 1983:118
New York Times III, page 14, Nov 21, 1983
New Yorker 59:180+, Dec 5, 1983
People 20:42-3, Dec 5, 1983

Marinka
```
book:              George Marion, Jr. and Karl Farkas
music:             Emmerich Kalman
lyrics:            George Marion, Jr. and Karl Farkas
staging:           Hassard Short
sets:              Howard Bay
costumes:          Mary Grant
choreography:      Albertina Rasch
```
Productions:
Opened July 18, 1945 for 165 performances
Reviews:
Catholic World 161:509-10, Sep 1945
Commonweal 42:381, Aug 3, 1945
New York Theatre Critics' Reviews 1945:186+
New York Times page 19, Jul 1945
            II, page 1, Sep 16, 1945
New Yorker 21:40, Jul 28, 1945
Newsweek 26:65, Jul 30, 1945
Saturday Review 28:22-3, Sep 29, 1945
Theatre Arts 29:551, Oct 1945
Time 46:72, Jul 30, 1945

Marjolaine
```
book:              Catherine Chisholm Cushing; based on L. N.
                   Parker's Pomander Walk
music:             Hugo Felix
lyrics:            Brian Hooker
```

Productions:
  Opened January 24, 1922 for 136 performances
Reviews:
  Dramatic Mirror 95:63, Mar 1922
  Life (New York) 79:18, Feb 16, 1922
  New York Clipper 69:20, Feb 1, 1922
  New York Times page 16, Jan 25, 1922
              page 17, Feb 21, 1922
  Theatre Magazine 35:229, Apr 1922
              35:268, Apr 1922

Marjorie
  book: Fred Thompson, Clifford Grey and Harold At-
               teridge
  music: Sigmund Romberg, Herbert Stothart, Philip
               Kulkin and Stephen Jones
Productions:
  Opened August 11, 1924 for 144 performances
Reviews:
  New York Times page 12, Aug 12, 1924
  Theatre Magazine 40:15, Oct 1924

Marjorie Daw
  book: Sally Dixon Weiner
  music: Sally Dixon Weiner
  lyrics: Sally Dixon Weiner
  staging: Miriam Fond
Productions:
  (Off-Off-Broadway) Season of 1973-1974
No Reviews.

Marlene Dietrich
  staging: Burt Bacharach
Productions:
  Opened October 9, 1967 for 48 performances
  Opened October 3, 1968 for 67 performances
Reviews:
  Life 65:6, Nov 8, 1968
  New York Theatre Critics' Reviews 1967:267
  New York Times page 26, Aug 25, 1967
              page 55, Sep 26, 1967
              page 52, Oct 10, 1967
              page 36, Oct 4, 1968
              page 36, Dec 1, 1968
  Newsweek 70:113, Oct 23, 1967
  Time 90:84, Oct 20, 1967

Marlowe
  book: Leo Rost
  music: Jimmy Horowitz
  lyrics: Leo Rost and Jimmy Horowitz

```
staging:          Don Price
sets:             Cary Chalmers
costumes:         Natalie Walker
choreography:     Peter Moore
```
Productions:
Opened October 12, 1981 for 48 performances
Reviews:
New York Theatre Critics' Reviews 1981:151
New York Times III, page 7, Oct 13, 1981

Marriage a la Carte
```
book:             C. M. S. McLellan
music:            Ivan Caryll
lyrics:           C. M. S. McLellan
staging:          Austin Hurgon
```
Productions:
Opened January 2, 1911 for 64 performances
Reviews:
Columbian 3:1080-1, Mar 1911
Dramatic Mirror 65:7, Jan 4, 1911
     65:9, Feb 8, 1911
Everybody's 24:561, Apr 1911
Green Book Album 5:474-5+, Mar 1911
New York Times page 12, Jan 3, 1911
Red Book 16:956-60, Mar 1911
Theatre Magazine 13:iii, Feb 1911
     13:xv, Feb 1911
     13:99, Mar 1911

The Marriage Market
```
book:             M. Brody and F. Martos; adapted for the English
                  stage by Gladys Unger
music:            Victor Jacobi
lyrics:           Arthur Anderson and Adrian Ross
staging:          Edward Royce
```
Productions:
Opened September 22, 1913 for 80 performances
Reviews:
Dramatic Mirror 70:10, Sep 24, 1913
     70:2, Oct 8, 1913
     70:2, Nov 5, 1913
Green Book 10:966-7, Dec 1913
Munsey 49:878-79, Aug 1913
   50:476, Dec 1913
New York Dramatic News 58:18-19, Sep 27, 1913
New York Times page 11, Sep 16, 1913
     page 11, Sep 23, 1913
Theatre Magazine 18:145, Nov 1913
     18:156, Nov 1913

Marry Me a Little
```
conceived:        Craig Lucas and Norman Rene
```

songs:	Stephen Sondheim
staging:	Norman Rene
sets:	Jane Thurn
costumes:	Oleksa
choreography:	Don Johanson

Productions:
    (Off-Off-Broadway) Opened November 1980
    (Off-Broadway) Opened March 21, 1981 for 96 performances
    (Off-Off-Broadway) Opened January 16, 1987
Reviews:
    Los Angeles 30:48+, May 1985
    New York Times page 76, Nov 2, 1980
                  page 12, Mar 14, 1981
                  III, page 15, Jan 27, 1987
    New Yorker 57:126, Mar 23, 1981

Mary

book:	Otto Harbach and Frank Mandel
music:	Lou Hirsch
lyrics:	Otto Harbach and Frank Mandel
staging:	George M. Cohan, Julian Mitchell and Sam Forrest

Productions:
    Opened October 18, 1920 for 219 performances
    (Off-Off-Broadway) Opened March 1, 1979
Reviews:
    Dramatic Mirror 82:733, Apr 17, 1920
                     page 743, Oct 23, 1920
    Life (New York) 76:820-1, Nov 4, 1920
    New York Clipper 68:19, Oct 27, 1920
    New York Times page 12, Oct 19, 1920
                  III, page 25, Mar 7, 1979
    New Yorker 55:56+, Mar 19, 1979
    Theatre Magazine 33:32-4, Jan 1921

Mary Jane McKane

book:	William Cary Duncan and Oscar Hammerstein II
music:	Herbert Stothart and Vincent Youmans
lyrics:	William Cary Duncan and Oscar Hammerstein II

Productions:
    Opened December 25, 1923 for 151 performances
Reviews:
    New York Times page 13, Dec 26, 1923
    Theatre Magazine 39:19, Mar 1924

Mask and Gown

conceived by:	Leonard Sillman
continuity by:	Ronny Graham and Sidney Carroll
music and lyrics:	Ronny Graham, June Carroll, Arthur Siegel, Dorothea Freitag

staging: Leonard Sillman
choreography: Jim Russell
Productions:
Opened September 10, 1957 for 39 performances
Reviews:
New York Theatre Critics' Reviews 1957:259+
New York Times page 29, Sep 11, 1957
Theatre Arts 41:17-18, Nov 1957

Mata Hari (see Ballad for a Firing Squad)

The Matinee Girl
book: McElbert Moore and Bide Dudley
music: Frank Grey
lyrics: McElbert Moore and Bide Dudley
staging: Oscar Eagle
Productions:
Opened February 1, 1926 for 24 performances
Reviews:
New York Times page 20, Feb 2, 1926

A Matinee Idol
book: Armand Barnard
music: Silvio Hein
lyrics: E. Ray Goetz and Seymour Brown
Productions:
Opened April 28, 1910 for 68 performances
Reviews:
Dramatic Mirror 63:8, May 7, 1910
Harper's Weekly 54:24, May 14, 1910
Metropolitan Magazine 32:544, Jul 1910
Theatre Magazine 11:177, Jun 1910

A Matter of Opinion
book: Mary Elizabeth Hauer
music: Harold Danko and John Jacobson
lyrics: Mary Elizabeth Hauer
staging: Shari Upbin
sets: John Arnone
costumes: John Arnone
choreography: Shari Upbin
Productions:
(Off-Broadway) Opened September 30, 1980 for 8 performances
Reviews:
New York Times III, page 18, Oct 2, 1980

A Matter of Time
book: Hap Schlein and Russell Leib
music: Philip F. Margo
lyrics: Philip F. Margo
staging: Tod Jackson

sets: David Guthrie
choreography: Tod Jackson
Productions:
  (Off-Broadway) Opened April 27, 1975 for one performance
Reviews:
  New York Times page 37, Apr 28, 1975

Maurice Chevalier (1932)
Productions:
  Opened February 9, 1932 for 17 performances
Reviews:
  Commonweal 15: 470, Feb 24, 1932
  New York Times page 26, Feb 10, 1932

Maurice Chevalier (1947)
Productions:
  Opened March 10, 1947 for 46 performances
Reviews:
  Life 22: 94, Apr 14, 1947
      23: 67-8, Nov 10, 1947
  Newsweek 29: 84, Mar 24, 1947
  Theatre Arts 31: 49, Dec 1947
  Time 49: 66, Mar 24, 1947

Maurice Chevalier (1948)
Productions:
  Opened February 29, 1948 for 33 performances
Reviews:
  New York Times page 16, Mar 1, 1948

Maurice Chevalier (1963)
  sketches: Maurice Chevalier
  songs: Alan Jay Lerner, Frederick Loewe, George
                    Gershwin, Johnny Mercer, George M. Cohan and
                    others
  staging: Maurice Chevalier
  sets: Raoul Pene du Bois
Productions:
  Opened January 28, 1963 for 29 performances
Reviews:
  New York Times page 7, Jan 30, 1963
  Theatre Arts 46: 13+, Nov 1962

Maurice Chevalier at 77
  sketches: Maurice Chevalier and others
  songs: Alan Jay Lerner, Frederick Loewe, Cole Porter,
                    Jerry Herman, Johnny Mercer and others
Productions:
  Opened May 1, 1975 for 31 performances
Reviews:
  America 112: 590, Apr 17, 1965

Commonweal 82:155-7, Apr 23, 1965
New York Theatre Critics' Reviews 1965:354
New York Times page 26, Apr 2, 1965
Newsweek 65:100-101, Apr 12, 1965
Saturday Review 48:44, Apr 17, 1965

Maurice Chevalier in Songs and Impressions
music: Maurice Chevalier, Fred Freed and others
lyrics: Maurice Chevalier, Fred Freed and others
Productions:
Opened September 28, 1955 for 46 performances
Reviews:
America 94:81, Oct 15, 1955
Catholic World 182:143, Nov 1955
Commonweal 63:62-3, Oct 21, 1955
New York Times page 38, Sep 29, 1955
New Yorker 31:97, Oct 8, 1955
Newsweek 46:75, Oct 10, 1955
Theatre Arts 39:20, Dec 1955
Time 66:53, Oct 10, 1955

Max Morath   (see An Evening with Max Morath at the Turn of the Century)

May Wine
book: Frank Mandel, adapted from The Happy Alienist
            by Erich von Stroheim and Wallace Smith
music: Sigmund Romberg
lyrics: Oscar Hammerstein II
staging: Jose Ruben
sets: Raymond Sovey
costumes: Kay Morrison
Productions:
Opened December 5, 1935 for 213 performances
Reviews:
Catholic World 142:601, Feb 1936
Commonweal 23:218, Dec 20, 1935
Literary Digest 120:20, Dec 21, 1935
New York Times page 23, Nov 23, 1935
            page 30, Dec 6, 1935
Newsweek 6:38, Dec 14, 1935
Theatre Arts 20:103, Feb 1936
Time 26:61, Dec 16, 1935

Maybe I'm Doing It Wrong
conceived: Joan Micklin Silver
music: Randy Newman
lyrics: Randy Newman
staging: Joan Micklin Silver
sets: Heidi Landesman
costumes: Hilary Rosenfeld
choreography: Eric Elice

Productions:
   (Off-Broadway)   Opened March 14, 1982 for 33 performances
Reviews:
   New York Times III, page 14, Mar 15, 1982
   Newsweek 99:52, Mar 29, 1982

Mayflowers
   book: Clifford Grey; from a play by Arthur Richman
   music: Edward Kunneke
   lyrics: Clifford Grey
   staging: William J. Wilson and Joseph Santley
Productions:
   Opened November 24, 1925 for 81 performances
Reviews:
   New York Times page 14, Nov 25, 1925

Mayor
   book: Warren Leight, based on Mayor by Edward I.
                    Koch
   music: Charles Strouse
   lyrics: Charles Strouse
   staging: Jeffrey B. Moss
   sets: Randy Barcelo
   costumes: Randy Barcelo
   choreography: Barbara Siman
Productions:
   (Off-Broadway)   Opened May 13, 1985 for 185 performances
   Opened October 23, 1985 for 70 performances
Reviews:
   New York 18:101, May 27, 1985
   New York Theatre Critics' Reviews 1985:271
   New York Times III, page 11, May 14, 1985

Maytime
   book: Rida Johnson Young
   music: Sigmund Romberg
   lyrics: Rida Johnson Young
   staging: Edward P. Temple, Allen K. Foster and J. J.
                    Shubert
Productions:
   Opened August 16, 1917 for 492 performances
Reviews:
   Dramatic Mirror 77:8, Aug 25, 1917
   Green Book 20:202+, Aug 1918
   Life (New York) 70:283, Sep 6, 1917
   Munsey 62:305-6, Nov 1917
          64:427, Jul 1918
   New York Times page 7, Aug 17, 1917
                    IX, page 5, Aug 26, 1917
                    IV, page 5, Sep 2, 1917
   Stage 14:68-9, Aug 1937
   Theatre Magazine 26:205+, Oct 1917

Me and Bessie
-----
    conceived: Will Holt and Linda Hopkins
    written: Will Holt and Linda Hopkins
    staging: Robert Greenwald
    sets: Donald Harris
    costumes: Pete Menefee
    choreography: Lester Wilson
Productions:
    Opened October 22, 1975 for 453 performances
Reviews:
    Essence 6:31, Feb 1976
    New York 8:84, Nov 10, 1975
    New York Theatre Critics' Reviews 1975:184
    New York Times page 46, Oct 23, 1975
                 II, page 5, Nov 2, 1975
    New Yorker 51:151-2, Nov 10, 1975
    Time 106:66, Nov 3, 1975

Me and Juliet
-----
    book: Oscar Hammerstein II
    music: Richard Rodgers
    lyrics: Oscar Hammerstein II
    staging: George Abbott
    sets: Jo Mielziner
    costumes: Irene Sharaff
    choreography: Robert Alton
Productions:
    Opened May 28, 1953 for 358 performances
    (Off-Broadway) Opened May 7, 1970 for 19 performances
Reviews:
    America 89:305, Jun 13, 1953
    Catholic World 177:308, Jul 1953
    Commonweal 58:273, Jun 19, 1953
    Life 34:89-90+, Jun 15, 1953
    Look 17:34-6, Jun 16, 1953
    Nation 176:530, Jun 20, 1953
    New York Theatre Critics' Reviews 1953:298+
    New York Times page 33, Apr 21, 1953
                 II, page 1, May 24, 1953
                 VI, page 28, May 24, 1953
                 page 17, May 29, 1953
                 II, page 1, Jun 7, 1953
                 page 42, May 15, 1970
    New York Times Magazine pages 28-9, May 24, 1953
    New Yorker 29:64+, Jun 6, 1953
    Newsweek 41:72, Jun 8, 1953
                42:60, Dec 21, 1953
    Saturday Review 36:26-7, Jun 13, 1953
                    36:37, Jul 11, 1953
    Theatre Arts 37:15-16, Aug 1953
                37:28-9, Sep 1953

Time 61:93, Jun 8, 1953
Vogue 121:90-1, Jun 1953

Me and My Girl
    book: L. Arthur Rose and Douglas Furber, revised by
                     Stephen Fry and Mike Ockrent
    music: Noel Gay
    lyrics: L. Arthur Rose and Douglas Furber
    staging: Mike Ockrent
    sets: Martin Johns
    costumes: Ann Curtis
    choreography: Gillian Gregory
Productions:
    Opened August 10, 1986 for *1,595 performances (still running
    6/1/89)
Reviews:
    America 155:122+, Sep 13-20, 1986
    Commonweal 113:501, Sep 26, 1986
    Dance Magazine 60:72, Dec 1986
    Los Angeles 31:40, Jul 1986
    New Leader 69:22-3, Sep 8, 1986
    New York 19:113-14, Aug 25, 1986
    New York Theatre Critics' Reviews 1986:244
    New York Times III, page 13, Aug 11, 1986
                    II, page 5, Aug 17, 1986
                    II, page 2, Sep 28, 1986
                    III, page 19, Sep 29, 1987
    New Yorker 62:90-1, Aug 25, 1986
    Newsweek 108:60-1, Aug 25, 1986
    Saturday Evening Post 259:22+, Oct 1987
    Time 128:69, Aug 25, 1986
    Vogue 176:104, Aug 1986

The Me Nobody Knows
    book: Stephen M. Joseph; edited from the book The
                     Me Nobody Knows; and adapted by Robert H.
                     Livingston and Herb Schapiro
    music: Gary William Friedman
    lyrics: Will Holt
    staging: Robert H. Livingston
    sets: Clarke Dunham
    costumes: Patricia Quinn Stuart
    choreography: Patricia Birch
Productions:
    (Off-Broadway) Opened May 18, 1970 for 208 performances
    Opened December 18, 1970 for 586 performances
Reviews:
    America 122:638, Jun 13, 1970
    Commonweal 93:396, Jan 22, 1971
    Dance Magazine 44:80, Sep 1970
    Life 69:34-42, Sep 4, 1970

Nation 210:701, Jun 8, 1970
New Republic 162:312, Jun 13, 1970
New York Theatre Critics' Reviews 1970:203
New York Times II, page 22, Feb 22, 1970
    page 42, May 19, 1970
    II, page 3, May 31, 1970
    II, page 36, Oct 18, 1970
    page 48, Dec 18, 1970
    page 16, Jan 1, 1971
    page 51, Sep 8, 1971
    page 58, Nov 12, 1971
New Yorker 46:70+, May 30, 1970
Newsweek 75:104, Jun 1, 1970

Mecca
  book: Oscar Asche
  music: Percy E. Fletcher
  staging: E. Lyall Swete
  choreography: Michel Fokine
Productions:
  Opened October 4, 1920 for 128 performances
Reviews:
  Dramatic Mirror page 635, Oct 9, 1920
  New York Clipper 68:19, Oct 13, 1920
  New York Times page 12, Oct 5, 1920
    page 14, Oct 13, 1920
    III, page 8, Oct 24, 1920
    VI, page 1, Oct 24, 1920
  Theatre Magazine 32:349, Dec 1920
    32:369, Dec 1920

The Medium (Presented with The Telephone)
  book: Gian-Carlo Menotti
  music: Gian-Carlo Menotti
  lyrics: Gian-Carlo Menotti
  staging: Gian-Carlo Menotti
  sets: Horace Armistead
  costumes: Horace Armistead
Productions:
  Opened May 1, 1947 for 212 performances
  Opened December 7, 1948 for 40 performances
  Opened July 19, 1950 for 110 performances
  (Off-Off-Broadway) Opened December 16, 1976
Reviews:
  Catholic World 165:265-6, Jun 1947
    171:469, Sep 1950
  Life 22:95-6+, Jun 9, 1947
  Nation 164:637+, May 4, 1947
  New York Theatre Critics' Reviews 1947:379
    1950:280
  New York Times page 28, May 2, 1947

                              II, page 2, May 11, 1947
                              page 26, Apr 30, 1948
                              page 41, Dec 8, 1948
          New Yorker 23:50+, May 10, 1947
          Newsweek 29:76, Mar 3, 1947
          Saturday Review 30:22-4, May 31, 1947
                           31:44, Feb 28, 1948
          School and Society 66:66, Jul 26, 1947
                           69:86, Jan 29, 1949
          Theatre Arts 31:24, Apr 1947
                     31:60, May 1947
          Time 49:69, Jun 30, 1947

Meet My Sister
     book: Harry Wagstaffe Gribble, from the French of
                        Berr, Verneuil, and Blum
     music: Ralph Benatsky
     lyrics: Ralph Benatsky
     staging: William Mollison
     choreography: John Pierce
Productions:
     Opened December 30, 1930 for 167 performances
Reviews:
     Catholic World 132:596, Feb 1931
     New York Times page 11, Dec 31, 1930
     Theatre Magazine 53:60, Mar 1931

Meet Peter Grant
     book: Elliot Arluck; based on Henrik Ibsen's Peer Gynt
     music: Ted Harris
     lyrics: Elliot Arluck
Productions:
     (Off-Broadway) Season of 1960-1961
Reviews:
     New York Times page 41, May 11, 1961
     New Yorker 37:120, May 29, 1961

Meet the People
     assembled: Henry Myers
     sketches: Ben and Sol Barzman, Mortimer Offner, Edward
                        Eliscu, Danny Dare, Henry Blankfort, Bert
                        Lawrence, Sid Kuller, Ray Golden, Milt Gross,
                        Mike Quin, Arthur Ross
     music: Jay Gorney and George Bassman
     staging: Danny Dare
     sets: Frederick Stover
     costumes: Gerda Vanderneers and Kate Lawson
Productions:
     Opened December 25, 1940 for 160 performances
Reviews:
     Catholic World 152:598, Feb 1941

Collier's 107:24-5+, Mar 22, 1941
Life 8:39-41, Feb 26, 1940
New York Theatre Critics' Reviews 1940:170+
                                  1941:440+
New York Times IX, page 3, Oct 20, 1940
               page 22, Dec 26, 1940
               IX, page 3, Jan 5, 1941
               IX, page 1, Jan 12, 1941
               II, page 1, Aug 22, 1943
Theatre Arts 25:184, Mar 1941
             28:123, Feb 1944
             39:93, Jun 1955
Time 35:36, Jan 29, 1941

The Megilla of Itzik Manger

book: Schmuel Bunim, adapted from the Israeli version
                by Schmuel Bunim, Hayim Hefer, Itzik Manger,
                and Dov Seltzer
music: Dov Seltzer
staging: Schmuel Bunim
sets: Schlomo Vitkin

Productions:
Opened October 9, 1968 for 78 performances
Opened April 19, 1969 for 12 performances
Reviews:
New York Times page 60, Oct 10, 1968
               page 55, Apr 21, 1969

Melody

book: Edward Childs Carpenter
music: Sigmund Romberg
lyrics: Irving Caesar
staging: Bobby Connelly
sets: Joseph Urban
choreography: Bobby Connelly

Productions:
Opened February 14, 1933 for 79 performances
Reviews:
Arts and Decoration 38:59+, Apr 1933
Catholic World 137:81-2, Apr 1933
Nation 136:244, Mar 1, 1933
New Outlook 161:48, Mar 1933
New York Times page 17, Feb 15, 1933
Newsweek 1:26, Feb 17, 1933
Stage 10:16-17, Mar 1933

The Melting of Molly

book: Edgar Smith; from the novel of Maria Thompson
                Davies
music: Sigmund Romberg
lyrics: Cyrus Wood
staging: Oscar Eagle

Productions:
    Opened December 30, 1918 for 88 performances
Reviews:
    Dramatic Mirror 80:48, Jan 11, 1919
    New York Times page 9, Dec 31, 1918
                    IV, page 2, Jan 5, 1919
    Theatre Magazine 29:80, Feb 1919
                    29:87, Feb 1919

Memorial Liquid Theatre   (see The James Joyce Memorial Liquid
    Theatre)

Memphis Bound!
    book: Albert Barker and Sally Benton, a swing version
                    of Gilbert and Sullivan's H. M. S. Pinafore
    music: Don Walker and Clay Warnick
    lyrics: Don Walker and Clay Warnick
    staging: Robert Ross
    sets: George Jenkins
    costumes: Lucinda Ballard
    choreography: Al White
Productions:
    Opened May 24, 1945 for 36 performances
Reviews:
    Catholic World 161:350, Jul 1945
    Commonweal 42:191, Jun 8, 1945
    Life 18:57-8+, Jun 25, 1945
    Nation 160:705, Jun 23, 1945
    New York Theatre Critics' Reviews 1945:207+
    New York Times page 23, May 25, 1945
                    II, page 1, Jun 10, 1945
    New Yorker 21:36+, Jun 2, 1945
    Newsweek 25:90, Jun 4, 1945
    Theatre Arts 29:389, Jul 1945
    Time 45:85, Jun 4, 1945

Memphis Store-Bought Teeth
    book: E. Don Alldredge
    music: William Fisher
    lyrics: D. Brian Wallach
    staging: Marvin Gordon
    sets: Robert O'Hearn
    costumes: William Pitkin
Productions:
    (Off-Broadway) Opened December 29, 1971 for one performance
Reviews:
    New York Times page 18, Dec 30, 1971

The Mental Cure   (see Doctor Selavy's Magic Theater)

Mercenary Mary
    book: William B. Friedlander and Isabel Leighton;

based on a farce by E. Nyitray and H. H.
Winslow

music: William B. Friedlander and Con Conrad
lyrics: William B. Friedlander and Con Conrad
staging: William B. Friedlander

Productions:

Opened April 13, 1925 for 32 performances

Reviews:

New York Times page 27, Apr 14, 1925
Theatre Magazine 42:7, Dec 1925

Mercy Drop

book: Robert Patrick
music: Richard Weinstock
staging: Hugh Gittens

Productions:

(Off-Off-Broadway) Opened February 4, 1973

No Reviews.

Merlin

book: Richard Levinson and William Link, based on an
original concept by Doug Henning and Barbara
DeAngelis

songs and inci-
  dental music: Elmer Bernstein
lyrics: Don Black
magic illusions: created by Doug Henning
staging: Ivan Reitman
sets: Robin Wagner
costumes: Theoni V. Aldredge
choreography: Christopher Chadman and Billy Wilson

Productions:

Opened February 13, 1983 for 199 performances

Reviews:

Dance Magazine 57:92-3+, Apr 1983
Harper's Bazaar 116:204-5+, Dec 1982
Los Angeles 28:58+, Apr 1983
New Leader 66:20, Mar 7, 1983
New York 16:77-8, Feb 28, 1983
New York Theatre Critics' Reviews 1983:370
New York Times III, page 22, Jan 31, 1983
               II, page 3, Feb 20, 1983
New Yorker 59:82, Feb 28, 1983
Time 121:63, Feb 7, 1983

Merrily We Roll Along

book: George Furth, based on the play by George S.
Kaufman and Moss Hart
music: Stephen Sondheim
lyrics: Stephen Sondheim
staging: Harold Prince
sets: Eugene Lee

costumes: Judith Dolan
choreography: Larry Fuller
Productions:
Opened November 16, 1981 for 16 performances
Reviews:
Los Angeles 28:60+, Jun 1983
New York 14:87-8, Nov 30, 1981
New York Theatre Critics' Reviews 1981:104
New York Times III, page 9, Nov 17, 1981
New Yorker 57:110, Dec 7, 1981
Newsweek 98:109, Nov 30, 1981
Theatre Crafts 19:18-19, Oct 1985
Time 118:90, Nov 30, 1981

Merry-Go-Round
book: Morrie Ryskind and Howard Dietz
music: Henry Souvaine and Jay Gorney
lyrics: Morrie Ryskind and Howard Dietz
staging: Allan Dinehart
Productions:
Opened May 31, 1927 for 136 performances
Reviews:
Bookman 65:705-6, Aug 1927
New York Times page 25, Jun 1, 1927
             VII, page 1, Jun 5, 1927
             page 19, Jul 5, 1927
             VII, page 1, Jul 10, 1927
Theatre Magazine 46:18, 1927
Vogue 70:66, Aug 15, 1927

Merry Malones
book: George M. Cohan
staging: Edward Royce
Productions:
Opened September 26, 1927 for 192 performances
Opened Season of 1927-28 for 16 performances
Reviews:
National Magazine 56:87+, Oct 1927
New York Times VIII, page 1, Sep 11, 1927
             page 30, Sep 27, 1927
Theatre Magazine 46:74, Nov 1927

Merry, Merry
book: Harlan Thompson
music: Harry Archer
lyrics: Harlan Thompson
staging: Harlan Thompson
Productions:
Opened September 24, 1925 for 176 performances
Reviews:
New York Times page 24, Sep 25, 1925
Theatre Magazine 41:16, Feb 1925

The Merry Whirl
    book: Don Roth
    music: Leo Edwards
    choreography: Jack Mason
Productions:
    Opened May 30, 1910 for 24 performances
No Reviews.

Merry Widow
    book: Victor Leon and Leo Stein
    music: Franz Lehar
    English lyrics: Adrian Ross
    staging: William Mount-Burke
Productions:
    (Off-Broadway) Opened December 8, 1976 for 40 performances
    (Off-Broadway) Opened July 13, 1977 for 49 performances
Reviews:
    New York Times page 15, Dec 11, 1976
                   III, page 19, Apr 3, 1978

The Merry World
    music: Maurice Rubens, J. Fred Coots, Herman Hupfeld
                and Sam Timber
    lyrics: Clifford Grey
    staging: J. J. Shubert
Productions:
    Opened June 8, 1926 for 85 performances
Reviews:
    New York Times page 18, Jun 9, 1926
                   VII, page 1, Jun 13, 1926
                   page 15, Jul 30, 1926
    Theatre Magazine 44:15, Aug 1926

Messin' Around
    music: Jimmy Johnson
    lyrics: Perry Bradford
    staging: Louis Isquith and Eddie Rector
Productions:
    Opened April 22, 1929 for 33 performances
Reviews:
    Life (New York) 93:28, May 17, 1929
    New York Times page 26, Apr 23, 1929
                   page 27, May 23, 1929
    Theatre Magazine 50:41, Jul 1929

Mexican Hayride
    book: Herbert and Dorothy Fields
    music: Cole Porter
    lyrics: Cole Porter
    staging: Hassard Short
    sets: George Jenkins

costumes: Mary Grant
choreography: Paul Haakon
Productions:
Opened January 28, 1944 for 481 performances
Reviews:
Catholic World 158: 586, Mar 1944
Collier's 113: 18-21, Feb 5, 1944
Commonweal 39: 446, Feb 18, 1944
Life 16: 83-4+, Feb 21, 1944
Nation 158: 197, Feb 12, 1944
New York Theatre Critics' Reviews 1944: 271+
New York Times page 9, Jan 29, 1944
           II, page 1, Feb 6, 1944
           II, page 8, Mar 26, 1944
           II, page 1, Jul 2, 1944
Saturday Review 27: 18, Feb 19, 1944
Theatre Arts 28: 202+, Apr 1944
Time 43: 94, Feb 7, 1944

Mexicana
staging: Celestino Gorostiza
sets: Julio Castellanos
costumes: Augustin Lazo
Productions:
Opened April 21, 1939 for 35 performances
Reviews:
Catholic World 149: 346-7, Jun 1939
Modern Music 16: 268-9, May-Jun 1939
Nation 148: 538, May 6, 1939
New York Times page 14, Apr 22, 1939
           X, page 3, May 7, 1939
Theatre Arts 28: 404, Jun 1939

Michael Feinstein in Concert: Isn't It Romantic
conceived: Michael Feinstein and Christopher Chadman
music: various composers
lyrics: various authors
staging: Christopher Chadman
sets: Andrew Jackness
Productions:
Opened April 19, 1988 for 62 performances
Opened October 5, 1988 for 38 performances
Reviews:
New York Theatre Critics' Reviews 1988: 304
New Yorker 64: 100-1, May 9, 1988

Michael Todd's Peep Show
sketches: Bobby Clark, H. I. Phillips, William Roos, Billy
                K. Wells
music and
lyrics: Bhumibal and Chakraband, Sammy Fain and

```
                        Herb Magidson, Harold Rome, Raymond Scott,
                        Sammy Stept and Dan Shapiro, Jule Styne and
                        Bob Hilliard
    staging:            Hassard Short
    sets:               Howard Bay
    costumes:           Irene Sharaff
    choreography:       James Starbuck
Productions:
  Opened June 28, 1950 for 278 performances
Reviews:
  Life 29:67-70, Jul 10, 1950
  New Republic 123:21, Jul 17, 1950
  New York Theatre Critics' Reviews 1950:285+
  New York Times page 34, Jun 7, 1950
                      VI, page 28, Jun 18, 1950
                      VI, page 29, Jun 18, 1950
                      II, page 2, Jun 25, 1950
                      page 37, Jun 29, 1950
                      II, page 1, Jul 9, 1950
  New York Times Magazine pages 28-9, Jun 18, 1950
  New Yorker 26:44+, Jul 8, 1950
  Newsweek 36:77, Jul 10, 1950
  Theatre Arts 34:26-31+, Jul 1950
                      34:9, Sep 1950
  Time 56:58, Jul 10, 1950
        56:59-60, Jul 17, 1950
```

The Middle of Nowhere
```
    conceived:          Tracy Friedman
    by:                 Tracy Friedman, based on songs by Randy New-
                        man
    songs:              Randy Newman
    staging:            Tracy Friedman
    sets:               Loren Sherman
    costumes:           Juliet Polcsa and Loren Sherman
    choreography:       Tracy Friedman
Productions:
  (Off-Broadway) Opened November 20, 1988 for 24 performances
Reviews:
  New York Times III, page 17, Nov 22, 1988
```

The Midnight Girl
```
    book:               Paul Herve; American version by Adolph Philipp
                        and Edward A. Paulton
    music:              Jean Briquet and Adolph Philipp
    staging:            Ben Teal
Productions:
  Opened February 23, 1914 for 104 performances
Reviews:
  Dramatic Mirror 71:6-7, Feb 25, 1914
                  71:4, Mar 11, 1914
                  71:2, Mar 18, 1914
```

Green Book 11:718-19, May 1914
11:776-7, May 1914
Munsey 51:581-8, Apr 1914
New York Times page 12, Feb 24, 1914
Theatre Magazine 19:182, Apr 1914
19:212, Apr 1914

The Midnight Rounders of 1921
    music: Jean Schwartz and Lew Pollack
    lyrics: Alfred Bryan
    staging: J. J. Shubert
Productions:
    Opened February 5, 1921 for 120 performances
Reviews:
    Theatre Magazine 33:264, Apr 1921

Midnight Whirl   (see Morris Gest Midnight Whirl)

Milk and Honey
    book: Don Appell
    music: Jerry Herman
    lyrics: Jerry Herman
    staging: Albert Marre
    sets: Howard Bay
    costumes: Miles White
    choreography: Donald Saddler
Productions:
    Opened October 10, 1961 for 543 performances
Reviews:
    America 106:376+, Dec 9, 1961
    Commonweal 75:154, Nov 3, 1961
    Dance Magazine 35:28-30, Nov 1961
    Nation 193:361, Nov 4, 1961
    New York Theatre Critics' Reviews 1961:238+
    New York Times page 52, Oct 11, 1961
    New Yorker 37:130, Oct 21, 1961
    Newsweek 58:60+, Oct 23, 1961
    Saturday Review 44:32, Nov 4, 1961
    Theatre Arts 45:10-11, Dec 1961
    Time 78:64, Oct 20, 1961

The Mimic World
    dialogue: Harold Atteridge, James Hussey and Owen
                    Murphy
    music: Jean Schwartz, Lew Pollack and Owen Murphy
    staging: Allen K. Foster
Productions:
    Opened August 15, 1921 for 27 performances
Reviews:
    New York Times page 22, Aug 14, 1921
                    page 9, Aug 18, 1921
    Theatre Magazine 34:279, Oct 1921

Minnie Field (see American Legend)

Minnie's Boys
    book: Arthur Marx and Robert Fisher; suggested by
                            the life of the Marx Brothers
    music: Larry Grossman
    lyrics: Hal Hackady
    staging: Stanley Prager
    sets: Peter Wexler
    costumes: Donald Brooks
    choreography: Marc Breaux
Productions:
    Opened March 26, 1970 for 76 performances
Reviews:
    Commonweal 92:222, May 15, 1970
    Dance Magazine 44:84, Jun 1970
    New York Theatre Critics' Reviews 1970:325
    New York Times II, page 1, Mar 1, 1970
                    page 27, Mar 27, 1970
                    II, page 3, Apr 5, 1971
                    II, page 16, May 17, 1970
    New Yorker 46:61, Apr 4, 1970
    Newsweek 75:98-9, Apr 6, 1970
    Saturday Review 53:20, Apr 11, 1970
    Time 95:98+, Apr 13, 1970

The Misanthrope
    book: Richard Wilbur, adapted from the play by Moliere
    music: Jobriath Boone
    songs: Jobriath Boone, additional songs by Margaret
                            Pine and Arthur Bienstock
    staging: Bill Gile
    sets: Bill Stabile
    costumes: Carrie F. Robbins
    choreography: Rachel Lampert
Productions:
    (Off-Broadway) Opened October 5, 1977 for 63 performances
Reviews:
    Los Angeles 27:253, Jul 1982
    New York 8:64+, Mar 31, 1975
    New York Review of Books 24:47+, Dec 8, 1977
    New York Theatre Critics' Reviews 1975:306
                                       1983:386
    New York Times III, page 15, Nov 24, 1977

Miserables, Les (see Les Miserables)

Miss Daisy
    book: Philip Bartholomae
    music: Silvio Hein
    lyrics: Philip Bartholomae
    staging: Philip Bartholomae

Productions:
    Opened September 9, 1914 for 29 performances
Reviews:
    Dramatic Mirror 72:8, Sep 16, 1914
    Green Book 12:905, Nov 1914
    New York Times page 9, Sep 10, 1914
    Theatre Magazine 20:201, Nov 1914
                    20:206, Nov 1914

Miss Emily Adam
    material: James Lipton and Paul E. Davies; based on
                        Winthrop Palmer's Rosemary and the Planet
Productions:
    (Off-Broadway) Season of 1959-20
Reviews:
    New York Times page 43, Mar 30, 1960
                    page 12, Apr 15, 1960

Miss Information
    book: Paul Dickey and Charles W. Goddard
    music: Jerome Kern
    staging: Robert Milton
Productions:
    Opened October 5, 1915 for 47 performances
Reviews:
    Dramatic Mirror 74:8, Oct 16, 1915
    New York Dramatic News 61:18, Oct 9, 1915
    New York Times page 11, Oct 6, 1915
    Smart Set 47:146-7, Dec 1915
    Theatre Magazine 22:223-4+, Nov 1915

Miss Jack
    book: Mark E. Swan
    music: William F. Peters
    lyrics: Mark E. Swan
Productions:
    Opened September 4, 1911 for 16 performances
Reviews:
    Dramatic Mirror 66:11, Sep 6, 1911
                    66:4, Sep 13, 1911
    Green Book Album 6:925-7, Nov 1911
                    6:965, Nov 1911
    Life (New York) 58:479, Sep 21, 1911
    Theatre Magazine 14:113, Oct 1911

Miss Liberty
    book: Robert E. Sherwood
    music: Irving Berlin
    lyrics: Irving Berlin
    staging: Moss Hart
    sets: Oliver Smith

costumes: Motley
choreography: Jerome Robbins
Productions:
   Opened July 15, 1949 for 308 performances
Reviews:
   Catholic World 170:67-8, Oct 1949
   Commonweal 50:414, Aug 5, 1949
   Good Housekeeping 129:121, Dec 1949
   Holiday 6:16-17+, Nov 1949
   Life 27:56-8, Jul 4, 1949
   New Republic 121:27-8, Aug 1, 1949
   New York Theatre Critics' Reviews 1949:279+
   New York Times page 23, Feb 13, 1949
                 VI, page 16, May 29, 1949
                 page 26, Jun 14, 1949
                 page 39, Jun 15, 1949
                 page 6, Jul 16, 1949
                 II, page 6, Aug 7, 1949
   New York Times Magazine pages 16-17, May 29, 1949
                          pages 22-3, Jun 26, 1949
   New Yorker 25:18, Jun 25, 1949
            25:44, Jul 23, 1949
   Newsweek 34:70-1, Jul 25, 1949
   Saturday Review 32:28-9, Aug 13, 1949
   Theatre Arts 33:10, Sep 1949
   Time 54:66, Jul 25, 1949

Miss Millions
   book: R. H. Burnside
   music: Raymond Hubbell
Productions:
   Opened December 9, 1919 for 47 performances
Reviews:
   Dramatic Mirror 80:1981, Dec 25, 1919
   New York Times page 11, Dec 10, 1919
               VIII, page 2, Dec 14, 1919

Miss Moffat
   book: Emlyn Williams, and Joshua Logan, based on
               Williams' play The Corn is Green
   music: Albert Hague
   lyrics: Emlyn Williams
   staging: Joshua Logan
   sets: Jo Mielziner
   costumes: Robert Mackintosh
   choreography: Donald Saddler
Productions:
   Closed in pre-Broadway production, October, 1974.
Reviews:
   Playboy 21:24, Sep 1974

Ms. Nefertiti

book: Tom Eyen
music: Ilene Berson and Tom Eyen
staging: Tom Eyen

Productions:
(Off-Off-Broadway) Opened February 9, 1973
No Reviews.

Miss 1917

book: Guy Bolton and P. G. Wodehouse
music: Victor Herbert
lyrics: Guy Bolton and P. G. Wodehouse
staging: Ned Wayburn

Productions:
Opened November 5, 1917 for 48 performances
Reviews:
Dramatic Mirror 77:5, Nov 17, 1917
                77:5, Dec 8, 1917
Green Book 19:4+, Jan 1918
New York Dramatic News 64:11, Nov 10, 1917
New York Times page 11, Nov 6, 1917
                VIII, page 6, Nov 11, 1917
Theatre Magazine 27:350-51, Dec 1917

Miss Springtime

book: Guy Bolton
music: Emmerich Kalman
staging: Herbert Gresham

Productions:
Opened September 25, 1916 for 224 performances
Reviews:
Dramatic Mirror 76:7, Sep 30, 1916
                76:5, Oct 7, 1916
                76:1, Oct 14, 1916
Green Book 16:974-5+, Dec 1916
Leslie's Weekly 124:327, Mar 22, 1917
New York Dramatic News 63:3, Sep 30, 1916
New York Times page 9, Sep 26, 1916
Theatre Magazine 24:280+, Nov 1916

Mr. Lode of Koal

book: J. A. Shipp and Alexander Rogers
music: J. Rosamond and Bert A. Williams
lyrics: J. A. Shipp and Alexander Rogers

Productions:
Opened November 1, 1909 for 40 performances
No Reviews.

Mr. President

book: Howard Lindsay and Russel Crouse
music: Irving Berlin

lyrics: Irving Berlin
staging: Joshua Logan
sets: Jo Mielziner
costumes: Theoni V. Aldredge
choreography: Peter Gennaro
Productions:
    Opened October 20, 1962 for 265 performances
Reviews:
    America 107:1230, Dec 8, 1962
    Business Week page 31, Sep 29, 1962
    Commonweal 77:279, Dec 7, 1962
    Dance Magazine 36:98, Dec 1962
    National Review 14:78-9, Jan 29, 1963
    New York Theatre Critics' Reviews 1962:238+
    New York Times page 18, Aug 29, 1962
                     page 36, Sep 26, 1962
                     II, page 1, Oct 14, 1962
                     page 34, Oct 22, 1962
                     page 38, May 29, 1963
    New Yorker 38:147, Oct 27, 1962
    Newsweek 60:74, Nov 5, 1962
    Reporter 27:43, Dec 20, 1962
    Saturday Review 45:40, Nov 3, 1962
    Theatre Arts 46:14-16, Nov 1962
                 46:14, Dec 1962
    Time 80:62, Sep 7, 1962
         80:82, Nov 2, 1962
    Vogue 140:144-7+, Nov 1, 1962

Mr. Strauss Goes to Boston
    book: Leonard L. Levenson from a story by Alfred
                      Grunwald and Geza Herczeg
    music: Robert Stolz
    lyrics: Robert Sour
    staging: Felix Brentano
    sets: Stewart Chaney
    costumes: Walter Florell
    choreography: George Balanchine
Productions:
    Opened September 6, 1945 for 12 performances
Reviews:
    Catholic World 162:70, Oct 1945
    New York Theatre Critics' Reviews 1945:180+
    New York Times page 20, Sep 7, 1945
                     II, page 1, Sep 16, 1945
    New Yorker 21:46, Sep 15, 1945
    Newsweek 26:103, Sep 17, 1945
    Time 46:74, Sep 17, 1945

Mr. Wonderful
    book: Joseph Stein and Will Glickman

music:	Jerry Bock, Larry Holofcener, George Weiss
lyrics:	Jerry Bock, Larry Holofcener, George Weiss
staging:	Jack Donohue
sets:	Oliver Smith
costumes:	Robert Mackintosh
choreography:	Jack Donohue

Productions:
  Opened March 22, 1956 for 383 performances
Reviews:
  America 95:42, Apr 7, 1956
  Catholic World 183:150, May 1956
  New York Theatre Critics' Reviews 1956:339+
  New York Times page 23, Mar 23, 1956
  New Yorker 32:62+, Mar 31, 1956
  Saturday Review 39:34, Apr 14, 1956
  Theatre Arts 40:14, Jun 1956
  Time 67:91, Apr 2, 1956

Mixed Doubles

book:	Rod Warren
music:	Michael Cohen and Edward Morris
lyrics:	Rod Warren
staging:	Robert Audy
choreography:	Robert Audy

Productions:
  (Off-Broadway) Opened October 19, 1966 for 428 performances
No Reviews.

Mlle. Colombe

book:	Edwin Dulchin, Albert Harris, and Michael Valenti, based on Louis J. Kronenberger's English adaptation of Jean Anouilh's play
music:	Michael Valenti
lyrics:	Edwin Dulchin
staged:	Albert Harris
sets:	Philipp Yung
costumes:	Lindsay Davis
choreography:	William Fleet Lively

Productions:
  (Off-Off-Broadway) Opened December 9, 1987 for 42 performances
Reviews:
  New York 21:84-5, Jan 18, 1988
  New York Times III, page 28, Dec 10, 1987

Mlle. Modiste

book:	Henry Blossom
music:	Victor Herbert
lyrics:	Henry Blossom
staging:	William Mount-Burke
sets:	Louise Krozek
costumes:	James Nadeaux
choreography:	Jerry Gotham

Productions:
    (Off-Broadway)   Opened January 11, 1978 for 35 performances
    (Off-Broadway)   Opened June 7, 1978 for 49 performances
No Reviews.

Mod Donna
    book: Myrna Lamb
    music: Susan Hulsman Bingham
    lyrics: Myrna Lamb
    staging: Joseph Papp
    costumes: Milo Morrow
    choreography: Ze-eva Cohen
Productions:
    (Off-Broadway)   Opened April 24, 1970 for 56 performances
Reviews:
    Harper's 103:6+, Jul 1970
    New York Times page 60, Mar 26, 1970
                     page 48, May 4, 1970
                     II, page 1, May 10, 1970
    New Yorker 46:107, May 16, 1970
    Newsweek 75:121, May 18, 1970
    Time 95:62, May 25, 1970

A Modern Eve
    book: Adapted by William M. Hough and Benjamin Hapgood Burt
    music: Jean Gilbert and Victor Hollaender
    choreography: Julian Alfred
Productions:
    Opened May 3, 1915 for 56 performances
Reviews:
    Dramatic Mirror 73:8, May 5, 1915
                     73:2, May 12, 1915
                     73:2, May 26, 1915
                     73:2, Jun 2, 1915
    Green Book 14:63-5, Jul 1915
              14:192, Jul 1915
    Life (New York) 65:860-1, May 13, 1915
    New York Dramatic News 61:17, May 8, 1915
    Theatre Magazine 21:279+, Jun 1915

A Modern Hamlet
    book: John Guenther
    music: Dennis Deal
    staging: Michael Dennis Moore
Productions:
    (Off-Off-Broadway) Opened April 3, 1973
No Reviews.

Molly
    book: Louis Garfinkle and Leonard Adelson; based on

                    characters from "The Goldbergs" by Gertrude
                    Berg
music: Jerry Livingston
lyrics: Leonard Adelson and Mack David
staging: Alan Arkin
sets: Marsha L. Eck
costumes: Carrie F. Robbins
choreography: Grover Dale
Productions:
    Opened November 1, 1973 for 68 performances
Reviews:
    New York 6:114, Nov 19, 1973
    New York Theatre Critics' Reviews 1973:206
    New York Times page 45, Jun 11, 1973
                    page 28, Aug 9, 1973
                    page 46, Nov 2, 1973
                    II, page 1, Nov 11, 1973
                    page 21, Dec 28, 1973
    New Yorker 49:114, Nov 12, 1973
    Newsweek 82:81, Nov 12, 1973
    Time 102:97, Nov 19, 1973

Molly Darling
    book: Otto Harbach and William Cary Duncan
    music: Tom Johnstone
    lyrics: Phil Cook
    staging: Julian Mitchell
Productions:
    Opened September 1, 1922 for 99 performances
Reviews:
    New York Clipper 70:39, Oct 4, 1922
    New York Times page 10, Sep 2, 1922

Moms
    by: Ben Caldwell, based on a concept by Clarice
                    Taylor (the life of Jackie "Moms" Mabley)
    music: Grenoldo Frazier
    lyrics: Grenoldo Frazier
    staging: Walter Dallas
    sets: Rosario Provenza
    costumes: Judy Dearing
Productions:
    (Off-Broadway) Opened August 4, 1987 for 152 performances
Reviews:
    New York Times III, page 16, Feb 10, 1987

Money
    book: David Axlerod and Tom Whedon
    music: Sam Pottle
    lyrics: David Axlerod and Tom Whedon
    staging: Ronny Graham

sets: Peter Harvey
costumes: Mr. William
Productions:
   (Off-Broadway)   Opened July 9, 1963 for 214 performances
No Reviews.

Montand, Yves   (see An Evening with Yves Montand)

Monte Cristo, Jr.
   book: Harold Atteridge
   music: Sigmund Romberg and Jean Schwartz
   lyrics: Harold Atteridge
   staging: J. C. Huffman
Productions:
   Opened February 12, 1919 for 254 performances
Reviews:
   Dramatic Mirror 80:305, Mar 1, 1919
   Forum 61:506, Apr 1919
   New York Times page 13, Feb 13, 1919
   Theatre Magazine 29:201, Apr 1919
                     29:208, Apr 1919

Month of Sundays
   book: Romeo Muller; based on his play The Great
                     Git-Away
   music: Maury Laws
   lyrics: Jules Bass
   staging: Stone Widney
   sets: Robert T. Williams
   costumes: Sara Brook
Productions:
   (Off-Broadway)   Opened September 16, 1968 for 8 performances
Reviews:
   New York Times page 50, Sep 17, 1968
   New Yorker 44:89, Sep 28, 1968

Moonlight
   book: William Le Baron
   music: Con Conrad
   lyrics: William B. Friedlander
Productions:
   Opened January 30, 1924 for 149 performances
Reviews:
   New York Times page 13, Jan 31, 1924

The Moony Shapiro Songbook
   book: Monty Norman and Julian More
   music: Monty Norman
   lyrics: Julian More
   staging: Jonathon Lynn
   sets: Saul Radomsky

costumes: Franne Lee
choreography: George Faison
Productions:
Opened May 3, 1981 for one performance
Reviews:
New York Theatre Critics' Reviews 1981:248
New York Times III, page 13, May 4, 1981

Morath, Max   (see An Evening with Max Morath at the Turn of the
Century)

Morning Sun
book: Fred Ebb; based on a story by Mary Deasy
music: Paul Klein
lyrics: Fred Ebb
staging: Daniel Petrie
sets: Eldon Elder
costumes: Patricia Zipprodt
choreography: Donald Saddler
Productions:
(Off-Broadway) Opened October 6, 1963 for 9 performances
Reviews:
New York Times page 36, Oct 7, 1963
              page 34, Oct 14, 1963
Theatre Arts 48:11+, Jan 1964

Morris Gest Midnight Whirl
music: George Gershwin
lyrics: Bud DeSylva and John Henry Mears
staging: Julian Mitchell
Productions:
Opened December 27, 1919 (number of performances unknown)
Reviews:
New York Times page 7, Dec 29, 1919

The Most Happy Fella
book: Frank Loesser, based on Sidney Howard's play
                 They Knew What They Wanted
music: Frank Loesser
lyrics: Frank Loesser
staging: Joseph Anthony
sets: Jo Mielziner
costumes: Motley
choreography: Dania Krupska
Productions:
Opened May 3, 1956 for 676 performances
Opened February 10, 1959 for 16 performances
Opened May 11, 1966 for 15 performances
Opened October 11, 1979 for 52 performances
Reviews:
America 95:209, May 19, 1956

100:670, Mar 7, 1959
141:281, Nov 10, 1979
Catholic World 183:309, Jul 1956
Christian Century 73:1453, Dec 12, 1956
Collier's 138:8, Jul 6, 1956
Commonweal 64:226, Jun 1, 1956
Dance Magazine 40:25, Jul 1966
High Fidelity 30:MA16-17, Feb 1980
            30:MA 36-8, Feb 1980
Holiday 20:75+, Oct 1956
Life 40:68+, Apr 23, 1956
     60:18, Jun 17, 1966
Musical America 76:13, Jul 1956
Nation 182:439, May 19, 1956
New York 12:86, Oct 29, 1979
New York Theatre Critics' Reviews 1956:308+
                                  1979:124
New York Times VI, page 62, Apr 22, 1956
               II, page 1, Apr 29, 1956
               page 20, May 4, 1956
               II, page 1, May 13, 1956
               II, page 7, Jun 10, 1956
               page 50, Feb 11, 1959
               page 25, Apr 22, 1960
               page 55, May 12, 1966
               XII, page 8, Feb 12, 1978
               III, page 3, Oct 12, 1979
               II, page 3, Nov 4, 1979
New York Times Magazine page 62, Apr 22, 1956
New Yorker 32:84+, May 12, 1956
           55:142+, Oct 22, 1979
Newsweek 47:82, May 14, 1956
         94:130, Oct 22, 1979
Reporter 14:34-5, Jun 28, 1956
Saturday Review 39:46, May 19, 1956
                39:39, Aug 25, 1956
Theatre Arts 40:17-19, Jul 1956
             43:67-8, Apr 1959
Time 67:102, May 14, 1956
     114:98, Oct 22, 1979

Mother Earth
    sketches: Ron Thronson
    music: Toni Shearer
    lyrics: Ron Thronson
    staging: Ray Golden
    sets: Alan Kimmel
    costumes: Mary McKinley
    choreography: Lynn Morris
Productions:
    Opened October 19, 1972 for 12 performances

Reviews:
    National Review 23:1481, Dec 31, 1971
    New York Theatre Critics' Reviews 1972:214
    New York Times page 33, Oct 20, 1972
    New Yorker 48:119, Oct 28, 1972
    Time 100:83, Nov 6, 1972

The Motor Girl
    book: Charles J. Campbell and Ralph M. Skinner
    music: Julian Edwards
    lyrics: Charles J. Campbell and Ralph M. Skinner
    staging: Frank Smithson
Productions:
    Opened June 15, 1909 for 95 performances
Reviews:
    Theatre Magazine 10:36, Aug 9, 1909
                     10:63, Aug 9, 1909

Mourning Pictures
    book: Honor Moore
    music: Susan Ain
    lyrics: Honor Moore
    staging: Kay Carney
    sets: John Jacobsen
    costumes: Whitney Blausen
Productions:
    Opened November 10, 1974 for one performance
Reviews:
    New York 7:101, Nov 25, 1974
    New York Theatre Critics' Reviews 1974:195
    New York Times page 41, Nov 11, 1974

Movie Buff
    book: Hiram Taylor
    music: John Raniello
    lyrics: Hiram Taylor and John Raniello
    staging: Jim Payne
    sets: Jimmy Cuomo
    costumes: Carol Wenz
    choreography: Jack Dyville
Productions:
    (Off-Broadway) Opened March 14, 1977 for 21 performances
Reviews:
    New York Times page 42, Mar 15, 1977

The Muffled Report
    material: Peter Cook
Productions:
    (Off-Broadway) Opened April 8, 1964 for 92 performances
No Reviews.

Murder at the Vanities
    book: Earl Carroll and Rufus King
    music and
       lyrics: John Green, Edward Heyman, Richard Meyers,
                   Ned Washington, Victor Young, Herman Hupfeld,
                   John J. Loeb, Paul Francis Webster
    staging: Earl Carroll
Productions:
    Opened September 8, 1933 for 207 performances
Reviews:
    Nation 137:362-3, Sep 27, 1933
    New Outlook 162:49, Oct 1933
    New York Times page 20, Aug 31, 1933
                    page 22, Sep 13, 1933
    Theatre Arts 17:839, Nov 1933

Murray Anderson's Almanac
    book: Noel Coward, Rube Goldberg, Ronald Jeans,
                   Paul Gerard Smith, Harry Ruskin, John McGowan,
                   Peter Arno, Ed Wynn
    music: Milton Ager and Henry Sullivan
    lyrics: Jack Yellen
    staging: John Murray Anderson, William Holbrook, Harry
                   Ruskin
Productions:
    Opened August 14, 1929 for 69 performances
Reviews:
    Life (New York) 94:24, Sep 6, 1929
    New York Times VIII, page 1, Aug 4, 1929
                    page 20, Aug 15, 1929
    Outlook 152:712, Aug 28, 1929
    Theatre Magazine 50:42, Oct 1929

Murray, Ken (see Ken Murray)

Music and Miracles for a New Age (see Genesis: Music and Miracles
       for a New Age)

Music Box Revue (1921)
    book: Irving Berlin
    music: Irving Berlin
    lyrics: Irving Berlin
    staging: Hassard Short
    choreography: I. Tarasoff
Productions:
    Opened September 22, 1921 for 440 performances
Reviews:
    Independent 107:856, Dec 31, 1921
    Life (New York) 78:18, Oct 20, 1921
    New York Times page 18, Sep 23, 1921
    Theatre Magazine 34:387, Dec 1921

Music Box Revue (1922)

book:	Irving Berlin
music:	Irving Berlin
lyrics:	Irving Berlin
staging:	Hassard Short
choreography:	William Seabury

Productions:
  Opened October 23, 1922 for 273 performances
Reviews:
  Forum 68:1037-8, Dec 1922
  New York Times page 18, Oct 24, 1922

Music Box Revue (1923)

book:	Irving Berlin
music:	Irving Berlin
lyrics:	Irving Berlin
staging:	Hassard Short

Productions:
  Opened September 22, 1923 for 273 performances
Reviews:
  New York Times page 5, Sep 24, 1923
  Theatre Magazine 38:54, Nov 1923

Music Box Revue (1924)

book:	Irving Berlin
music:	Irving Berlin
lyrics:	Irving Berlin
staging:	John Murray Anderson

Productions:
  Opened December 1, 1924 for 184 performances
Reviews:
  New York Times page 23, Dec 2, 1924
  Theatre Magazine 41:19, Feb 1925

Music Hall Varieties   (see George White's Music Hall Varieties)

Music Hath Charms

book:	Rowland Leigh, George Rosener, John Shubert
music:	Rudolf Friml
lyrics:	Rowland Leigh and John Shubert
staging:	George Rosener
sets:	Watson Barratt
choreography:	Alex Yakovleff

Productions:
  Opened December 29, 1934 for 29 performances
Reviews:
  Catholic World 140:601, Feb 1935
  New York Times page 8, Dec 31, 1934

Music in May

book:	Fanny Todd Mitchell, adapted from the original by Heinz Merley and Kurt Breuer

music: Emile Berte and Maury Rubens
lyrics: J. Kiern Brennan
staging: Lew Morton and Stanley Logan
Productions:
  Opened April 1, 1929 for 80 performances
Reviews:
  New York Times IX, page 1, Jan 7, 1929
                page 29, Apr 2, 1929

Music in My Heart

book: Patsy Ruth Miller, based on the life of
                  Tchaikovsky
music: Franz Steininger, adapted from Tchaikovsky
lyrics: Forman Brown
staging: Hassard Short
sets: Alvin Colt
costumes: Alvin Colt
choreography: Ruth Page
Productions:
  Opened October 2, 1947 for 125 performances
Reviews:
  Catholic World 166:171, Nov 1947
  New York Theatre Critics' Reviews 1947:324+
  New York Times II, page 1, Sep 28, 1947
                page 30, Oct 3, 1947
                II, page 6, Nov 9, 1947
                II, page 4, Dec 21, 1947
  New Yorker 23:54, Oct 11, 1947
  Newsweek 30:81, Oct 13, 1947
  School and Society 66:508-9, Dec 27, 1947
  Theatre Arts 31:16, Nov 1947

Music in the Air

book: Oscar Hammerstein II
music: Jerome Kern
lyrics: Oscar Hammerstein II
staging: Oscar Hammerstein II and Jerome Kern
sets: Joseph Urban
Productions:
  Opened November 8, 1932 for 342 performances
  Opened October 8, 1951 for 56 performances
Reviews:
  Arts and Decoration 38:50, Jan 1933
  Catholic World 136:462-3, Jan 1933
                174:228, Dec 1951
  Commonweal 17:131, Nov 30, 1932
                55:62, Oct 26, 1951
  New Republic 125:22, Nov 12, 1951
  New York Theatre Critics' Reviews 1951:215
  New York Times IX, page 3, Oct 23, 1932
                page 28, Nov 9, 1932

IX, page 1, Nov 20, 1932
page 11, May 20, 1933
II, page 1, Oct 7, 1951
page 32, Oct 9, 1951
II, page 1, Oct 21, 1951
New Yorker 27: 60+, Oct 20, 1951
Newsweek 38: 93, Oct 22, 1951
Stage 10: 32-3, Dec 1932
Theatre Arts 17: 4-5, Jan 1933
35: 3+, Dec 1951
Time 58: 56, Oct 22, 1951

Music Is

book:	George Abbott, based on William Shakespeare's Twelfth Night
music:	Richard Adler
lyrics:	Will Holt
staging:	George Abbott
sets:	Eldon Elder
costumes:	Lewis D. Rampino
choreography:	Patricia Birch

Productions:
Opened December 20, 1976 for 8 performances
Reviews:
New York 10: 63, Jan 10, 1977
New York Theatre Critics' Reviews 1976: 58
New York Times page 44, Dec 21, 1976

The Music Man

book:	Meredith Willson
music:	Meredith Willson
lyrics:	Meredith Willson
staging:	Morton Da Costa
sets:	Howard Bay
costumes:	Raoul Pene du Bois
choreography:	Onna White

Productions:
Opened December 19, 1957 for 1,375 performances
Opened June 16, 1965 for 15 performances
Opened June 5, 1980 for 21 performances
(Off-Off-Broadway) Opened October 27, 1983
Reviews:
America 98: 550, Feb 8, 1958
Catholic World 186: 468, Mar 1958
Dance Magazine 32: 17, Jan 1958
39: 24, Aug 1965
54: 108-9, Sep 1980
Life 44: 103-6, Jan 20, 1958
Look 22: 53-5, Mar 4, 1958
Los Angeles 24: 236+, Feb 1980
Nation 186: 126, Feb 8, 1959

New York 13:49, Jun 23, 1980
New York Theatre Critics' Reviews 1957:146+
                                    1980:214
New York Times VI, page 128, Dec 1, 1957
               II, page 3, Dec 15, 1957
               page 31, Dec 20, 1957
               II, page 16, Jan 19, 1958
               page 22, Aug 20, 1958
               II, page 1, Sep 28, 1958
               page 17, Mar 18, 1961
               page 32, Mar 21, 1961
               page 26, Jun 17, 1965
               XXII, page 18, Dec 17, 1978
               III, page 3, Jun 6, 1980
               III, page 14, Oct 31, 1983
New Yorker 33:48+, Jan 4, 1958
           56:96, Jun 16, 1980
           64:103, Mar 21, 1988
Newsweek 50:41, Dec 30, 1957
Opera News 52:4, Mar 26, 1988
Saturday Review 41:21, Jan 4, 1958
Theatre Arts 42:10-11, Mar 1958
Theatre Crafts 20:20-1+, May 1986
Time 70:62-4, Dec 30, 1957
     72:42-6, Jul 21, 1958

Music Moves Me   (see Ann Reinking ... Music Moves Me)

Music! Music!
     commentary: Alan Jay Lerner
     staging: Martin Charnin
     sets: David Chapman
     costumes: Theoni V. Aldredge
Productions:
     Opened April 11, 1974 for 37 performances
Reviews:
     New York 7:81, Apr 29, 1974
     New York Theatre Critics' Reviews 1974:314
     New York Times page 22, Apr 12, 1974
                     II, page 1, Apr 21, 1974
     New Yorker 50:103, Apr 22, 1974
     Time 103:84, Apr 22, 1974

Musical Chairs
     book: Barry Berg, Ken Donnelly and Tom Savage, based
                     on an original story concept by Larry P. Pontillo
     music: Tom Savage
     lyrics: Tom Savage
     staging: Rudy Tronto
     sets: Ernest Allen Smith
     costumes: Michael J. Cesario
     choreography: Rudy Tronto

Productions:
  Opened May 14, 1980 for 14 performances
Reviews:
  New York Theatre Critics' Reviews 1980:238
  New York Times III, page 19, May 15, 1980

A Musical Jubilee
  conceived: Marilyn Clark and Charles Burr
  continuity: Max Wilk
  songs: Various authors and composers
  staging: Morton Da Costa
  sets: Herbert Senn
  costumes: Donald Brooks
  choreography: Robert Tucker
Productions:
  Opened November 13, 1975 for 92 performances
Reviews:
  Dance Magazine 50:74-5, Feb 1976
  New York 8:90, Dec 1, 1975
  New York Theatre Critics' Reviews 1975:149
  New York Times page 24, Nov 14, 1975
                  II, page 7, Nov 23, 1975
  New Yorker 51:93, Nov 24, 1975
  Time 106:67, Dec 1, 1975

A Musical Tragedy   (see Lady Day: A Musical Tragedy)

My Best Girl
  book: Channing Pollock and Rennold Wolf
  music: Clifton Crawford and Augustus Barratt
  lyrics: Channing Pollock and Rennold Wolf
  staging: Sidney Ellison
Productions:
  Opened September 12, 1912 for 68 performances
Reviews:
  Blue Book 16:470-73, Jan 1913
  Dramatic Mirror 68:7+, Sep 18, 1912
                  68:2, Sep 25, 1912
  Green Book 8:1005, Dec 1912
  Harper's Weekly 56:21, Oct 1912
  Munsey 48:353-4, Nov 1912
  New York Dramatic News 56:12, Sep 21, 1912
  Red Book 20:381-2+, Dec 1912
  Theatre Magazine 16:iii, Oct 1912
                   16:xiv, Oct 1912

My Darlin' Aida
  book: Charles Friedman, based on Verdi's opera
  music: Giuseppe Verdi
  staging: Charles Friedman
  sets: Lemuel Ayers

```
    costumes:        Lemuel Ayers
    choreography:    Hanya Holm
Productions:
    Opened October 27, 1952 for 89 performances
Reviews:
    Catholic World 176:228, Dec 1952
    Commonweal 57:164, Nov 21, 1952
    Musical America 72:9, Dec 15, 1952
    New York Theatre Critics' Reviews 1952:218+
    New York Times II, page 1, Oct 26, 1952
                    page 36, Oct 28, 1952
                    II, page 7, Nov 9, 1952
                    II, page 1, Nov 9, 1952
    New Yorker 28:86+, Nov 8, 1952
    Newsweek 40:94-5, Nov 10, 1952
    Theatre Arts 37:24-5, Jan 1953
    Time 60:72, Nov 10, 1952
```

My Dear Public

```
    book:            Irving Caesar and Chuno Gottesfeld
    songs:           Irving Caesar, Sam Lerner, Gerald Marks
    staging:         Edgar MacGregor
    sets:            Albert Johnson
    costumes:        Lucinda Ballard
    choreography:    Felicia Sorel and Henry LeTang
Productions:
    Opened September 9, 1943 for 45 performances
Reviews:
    Commonweal 38:562, Sep 24, 1943
    New York Theatre Critics' Reviews 1943:281+
    New York Times page 28, Sep 10, 1943
                    page 10, Oct 18, 1943
    Theatre Arts 27:645-6, Nov 1943
```

My Fair Lady

```
    book:            Alan Jay Lerner, based on George Bernard
                     Shaw's Pygmalion
    music:           Frederick Loewe
    lyrics:          Alan Jay Lerner
    staging:         Moss Hart
    sets:            Oliver Smith
    costumes:        Cecil Beaton
    choreography:    Hanya Holm
Productions:
    Opened March 15, 1956 for 2,717 performances
    Opened May 20, 1964 for 47 performances
    Opened June 13, 1968 for 22 performances
    Opened March 25, 1976 for 377 performances
    Opened August 18, 1981 for 119 performances
Reviews:
    America 94:723, Mar 31, 1956
            145:163, Sep 26, 1981
```

Business World pages 28-30, Jul 28, 1956
Catholic World 183:148, May 1956
Collier's 137:6+, May 25, 1956
Commonweal 64:95, Apr 27, 1956
Coronet 41:54-63, Dec 1956
        45:16+, Apr 1959
Dance Magazine 32:15, Apr 1958
              38:16, Aug 1964
              42:18-19, Aug 1968
              50:73-4, Aug 1976
              55:112, Nov 1981
Etude 74:57, Jul 1956
Holiday 20:75+, Oct 1956
Life 40:58-60+, Mar 26, 1956
Look 20:47-8+, Apr 17, 1956
Los Angeles 26:214+, Jan 1981
Nation 182:264-5, Mar 31, 1956
      222:476, Apr 17, 1976
      233:249+, Sep 19, 1981
National Review 28:686+, Jun 25, 1976
New Republic 134:29-30, Apr 9, 1956
New York 9:70, Apr 12, 1976
        14:56, Aug 31, 1981
New York Theatre Critics' Reviews 1956:345+
                            1976:315
                            1981:194
New York Times page 30, Feb 13, 1956
                VI, pages 28-9, Mar 4, 1956
                II, page 1, Mar 11, 1956
                page 20, Mar 16, 1956
                II, page 1, Mar 25, 1956
                VI, page 24, Apr 1, 1956
                II, page 17, Apr 29, 1956
                II, page 1, Jun 3, 1956
                II, page 1, Aug 12, 1956
                VI, page 27, Sep 9, 1956
                II, page 1, Sep 23, 1956
                page 27, Feb 5, 1957
                II, page 3, Mar 10, 1957
                page 33, Mar 20, 1957
                page 22, Jul 10, 1957
                II, page 1, Mar 9, 1958
                VI, page 22, Mar 9, 1958
                page 34, May 1, 1958
                II, page 3, May 4, 1958
                page 26, Jan 27, 1959
                page 24, Feb 16, 1959
                page 25, Feb 21, 1959
                VI, pages 16-17, Mar 15, 1959
                page 12, Apr 4, 1959
                page 24, Aug 10, 1959

page 35, Aug 12, 1959
page 52, Dec 15, 1959
page 31, Jan 9, 1961
page 24, Jul 13, 1961
page 40, Oct 26, 1961
page 22, Jan 9, 1962
II, page 3, Mar 11, 1962
VI, page 55, Mar 11, 1962
page 28, Mar 15, 1962
page 24, Jun 14, 1962
page 27, Sep 11, 1962
page 15, Sep 29, 1962
page 38, Oct 1, 1962
page 34, May 1, 1963
page 32, Jun 3, 1963
page 8, Jul 4, 1963
page 37, Aug 21, 1963
page 19, Sep 2, 1963
page 13, Sep 21, 1963
page 16, Nov 16, 1963
page 40, Dec 13, 1963
page 24, Feb 20, 1964
page 43, May 21, 1964
page 29, Oct 31, 1965
page 42, Jun 14, 1968
page 20, Mar 26, 1976
II, page 1, Apr 4, 1976
III, page 3, Sep 17, 1976
III, page 17, Aug 19, 1981
III, page 15, Sep 3, 1981
New York Times Magazine pages 28-9, Mar 4, 1956
                  page 27+, Sep 9, 1956
                  page 14+, Mar 10, 1957
                  pages 16-17+, Mar 15, 1959
New Yorker 32:80+, Mar 24, 1956
        52:96, Apr 5, 1976
        52:32-3, May 3, 1976
        57:78, Aug 31, 1981
Newsweek 47:94, Mar 26, 1956
        47:80-1, Apr 2, 1956
        51:94+, May 12, 1958
        87:78, Apr 5, 1976
        98:56, Aug 31, 1981
Reporter 14:34, Jun 28, 1956
Saturday Evening Post 231:34-5+, May 2, 1959
Saturday Review 39:26-7, Mar 31, 1956
        3:36-8, Apr 3, 1976
        8:66-7, Nov 1981
Senior Scholastic 85:5, Oct 21, 1964
Theatre Arts 40:18-19, May 1956
        40:68-9, Jun 1956

                    40:14, Nov 1956
                    40:26-8, Dec 1956
                    41:29+, Mar 1957
                    41:63-4+, Oct 1957
                    42:70-1, May 1958
        Time 67:89, Mar 26, 1956
             68:42-6, Jul 23, 1956
             73:44-5, Mar 2, 1959
             107:55-6, Apr 5, 1976
             118:70, Aug 31, 1981
        Vogue 127:116, Apr 1, 1956
              127:52-5, Jun 1956
              144:152-5, Nov 1, 1964

My Girl
    book: Harlan Thompson
    music: Harry Archer
    lyrics: Harlan Thompson
Productions:
    Opened November 24, 1924 for 192 performances
Reviews:
    New York Times page 27, Nov 25, 1924
                    page 24, Apr 1, 1925
    Theatre Magazine 41:64, Jan 1925

My Golden Girl
    book: Frederic Arnold Kummer
    music: Victor Herbert
    lyrics: Frederic Arnold Kummer
Productions:
    Opened February 2, 1920 for 105 performances
Reviews:
    Dramatic Mirror 82:206, Feb 7, 1920
    New York Clipper 68:21, Feb 11, 1920
    New York Times page 18, Feb 3, 1920
    Theatre Magazine 31:220+, Mar 1920

My Little Friend
    book: Harry B. Smith; adapted from the German of
                        Willner and Stein
    music: Oscar Straus
    lyrics: Robert B. Smith
    staging: Herbert Gresham
Productions:
    Opened May 19, 1913 for 24 performances
Reviews:
    Dramatic Mirror 69:6, May 21, 1913
    New York Dramatic News 57:17, May 24, 1913
    New York Times page 11, May 20, 1913
    Theatre Magazine 18:xx, Jul 1913

My Magnolia
- book: Alex C. Rogers and Eddie Hunter
- music: C. Luckey Roberts
- lyrics: Alex C. Rogers
- staging: Alex C. Rogers and Eddie Hunter

Productions:
Opened July 8, 1926 for 4 performances

Reviews:
New York Times page 19, Jul 13, 1926

My Maryland
- book: Dorothy Donnelly
- music: Sigmund Romberg
- lyrics: Dorothy Donnelly
- staging: J. J. Shubert

Productions:
Opened September 12, 1927 for 312 performances

Reviews:
New York Times page 37, Sep 13, 1927
Time 49:40, Mar 17, 1947
Vogue 70:126, Nov 1, 1927

My Old Friends
- book: Mel Mandel and Norman Sachs
- music: Mel Mandel and Norman Sachs
- lyrics: Mel Mandel and Norman Sachs
- staging: Philip Rose
- sets: Leon Munier
- costumes: George Drew
- choreography: Bob Tucker

Productions:
(Off-Broadway) Opened January 12, 1979 for 100 performances
Opened April 12, 1979 for 53 performances
(Off-Off-Broadway) Opened May 1, 1985

Reviews:
New York Times II, page 13, Feb 13, 1979
III, page 20, May 9, 1985
Time 113:142, Feb 5, 1979

My One and Only
- book: Peter Stone and Timothy S. Mayer
- music: George Gershwin, from Funny Face and other shows
- lyrics: Ira Gershwin
- staging: Thommie Walsh and Tommy Tune
- sets: Adrianne Lobel
- costumes: Rita Ryack
- choreography: Thommie Walsh, Tommy Tune, and Baayork Lee

Productions:
Opened May 1, 1983 for 767 performances

Reviews:
America 148:460, Jun 11, 1983

Dance Magazine 57:106, Jul 1983
                 57:66-73, Sep 1983
                 59:70-1, Feb 1985
Harper's Bazaar 116:20, Mar 1983
Los Angeles 30:50+, Sep 1985
Nation 236:746, Jun 11, 1983
        237:25-6, Jul 2, 1983
New Leader 66:22, May 30, 1983
New Republic 188:27-8, Jun 6, 1983
New York 16:57-8+, Feb 1983
           16:78-9, May 16, 1983
New York Theatre Critics' Reviews 1983:261
New York Times III, page 13, May 2, 1983
                II, page 3, May 15, 1983
New Yorker 59:108-9, May 9, 1983
Newsweek 101:97-8, May 16, 1983
People 19:50-2, May 2, 1983
Time 121:76, May 16, 1983

My Romance
book:	Rowland Leigh, based on Edward Sheldon's Romance
music:	Sigmund Romberg
lyrics:	Rowland Leigh
staging:	Rowland Leigh
sets:	Watson Barratt
costumes:	Lou Eisele
choreography:	Fredric N. Kelly

Productions:
    Opened October 19, 1948 for 95 performances
Reviews:
    Catholic World 168:242, Dec 1948
    New Republic 119:26, Nov 8, 1948
    New York Theatre Critics' Reviews 1948:186+
    New York Times page 38, Oct 20, 1948
    New Yorker 24:44, Oct 30, 1948
    Time 52:52, Nov 1, 1948
    Vogue 112:154+, Dec 1948

My Wife and I
book:	Bill Mahoney
music:	Bill Mahoney
lyrics:	Bill Mahoney
staging:	Tom Ross Pather
sets:	Robert Green

Productions:
    (Off-Broadway) Opened October 10, 1966 for 8 performances
Reviews:
    New York Times page 53, Oct 11, 1966

Mystery Moon
book:	Fred Herendeen

music: Carlo and Sanders
lyrics: Carlo and Sanders
Productions:
  Opened June 23, 1930 for one performance
Reviews:
  New York Times page 23, Jun 24, 1930

The Mystery of Edwin Drood
  by: Rupert Holmes, suggested by the unfinished
                novel by Charles Dickens
  music: Rupert Holmes
  lyrics: Rupert Holmes
  staging: Wilford Leach
  sets: Bob Shaw
  costumes: Lindsay W. Davis
  choreography: Graciela Daniele
Productions:
  (Off-Broadway) Opened August 4, 1985 for 24 performances
  Opened December 2, 1985 for 608 performances
Reviews:
  America 154:53, Jan 25, 1986
  Dance Magazine 60:78, Feb 1986
  Los Angeles 31:260+, Aug 1986
  New Leader 68:18-19, Nov 4-18, 1985
  New Republic 193:28-9, Oct 14, 1985
  New York 18:57-8, Sep 2, 1985
          18:100-1, Dec 16, 1985
          18:34, Dec 23-30, 1985
  New York Theatre Critics' Reviews 1985:142, 234
  New York Times III, page 3, Aug 23, 1985
              II, page 3, Sep 1, 1985
              III, page 4, Nov 29, 1985
              III, page 21, Dec 3, 1985
              II, page 3, Dec 8, 1985
              II, page 1, Jan 5, 1986
  New Yorker 61:71, Sep 2, 1985
          61:140, Dec 16, 1985
  Newsweek 106:66, Sep 2, 1985
  Theatre Crafts 23:52-5+, Apr 1989
  Time 126:83, Dec 16, 1985
  Vogue 175:88, Dec 1985

-N-

Nash at Nine
  conceived: Martin Charnin
  words: Ogden Nash
  music: Milton Rosenstock
  lyrics: Ogden Nash
  staging: Martin Charnin

    sets: David Chapman
    costumes: Theoni V. Aldredge
Productions:
    Opened May 17, 1973 for 21 performances
Reviews:
    New York 6:72, Jun 4, 1973
    New York Theatre Critics' Reviews 1973:268+
    New York Times page 31, May 18, 1973

The National Lampoon Show
    book: Sean Kelly, with John Belushi, Brian Doyle-
                     Murray, Bill Murray, Gilda Radner, and Harold
                     Ramis
    music: Paul Jacobs
    lyrics: Paul Jacobs
    staging: Martin Charnin
Productions:
    (Off-Broadway) Opened March 2, 1975 for 180 performances
Reviews:
    New York 8:94, May 5, 1975
    New York Times page 34, Mar 3, 1975

National Lampoon's Class of '86
    written: Andrew Simmons (head writer), John Belushi,
                     Chevy Chase, Stephen Collins, Lance Contrucci,
                     Christopher Guest, Dave Hanson, Matty Simmons,
                     Michael Simmons, Larry Sloman, plus Rodger
                     Bumpass, Veanne Cox, Annie Golden, John Michael
                     Higgins, Tommy Koenig, and Brian Brucker
                     O'Connor
    songs: Various authors and composers
    staging: Jerry Adler
    sets: Daniel Proett
    costumes: Nancy Konrardy
    choreography: Nora Brennan
Productions:
    (Off-Broadway) Opened May 22, 1986 for 53 performances
Reviews:
    New York Theatre Critics' Reviews 1986:209
    New York Times I, page 56, May 25, 1986
    Newsweek 107:78, Jun 2, 1986

National Lampoon's Lemmings
    music: Paul Jacobs and Christopher Guest
    words and
      lyrics: David Axlerod, Anne Beatts, Henry Beard,
                     John Boni, Tony Hendra, Sean Kelly, Doug
                     Kenny, P. G. O'Rourke and the cast
    staging: Tony Hendra
Productions:
    (Off-Broadway) Opened January 25, 1973 for 350 performances

Reviews:
New York Times page 43, Jan 2, 1973
page 46, Jan 26, 1973
II, page 3, Feb 4, 1973
II, page 1, May 27, 1973
II, page 34, Sep 9, 1973
New Yorker 48:59, Feb 3, 1973
Playboy 20:52, May 1973
Time 108:58+, Feb 19, 1973

Naughty Marietta
book: Rida Johnson Young
music: Victor Herbert
lyrics: Rida Johnson Young
Productions:
Opened November 7, 1910 for 136 performances
Opened November 16, 1931 for 24 performances
(Off-Broadway) Opened November 12, 1975 for 12 performances
(Off-Broadway) Opened December 29, 1976 for 19 performances
(Off-Broadway) Opened August 3, 1977 for 14 performances
(Off-Broadway) Opened April 23, 1980 for 14 performances
(Off-Broadway) Opened May 26, 1985 for 28 performances
Reviews:
Blue Book 12:888-9, Mar 1911
13:1140-41, Oct 1911
Columbian 3:899, Feb 1911
Leslie's Weekly 111:541, Nov 24, 1910
Metropolitan Magazine 33:799, Mar 1911
Munsey 44:707, Feb 1911
Musical Courier 106:10, May 27, 1933
New York Times page 31, Nov 17, 1931
page 18, May 10, 1975
II, page 1, May 11, 1975
page 117, Sep 2, 1978
page 55, Nov 6, 1978
III, page 29, May 16, 1985
Pearson 25:121, Jan 1911
Stage 13:56, Aug 1936
Theatre Magazine 12:165-6, Dec 1910

Naughty Naught '00
book: John Van Antwerp
music: Richard Lewine
lyrics: Ted Fetter
staging: Morgan Lewis
sets: Eugene Dunkel
Productions:
Opened January 23, 1937 for 173 performances
Opened October 19, 1946 for 17 performances
Reviews:
New York Times page 23, Jan 25, 1937
page 27, Oct 21, 1946

Newsweek 9:35, Feb 6, 1937
Time 48:63, Oct 28, 1946

Naughty Riquette
book: Harry B. Smith; adapted from the German of
                       R. Schanzer and E. Welisch
lyrics: Harry B. Smith
staging: J. J. Shubert
Productions:
Opened September 13, 1926 for 88 performances
Reviews:
Life (New York) 88:23, Oct 7, 1926
New York Times page 25, Sep 14, 1926
                     IX, page 1, Sep 19, 1926
Theatre Magazine 44:23, Nov 1926

Ned Wayburn's Gambols
book: Ned Wayburn
music: Walter G. Samuels
lyrics: Morrie Ryskind
staging: Ned Wayburn
Productions:
Opened January 15, 1929 for 31 performances
Reviews:
New York Times page 22, Jan 16, 1929

Ned Wayburn's Town Topics
book: Harry B. Smith, Thomas J. Gray and Robert B.
                     Smith
music: Harold Orlob
lyrics: Harry B. Smith, Thomas J. Gray and Robert
                     B. Smith
staging: Ned Wayburn
Productions:
Opened September 23, 1915 for 68 performances
Reviews:
Current Opinion 59:326-7, Nov 1915
Dramatic Mirror 74:8, Sep 29, 1915
                 74:2, Oct 6, 1915
                 74:2, Oct 16, 1915
Green Book 14:983-6, Dec 1915
Life (New York) 66:662, Oct 7, 1915
New York Dramatic News 61:19, Oct 16, 1915
Opera Magazine 2:29, Oct 1915
Theatre Magazine 22:301, Dec 1915

Nellie Bly
book: Joseph Quillan, based on a story by Jack Em-
                     manuel
music: James Van Heusen
lyrics: Johnny Burke

staging: Edgar McGregor
sets: Nat Karson
choreography: Lee Sherman
Productions:
Opened January 21, 1946 for 16 performances
Reviews:
New York Theatre Critics' Reviews 1946: 481+
New York Times page 32, Jan 22, 1946
                II, page 1, Jan 27, 1946
Newsweek 27:80, Feb 4, 1946
Theatre Arts 30:137, Mar 1946
Time 47:63, Feb 4, 1946

The Nervous Set
book: Jay Landesman and Theodore J. Flicker, based
            on the novel by Jay Landesman
music: Tommy Wolf
lyrics: Fran Landesman
staging: Theodore J. Flicker
sets: Paul Morrison
costumes: Theoni V. Aldredge
Productions:
Opened May 12, 1959 for 23 performances
Reviews:
Nation 188:483, May 23, 1959
New York Theatre Critics' Reviews 1959:306+
New York Times page 43, May 13, 1959
New Yorker 35:72+, May 23, 1959
Reporter 20:35-6, Jun 11, 1959
Saturday Review 42:26, May 30, 1959
Theatre Arts 43:10-11, Jul 1959
Time 73:50, May 25, 1959

The Never Homes
words: Glen MacDonough
rhymes: E. Ray Goetz
music: A. Baldwin Sloane
staging: Ned Wayburn
sets: Arthur Volgtlin
Productions:
Opened October 5, 1911 for 92 performances
Reviews:
Blue Book 14:680-2, Feb 1912
Dramatic Mirror 66:7+, Oct 11, 1911
                66:2, Oct 25, 1911
                66:4, Nov 11, 1911
Green Book Album 6:1126-9, Dec 1911
                6:1201, Dec 1911
Leslie's Weekly 113:447, Oct 26, 1911
Life (New York) 58:662, Oct 19, 1911
Theatre Magazine 14:ix, Nov 1911
                14:175, Nov 1911

New Cole Porter Revue
    conceived: Ben Bagley
    songs: Cole Porter
    staging: Ben Bagley
    costumes: Charles Fatone
    choreography: Buddy Schwab
Productions:
    (Off-Broadway)   Opened December 22, 1965 for 76 performances
No Reviews.

New Faces (1934)
    sketches: Viola Brothers Shore, Nancy Hamilton, June
                      Sillman
    music: Warburton Guilbert, Donald Honrath, Martha
                      Caples, James Shelton, Morgan Lewis
    lyrics: Viola Brothers Shore, Nancy Hamilton, June
                      Sillman
    staging: Elsie Janis
    sets: Sergei Soudeikine
Productions:
    Opened March 15, 1934 for 149 performances
Reviews:
    Catholic World 139:215, May 1934
    Commonweal 19:609, Mar 30, 1934
    Nation 138:370, Mar 28, 1934
    New Outlook 163:45, Apr 1934
    New York Times page 24, Mar 16, 1934
                    X, page 2, Apr 1, 1934
    Newsweek 3:39, Mar 24, 1934
    Stage 11:10-11, May 1934

New Faces of 1936
    sketches: Mindret Lord and Everett Marcy
    music: Alexander Fogarty and Irvin Graham
    lyrics: June Sillman, Edwin Gilbert, Bickley Reichner
    staging: Leonard Sillman
    sets: Stewart Chaney
    costumes: Stewart Chaney
    choreography: Ned McGurn
Productions:
    Opened May 19, 1936 for 193 performances
Reviews:
    Catholic World 143:474, 602, Jul-Aug 1936
    Commonweal 24:160, Jun 5, 1936
    Literary Digest 121:26, May 30, 1936
    New York Times page 24, May 20, 1936
                    IX, page 2, Jun 21, 1936

New Faces of 1943
    sketches: John Lund, additional sketches by June Carroll
                      and J. B. Rosenberg

music:	John Lund
lyrics:	John Lund, additional lyrics by June Carroll and J. B. Rosenberg
staging:	Leonard Sillman
choreography:	Charles Weidman

Productions:
Opened December 22, 1942 for 94 performances
Reviews:
New York Theatre Critics' Reviews 1942:140+
New York Times page 22, Dec 23, 1942

New Faces of 1952

sketches:	not credited
music:	Francis Lemarque, Sheldon Harnick, Murray Grand, Elisse Boyd, Arthur Siegel, Ronald Graham, Michael Brown
lyrics:	Francis Lemarque, Sheldon Harnick, Murray Grand, Elisse Boyd, June Carroll, Ronald Graham, Michael Brown
staging:	John Murray Anderson
sets:	Raoul Pene du Bois
costumes:	Thomas Becher
choreography:	Richard Barstow

Productions:
Opened May 16, 1952 for 365 performances
Reviews:
Catholic World 175:310, Jul 1952
Commonweal 56:224, Jun 6, 1952
Life 32:91-2, Jun 2, 1952
New York Theatre Critics' Reviews 1952:278+
New York Times page 23, May 17, 1952
　　　　　　　II, page 1, May 25, 1952
　　　　　　　II, page 2, Nov 2, 1952
New Yorker 28:88, May 24, 1952
Newsweek 39:84, May 26, 1952
Saturday Review 35:26, May 31, 1952
Theatre Arts 36:82, Jul 1952
　　　　　　36:18-21, Aug 1952
Time 59:56, May 26, 1952

New Faces of '56

sketches:	Paul Lynde, Richard Maury, Louis Botto
music and lyrics:	June Carroll, Arthur Siegel, Marshall Barer, Dean Fuller, Murray Grand, Matt Dubey, Harold Karr, Irvin Graham, Paul Nassau, John Rox, Michael Brown
staging:	Paul Lynde
sets:	Peter Larkin
costumes:	Thomas Becher
choreography:	David Tihmar

Productions:
    Opened June 14, 1956 for 220 performances
Reviews:
    America 95:332, Jun 30, 1956
    Catholic World 183:387, Aug 1956
    Commonweal 64:396, Jul 20, 1956
    New York Theatre Critics' Reviews 1956:290+
    New York Times page 32, Jun 15, 1956
    New Yorker 32:62+, Jun 23, 1956
    Saturday Review 39:22, Jun 30, 1956
    Theatre Arts 40:17-18, Aug 1956
    Time 67:86, Jun 25, 1956

New Faces of 1962
    conceived by: Leonard Sillman
    sketches: Ronny Graham, Paul Lynde, Jean Shepherd,
                        Richard Maury, Joey Carter, R. G. Brown, and
                        others
    music and
      lyrics: June Carroll, Arthur Siegel, David Rogers,
                        Mark Bucci, Jack Holmes, Ronny Graham, and
                        others
    staging: Leonard Sillman and Richard Maury
    sets: Marvin Reiss
    costumes: Thomas Becher
    choreography: James Moore and others
Productions:
    Opened February 1, 1962 for 28 performances
Reviews:
    America 106:737, Mar 3, 1962
    New York Theatre Critics' Reviews 1962:366+
    New York Times page 25, Feb 2, 1962
                   page 22, Feb 9, 1962
                   page 21, Feb 22, 1962
    Theatre Arts 46:63, Apr 1962

New Faces of 1968   (see Leonard Sillman's New Faces of 1968)

New Girl in Town
    book: George Abbott, based on Eugene O'Neill's play
                        Anna Christie
    music: Bob Merrill
    lyrics: Bob Merrill
    staging: George Abbott
    sets: Helene Pons
    costumes: Rouben Ter-Arutunian
    choreography: Bob Fosse
Productions:
    Opened May 14, 1957 for 431 performances
    (Off-Broadway) Opened February 15, 1963 for 10 performances
Reviews:
    America 97:311, Jun 8, 1957

Catholic World 185:307, Jul 1957
Life 42:109+, Jun 24, 1957
Nation 184:486, Jun 1, 1957
New York Theatre Critics' Reviews 1957:268+
New York Times VI, pages 30-31, Apr 14, 1957
             II, page 1, May 12, 1957
             page 50, May 15, 1957
             II, page 1, May 26, 1957
             VI, page 25, May 26, 1957
New York Times Magazine pages 30-1, Apr 14, 1957
                        page 25+, May 26, 1957
New Yorker 33:82+, May 25, 1957
Newsweek 49:70, May 27, 1957
Saturday Review 40:22, Jun 1, 1957
Theatre Arts 41:25-6, Jun 1957
             41:14-15, Jul 1957
Time 69:60, May 27, 1957

The New Moon
    book: Oscar Hammerstein II, Frank Mandel, Laurence
                   Schwab
    music: Sigmund Romberg
    lyrics: Oscar Hammerstein II
    staging: Bobby Connelly
    choreography: Bobby Connelly
Productions:
    Opened September 19, 1928 for 509 performances
    Opened August 18, 1942 for 24 performances
    Opened May 17, 1944 for 53 performances
    (Off-Broadway) Opened October 10, 1984 for 42 performances
Reviews:
    Life (New York) 92:28, Oct 5, 1928
    New York Times VII, page 4, Sep 2, 1928
                   page 33, Sep 20, 1928
                   IX, page 2, Sep 20, 1928
                   IX, page 2, Sep 15, 1929
                   page 14, Aug 19, 1942
                   page 12, Aug 31, 1942
                   page 16, May 18, 1944
                   page 26, Jul 5, 1950
                   page 13, Jul 1, 1955
                   III, page 12, Apr 30, 1976
    New Yorker 20:40, May 27, 1944
    Theatre Magazine 48:80, Nov 1928
    Vogue 72:100, Nov 10, 1928

The New Music Hall of Israel
    staging: Jonathon Karmon
    costumes: Lydia Pincus Ganay
    choreography: Jonathon Karmon
Productions:
    Opened October 2, 1969 for 68 performances

Reviews:
    America 121:342, Oct 18, 1969
    New York Times page 40, Oct 3, 1969
    New Yorker 45:88, Oct 11, 1969

New Priorities of 1943
    assembled: Clifford C. Fischer
    music: Lester Lee and Jerry Seelen
    lyrics: Lester Lee and Jerry Seelen
    staging: Jean LeSeyeux
    choreography: Truly McGee
Productions:
    Opened September 15, 1942 for 54 performances
Reviews:
    New York Theatre Critics' Reviews 1942:236
    New York Times page 28, Sep 16, 1942

New York City Street Show
    conceived: Peter Copani
    book: Peter Copani
    music: Peter Copani
    lyrics: Peter Copani
    staging: Peter Copani
    sets: Jim Chestnut
Productions:
    (Off-Broadway) Opened April 28, 1977 for 20 performances
Reviews:
    New Yorker 53:59+, May 9, 1977

New York Coloring Book
    music: Jerry Powell
    lyrics: Michael McWhinney
    staging: Bill Penn
    choreography: Bill Miller
Productions:
    (Off-Broadway) Opened April 2, 1963 for 84 performances
No Reviews.

A New York Summer
    created: Tom Bahler
    words: Stanley Hart
    songs: Mark Vieha and Tom Bahler
    staging: Robert F. Jani
    costumes: Frank Spencer
    choreography: Dru Davis, Violet Holmes, Louis Johnson, Linda
                        Lemac and Howard Parker
Productions:
    Opened May 31, 1979 for 136 performances
Reviews:
    New York Theatre Critics' Reviews 1979:224

The New Yorkers (1927)
    book: Jo Swerling and Henry Myers
    music: Arthur Schwartz, Edgar Fairchild and Charlie
                      M. Schwab
    lyrics: Jo Swerling and Henry Myers
Productions:
    Opened March 10, 1927 for 52 performances
Reviews:
    New York Times page 24, Mar 11, 1927
    Theatre Magazine 45:21, May 1927

The New Yorkers (1930)
    book: Herbert Fields, suggested by Peter Arno and
                      Ray Goetz
    music: Cole Porter
    lyrics: Cole Porter
    staging: Monty Woolley
    choreography: George Hale
Productions:
    Opened December 8, 1930 for 168 performances
Reviews:
    Catholic World 132:596, Feb 1931
    Life (New York) 96:18, Dec 26, 1930
    New York Times VIII, page 3, Nov 16, 1930
                     page 31, Dec 9, 1930
    Outlook 156:671, Dec 24, 1930

The Newcomers
    book: Joe Burrows and Will Morrissey
    staging: Will Morrissey
Productions:
    Opened August 8, 1923 for 21 performances
No Reviews.

The News
    book: Paul Schierhorn, David Rotenberg and R. Vin-
                      cent Park
    music: Paul Schierhorn
    lyrics: Paul Schierhorn
    staging: David Rotenberg
    sets: Jane Musky
    costumes: Richard Hornung
    choreography: Wesley Fata
Productions:
    Opened November 7, 1985 for 4 performances
Reviews:
    New York 18:99, Nov 18, 1985
    New York Theatre Critics' Reviews 1985:150
    New York Times III, page 3, Nov 8, 1985
    New Yorker 61:144, Nov 18, 1985

Nic Nax of 1926
          words: Paul W. Porter, Matt Kennedy and Roger Gray
          music: Gitz Rice and Werner Janssen
          staging: Paul W. Porter and Jack Conners
Productions:
     Opened August 2, 1926 for 13 performances
Reviews:
     New York Times page 19, Aug 5, 1926

Nifties of 1923
          book: Sam Bernard and William Collier
Productions:
     Opened September 25, 1923 for 47 performances
Reviews:
     Life (New York) 82:18, Oct 18, 1923
     New York Times page 10, Sep 26, 1923
     Theatre Magazine 38:54, Nov 1923

The Night Boat
          book: Anne Caldwell; adapted from a farce by A. Bis-
                        son
          music: Jerome Kern
          lyrics: Anne Caldwell
Productions:
     Opened February 2, 1920 for 148 performances
Reviews:
     Dramatic Mirror 82:210, Feb 7, 1920
     New York Clipper 68:21, Feb 11, 1920
     New York Times page 18, Feb 3, 1920
     Theatre Magazine 31:220, Mar 1920
                       31:275, Apr 1920

A Night in Paris
          dialogue: Harold Atteridge
          music: J. Fred Coots and Maurice Rubens
          lyrics: Clifford Grey and McElbert Moore
          staging: J. C. Huffman
Productions:
     Opened January 5, 1926 for 196 performances
Reviews:
     New Republic 46:145, Mar 24, 1926
     New York Times page 16, Jan 6, 1926
     Theatre Magazine 43:18, Mar 1926
     Vogue 68:124+, Oct 1, 1926

Night in Spain (1917)
          assembled: Charles Dillingham and Florenz Ziegfeld
          music: Quinito Valverde
Productions:
     Opened December 6, 1917 for 33 performances
Reviews:
     Life (New York) 89:20, May 26, 1927

Theatre Magazine 46:20, Jul 1927
Vogue 70:62-3, Jul 1, 1927

A Night in Spain (1927)
>   book: Harold Atteridge
>   music: Jean Schwartz
>   lyrics: Al Byram
>   staging: Gertrude Hoffman and Charles Judels

Productions:
Opened May 3, 1927 for 222 performances
Reviews:
Life (New York) 89-20, May 26, 1927
New York Times page 28, May 4, 1927
>   VIII, page 1, May 22, 1927
>   VIII, page 1, Jul 3, 1927

Theatre Magazine 46:20, Jul 1927
Vogue 70:62-3, Jul 1, 1927

A Night in Spain (1949) (see Cabalgata)

A Night in the Ukraine   (see A Day in Hollywood/A Night in the
>   Ukraine)

A Night in Venice (1929)
>   music: Lee Davis and Maury Rubens
>   lyrics: J. Keirn Brennan and Moe Jaffe
>   staging: Lew Morton and Thomas A. Hart
>   choreography: Busby Berkeley

Productions:
Opened May 21, 1929 for 175 performances
Reviews:
Life (New York) 93:26, Jun 14, 1929
New York Times IX, page 1, May 12, 1929
>   page 30, May 22, 1929

Outlook 152:234, Jun 5, 1929
Theatre Magazine 50:42, Sep 1929

A Night in Venice (1982)
>   book: William Mount-Burke and Alice Hammerstein
>   Mathias, based freely on an idea by Zell & Genee
>   music: Johann Strauss
>   lyrics: Alice Hammerstein Mathias
>   staging: William Mount-Burke
>   sets: Jeremy Conway
>   costumes: James Brega

Productions:
>   (Off-Broadway) Opened May 5, 1982 for 28 performances

No Reviews.

Night of Love
>   book: Rowland Leigh, based on Lili Hatvany's Tonight
>   or Never

music: Robert Stolz
lyrics: Rowland Leigh
staging: Barrie O'Daniels
sets: Watson Barratt
costumes: Ernest Schraps
Productions:
Opened January 7, 1941 for 7 performances
Reviews:
New York Theatre Critics' Reviews 1941: 421+
New York Times page 14, Jan 8, 1941

Night Song
music: Dave Bobrowits
lyrics: Gene Rempel
staging: Andy Thomas and Luba Ash
Productions:
(Off-Off-Broadway) Opened April 3, 1974
No Reviews.

The Night That Made America Famous
music: Harry Chapin
lyrics: Harry Chapin
staging: Gene Frankel
sets: Kert Lundell
costumes: Randy Barcelo
choreography: Doug Rogers
Productions:
Opened February 26, 1975 for 47 performances
Reviews:
Essence 6: 9, Jun 1975
New York 8: 68, Mar 17, 1975
New York Theatre Critics' Reviews 1975: 350
New York Times page 30, Feb 27, 1975
New Yorker 51: 64, Mar 10, 1975

Nightclub Cantata
conceived: Elizabeth Swados
composed: Elizabeth Swados
staging: Elizabeth Swados
sets: Patricia Woodbridge
costumes: Kate Carmel
Productions:
(Off-Broadway) Opened January 9, 1977 for 145 performances
Reviews:
Ms. 5: 18+, Jun 1977
Nation 224: 124-5, Jan 29, 1977
New Republic 176: 24+, Feb 5, 1977
New York 10: 68, Jan 31, 1977
New York Theatre Critics' Reviews 1977: 359
New York Times page 29, Jan 10, 1977
New Yorker 52: 64, Jan 24, 1977
Psychology Today 10: 22+, May 1977

The Nightingale
    book: Guy Bolton and P. G. Wodehouse; based on the life of Jenny Lind
    music: Armand Vecsey
    lyrics: Guy Bolton and P. G. Wodehouse
    staging: Lewis Morton
Productions:
    Opened January 3, 1927 for 96 performances
Reviews:
    Theatre Magazine 45:21, Mar 1927

Nightsong
    words: Ron Eliran
    songs: Ron Eliran
    staging: Dan Early
    sets: Harry Silverglat
    costumes: Ron Whitehead and Margot Miller
Productions:
    (Off-Broadway) Opened November 1, 1977 for 34 performances
No Reviews.

Nikki
    book: John Monk Saunders
    music: Philip Charig
    lyrics: John Monk Saunders
    staging: William B. Friedlander
Productions:
    Opened September 29, 1931 for 39 performances
Reviews:
    New York Times page 23, Sep 30, 1931

Nina Rosa
    book: Otto Harbach
    music: Sigmund Romberg
    lyrics: Irving Caesar
    staging: J. J. Shubert and J. C. Huffman
Productions:
    Opened September 20, 1930 for 137 performances
Reviews:
    Life (New York) 96:18, Oct 10, 1930
    National Magazine 59:107, Nov 1930
    New York Times page 13, May 30, 1930
                     page 19, May 31, 1930
                     page 22, Sep 22, 1930
    Theatre Magazine 52:26, Nov 1930
    Vogue 76:118, Nov 10, 1930

Nine
    book: Arthur Kopit, adapted from the Italian by Mario Fratti
    music: Maury Yeston

lyrics: Maury Yeston
staging: Tommy Tune
sets: Lawrence Miller
costumes: William Ivey Long
Productions:
  Opened May 9, 1982 for 739 performances
Reviews:
  America 147:13, Jun 26-Jul 3, 1982
  Dance Magazine 56:76, Aug 1982
                  56:52-7, Sep 1982
  Los Angeles 28:58, Apr 1983
  Nation 235:28-9, Jul 3, 1982
  New Republic 186:24-6, Jun 9, 1982
  New York 15:88-9, May 24, 1982
  New York Theatre Critics' Reviews 1982:288
  New York Times III, page 13, May 10, 1982
                   II, page 3, May 23, 1982
  New Yorker 58:100+, May 24, 1982
  Newsweek 99:74, May 24, 1982
  Theatre Crafts 16:16-19+, Aug/Sep 1982
                  19:17+, May 1985
  Time 119:73, May 24, 1982
  Working Woman 7:156-7, Dec 1982

Nine-Fifteen Revue
  staging: Alexander Leftwich
  choreography: Busby Berkeley and Leon Leonidoff
Productions:
  Opened February 11, 1930 for 7 performances
Reviews:
  New York Times page 26, Feb 12, 1930
                   IX, page 4, Feb 16, 1930
                   page 19, Feb 18, 1930

9 O'Clock Revue   (see Hammerstein's 9 O'Clock Revue)

Nine O'Clock Revue
  sketches: Jay Strong, Dorothy Quick, Larry Shaw and
                    Richard Fehr
  music: Arthur Jones and Paul Stackpole
  staging: Mabel Rowland
  sets: John P. Ludlum
Productions:
  (Off-Broadway) Opened June 1936
Reviews:
  New York Times page 14, Jul 8, 1936

The 1940's Radio Hour
  book: Walton Jones
  music: Walton Jones
  lyrics: Walton Jones

```
staging:          Walton Jones
sets:             David Gropman
costumes:         William Ivey Long
choreography:     Thommie Walsh
```
Productions:
  Opened October 7, 1979 for 105 performances
Reviews:
  America 141:237, Oct 27, 1979
  Horizon 22:4+, Dec 1979
  New York 12:97, Oct 22, 1979
  New York Theatre Critics' Reviews 1979:138
  New York Times III, page 13, Oct 8, 1979
                  III, page 6, Oct 26, 1979
                  II, page 27, Nov 4, 1979
  New Yorker 55:147-8, Oct 15, 1979
  Newsweek 94:130, Oct 22, 1979

90 in the Shade
```
book:             Guy Bolton
music:            Jerome Kern
staging:          Robert Milton
choreography:     Julian Alfred
```
Productions:
  Opened January 25, 1915 for 40 performances
Reviews:
  Dramatic Mirror 73:8, Feb 3, 1915
                  73:2, Feb 17, 1915
  Green Book 13:766, Apr 1915
  New York Dramatic News 60:17, Jan 30, 1915
  New York Times page 11, Jan 26, 1915
  Theatre Magazine 21:120, Mar 1915
                   21:150, Mar 1915

Nite Club Confidential
```
conceived:        Dennis Deal, with Albert Evans and Jamie Rocco
book:             Dennis Deal
songs:            Various authors and composers, with new songs
                  by Dennis Deal
staging:          Dennis Deal with Albert Evans and Jamie Rocco
sets:             Christopher Cole
costumes:         Stephen Rotondaro
```
Productions:
  (Off-Broadway) Opened May 10, 1984 for 156 performances
Reviews:
  New York Times I, page 12, May 12, 1984

No Foolin' (Ziegfeld's American Revue of 1926) (Glorifying the American Girl)
```
sketches:         J. P. McEvoy and James Barton
music:            Rudolf Friml and James Hanley
lyrics:           Gene Buck and Irving Caesar
staging:          Florenz Ziegfeld and John Boyle
```

Productions:
    Opened June 24, 1926 for 108 performances
Reviews:
    Bookman 64:86, Sep 1926
    New York Times page 25, Jun 25, 1926
    Theatre Magazine 44:23, Aug 1926
    Vogue 68:122, Sep 1, 1926

No for an Answer
    book: Marc Blitzstein
    music: Marc Blitzstein
    lyrics: Marc Blitzstein
    staging: W. E. Watts
Productions:
    (Off-Broadway) Opened January 5, 1941 for 3 performances
Reviews:
    Modern Music 18:70+, Jan-Feb 1941
    Musical Courier 123:9, Jan 15, 1941
    Theatre Arts 25:183, Mar 1941

The No-Frills Revue
    conceived: Martin Charnin
    dialogue and
       segues: Martin Charnin, Douglas Bernstein and Denis
                 Markell
    sketches: Various authors
    songs: Various authors and composers
    staging: Martin Charnin
    sets: Evelyn Sakash
    clothing: Perry Ellis
    choreography: Frank Ventura
Productions:
    (Off-Broadway) Opened November 25, 1987 for 207 performances
Reviews:
    New York Times I, page 79, Oct 18, 1987
    New Yorker 64:96, Feb 22, 1988
    Vogue 178:132, Mar 1988

No! No! Nanette!
    book: Otto Harbach and Frank Mandel
    music: Vincent Youmans
    lyrics: Otto Harbach and Irving Caesar
    staging: H. H. Frazee
Productions:
    Opened September 16, 1925 for 321 performances
    Opened January 19, 1971 for 861 performances
    (Off-Off-Broadway) Opened May 12, 1988
Reviews:
    Dance Magazine 45:27, Mar 1971
    Life 70:40-1, Feb 19, 1971
    National Review 23:440, Apr 20, 1971

New York Theatre Critics' Reviews 1971:382
New York Times page 17, Mar 12, 1925
               page 28, Nov 17, 1925
               page 23, Mar 8, 1926
               page 25, Oct 18, 1926
               VIII, page 2, Feb 26, 1928
               page 38, Mar 17, 1970
               page 56, Jun 25, 1970
               page 36, Sep 29, 1970
               II, page 1, Jan 10, 1971
               page 24, Jan 20, 1971
               page 26, Jan 21, 1971
               II, page 1, Jan 31, 1971
               II, page 1, Feb 21, 1971
               VI, page 14, Apr 11, 1971
               page 46, Mar 1, 1972
               VII, page 29, May 21, 1972
               page 58, Nov 9, 1972
               page 25, Jan 30, 1973
               XXIII, page 4, Jan 1, 1978
               I, page 49, May 22, 1988
New Yorker 46:54, Jan 30, 1971
Newsweek 77:73-4, Feb 1, 1971
Saturday Review 54:62+, Feb 6, 1971
             54:14, Apr 24, 1971
Theatre Magazine 44:17, Aug 1926
Time 47:90, Apr 15, 1946
     97:76, Feb 1, 1971

No Other Girl
    book: Aaron Hoffman
    music: Bert Kalmar and Harry Ruby
    lyrics: Bert Kalmar and Harry Ruby
Productions:
    Opened August 13, 1924 for 52 performances
Reviews:
    New York Times page 10, Aug 14, 1924
    Theatre Magazine 40:16, Oct 1924

No Shoestrings
    conceived: Ben Bagley
    staging: Robert Haddad
    costumes: Dick Granger
    choreography: Robert Haddad
Productions:
    (Off-Broadway) Opened October 11, 1962 for 66 performances
No Reviews.

No Strings
    book: Samuel Taylor
    music: Richard Rodgers

lyrics: Richard Rodgers
staging: Joe Layton
sets: David Hays
costumes: Fred Voelpel and Donald Brooks
choreography: Joe Layton and Buddy Schwab
Productions:
Opened March 15, 1962 for 580 performances
Reviews:
America 106:869, Mar 31, 1962
Christian Century 79:493, Apr 18, 1962
Dance Magazine 36:19-21, May 1962
Ebony 17:40-2+, Jul 1962
Nation 194:337-8, Apr 14, 1962
New Republic 146:26-7+, Apr 9, 1962
New York Theatre Critics' Reviews 1962:328+
New York Times page 24, Mar 16, 1962
                 II, page 1, Mar 25, 1962
                 page 17, Jan 1, 1964
New Yorker 38:100+, Mar 31, 1962
Newsweek 59:85, Mar 26, 1962
Saturday Review 45:27, Mar 31, 1962
Theatre Arts 46:57-9, May 1962
Time 79:51, Mar 23, 1962

No Way to Treat a Lady
book: David J. Cohen, based on William Goldman's
                 novel
music: David J. Cohen
lyrics: David J. Cohen
staging: Jack Hofsiss
sets: David Jenkins
costumes: Michael Kaplan
Productions:
(Off-Off-Broadway) Opened May 27, 1987 for 28 performances
Reviews:
New York 20:68+, Jun 22, 1987
New York Times III, page 6, Jun 12, 1987
New Yorker 63:69, Jun 22, 1987

Nobody Home
book: Guy Bolton and Paul Rubens
music: Jerome Kern
staging: J. C. Benrimo
Productions:
Opened April 20, 1915 for 135 performances
Reviews:
Dramatic Mirror 73:8, Apr 28, 1915
                73:2, May 12, 1915
                73:1, Jun 16, 1915
Green Book 14:59-60, Jul 1915
           14:191-2, Jul 1915

Life (New York) 65:808, May 16, 1915
Theatre Magazine 21:280, Jun 1915
  21:297, Jun 1915

Noel Coward's Sweet Potato
    music: Noel Coward
    lyrics: Noel Coward
    staging: Lee Theodore
    sets: Helen Pond and Herbert Senn
    costumes: David Toser
    choreography: Lee Theodore
Productions:
    Opened September 29, 1968 for 44 performances
Reviews:
    Dance Magazine 42:106, Dec 1968
    New York Theatre Critics' Reviews 1968:232
    New York Times page 59, Sep 30, 1968
        II, page 5, Oct 13, 1968
        page 39, Oct 15, 1968
        page 39, Oct 16, 1968
    New Yorker 44:97, Oct 5, 1968

Not Tonight, Benvenuto
    book: Virgil Engeran
    music: Virgil Engeran
    lyrics: Virgil Engeran
    staging: Jim Payne
    sets: James Morgan and Peter A. Scheu
    costumes: Sherri Bucks
    choreography: Robin Reseen
Productions:
    (Off-Broadway) Opened June 5, 1979 for one performance
No Reviews.

Nothing But Love
    book: Frank Stammers
    music: Harold Orlob
    lyrics: Frank Stammers
Productions:
    Opened October 14, 1919 for 39 performances
Reviews:
    Dramatic Mirror 80:1653, Oct 23, 1919
    New York Times page 20, Oct 15, 1919
    Theatre Magazine 30:356, Nov 1919

Now
    conceived: Marvin Gordon
    sketches: George Haimsohn
    music: John Aman; additional material by Steve Holden,
                    John Kuntz, Sue Lawless and Mart Panzer
    lyrics: George Haimsohn

```
staging:            Marvin Gordon
sets:               Jack Robinson
costumes:           Betsey Johnson, Michael Mott and The Different
                    Drummer
```
Productions:
    (Off-Broadway)   Opened June 5, 1968 for 22 performances
Reviews:
    New York Times page 53, Jun 6, 1968

Now Is the Time for All Good Men

```
book:               Gretchen Cryer
music:              Nancy Ford
lyrics:             Gretchen Cryer
staging:            Word Baker
sets:               Holly Haas
costumes:           Jeanne Button
```
Productions:
    (Off-Broadway)   Opened September 26, 1967 for 112 performances
    (Off-Broadway)   Opened Season of 1970-1971
Reviews:
    America 117:421-2, Oct 14, 1967
    New York Times page 42, Sep 27, 1967
                   page 49, Oct 27, 1967
                    page 13, Dec 29, 1967
                    page 73, May 2, 1971
    New Yorker 43:133-4, Oct 7, 1967

Nowhere to Go But Up

```
book:               James Lipton
music:              Sil Berkowitz
lyrics:             James Lipton
staging:            Sidney Lumet
sets:               Peter Larkin
costumes:           Robert Fletcher
choreography:       Ronald Field
```
Productions:
    Opened November 10, 1962 for 9 performances
Reviews:
    Dance Magazine 37:24, Jan 1963
                     37:28-9, Feb 1963
    New York Theatre Critics' Reviews 1962:209+
    New York Times page 46, Oct 9, 1962
                   page 36, Nov 12, 1962
                   page 46, Nov 15, 1962
    New Yorker 38:147, Nov 17, 1962
    Theatre Arts 46:15, Dec 1962

Nunsense

```
book:               Dan Goggin
music:              Dan Goggin
lyrics:             Dan Goggin
```

staging: Dan Goggin
sets: Barry Axtell
choreography: Felton Smith
Productions:
(Off-Broadway) Opened December 12, 1985 for *1,431 performances
(still running 6/1/89)
Reviews:
America 156:283-4, Apr 4, 1987
Dance Magazine 60:103-4, Mar 1986
New York Times I, page 99, Dec 15, 1985
People 26:148-9, Dec 15, 1986

-O-

O Marry Me
book: Lola Pergament; based on Goldsmith's She Stoops
                to Conquer
music: Robert Kessler
lyrics: Lola Pergament
staging: Michael Howard
sets: Herbert Senn and Helen Pond
costumes: Sonia Lowenstein
Productions:
(Off-Broadway) Opened October 27, 1961 for 21 performances
Reviews:
New York Times page 13, Oct 28, 1961
                page 42, Nov 13, 1961
New Yorker 37:130-2, Nov 4, 1961

O, Oysters!
book: Eric Blau
music: Doris Schwerin
Productions:
(Off-Broadway) Season of 1960-61
Reviews:
America 104:714, Feb 25, 1961
New York Times page 23, Jan 31, 1961

O Say Can You See!
book: Bill Conklin and Bob Miller
music: Jack Holmes
lyrics: Bill Conklin and Bob Miller
staging: Ray Harrison and Cynthia Baer
sets: Jack H. Cornwell
costumes: Jane K. Stevens
choreography: Ray Harrison
Productions:
(Off-Broadway) Opened October 8, 1962 for 24 performances
Reviews:
New York Times page 45, Oct 9, 1962
New Yorker 38:86+, Oct 20, 1962

Oba Oba
    produced: Franco Fontaine
    songs: Popular music and folksongs of Brazil
    musical
        director: Wilson Mauro
    choreography: Roberto Abrahao
Productions:
    Opened March 29, 1988 for 46 performances
Reviews:
    New York Theatre Critics' Reviews 1988: 313
    New York Times III, page 26, Mar 30, 1988

The O'Brien Girl
    book: Otto Harbach and Frank Mandel
    music: Lou Hirsch
    lyrics: Otto Harbach and Frank Mandel
    staging: Julian Mitchell
Productions:
    Opened October 3, 1921 for 164 performances
Reviews:
    Dramatic Mirror 83: 893, May 21, 1921
                   84: 520, Oct 8, 1921
    Life (New York) 78: 18, Oct 20, 1921
    New York Clipper 69: 26, Oct 12, 1921
    New York Times page 10, Oct 4, 1921
                   page 18, Oct 21, 1921
    Theatre Magazine 34: 440, Dec 1921

Odds and Ends of 1917
    book: Bide Dudley and John Godfrey
    music: Bide Dudley, John Godfrey and James Byrnes
    lyrics: Bide Dudley, John Godfrey and James Byrnes
    staging: Julian Alfred
Productions:
    Opened November 19, 1917 for 112 performances
Reviews:
    Dramatic Mirror 77: 5+, Dec 1, 1917
    Green Book 19: 205+, Feb 1918
    New York Times page 11, Nov 20, 1917

Ododo
    book: Joseph A. Walker
    music: Dorothy A. Dinroe
    staging: Joseph A. Walker
    sets: Edward Burbridge
    costumes: Dorothy A. Dinroe
    choreography: Syvilla Fort
Productions:
    (Off-Broadway) Opened November 17, 1970 for 48 performances
Reviews:
    New York Theatre Critics' Reviews 1970: 124

New York Times page 26, Nov 25, 1970
II, page 7, Dec 6, 1970
New Yorker 46:162, Dec 5, 1970

Odyssey (see Home Sweet Homer)

Of Thee I Sing
book: George S. Kaufman and Morrie Ryskind
music: George Gershwin
lyrics: Ira Gershwin
staging: George S. Kaufman
choreography: Chester Hale
Productions:
Opened December 26, 1931 for 441 performances
Opened May 15, 1933 for 32 performances
Opened May 5, 1952 for 72 performances
(Off-Broadway) Opened October 18, 1968 for 15 performances
(Off-Broadway) Opened March 7, 1969 for 21 performances
Reviews:
Arts and Decoration 36:39+, Feb 1932
                    37:43+, Sep 1932
Bookman 74:561-2, Jan 1932
Catholic World 134:587-8, Feb 1932
               175:310, Jul 1952
Commonweal 15:302, Jan 13, 1932
           56:196-7, May 30, 1952
Harper's 205:92, Jul 1952
Literary Digest 112:18, Jan 16, 1932
Nation 134:56, Jan 13, 1932
       134:294, Mar 9, 1932
       174:486, May 17, 1952
New Republic 69:243, Jan 13, 1932
             70:97, Mar 9, 1932
New York Theatre Critics' Reviews 1952:289
New York Times VIII, page 2, Dec 13, 1931
               VIII, page 1, Mar 20, 1932
               page 1, May 3, 1932
               VIII, page 1, May 8, 1932
               page 28, Jan 2, 1933
               page 23, Jan 6, 1933
               page 22, Aug 10, 1937
               page 14, Aug 18, 1937
               II, page 1, May 4, 1952
               page 34, May 6, 1952
               II, page 1, May 11, 1952
               page 19, Mar 8, 1969
               page 39, Mar 25, 1969
New Yorker 28:87, May 17, 1952
Newsweek 39:101, May 19, 1952
Outlook 160:54+, Jan 13, 1932
Saturday Review 9:385-6, Jan 21, 1933
                35:30-2, May 24, 1952

Theatre Arts 36:17+, Jul 1952
Theatre Guild Magazine 9:16-20, Feb 1932
                       9:23, Apr 1932
Time 59:83, May 19, 1952
Vogue 79:73+, Feb 15, 1932

Of V We Sing
sketches: Al Geto, Sam D. Locke, Mel Tolkin
music: Alex North, George Kleinsinger, Ned Lehak,
               Beau Bergersen, Lou Cooper and Tony Sacher
lyrics: Alfred Hayes, Lewis Allen, Roslyn Harvey,
               Mike Stratton, Bea Goldsmith, Joe Barian and
               Arthur Zipser
staging: Perry Bruskin
choreography: Susanne Remos
Productions:
   Opened February 11, 1942 for 76 performances
Reviews:
   New York Times page 20, Feb 16, 1942

Ogden Nash (see Nash at Nine)

Oh, Boy
book: Guy Bolton and P. G. Wodehouse
music: Jerome Kern
lyrics: Guy Bolton and P. G. Wodehouse
staging: Edward Royce
Productions:
   Opened February 20, 1917 for 463 performances
   (Off-Off-Broadway) Opened December 1979
   (Off-Off-Broadway) Opened December 1980
Reviews:
   Book News 35:317+, Apr 1917
   Dramatic Mirror 77:7, Mar 3, 1917
                   77:4, Mar 17, 1917
                   77:9, Mar 31, 1917
                   77:5, Jun 2, 1917
   Green Book 17:785-6+, May 1917
   Nation 104:250, Mar 1, 1917
   New York 18:56-8, Feb 11, 1985
             18:78+, Feb 11, 1985
   New York Dramatic News 64:11, Feb 24, 1917
   New York Times page 7, Feb 20, 1917
                   III, page 9, Dec 18, 1979
   Theatre Magazine 25:214-15+, Apr 1917
                    25:199, Apr 1917
                    26:157, Sep 1917

Oh, Brother!
book: Donald Driver, based on Shakespeare's Comedy
           of Errors

music: Michael Valenti
lyrics: Donald Driver
staging: Donald Driver
sets: Michael J. Hotopp and Paul De Pass
costumes: Ann Emonts
choreography: Marvin Laird
Productions:
Opened November 10, 1981 for 3 performances
Reviews:
New York 14:86-7, Nov 23, 1981
New York Theatre Critics' Reviews 1981:124
New York Times III, page 23, Nov 11, 1981

Oh, Calcutta!
devised: Kenneth Tynan
contributors: Samuel Beckett, Jules Feiffer, Dan Greenburg,
                 John Lennon, Jacques Levy, Leonard Melfi,
                 David Newman, Robert Benton, Sam Shepard,
                 Clovis Trouille, Kenneth Tynan and Sherman
                 Yellen
music: The Open Window
lyrics: The Open Window
staging: Jacques Levy
sets: James Tilton
costumes: Fred Voelpel
choreography: Margo Sappington
Productions:
(Off-Broadway) Opened June 17, 1969 for 704 performances
Transferred to Broadway February 26, 1971 for 610 performances
Opened September 24, 1976 for *5,856 performances (still running
   6/1/89)
Reviews:
America 121:146, Sep 6, 1969
Commonweal 90:463-4, Jul 25, 1969
Commentary 48:24+, Nov 1969
Esquire 72:44, Dec 1969
Holiday 46:39+, Dec 1969
New York Theatre Critics' Reviews 1969:208
New York Times page 54, Apr 9, 1969
              II, page 1, Jun 15, 1969
              page 33, Jun 18, 1969
              II, page 1, Jun 29, 1969
              page 32, Oct 24, 1969
              page 30, Jul 29, 1970
              page 32, Sep 12, 1970
              page 37, Sep 29, 1970
              II, page 5, Dec 6, 1970
              page 40, Feb 8, 1971
              VI, page 2, Jun 20, 1971
              page 20, Jul 23, 1971
              page 46, Oct 26, 1976
              III, page 13, Aug 8, 1989

New Yorker 45:72+, Jun 28, 1969
Newsweek 73:107, Jun 16, 1969
          73:81, Jun 30, 1969
Saturday Review 52:51, Apr 26, 1969
                52:20, Jul 26, 1969
Time 93:59, Jun 27, 1969
     127:89, Mar 24, 1986
Vogue 154:60, Aug 1, 1969

Oh Captain!
    book: Al Morgan and José Ferrer, based on an original
                       screenplay by Alec Coppel
    music: Jay Livingston and Ray Evans
    lyrics: Jay Livingston and Ray Evans
    staging: José Ferrer
    sets: Jo Mielziner
    costumes: Miles White
    choreography: James Starbuck
Productions:
    Opened February 4, 1958 for 192 performances
Reviews:
    America 99:26, Apr 5, 1958
    Catholic World 187:70, Apr 1958
    Dance Magazine 32:15, Mar 1958
    New Republic 138:22-3, Mar 3, 1958
    New York Theatre Critics' Reviews 1958:370+
    New York Times page 21, Feb 5, 1958
    New Yorker 33:55, Feb 15, 1958
    Newsweek 51:66, Feb 17, 1958
    Theatre Arts 42:20-1, Apr 1958
    Time 71:84, Feb 17, 1958

Oh Coward!
    devised: Roderick Cook
    words: Noel Coward
    music: Noel Coward
    staging: Roderick Cook
    sets: Helen Pond and Herbert Senn
Productions:
    (Off-Broadway) Opened October 4, 1972 for 294 performances
    (Off-Off-Broadway) Opened October 13, 1979
    (Off-Off-Broadway) Opened June 1981
    Opened November 17, 1986 for 56 performances
Reviews:
    America 127:323-4, Oct 21, 1972
    New Leader 69:22, Nov 17, 1986
    New York Theatre Critics' Reviews 1972:167
                                      1986:166
    New York Times page 55, Oct 5, 1972
                    II, page 1, Oct 15, 1972
                    II, page 31, Nov 19, 1972

page 37, Jun 6, 1973
XI, page 16, May 11, 1980
III, page 18, Jun 11, 1981
III, page 17, Nov 18, 1986
New Yorker 48:125, Oct 14, 1972
62:136, Dec 8, 1986
Playboy 20:44, Jan 1973
Time 100:80, Oct 23, 1972

Oh, Ernest!
book: Francis DeWill
music: Robert Hood Bowers
lyrics: Francis DeWill
staging: William J. Wilson
Productions:
Opened May 9, 1927 for 56 performances
Reviews:
New York Times page 24, May 10, 1927

Oh Glorious Tintinnabulation
book: June Havoc
music: Cathy MacDonald
lyrics: June Havoc
staging: June Havoc
Productions:
(Off-Off-Broadway) Opened May 23, 1974
No Reviews.

Oh, I Say!   (The Wedding Night)
book: Keroul and Barre; adapted by Sydney Blow and
                  Douglas Hoare
music: Jerome D. Kern
staging: J. C. Huffman
choreography: Julian Alfred
Productions:
Opened October 30, 1913 for 68 performances
Reviews:
Dramatic Mirror 70:10, Nov 5, 1913
Green Book 11:163-4, Jan 1914
New York Times page 11, Oct 28, 1913
                 page 11, Oct 31, 1913
Theatre Magazine 18:xx, Dec 1913

Oh, Johnny
book: Paul Streitz
music: Gary Cherpakov
lyrics: Paul Streitz and Gary Cherpakov
staging: Alan Weeks
sets: Jim Chesnutt
costumes: Gene Galvin
choreography: Alan Weeks

Productions:
    (Off-Broadway)   Opened January 10, 1982 for one performance
No Reviews.

Oh, Kay
    book: Guy Bolton and P. G. Wodehouse
    music: George Gershwin
    lyrics: Ira Gershwin
    staging: John Harwood and Sammy Lee
Productions:
    Opened November 8, 1926 for 256 performances
    Opened January 2, 1928 for 16 performances
    (Off-Broadway)   Season of 1959-60
Reviews:
    New York Times page 31, Nov 9, 1926
                    page 33, Sep 22, 1927
                    page 29, Jan 3, 1928
                    page 37, Apr 18, 1960
                    page 28, Jun 29, 1960
    Vogue 69:100+, Jan 1, 1927

Oh, Lady! Lady!
    book: Guy Bolton and P. G. Wodehouse
    music: Jerome Kern
    lyrics: Guy Bolton and P. G. Wodehouse
    staging: Robert Milton and Edward Royce
Productions:
    Opened February 1, 1918 for 219 performances
    (Off-Off-Broadway) Opened March 13, 1974
Reviews:
    Dramatic Mirror 78:7, Feb 16, 1918
                 78:7, Mar 2, 1918
                 79:949, Jul 6, 1918
    Green Book 19:588+, Apr 1918
    Life (New York) 71:262, Feb 14, 1918
    New York Times page 7, Feb 1, 1918
                    page 41, Mar 18, 1974
    New Yorker 50:108, Mar 25, 1974
    Stage 12:29, Oct 1934
    Theatre Magazine 27:143, Feb 1918

Oh, Look!
    book: Suggested by James Montgomery's Ready Money
    music: Harry Carroll
    lyrics: Joseph McCarthy
Productions:
    Opened March 7, 1918 for 68 performances
Reviews:
    Dramatic Mirror 78:5, Mar 16, 1918
    Green Book 19:785-7, May 1918
    New York Times page 9, Mar 8, 1918
    Theatre Magazine 27:216+, Apr 1918

Oh, My Dear!
　　book:　　　　　　Guy Bolton and P. G. Wodehouse
　　music:　　　　　　Louis A. Hirsch
　　lyrics:　　　　　　Guy Bolton and P. G. Wodehouse
　　staging:　　　　　Robert Milton and Edward Royce
Productions:
　　Opened November 27, 1918 for 189 performances
Reviews:
　　Dramatic Mirror 79:865, Dec 14, 1918
　　New York Times page 11, Nov 27, 1918
　　Theatre Magazine 29:37, Jan 1919

Oh! Oh! Delphine
　　book:　　　　　　C. M. S. McLellan; based on Georges Berr and
　　　　　　　　　　　Marcel Guillemaud's Villa Primrose
　　music:　　　　　　Ivan Caryll
　　lyrics:　　　　　　C. M. S. McLellan
　　staging:　　　　　Herbert Gresham
Productions:
　　Opened September 30, 1912 for 248 performances
Reviews:
　　Blue Book 16:467-9, Jan 1913
　　Dramatic Mirror 68:6-7, Oct 2, 1912
　　　　　　　　　　 68:2, Nov 6, 1912
　　　　　　　　　　 68:1, Nov 27, 1912
　　Green Book 8:929-31+, Dec 1912
　　Harper's Weekly 55:19, Oct 26, 1912
　　　　　　　　　　 57:20, Apr 19, 1913
　　Life (New York) 60:2005, Oct 17, 1912
　　Munsey 48:521-5, Dec 1912
　　New York Dramatic News 56:25, Oct 5, 1912
　　Theatre Magazine 16:155+, Nov 1912
　　　　　　　　　　 18:71, Apr 1913

Oh! Oh! Oh! Nurse
　　book:　　　　　　George E. Stoddard
　　music:　　　　　　Carlo and Sanders
　　lyrics:　　　　　　Carlo and Sanders
　　staging:　　　　　Walter Brooks
Productions:
　　Opened December 7, 1925 for 32 performances
Reviews:
　　New York Times page 28, Dec 8, 1925

Oh, Please
　　book:　　　　　　Otto Harbach and Anne Caldwell, based on a
　　　　　　　　　　　story by Maurice Hennequin and Pierre Veber
　　music:　　　　　　Vincent Youmans
　　lyrics:　　　　　　Clifford Grey and Leo Robin
　　staging:　　　　　Hassard Short
Productions:
　　Opened December 17, 1926 for 75 performances

Reviews:
    Life (New York) 89:21, Jan 13, 1927
    New York Times page 24, Dec 22, 1926

Oh, What a Girl!
book:	Edgar Smith and Edward Clark
music:	Charles Jules and Jacques Presburg
lyrics:	Edgar Smith and Edward Clark
staging:	Edward Clark

Productions:
    Opened July 28, 1919 for 68 performances
Reviews:
    New York Times page 20, Jul 29, 1919
    Theatre Magazine 30:151-2, Sep 1919

Oh What a Lovely War
book:	The Theatre Workshop, Charles Chilton, and members of the cast
music:	The Theatre Workshop, Charles Chilton, and members of the cast
lyrics:	The Theatre Workshop, Charles Chilton, and members of the cast
staging:	Joan Littlewood
sets:	John Bury
costumes:	Una Collins
choreography:	Bob Stevenson

Productions:
    Opened September 30, 1964 for 125 performances
Reviews:
    America 111:497-8, Oct 24, 1964
    Catholic World 200:131-2, Nov 1964
    Commonweal 81:134, Oct 23, 1964
    Dance Magazine 38:56-7, Nov 1964
    Esquire 60:34+, Dec 1963
    Nation 196:450+, May 25, 1963
          199:256, Oct 19, 1964
    New Republic 151:26, Oct 24, 1964
    New York Theatre Critics' Reviews 1964:209+
    New Yorker 39:76-7, Jun 29, 1963
          39:98, Sep 7, 1963
          40:95, Oct 10, 1964
    Newsweek 64:104, Oct 12, 1964
    Saturday Review 47:29, Oct 17, 1964
    Theatre Arts 47:31-2+, Jun 1963
    Time 84:92, Oct 9, 1964
    Vogue 144:64, Nov 15, 1964

Oil City Symphony
written:	Mike Cravar, Mark Hardwick, Debra Monk, and Mary Murfitt
staging:	Larry Forde
sets:	Jeffrey Schissler

Productions:
  (Off-Broadway) Opened November 5, 1987 for 626 performances
Reviews:
  Nation 246:175-6, Feb 6, 1988
  New York Times I, page 11, Nov 7, 1987
  New Yorker 63:74-5, Jan 18, 1988
  People 29:60, Mar 21, 1988
  Theatre Crafts 22:28-9, Mar 1988
  Time 130:67, Dec 21, 1987

Oklahoma!
  book: Oscar Hammerstein II, based on Lynn Riggs'
                   play Green Grow the Lilacs
  music: Richard Rodgers
  lyrics: Oscar Hammerstein II
  staging: Rouben Mamoulian
  sets: Lemuel Ayers
  costumes: Miles White
  choreography: Agnes de Mille
Productions:
  Opened March 31, 1943 for 2,212 performances
  Opened May 29, 1951 for 100 performances
  Opened August 31, 1953 for 40 performances
  Opened March 19, 1958 for 16 performances
  Opened February 27, 1963 for 15 performances
  Opened May 15, 1963 for 15 performances
  Opened December 15, 1965 for 24 performances
  Opened June 23, 1969 for 88 performances
  (Off-Off-Broadway) Opened June 26, 1975
  Opened December 13, 1979 for 293 performances
Reviews:
  America 89:609+, Sep 19, 1953
         121:76-7, Aug 2, 1969
  Americana 15:15, May/Jun 1987
  Catholic World 157:186-7, May 1943
                 173:308, Jul 1951
                 178:67, Oct 1953
  Commonweal 54:285, Jun 29, 1951
  Cosmopolitan 134:24-7, May 1953
  Dance Magazine 32:17, May 1958
                 37:32-4, Mar 1963
                 40:14-15+, Feb 1966
  Holiday 20:75+, Oct 1956
  Independent Woman 22:144, May 1943
  Life 14:56-8+, May 24, 1943
       16:82-5, Mar 6, 1944
  Look 17:4, Apr 7, 1953
  Los Angeles 24:249+, Jun 1979
  Mademoiselle 41:125+, May 1955
  Nation 156:572, Apr 17, 1943
  New Republic 108:508-9, Apr 19, 1943

New York 13:69, Dec 31, 1979
New York Theatre Critics' Reviews 1943:341+
                                   1951:257+
                                   1953:294+
                                   1979:68
New York Times page 27, Apr 1, 1943
                 II, page 1, Apr 11, 1943
                 II, page 6, May 9, 1943
                 II, page 5, Jun 6, 1943
                 VI, page 10, Jul 25, 1943
                 II, page 1, Aug 1, 1943
                 II, page 2, Sep 5, 1943
                 VI, page 39, Jan 21, 1945
                 II, page 5, Feb 4, 1945
                 VI, page 18, Mar 25, 1945
                 page 14, Jul 13, 1945
                 II, page 1, Mar 31, 1946
                 page 19, Oct 5, 1946
                 II, page 1, Mar 30, 1947
                 page 35, May 1, 1947
                 II, page 3, May 11, 1947
                 page 18, Jun 20, 1947
                 page 31, May 19, 1948
                 II, page 1, Jun 6, 1948
                 page 35, Mar 29, 1950
                 page 23, Sep 5, 1950
                 page 78, Oct 22, 1950
                 page 15, May 30, 1951
                 page 38, Sep 13, 1951
                 II, page 3, Sep 23, 1951
                 page 79, Feb 15, 1953
                 II, page 1, Mar 29, 1953
                 page 22, Aug 31, 1953
                 page 19, Sep 1, 1953
                 II, page 1, Sep 6, 1953
                 page 19, Aug 15, 1955
                 page 15, Mar 8, 1958
                 page 32, Mar 20, 1958
                 page 8, Feb 28, 1963
                 VI, pages 30-31, May 12, 1963
                 page 40, May 16, 1963
                 page 62, Dec 16, 1965
                 page 37, Jun 24, 1969
                 II, page 5, Jul 6, 1969
                 page 19, Jul 17, 1975
                 III, page 5, Dec 14, 1979
New York Times Magazine pages 18-19, Mar 25, 1945
                         pages 30-1, May 12, 1963
New Yorker 19:61, May 29, 1943
           55:70+, Dec 24, 1979
Newsweek 61:86, Mar 11, 1963
         94:56, Dec 24, 1979

Saturday Review 26:14, Sep 4, 1943
School and Society 67:475, Jun 26, 1948
Theatre Arts 27:329-31, Jun 1943
     35:5, Sep 1951
     37:17, Nov 1953
Theatre Crafts 20:36-7+, May 1986
Time 51:75, Apr 12, 1948
    114:77, Dec 24, 1979

Old Bucks and New Wings
book: Harvey Lasker
music: Eddie Stuart
lyrics: Harvey Lasker
staging: Harvey Lasker
costumes: Phyllis Uzill
choreography: Buster Burnell
Productions:
(Off-Broadway) Opened November 5, 1962 for 16 performances
Reviews:
New York Times page 36, Nov 5, 1962
            page 39, Nov 6, 1962
New Yorker 38:148, Nov 17, 1962

Old Dutch
book: Edgar Smith
music: Victor Herbert
lyrics: George V. Hobart
staging: Ned Wayburn
Productions:
Opened November 22, 1909 for 88 performances
Reviews:
Dramatic Mirror 62:5, Dec 4, 1909
Hampton 24:273-5, Feb 1910
Harper's Weekly 54:24, Jan 29, 1910
Life (New York) 54:854, Dec 9, 1909
Metropolitan Magazine 31:820-1, Mar 1910
Theatre Magazine 11:xi, Jan 1910
           11:30, Jan 1910

The Old Town
book: George Ade
music: Gustav Luders
Productions:
Opened January 10, 1910 for 171 performances
Reviews:
Dramatic Mirror 63:5, Jan 22, 1910
Green Book 8:382-3, Sep 1912
Hampton 24:410, Mar 1910
Leslie's Weekly 110:136, Feb 10, 1910
Life (New York) 55:128, Jan 20, 1910
Metropolitan Magazine 32:120-1, Apr 1910

Pearson 24:93, Jul 1910
Theatre Magazine 11:xv, Feb 1910
                    11:86, Mar 1910

The Oldest Trick in the World (with The Bible Salesman, billed as
    Double Entry)
    book: Jay Thompson
    music: Jay Thompson
    lyrics: Jay Thompson
    staging: Bill Penn
    sets: Howard Becknell
Productions:
    (Off-Broadway) Opened February 20, 1961 for 56 performances
Reviews:
    New York Times page 40, Feb 21, 1961
    New Yorker 37:115-16, Mar 11, 1961

Oliver!
    book: Lionel Bart, adapted from Charles Dickens'
                    Oliver Twist
    music: Lionel Bart
    lyrics: Lionel Bart
    staging: Peter Coe
    sets: Sean Kenny
    costumes: Sean Kenny
Productions:
    Opened January 6, 1963 for 774 performances
    Opened August 2, 1965 for 64 performances
    Opened April 29, 1984 for 17 performances
Reviews:
    Commonweal 77:493, Feb 1, 1963
    Life 54:75-7, Jan 18, 1963
    New York 17:81, May 14, 1984
    New York Theatre Critics' Reviews 1963:397+
                                      1984:295
    New York Times page 34, Aug 8, 1962
                    page 32, Sep 27, 1962
                    page 27, Nov 2, 1962
                    VI, page 60, Dec 9, 1962
                    page 5, Jan 8, 1963
                    page 35, Aug 3, 1965
                    page 85, Nov 21, 1965
                    page 32, Feb 5, 1966
                    page 19, Sep 10, 1966
                    III, page 11, Apr 30, 1984
    New York Times Magazine page 60, Dec 9, 1962
    New Yorker 36:145, Oct 8, 1960
               38:85-6, Jun 2, 1962
               38:60, Jan 19, 1963
    Newsweek 60:87, Aug 20, 1962
             61:65, Jan 14, 1963

Saturday Review 46:26, Jan 19, 1963
Theatre Arts 46:19-20, Dec 1962
47:10-11+, Feb 1963
Time 81:52, Jan 11, 1963

Olympus on My Mind

book:	Barry Harman, suggested by Amphitryon by Heinrich Von Kleist
music:	Grant Sturiale
lyrics:	Barry Harman
staging:	Barry Harman
sets:	Christopher Stapleton
costumes:	Steven Jones
choreography:	Pamela Sousa

Productions:
  (Off-Off-Broadway) Opened May 1986
  (Off-Broadway) Opened July 15, 1986 for 207 performances
Reviews:
  New York Theatre Critics' Reviews 1986:212
  New York Times III, page 3, May 23, 1986
  New Yorker 62:58, Aug 18, 1986

On a Clear Day You Can See Forever

book:	Alan Jay Lerner
music:	Burton Lane
lyrics:	Alan Jay Lerner
staging:	Robert Lewis
sets:	Oliver Smith
costumes:	Freddy Wittop
choreography:	Herbert Ross

Productions:
  Opened October 17, 1965 for 272 performances
Reviews:
  Dance Magazine 39:138-9, Dec 1965
  Holiday 39:118+, Jan 1966
  Nation 201:398, Nov 22, 1965
  New York Theatre Critics' Reviews 1965:308
  New York Times page 44, Oct 18, 1965
                 page 53, Jun 7, 1966
                 page 40, Jun 8, 1966
  New Yorker 41:108, Oct 30, 1965
  Newsweek 66:84+, Nov 1, 1965
  Saturday Review 48:41-2, Nov 6, 1965
  Time 86:84, Oct 29, 1965

On the Lock-In

conceived:	Robert Macbeth
book:	David Langston Smyrl
music:	David Langston Smyrl
lyrics:	David Langston Smyrl
staging:	Robert Macbeth

sets:	Karl Eigsti
costumes:	Grace Williams

Productions:
    (Off-Broadway) Opened April 14, 1977 for 62 performances
Reviews:
    New York 10:68, Jan 31, 1977
    New York Theatre Critics' Reviews 1977:225
    New York Times II, page 23, Apr 28, 1977
    New Yorker 53:59, May 9, 1977

On the Town

book:	Betty Comden and Adolph Green, based on an idea by Jerome Robbins
music:	Leonard Bernstein
lyrics:	Betty Comden and Adolph Green
staging:	George Abbott
sets:	Oliver Smith
costumes:	Alvin Colt
choreography:	Jerome Robbins

Productions:
    Opened December 28, 1944 for 463 performances
    Opened October 31, 1971 for 73 performances
Reviews:
    America 125:428, Nov 20, 1971
    Catholic World 160:453, Feb 1945
    Commonweal 41:332, Jan 12, 1945
    Dance Magazine 33:22-3, Apr 1959
    Life 18:49-51, Jan 15, 1945
    Nation 160:48, Jan 13, 1945
            213:538-9, Nov 22, 1971
    New Republic 112:85, Jan 15, 1945
    New York Theatre Critics' Reviews 1944:45+
                       1971:199
    New York Times page 11, Dec 29, 1944
               II, page 1, Jan 7, 1945
               II, page 5, Feb 4, 1945
               II, page 1, Feb 18, 1945
               II, page 2, Oct 17, 1945
               page 36, Jan 16, 1959
               II, page 1, Jan 25, 1959
               page 15, Feb 14, 1959
               page 30, May 31, 1963
               page 52, Apr 14, 1971
               page 14, Aug 13, 1971
               page 46, Sep 1, 1971
               II, page 1, Oct 31, 1971
               page 54, Nov 1, 1971
               II, page 1, Nov 7, 1971
               II, page 26, Nov 14, 1971
               page 27, Jan 4, 1972
    New Yorker 20:40, Jan 6, 1945
               47:115, Nov 6, 1971

Newsweek 25:72+, Jan 8, 1945
        78:106, Nov 15, 1971
Saturday Review 28:26-7, Feb 17, 1945
Theatre Arts 29:133-4, Mar 1945
Time 45:67-8, Jan 8, 1945
        98:51, Nov 15, 1971

On the Twentieth Century
    book: Betty Comden and Adolph Green, based on plays
                        by Ben Hecht and Charles MacArthur and by
                        Bruce Millholland
    music: Cy Coleman
    lyrics: Betty Comden and Adolph Green
    staging: Harold Prince
    sets: Robin Wagner
    costumes: Florence Klotz
    choreography: Larry Fuller
Productions:
    Opened February 19, 1978 for 453 performances
Reviews:
    America 138:191, Mar 11, 1978
    Nation 226:282-3, Mar 11, 1978
    New Leader 61:27-8, Mar 27, 1978
    New Republic 178:24-5, Mar 18, 1978
    New York 11:90-1, Mar 6, 1978
    New York Theatre Critics' Reviews 1978:376
    New York Times III, page 18, Feb 20, 1978
                    II, page 5, Feb 26, 1978
    New Yorker 54:67, Mar 6, 1978
                54:30-3, Mar 27, 1978
    Newsweek 91:79+, Mar 6, 1978
    Saturday Review 5:50-1, Apr 15, 1978
    Theatre Crafts 12:12-13+, May 1978
    Time 111:75, Mar 6, 1978
        129:11-13, Apr 20, 1987

On Toby Time
    book: Harvey Hackett
    music: Herschel Dwellingham
    lyrics: Harvey Hackett
    staging: Robert M. Cooper
Productions:
    (Off-Off-Broadway) Opened January 1977
Reviews:
    New York Times III, page 3, Jan 21, 1977

On Your Toes
    book: George Abbott
    music: Richard Rodgers
    lyrics: Lorenz Hart
    staging: Worthington Miner

```
sets:              Jo Mielziner
costumes:          Irene Sharaff
choreography:      George Balanchine
```
Productions:
    Opened April 11, 1936 for 315 performances
    Opened October 11, 1954 for 64 performances
    Opened March 6, 1983 for 505 performances
Reviews:
    America 92:163, Nov 6, 1954
            148:441, Jun 4, 1983
    Catholic World 143:340, Jun 1936
                   180:228, Dec 1954
    Commonweal 23:724, Apr 24, 1936
               61:166, Nov 12, 1954
    Dance Magazine 57:60-7, Mar 1983
                   57:74-5, Jun 1983
                   57:121, Dec 1983
    Los Angeles 31:214+, Sep 1986
    Mademoiselle 40:142, Nov 1954
    Nation 142:559, Apr 29, 1936
           179:390, Oct 30, 1954
           236:409-10, Apr 2, 1983
    New Republic 131:22-3, Nov 1, 1954
    New York 16:85, Jan 3, 1983
             16:67, Mar 21, 1983
    New York Theatre Critics' Reviews 1983:259
    New York Times page 22, Mar 23, 1936
                    page 14, Apr 13, 1936
                    page 15, Feb 6, 1937
                    page 21, Aug 3, 1937
                    II, page 1, Oct 10, 1954
                    page 24, Oct 12, 1954
                    III, page 13, Mar 7, 1983
                    II, page 5, Mar 27, 1983
                    III, page 11, Mar 29, 1983
    New Yorker 30:84-6, Oct 23, 1954
               59:134-5, Mar 14, 1983
               59:112-14, Mar 21, 1983
    Newsweek 7:28-9, Apr 25, 1936
             44:93, Oct 25, 1954
             101:67-8, Mar 21, 1983
    People 19:98-9, Apr 4, 1983
    Theatre Arts 20:415, Jun 1936
                 38:22-3+, Dec 1954
    Time 37:56, Apr 20, 1936
         64:41, Oct 25, 1954
         121:83, Mar 21, 1983
    Vogue 124:100-1, Oct 15, 1954

Once Over Lightly
    book: Laszlo Halasz; adapted from Beaumarchais' The
                       Barber of Seville

music: G. Rossini
dialogues: Louis Garden and Robert Pierpont Forshaw
solos: Louis Garden and Robert Pierpont Forshaw
ensembles: George Mead
staging: Robert H. Gordon
sets: Richard Rychtarick
Productions:
Opened November 19, 1942 for 6 performances
Reviews:
New York Times page 26, Nov 20, 1942

Once upon a Mattress
book: Jay Thompson, Marshall Barer, Dean Fuller
music: Mary Rodgers
lyrics: Marshall Barer
staging: George Abbott
sets: William and Jean Eckart
costumes: William and Jean Eckart
choreography: Joe Layton
Productions:
Opened May 11, 1959 for 460 performances
(Off-Broadway) Season of 1966-67 for 14 performances
Reviews:
America 101:397-8, May 30, 1959
Nation 188:484, May 23, 1959
New York Theatre Critics' Reviews 1959:309+
New York Times page 40, May 12, 1959
                II, page 1, May 17, 1959
                II, page 3, May 8, 1960
                page 14, Jul 1, 1960
                page 43, Sep 21, 1960
                page 55, Oct 11, 1960
New Yorker 35:80-1, May 23, 1959
Newsweek 53:78, May 25, 1959
Saturday Review 42:26, May 30, 1959
Theatre Crafts 20:30-1+, May 1986
Time 73:50, May 25, 1959

One for the Money
book: Nancy Hamilton
music: Morgan Lewis
lyrics: Nancy Hamilton
staging: John Murray Anderson
sets: Raoul Pene du Bois
choreography: Robert Alton
Productions:
Opened February 4, 1939 for 132 performances
Reviews:
Catholic World 148:730, Mar 1939
New York Times page 9, Feb 6, 1939
Stage 16:11-12, Feb 1939

110 in the Shade
    book: N. Richard Nash, based on his play The Rain-
                         maker
    music: Harvey Schmidt
    lyrics: Tom Jones
    staging: Joseph Anthony
    sets: Oliver Smith
    costumes: Motley
    choreography: Agnes de Mille
Productions:
    Opened October 24, 1963 for 330 performances
    (Off-Off-Broadway) Opened May 19, 1982
Reviews:
    America 109: 644, Nov 16, 1963
    New York Theatre Critics' Reviews 1963: 218+
    New York Times page 33, Sep 12, 1963
                   page 37, Oct 25, 1963
                   III, page 10, Jun 8, 1982
    New Yorker 39: 93, Nov 2, 1963
    Newsweek 62: 63, Nov 4, 1963
    Saturday Review 46: 32, Nov 9, 1963
    Theatre Arts 48: 68, Jan 1964
    Time 82: 74, Nov 1, 1963

One Kiss
    book: Clare Kummer; from the French Ta Bouche by
                         Y. Mirande and A. Willemetz
    music: Maurice Yvain
Productions:
    Opened November 27, 1923 for 95 performances
Reviews:
    New York Times page 14, Nov 28, 1923

One Mo' Time
    conceived: Vernel Bagneris
    staging: Vernel Bagneris
    sets: Elwin Charles Terrel II
    costumes: Joann Clevenger
Productions:
    (Off-Broadway) Opened October 22, 1979 for 1,372 performances
Reviews:
    Down Beat 47: 53, Oct 1980
    Ebony 38: 69-72, Nov 1982
    Encore 8: 44, Dec 3, 1979
    Essence 11: 15-16+, Mar 1981
    New York 13: 42, Aug 4, 1980
    New York Theatre Critics' Reviews 1979: 101
    New York Times III, page 20, Oct 24, 1979
    Southern Living 18: 80, May 1983
    Time 114: 76, Nov 5, 1979

One Touch of Venus
        book: S. J. Perelman and Ogden Nash, suggested by
                            "The Tinted Venus" by F. Anstey (Thomas Anstey
                            Guthrie)
        music: Kurt Weill
        lyrics: Ogden Nash
        staging: Elia Kazan
        sets: Howard Bay
        costumes: Paul Du Pont, Kermit Love, Mainbocher
        choreography: Agnes de Mille
Productions:
    Opened October 7, 1943 for 567 performances
Reviews:
    Catholic World 158:185-7, Nov 1943
    Commonweal 39:14-15, Oct 22, 1943
    Life 15:61-4, Oct 25, 1943
    Nation 157:479, Oct 23, 1943
    New York Theatre Critics' Reviews 1943:264+
    New York Times page 14, Oct 8, 1943
                    II, page 1, Oct 17, 1943
                    II, page 1, Feb 20, 1944
    New Yorker 19:41, Oct 16, 1943
    Newsweek 22:86+, Oct 18, 1943
    Theatre Arts 27:703-7, Dec 1943
    Time 42:50, Oct 18, 1943
    Vogue 102:60-1, Nov 1, 1943

Only Fools Are Sad
        book: Dan Almagor; based on old Hassidic stories and
                            parables
        music: Derived from Hassidic songs
        lyrics: Translated by Robert Friend
        staging: Yossi Yzraely
        sets: Dani Karavan and Herbert Senn
        costumes: Helen Pond
Productions:
    Opened November 22, 1971 for 144 performances
Reviews:
    New York Theatre Critics' Reviews 1971:176
    New York Times page 59, Nov 11, 1971
                    page 53, Nov 23, 1971

The Only Girl
        book: Henry Blossom; adapted from Our Wives by
                            Frank Mandel
        music: Victor Herbert
        staging: Fred G. Latham
Productions:
    Opened November 2, 1914 for 240 performances
    Opened May 21, 1934 for 16 performances
Reviews:
    Dramatic Mirror 72:8, Nov 11, 1914

                    73:1, Feb 24, 1915
Dramatist 7:622-3, Oct 1915
Leslie's Weekly 120:107, Feb 4, 1915
Munsey 53:811, Jan 1915
        55:104, Jun 1915
Musical Courier 106:10, May 27, 1933
New York Dramatic News 60:19, Nov 7, 1914
New York Times page 11, Oct 2, 1914
                page 11, Nov 3, 1914
                VII, page 8, Nov 15, 1914
                page 28, May 22, 1934
Theatre Magazine 20:263+, Dec 1914
                20:303, Dec 1914

Onward Victoria
    book: Charlotte Anker and Irene Rosenberg
    music: Keith Herrmann
    lyrics: Charlotte Anker and Irene Rosenberg
    staging: Julianne Boyd
    sets: William Ritman
    costumes: Theoni V. Aldredge
    choreography: Michael Shawn
Productions:
Opened December 14, 1980 for one performance
Reviews:
New York Theatre Critics' Reviews 1980:71
New York Times III, page 15, Dec 15, 1980
New Yorker 56:55, Dec 22, 1980

The Opera Ball
    book: Sydney Rosenfeld and Clare Kummer; adapted
                   from the German of Victor Leon and H. Von
                   Waldberg
    music: Richard Heuberger
Productions:
Opened Febraury 12, 1912 for 32 performances
Reviews:
Dramatic Mirror 67:6-7, Feb 14, 1912
                67:8, Feb 21, 1912
Green Book 7:459-61+, Mar 1912
Hampton 28:203, Apr 1912
Theatre Magazine 15:xi, Mar 1912

The Opposite Side of Sonny
    book: Peter Copani
    music: John Roman and Peter Copani
    lyrics: Peter Copani
Productions:
(Off-Off-Broadway) Season of 1973-74
No Reviews.

The Optimists
    sketches: Clifford Grey, Greatrex Newman and Austin
                    Melford
    lyrics: Clifford Grey, Greatrex Newman and Austin
                    Melford
    staging: Melville Gideon
Productions:
    Opened January 30, 1928 for 24 performances
Reviews:
    Life 91:23, Mar 1, 1928
    New York Times page 28, Jan 31, 1928

Options
    book: Walter Willison
    music: Jeffrey Silverman
    lyrics: Walter Willison
    staging: Michael Shawn
    sets: Ron Placzek
    costumes: Dona Granata
Productions:
    (Off-Broadway) Opened July 11, 1985 for 2 performances
Reviews:
    New York Times III, page 18, Jul 11, 1985

Orange Blossoms
    book: Fred deGresac, based on Fred deGresac and
                    Francis deCroisset's play The Marriage of Kitty
    music: Victor Herbert
    lyrics: B. G. DeSylva
    staging: Edward Royce
Productions:
    Opened September 19, 1922 for 95 performances
Reviews:
    New York Clipper 70:20, Oct 25, 1922
    New York Times page 18, Sep 20, 1922

Orchids Preferred
    book: Fred Herendeen
    music: Dave Stamper
    lyrics: Fred Herendeen
    staging: Alexander Leftwich
    sets: Frederick Fox
    choreography: Robert Sanford
Productions:
    Opened May 11, 1937 for 7 performances
Reviews:
    New York Times page 26, May 12, 1937
                     page 16, Aug 29, 1937

Orwell That Ends Well
    words: The Original Chicago Second City Company

music: Fred Kaz
staging: Bernard Sahlins
Productions:
 (Off-Broadway) Opened March 4, 1984 for 110 performances
Reviews:
 New Leader 67:22, Apr 2, 1984
 New York Times III, page 3, Mar 2, 1984
       II, page 5, Mar 11, 1984

Oscar Brown, Jr. (see Worlds of Oscar Brown, Jr.)

Our Miss Gibbs
 book: James T. Tanner
 music: Ivan Caryll and Lionel Monckton
 staging: Thomas Reynolds
Productions:
 Opened August 29, 1910 for 64 performances
Reviews:
 Cosmopolitan 47:628-32, Oct 1909
      50:70, Dec 1910
 Dramatic Mirror 64:6, Sep 10, 1910
 Hampton 25:674+, Nov 1910
 Leslie's Weekly 111:317, Sep 22, 1910
 Munsey 41:907, Sep 1909
 Theatre Magazine 12:101-2, Oct 1910
      12:126, Oct 1910

Our Nell
 book: A. E. Thomas and Brian Hooker
 music: George Gershwin and William Daly
 lyrics: Brian Hooker
 staging: W. H. Gilmore, Edgar MacGregor, Julian Mason
Productions:
 Opened December 4, 1922 for 40 performances
Reviews:
 New York Clipper 70:20, Dec 13, 1922
 New York Times page 24, Dec 5, 1922

Out of this World
 book: Dwight Taylor and Reginald Lawrence
 music: Cole Porter
 lyrics: Cole Porter
 staging: Agnes de Mille
 sets: Lemuel Ayers
 costumes: Lemuel Ayers
 choreography: Hanya Holm
Productions:
 Opened December 21, 1950 for 157 performances
 (Off-Broadway) Season of 1955-56
 (Off-Broadway) Opened November 30, 1962 for 9 performances
 (Off-Off-Broadway) Opened March 8, 1973

Reviews:
Catholic World 173:69, Apr 1951
Christian Science Monitor Magazine page 9, Dec 30, 1950
Commonweal 53:349, Jan 12, 1951
New York Theatre Critics' Reviews 1950:166+
New York Times VI, page 62, Dec 10, 1950
                II, page 3, Dec 17, 1950
                page 17, Dec 22, 1950
                II, page 8, Jan 14, 1951
                page 35, Oct 13, 1955
                page 44, Nov 10, 1955
                page 39, Mar 12, 1973
New Yorker 26:44, Dec 30, 1950
            49:94, Mar 17, 1973
Newsweek 37:35, Jan 1, 1951
Theatre Arts 35:19, Feb 1951
Time 57:42, Jan 1, 1951

Over Here!
    book: Will Holt
    music: Richard M. Sherman and Robert B. Sherman
    lyrics: Richard M. Sherman and Robert B. Sherman
    staging: Tom Moore
    sets: Douglas W. Schmidt
    costumes: Carrie F. Robbins
    choreography: Patricia Birch
Productions:
    Opened March 6, 1974 for 348 performances
Reviews:
    America 130:262, Apr 6, 1974
    Nation 218:410, Mar 20, 1974
    New York 7:80, Mar 25, 1974
    New York Theatre Critics' Reviews 1974:347
    New York Times page 51, Mar 7, 1974
                II, page 5, Mar 17, 1974
    New Yorker 50:107, Mar 11, 1974
    Newsweek 83:83, Mar 13, 1974
    Playboy 21:239, Jan 1974
            21:40, Mar 1974
            21:48, Jun 1974
    Time 103:66, Mar 18, 1974

Over the River
    book: George V. Hobart and H. A. DuSouchet; based
                       on The Man from Mexico
    music: John Golden
Productions:
    Opened January 8, 1912 for 120 performances
Reviews:
    Blue Book 15:18-21, May 1912
    Dramatic Mirror 67:6, Jan 10, 1912

          67:4, Jan 24, 1912
          67:4, Feb 14, 1912
Green Book 7:455-8+, Mar 1912
          7:566-7, Mar 1912
          8:1020-21, Dec 1912
Hampton 28:117, Mar 1912
Harper's Weekly 56:19, Feb 3, 1912
Munsey 47:128, Apr 1912
Theatre Magazine 15:xii, Feb 1912
          15:40, Feb 1912
          15:136, Apr 1912

Over the Top
    book: Philip Bartholomae and Sigmund Romberg
    music: Sigmund Romberg and Herman Timberg
    staging: J. C. Huffman
Productions:
    Opened November 28, 1917 for 78 performances
Reviews:
    Dramatic Mirror 77:7, Dec 8, 1917
    New York Times page 11, Dec 3, 1917
    Theatre Magazine 27:89, Feb 1918

Oy Is Dus a Leben!
    book: Jacob Kalich
    music: Joseph Rumshinsky
    lyrics: Molly Picon
    staging: Jacob Kalich
    sets: Harry Gordon Bennett
    choreography: David Lubritzky and Lillian Shapero
Productions:
    Opened October 12, 1942 for 139 performances
Reviews:
    New York Times page 19, Oct 13, 1942

                          -P-

Pacific Overtures
    book: John Weidman
    music: Stephen Sondheim
    lyrics: Stephen Sondheim
    additional
      material: Hugh Wheeler
    staging: Harold Prince
    sets: Boris Aronson
    costumes: Florence Klotz
    choreography: Patricia Birch
Productions:
    Opened January 11, 1976 for 193 performances
    (Off-Broadway) Opened October 25, 1984 for 109 performances

Reviews:

America 134:128, Feb 14, 1976
Commonweal 112:85, Feb 8, 1985
Dance Magazine 59:74, Jan 1985
Essence 7:42, May 1976
Los Angeles 21:202+, Oct 1976
Nation 222:124, Jan 31, 1976
New Republic 174:20, Feb 7, 1976
192:27-9, Jan 7-14, 1985
New York 9:54, Jan 26, 1976
17:79-80, Nov 5, 1984
New York Theatre Critics' Reviews 1976:388
1984:157
New York Times page 39, Jan 12, 1976
II, page 1, Jan 18, 1976
III, page 19, Apr 4, 1984
III, page 3, Oct 26, 1984
II, page 5, Nov 11, 1984
New Yorker 51:44, Jan 19, 1976
60:155-6, Nov 5, 1984
Newsweek 87:59, Jan 26, 1976
Opera News 40:45-6, Feb 28, 1976
Saturday Review 3:43-4, Apr 3, 1976
Time 107:46-8, Jan 26, 1976
Theatre Crafts 19:24-5+, May 1985
Vogue 174:86, Dec 1984

Pacific Paradise
staging: Jack Regas
Productions:
Opened October 16, 1972 for 7 performances
No Reviews.

Padlocks of 1927
sketches: Paul Gerard Smith and Ballard Macdonald
music: Lee David, Jesse Greer and Henry H. Tobias
lyrics: Billy Rose
staging: W. J. Wilson
Productions:
Opened July 5, 1927 for 95 performances
Reviews:
New York Times page 23, Jul 6, 1927
page 33, Sep 23, 1927

Paint Your Wagon
book: Alan Jay Lerner
music: Frederick Loewe
lyrics: Alan Jay Lerner
staging: Daniel Mann
sets: Oliver Smith
costumes: Motley
choreography: Agnes de Mille

Productions:
    Opened November 12, 1951 for 289 performances
    (Off-Broadway) Opened February 24, 1962 for 9 performances
Reviews:
    Catholic World 174:308, Jan 1952
    Commonweal 55:199, Nov 30, 1951
    Nation 173:484-5, Dec 1, 1951
    New Republic 126:22, Jan 7, 1952
    New York Theatre Critics' Reviews 1951:172+
    New York Times II, page 1, Nov 11, 1951
                    page 32, Nov 13, 1951
                    II, page 1, Nov 18, 1951
                    XXIII, page 6, Dec 24, 1978
    New Yorker 27:67, Nov 24, 1951
    Newsweek 38:84, Nov 26, 1951
    Saturday Review 35:27, Jul 5, 1952
    School and Society 75:246, Apr 19, 1952
    Theatre Arts 36:72, Feb 1952
                  36:33-5, Dec 1952
    Time 58:87, Nov 26, 1951

The Pajama Game
    book: George Abbott and Richard Bissell, based on
                    Bissell's novel 7-1/2 Cents
    music: Richard Adler and Jerry Ross
    lyrics: Richard Adler and Jerry Ross
    staging: George Abbott and Jerome Robbins
    sets: Lemuel Ayers
    costumes: Lemuel Ayers
    choreography: Bob Fosse
Productions:
    Opened May 13, 1954 for 1,063 performances
    Opened May 15, 1957 for 23 performances
    Opened December 9, 1973 for 65 performances
    (Off-Off-Broadway) Opened October 30, 1986
Reviews:
    America 91:306, Jun 12, 1954
    Business Week page 76+, Jun 5, 1954
    Catholic World 179:307-8, Jul 1954
    Life 36:125-6+, Jun 7, 1954
    Nation 178:470, May 29, 1954
    New York 6:72, Dec 24, 1973
               22:66, Mar 27, 1989
    New York Theatre Critics' Reviews 1954:324+
                                       1973:152
    New York Times page 20, May 14, 1954
                    II, page 1, May 30, 1954
                    page 87, Jan 30, 1955
                    II, page 3, May 8, 1955
                    page 27, May 16, 1957
                    II, page 1, May 26, 1957

page 61, Oct 23, 1973
page 58, Dec 10, 1973
II, page 3, Dec 16, 1973
III, page 28, Nov 5, 1986
New Yorker 30:68+, May 22, 1954
49:56, Dec 24, 1973
65:87, Mar 20, 1989
Newsweek 43:64, May 24, 1954
Saturday Review 37:24-5, Jun 12, 1954
39:12, Sep 15, 1956
Theatre Arts 38:18-19, Jul 1954
38:14, Sep 1954
41:17, Jul 1957
Time 63:66, May 24, 1954

Pal Joey
book: John O'Hara
music: Richard Rodgers
lyrics: Lorenz Hart
staging: George Abbott
sets: Jo Mielziner
costumes: John Koenig
choreography: Robert Alton
Productions:
Opened December 25, 1940 for 374 performances
Opened October 21, 1941 for 104 performances
Opened January 3, 1952 for 540 performances
Opened May 31, 1961 for 31 performances
Opened May 29, 1963 for 15 performances
Opened June 27, 1976 for 73 performances
(Off-Off-Broadway) Opened May 10, 1984
Reviews:
Catholic World 152:598, Feb 1941
174:391, Feb 1952
Commonweal 55:398-9, Jan 25, 1952
74:379-80, Jul 7, 1961
Dance Magazine 35:21, Jul 1961
Life 10:44, Feb 17, 1941
32:67-8+, Jan 21, 1952
Nation 152:81, Jan 18, 1941
New Republic 126:23, Jan 21, 1952
New York 9:64+, Jul 12, 1976
New York Theatre Critics' Reviews 1940:172+
1941:442+
1952:398+
1976:213
New York Times page 22, Dec 26, 1940
IX, page 8, Jun 8, 1941
page 20, Sep 2, 1941
page 17, Mar 7, 1949
II, page 1, Dec 30, 1951

               page 17, Jan 4, 1952
               II, page 1, Jan 13, 1952
               II, page 13, Feb 17, 1952
               page 23, Jun 17, 1952
               II, page 3, Nov 23, 1952
               page 40, Apr 1, 1954
               II, page 2, Apr 11, 1954
               page 32, Jun 1, 1961
               page 21, May 30, 1963
               page 22, Jun 28, 1976
               XXII, page 14, Jun 19, 1977
               III, page 12, May 14, 1984
New Yorker 27:38, Jan 12, 1952
          52:83, Jul 12, 1976
Newsweek 17:42, Jan 6, 1941
        39:73, Jan 14, 1952
Saturday Review 35:28-9, Feb 2, 1952
School and Society 76:404, Dec 20, 1952
Stage 1:17, Dec 1940
      1:22-3, Feb 1941
Theatre Arts 25:95, Feb 1941
Time 37:41, Jan 6, 1941
    59:62, Jan 14, 1952
    108:68, Jul 12, 1976

Panama Hattie
    book: Herbert Fields and B. G. DeSylva
    music: Cole Porter
    lyrics: Cole Porter
    staging: Edgar MacGregor
    sets: Raoul Pene du Bois
    costumes: Raoul Pene du Bois
    choreography: Robert Alton
Productions:
    Opened October 30, 1940 for 501 performances
    (Off-Off-Broadway) Opened January 15, 1976
Reviews:
    Catholic World 152:335, Dec 1940
    Commonweal 33:103, Nov 15, 1940
    Life 9:67-8, Oct 28, 1940
    Nation 151:513, Nov 23, 1940
    New York Theatre Critics' Reviews 1940:233+
                           1941:460+
    New York Times page 28, Oct 4, 1940
                    page 28, Oct 31, 1940
                    IX, page 1, Nov 10, 1940
                    II, page 5, Dec 5, 1943
                    page 16, Jan 21, 1976
    Newsweek 16:60, Nov 11, 1940
    Stage 1:40-41, Nov 1940
    Theatre Arts 25:12-13, Jan 1941
    Time 36:65, Oct 28, 1940

Pansy
    book: Alex Belledna
    music: Maceo Pinkard
Productions:
    Opened May 14, 1929 for 3 performances
Reviews:
    Life (New York) 93:28, Jun 7, 1929
    New York Times page 36, May 15, 1929
                  page 24, May 17, 1929
                  III, page 4, May 19, 1929
    Theatre Magazine 50:42, Jul 1929

Papa's Darling
    book: Harry B. Smith; based on Grenet d'Ancourt and
                  Maurice Vaucaire's Le Fils Surnaturel
    music: Ivan Caryll
    lyrics: Harry B. Smith
    staging: Julian Mitchell
Productions:
    Opened November 2, 1914 for 40 performances
Reviews:
    Dramatic Mirror 72:8, Nov 11, 1914
                  72:2, Nov 18, 1914
    Green Book 13:377-8, Feb 1915
    New York Dramatic News 60:19-20, Nov 7, 1914
    New York Times I, page 7, Nov 4, 1914
    Theatre Magazine 20:314, Dec 1914

Parade
    sketches: Paul Peters, George Sklar, Frank Gabrielson,
                  David Lesan, Kyle Crichton
    music: Jerome Moross
    staging: Philip Loeb
    sets: Lee Simonson
    choreography: Robert Alton
Productions:
    Opened May 20, 1935 for 40 performances
Reviews:
    Commonweal 22:160, Jun 7, 1935
    Nation 140:666+, Jun 5, 1935
    New Republic 83:106, Jun 5, 1935
    New York Times page 26, May 7, 1935
                  X, page 2, May 12, 1935
                  page 22, May 21, 1935
                  XI, page 22, May 26, 1935
    Newsweek 5:24-5, Jun 1, 1935
    Time 25:26+, Jun 3, 1935

Paradise!
    book: George C. Wolfe
    music: Robert Forrest

lyrics:	George C. Wolfe
staging:	Theodore Pappas
sets:	James Noone
costumes:	David C. Woolard
choreography:	Theodore Pappas

Productions:
   (Off-Broadway) Opened September 28, 1985 for 14 performances
Reviews:
   New York Times III, page 24, Sep 27, 1985

Paradise Alley

book:	Charles W. Bell and Edward Clark
music:	Carl Carlton, Harry Archer and A. Otvos
lyrics:	Howard Johnson

Productions:
   Opened March 31, 1924 for 64 performances
Reviews:
   New York Times VIII, page 2, Mar 16, 1924
               page 17, Apr 2, 1924
   Theatre Magazine 39:68, Jun 1924

Paradise Island

book:	Carmen Lombardo and John Jacob Loeb
music:	Carmen Lombardo and John Jacob Loeb
lyrics:	Carmen Lombardo and John Jacob Loeb
staging:	Francis Swann
sets:	George Jenkins
choreography:	June Taylor

Productions:
   (Off-Broadway) Opened June 22, 1961 for 75 performances
   (Off-Broadway) Opened June 27, 1962 for 68 performances
Reviews:
   America 105:532, Jul 15, 1961
   New York Times page 11, Jun 24, 1961
               page 22, Jun 28, 1962

Pardon My English

book:	Herbert Fields
music:	George Gershwin
lyrics:	Ira Gershwin
staging:	George Hale
sets:	John Wenger

Productions:
   Opened January 20, 1933 for 46 performances
Reviews:
   New Outlook 161:48, Mar 1933
   New York Times IX, page 5, Dec 11, 1932
               page 11, Jan 21, 1933

Pardon Our French

sketches:	Ole Olsen and Chic Johnson

music:	Victor Young
lyrics:	Edward Heyman
sets:	Albert Johnson
costumes:	Jack Mosser

Productions:
  Opened October 5, 1950 for 100 performances
Reviews:
  Catholic World 172:228, Dec 1950
  Commonweal 53:62, Oct 27, 1950
  New York Theatre Critics' Reviews 1950:254+
  New York Times page 22, Oct 6, 1950
  New Yorker 26:52+, Oct 14, 1950
  Newsweek 36:86, Oct 16, 1950
  Theatre Arts 34:12, Dec 1950
  Time 56:54, Oct 16, 1950

Paris

book:	Martin Brown
music:	Cole Porter; additional words and music by Ray Goetz and Walter Kollo
lyrics:	Cole Porter; additional words and music by Ray Goetz and Walter Kollo
staging:	W. H. Gilmore

Productions:
  Opened October 8, 1928 for 195 performances
Reviews:
  Life (New York) 92:17, Oct 28, 1928
  New York Times VIII, page 4, Apr 8, 1928
                page 34, Oct 9, 1928
  Outlook 150:1124, Nov 7, 1928
  Theatre Magazine 48:81, Dec 1928

Paris Lights: The All-Star Literary Genius Expatriate Revue

conceived:	William Russo, developed by Michael Zettler and George Ferencz
book:	Michael Zettler
music:	William Russo
lyrics:	writings of American poets in 1920s Paris
spoken words:	writings of Americans in 1920s Paris
staging:	George Ferencz
sets:	Bill Stabile
costumes:	Kathleen Smith and Sally Lesser
choreography:	George Ferencz

Productions:
  (Off-Broadway) Opened January 11, 1980 for 23 performances
Reviews:
  New York 13:58, Feb 4, 1980
  New York Times III, page 3, Jan 25, 1980
  New Yorker 55:96, Feb 4, 1980

Parisiana

book:	Vincent Valentini

staging: Vincent Valentini
Productions:
   Opened February 9, 1928 for 28 performances
Reviews:
   New York Times page 26, Feb 10, 1928
   Theatre Magazine 17:159, May 1913

Park

book:	Paul Cherry
music:	Lance Mulcahy
lyrics:	Paul Cherry
staging:	John Stix
sets:	Peter Harvey
costumes:	Peter Harvey
choreography:	Lee Theodore

Productions:
   Opened April 22, 1970 for 5 performances
Reviews:
   New York Theatre Critics' Reviews 1970:270
   New York Times page 47, Apr 23, 1970

Park Avenue

book:	Nunnally Johnson and George S. Kaufman, based on the story "Holy Matrimony"
music:	Arthur Schwartz
lyrics:	Ira Gershwin
staging:	George S. Kaufman
sets:	Donald Oenslager
choreography:	Helen Tamiris

Productions:
   Opened November 4, 1946 for 72 performances
Reviews:
   Catholic World 164:361, Jan 1946
   Nation 163:629, Nov 30, 1946
   New York Theatre Critics' Reviews 1946:275+
   New York Times VI, page 26, Sep 22, 1946
                  page 31, Nov 5, 1946
                  II, page 3, Dec 15, 1946
   New Yorker 22:59, Nov 16, 1946
   Newsweek 28:98, Nov 18, 1946
   Time 48:64+, Nov 18, 1946
   Vogue 108:196, Nov 15, 1946

A Party with Betty Comden and Adolph Green

music and lyrics:	Betty Comden, Adolph Green, Andre Previn, Leonard Bernstein, Morton Gould, Roger Edens, Jule Styne and Saul Chaplin
sets:	Marvin Reiss

Productions:
   (Off-Broadway) Opened Season of 1958-59

Opened December 23, 1958 for 38 performances
Opened April 16, 1959 for 44 performances
Revised version opened on Broadway February 10, 1977 for 92
performances
Reviews:
   Nation 188:77, Jan 24, 1959
        224:573-4, May 7, 1977
   New York Theatre Critics' Reviews 1958:159
                          1977:374
   New York Times page 2, Dec 24, 1958
               page 30, May 18, 1959
               page 22, Feb 28, 1977
   New Yorker 34:70, Jan 10, 1959
        53:77, Feb 21, 1977
   Newsweek 53:61, Jan 5, 1959
        89:57, Feb 21, 1977
   Saturday Review 42:67, Jan 10, 1959
   Theatre Arts 43:67-8, Mar 1959
   Time 73:56, Jan 5, 1959
      109:57, Feb 21, 1977

The Passing Show of 1913
   dialogue: Harold Atteridge
   music: Jean Schwartz and Al W. Brown
   special music: Melville Ellis
   lyrics: Harold Atteridge
   staging: Ned Wayburn
Productions:
   Opened July 24, 1913 for 116 performances
Reviews:
   Dramatic Mirror 70:7, Aug 6, 1913
   Munsey 50:90, Oct 1913
   New York Times page 7, Jul 25, 1913
   Theatre Magazine 18:83, Sep 1913
                  18:89, Sep 1913

The Passing Show of 1914
   dialogue: Harold Atteridge
   music: Harry Carroll and Sigmund Romberg
   special music: Melville Ellis
   lyrics: Harold Atteridge
   staging: J. C. Huffman
   costumes: Melville Ellis
   choreography: Jack Mason
Productions:
   Opened June 10, 1914 for 133 performances
Reviews:
   Dramatic Mirror 71:8, Jun 17, 1914
   Munsey 53:92-4, Oct 1914
   New York Times page 11, Jun 11, 1914
   Theatre Magazine 20:37, Jul 1914
                  20:230, Nov 1914

The Passing Show of 1915
    dialogue: Harold Atteridge
    music: Leo Edwards, William F. Peters and J. Leubrie
                       Hill
    lyrics: Harold Atteridge
    staging: J. C. Huffman
    choreography: Jack Mason and Theodor Kosloff
Productions:
    Opened May 29, 1915 for 145 performances
Reviews:
    Dramatic Mirror 73:8, Jun 2, 1915
                    73:2, Jun 30, 1915
                    74:4, Jul 7, 1915
    Green Book 14:221-3, Aug 1915
    Harper's Bazaar 50:49, Jul 1915
    Smart Set 46:146-8, Aug 1915
    Theatre Magazine 22:27, Jun 1915
                     22:39, Jun 1915
                     22:57, Aug 1915

The Passing Show of 1916
    book: Harold Atteridge
    music: Sigmund Romberg, Otto Motzan and George
                       Gershwin
    staging: J. J. Shubert, J. C. Huffman
    choreography: Allen K. Foster
Productions:
    Opened June 22, 1916 for 140 performances
Reviews:
    Dramatic Mirror 76:8, Jul 1, 1916
                    76:4, Jul 8, 1916
                    76:2, Jul 15, 1916
                    76:4, Jul 22, 1916
    Green Book 16:422-3, Sep 1916
    New York Times page 9, Jun 23, 1916
    Theatre Magazine 24:63, Aug 1915
                     24:94, Aug 1915

The Passing Show of 1917
    dialogue: Harold Atteridge
    music: Sigmund Romberg and Otto Motzan
    lyrics: Harold Atteridge
    staging: J. C. Huffman
    choreography: Allen K. Foster
Productions:
    Opened April 26, 1917 for 196 performances
Reviews:
    Dramatic Mirror 77:7, May 5, 1917
                    77:4, May 12, 1917
    Green Book 18:16+, Jul 1917
    Life (New York) 69:816, May 10, 1917

New York Times page 9, Apr 27, 1917
Theatre Magazine 25:344+, Jun 1917

The Passing Show of 1918

dialogue: Harold Atteridge
music: Sigmund Romberg and Jean Schwartz
lyrics: Harold Atteridge
staging: J. C. Huffman and J. J. Shubert
sets: Watson Barratt
choreography: Jack Mason

Productions:
Opened July 25, 1918 for 124 performances

Reviews:
Dramatic Mirror 79:193, Aug 10, 1918
                79:683, Nov 9, 1918
Forum 60:365, Sep 1918
Green Book 20:582-6, Oct 1918
New York Times page 9, Jul 26, 1918
Theatre Magazine 28:144+, Sep 1918

The Passing Show of 1919

conceived: Lee Shubert and J. J. Shubert
book: Harold Atteridge
songs: Jean Schwartz
staging: J. J. Shubert
sets: Watson Barratt
costumes: Cora McGeachey and Homer Conant

Productions:
Opened October 23, 1919 for 280 performances

Reviews:
New York Times page 11, Oct 24, 1919

The Passing Show of 1921

book: Harold Atteridge
music: Jean Schwartz
staging: J. C. Huffman and J. J. Shubert
sets: William Weaver
choreography: Max Scheck

Productions:
Opened December 29, 1920 for 200 performances

Reviews:
Nation 112:126, Jan 26, 1921
New York Clipper 68:30, Jan 5, 1921
New York Times page 16, Dec 30, 1920
Theatre Magazine 33:165, Mar 1921
                33:177-8, Mar 1921

The Passing Show of 1923

book: Harold Atteridge
music: Jean Schwartz and Sigmund Romberg
lyrics: Harold Atteridge
staging: J. C. Huffman

Productions:
    Opened June 14, 1923 for 118 performances
Reviews:
    Life (New York) 82:20, Jul 5, 1923
    New York Clipper 71:30, Jun 20, 1923
    New York Times page 24, Jun 15, 1923
    Theatre Magazine 38:15, Aug 1923

The Passing Show of 1924
    book: Harold Atteridge
    music: Sigmund Romberg and Jean Schwartz
    lyrics: Harold Atteridge and Alex Gerber
    staging: J. C. Huffman
Productions:
    Opened September 3, 1924 for 106 performances
Reviews:
    New York Times page 13, Sep 4, 1924
    Theatre Magazine 40:16, Nov 1924

Peace
    book: Tim Reynolds; based on the play by Aristophanes
    music: Al Carmines
    lyrics: Tim Reynolds
    staging: Lawrence Kornfield
    costumes: Nancy Christofferson
    choreography: Arlene Rothlein
Productions:
    (Off-Broadway) Opened January 27, 1969 for 192 performances
Reviews:
    Dance Magazine 43:23+, Apr 1969
    New York Theatre Critics' Reviews 1969:276
    New York Times page 49, Jan 28, 1969
                   II, page 10, Feb 16, 1969
                   II, page 1, Feb 23, 1969
                   page 22, Jul 11, 1969
    New Yorker 44:98-100, Feb 8, 1969

The Pearl Maiden
    libretto: Earl C. Anthony
    music: Harry Auracher
    staging: Al Holbrook
Productions:
    Opened January 22, 1912 for 24 performances
Reviews:
    Dramatic Mirror 67:7, Jan 24, 1912
    Green Book 7:1205, Jun 1912
    Theatre Magazine 15:xv, Mar 1912

The Pearl Necklace
    book: Israel Bercovici; based on Jewish folk tales
    staging: Franz Auerbach

Productions:
  (Off-Broadway) Opened September 21, 1972 for 8 performances
Reviews:
  New York Times page 35, Sep 22, 1972

The Peasant Girl
  book: Leo Stein; adapted by Edgar Smith
  music: Oskar Nedbal; additional numbers by Rudolph
                  Friml
  lyrics: Herbert Reynolds and Harold Atteridge
  staging: J. H. Benrimo
Productions:
  Opened March 2, 1915 for 111 performances
Reviews:
  Dramatic Mirror 73:8, Mar 10, 1915
                  73:2, Mar 31, 1915
  Green Book 13:826, May 1915
             13:1144-5, Jun 1915
  Munsey 54:731, May 1915
  New York Dramatic News 60:17, Mar 13, 1915
  New York Times page 11, Mar 3, 1915
  Theatre Magazine 21:171, Apr 1915
                   21:192, Apr 1915
                   22:78, Aug 1915

Peg
  story: Peggy Lee (her musical biography)
  music: Paul Horner and various composers
  lyrics: Peggy Lee and various authors
  staging: Robert Drivas
  sets: Tom H. John
  costumes: Florenze Klotz
Productions:
  Opened December 14, 1983 for 5 performances
Reviews:
  New York 17:104+, Dec 26, 1983-Jan 2, 1984
  New York Theatre Critics' Reviews 1983:57
  New York Times III, page 17, Dec 15, 1983

Peg-o'-My-Dreams
  book: J. Hartley Manners
  music: Hugo Felix
  lyrics: Anne Caldwell
Productions:
  Opened May 5, 1924 for 32 performances
Reviews:
  Life (New York) 83:18, May 29, 1924
  New York Times page 25, May 6, 1924
                  VIII, page 1, May 18, 1924

Peggy
  book: George Grossmith, Jr.

music: Leslie Stuart
lyrics: C. H. Bovill
staging: Ned Wayburn
Productions:
   Opened December 7, 1911 for 36 performances
Reviews:
   Blue Book 14:900-903, Mar 1912
   Dramatic Mirror 66:7, Dec 13, 1911
   New York Times page 8, Dec 8, 1911
   Theatre Magazine 15:xi, Jan 1912

Peggy-Ann
   book: Herbert Fields
   music: Richard Rodgers
   lyrics: Lorenz Hart
   staging: Robert Milton
Productions:
   Opened December 27, 1926 for 333 performances
Reviews:
   New York Times page 16, Dec 28, 1926
                    VII, page 2, Mar 27, 1927
                    VII, page 1, Jul 3, 1927
                    VIII, page 4, Jan 29, 1928

The Penny Friend
   book: William Roy; based on J. M. Barrie's A Kiss for
                     Cinderella
   music: William Roy
   lyrics: William Roy
   staging: Benno D. Frank
   sets: Ben Shecter
   choreography: Lou Kristofer
Productions:
   (Off-Broadway) Opened December 26, 1966 for 32 performances
Reviews:
   New York Times page 46, Dec 27, 1966

The Pepper Mill
   sketches: W. H. Auden, Klaus Mann, Erich Muhsam,
                     Ernst Toller, Erica Mann; English adaptation by
                     John Latouche and Edwin Denby
   music: Magnus Henning, Aaron Copland, Peter Krender,
                     Herbert Murril, Werner Kruse
   staging: Therese Giehse
   sets: Anton Refregier
Productions:
   Opened January 5, 1937 for 6 performances
Reviews:
   New York Times page 19, Jan 6, 1937
   Theatre Arts 21:6, Jan 1937

The Perfect Fool
    book: Ed Wynn
    music: Ed Wynn
    lyrics: Ed Wynn
    staging: Ed Wynn
Productions:
Opened November 7, 1921 for (256) performances
Reviews:
Dramatic Mirror 84:593, Oct 22, 1921
Life (New York) 78:18, Dec 15, 1921
New York Clipper 69:20, Nov 16, 1921
New York Times page 28, Nov 8, 1921
              VI, page 1, Nov 27, 1921
Theatre Magazine 35:32, Jan 1922

Perfectly Frank
    book: Kenny Solms
    music: Frank Loesser
    lyrics: Frank Loesser
    staging: Fritz Holt
    sets: John Falabella
    costumes: John Falabella
    choreography: Tony Stevens
Productions:
Opened November 30, 1980 for 17 performances
Reviews:
Los Angeles 25:258, Oct 1980
New York 13:58-9, Dec 15, 1980
New York Theatre Critics' Reviews 1980:74
New York Times III, page 14, Dec 1, 1980
              II, page 3, Dec 7, 1980
Time 116:86, Dec 15, 1980

Personals
    words: David Crane, Seth Friedman and Marta Kauffman
    music: William Dreskin, Joel Phillip Friedman, Seth
                  Friedman, Alan Menken, Stephen Schwartz and
                  Michael Skloff
    lyrics: David Crane, Seth Friedman and Marta Kauffman
    staging: Paul Lazarus
    sets: Loren Sherman
    costumes: Ann Hould-Ward
    choreography: D. J. Giagni
Productions:
(Off-Broadway) Opened November 24, 1985 for 265 performances
Reviews:
New York 18:109-10, Dec 9, 1985
New York Times III, page 16, Nov 25, 1985
New Yorker 61:143-4, Dec 16, 1985

Peter Allen Up in One
    conceived: Peter Allen and Craig Zadan

music: various artists
lyrics: various authors
staging: Craig Zadan
sets: Douglas W. Schmidt
costumes: Charles Suppon
choreography: Betsy Haug
Productions:
Opened May 23, 1979 for 46 performances
Reviews:
New York Times III, page 18, May 24, 1979

Peter Pan, Or The Boy Who Wouldn't Grow Up
    book: Richard Halliday, adapted from James M. Barrie's
                    play
    music: Mark Charlap and Jule Styne
    lyrics: Carolyn Leigh, Betty Comden, Adolph Green
    staging: Jerome Robbins
    sets: Peter Larkin
    costumes: Motley
    choreography: Jerome Robbins
Productions:
Opened October 20, 1954 for 152 performances
Opened September 6, 1979 for 551 performances
Reviews:
    America 92:259, Nov 27, 1954
    Catholic World 180:225, Dec 1954
    Commonweal 61:223, Nov 26, 1954
    Dance Magazine 28:24-5, Dec 1954
    Horizon 22:20-1, Dec 1979
    Life 37:109-10+, Nov 8, 1954
        38:97-100, Apr 4, 1955
    Look 18:54-5, Dec 14, 1954
    Los Angeles 26:411, Dec 1981
    Nation 179:428, Nov 13, 1954
        229:382, Oct 20, 1979
    New Republic 131:23, Nov 1, 1954
    New York 12:92, Sep 24, 1979
    New York Theatre Critics' Reviews 1954:273+
                                      1979:158
    New York Times page 15, Jul 20, 1954
                    II, page 1, Oct 17, 1954
                    page 30, Oct 21, 1954
                    II, page 1, Oct 31, 1954
                    III, page 3, Sep 7, 1979
                    VII, page 3, Jan 13, 1980
    New York Times Magazine page 60, Oct 10, 1954
    New Yorker 30:66+, Oct 30, 1954
        55:124, Sep 17, 1979
    Newsweek 44:60, Nov 1, 1954
        94:111, Sep 17, 1979
    Saturday Review 37:29, Nov 20, 1954

Theatre Arts 38:18-19+, Nov 1954
39:12-13+, Jan 1955
Time 64:80, Nov 1, 1954
114:93, Sep 17, 1979
Vogue 124:124, Dec 1954

The Phantom of the Opera
book: Richard Stilgoe and Andrew Lloyd Webber, adapted from the novel by Gaston Leroux
music: Andrew Lloyd Webber
lyrics: Charles Hart
additional
  lyrics: Richard Stilgoe
staging: Harold Prince
sets: Maria Bjornson
costumes: Maria Bjornson
choreography: Gillian Lynne
Productions:
Opened January 26, 1988 for *563 performances (still running 6/1/89)
Reviews:
Dance Magazine 62:82-3, Apr 1988
Life 11:88-92, Feb 1988
Los Angeles 33:160+, Jul 1988
Maclean's 101:51, Feb 8, 1988
102:11, Feb 6, 1989
102:40-4, Mar 27, 1989
102:62-4, Oct 2, 1989
Nation 246:244, Feb 20, 1988
New Leader 71:21-2, Feb 22, 1988
New Republic 198:33-4+, Mar 14, 1988
New York 21:26-34, Jan 18, 1988
21:89-90, Feb 8, 1988
New York Theatre Critics' Reviews 1988:389
New York Times II, page 1, Jan 24, 1988
III, page 19, Jan 27, 1988
III, page 24, Jan 28, 1988
II, page 5, Jan 31, 1988
II, page 5, Feb 14, 1988
III, page 21, Jun 9, 1988
New Yorker 63:97-8, Feb 8, 1988
Newsweek 109:64, Mar 30, 1987
111:68-70+, Feb 8, 1988
Opera News 52:22+, Jan 16, 1988
52:32, Jun 1988
Rolling Stone page 26, Feb 25, 1988
Theatre Crafts 22:42-9, Jan 1988
22:32-7+, Feb 1988
Time 128:103, Oct 27, 1986
131:54-61, Jan 18, 1988
131:83-4, Feb 8, 1988

USA Today 116:34-9, May 1988
World Press Review 33:58, Jul 1986

Philemon
    book: Tom Jones
    music: Harvey Schmidt
    lyrics: Tom Jones
    staging: Lester Collins
    costumes: Charles Blackburn
Productions:
    (Off-Broadway) Opened April 8, 1975 for 48 performances
Reviews:
    New York 8:96, Apr 28, 1975
    New York Theatre Critics' Reviews 1975:256
    New York Times page 28, Jan 7, 1975
                      II, page 5, May 4, 1975

Phoebe of Quality Street
    adapted: Edward Delaney Dunn; adapted from Sir James
                  M. Barrie's Quality Street
    music: Walter Kollo
    staging: W. H. Gilmore
Productions:
    Opened May 9, 1921 for 16 performances
Reviews:
    New York Times page 20, May 10, 1921

Phoenix '55
    sketches: Ira Wallach
    music: David Baker
    lyrics: David Craig
    staging: Marc Daniels
    sets: Eldon Elder
    costumes: Alvin Colt
    choreography: Boris Runanin
Productions:
    Opened April 23, 1955 for 97 performances
    (Off-Broadway) Season of 1954-55
Reviews:
    America 92:545+, Feb 19, 1955
            93:191, May 14, 1955
    Catholic World 181:67-8, Apr 1955
                181:228, Jun 1955
    Commonweal 61:551, Feb 25, 1955
    Life 38:75-6+, Feb 21, 1955
        38:130, May 23, 1955
    Nation 180:430, May 14, 1955
    New York Theatre Critics' Reviews 1955:317+
    New York Times page 20, Apr 25, 1955
    New Yorker 30:52, Feb 5, 1955
            31:67-9, Apr 30, 1955

Newsweek 45:72, Feb 7, 1955
    46:55, Jul 18, 1955
Saturday Review 38:24, Feb 12, 1955
    39:12-13, Sep 15, 1956
Theatre Arts 39:18-19+, Apr 1955
    39:86+, Jul 1955
Time 65:50, Feb 7, 1955

Piaf ... a Remembrance

conceived:	Milli Janz
book:	David Cohen
songs:	David Cohen
staging:	Lee Rachman
sets:	Ralph Alswang
costumes:	Robert Troie

Productions:

Opened February 14, 1977 for 21 performances

Reviews:

New York 10:61, Feb 28, 1977
New York Theatre Critics' Reviews 1977:369
New York Times page 18, Feb 15, 1977
    XI, page 7, Feb 27, 1977

(See also Edith Piaf)

Piano Bar

book:	Doris Willens and Rob Fremont
music:	Rob Fremont
lyrics:	Doris Willens
staging:	Albert Takazauckas
sets:	Michael Massee
costumes:	Michael Massee
choreography:	Nora Peterson

Productions:

(Off-Broadway) Opened June 8, 1978 for 125 performances

Reviews:

New York 11:62, Jul 17, 1978
New York Theatre Critics' Reviews 1978:181
New York Times III, page 3, Jun 9, 1978
    II, page 10, Jun 18, 1978
New Yorker 54:54+, Jun 19, 1978

Pick a Number XV

conceived:	Julius Monk
sketches:	William F. Brown and others
songs:	Clark Gesner, Claibe Richardson and others
staging:	Julius Monk
choreography:	Frank Wagner

Productions:

(Off-Broadway) Opened October 14, 1965 for 400 performances

No Reviews.

Pickwick
  book: Wolf Mankowitz
  music: Cyril Ornadel
  lyrics: Leslie Bricusse
  staging: Peter Coe
  sets: Sean Kenny
  costumes: Roger Furse and Peter Rice
  choreography: Gillian Lynne
Productions:
  Opened October 4, 1965 for 55 performances
Reviews:
  America 113:509, Oct 30, 1965
  Dance Magazine 39:24. Nov 1965
  New York Theatre Critics' Reviews 1965:265
  New York Times page 5, Oct 6, 1965
                 page 57, Nov 16, 1965
  New Yorker 41:195, Oct 16, 1965
  Newsweek 66:114, Oct 18, 1965
  Saturday Review 48:74, Oct 23, 1965
  Time 86:75, Oct 15, 1965
  Vogue 146:71, Nov 15, 1965

Piggy
  book: Daniel Kusell and Alfred Jackson; adapted from
                   Harry B. Smith and Ludwig Englander's The
                   Rich Mr. Hoggenheimer
  staging: William B. Friedlander
Productions:
  Opened January 11, 1927 for 83 performances
Reviews:
  New York Times page 22, Jan 12, 1927
  Theatre Magazine 45:4, Mar 1927
(See also I Told You So)

Pigjazz, II
  conceived: Michael Nee
  sketches: Gretchen Alan Aurthur, Glenn Kramer, Michael
                   Nee and Stephen Pell
  songs: Various authors and composers
  staging: Michael Nee
  sets: Dorian Vernacchio
  costumes: Muriel Stockdale
Productions:
  (Off-Broadway)   Opened November 16, 1981 for 30 performances
No Reviews.

Pimpernel!
  book: William Kaye; based on The Scarlet Pimpernel by
                   Baroness Orczy
  music: Mimi Stone
  lyrics: William Kaye

staging: Malcolm Black
sets: Lloyd Burlingame
costumes: Sonia Lowenstein
choreography: Sandra Devlin
Productions:
(Off-Broadway) Opened January 7, 1964 for 3 performances
Reviews:
New York Times page 26, Jan 7, 1964

The Pink Lady
book: C. M. S. McLellan; adapted from the French of Georges Berr and Marcel Guillemaud
music: Ivan Caryll
lyrics: C. M. S. McLellan
staging: Herbert Gresham
choreography: Julian Mitchell
Productions:
Opened March 13, 1911 for 312 performances
Reviews:
Blue Book 13:4-8, May 1911
Dramatic Mirror 65:7, Mar 15, 1911
           65:2, Mar 22, 1911
           67:14+, Jan 31, 1912
Green Book Album 5:922-4, May 1911
Hampton 27:524, Oct 1911
Metropolitan Magazine 34:221, May 1911
Munsey 45:284, May 1911
New England Magazine 45:398, Dec 1911
New York Dramatic News 57:5, Dec 28, 1912
Pearson 25:666+, May 1911
Red Book 17:379+, Jun 1911
Theatre Magazine 13:xii, Apr 1911
             13:134, Apr 1911
             15:iii, May 1912

Pink Ships on Parade
book: Muni Diamond, Ben Ross, Kenneth Hunter and Peter Martin
music: Earl Robinson
lyrics: Muni Diamond, Ben Ross, Kenneth Hunter and Peter Martin
Productions:
(Off-Broadway) Opened January 30, 1937
Reviews:
New York Times page 14, Feb 1, 1937

Pins and Needles (1922)
book: Albert de Courville, Wal Pink and Edgar Wallace
music: James Hanley and Frederick Chappelle
lyrics: Ballard MacDonald, Rupert Hazel and I. Caesar
Productions:
Opened February 1, 1922 for 46 performances

Reviews:
New York Times page 20, Feb 2, 1922
Theatre Magazine 35:264+, Apr 1922

Pins and Needles (1937)
book: Arthur Arent, Marc Blitzstein, Emanuel Eisen-
                     berg, Charles Friedman, David Gregory
music: Harold J. Rome
lyrics: Harold J. Rome
staging: Charles Friedman
sets: S. Syrjala
choreography: Benjamin Zemach
Productions:
Opened November 27, 1937 for 1,108 performances
(Off-Broadway) Opened May 30, 1978 for 225 performances
Reviews:
Catholic World 147:215, May 1938
               150:86-7, Oct 1939
Collier's 102:34+, Nov 12, 1938
Commonweal 105:499, Aug 4, 1978
Independent Woman 17:52, Feb 1938
                  17:359, Nov 1938
Life 3:52-3, Dec 27, 1937
Literary Digest 125:34, Jan 1, 1938
Nation 145:698, Dec 18, 1937
New York Theatre Critics' Reviews 1940:497+
New York Times page 24, Jun 15, 1936
               page 18, Nov 29, 1937
               XI, page 1, Jan 23, 1938
               IX, page 3, Aug 21, 1938
               page 27, Dec 6, 1938
               X, page 3, Dec 11, 1938
               page 16, Jan 24, 1939
               page 26, Apr 21, 1939
               page 19, Nov 21, 1939
               page 10, Jul 8, 1978
New York Times Magazine pages 30-1+, Jun 4, 1978
Scholastic 32:19E, Mar 5, 1938
Stage 15:54-5, Feb 1938
Theatre Arts 22:4, Jan 1938
             23:403, Jun 1939
             24:20, Jan 1940
Time 31:32+, Mar 14, 1938
     112:83, Jul 17, 1978

Pipe Dream
book: Oscar Hammerstein II, based on John Steinbeck's
                     novel Sweet Thursday
music: Richard Rodgers
lyrics: Oscar Hammerstein II
staging: Harold Clurman

sets: Jo Mielziner
costumes: Alvin Colt
Productions:
   Opened November 30, 1955 for 246 performances
Reviews:
   America 94:417-18, Jan 7, 1956
   Catholic World 182:388, Feb 1956
   Commonweal 63:331, Dec 30, 1955
   Nation 181:544, Dec 17, 1955
   New York Theatre Critics' Reviews 1955:198+
   New York Times II, page 1, Nov 27, 1955
                 page 44, Dec 1, 1955
                 II, page 5, Dec 11, 1955
   New Yorker 31:104+, Dec 10, 1955
   Newsweek 46:110, Dec 12, 1955
   Saturday Review 38:24, Dec 17, 1955
                39:13, Sep 15, 1956
   Theatre Arts 40:12-13, Feb 1956
   Time 66:67, Dec 12, 1955

Pippin
   book: Roger O. Hirson
   music: Stephen Schwartz
   lyrics: Stephen Schwartz
   staging: Bob Fosse
   sets: Tony Walton
   costumes: Patricia Zipprodt
   choreography: Bob Fosse
Productions:
   Opened October 23, 1972 for 1,944 performances
Reviews:
   America 127:418, Nov 18, 1972
   Dance Magazine 49:90-1, Apr 1975
   Ebony 28:74-6+, May 1973
   Jet 70:15, May 19, 1986
   Life 73:54-7, Nov 17, 1972
        73:30, Nov 24, 1972
   Los Angeles 23:215, Aug 1978
   Nation 215:474-5, Nov 13, 1972
   New West 3:87, Aug 14, 1978
   New York Theatre Critics' Reviews 1972:208
   New York Times page 46, Feb 9, 1972
               page 37, Oct 24, 1972
               II, page 1, Oct 29, 1972
               II, page 1, Nov 5, 1972
               page 26, Nov 7, 1972
               II, page 27, Dec 3, 1972
               II, page 1, Jan 28, 1973
               III, page 4, Apr 1, 1977
               XXIII, page 18, May 21, 1978
   New Yorker 48:105, Nov 4, 1972

Newsweek 80:134-5, Nov 6, 1972
Playboy 20:34, Feb 1973
Saturday Review 55:92, Dec 2, 1972
Time 100:83, Nov 6, 1972

Pitter Patter
book: Will M. Hough; based on W. Collier and G. Stewart's Caught in the Rain
music: William B. Friedlander
lyrics: William B. Friedlander
Productions:
Opened September 28, 1920 for 111 performances
Reviews:
Dramatic Mirror page 621, Oct 2, 1920
New York Clipper 68:28, Oct 6, 1920
New York Times page 12, Sep 29, 1920

Plain and Fancy
book: Joseph Stein and Will Glickman
music: Albert Hague
lyrics: Arnold B. Horwitt
staging: Morton Da Costa
sets: Raoul Pene du Bois
costumes: Raoul Pene du Bois
choreography: Helen Tamiris
Productions:
Opened January 27, 1955 for 461 performances
(Off-Off-Broadway) Opened February 23, 1964 for 8 performances
Reviews:
America 92:545+, Feb 19, 1955
Catholic World 181:67-8, Apr 1955
Commonweal 61:551, Feb 25, 1955
Life 38:75-6+, Feb 21, 1955
New York Theatre Critics' Reviews 1955:382+
New York Times page 14, Jan 28, 1955
II, page 1, Feb 6, 1955
II, page 6, Feb 6, 1955
II, page 3, Feb 5, 1956
New Yorker 30:52, Feb 5, 1955
Newsweek 45:72, Feb 7, 1955
Saturday Review 38:24, Feb 12, 1955
39:12-13, Sep 15, 1956
Theatre Arts 39:18-19+, Apr 1955
Time 65:50, Feb 7, 1955

Plain Jane
book: Phil Cook and McElbert Moore
music: Tom Johnstone
lyrics: Phil Cook
Productions:
Opened May 12, 1924 for (40) performances

Reviews:
  New York Times page 24, May 13, 1924
  Theatre Magazine 40:16, Aug 1924

Plantation Revue
Productions:
  Opened July 17, 1922 for 40 performances
Reviews:
  New York Times page 18, Jul 18, 1922

Platinum
  conceived: Will Holt
  book: Will Holt and Bruce Vilanch
  music: Gary William Friedman
  lyrics: Will Holt
  staging: Joe Layton
  sets: David Hays
  costumes: Bob Mackie
  choreography: Joe Layton
Productions:
  Opened November 12, 1978 for 33 performances
Reviews:
  Encore 7:30-1, Dec 18, 1978
  New York Theatre Critics' Reviews 1978:191
  New York Times III, page 15, Nov 13, 1978
                  II, page 3, Nov 19, 1978
  New Yorker 54:117, Nov 20, 1978
  Newsweek 92:70, Nov 27, 1978
  Rolling Stone page 29, Feb 8, 1979

Play Me a Country Song
  book: Jay Broad
  music: John R. Briggs and Harry Manfredini
  lyrics: John R. Briggs and Harry Manfredini
  staging: Jerry Adler
  sets: David Chapman
  costumes: Carol Oditz
  choreography: Margo Sappington
Productions:
  Opened June 27, 1982 for one performance
Reviews:
  New York Theatre Critics' Reviews 1982:250
  New York Times III, page 14, Jan 28, 1982
  New Yorker 58:90, Jul 5, 1982

Pleasure Bound
  book: Harold Atteridge, Max and Nathaniel Lief
  music: Muriel Pollock
  lyrics: Harold Atteridge, Max and Nathaniel Lief
  staging: Lew Morton
  choreography: Busby Berkeley

Productions:
  Opened February 18, 1929 for 136 performances
Reviews:
  New York Times IX, page 2, Feb 10, 1929
                     page 22, Feb 19, 1929
                 X, page 4, Mar 17, 1929
  Theatre Magazine 49:47, Apr 1929

The Pleasure Seekers
  book: Edgar Smith
  music/lyrics: E. Ray Goetz
  staging: William J. Wilson
Productions:
  Opened November 3, 1913 for 72 performances
Reviews:
  Dramatic Mirror 70:11, Nov 5, 1913
  New York Times page 11, Oct 23, 1913
                 page 9, Nov 4, 1913
  Theatre Magazine 18:xx, Dec 1913

The Plot Against the Chase Manhattan Bank
  sketches: Carl Larsen, David Dozer, Ernest Leongrande,
                  Lawrence B. Eisenberg and Betty Freedman
  music: Richard R. Wolf
  lyrics: Frank Spiering, Jr.
  staging: Tom Gruenwald
  sets: Robert T. Williams
  costumes: Sylvia Kalegi
  choreography: Karen Kristen and Bick Goss
Productions:
  (Off-Broadway) Opened November 26, 1963 for 15 performances
Reviews:
  New York Times page 29, Nov 27, 1963

Plume de Ma Tante, La (see La Plume de Ma Tante)

Policy Kings
  book: Michael Ashwood
  music: Sam Manning
  songs: James P. Johnson
  staging: Winston Douglas
Productions:
  (Off-Broadway) Opened December 29, 1938
Reviews:
  New York Times page 6, Dec 31, 1938

A Political Party
  sketches: Daniel Ruslander, Kurt Moss, C. D. Bryan and
                  others
  songs: Daniel Ruslander, Kurt Moss, C. D. Bryan and
                  others

staging: Arch Lustberg
costumes: Jean Anne
Productions:
  (Off-Broadway) Opened September 26, 1963 for 8 performances
Reviews:
  New York Times page 17, Sep 27, 1963

Polly (1929)
  book: Guy Bolton and George Middleton, based on
                 David Belasco's Polly with a Past
  music: Herbert Stothart and Philip Charig
  lyrics: Irving Caesar
  staging: Jack Haskell
Productions:
  Opened January 8, 1929 for 15 performances
Reviews:
  Life (New York) 93:28, Jan 25, 1929
  New York Times X, page 2, Nov 11, 1928
               page 28, Jan 9, 1929

Polly (1975)
  book: Robert Kalfin, freely adapted from John Gay's
                 Beggar's Opera
  music: Adapted by Mel Marvin
  lyrics: John Gay
  staging: Robert Kalfin
  sets: Robert U. Taylor
  costumes: Carrie F. Robbins
Productions:
  (Off-Broadway) Opened April 29, 1975 for 32 performances
Reviews:
  Nation 220:635, May 24, 1975
  New York 8:58, Jun 2, 1975
  New York Times page 16, May 9, 1975
               II, page 5, May 18, 1975
  New Yorker 51:75-6, May 19, 1975

Polly of Hollywood
  book: Will Morrissey
  staging: Will Morrissey
Productions:
  Opened February 21, 1927 for 24 performances
Reviews:
  New York Times page 22, Feb 22, 1927

Polonaise
  book: Gottfried Reinhardt and Anthony Veiller
  music: Frederic Chopin (Adaptations by Bronislaw
                 Kaper)
  lyrics: John Latouche
  staging: Stella Adler

sets: Howard Bay
costumes: Mary Grant
choreography: David Lichine
Productions:
   Opened October 6, 1945 for 113 performances
Reviews:
   Catholic World 162:167, Nov 1945
   New York Theatre Critics' Reviews 1945:149+
   New York Times page 20, Oct 8, 1945
                     II, page 1, Oct 14, 1945
   New Yorker 21:50, Oct 13, 1945
   Newsweek 26:94, Oct 15, 1945
   Theatre Arts 29:687, Dec 1945
   Time 46:66, Oct 15, 1945

Poor Little Ritz Girl
   book: Lew Fields and George Campbell
   music: Richard Rodgers and Sigmund Romberg
   lyrics: Lorenz Hart and Alex Gerber
   staging: Ned Wayburn
Productions:
   Opened July 27, 1920 for 119 performances
Reviews:
   Dramatic Mirror page 23, Aug 4, 1920
   New York Clipper 68:25, Jun 2, 1920
   New York Times page 7, Jul 29, 1920
   Theatre Magazine 32:187, Oct 1920

Pop
   book: Larry Schiff and Chuck Knull
   music: Donna Cribari
   lyrics: Larry Schiff and Chuck Knull
   staging: Allen R. Belknap
   sets: Pat Gorman
   costumes: Pat Gorman
   choreography: Ron Spencer
Productions:
   (Off-Broadway) Opened April 3, 1974 for one performance
Reviews:
   New York Times page 54, Apr 4, 1974

Poppy
   book: Dorothy Donnelly
   music: Stephen Jones and Arthur Samuels
   lyrics: Dorothy Donnelly
   staging: Dorothy Donnelly and Julian Alfred
Productions:
   Opened September 3, 1923 for (328) performances
Reviews:
   Life (New York) 82:18, Sep 20, 1923
   Nation 119:304, Sep 19, 1923

New York Times page 14, Sep 4, 1923
          page 14, Sep 6, 1924
Theatre Magazine 38:19, Nov 1923

Porgy and Bess

book: Du Bose Heyward, adapted from Du Bose and
            Dorothy Heyward's play Porgy
music: George Gershwin
lyrics: Du Bose Heyward and Ira Gershwin
staging: Rouben Mamoulian
sets: Sergei Soudekine

Productions:

Opened October 10, 1935 for 124 performances
Opened January 22, 1942 for 286 performances
Opened September 13, 1943 for 24 performances
Opened February 7, 1944 for 16 performances
Opened February 28, 1944 for 48 performances
Opened March 10, 1953 for 305 performances
Opened May 17, 1961 for 16 performances
Opened May 6, 1964 for 15 performances
Opened September 25, 1976 for 122 performances
Opened April 7, 1983 for 45 performances

Reviews:

America 88:687, Mar 21, 1953
        105:473, Jun 24, 1961
Catholic World 142:340-1, Dec 1935
               177:148-9, May 1953
Commonweal 22:642, Oct 25, 1935
           57:624-5, Mar 27, 1953
Etude 74:14-15, Mar 1956
Good Housekeeping 141:17+, Oct 1955
Life 12:65, Feb 23, 1942
Literary Digest 120:18, Oct 26, 1935
Look 17:17, May 19, 1953
Modern Music 19:195, Mar-Apr 1942
Musical America 73:33, Apr 15, 1953
Musical Courier 111:7, Oct 12, 1935
Nation 141:518-19, Oct 30, 1935
       176:272, Mar 28, 1953
New Republic 84:338, Oct 30, 1935
             128:30-1, Apr 6, 1953
New York Theatre Critics' Reviews 1942:373+
                                  1953:337+
                                  1976:164
                                  1983:316
New York Times IX, page 2, Sep 15, 1935
               page 27, Oct 1, 1935
               XI, page 3, Oct 6, 1935
               page 30, Oct 11, 1935
               X, page 1, Oct 20, 1935
               X, page 7, Oct 20, 1935

page 25, Mar 17, 1936
page 16, Jan 23, 1942
IX, page 1, Feb 1, 1942
VIII, page 7, Nov 15, 1942
page 26, Sep 14, 1943
page 13, Feb 8, 1944
II, page 4, Jun 17, 1945
II, page 7, Nov 26, 1950
II, page 1, Sep 7, 1952
page 18, Sep 8, 1952
page 37, Sep 11, 1952
page 18, Sep 18, 1952
II, page 1, Sep 28, 1952
VI, page 20, Sep 28, 1952
page 29, Oct 31, 1952
page 21, Feb 17, 1953
page 25, Mar 10, 1953
II, page 1, Mar 15, 1953
page 42, Sep 23, 1954
page 36, Dec 17, 1954
page 30, Dec 22, 1954
page 19, Jan 21, 1955
page 22, Jan 31, 1955
page 23, Feb 8, 1955
page 26, Feb 16, 1955
page 23, Feb 23, 1955
page 20, Apr 22, 1955
page 14, Aug 5, 1955
page 38, Nov 22, 1955
page 29, Dec 27, 1955
page 36, Jan 11, 1956
II, page 3, Jan 15, 1956
page 40, May 18, 1961
page 53, Oct 20, 1965
page 40, Sep 27, 1976
II, page 5, Oct 10, 1976
II, page 2, Nov 7, 1976
II, page 1, Apr 3, 1983
III, page 3, Apr 8, 1983
II, page 5, May 1, 1983
New York Times Magazine page 58, Jan 30, 1955
New Yorker 29:71, Mar 7, 1953
          29:62+, Mar 21, 1953
          38:175-6, Apr 14, 1962
Newsweek 6:23-4, Oct 19, 1935
          19:56, Feb 2, 1942
          40:68, Sep 22, 1952
          41:98, Mar 23, 1953
          47:43-4, Jan 9, 1956
Pictorial Review 37:4+, Nov 1935
Saturday Review 34:50-1, Sep 29, 1951

```
                35:44, Jun 28, 1952
                36:27, Mar 28, 1953
                39:38, Jan 14, 1956
                44:30, Jun 17, 1961
Stage 13:25-8, Oct 1935
      13:31-3, Nov 1935
      13:36-8, Dec 1935
Theatre Arts 19:853-9+, Nov 1935
             19:893-4, Dec 1935
             37:89, Jun 1952
             37:64-5, May 1953
             39:66-7+, May 1955
             45:10-11, Jul 1961
Time 26:49-50, Sep 30, 1935
     26:48-9, Oct 21, 1935
     39:45, Feb 2, 1942
     61:80, Mar 23, 1953
     65:83, Mar 7, 1955
Vanity Fair 45:68, Dec 1935
```

Porter, Cole (see Cole Porter)

Portofino
```
    book:           Richard Ney
    music:          Louis Bellson and Will Irwin
    lyrics:         Richard Ney and Sheldon Harnick
    staging:        Karl Genus
    sets:           Wolfgang Roth
    costumes:       Michael Travis
    choreography:   Charles Weidman
```
Productions:
    Opened February 21, 1958 for 3 performances
Reviews:
    New York Theatre Critics' Reviews 1958:346+
    New York Times page 8, Feb 22, 1958
    New Yorker 34:58+, Mar 1, 1958

Potholes
```
    book:           Elinor Guggenheimer
    music:          Ted Simons
    lyrics:         Elinor Guggenheimer
    staging:        Sue Lawless
    sets:           Kenneth Foy
    costumes:       Ann Emonts
    choreography:   Wayne Cilento
```
Productions:
    (Off-Broadway) Opened October 9, 1979 for 15 performances
Reviews:
    New York Times III, page 22, Oct 10, 1979

Pousse-Café
    book: Jerome Weidman; based on the film The Blue
                         Angel
    music: Duke Ellington
    lyrics: Marshall Barer and Fred Tobias
    staging: José Quintero
    sets: Will Steven Armstrong
    costumes: Patricia Zipprodt and Albert Wolsky
    choreography: Valerie Bettis
Productions:
    Opened March 18, 1966 for 3 performances
Reviews:
    Dance Magazine 40:24, May 1966
    New York Theatre Critics' Reviews 1966:326
    New York Times page 19, Mar 19, 1966
                   page 36, Mar 21, 1966
    New Yorker 42:120, Mar 26, 1966
    Newsweek 67:88, Mar 28, 1966

Power
    book: Peter Copani
    music: David McHugh
    lyrics: Peter Copani
Productions:
    (Off-Off-Broadway) Opened Season of 1973-74
No Reviews.

Preppies
    book: David Taylor and Carlos Davis
    music: Gary Portnoy and Judy Hart Angelo
    lyrics: Gary Portnoy and Judy Hart Angelo
    staging: Tony Tanner
    sets: David Jenkins
    costumes: Patricia McGourty
    choreography: Tony Tanner
Productions:
    (Off-Broadway) Opened August 18, 1983 for 52 performances
Reviews:
    New York 16:104, Aug 29, 1983
    New York Theatre Critics' Reviews 1983:163
    New York Times III, page 3, Aug 19, 1983

Present Arms
    book: Herbert Fields
    music: Richard Rodgers
    lyrics: Lorenz Hart
    staging: Alexander Leftwich
Productions:
    Opened April 26, 1928 for 155 performances
Reviews:
    New York Times page 16, Apr 27, 1928

Outlook 149:185, May 30, 1928
Theatre Magazine 47:65, Jun 1928
Vogue 71:74, Jun 15, 1928

The Present Tense

book:	Stephen Rosenfield, Haila Strauss, Ralph Buckley, Jeff Sweet (head writer) and the cast
music and lyrics:	Allen Cohen, Bob Joseph, Alan Menken, Muriel Robinson, Don Siegel, Jeff Sweet and Lee S. Wilkof
staging:	Stephen Rosenfield
sets:	Paul DePass
costumes:	Paul DePass

Productions:
(Off-Broadway) Opened October 4, 1977 for 24 performances
Reviews:
New York Times III, page 20, Oct 5, 1977
New Yorker 53:94+, Oct 17, 1977

The President's Daughter

book:	H. Kalmanov
music:	Murray Rumshinsky
lyrics:	Jacob Jacobs
staging:	Jacob Jacobs
sets:	Barry Arnold
choreography:	Henrietta Jacobson

Productions:
Opened November 3, 1970 for 72 performances
Reviews:
New York Times page 41, Nov 4, 1970

Pretty Mrs. Smith

book:	Oliver Morosco and Elmer Harris
music:	Henry James and Alfred Robyn
lyrics:	Earl Carroll
staging:	T. Daniel Frawley

Productions:
Opened September 21, 1914 for 48 performances
Reviews:
Dramatic Mirror 72:8, Sep 30, 1914
                72:4, Oct 7, 1914
                72:2, Oct 21, 1914
Green Book 12:91+, Jul 1914
New York Dramatic News 60:20, Jan 2, 1915
New York Times page 11, Sep 22, 1914
Theatre Magazine 20:206-7, Nov 1914

Pretzels

book:	Jane Curtin, Fred Grandy, and Judy Kahan
music:	John Forster

lyrics: John Forster
staging: Patricia Carmichael
sets: Stuart Wurtzel
costumes: Clifford Capone
choreography: Francis Patrelle
Productions:
    (Off-Broadway) Opened December 16, 1974 for 120 performances
Reviews:
    New York Theatre Critics' Reviews 1974:120
    New York Times page 49, May 21, 1974
                    page 32, Dec 17, 1974

The Prince and the Pauper
    book: Verna Tomasson; based on the story by Mark
                    Twain
    music: George Fischoff
    lyrics: Verna Tomasson
    staging: David Shanstrom
    sets: Norman Womack
    costumes: Norman Womack
    choreography: Bick Goss
Productions:
    (Off-Broadway) Opened October 12, 1963 for 158 performances
No Reviews.

The Prince of Bohemia
    book: J. Hartley Manners
    music: A. Baldwin Sloane
    lyrics: E. Ray Goetz
    staging: Ned Wayburn
Productions:
    Opened January 13, 1910 for 20 performances
Reviews:
    Dramatic Mirror 63:6, Jan 22, 1910

The Prince of Grand Street
    book: Bob Merrill
    music: Bob Merrill
    lyrics: Bob Merrill
    staging: Gene Saks
    sets: David Mitchell
    costumes: Jane Greenwood
    choreography: Lee Theodore
Productions:
    Closed prior to Broadway opening (Philadelphia, March 1978)
Reviews:
    New York Times III, page 15, Jan 11, 1978

The Prince of Liederkranz   (see The Student Gypsy)

Princess April
    book: William Cary Duncan and Lewis Allen Browne;
                     adapted from a story by Frank R. Adams
    music: Carlo and Sanders
    lyrics: Carlo and Sanders
Productions:
    Opened December 1, 1924 for 24 performances
Reviews:
    New York Times page 23, Dec 2, 1924
    Theatre Magazine 41:16, Feb 1925

Princess Flavia
    book: Harry B. Smith; adapted from Anthony Hope's
                     The Prisoner of Zenda
    music: Sigmund Romberg
    lyrics: Harry B. Smith
    staging: J. J. Shubert
Productions:
    Opened November 2, 1925 for 152 performances
Reviews:
    New York Times page 34, Nov 3, 1925
                 VIII, page 2, Nov 8, 1925
    Theatre Magazine 43:4, Jan 1926

Princess Virtue
    book: B. C. Hilliam and Gitz Rice
    staging: Leon Errol
Productions:
    Opened May 4, 1921 for 16 performances
Reviews:
    Dramatic Mirror 83:660, Apr 16, 1921
                  83:817, May 14, 1921
    New York Clipper 69:19, May 11, 1921
    New York Times page 20, May 5, 1921

Priorities of 1942
    assembled: Clifford C. Fischer
    music: Marjorie Fielding and Charles Barnes
    lyrics: Marjorie Fielding and Charles Barnes
    choreography: Marjorie Fielding
Productions:
    Opened March 12, 1942 for 353 performances
Reviews:
    New Republic 106:430, Mar 30, 1942
    New York Theatre Critics' Reviews 1942:329
    New York Times page 23, Mar 13, 1942
                 VIII, page 1, Mar 29, 1942
                 VII, page 18, Apr 19, 1942
    Time 39:46, Mar 23, 1942

The Prodigal Sister
    book: J. E. Franklin

music: Micki Grant
lyrics: J. E. Franklin and Micki Grant
staging: Shauneille Perry
sets: C. Richard Mills
costumes: Judy Dearing
choreography: Rod Rogers
Productions:
    (Off-Broadway)   Opened November 25, 1974 for 40 performances
Reviews:
    New York 7:96, Dec 16, 1974
    New York Theatre Critics' Reviews 1974:124
    New York Times page 42, Jul 16, 1974
                     page 30, Nov 26, 1974
    New Yorker 50:69-70, Dec 9, 1974

Professionally Speaking

written: Peter Winkler, Ernst Muller and Frederic Block
songs: Peter Winkler, Ernst Muller and Frederic Block
staging: Tony Tanner
sets: Robert Alan Harper
costumes: P. Chelsea Harriman
Productions:
    (Off-Broadway)   Opened May 22, 1986 for 37 performances
Reviews:
    New York Times I, page 57, May 25, 1986

Promenade

book: Maria Irene Fornes
music: Al Carmines
lyrics: Maria Irene Fornes
staging: Lawrence Kornfield
sets: Rouben Ter-Arutunian
costumes: Willa Kim
Productions:
    (Off-Broadway)   Opened June 4, 1969 for 259 performances
Reviews:
    Life 67:8, Aug 1, 1969
    Nation 208:837, Jun 30, 1969
    New York Theatre Critics' Reviews 1969:213
    New York Times page 56, Jun 5, 1969
                     page 32, Jun 6, 1969
                     II, page 1, Jun 15, 1969
    New Yorker 45:63, Jul 5, 1969
    Newsweek 73:107, Jun 16, 1969

Promises, Promises

book: Neil Simon; based on the screenplay The Apart-
                      ment by Billy Wilder and I. A. L. Diamond
music: Burt Bacharach
lyrics: Hal David
staging: Robert Moore

sets:	Robin Wagner
costumes:	Donald Brooks
choreography:	Harold Wheeler

Productions:
Opened December 1, 1968 for 1,281 performances
(Off-Off-Broadway) Opened May 12, 1983
Reviews:
America 120:146, Feb 1, 1969
Dance Magazine 43:93-4, Jan 1969
Life 66:14, Jan 17, 1969
National Review 21:918, Sep 9, 1969
Nation 208:125, Jan 27, 1969
New York Theatre Critics' Reviews 1968:161
                                           1968:164
New York Times page 59, Dec 2, 1968
                page 52, Dec 3, 1968
                II, page 3, Dec 15, 1968
                page 26, Oct 4, 1969
                page 17, Jan 22, 1971
                page 21, Dec 29, 1971
                XXII, page 16, Jun 11, 1978
New Yorker 44:139, Dec 7, 1968
Newsweek 72:114, Dec 16, 1968
Saturday Review 51:13, Dec 21, 1968
Time 92:81, Dec 13, 1968

The Proposition
conceived:	Allan Albert
staging:	Allan Albert

Productions:
(Off-Broadway) Opened May 3, 1978 for 24 performances
Reviews:
New York Times page 50, May 9, 1978
New Yorker 54:116, May 15, 1978

Provincetown Follies
sketches:	Frederick Herendeen, Gwynn Langdon, Barrie Oliver, George K. Arthur
music:	Sylvan Green, Mary Schaeffer, Arthur Jones, Trevor Jones, Dave Stamper
lyrics:	Frederick Herendeen, Gwynn Langdon, Barrie Oliver, George K. Arthur
staging:	Lee Morrison
choreography:	Mary Read

Productions:
Opened November 3, 1935 for 63 performances
Reviews:
New York Times page 24, Nov 4, 1935

Prunella, or Love in a Garden
book:	Laurence Housman and Granville Barker

music: Joseph Moorat
Productions:
    Opened October 27, 1913 for 104 performances
Reviews:
    American Mercury 77:33-4, Mar 1914
    Bookman 38:363, Dec 1913
    Current Opinion 56:24-8, Jan 1914
    Dramatic Mirror 70:6, Oct 29, 1913
                    70:2, Nov 12, 1913
                    70:1, Dec 3, 1913
    Everybody's 30:264, Feb 1914
    Green Book 11:71-2, Jan 1914
               11:165-6, Jan 1914
    Harper's Bazaar 49:37+, Mar 1914
    International 7:364+, Dec 1913
    Leslie's Weekly 117:495, Nov 20, 1913
    Life (New York) 62:790-91, Nov 6, 1913
    Literary Digest 47:944-5, Nov 15, 1913
    Munsey 50:726-7, Jan 1914
    New York Times page 11, Oct 17, 1913
                    page 9, Oct 27, 1913
    Theatre Magazine 18:174-5, Dec 1913
                    18:197, Dec 1913

Prussian Suite
    book: Michael Smith
    music: John Smead
    staging: Michael Smith
Productions:
    (Off-Off-Broadway) Opened February 14, 1974
No Reviews.

Pugh, Ted   (see An Evening with Sue and Pugh)

Pump Boys and Dinettes
    book: Jim Wann
    music: Jim Wann
    lyrics: Jim Wann
    additional music
        and lyrics: John Foley, Mark Hardwick, Spider John Koerner,
                    Cass Morgan, Debra Monk, Charlie Rich, and B.
                    Simpson
    sets: Doug Johnson and Christopher Nowak
    costumes: Patricia McGourty
Productions:
    (Off-Broadway) Opened October 1, 1981 for 112 performances
    Opened February 4, 1982 for 573 performances
Reviews:
    Los Angeles 31:286+, Dec 1986
    New York Theatre Critics' Reviews 1982:338
    New York Times III, page 20, Oct 14, 1981

II, page 3, Dec 13, 1981
II, page 1, Mar 28, 1982
New Yorker 57:183, Nov 16, 1981
Time 119:78, Mar 1, 1982

Purlie
book: Ossie Davis, Philip Rose, Peter Udell; based on
                the play Purlie Victorious by Ossie Davis
music: Gary Geld
lyrics: Peter Udell
staging: Philip Rose
sets: Ben Edwards
costumes: Ann Roth
choreography: Louis Johnson
Productions:
Opened March 15, 1970 for 688 performances
Opened December 27, 1972 for 14 performances
Reviews:
America 122:510, May 9, 1970
Dance Magazine 44:89-90, May 1970
Life 68:18, Apr 24, 1970
Nation 210:414, Apr 6, 1970
New York Theatre Critics' Reviews 1970:340
New York Times page 53, Mar 16, 1970
              II, page 3, Mar 22, 1970
              II, page 1, Apr 5, 1970
              page 48, Apr 21, 1970
              II, page 5, Nov 29, 1970
              page 17, Apr 24, 1971
              page 37, Nov 25, 1972
              page 36, Dec 28, 1972
New Yorker 46:81, Mar 28, 1970
Newsweek 75:84, Mar 30, 1970
Time 95:77, Mar 30, 1970

Put It in Writing
staging: Bill Penn
sets: Peter Harvey
costumes: Audré
choreography: Joyce Trisler
Productions:
(Off-Broadway) Opened May 13, 1963 for 24 performances
Reviews:
New York Times page 31, May 14, 1963
New Yorker 39:59, May 25, 1963
Saturday Review 45:21, Aug 18, 1962
Theatre Arts 47:12, Jul 1963

-Q-

The Quaker Girl
    book: James T. Tanner
    music: Lionel Monckton
    lyrics: Adrian Ross and Percy Greenbank
    staging: T. A. E. Malone
Productions:
    Opened October 23, 1911 for 240 performances
Reviews:
    Blue Book 14:472-4, Jan 1912
    Canadian Magazine 38:280, Jan 1912
    Dramatic Mirror 66:10, Oct 25, 1911
                  66:4, Nov 8, 1911
                  66:4, Dec 13, 1911
                  67:19, Jan 31, 1912
    Green Book 7:13-15+, Jan 1912
    Hampton 27:825, Jan 1912
    Munsey 46:430, Dec 1911
    Red Book 18:957-60, Mar 1912

A Quarter for the Ladies Room
    music: John Clifton and Arthur Siegel
    lyrics: Ruth Batchelor
    staging: Darwin Knight
    sets: David R. Ballou
    costumes: Miles White
Productions:
    (Off-Broadway) Opened November 12, 1972 for one performance
Reviews:
    New York Theatre Critics' Reviews 1972:161
    New York Times page 47, Nov 13, 1972

Queen High
    book: Laurence Schwab and B. G. De Sylva; based on
                       E. Peple's A Pair of Sixes
    music: Lewis E. Gensler
    lyrics: B. G. DeSylva
    staging: Edgar McGregor and Sammy Lee
Productions:
    Opened September 8, 1926 for 378 performances
Reviews:
    Bookman 64:343, Nov 1926
    Life (New York) 88:23, Oct 7, 1926
    New York Times page 21, Sep 9, 1926
                   IX, page 1, Sep 19, 1926
    Theatre Magazine 44:66+, Nov 1926
                      44:21, Dec 1926
    Time 52:48, Oct 1930
    Vogue 68:91, Nov 1926

Queen of Hearts
    book: Frank Mandel and Oscar Hammerstein II
    music: Lewis Gensler and Dudley Wilkinson
    lyrics: Oscar Hammerstein II and Sydney Mitchell
    staging: Ira Hards
Productions:
    Opened October 10, 1922 for 39 performances
Reviews:
    New York Clipper 70:20, Oct 18, 1922
    New York Times page 22, Oct 11, 1922
    Theatre Magazine 32:31, Midsummer 1920
                    36:377, Dec 1922

The Queen of the Movies
    book: Glen Macdonough; based on Die Kino-Konigin by
                    Julius Freund and Georg Okonowski
    music: Jean Gilbert
    lyrics: Glen Macdonough
    staging: Herbert Gresham
    choreography: Julian Mitchell
Productions:
    Opened January 12, 1914 for 104 performances
Reviews:
    Dramatic Mirror 71:11, Jan 7, 1914
                    71:6, Jan 21, 1914
    Green Book 11:541-3, Apr 1914
               11:607-8, Apr 1914
               11:699-700, Apr 1914
    New York Times page 9, Jan 13, 1914
    Theatre Magazine 19:96, Feb 1914

Quick Change
    by: Bruce Belland, Roy M. Rogosin, and Michael
                    McGiveney
    lyrics: Bruce Belland
    staging: Roy M. Rogosin
    costumes: Mary Wills
Productions:
    Opened October 30, 1980 for 5 performances
Reviews:
    New York Theatre Critics' Reviews 1980:135
    New York Times III, page 4, Oct 31, 1980
    People 11:98-9, Apr 30, 1979

Quilters
    book: Molly Newman and Barbara Damashek, based on
                    The Quilters: Women and Domestic Art by
                    Patricia Cooper and Norma Bradley Allen
    music: Barbara Damashek
    lyrics: Barbara Damashek
    staging: Barbara Damashek

```
     sets:          Ursula Belden
     costumes:      Elizabeth Palmer
Productions:
     Opened September 25, 1984 for 24 performances
Reviews:
     Los Angeles 29:44+, Feb 1984
     New York 17:77-8, Oct 8, 1984
     New York Theatre Critics' Reviews 1984:206
     New York Times III, page 17, Sep 26, 1984
     New Yorker 60:116, Oct 8, 1984
     Saturday Review 10:58-9, Nov/Dec 1984
```

-R-

R.S.V.P.
```
     sketches:      Rick Crom
     music:         Rick Crom
     lyrics:        Rick Crom
     staging:       Word Baker and Rod Rogers
     sets:          Carleton Varney
     costumes:      Jerry Hart
Productions:
     (Off-Broadway)  Opened August 24, 1982 for 127 performances
No Reviews.
```

Rabboni
```
     book:          Jerimiah Ginsberg
     music:         Jerimiah Ginsberg
     lyrics:        Jerimiah Ginsberg
     staging:       Alan Weeks
Productions:
     (Off-Off-Broadway)  Opened June 13, 1985
Reviews:
     Christianity Today 29:94, Nov 8, 1985
     New York Times III, page 22, Jun 19, 1985
```

Raggedy Ann
```
     book:          William Gibson
     music:         Joe Raposo
     lyrics:        Joe Raposo
     staging:       Patricia Birch
     sets:          Gerry Hariton and Vicki Baral
     costumes:      Carrie Robbins
     choreography:  Patricia Birch
Productions:
     Opened October 16, 1986 for 5 performances
Reviews:
     New York 19:139-40, Oct 27, 1986
     New York Theatre Critics' Reviews 1986:184
     New York Times III, page 3, Oct 17, 1986
     New Yorker 62:116, Oct 27, 1986
```

Rags
book: Joseph Stein
music: Charles Strouse
lyrics: Stephen Schwartz
staging: Gene Saks
sets: Beni Montresor
costumes: Florence Klotz
choreography: Ron Field
Productions:
Opened August 21, 1986 for 4 performances
Reviews:
Maclean's 99:42, Aug 25, 1986
New York 19:46-7, Sep 1, 1986
New York Theatre Critics' Reviews 1986:238
New York Times XXI, page 21, Aug 17, 1986
                III, page 3, Aug 22, 1986
New Yorker 62:78+, Sep 1, 1986
Newsweek 108:86, Sep 1, 1986

Rain or Shine
book: James Gleason and Maurice Marks
music: Milton Ager and Owen Murphy
lyrics: Jack Yellen
Productions:
Opened February 9, 1928 for 356 performances
Reviews:
Life (New York) 91:23, Mar 8, 1928
                96:18, Aug 29, 1930
New York Times page 26, Feb 10, 1928
                VIII, page 1, Feb 19, 1928
Outlook 148:344, Feb 29, 1928
Theatre Magazine 48:38, Aug 1928
Vogue 71:140, Apr 1, 1928

Rainbow (1928)
book: Laurence Stallings and Oscar Hammerstein II
music: Vincent Youmans
lyrics: Oscar Hammerstein II
staging: Oscar Hammerstein II
choreography: Busby Berkeley
Productions:
Opened November 21, 1928 for 29 performances
Reviews:
New York Times page 1, Nov 4, 1928
                page 25, Nov 22, 1928
                IX, page 1, Dec 16, 1928
Theatre Magazine 49:60, Jan 1929

Rainbow (1972)
book: James and Ted Rado
music: James Rado

lyrics:	James Rado
staging:	Joe Donovan
sets:	James Tilton
costumes:	Nancy Potts

Productions:
  (Off-Broadway) Opened December 18, 1972 for 48 performances
Reviews:
New York 6:66, Jan 15, 1973
New York Times page 50, Dec 19, 1972
              II, page 1, Jan 7, 1973
New Yorker 48:47, Dec 30, 1972

The Rainbow Girl

book:	Rennold Wolf; based on a comedy by Jerome K. Jerome
music:	Louis A. Hirsch
lyrics:	Rennold Wolf
staging:	Julian Mitchell and Herbert Gresham

Productions:
Opened April 1, 1918 for 160 performances
Reviews:
Dramatic Mirror 77:32, Dec 8, 1917
             78:509, Apr 13, 1918
             78:549, Apr 20, 1918
             79:189, Aug 10, 1918
             79:261, Aug 24, 1918
Green Book 19:972+, Jun 1918
Munsey 64:438, Jul 1918
New York Times page 11, Apr 2, 1918
Theatre Magazine 27:277, May 1918
               27:316, May 1918

Rainbow Jones

book:	Jill Williams
music:	Jill Williams
lyrics:	Jill Williams
staging:	Gene Persson
sets:	Richard Ferrer
costumes:	James Berton-Harris
choreography:	Sammy Bayes

Productions:
Opened February 13, 1974 for one performance
Reviews:
New York Theatre Critics' Reviews 1974:390
New York Times page 57, Feb 14, 1974

Rainbow Rose

book:	Walter De Leon; based on Zelda Sears' A Lucky Break
music:	Harold Levey and Owen Murphy
lyrics:	Walter De Leon and Owen Murphy
staging:	Walter Wilson

Productions:
   Opened March 16, 1926 for 55 performances
Reviews:
   New York Times page 28, Mar 17, 1926
   Theatre Magazine 43:15, May 1926

Raisin
   book: Robert Nemiroff and Charlotte Zaltzberg; based
                    on Lorraine Hansberry's A Raisin in the Sun
   music: Judd Waldin
   lyrics: Robert Brittan
   staging: Donald McKayle
   sets: Robert U. Taylor
   costumes: Bernard Johnson
   choreography: Donald McKayle
Productions:
   Opened October 18, 1973 for 847 performances
   (Off-Off-Broadway) Opened May 14, 1981
Reviews:
   America 129:392, Nov 17, 1973
   Dance Magazine 49:90, Apr 1975
   Ebony 29:74-6+, May 1974
   Essence 4:15, Dec 1973
   Ms. 2:40+, Dec 1973
   Nation 217:508, Nov 12, 1973
   New York Theatre Critics' Reviews 1973:218
   New York Times page 49, May 31, 1973
                 page 59, Oct 19, 1973
                 page 20, Oct 27, 1973
                 II, page 1, Oct 28, 1973
                 II, page 3, Nov 4, 1973
                 III, page 12, May 18, 1981
   New Yorker 49:107, Oct 29, 1973
   Newsweek 82:67, Oct 29, 1973
   Playboy 21:38, Feb 1974
   Time 102:99, Oct 29, 1973

Rambler Rose
   book: Harry B. Smith
   music: Victor Jacobi
Productions:
   Opened September 10, 1917 for 72 performances
Reviews: .
   Dramatic Mirror 77:31, Sep 8, 1917
                   77:7, Sep 22, 1917
                   77:5, Sep 29, 1917
   New York Dramatic News 64:7, Sep 15, 1917
   New York Times page 11, Sep 11, 1917
   Theatre Magazine 26:277, Nov 1917
                    26:281, Nov 1917

The Ramblers
    book: Guy Bolton, Bert Kalmar and Harry Ruby
    music: Bert Kalmar and Harry Ruby
    lyrics: Bert Kalmar and Harry Ruby
    staging: Philip Goodman
Productions:
    Opened September 20, 1926 for 289 performances
Reviews:
    Life (New York) 88:23, Oct 7, 1926
    New York Times page 32, Sep 21, 1926
    Theatre Magazine 44:15, Nov 1926
                    45:19, Jan 1927
    Vogue 68:106+, Nov 15, 1926

Rang Tang
    book: Kaj Gynt
    lyrics: Jo Trent
    staging: Charles Davis and Miller and Lyles
Productions:
    Opened July 12, 1927 for 119 performances
Reviews:
    Life (New York) 90:19, Aug 18, 1927
    New York Times page 20, Jul 13, 1927

Rap Master Ronnie
    by: Elizabeth Swados, (Ronald Reagan satirized)
    music: Elizabeth Swados
    lyrics: Garry Trudeau and Elizabeth Swados
    staging: Caymichael Patten
    sets: Neil Peter Jampolis
    costumes: David Woolard
    choreography: Ronni Stewart
Productions:
    (Off-Broadway) Opened October 3, 1984 for 49 performances
Reviews:
    Los Angeles 30:42, Jul 1985
    Maclean's 101:53, Jan 18, 1988
    Nation 239:428-9, Oct 27, 1984
    New York Times III, page 2, Aug 24, 1984
                    II, page 3, Sep 30, 1984
                    III, page 16, Oct 4, 1984
    Time 128:107, Dec 8, 1986

Razzle Dazzle
    sketches: Mike Stewart
    music: Leo Schumer, Shelley Mowell, James Reed
                    Lawlor, Bernice Kroll, Irma Jurist
    lyrics: Mike Stewart
    sets: William Riva
    choreography: Nelle Fischer
Productions:
    Opened February 19, 1951 for 8 performances

Reviews:
Commonweal 53:542, Mar 9, 1951
New York Theatre Critics' Reviews 1951:339+
New York Times page 21, Feb 20, 1951
Newsweek 37:83, Mar 5, 1951
Theatre Arts 35:21, Apr 1951

Real Life Funnies
book: Howard Ashman, adapted from Stan Mack's comic strip
songs: Alan Menken
staging: Howard Ashman
choreography: Douglas Norwick
Productions:
(Off-Off-Broadway) Opened February 1981 for 35 performances
Reviews:
New York 14:44-5, Feb 23, 1981
New York Times III, page 23, Feb 12, 1981

Really Rosie
book: Maurice Sendak
music: Carole King
lyrics: Maurice Sendak
staging: Patricia Birch
sets: Douglas W. Schmidt
costumes: Carrie F. Robbins
choreography: Patricia Birch
Productions:
(Off-Broadway) Opened October 14, 1980 for 274 performances
Reviews:
New York 13:49-50, Oct 27, 1980
New York Times III, page 21, Oct 15, 1980

The Red Canary
book: William Le Baron and Alexander Johnstone
music: Harold Orlob
lyrics: Will B. Johnstone
staging: Ben Teal
Productions:
Opened April 13, 1914 for 16 performances
Reviews:
Dramatic Mirror 71:12, Apr 15, 1914
New York Times page 11, Apr 14, 1914
                   page 13, Apr 15, 1914
Theatre Magazine 19:319-20, Jun 1914

Red, Hot and Blue
book: Howard Lindsay and Russel Crouse
music: Cole Porter
lyrics: Cole Porter
staging: Howard Lindsay

```
sets:            Donald Oenslager
costumes:        Constance Ripley
choreography:    George Hale
```
Productions:
    Opened October 29, 1936 for 183 performances
Reviews:
    Catholic World 144:338-9, Dec 1936
    Nation 143:585, Nov 14, 1936
    New York Times page 28, Oct 8, 1936
                 X, page 3, Oct 11, 1936
                 page 26, Oct 30, 1936
                 X, page 1, Nov 8, 1936
    Newsweek 8:41, Nov 7, 1936
           34:88, Nov 14, 1949
    Photoplay 36:19, Dec 1949
    Stage 14:49, Oct 1936
    Time 28:21, Nov 9, 1936
       54:96, Nov 7, 1949

The Red Mill
```
book:            Henry Blossom
music:           Victor Herbert
lyrics:          Henry Blossom
additional
  lyrics:        Forman Brown
staging:         Billy Gilbert
sets:            Arthur Lonergan
costumes:        Walter Israel and Emile Santiago
choreography:    Aida Broadbent
```
Productions:
    Opened October 16, 1945 (Originally produced in 1906) for 531 performances
    (Off-Broadway) Opened October 28, 1981 for 35 performances
    (Off-Broadway) Opened July 2, 1986 for 21 performances
Reviews:
    Catholic World 162:262, Dec 1945
    Life 19:75-8+, Nov 12, 1945
    Nation 161:441, Oct 27, 1945
    New York Theatre Critics' Reviews 1945:141+
    New York Times page 16, Oct 17, 1945
                 II, page 1, Oct 28, 1945
                 II, page 1, Aug 11, 1946
                 VI, page 23, Dec 8, 1946
                 III, page 14, May 29, 1978
                 page 81, Nov 15, 1981
    New Yorker 21:42+, Oct 27, 1945
    Newsweek 26:90, Oct 29, 1945
    Theatre Arts 29:687, Dec 1945
    Time 46:62, Oct 29, 1945

Red Pepper
```
book:            Edgar Smith and Emily Young
```

music: Albert Gumble and Owen Murphy
lyrics: Howard Rogers and Owen Murphy
staging: Frank Smithson
Productions:
Opened May 29, 1922 for (22) performances
Reviews:
New York Clipper 70:24, Jun 7, 1922
New York Times page 8, May 30, 1922
Theatre Magazine 36:95, Aug 1922

The Red Petticoat
book: Rida Johnson Young
music: Jerome D. Kern
lyrics: Paul W. Herbert
staging: Joseph W. Herbert
Productions:
Opened November 13, 1912 for 61 performances
Reviews:
Blue Book 16:912-14, Mar 1913
Dramatic Mirror 68:7, Nov 20, 1912
              68:2, Dec 4, 1912
              68:2, Dec 25, 1912
Green Book 9:183-4, Jan 1913
Harper's Weekly 56:19, Nov 30, 1912
Munsey 48:683-4, Jan 1913
New York Dramatic News 56:22, Nov 23, 1912

The Red Rose
book: Harry B. and Robert B. Smith
music: Robert Hood Bowers
lyrics: Harry B. and Robert B. Smith
staging: R. H. Burnside
sets: Valeska Suratt
costumes: Valeska Suratt
Productions:
Opened June 22, 1911 for 76 performances
Reviews:
Blue Book 13:684-7, Aug 1911
Dramatic Mirror 65:11+, Jun 28, 1911
Hampton 27:522, Oct 1911
Red Book 17:959, Sep 1911
Theatre Magazine 14:40-1+, Aug 1911

The Red, White and Black
book: Eric Bentley
music: Brad Burg
lyrics: Eric Bentley
staging: John Dillon and Eric Bentley
sets: Bill Mikeulewicz
costumes: Margaret Tobin
Productions:
(Off-Broadway) Opened March 30, 1971 for one performance

Reviews:
    New York Times page 20, Mar 6, 1971
                  page 37, Mar 31, 1971

Red, White and Maddox
    book: Don Tucker and Jay Broad
    music: Don Tucker
    lyrics: Don Tucker
    staging: Jay Broad and Don Tucker
    sets: David Chapman
    costumes: David Chapman
Productions:
    Opened January 26, 1969 for 41 performances
Reviews:
    America 120:232, Feb 22, 1969
    Nation 208:221, Feb 17, 1969
    New Republic 160:29-30, Feb 22, 1969
    New York Theatre Critics' Reviews 1969:379
    New York Times page 29, Jul 25, 1968
                  page 71, Oct 5, 1968
                  VI, page 61, Nov 24, 1968
                  page 27, Jan 27, 1969
                  II, page 3, Feb 2, 1969
                  page 33, Mar 4, 1969
                  page 75, Feb 13, 1970
    New Yorker 44:49, Feb 1, 1969
    Saturday Review 51:32, Oct 26, 1968
                  52:33, Feb 1, 1969
    Time 92:73, Nov 29, 1968
    Vogue 153:42, Mar 15, 1969

The Red Widow
    book: Channing Pollock and Rennold Wolf
    music: Charles J. Gebest
    lyrics: Channing Pollock and Rennold Wolf
    staging: Frederick G. Latham
Productions:
    Opened November 6, 1911 for 128 performances
Reviews:
    Blue Book 14:240-3, Dec 1911
    Dramatic Mirror 66:7, Nov 15, 1911
    Green Book 7:16-18+, Jan 1912
    Hampton 28:116, Mar 1912
    Munsey 46:586, Jan 1912
    New York Times page 13, Nov 7, 1911
    Theatre Magazine 14:xii, Dec 1911
                     14:186, Dec 1911

Redhead
    book: Herbert and Dorothy Fields, Sidney Sheldon,
                  David Shaw

music: Albert Hague
lyrics: Dorothy Fields
staging: Bob Fosse
sets: Rouben Ter-Arutunian
costumes: Rouben Ter-Arutunian
choreography: Bob Fosse
Productions:
    Opened February 5, 1959 for 452 performances
    (Off-Broadway) Opened January 12, 1968 for 15 performances
Reviews:
    America 100:671, Mar 7, 1959
    Catholic World 189:58-9, Apr 1959
    Dance Magazine 33:40-5, May 1959
    Life 46:81-3, Feb 23, 1959
    Nation 188:234, Mar 14, 1959
    New York Theatre Critics' Reviews 1959:384+
    New York Times page 21, Feb 6, 1959
               II, page 1, Feb 15, 1959
               II, page 1, Mar 20, 1960
    New Yorker 35:98+, Feb 21, 1959
    Newsweek 53:94, Feb 16, 1959
    Saturday Review 42:25, Feb 28, 1959
    Theatre Arts 43:10-11, Apr 1959
    Time 73:77, Feb 16, 1959

Reety in Hell
    book: Stephen Holt
    music: Don Arrington
    staging: Peter Schneider
Productions:
    (Off-Off-Broadway) Opened May 8, 1973
No Reviews.

Reggae
    conceived: Michael Butler
    story: Kendrew Lascelles
    book: Melvin Van Peebles, Kendrew Lascelles and
                    Stafford Harrison
    music and
    lyrics: Ras Karbi, Michael Kamen, Kendrew Lascelles,
                    Max Romeo, Randy Bishop, Jackie Mittoo and
                    Stafford Harrison
    staging: Glenda Dickerson
    sets: Ed Burbridge
    costumes: Raoul Pene du Bois
    choreography: Mike Malone
Productions:
    Opened March 27, 1980 for 21 performances
Reviews:
    New York Theatre Critics' Reviews 1980:307
    New York Times III, page 3, Mar 28, 1980
    Newsweek 95:93+, Apr 7, 1980

Regina
    book: Marc Blitzstein, based on Lillian Hellman's The
                          Little Foxes
    music: Marc Blitzstein
    lyrics: Marc Blitzstein
    staging: Robert Lewis
    sets: Horace Armistead
    costumes: Aline Bernstein
    choreography: Anna Abravanel
Productions:
Opened October 31, 1949 for 56 performances
Reviews:
  American Mercury 70:172-3, Feb 1950
  Catholic World 170:228-9, Dec 1949
  Commonweal 51:238, Dec 2, 1949
  Musical America 69:9, Dec 1, 1949
                73:5, Apr 15, 1953
  Nation 169:478, Nov 12, 1949
       177:118-19, Aug 8, 1953
       186:399, May 3, 1958
  New Republic 121:22, Dec 5, 1949
  New York Theatre Critics' Reviews 1949:237+
  New York Times II, page 1, Oct 30, 1949
              page 32, Nov 1, 1949
              II, page 1, Nov 13, 1949
              VI, page 14, Dec 11, 1949
              page 25, Jun 2, 1952
              page 18, Apr 3, 1953
              II, page 7, Apr 12, 1953
              page 12, Oct 10, 1953
              page 19, Apr 19, 1958
              page 10, May 3, 1958
              page 36, Apr 20, 1959
  New Yorker 25:56-8, Nov 12, 1949
          29:103-5, Jun 14, 1952
          29:113, Oct 17, 1953
          34:80, Apr 26, 1958
  Newsweek 34:84-5, Nov 14, 1949
          41:96, Apr 13, 1953
  Reporter 8:36-7, Jun 23, 1953
  Saturday Review 32:54-5, Nov 19, 1949
              36:41-2, Apr 4, 1953
              36:33, Apr 18, 1953
  School and Society 71:24-5, Jan 14, 1950
  Theatre Arts 34:12, Jan 1950
  Time 54:46, Nov 14, 1949
      61:79, Apr 13, 1953

Religion
    oratorio: Al Carmines
    staging: Al Carmines

Productions:
   (Off-Off-Broadway) Opened October 28, 1973
Reviews:
   New York Times page 37, Oct 30, 1973

Reunion in New York
   conceived by: Lothar Metzl and Werner Michel
   sketches: Carl Don, Richard Alma, Richard Holden, Hans
                    Lefebre
   music: André Singer, Bert Silving, Berenice Kazouneff,
                    M. Cooper Paul
   lyrics: David Gregory, Peter Barry, Stewart Arthur
   staging: Herbert Berghof and Ezra Stone
   sets: Harry Horner
   costumes: Lester Polakov
   choreography: Lotte Gosler
Productions:
   Opened February 21, 1940 for 89 performances
Reviews:
   New York Theatre Critics' Reviews 1940: 388+
   New York Times page 28, Feb 22, 1940
                   X, page 1, Mar 3, 1940
   Theatre Arts 24: 237, Apr 1940
   Time 35: 34, Mar 4, 1940

Revenge with Music
   book: Howard Dietz and Arthur Schwartz, from the
                    Spanish fable "The Three Cornered Hat"
   music: Arthur Schwartz
   lyrics: Howard Dietz
   staging: Komisarjevsky
   sets: Albert Johnson
   choreography: Michael Mordkin
Productions:
   Opened November 28, 1934 for 158 performances
Reviews:
   Catholic World 140: 469, Jan 1935
   Golden Book Magazine 21: 32a, Feb 1935
   New York Times page 33, Nov 29, 1934
                   IX, page 2, Dec 23, 1934
   Time 24: 50, Dec 10, 1934

Revue of 1924 (see Andre Charlot's Revue of 1924)

The Revue of Revues
   produced by: The Shuberts
Productions:
   Opened September 27, 1911 for 55 performances
No Reviews.

Rex
   book: Sherman Yellen

music: Richard Rodgers
lyrics: Sheldon Harnick
staging: Edwin Sherin
sets: John Conklin
costumes: John Conklin
choreography: Dania Krupska
Productions:
    Opened April 25, 1976 for 49 performances
Reviews:
    New York 9:78, May 10, 1976
    New York Theatre Critics' Reviews 1976:286
    New York Times page 38, Apr 26, 1976
                II, page 5, May 9, 1976
    New Yorker 52:75, May 3, 1976
    Newsweek 87:76, May 10, 1976
    Saturday Review 3:44, Apr 3, 1976
    Time 107:87, May 10, 1976

Rhapsody in Black
    assembled by: Lew Leslie
    music: Alberta Nichols
    lyrics: Mann Holiner
    staging: Lew Leslie
Productions:
    Opened May 4, 1931 for 80 performances
Reviews:
    New York Times page 33, May 5, 1931

Richard Farina; Long Time Coming and a Long Time Gone
    material: Nancy Greenwald, adapted from the works of
                    Richard Farina
    staging: Robert Greenwald
    sets: Richard Hammer and Patrick Sullivan
    costumes: Joyce and Jerry Marcel
Productions:
    (Off-Broadway) Opened November 17, 1971 for 7 performances
Reviews:
    New York Times page 58, Nov 18, 1971

Ride the Winds
    book: John Driver
    music: John Driver
    lyrics: John Driver
    staging: Lee D. Sankowich
    sets: Samuel C. Ball
    costumes: Samuel C. Ball
    choreography: Jay Norman
Productions:
    Opened May 16, 1974 for 3 performances
Reviews:
    New York 7:90, Jun 3, 1974
    New York Theatre Critics' Reviews 1974:266

The Right Girl
  book: Raymond Peck
  music: Percy Wenrich
  lyrics: Raymond Peck
  staging: Walter Wilson
Productions:
  Opened March 15, 1921 for 98 performances
Reviews:
  Dramatic Mirror 83:508, Mar 19, 1921
  New York Clipper 69:19, Mar 23, 1921
  New York Times page 12, Mar 16, 1921
  Theatre Magazine 33:370, May 1921
                  33:421, Jun 1921

Right This Way
  book: Marianne Brown Waters; additional dialogue by
                  Parke Levy and Allen Lipscott; additional songs
                  by Sammy Fain and Irving Kahal
  music: Brad Greene and Fabian Storey
  lyrics: Marianne Brown Waters
  staging: Bertram Robinson and Alice Alexander
  sets: Nat Karson
  costumes: Miles White
  choreography: Marjorie Fielding
Productions:
  Opened January 4, 1938 for 15 performances
Reviews:
  New York Times VI, page 6, Oct 31, 1937
                 page 22, Jan 6, 1938

Ring Gott Farblonjet, Der   (see Der Ring Gott Farblonjet)

The Rink
  book: Terrence McNally
  music: John Kander
  lyrics: Fred Ebb
  staging: A. J. Antoon
  sets: Peter Larkin
  costumes: Theoni V. Aldredge
  choreography: Graciela Daniele
Productions:
  Opened Febraury 9, 1984 for 204 performances
Reviews:
  America 150:216, Mar 24, 1984
  Dance Magazine 58:146-8, May 1984
  New Leader 67:21-2, Apr 2, 1984
  New York 17:89-90, Feb 20, 1984
  New York Theatre Critics' Reviews 1984:374
  New York Times III, page 3, Feb 10, 1984
                    II, page 5, Feb 19, 1984
  New Yorker 60:104, Feb 20, 1984

People 21:61+, Mar 5, 1984
Time 123:84, Feb 20, 1984

Rio Rita
    book: Guy Bolton and Fred Thompson
    staging: John Harwood
Productions:
Opened February 2, 1927 for 494 performances
Reviews:
    Life (New York) 89:21, Feb 24, 1927
    New York Times page 18, Feb 3, 1927
                     VII, page 1, Feb 13, 1927
                     IX, page 2, May 13, 1928
                     page 25, May 21, 1928
    Theatre Magazine 46:16, Aug 1927
    Vogue 69:132+, Apr 1, 1927

Ripples
    book: William Anthony McGuire
    music: Oscar Levant and Albert Sirmay
    lyrics: Irving Caesar and Graham John
    staging: William Anthony McGuire
    choreography: William Holbrook
Productions:
Opened February 11, 1930 for 55 performances
Reviews:
    Life (New York) 95:18, Mar 14, 1930
    New York Times VIII, page 2, Feb 2, 1930
                    page 26, Feb 12, 1930
                    page 31, Mar 18, 1930
    Outlook 154:512, Mar 26, 1930
    Theatre Magazine 51:46, Apr 1930
    Vogue 75:55+, Mar 29, 1930

The Rise and Fall of the City of Mahagonny (see Mahagonny)

The Rise of David Levinsky
    book: Isaiah Sheffer, based on the novel by Abraham
                    Cahan
    music: Bobby Paul
    lyrics: Isaiah Sheffer
    staging: Sue Lawless
    sets: Kenneth Foy
    costumes: Mimi Maxmen
Productions:
    (Off-Off-Broadway) Opened November 1976
    (Off-Off-Broadway) Opened March 12, 1983
    (Off-Broadway) Opened January 12, 1987 for 31 performances
Reviews:
    New York Theatre Critics' Reviews 1987:352

New York Times page 41, Nov 23, 1976
I, page 52, Mar 27, 1983
III, page 30, Jan 15, 1987

The Rise of Rosie O'Reilly
    book: George M. Cohan
    staging: Julian Mitchell and John Meehan
Productions:
    Opened December 25, 1923 for 87 performances
Reviews:
    New York Times page 13, Dec 26, 1923
    Theatre Magazine 39:19, Mar 1924

Ritz Revue (see Hassard Short's Ritz Revue)

The River
    book: Peter Link
    music: Peter Link
    lyrics: Peter Link
    staging: Michael Shawn
    sets: William Barclay
    costumes: David Dille
    choreography: Michael Shawn
Productions:
    (Off-Broadway) Opened January 13, 1988 for 41 performances
Reviews:
    New York Theatre Critics' Reviews 1988:373
    New York Times III, page 28, Jan 14, 1988

Riverwind
    book: John Jennings
    music: John Jennings
    lyrics: John Jennings
    staging: Adrian Hall
    sets: Robert Soule
    costumes: Robert Soule
Productions:
    (Off-Broadway) Opened December 12, 1962 for 433 performances
    (Off-Off-Broadway) Opened May 3, 1973
Reviews:
    New York Times page 5, Dec 14, 1962
                  page 33, Jan 2, 1964
                  page 53, May 7, 1973
    New Yorker 38:66-7, Dec 22, 1962

The Riviera Girl
    book: Guy Bolton and P. G. Wodehouse
    music: Emmerich Kalman
    lyrics: Guy Bolton and P. G. Wodehouse

Productions:
  Opened September 24, 1917 for 78 performances
Reviews:
  Dramatic Mirror 77:4-5, Oct 6, 1917
  New York Dramatic News 64:10, Sep 29, 1917
  New York Times page 9, Sep 25, 1917
              III, page 8, Sep 30, 1917
  Theatre Magazine 26:265, Nov 1917
                26:328, Nov 1917

The Roar of the Greasepaint--The Smell of the Crowd
    book: Leslie Bricusse and Anthony Newley
    music: Leslie Bricusse and Anthony Newley
    lyrics: Leslie Bricusse and Anthony Newley
    staging: Anthony Newley
    sets: Sean Kenny
    costumes: Freddy Wittop
    choreography: Gillian Lynne
Productions:
  Opened May 16, 1965 for 231 performances
Reviews:
  America 112:867-8, Jun 12, 1965
  Catholic World 201:151-2, May 1965
  Dance Magazine 39:22-3, Jul 1965
  New York Theatre Critics' Reviews 1965:326+
  New York Times page 46, May 17, 1965
  New Yorker 41:56, May 29, 1965
  Newsweek 65:76, May 31, 1965
  Reporter 32:45-6, Apr 8, 1965
  Saturday Review 48:38, Jun 5, 1965
  Time 85:83, May 28, 1965

Robber Bridegroom
    book: Alfred Uhry, based on novella by Eudora Welty
    music: Robert Waldman
    lyrics: Alfred Uhry
    staging: Gerald Freedman
    sets: Douglas W. Schmidt
    costumes: Jeanne Button
    choreography: Donald Saddler
Productions:
  Opened October 7, 1975 for 15 performances
  Opened October 9, 1976 for 145 performances
  (Off-Off-Broadway) Opened January 6, 1983
Reviews:
  America 133:inside back cover, Nov 15, 1975
  New York 8:82+, Oct 20, 1975
          9:77, Oct 25, 1976
  New York Theatre Critics' Reviews 1975:206
                                    1976:156
  New York Times page 27, Oct 8, 1975
              II, page 5, Oct 19, 1975

page 35, Oct 11, 1976
I, page 48, Jan 9, 1983
New Yorker 51:102, Oct 20, 1975
52:61, Oct 25, 1976
Time 108:87, Oct 25, 1976

Roberta
    book: Otto Harbach, adapted from Alice Duer Miller's
                       novel Gowns
    music: Jerome Kern
    lyrics: Otto Harbach
    staging: Hassard Short
    sets: Clark Robinson
    choreography: John Lonergan
Productions:
    Opened November 18, 1933 for 295 performances
Reviews:
    Catholic World 138:733-4, Mar 1934
    Fortune 9:69-76+, May 1934
    New Outlook 163:43, Jan 1934
    New York Times page 18, Nov 20, 1933
                     IX, page 3, Jan 13, 1935
                     II, page 3, Aug 18, 1935
    Newsweek 2:32, Nov 25, 1933
    Review of Reviews 89:48, Mar 1934
    Stage 11:8-9+, Dec 1933
    Time 22:45, Nov 27, 1933

Robinson Crusoe, Jr.
    book: Harold Atteridge and Edgar Smith
    music: Sigmund Romberg and James Hanley
    lyrics: Harold Atteridge and Edgar Smith
    staging: J. C. Huffman
    choreography: Allen K. Foster
Productions:
    Opened February 17, 1916 for 139 performances
Reviews:
    Dramatic Mirror 75:8, Feb 26, 1916
                    75:2, Mar 25, 1916
    Munsey 57:700, May 1916
    New York Dramatic News 62:17-18, Feb 26, 1916
    Theatre Magazine 23:196, Apr 1916
                     23:238, Apr 1916

Rock-a-Bye Baby
    book: Edgar Allan Woolf and Margaret Mayo
    music: Jerome Kern
    lyrics: Herbert Reynolds
    staging: Edward Royce
Productions:
    Opened May 22, 1918 for 85 performances

Reviews:
    Dramatic Mirror 78:608, Apr 27, 1918
                  78:802, Jun 8, 1918
                  78:873, Jun 22, 1918
    Green Book 20:202-3+, Aug 1918
    New York Times page 11, May 23, 1918
    Theatre Magazine 28:23, Jul 1918
                    28:31, Jul 1918

Rock 'n Roll! The First 5,000 Years

conceived: Bob Gill and Robert Rabinowitz
songs: Various authors and composers
staging: Joe Layton
sets: Mark Ravitz
costumes: Franne Lee
choreography: Joe Layton and Jerry Grimes
Productions:
    Opened October 24, 1982 for 9 performances
Reviews:
    New York Theatre Critics' Reviews 1982:176
    New York Times III, page 15, Oct 14, 1982
                 III, page 14, Oct 25, 1982

Rockabye Hamlet

book: Cliff Jones, based on Hamlet by William Shakespeare
music: Cliff Jones
lyrics: Cliff Jones
staging: Gower Champion
sets: Kert F. Lundell
costumes: Joseph G. Aulisi
choreography: Gower Champion and Tony Stevens
Productions:
    Opened May 4, 1980 for 89 performances
Reviews:
    New York Theatre Critics' Reviews 1980:246

A Rockette Spectacular

dialogue: Stan Hart
original music: Donald Pippin and Sammy Cahn
original lyrics: Donald Pippin and Sammy Cahn
staging: Robert F. Jani
sets: John W. Keck
costumes: Frank Spencer
choreography: Violet Holmes and Howard Parker
Productions:
    Opened February 17, 1976 for 7 performances
Reviews:
    New York 9:59+, Mar 1, 1976
    New York Theatre Critics' Reviews 1976:368
    New York Times page 23, Feb 18, 1976

New Yorker 52:76, Mar 1, 1976
Rolling Stone 209:22, Mar 25, 1976

The Rocking 60's Musical Soap Opera   (see Suds: The Rocking 60's
    Musical Soap Opera

The Rocky Horror Show
    book: Richard O'Brien
    music: Richard O'Brien
    lyrics: Richard O'Brien
    staging: Jim Sharman
    sets: Brian Thompson, supervised by Peter Harvey
    costumes: Sue Blane, supervised by Pearl Somner
Productions:
    Opened March 10, 1975 for 32 performances
Reviews:
    Dance Magazine 49:28+, May 1975
    New York Theatre Critics' Reviews 1975:311
    New York Times page 26, Mar 11, 1975
    Playboy 22:40+, Jun 1975
    Rolling Stone 157:26, Mar 28, 1974
    Time 105:85, Mar 24, 1975

Rodgers & Hart
    conceived: Richard Lewine and John Fearnley
    music: Richard Rodgers
    lyrics: Lorenz Hart
    staging: Burt Shevelove
    sets: David Jenkins
    costumes: Stanley Simmons
    choreography: Donald Saddler
Productions:
    Opened May 13, 1975 for 111 performances
Reviews:
    New York 8:58+, Jun 2, 1975
    New York Theatre Critics' Reviews 1975:260
    New York Times page 34, May 14, 1975
                    II, page 5, May 25, 1975
    New Yorker 51:77, May 26, 1975
    Playboy 22:30, Sep 1975

Roly-Boly Eyes
    book: Edgar Allan Woolf
    music: Eddy Brown and Louis Gruenberg
    lyrics: Edgar Allan Woolf
Productions:
    Opened September 25, 1919 for 100 performances
Reviews:
    Dramatic Mirror 80:1578, Oct 9, 1919
    Musical Courier 79:39, Oct 2, 1919
    New York Times page 11, Sep 26, 1919

Theatre Magazine 30: 344, Nov 1919
30: 371, Dec 1919

Romance Romance (two one-act musicals)
    book: Barry Harman, The Little Comedy based on the
                 short story by Arthur Schnitzler and Summer
                 Share based on the play Pain de Menage by Jules
                 Renard
    music: Keith Herrmann
    lyrics: Barry Harman
    staging: Barry Harman
    sets: Steven Rubin
    costumes: Steven Jones
    choreography: Pamela Sousa
Productions:
    (Off-Off-Broadway) Opened November 16, 1987
    Opened May 1, 1988 for 297 performances
Reviews:
    America 158: 536, May 21, 1988
    Nation 246: 727-8, May 21, 1988
    New York 21: 106+, May 16, 1988
    New York Theatre Critics' Reviews 1988: 284
    New York Times III, page 15, Nov 17, 1987
                    II, page 5, May 1, 1988
                     III, page 15, May 2, 1988
    New Yorker 64: 95, May 16, 1988

Romberg, Sigmund (see Evening with Romberg)

Rondelay
    book: Jerry Douglass; based on Arthur Schnitzler's
                 La Ronde
    music: Hal Jordon
    lyrics: Jerry Douglass
    staging: William Francisco
    sets: Raoul Pene du Bois
    choreography: Jacques d'Amboise
Productions:
    (Off-Broadway) Opened November 5, 1969 for 11 performances
Reviews:
    New York Times page 55, Nov 6, 1969

Rosalie
    book: William Anthony McGuire and Guy Bolton
    music: George Gershwin and Sigmund Romberg
    lyrics: P. G. Wodehouse and Ira Gershwin
    staging: Florenz Ziegfeld, Seymour Felix, William A.
                 McGuire
Productions:
    Opened January 10, 1928 for 335 performances
Reviews:
    New York Times IX, page 2, Dec 18, 1927

page 26, Jan 11, 1928
Outlook 148:344, Feb 29, 1928
Vogue 71:114, Mar 1, 1928

Rose, Billy   (see Billy Rose)

The Rose Girl
    book: William Cary Duncan
    music: Anselm Goetzl
    lyrics: William Cary Duncan
    staging: Hassard Short
Productions:
    Opened February 11, 1921 for 110 performances
Reviews:
    Dramatic Mirror 83:328, Feb 19, 1921
    New York Clipper 69:23, Feb 23, 1921
    New York Times page 11, Feb 12, 1921
    Theatre Magazine 33:304, Apr 1921
                     33:329, May 1921

Rose-Marie
    book: Otto Harbach and Oscar Hammerstein II
    music: Rudolf Friml and Herbert Stothart
    lyrics: Otto Harbach and Oscar Hammerstein II
    staging: Paul Dickey
    choreography: David Bennett
Productions:
    Opened September 2, 1924 for 557 performances
    Opened January 24, 1927 for 48 performances
    (Off-Broadway) Opened May 4, 1983 for 49 performances
Reviews:
    Canadian Magazine 64:164-6, Jul 1925
    New York Times VII, page 1, Aug 24, 1924
                    page 12, Sep 3, 1924
                    page 16, Mar 21, 1925
                    page 26, Dec 4, 1925
                    page 17, Apr 1, 1926
                    page 1, Sep 14, 1926
                    page 16, Sep 16, 1926
                    page 19, Jan 25, 1927
                    II, page 8, Apr 17, 1927
                    VII, page 2, May 8, 1927
                    page 15, Jul 17, 1927
                    page 23, Mar 31, 1928
                    IX, page 2, Apr 29, 1928
    Theatre Magazine 40:16, Nov 1924

The Rose of Algeria
    book: Glen MacDonough
    music: Victor Herbert
    lyrics: Glen MacDonough
    staging: Ned Wayburn

Productions:
Opened September 20, 1909 for 40 performances
Reviews:
Dramatic Mirror 62:7, Oct 2, 1909
Leslie's Weekly 109:391, Oct 21, 1909
109:415, Oct 28, 1909
Life (New York) 54:477, Oct 7, 1909
Metropolitan Magazine 31:268-9, Nov 1909
Theatre Magazine 10:v, Nov 1909
10:xiv, Nov 1909

The Rose of China
book: Guy Bolton
music: Armand Vecsey
lyrics: P. G. Wodehouse
Productions:
Opened November 25, 1919 for 47 performances
Reviews:
Dramatic Mirror 80:1909, Dec 11, 1919
Forum 63:113-14, Jan 1920
Munsey 69:314, Mar 1920
New York Times page 11, Nov 26, 1919
Theatre Magazine 31:61, Jan 1920
31:99, Feb 1920

Rosewood
book: Joel Gross
music: Brian Hurley
lyrics: Brian Hurley
staging: David Black
Productions:
(Off-Off-Broadway) Opened December 1975
Reviews:
New York Times page 12, Dec 30, 1976

Ross, Diana (see Evening with Diana Ross)

The Rothschilds
book: Sherman Yellen; based on The Rothschilds by
               Frederic Morton
music: Jerry Bock
lyrics: Sheldon Harnick
staging: Michael Kidd
sets: John Bury
costumes: John Bury
choreography: Michael Kidd
Productions:
Opened October 19, 1970 jor 507 performances
Reviews:
America 124:125, Feb 6, 1971
Dance Magazine 45:77-8, Jan 1971

Nation 211:506, Nov 16, 1970
New York Theatre Critics' Reviews 1970:181
                                  1970:184
New York Times page 26, Aug 11, 1970
              page 60, Oct 15, 1970
              II, page 1, Oct 18, 1970
              page 40, Oct 20, 1970
              II, page 1, Nov 1, 1970
              II, page 17, Nov 15, 1970
              page 34, Nov 5, 1971
              page 26, Dec 22, 1971
              page 21, Dec 29, 1971
              page 29, Feb 7, 1972
              VII, page 4, Mar 5, 1972
New Yorker 46:101, Oct 31, 1970
Newsweek 76:104, Nov 2, 1970
Saturday Review 53:6+, Nov 28, 1970
Time 96:77, Nov 2, 1970

Round the Town
    assembled: Herman Mankiewiez and S. Jay Kaufman
Productions:
Opened May 21, 1924 for 13 performances
Reviews:
New York Times page 14, May 22, 1924

Roza
    book: Julian More, based on La Vie Devant Soi by
                      Romain Gary
    music: Gilbert Becaud
    lyrics: Julian More
    staging: Harold Prince
    sets: Alexander Okun
    costumes: Florence Klotz
    choreography: Patricia Birch
Productions:
Opened October 1, 1987 for 12 performances
Reviews:
Los Angeles 32:207+, Jun 1987
Nation 245:460-1, Oct 24, 1987
New Leader 70:21, Nov 16, 1987
New York 20:98, Oct 12, 1987
New Yorker 63:118+, Oct 12, 1987
New York Theatre Critics' Reviews 1987:174
New York Times III, page 3, Oct 2, 1987

Rufus LeMaire's Affairs
    book: Ballard Macdonald; additional skits by Andy Rice
    music: Martin Broones
    lyrics: Ballard Macdonald
    staging: William Halligan, Jack Haskell and Albertina Rasch

Productions:
Opened March 28, 1927 for 56 performances
Reviews:
New York Times page 22, Mar 29, 1927
VIII, page 1, Apr 10, 1927
Theatre Magazine 45:24, Jun 27, 1927
Vogue 69:122, May 15, 1927

Rugantino
book: Pietro Garinei and Sandro Giovannini, with
                 Festa Campanile and Franciosa; English version
                 by Alfred Drake
music: Armando Trovaioli
lyrics: Pietro Garinei and Sandro Giovannini; English
                 version by Edward Eager
staging: Pietro Garinei and Sandro Giovannini
sets: Giulio Coltellacci
costumes: Giulio Coltellacci
choreography: Dania Krupska
Productions:
Opened February 6, 1964 for 28 performances
Reviews:
Nation 198:204, Feb 24, 1964
New York Theatre Critics' Reviews 1964:362+
New York Times page 25, Jan 17, 1964
II, page 1, Feb 2, 1964
page 24, Feb 20, 1964
New Yorker 39:113, Feb 15, 1964
Newsweek 63:90-1, Feb 17, 1964
Time 83:69, Feb 14, 1964

Ruggles of Red Gap
book: Harrison Rhodes; from stories by Harry Leon
                 Wilson
music: Sigmund Romberg
lyrics: Harold Atteridge
staging: J. H. Benrimo
Productions:
Opened December 25, 1915 for 33 performances
Reviews:
Dramatic Mirror 75:8, Jan 1, 1916
75:4, Jan 8, 1916
Life (New York) 67:26-7, Jan 6, 1916
Nation 101:786-7, Dec 30, 1915
New York Dramatic News 62:17-18, Jan 1, 1916
New York Times page 7, Dec 25, 1915
Theatre Magazine 23:65-6, Feb 1916

Rumple
book: Irving Phillips
music: Ernest G. Schweikert

lyrics: Frank Reardon
staging: Jack Donohue
sets: George Jenkins
costumes: Alvin Colt
choreography: Bob Hamilton
Productions:
  Opened November 6, 1957 for 45 performances
Reviews:
  New York Theatre Critics' Reviews 1957:188+
  New York Times page 42, Nov 7, 1957
  New Yorker 33:104+, Nov 16, 1957
  Newsweek 50:90, Nov 18, 1957
  Theatre Arts 42:22, Jan 1958
  Time 70:78, Nov 18, 1957

Rumstick Road
  by: Spalding Gray and Elizabeth LeCompte in col-
                   laboration with Libby Howes, Bruce Porter, and
                   Ron Vawter
  staging: Elizabeth LeCompte
  design: Jim Clayburgh and Elizabeth LeCompte
Productions:
  (Off-Off-Broadway) Opened March 1977
  (Off-Off-Broadway) Opened December 1978
  (Off-Broadway) Opened March 27, 1980 for 38 performances
Reviews:
  New York Times III, page 2, Mar 25, 1977
                 page 38, Apr 5, 1977
                 III, page 7, Dec 19, 1978
                 page 48, Mar 30, 1980

Runaways
  book: Elizabeth Swados
  music: Elizabeth Swados
  lyrics: Elizabeth Swados
  staging: Elizabeth Swados
  sets: Douglas W. Schmidt and Woods Mackintosh
  costumes: Hilary Rosenfeld
Productions:
  (Off-Broadway) Opened February 21, 1978 for 80 performances
  Opened May 13, 1978 for 267 performances
Reviews:
  America 138:349, Apr 29, 1978
  Commonweal 105:498, Aug 4, 1978
  Crawdaddy p. 20, Jul 1978
  Cycle page 20, Jul 1978
  Encore 7:30, May 22, 1978
  Nation 226:379-80, Apr 1, 1978
  New Republic 178:24, Apr 22, 1978
  New York 11:70-1, Mar 27, 1978
            11:77, May 29, 1978

New York Theatre Critics' Reviews 1978:278
New York Times III, page 3, Mar 10, 1978
            III, page 17, Mar 22, 1978
            III, page 15, May 15, 1978
            II, page 5, May 21, 1978
            II, page 4, Jun 4, 1978
New Yorker 54:88, Mar 20, 1978
Newsweek 91:74-5, Mar 27, 1978
Rolling Stone pages 54-6, Jun 15, 1978
Saturday Review 5:24, May 13, 1978
            5:24, Jul 8, 1978
Time 111:84, Mar 20, 1978

Runnin' Wild
    book: F. E. Miller and A. L. Lyles
    music: James Johnson and Cecil Mack
    lyrics: James Johnson and Cecil Mack
Productions:
    Opened October 29, 1923 for 213 performances
Reviews:
    New York Times page 17, Oct 30, 1923

Russell, Anna   (see Anna Russell's Little Show)

-S-

Sacco-Vanzetti
    book: Armand Aulicino
    music: Frank Gaskin Fields
    lyrics: Armand Aulicino
    staging: Allan Lokos
    choreography: Diane Adler
Productions:
    (Off-Broadway) Opened February 7, 1969 for 15 performances
Reviews:
    New York Times page 78, Feb 9, 1969
(See also The Shoemaker and the Peddler)

Sacred Guard
    conceived: Ken Rubenstein
    music: John Smead
    staging: Ken Rubenstein
Productions:
    (Off-Off-Broadway) Opened April 11, 1973
No Reviews.

Sadie Thompson
    book: Howard Dietz and Rouben Mamoulian, adapted
                        from Rain, a drama by John Colton and Clemence
                        Randolph, based on a story by Somerset Maugham

music: Vernon Duke
lyrics: Howard Dietz and Rouben Mamoulian
staging: Rouben Mamoulian
sets: Boris Aronson
costumes: Motley and Azadia Newman
choreography: Edward Caton
Productions:
Opened November 16, 1944 for 60 performances
Reviews:
Catholic World 160:357, Jan 1945
Collier's 115:12-13, Jan 6, 1945
Commonweal 41:174-5, Dec 1, 1944
Life 17:43-6+, Dec 11, 1944
Nation 159:698, Dec 2, 1944
New York Theatre Critics' Reviews 1944:84+
New York Times VI, page 28, Nov 12, 1944
                page 25, Nov 17, 1944
                II, page 1, Nov 26, 1944
New Yorker 20:46, Nov 25, 1944
Newsweek 24:100, Nov 27, 1944
Theatre Arts 29:12+, Jan 1945
Time 44:48, Nov 27, 1944

Safari 300
book: Tad Truesdale
staging: Hugh Gittens
sets: Bob Olsen
costumes: Lee Lynn
choreography: Lari Becham and Phil Black
Productions:
(Off-Broadway) Opened July 12, 1972 for 17 performances
Reviews:
New York Times page 27, Jul 13, 1972

Sail Away
book: Noel Coward
music: Noel Coward
lyrics: Noel Coward
staging: Noel Coward
sets: Oliver Smith
costumes: Helene Pons and Oliver Smith
choreography: Joe Layton
Productions:
Opened October 3, 1961 for 167 performances
Reviews:
Commonweal 75:154, Nov 3, 1961
Dance Magazine 35:28, Nov 1961
Nation 193:361, Nov 4, 1961
New Republic 145:22, Nov 6, 1961
New York Theatre Critics' Reviews 1961:251+
New York Times page 17, Aug 10, 1961

II, page 1, Oct 1, 1961
page 48, Oct 4, 1961
page 14, Jun 23, 1962
New Yorker 37:162+, Oct 14, 1961
Newsweek 58:101, Oct 16, 1961
Reporter 25:53, Oct 26, 1961
Saturday Review 44:34, Oct 21, 1961
Theatre Arts 45:10-11, Dec 1961
Time 78:58, Oct 13, 1961

St. Louis Woman

book: Arna Bontemps and Countee Cullen based on
               Arna Bontemps' God Sends Sunday
music: Harold Arlen
lyrics: Johnny Mercer
staging: Rouben Mamoulian
sets: Lemuel Ayers
costumes: Lemuel Ayers
choreography: Charles Walters
Productions:
Opened March 30, 1946 for 113 performances
Reviews:
Catholic World 163:170, May 1946
Commonweal 44:14, Apr 19, 1946
Forum 105:937-8, Jun 1946
Life 20:63-4, Apr 29, 1946
Modern Music 23 no2:146, Apr 1946
New York Theatre Critics' Reviews 1946:415+
New York Times page 22, Apr 1, 1946
page 20, Jul 3, 1946
New Yorker 22:46+, Apr 6, 1946
Newsweek 27:84, Apr 15, 1946
Saturday Review 29:24, Apr 27, 1946
Time 47:47, Apr 8, 1946

The Saint of Bleecker Street

book: Gian-Carlo Menotti
music: Gian Carlo Menotti
lyrics: Gian-Carlo Menotti
staging: Gian-Carlo Menotti
sets: Robert Randolph
costumes: Robert Randolph
Productions:
Opened December 27, 1954 for 92 performances
Opened September 29, 1965 for 2 performances
Reviews:
America 92:434, Jan 22, 1955
Catholic World 180:385, Feb 1955
Commonweal 61:476-7, Feb 4, 1955
Life 38:62-3, Feb 14, 1955
Musical America 75:3+, Jan 15, 1955

Nation 180:83, Jan 22, 1955
New York Theatre Critics' Reviews 1954:199+
New York Times page 21, Dec 28, 1954
                 II, page 1, Jan 2, 1955
                 II, page 1, Mar 6, 1955
                 page 26, May 9, 1955
                 page 76, Sep 18, 1955
                 page 26, Nov 1, 1955
                 page 38, Nov 22, 1955
                 page 78, Jun 10, 1956
                 page 40, Sep 4, 1957
New Yorker 30:74-6, Jan 8, 1955
           30:77, Jun 2, 1955
Newsweek 45:62, Jan 10, 1955
Reporter 12:40, Apr 7, 1955
Saturday Review 38:28, Jan 8, 1955
Theatre Arts 39:17+, Mar 1955
Time 65:42, Jan 10, 1955

Sally
    book: Guy Bolton
    music: Jerome Kern and Victor Herbert
    lyrics: Clifford Grey, additional lyrics by B. G. DeSylva
    staging: Edward Royce
Productions:
    Opened December 21, 1920 for 570 performances
    Opened May 6, 1948 for 36 performances
Reviews:
    Catholic World 167:268, Jun 1948
    Dramatic Mirror page 1241, Dec 25, 1920
    New Republic 118:34, May 31, 1948
    New York Clipper 68:18, Dec 29, 1920
    New York Theatre Critics' Reviews 1948:271+
    New York Times page 16, Dec 22, 1920
                    page 20, Sep 11, 1921
                    page 20, Mar 30, 1922
                    page 31, May 7, 1948
    New Yorker 24:48+, May 15, 1948
    Newsweek 31:90, May 17, 1948
    Theatre Arts 32:14, Jun 1948
    Theatre Magazine 33:178, Mar 1921
    Time 51:88, May 17, 1948

Sally, Irene and Mary
    book: Eddie Dowling and Cyrus Wood
    music: J. Fred Coots
    lyrics: Raymond Klages
    staging: Frank Smithson
Productions:
    Opened September 4, 1922 for 312 performances
    Opened March 23, 1925 for 16 performances

Reviews:
    New York Clipper 70:20, Sep 27, 1922
    New York Times page 21, Sep 5, 1922

Saluta
    book: Will Morrissey, revised by Eugene Conrad and
                       Maurice Marks
    music: Frank D'Armond
    lyrics: Will Morrissey
    staging: Will Morrissey and Edwin Saulpaugh
    sets: Hugh Willoughby
    choreography: Boots McKenna
Productions:
    Opened August 28, 1934 for 39 performances
Reviews:
    New York Times page 13, Aug 29, 1934

Salvation
    book: Peter Link and C. C. Courtney
    music: Peter Link and C. C. Courtney
    lyrics: Peter Link and C. C. Courtney
    staging: Paul Aaron
    choreography: Kathryn Posin
Productions:
    (Off-Broadway) Opened September 24, 1969 for 239 performances
Reviews:
    Christian Century 86:1646-7, Dec 24, 1969
    Commonweal 91:534-5, Feb 13, 1970
    Dance Magazine 43:84, Nov 1969
    New York Theatre Critics' Reviews 1969:198
    New York Times page 53, Mar 13, 1969
                    page 55, Sep 25, 1969
                    page 24, Sep 27, 1969
                    II, page 1, Oct 5, 1969
    New Yorker 45:114, Oct 4, 1969
    Newsweek 74:133, Oct 6, 1969
    Saturday Review 52:26, Oct 11, 1969

Sambo
    music: Ron Steward and Neal Tate
    lyrics: Ron Steward
    staging: Gerald Freedman
    sets: Ming Cho Lee and Marjorie Kellogg
    costumes: Milo Morrow
Productions:
    (Off-Broadway) Opened December 12, 1969 for 37 performances
    (Off-Broadway) Opened July 14, 1970 for 22 performances
Reviews:
    New York Theatre Critics' Reviews 1969:130
    New York Times page 42, Dec 22, 1969
                    II, page 3, Jan 11, 1970

page 24, Jul 23, 1970
page 20, Jul 24, 1970
New Yorker 45:43, Jan 3, 1970

Sancho Panza

book: Melchior Lengyel; based on Cervantes' Don
                 Quixote de la Mancha
music: Hugo Felix
lyrics: Hugo Felix
Productions:
Opened November 26, 1923 for 40 performances
Reviews:
American Mercury 1:119, Jan 1924
New York Times VIII, page 2, Oct 21, 1923
              page 23, Nov 27, 1923
              VIII, page 1, Dec 2, 1923
              IX, page 2, Dec 16, 1923
Theatre Magazine 39:16, Feb 1924

Sancocho

book: Ramiro Ramirez
music: Jimmy Justice and Ramiro Ramirez
lyrics: Jimmy Justice and Ramiro Ramirez
staging: Miguel Godreau
sets: Frank J. Boros
costumes: Frank J. Boros
choreography: Miguel Godreau
Productions:
(Off-Broadway) Opened March 28, 1979 for 7 performances
Reviews:
New York 12:66, Aug 6, 1979
New York Theatre Critics' Reviews 1979:256
New York Times III, page 15, Mar 29, 1979
New Yorker 55:100, Apr 9, 1979

Sandhog

book: Earl Robinson and Waldo Salt; based on Theodore
                 Dreiser's St. Columba and the River
music: Earl Robinson and Waldo Salt
lyrics: Earl Robinson and Waldo Salt
staging: Howard Da Silva
sets: Howard Bay
costumes: Toni Ward
choreography: Sophie Maslow
Productions:
Opened November 23, 1954 for 48 performances
Reviews:
America 92:326, Dec 18, 1954
Catholic World 180:308-9, Jan 1955
Nation 179:518, Dec 11, 1954
Newsweek 44:84, Dec 6, 1954

New York Theatre Critics' Reviews 1954:239
New York Times page 17, Nov 24, 1954
New Yorker 30:86+, Dec 4, 1954
Saturday Review 38:62, Jan 1, 1955
Theatre Arts 39:76+, Feb 1955

The Sap of Life
    book: Richard Maltby, Jr.
    music: David Shire
    lyrics: Richard Maltby, Jr.
    staging: William Francisco
    sets: John Conklin
    costumes: John Conklin
Productions:
    (Off-Broadway) Opened October 2, 1961 for 49 performances
Reviews:
    New York Times page 44, Oct 3, 1961
                   page 15, Nov 4, 1961
                   page 48, Nov 6, 1961
    New Yorker 37:166, Oct 14, 1961

Sarafina!
    conceived: Mbongeni Ngema
    written: Mbongeni Ngema
    music: Mbongeni Ngema and Hugh Masekela
    staging: Mbongeni Ngema
    sets: Sarah Roberts
    costumes: Sarah Roberts
    choreography: Ndaba Mhlongo
Productions:
    (Off-Broadway) Opened October 25, 1987 for 81 performances
    Opened January 28, 1988 for *560 performances (still running
    6/1/89)
Reviews:
    Nation 245:694, Dec 5, 1987
    New York 20:124, Nov 9, 1987
    New York Theatre Critics' Reviews 1988:384
    New York Times II, page 5, Oct 25, 1987
                   III, page 15, Oct 26, 1987
                   III, page 15, Feb 9, 1988
    New Yorker 63:130, Nov 9, 1987
    Newsweek 110:82, Nov 9, 1987
    Opera News 52:41, Jun 1988
    Time 131:10-11, Jun 13, 1988

Saratoga
    book: Morton Da Costa, based on Edna Ferber's
                      Saratoga Trunk
    music: Harold Arlen
    lyrics: Johnny Mercer
    staging: Morton Da Costa

```
    sets:              Cecil Beaton
    costumes:          Cecil Beaton
    choreography:      Ralph Beaumont
Productions:
    Opened December 7, 1959 for 80 performances
Reviews:
    America 102:594+, Feb 13, 1960
    New York Theatre Critics' Reviews 1959:195+
    New York Times page 59, Dec 8, 1959
                     page 23, Feb 1, 1960
    New Yorker 35:81, Dec 19, 1959
    Newsweek 54:83, Dec 21, 1959
    Saturday Review 42:25, Dec 26, 1959
    Theatre Arts 44:17-21, Jan 1960
    Time 74:34, Dec 21, 1959
    Vogue 135:114-15, Feb 1, 1960
```

Sarava
```
    book:              N. Richard Nash, based on Jorge Amado's novel
                       Dona Flor and Her Two Husbands and the film of
                       the same title
    music:             Mitch Leigh
    lyrics:            N. Richard Nash
    staging:           Rick Atwell
    sets:              Santo Loquasto
    costumes:          Santo Loquasto
    choreography:      Rick Atwell
Productions:
    Opened January 11, 1979 for 177 performances
Reviews:
    New Leader 62:21-2, Mar 12, 1979
    New York Theatre Critics' Reviews 1979:364
    New York Times III, page 12, Feb 12, 1979
                    II, page 5, Mar 4, 1979
    New Yorker 55:92, Mar 5, 1979
```

Satchmo: America's Musical Legend
```
    book:              Jerry Bilik, based on the life and career of
                       Louis Armstrong
    music:             Jerry Bilik
    lyrics:            Jerry Bilik
    staging:           Jerry Bilik
    sets:              Edward Burbridge
    costumes:          Judy Dearing
    choreography:      Maurice Hines
Productions:
    Closed prior to Broadway opening (New Orleans and Boston, July
    1987)
Reviews:
    Jet 72:18, Aug 24, 1987
```

Saturday Night (see American Legend)

Say, Darling
book: Richard Bissell, Abe Burrows, and Marian Bissell, based on the novel by Richard Bissell
music: Jule Styne
lyrics: Betty Comden and Adolph Green
staging: Abe Burrows
sets: Oliver Smith
costumes: Alvin Colt
choreography: Matt Mattox
Productions:
    Opened April 3, 1958 for 332 performances
    Opened February 25, 1959 for 16 performances
    (Off-Broadway) Opened November 12, 1965 for 15 performances
Reviews:
    America 99:178, May 3, 1958
    Catholic World 187:225, Jun 1958
    Commonweal 68:351, Jul 4, 1958
    New York Theatre Critics' Reviews 1958:317+
    New York Times II, page 1, Mar 30, 1958
               page 17, Apr 4, 1958
               II, page 1, Apr 13, 1958
               II, page 1, Jan 18, 1959
               page 38, Feb 26, 1959
    New Yorker 34:67, Apr 12, 1958
    Newsweek 51:87, Apr 14, 1958
    Saturday Review 41:28, Apr 19, 1958
    Time 71:66, Apr 14, 1958

Say When (1928)
book: Calvin Brown, based on Amelie Rives and Gilbert Emery's Love in a Mist
music: Jesse Greer
lyrics: Raymond Klages
staging: Bertram Harrison and Max Scheck
Productions:
    Opened June 26, 1928 for 24 performances
Reviews:
    Golden Book Magazine 21:30a, Feb 1935
    New York Times page 29, Jun 27, 1928
    Outlook 149:425, Jul 11, 1928

Say When (1934)
book: Jack McGowan
music: Ray Henderson
lyrics: Ted Koehler
staging: Bertram Harrison and Russell Markert
sets: Clark Robinson
Productions:
    Opened November 8, 1934 for 76 performances

Reviews:
  New York Times page 24, Nov 9, 1934
  Stage 12:9, Dec 1934

Say When (1972)
  book: Keith Winter
  music: Arnold Goland
  lyrics: Keith Winter
  staging: Zoya Leporska
  sets: William James Wall
  costumes: Leilia Larmon
  choreography: Zoya Leporska
Productions:
  (Off-Broadway) Opened December 4, 1972 for 7 performances
Reviews:
  New York Times page 61, Dec 5, 1972

Scandals (see George White's Scandals)

Scenes from Country Life
  book: Norman Plotkin
  music: Michael S. Roth
  lyrics: Norman Plotkin and Michael S. Roth
  staging: Carl Weber
  sets: Jonathan Arkin
  costumes: Perry McLamb
Productions:
  (Off-Off-Broadway) Opened March 8, 1978 for 12 performances
Reviews:
  New York Times page 29, Mar 14, 1978

Scrambled Feet
  by: John Driver and Jeffrey Haddow
  staging: John Driver
  sets: Ernest Allen Smith
  costumes: Kenneth M. Yount
Productions:
  (Off-Broadway) Opened June 11, 1979 for 831 performances
Reviews:
  Los Angeles 26:274, Sep 1981
  New York 12:66, Aug 6, 1979
  New York Theatre Critics' Reviews 1979:181
  New York Times III, page 6, Jun 12, 1979
              II, page 1, Sep 9, 1979
  Newsweek 94:77, Aug 20, 1979
  Time 114:65, Jul 2, 1979

Sea Legs
  book: Arthur Swanstrom
  music: Michael H. Cleary
  lyrics: Arthur Swanstrom

staging: Bertram Harrison
sets: Mabel Buell
choreography: Johnny Mattison
Productions:
  Opened May 18, 1937 for 15 performances
Reviews:
  New York Times page 26, May 19, 1937

Second Little Show
  assembled by: Dwight Deere Wiman
  music: Arthur Schwartz
  lyrics: Howard Dietz
  staging: Dwight Deere Wiman, David Gould, Monty Woolley
Productions:
  Opened September 2, 1930 for 63 performances
Reviews:
  Life (New York) 96:16, Sep 19, 1930
  New York Times VIII, page 2, Aug 17, 1930
                 page 36, Sep 3, 1930
  Vogue 76:60+, Oct 27, 1930

The Secret Life of Walter Mitty
  book: Joe Manchester; based on the short story by
                  James Thurber
  music: Leon Carr
  lyrics: Earl Shuman
  staging: Mervyn Nelson
  sets: Lloyd Burlingame
  costumes: Al Lehman
  choreography: Bob Arlen
Productions:
  (Off-Broadway) Opened October 26, 1964 for 96 performances
Reviews:
  New York Times page 44, Oct 27, 1964
                 page 34, Dec 28, 1964

Seduction Scene from a Musical Play in Progress
  book: Stuart Richard Townsend
  music: John Wallowitch
  staging: Robert Haddad
Productions:
  (Off-Off-Broadway) Opened May 10, 1964 for 3 performances
No Reviews.

See-Saw
  book: Earl Derr Biggers; adapted from the novel Love
                  Insurance
  music: Louis A. Hirsch
  lyrics: Earl Derr Biggers
Productions:
  Opened September 23, 1919 for 89 performances

Reviews:
Dramatic Mirror 80:1538, Oct 2, 1919
New York Times page 21, Sep 24, 1919
Theatre Magazine 30:371, Dec 1919

Seeniaya Ptitza (The Blue Bird)
  material: Yasha Yushua
Productions:
Opened December 29, 1924 for 80 performances
Reviews:
Life (New York) 85:18, Jan 15, 1925
New York Times page 11, Dec 29, 1924

Seesaw
  book: Michael Bennett; based on the play Two for the
                   Seesaw by William Gibson
  music: Cy Coleman
  lyrics: Dorothy Fields
  staging: Michael Bennett
  sets: Robin Wagner
  costumes: Ann Roth
  choreography: Michael Bennett
Productions:
Opened March 18, 1973 for 296 performances
(Off-Off-Broadway) Opened October 29, 1981
Reviews:
America 128:336, Apr 14, 1973
Dance Magazine 47:58A-58C, Jun 1973
Harper's 106:153, Mar 1973
Nation 216:508, Apr 16, 1973
New York 6:66, Apr 2, 1973
New York Theatre Critics' Reviews 1973:324
New York Times page 46, Mar 19, 1973
               II, page 1, Mar 25, 1973
               II, page 1, Apr 8, 1973
               page 53, Sep 11, 1973
               page 73, Nov 8, 1981
New Yorker 49:74, Mar 24, 1973
Newsweek 81:83, Apr 2, 1973
Playboy 20:48, Jun 1973
Time 101:71, Apr 2, 1973

The Selling of the President
  book: Jack O'Brien and Stuart Hample; based on the
                   book by Joe McGinniss
  music: Bob James
  lyrics: Jack O'Brien
  staging: Robert H. Livingston
  sets: Tom John
  costumes: Nancy Potts

Productions:
Opened March 22, 1972 for 5 performances
Reviews:
Life 35:52-3, Sep 7, 1971
New York Theatre Critics' Reviews 1972:351
New York Times page 30, Jan 19, 1972
               page 37, Feb 7, 1972
               page 28, Mar 3, 1972
               page 50, Mar 23, 1972
Newsweek 77:121, Apr 12, 1971

Sensations
   book: Paul Zakrzweski; suggested by William Shake-
                        speare's Romeo and Juliet
   music: Wally Harper
   lyrics: Paul Zakrzweski
   staging: Jerry Dodge
   sets: William and Jean Eckart
   costumes: Jeanne Button
Productions:
(Off-Broadway) Opened October 25, 1970 for 16 performances
Reviews:
New York Times page 48, Oct 26, 1970
New Yorker 46:135, Nov 7, 1970

The Serenade
   book: Harry B. Smith
   music: Victor Herbert
   staging: Milton Aborn
Productions:
Opened March 4, 1930 for 15 performances
Reviews:
New York Times page 23, Feb 20, 1930

Sgt. Pepper's Lonely Hearts Club Band on the Road
   book: Conceived and adapted by Robin Wagner and Tom
                        O'Horgan, based on the album by the Beatles
   music: John Lennon and Paul McCartney
   lyrics: John Lennon and Paul McCartney
   staging: Tom O'Horgan
   sets: Robin Wagner
   costumes: Randy Barcelo
Productions:
Opened November 17, 1974 for 66 performances
Reviews:
Cycle page 30+, Feb 1975
New York 7:86, Dec 2, 1974
New York Theatre Critics' Reviews 1974:182
New York Times page 46, Nov 18, 1974
Rolling Stone 175:10, Dec 5, 1974
Time 104:75, Dec 2, 1974

Serious Bizness
   by: Jennifer Allen, David Babcock, Don Perman and
                    Winnie Holzman
   music: David Evans
   staging: Phyllis Newman
   sets: Loren Sherman
   costumes: Cynthia O'Neal
Productions:
   (Off-Broadway) Opened September 26, 1983 for 189 performances
Reviews:
   New York Times III, page 3, Sep 30, 1983

Seven Brides for Seven Brothers
   book: Lawrence Kasha and David Landay, based on the
                    M-G-M film and The Sobbin' Women by Stephen
                    Vincent Benet
   music: Gene de Paul
   lyrics: Johnny Mercer
   new songs: Al Kasha and Joel Hirschhorn
   staging: Lawrence Kasha
   sets: Robert Randolph
   costumes: Robert Fletcher
   choreography: Jerry Jackson
Productions:
   Opened July 8, 1982 for 5 performances
Reviews:
   New York 15:60-1, Jul 19, 1982
   New York Theatre Critics' Reviews 1982:247
   New York Times III, page 3, Jul 9, 1982
                    II, page 3, Jul 13, 1982
   New Yorker 58:69, Jul 19, 1982

The Seven Deadly Sins
   book: Bertolt Brecht
   music: Kurt Weill
   lyrics: Bertolt Brecht
Productions:
   (Off-Broadway) Opened Season of 1958-59
Reviews:
   Time 72:42, Dec 29, 1958

Seven Lively Arts
   assembled: Billy Rose
   sketches: Moss Hart, George S. Kaufman, Robert Pirosh,
                    Joseph Schrank, Charles Sherman, Ben Hecht
   music: Cole Porter and Igor Stravinsky
   lyrics: Cole Porter
   staging: Hassard Short
   sets: Norman Bel Geddes
   costumes: Mary Shaw and Valentina
   choreography: Anton Dolin

Productions:
    Opened December 7, 1944 for 183 performances
Reviews:
    Catholic World 160:356, Jan 1945
    Commonweal 41:253-4, Dec 22, 1944
    Life 17:24-6, Dec 25, 1944
    Nation 159:781, Dec 23, 1944
    New Republic 111:867, Dec 25, 1944
    New York Theatre Critics' Reviews 1944:62+
    New York Times page 26, Dec 8, 1944
                    II, page 5, Dec 10, 1944
                    II, page 3, Dec 17, 1944
    New Yorker 20:42+, Dec 16, 1944
    Newsweek 24:76+, Dec 18, 1944
    Saturday Review 28:26, Jan 20, 1945
                    28:19-20, Mar 10, 1945

    Theatre Arts 29:66+, Feb 1945
    Time 44:72+, Dec 18, 1944

Seventeen
    book: Sally Benson, based on Booth Tarkington's novel
    music: Walter Kent
    lyrics: Kim Gannon
    staging: Hassard Short
    sets: Stewart Chaney
    costumes: David Ffolkes
    choreography: Dania Krupska
Productions:
    Opened June 21, 1951 for 182 performances
    (Off-Broadway) Opened May 5, 1962 for 9 performances
Reviews:
    Catholic World 173:386, Aug 1951
    Commonweal 54:309, Jul 6, 1951
    Life 31:57-8, Jul 23, 1951
    Musical America 71:34, Jul 1951
    New York Theatre Critics' Reviews 1951:250+
    New York Times II, page 2, Jun 10, 1951
                    page 16, Jun 22, 1951
                    II, page 1, Jul 1, 1951
                    II, page 9, Jul 1, 1951
    New Yorker 27:39, Jun 30, 1951
    Newsweek 38:74, Jul 2, 1951
    Theatre Arts 35:6-7, Sep 1951
    Time 58:55, Jul 2, 1951

1776
    book: Peter Stone; based on a conception of Sherman
                    Edwards'
    music: Sherman Edwards
    lyrics: Sherman Edwards
    staging: Peter Hunt

sets:	Jo Mielziner
costumes:	Patricia Zipprodt
choreography:	Onna White and Martin Allen

Productions:

Opened March 16, 1969 for 1,217 performances

Reviews:

America 120:512-14, Apr 26, 1969
Dance Magazine 43:92-3, May 1969
Nation 208:443-4, Apr 7, 1969
National Review 21:919, Sep 9, 1969
New York Theatre Critics' Reviews 1969:324
New York Times page 46, Mar 17, 1969
            page 38, Mar 18, 1969
            II, page 1, Mar 23, 1969
            II, page 1, Apr 6, 1969
            page 1, Feb 23, 1970
            page 54, Jun 18, 1970
            page 17, Apr 3, 1971
            II, page 9, Jan 30, 1972
            page 23, Feb 8, 1972
New Yorker 45:87, Mar 22, 1969
Newsweek 73:105, Mar 31, 1969
Reader's Digest 96:199-200+, Feb 1970

Saturday Review 52:20, Apr 5, 1969
Time 93:55, Mar 28, 1969
Vogue 153:118-19, Jun 1969

The Seventh Heart

book:	Sarah Ellis Hyman
staging:	Edward Elsner

Productions:

Opened May 2, 1927 for 8 performances

No Reviews.

Seventh Heaven

book:	Victor Wolfson and Stella Unger, based on Austin Strong's play Seventh Heaven
music:	Victor Young
lyrics:	Stella Unger
staging:	John C. Wilson
sets:	Marcel Vertes
costumes:	Marcel Vertes
choreography:	Peter Gennaro

Productions:

Opened May 26, 1955 for 44 performances

Reviews:

America 93:298, Jun 11, 1955
Catholic World 181:307-8, Jul 1955
Commonweal 62:329, Jul 1, 1955
Nation 180:510, Jun 11, 1955
New York Theatre Critics' Reviews 1955:302+

New York Times VI, page 19, May 15, 1955
                II, page 1, May 22, 1955
                page 16, May 27, 1955
New York Times Magazine page 19, May 15, 1955
Saturday Review 38:25, Jun 11, 1955
Theatre Arts 39:18-19, Aug 1955
Time 65:57, Jun 6, 1955

70, Girls, 70
    book: Fred Ebb and Norman L. Martin; adaption by
                     by Joseph Masteroff
    music: John Kander
    lyrics: Fred Ebb
    staging: Paul Aaron
    sets: Robert Randolph
    costumes: Jane Greenwood
    choreography: Onna White and Martin Allen
Productions:
    Opened April 15, 1971 for 36 performances
Reviews:
    America 124:615-16, Jun 12, 1971
    Dance Magazine 45:81-2, Jun 1971
    Nation 212:570-1, May 3, 1971
    New York Theatre Critics' Reviews 1971:302
    New York Times page 28, Feb 16, 1971
                    page 29, Apr 16, 1971
                    II, page 1, Apr 25, 1971
    New Yorker 47:93-4, Apr 24, 1971

Sex Tips for Modern Girls
    created: Edward Astley, Susan Astley, Kim Seary, John
                     Sereda, Hilary Strang, Christine Willes and
                     Peter Eliot Weiss
    songs: John Sereda and others
    staging: Susan Astley
    sets: Pearl Bellesen
    costumes: Pearl Bellesen
Productions:
    (Off-Broadway) Opened October 5, 1986 for 198 performances
Reviews:
    New York Times III, page 23, Oct 8, 1986

Sextet
    book: Harvey Perr and Lee Goldsmith
    music: Lawrence Hurwit
    lyrics: Lee Goldsmith
    staging: Jered Barclay
    sets: Peter Harvey
    costumes: Zoe Brown
    choreography: Jered Barclay
Productions:
    Opened March 3, 1974 for 9 performances

Reviews:
New York Theatre Critics' Reviews 1974:352
New York Times page 36, Mar 4, 1974

Shades of Harlem
  created: Jeree Palmer, ("A re-creation of an evening at
                   the Cotton Club in the 1920s.")
  songs: Various authors and composers
  staging: Mical Whitaker
  sets: Linda Lombardi
  costumes: Sharon Alexander
  choreography: Ty Stephens
Productions:
  (Off-Broadway) Opened August 21, 1984 for 258 performances
Reviews:
  Dance Magazine 58:76-7, Nov 1984
  New York Times III, page 13, Aug 22, 1984

Shady Lady
  book: Estelle Morando, revised by Irving Caesar
  music and
    lyrics: Sam H. Stept, Bud Green, Jesse Greer, Stanley
                   Adams
  staging: Theodore Hammerstein
  sets: Tom Adrian Cracraft
  choreography: Jack Donohue
Productions:
  Opened July 5, 1933 for 30 performances
Reviews:
  New York Times page 26, Jul 26, 1933

Shakespeare's Cabaret
  conceived: Lance Mulcahy, with words by William Shake-
                   speare
  music: Lance Mulcahy
  staging: John Driver
  sets: Frank J. Boros
  costumes: Frank J. Boros
  choreography: Lynne Taylor-Corbett
Productions:
  (Off-Broadway) Opened February 1, 1980 for 40 performances
  Opened January 21, 1981 for 54 performances
Reviews:
  New York 14:43+, Feb 2, 1981
  New York Theatre Critics' Reviews 1981:380
  New York Times III, page 15, Feb 11, 1980
                   III, page 15, Jan 22, 1981

Shangri-La
  book: James Hilton, Jerome Lawrence, Robert E. Lee,
                   based on James Hilton's novel Lost Horizon
  music: Harry Warren

lyrics:	James Hilton, Jerome Lawrence, Robert E. Lee
staging:	Albert Marre
costumes:	Irene Sharaff
choreography:	Donald Saddler

Productions:
Opened June 13, 1956 for 21 performances
Reviews:
America 95:330, Jun 30, 1956
Catholic World 183:388, Aug 1956
New York Theatre Critics' Reviews 1956:293+
New York Times page 40, Jun 14, 1956
Saturday Review 39:22, Jun 30, 1956
Theatre Arts 40:16, Aug 1956
Time 67:86+, Jun 25, 1956

Sharlee

book:	Harry L. Cort and George E. Stoddard
music:	C. Luckyeth Roberts
lyrics:	Alex Rogers

Productions:
Opened November 22, 1923 for 36 performances
Reviews:
New York Times page 20, Nov 23, 1923

She Loves Me

book:	Joe Masteroff, based on Miklos Laszlo's play Parfumerie
music:	Jerry Bock
lyrics:	Sheldon Harnick
staging:	Harold Prince
sets:	William and Jean Eckart
costumes:	Patricia Zipprodt
choreography:	Carol Haney

Productions:
Opened April 23, 1963 for 301 performances
(Off-Broadway) Opened April 18, 1969 for 15 performances
(Off-Off-Broadway) Opened November 19, 1976
(Off-Off-Broadway) Opened October 31, 1985
Reviews:
Commonweal 78:225, May 17, 1963
Life 55:49-50+, Jul 12, 1963
Los Angeles 32:310+, Aug 1987
New York Theatre Critics' Reviews 1963:330+
1977:292
New York Times page 39, Apr 24, 1963
II, page 1, May 5, 1963
page 20, Jan 10, 1964
III, page 19, Mar 30, 1977
III, page 3, Nov 8, 1985
New Yorker 39:90, May 4, 1963
61:138, Nov 25, 1985

Newsweek 61:83, May 6, 1963
Saturday Review 46:26, May 11, 1963
Theatre Arts 47:12-13, Jun 1963
Theatre Crafts 20:26-7+, May 1986
Time 81:76, May 3, 1963
     109:88, Apr 11, 1977

Sheba
    book: Hazel Bryant
    music: Jimmy Justice
    staging: Helaine Head
    choreography: Milo Timmons
Productions:
    (Off-Off-Broadway) Opened April 19, 1974
No Reviews.

Shelter
    book: Gretchen Cryer
    music: Nancy Ford
    lyrics: Gretchen Cryer
    staging: Austin Pendleton
    sets: Tony Walton
    costumes: Tony Walton
    choreography: Sammy Bayes
Productions:
    Opened February 6, 1973 for 31 performances
Reviews:
    New York 6:66, Feb 26, 1973
    New York Theatre Critics' Reviews 1973:370
    New York Times page 31, Feb 7, 1973
                 II, page 1, Feb 18, 1973
    New Yorker 48:79, Feb 17, 1973

Shenandoah
    book: James Lee Barrett, Peter Udell, and Philip Rose,
                      based on the original screenplay by James Lee
                      Barrett
    music: Gary Geld
    lyrics: Peter Udell
    staging: Philip Rose
    sets: C. Murawski
    costumes: Pearl Somner
    choreography: Robert Tucker
Productions:
    Opened January 7, 1975 for 1,050 performances
Reviews:
    America 132:93, Feb 8, 1975
    Dance Magazine 49:34+, Mar 1975
    New York 8:51, Jan 27, 1975
               22:134-5, Aug 21, 1989
    New York Theatre Critics' Reviews 1975:380
                                  1989:246

New York Times II, page 1, Sep 8, 1974
                page 30, Jan 8, 1975
                II, page 1, Jul 20, 1975
                II, page 5, Aug 10, 1975
                III, page 4, Apr 1, 1977
                XXII, page 14, May 28, 1978
                XXIII, page 18, Jun 11, 1978
New Yorker 50:61, Jan 20, 1975
Newsweek 85:82-3, Jan 20, 1975
Playboy 21:40, Mar 1974
        22:46, Apr 1975
Time 105:76, Jan 20, 1975

Sherry!
    book: James Lipton; based on The Man Who Came to
                    Dinner by George S. Kaufman and Moss Hart
    music: Laurence Rosenthal
    lyrics: James Lipton
    staging: Joe Layton
    sets: Robert Randolph
    costumes: Robert Mackintosh
    choreography: John Morris
Productions:
    Opened March 27, 1967 for 72 performances
Reviews:
    America 116:736-7, May 13, 1967
    Christian Century 84:870-1, Jul 5, 1967
    Commonweal 86:208-10, May 5, 1967
    Dance Magazine 41:27-8, May 1967
    New York Theatre Critics' Reviews 1967:332
    New York Times page 39, Mar 29, 1967
                    II, page 5, Apr 9, 1967
                    page 55, May 24, 1967
    New Yorker 43:138, Apr 8, 1967
    Newsweek 69:109, Apr 10, 1967
    Vogue 149:142, May 1967

She's a Good Fellow
    music: Jerome Kern
    libretto: Anne Caldwell
    lyrics: Anne Caldwell
    staging: Fred G. Latham and Edward Royce
Productions:
    Opened May 5, 1919 for 120 performances
Reviews:
    Forum 61:755, Jun 1919
    Life (New York) 73:904, May 22, 1919
    New York Times page 16, May 6, 1919
    Theatre Arts 29:343, Jun 1919
                   29:19, Jul 1919

She's My Baby
book: Bert Kalmar and Harry Ruby
music: Richard Rodgers
lyrics: Lorenz Hart
staging: Edward Royce
Productions:
  Opened January 3, 1928 for 71 performances
Reviews:
  Life (New York) 91:21, Jan 19, 1928
  New York Times page 22, Jan 4, 1928

Shinbone Alley
book: Joe Darion and Mel Brooks, based on the "archy
                         and mehitabel" stories of Don Marquis
music: George Kleinsinger
lyrics: Joe Darion
sets: Eldon Elder
costumes: Motley
choreography: Rod Alexander
Productions:
  Opened April 13, 1957 for 49 performances
Reviews:
  America 97:216, May 11, 1957
  Catholic World 185:228-9, Jun 1957
  Christian Century 74:762, Jun 19, 1957
  Commonweal 66:204, May 24, 1957
  New York Theatre Critics' Reviews 1957:292+
  New York Times page 23, Apr 15, 1957
                  II, page 1, Apr 28, 1957
  New Yorker 33:82+, Apr 20, 1957
  Newsweek 49:69-70, Apr 22, 1957
  Theatre Arts 41:15-16, Jun 1957
  Time 69:90, Apr 22, 1957

Shirley MacLaine
written: Frank Ebb
additional
  material: Bob Wells
music: Cy Coleman
staging: Tony Charmoli
choreography: Alan Johnson
Productions:
  Opened April 19, 1976 for 14 performances
  Opened July 9, 1976 for 20 performances
Reviews:
  New York Theatre Critics' Reviews 1976:293

Shirley MacLaine on Broadway
songs: Marvin Hamlisch and Christopher Adler
additional
  material: Larry Grossman and Buz Kohan

staging: Alan Johnson
costumes: Pete Menefee
choreography: Alan Johnson
Productions:
Opened April 19, 1984 for 47 performances
Reviews:
New York Theatre Critics' Reviews 1984: 308
New York Times III, page 3, Apr 20, 1984

The Shoemaker and the Peddler
    book: Armand Aulicino; based on the story of Sacco
                    and Vanzetti
    music: Frank Fields
    lyrics: Armand Aulicino
    staging: Lee Nametz
    sets: David Ballou
    costumes: David Ballou
    choreography: Sophie Maslow
Productions:
    (Off-Broadway) Opened October 14, 1960 for 43 performances
Reviews:
    New York Times page 27, Oct 15, 1960
                   page 12, Nov 12, 1960
    New Yorker 36:92, Oct 22, 1960
(See also Sacco-Vanzetti)

Shoemaker's Holiday
    book: Ted Berger
    music: Mel Marvin
    lyrics: Ted Berger
    staging: Ken Costigan
    sets: Robert Conley
    costumes: Whitney Blausen
    choreography: Myrna Gallé
Productions:
    (Off-Broadway) Opened March 3, 1967 for 6 performances
Reviews:
    New York Times page 25, Mar 3, 1967
                   page 15, Mar 4, 1967
    New Yorker 43:127-8+, Mar 11, 1967

Shoestring Revue
    conceived: Ben Bagley
Productions:
    (Off-Broadway) Season of 1954-55
Reviews:
    America 93:26, Apr 2, 1955
    Catholic World 181:68, Apr 1955
    Nation 180:294, Apr 2, 1955
    New York Times page 22, Mar 1, 1955
    New Yorker 31:67, Mar 12, 1955

Saturday Review 38:25, Apr 23, 1955
Theatre Arts 39:87, May 1955

Shoot the Works
    assembled by: Heywood Broun and Milton Raison
    contributors: Heywood Broun, H. I. Phillips, Peter Arno,
                    Sig Herzig, Edward J. McNamara, Michael H.
                    Cleary, Philip Charig, Jay Gorney, Dorothy
                    Fields, Ira Gershwin, Alexander Williams, Robert
                    Stolz, A. Robinson, Dorothy Parker, Nunnally
                    Johnson, E. B. White, Jack Hazzard, Irving Ber-
                    lin, Max Lief, Nathaniel Lief, E. Y. Harburg,
                    Jimmie McHugh, Vernon Duke, Herbert Goode,
                    Walter Reisch
Productions:
  Opened July 21, 1931 for 87 performances
Reviews:
    Arts and Decoration 35:45+, Oct 1931
    Commonweal 14:346, Aug 5, 1931
    Nation 133:148, Aug 12, 1931
    New Republic 67:317-18, Aug 5, 1931
    New York Times page 19, Jul 22, 1931
                    VIII, page 2, Jul 26, 1931
                    VIII, page 2, Aug 16, 1931
                    page 35, Oct 6, 1931
    Outlook 158:437, Aug 5, 1931
    Saturday Evening Post 204:16-17+, Nov 14, 1931

Short, Hassard   (see Hassard Short)

Show Boat
    book: Oscar Hammerstein II, adapted from Edna
                  Ferber's novel
    music: Jerome Kern
    lyrics: Oscar Hammerstein II
    staging: Florenz Ziegfeld and Zeke Cohan
    sets: Joseph Urban
    costumes: John Harkrider
    choreography: Sammy Lee
Productions:
  Opened December 27, 1927 for 572 performances
  Opened May 19, 1932 for 180 performances
  Opened January 5, 1946 for 418 performances
  Opened September 1948 for 15 performances
  Opened May 5, 1954 for 15 performances
  Opened April 12, 1961 for 14 performances
  Opened July 19, 1966 for 63 performances
  (Off-Off-Broadway) Opened July 1, 1976
  Opened April 24, 1983 for 73 performances
Reviews:
    America 91:227+, May 22, 1954

95:351, Jul 7, 1956
97:490, Aug 10, 1957
115:140-1, Aug 6, 1966
Arts and Decoration 37:43+, Sep 1932
Catholic World 162:456, Feb 1946
     168:77, Oct 1948
     179:308, Jul 1954
     183:388, Aug 1956
     185:469, Sep 1957
Commonweal 74:379, Jul 7, 1961
Cosmopolitan 120:32-3+, Apr 1946
Dance Magazine 40:34+, Sep 1966
     57:88+, Aug 1983
Life (New York) 91:21, Jan 12, 1928
Life 20:71-2+, Jan 28, 1946
Musical America 74:10, May 1954
Nation 134:660, Jun 8, 1932
  162:138, Feb 2, 1946
  178:390, May 1, 1954
  192:378, Apr 29, 1961
  236:746, Jun 11, 1983
New Leader 66:22, May 2, 1983
New Republic 119:38, Sep 27, 1948
New York 16:89-90, May 9, 1983
New York Theatre Critics' Reviews 1946:496+
           1983:270
New York Times page 26, Dec 18, 1927
      VIII, page 1, Jan 8, 1928
      page 31, May 4, 1928
      page 9, May 5, 1928
      page 14, Dec 26, 1928
      VIII, page 4, Dec 30, 1928
      page 22, May 20, 1932
      VIII, page 5, May 29, 1932
      II, page 5, Jul 3, 1938
      page 17, Jan 7, 1946
      II, page 1, Jan 13, 1946
      II, page 1, Feb 24, 1946
      II, page 1, Jun 23, 1946
      VI, page 25, Sep 29, 1946
      VI, page 23, Dec 8, 1946
      page 33, Sep 9, 1948
      II, page 1, Sep 19, 1948
      page 19, Jun 6, 1952
      page 19, Apr 9, 1954
      page 72, Apr 18, 1954
      page 21, May 3, 1954
      page 44, May 6, 1954
      page 28, Oct 29, 1954
      page 27, Nov 1, 1954
      page 16, Jun 22, 1956

page 30, Jun 28, 1957
page 32, Apr 13, 1961
II, page 1, Jul 17, 1966
page 48, Jul 20, 1966
page 18, Jul 6, 1976
XXI, page 3, Jul 11, 1976
VII, page 10, Nov 13, 1977
XXII, page 2, Dec 18, 1977
III, page 12, Apr 25, 1983
II, page 3, May 8, 1983
New Yorker 21:40+, Jan 12, 1946
         30:116, Apr 17, 1954
         59:109, May 9, 1983
         65:79-94, Jul 3, 1989
Newsweek 27:77, Jan 14, 1946
       43:52-3, Apr 19, 1954
       101:76, May 9, 1983
Outlook 148:265, Feb 15, 1928
Saturday Review 29:30-2, Jan 26, 1946
               37:27, Apr 24, 1954
               49:34, Aug 6, 1966
Stage 9:4, Jul 1932
Theatre Arts 27:246, Apr 1943
           30:138, Mar 1946
Theatre Magazine 47:58, Feb 1928
               47:35, May 1928
Time 47:47, Jan 14, 1946
Vogue 71:122, Feb 15, 1928

Show Girl (1929)
    book: William Anthony McGuire, based on the novel
                        by J. P. McEvoy
    music: George Gershwin
    lyrics: Ira Gershwin and Gus Kahn
    staging: Florenz Ziegfeld, Bobby Connelly, Albertina
                        Rasch
Productions:
    Opened July 2, 1929 for 111 performances
Reviews:
    Life (New York) 94:22, Aug 30, 1929
    New Republic 59:262-3, Jul 24, 1929
    New York Times page 19, Jul 3, 1929
                   page 29, Aug 8, 1929
    Outlook 152:515, Jul 24, 1929
    Theatre Magazine 50:39, Sep 1929

Show Girl (1961)
    sketches: Charles Gaynor (additional sketches by Ernest
                        Chambers)
    music: Charles Gaynor
    lyrics: Charles Gaynor

staging: Charles Gaynor
sets: Oliver Smith
costumes: Miles White
choreography: Richard D'Arcy
Productions:
Opened January 12, 1961 for 100 performances
Reviews:
America 104:557, Jan 28, 1961
New York Theatre Critics' Reviews 1961:394+
New York Times page 37, Jan 13, 1961
      II, page 1, Jan 29, 1961
      page 27, Apr 3, 1961
Newsweek 57:57, Jan 23, 1961
Saturday Review 44:27, Jan 28, 1961
Time 77:77, Jan 20, 1961

The Show Is On
assembled by: Vincente Minnelli
contributors: David Freedman, Moss Hart, Vernon Duke, Ted
      Fetter, Howard Dietz, Arthur Schwartz, Richard
      Rodgers, Lorenz Hart
staging: Vincente Minnelli
sets: Vincente Minnelli
choreography: Harry Losee
Productions:
Opened December 25, 1936 for 237 performances
Opened September 18, 1937 for 17 performances
Reviews:
Arts and Decoration 46:22-3, Jul 1937
Catholic World 144:729-30, Mar 1937
Nation 144:80, Jan 16, 1937
New York Times page 22, Nov 9, 1936
      XI, page 2, Nov 15, 1936
      page 14, Dec 26, 1936
      X, page 1, Jan 10, 1937
      X, page 2, Feb 14, 1937
      XI, page 8, Feb 28, 1937
      page 18, Sep 20, 1937
      X, page 3, Oct 31, 1937
Newsweek 9:22, Jan 2, 1937
Stage 13:33-5, Sep 1936
Theatre Arts 21:97, Feb 1937
Time 29:30-1, Jan 4, 1937
Vogue 89:64, Feb 1, 1937

Show Me Where the Good Times Are
book: Lee Thuna; based on Molière's The Imaginary
      Invalid
music: Kenneth Jacobson
lyrics: Rhoda Roberts
staging: Morton Da Costa

sets: Tom John
costumes: Gloria Gresham
choreography: Bob Herget
Productions:
(Off-Broadway) Opened March 5, 1970 for 29 performances
Reviews:
America 122:398, Apr 11, 1970
New York Times page 32, Mar 6, 1970
                page 35, Mar 31, 1970
New Yorker 46:122, Mar 14, 1970

The Show of Wonders
book: Harold Atteridge
music: Sigmund Romberg, Otto Motzan and Herman
               Timberg
lyrics: Harold Atteridge
staging: J. J. Shubert, J. C. Huffman and Allen K.
               Foster
Productions:
Opened October 26, 1916 for 209 performances
Reviews:
Dramatic Mirror 76:7, Nov 4, 1916
New York Dramatic News 63:10, Nov 4, 1916
New York Times page 7, Oct 27, 1916
                II, page 6, Nov 12, 1916
Theatre Magazine 26:357, Sep 1917

Showing Off
sketches: Douglas Bernstein and Denis Markell
songs: Douglas Bernstein and Denis Markell
staging: Michael Leeds
sets: Joseph Varga and Penny Holpit
costumes: Jeanne Button
choreography: Michael Leeds
Productions:
(Off-Broadway) Opened May 18, 1989
Reviews:
New York 22:57, Jun 26, 1989
New York Times I, page 57, May 28, 1989

The Shrinking Bride
book: Jonathan Levy
music: William Bolcom
lyrics: Jonathan Levy
staging: Marvin Gordon
sets: T. E. Mason
costumes: Joseph G. Aulisi
Productions:
(Off-Broadway) Opened January 17, 1971 for one performance
Reviews:
New York Times page 28, Jan 18, 1971

Shubert Gaieties 1919
    words: J. J. Shubert and Lee Shubert
    music: J. J. Shubert and Lee Shubert
    staging: J. C. Huffman
Productions:
    Opened July 17, 1919 for 87 performances
Reviews:
    New York Times page 9, Jul 8, 1919

Shuffle Along
    book: Flourney E. Miller
    music: Eubie Blake
    lyrics: Noble Sissle
    staging: Walter Brooks
Productions:
    Opened May 23, 1921 for 504 performances
    Opened December 26, 1932 for 17 performances
    Opened May 8, 1952 for 4 performances
    (Off-Off-Broadway) Opened February 2, 1978 for 12 performances
Reviews:
    Commonweal 56:197, May 30, 1952
    Encore 7:34, Mar 20, 1978
    National Magazine 51:244, Oct 1922
    New Republic 27:171, Jul 6, 1921
    New York Clipper 69:19, May 25, 1921
    New York Theatre Critics' Reviews 1952:286
    New York Times page 16, May 23, 1921
                   page 11, Dec 27, 1932
                   page 20, May 9, 1952
                   page 12, Feb 11, 1978
    New Yorker 28:87, May 17, 1952
    Theatre Magazine 34:98, Aug 1921
    Time 59:83, May 19, 1952

Side by Side by Sondheim
    music: Stephen Sondheim, Leonard Bernstein, Mary
                    Rodgers, Richard Rodgers and Jule Styne
    lyrics: Stephen Sondheim
    staging: Ned Sherrin
    sets: Peter Cocherty
    costumes: Florence Klotz
Productions:
    Opened April 18, 1977 for 384 performances
    (Off-Off-Broadway) Opened January 7, 1988
Reviews:
    Los Angeles 23:249+, May 1978
    Nation 224:573-4, May 7, 1977
    New York 9:62, Sep 13, 1976
             10:68+, May 2, 1977
    New York Theatre Critics' Reviews 1977:269
    New York Times II, page 5, Sep 12, 1976

page 30, Apr 19, 1977
II, page 5, May 1, 1977
page 36, Oct 24, 1977
XXI, page 13, Oct 14, 1979
III, page 20, Jan 12, 1988
New Yorker 53:89, May 2, 1977
53:26-7, Jun 13, 1977
Theatre Crafts 20:24+, May 1986
Time 109:88, May 2, 1977

Sidewalks of New York
book: Eddie Dowling and Jimmy Hanley
music: Eddie Dowling and Jimmy Hanley
lyrics: Eddie Dowling and Jimmy Hanley
staging: Edgar MacGregor
Productions:
Opened October 3, 1927 for 112 performances
Reviews:
Life (New York) 90:23, Nov 3, 1927
New York Times page 33, Oct 4, 1927
Theatre Magazine 46:44, Dec 1927

Signs Along the Cynic Route
sketches: Will Holt and Dolly Jonah
music: Will Holt
lyrics: Will Holt
staging: Walt Witcover
Productions:
(Off-Broadway) Opened December 14, 1961 for 93 performances
Reviews:
Commonweal 75:389, Jan 5, 1962
New York Times page 49, Dec 15, 1961
page 29, Feb 28, 1962
New Yorker 37:68, Jan 20, 1962

Silk Stockings
book: George S. Kaufman, Leueen MacGrath, and Abe
             Burrows, suggested by Melchior Lengyel's
             Ninotchka
music: Cole Porter
lyrics: Cole Porter
staging: Cy Feuer
sets: Jo Mielziner
costumes: Lucinda Ballard and Robert Mackintosh
choreography: Eugene Loring
Productions:
Opened February 24, 1955 for 478 performances
(Off-Off-Broadway) Opened May 5, 1977
Reviews:
America 93:109, Apr 23, 1955
Catholic World 181:67, Apr 1955

Commonweal 61:676, Apr 1, 1955
Life 38:93-4+, Mar 21, 1955
Look 19:66-8, Feb 8, 1955
Mademoiselle 40:142, Nov 1954
Nation 180:226, Mar 12, 1955
New York Theatre Critics' Reviews 1952:354+
New York Times page 17, Feb 25, 1955
                        II, page 1, Mar 27, 1955
                        page 26, May 9, 1977
New Yorker 31:68, Mar 5, 1955
Newsweek 45:85, Mar 7, 1955
Saturday Review 38:26, Mar 12, 1955
                      39:13+, Sep 15, 1956
Theatre Arts 39:18+, May 1955
Time 65:92, Mar 7, 1955
Vogue 125:124, Jan 1955

Silks and Satins
    book: Thomas Duggan
    music: Leon Rosebrook
    lyrics: Louis Weslyn
Productions:
    Opened July 15, 1920 for 53 performances
Reviews:
    New York Clipper 68:23, Jul 21, 1920
    New York Times page 19, Jul 1920
    Theatre Magazine 32:105, Sep 1920

Sillman, Leonard (see Leonard Sillman)

Silver Queen
    book: Paul Foster
    music: John Braden
    staging: Robert Patrick
Productions:
    (Off-Off-Broadway) Opened April 11, 1973
No Reviews.

The Silver Star
    book: Harry B. Smith
    staging: Herbert Gresham
    choreography: Julian Mitchell
Productions:
    Opened November 1, 1909 for 80 performances
Reviews:
    Dramatic Mirror 62:7, Nov 13, 1909
    Hampton 24:133-4, Jan 1910
    Leslie's Weekly 110:37, Jan 13, 1910
    Metropolitan Magazine 31:674-5, Feb 1910
    Theatre Magazine 10:xv, Dec 1909

The Silver Swan
    book: William S. Brady and Alonzo Price
    music: H. Maurice Jacquet
    lyrics: William S. Brady and Alonzo Price
    staging: Alonzo Price and Leroy J. Prinz
Productions:
    Opened November 27, 1929 for 21 performances
Reviews:
    New York Times IX, page 1, Nov 3, 1929
                   page 34, Nov 28, 1929

Simple Simon
    book: Ed Wynn and Guy Bolton
    music: Richard Rodgers
    lyrics: Lorenz Hart
    staging: Zeke Colvan
    choreography: Seymour Felix
Productions:
    Opened February 18, 1930 for 135 performances
    Opened March 9, 1931 for 16 performances
Reviews:
    Life (New York) 95:18, Mar 28, 1930
    New York Times VIII, page 2, Feb 2, 1930
                   page 22, Feb 19, 1930
                   page 23, Mar 10, 1931
    Theatre Magazine 51:46, Apr 1930

Simply Heavenly
    book: Langston Hughes
    music: David Martin
    lyrics: Langston Hughes
    staging: Joshua Shelley
    sets: Raymond Sovey
Productions:
    (Off-Broadway) Season of 1956-57
    Opened August 20, 1957 for 62 performances
Reviews:
    Catholic World 185:388-9, Aug 1957
    Nation 185:230, Oct 5, 1957
    New York Theatre Critics' Reviews 1957:264+
    New York Times page 28, May 22, 1957
                 II, page 1, Jun 2, 1957
                 page 36, Jan 2, 1958
    Saturday Review 40:24, Sep 7, 1957

Sinbad
    dialogue: Harold Atteridge
    music: Sigmund Romberg and Al Jolson
    lyrics: Harold Atteridge
    staging: J. C. Huffman and J. J. Shubert
Productions:
    Opened February 14, 1918 for 164 performances

Reviews:
    Dramatic Mirror 78:5, Mar 2, 1918
    Life (New York) 71:343, Feb 28, 1918
    New York Times page 7, Feb 18, 1918
    Theatre Magazine 37:227, Apr 1918
                  37:316, May 1918

Sing for Your Supper
    compiled by: Harold Hecht
    sketches: Dave Lesan, Turner Bullock, Charlotte Kent,
                      John Latouche
    music: Lee Wainer and Ned Lehak
    lyrics: Robert Sour
    staging: H. Gordon Graham and Harold Hecht
    sets: Herbert Andrews
    costumes: Mary Merrill
    choreography: Anna Sokolow
Productions:
    Opened April 24, 1939 for 44 performances
Reviews:
    Catholic World 149:345-6, Jun 1939
    New York Times page 18, Apr 25, 1939
    Newsweek 13:22, May 8, 1939
    Theatre Arts 23:404, Jun 1939

Sing Hallelujah! (gospel musical)
    conceived: Worth Gardner and Donald Lawrence
    songs: Various authors and composers
    staging: Worth Gardner
    sets: Joseph P. Tilford
    costumes: Rebecca Senske
Productions:
    (Off-Broadway) Opened November 3, 1987 for 72 performances
Reviews:
    New York Times III, page 28, Nov 4, 1987

Sing Israel Sing
    book, music,
        lyrics: Asaf Halevi, Moishe Broderson, M. M. Warshav-
                      sky, Wolf Younin, M. Neu, Shlomo Weisfisch, Joel
                      Chayes, E. Kishon and H. Kon
    special
       materials: M. Nudelman
    staging: Mina Bern and Felix Fibich
    costumes: Judith Fibich
    choreography: Felix and Judith Fibich
Productions:
    Opened May 11, 1967 for 14 performances
    Opened June 7, 1967 for 8 performances
Reviews:
    New York Times page 50, May 12, 1967
                     page 57, Jun 13, 1967

Sing Muse!
book:	Erich Segal
music:	Joseph Raposo
lyrics:	Erich Segal
staging:	Bill Penn
sets:	Boyd Dumrose

Productions:

(Off-Broadway) Opened December 6, 1961 for 39 performances

Reviews:

New York Times page 52, Dec 7, 1961
New Yorker 37:100+, Dec 16, 1961

Sing Out Sweet Land
book:	Walter Kerr
special music:	Elie Siegmeister (other music folk and popular)
staging:	Leon Leonidoff
sets:	Albert Johnson
costumes:	Lucinda Ballard
choreography:	Doris Humphrey and Charles Weidman

Productions:

Opened December 27, 1944 for 102 performances

Reviews:

Catholic World 160:452, Feb 1945
Collier's 115:22-3, Apr 7, 1945
Commonweal 41:331, Jan 12, 1945
Nation 160:52, Jan 13, 1945
New Republic 112:85, Jan 15, 1945
New York Theatre Critics' Reviews 1944:48+
New York Times page 24, Nov 10, 1944
               VI, page 14, Dec 24, 1944
               page 24, Dec 28, 1944
               II, page 1, Jan 7, 1945
               II, page 1, Jan 14, 1945
               II, page 5, Jan 21, 1945
New York Times Magazine pages 14-15, Dec 24, 1944
New Yorker 20:40, Jan 6, 1945
Newsweek 25:72, Jan 8, 1945
Theatre Arts 29:79, Feb 1945
           29:134-6, Mar 1945
Time 45:67, Jan 8, 1945

Sing Out the News
book:	Harold Rome and Charles Friedman
music:	Will Irwin
lyrics:	Harold Rome
staging:	Charles Friedman
sets:	Jo Mielziner
costumes:	John Hambleton
choreography:	Ned McGurn, Dave Gould, Charles Walters

Productions:

Opened September 24, 1938 for 105 performances

Reviews:
    Catholic World 148:214-15, Nov 1938
    Commonweal 28:615, Oct 7, 1938
    New Republic 96:271, Oct 12, 1938
    New York Times page 12, Sep 26, 1938
                    IX, page 1, Oct 2, 1938
    Stage 16:6+, Oct 1938
    Theatre Arts 22:784, Nov 1938
    Time 32:30, Oct 3, 1938

Singin' in the Rain
    book: Betty Comden and Adolph Green, based on the
                    M-G-M film
    songs: Nacio Herb Brown and Arthur Freed
    staging: Twyla Tharp
    sets: Santo Loquasto
    costumes: Ann Roth
    choreography: Twyla Tharp (original choreography by Gene
                    Kelly and Stanley Donen)
Productions:
    Opened July 2, 1985 for 367 performances
Reviews:
    Dance Magazine 59:4, Jun 1985
                   59:40-1, Aug 1985
    New Leader 68:22, Sep 23, 1985
    New York 18:67, Jul 15, 1985
             18:40-7, Oct 14, 1985
    New York Theatre Critics' Reviews 1985:239
    New York Times III, page 9, Jul 3, 1985
                    II, page 1, Aug 11, 1985
    New Yorker 61:64, Jul 15, 1985
               61:77-9, Jul 22, 1985
    Newsweek 106:72, Jul 15, 1985
    Theatre Crafts 19:42-3+, Oct 1985
    Time 126:79, Jul 15, 1985
    Vogue 175:242-3, Jun 1985

The Singing Rabbi
    book: Boris and Harry Thomashefsky
    music: J. Rumshinsky and Harry Lubin
    staging: William E. Morris
Productions:
    Opened September 10, 1931 for 4 performances
Reviews:
    New York Times page 24, Sep 11, 1931

The Siren
    book: Leo Stein and A. M. Willner; English version by
                Harry B. Smith
    music: Leo Fall
Productions:
    Opened August 28, 1911 for 136 performances

Reviews:
    Blue Book 14:19-21, Nov 1911
    Dramatic Mirror 66:11, Aug 30, 1911
                    66:8, Sep 6, 1911
    Everybody's 25:691, Nov 1911
    Green Book Album 6:963-4, Nov 1911
                    6:999, Nov 1911
    Life (New York) 58:430, Sep 14, 1911
    Munsey 46:279-80, Nov 1911
    New York Times page 7, Aug 29, 1911
                    I, page 4, Sep 10, 1911
    Pearson 26:651, Nov 1911
    Red Book 17:1140-42+, Oct 1911
    Theatre Magazine 14:xii, Oct 1911
                    14:120, Oct 1911

Sissy
    book: Seth Allen
    music: Michael Meadows and Seth Allen
    staging: John Vaccaro
Productions:
    (Off-Off-Broadway) Opened November 9, 1972
No Reviews.

Sisters of Mercy
    conceived: Gene Lesser
    words: Leonard Cohen
    music: Leonard Cohen
    additional
      music: Zizi Mueller
    staging: Gene Lesser
    sets: Robert U. Taylor
    costumes: Carrie F. Robbins
Productions:
    (Off-Broadway) Opened September 25, 1973 for 15 performances
Reviews:
    New York 6:90, Oct 8, 1973
    New York Times page 46, Sep 26, 1973

Sitting Pretty
    book: Guy Bolton and P. G. Wodehouse
    music: Jerome Kern
    lyrics: P. G. Wodehouse
Productions:
    Opened April 8, 1924 for 95 performances
Reviews:
    New York Times VIII, page 2, Mar 30, 1924
                    page 24, Apr 9, 1924
    Theatre Magazine 39:19, Jun 1924

Six
    book: Charles Strouse

music: Charles Strouse
lyrics: Charles Strouse
staging: Peter Coe
sets: Richard Nelson
Productions:
  (Off-Broadway) Opened April 12, 1971 for 8 performances
Reviews:
  New York Times page 29, Apr 13, 1971
  New Yorker 47:95, Apr 24, 1971

1600 Pennsylvania Avenue
  book: Alan Jay Lerner
  music: Leonard Bernstein
  lyrics: Alan Jay Lerner
  staging: Gilbert Moses and George Faison
  sets: Kert Lundell
  costumes: Whitney Blausen
  choreography: Gilbert Moses and George Faison
Productions:
  Opened May 4, 1976 for 7 performances
Reviews:
  New York 9:77, May 17, 1976
  New York Theatre Critics' Reviews 1976:244
  New York Times page 48, May 5, 1976
  New Yorker 52:124, May 17, 1976
  Newsweek 87:96, May 17, 1976
  Saturday Review 3:44-5, Apr 3, 1976
  Time 107:69-70, May 31, 1976

Skating Vanities of 1942
Productions:
  (Off-Broadway) Opened June 1942
Reviews:
  New York Times VII, page 39, Apr 26, 1942

Sketch Book   (see Earl Carroll's Sketch Book)

Skits-oh-Frantics!
  words, music: Bernie Wayne; additional material by Charles
                      Naylor and Ken Welch
  staging: Hank Ladd
  sets: Carleton Snyder
  costumes: Eve Henriksen
  choreography: Frank Westbrook and Patti Karr
Productions:
  (Off-Broadway) Opened April 2, 1967 for 17 performances
Reviews:
  New York Times page 39, Apr 3, 1967

Sky High (1925)
  book: Harold Atteridge and Captain Harry Graham

music:	Robert Stolz, Alfred Goodman, Carlton Kelsey and Maurie Rubens
staging:	J. J. Shubert

Productions:

Opened March 2, 1925 for 80 performances

Reviews:

Life (New York) 85:18, Mar 19, 1925

New York Times page 21, Mar 3, 1925

Theatre Magazine 41:34, May 1925

Sky High (1979)

book:	Brian O'Hara
music:	Ann Harris
lyrics:	Ann Harris
staging:	Brian O'Hara
sets:	Angel Jack
costumes:	Angel Jack
choreography:	the Harris sisters

Productions:

(Off-Broadway) Opened June 28, 1979 for 38 performances

Reviews:

New York Times III, page 10, Jun 29, 1979

Skye

book:	Avery Corman and Dan Rustin
music:	Ben Finn
lyrics:	Avery Corman and Dan Rustin
staging:	James Curtan

Productions:

Opened Season of 1970-71 (Equity Theatre Informal)

Reviews:

New York Times page 29, Feb 4, 1971

A Skylark

book:	William Harris, Jr.
music:	Frank G. Dossert
lyrics:	William Harris, Jr.
staging:	Ben Teal

Productions:

Opened April 4, 1910 for 24 performances

Reviews:

Dramatic Mirror 63:5, Apr 16, 1910

Leslie's Weekly 110:336, Apr 7, 1910

110:385, Apr 21, 1910

Theatre Magazine 11:xxvii, May 1910

Skyscraper

book:	Peter Stone; based on Elmer Rice's Dream Girl
music:	James Van Heusen
lyrics:	Sammy Cahn
staging:	Cy Feuer

sets: Robert Randolph
costumes: Theoni V. Aldredge
choreography: Michael Kidd
Productions:
    Opened November 13, 1965 for 241 performances
Reviews:
    America 114:180, Jan 29, 1966
    Commonweal 83:316, Dec 1, 1965
    Dance Magazine 40:16, Jan 1966
    Holiday 39:118+, Jan 1966
    Life 60:90-2, Feb 4, 1966
    New York Theatre Critics' Reviews 1965:274
    New York Times page 48, Nov 15, 1965
                     page 57, Nov 16, 1965
                     page 31, Jun 3, 1966
                     page 50, Jun 6, 1966
    New Yorker 41:149, Nov 20, 1965
    Newsweek 66:91, Nov 29, 1965
    Saturday Review 48:76, Dec 4, 1965
    Time 86:87, Nov 26, 1965

Sleepy Hollow
    book: Russell Maloney and Miriam Battista, based on
                      Washington Irving's "The Legend of Sleepy Hol-
                      low"
    music: George Lessner
    lyrics: Russell Maloney and Miriam Battista
    staging: John O'Shaughnessy and Marc Connelly
    sets: Jo Mielziner
    costumes: David Ffolkes
    choreography: Anna Sokolow
Productions:
    Opened June 3, 1948 for 12 performances
Reviews:
    New Republic 118:29, Jun 21, 1948
    New York Theatre Critics' Reviews 1948:258+
    New York Times page 26, Jun 4, 1948
    New Yorker 24:44, Jun 12, 1948
    Newsweek 31:86, Jun 14, 1948
    Time 51:64, Jun 14, 1948

The Slim Princess
    book: Henry Blossom; adapted from a story of George
                      Ade
    music: Leslie Stuart
    lyrics: Henry Blossom
    staging: Austin Hurgon
Productions:
    Opened January 2, 1911 for 104 performances
Reviews:
    Dramatic Mirror 65:6, Jan 4, 1911

Green Book Album 5:471-3+, Mar 1911
Life (New York) 57:109, Jan 19, 1911
Munsey 44:864-6, Mar 1911
New York Dramatic News 56:3, Nov 30, 1912
New York Times page 12, Jan 3, 1911
           I, page 2, Jan 22, 1911
Pearson 25:495, Apr 1911
Red Book 16:945+, Mar 1911
Theatre Magazine 13:x, Feb 1911

Small Wonder

sketches:	Charles Spalding, Max Wilk, George Axelrod, Louis Laun
music:	Baldwin Bergersen and Albert Selden
lyrics:	Phyllis McGinley and Billings Brown
staging:	Burt Shevelove
sets:	Ralph Alswang
costumes:	John Derro
choreography:	Gower Champion

Productions:
  Opened September 15, 1948 for 134 performances
Reviews:
  Catholic World 168:160, Nov 1948
  New Republic 119:26-7, Oct 4, 1948
  New York Theatre Critics' Reviews 1948:244+
  New York Times page 33, Sep 16, 1948
           II, page 1, Sep 26, 1948
  New York Times Magazine pages 40-1, Sep 12, 1948
  New Yorker 24:53, Sep 25, 1948
  Newsweek 32:79, Sep 27, 1948
  School and Society 68:302, Oct 30, 1948
  Theatre Arts 33:17, Jan 1949
  Time 52:63, Sep 27, 1948

Smile

book:	Howard Ashman, based on the screenplay by Jerry Belson
music:	Marvin Hamlisch
lyrics:	Howard Ashman
staging:	Howard Ashman
sets:	Douglas W. Schmidt
costumes:	William Ivey Long
choreography:	Mary Kyte

Productions:
  Opened November 24, 1986 for 48 performances
Reviews:
  New York 19:113-15, Dec 8, 1986
  New York Theatre Critics' Reviews 1986:152
  New York Times III, page 20, Nov 25, 1986
  New Yorker 62:135-6, Dec 8, 1986
  Smithsonian 17:92-4+, Feb 1987

Theatre Crafts 21:18-23+, Jan 1987
Time 128:83, Dec 8, 1986

Smile at Me

sketches:	Edward J. Lambert
music:	Gerald Dolin
lyrics:	Edward J. Lambert
staging:	Frank Merlin
sets:	Karl Amend
costumes:	Dorothy Van Winkle
choreography:	Paul Florenz

Productions:
Opened August 23, 1935 for 27 performances
Reviews:
New York Times page 18, Aug 24, 1935

Smile, Smile, Smile

book:	Robert Russell
music:	Hugo Peretti, Luigi Creatore and George David Weiss
lyrics:	Hugo Peretti, Luigi Creatore and George David Weiss
staging:	Robert Simpson
sets:	Philip Gilliam
costumes:	Patricia McGourty

Productions:
(Off-Broadway) Opened April 4, 1973 for 7 performances
Reviews:
New York Times II, page 1, Feb 11, 1973
page 51, Apr 5, 1973

Smiles

book:	William Anthony McGuire
music:	Vincent Youmans
lyrics:	Clifford Grey, Harold Adamson, Ring Lardner
staging:	Ned Wayburn and William Anthony McGuire

Productions:
Opened November 18, 1930 for 63 performances
Reviews:
Life (New York) 96:18, Dec 12, 1930
New York Times page 19, Nov 19, 1930

Smiling Faces

book:	Harry Clarke
music:	Harry Revel
lyrics:	Mark Gordon
staging:	R. H. Burnside

Productions:
Opened August 30, 1932 for 33 performances
Reviews:
Catholic World 136:84-5, Oct 1932

Smiling the Boy Fell Dead
book:	Ira Wallach
music:	David Baker
lyrics:	Sheldon Harnick
staging:	Theodore Mann
sets:	Herbert Senn and Helen Pond
costumes:	Theoni V. Aldredge

Productions:
(Off-Broadway) Opened April 19, 1961 for 22 performances
Reviews:
New York Times page 28, Apr 20, 1961
page 22, May 5, 1961
New Yorker 37:94, Apr 29, 1961
Theatre Arts 45:32, Jun 1961

Smith
book:	Dean Fuller, Tony Hendra and Matt Dubey
music:	Matt Dubey and Dean Fuller
lyrics:	Matt Dubey and Dean Fuller
staging:	Neal Kenyon
sets:	Fred Voelpel
costumes:	Winn Morton
choreography:	Michael Shawn

Productions:
Opened May 19, 1973 for 17 performances
Reviews:
New York 6:72, Jun 4, 1973
New York Theatre Critics' Reviews 1973:265
New York Times page 43, May 21, 1973
New Yorker 49:54, May 26, 1973

Snoopy
book:	Charles M. Schulz Creative Associates, Warren Lockhart, Arthur Whitelaw and Michael L. Grace, based on the comic strip Peanuts
music:	Larry Grossman
lyrics:	Hal Hackady
staging:	Arthur Whitelaw
sets:	David Graden
costumes:	David Graden
choreography:	Marc Breaux

Productions:
(Off-Broadway) Opened December 20, 1982 for 152 performances
Reviews:
Los Angeles 29:52+, Feb 1984
New York 16:79, Jan 17, 1983
New York Times III, page 17, Mar 11, 1982
II, page 3, Mar 21, 1982

Snow White and the Seven Dwarfs
by:	Joe Cook, adapted from Walt Disney's Snow White

music: Jay Blackton, and movie score music by Frank
                    Churchill
lyrics: Joe Cook, and movie score lyrics by Larry Morey
staging: Frank Wagner
sets: John William Keck
costumes: Frank Spencer
choreography: Frank Wagner
Productions:
    Opened October 18, 1979 for 38 performances
    Opened January 11, 1980 for 68 performances
Reviews:
    New York Theatre Critics' Reviews 1979:119
    New York Times III, page 5, Oct 19, 1979

So Long, Letty
    book: Oliver Morosco and Elmer Harris
    music: Earl Carroll
    lyrics: Earl Carroll
    staging: Oliver Morosco
    choreography: Julian Alfred
Productions:
    Opened October 23, 1916 for 96 performances
Reviews:
    Dramatic Mirror 76:7, Oct 28, 1916
                   76:8, Nov 11, 1916
    Life (New York) 68:767, Nov 2, 1916
    New York Dramatic News 63:11, Oct 28, 1916
    New York Times page 14, Oct 24, 1916
    Theatre Magazine 24:355, Dec 1916

So Long, 174th Street
    book: Joseph Stein, based on Joseph Stein's Enter
                    Laughing from the novel by Carl Reiner
    music: Stan Daniels
    lyrics: Stan Daniels
    staging: Burt Shevelove
    sets: James Riley
    costumes: Stanley Simmons
    choreography: Alan Johnson
Productions:
    Opened April 27, 1976 for 16 performances
Reviews:
    New York 9:72+, May 17, 1976
    New York Theatre Critics' Reviews 1976:282
    New York Times page 34, Apr 28, 1976
                   II, page 5, May 9, 1976
    New Yorker 52:104, May 10, 1976
    Newsweek 87:76, May 10, 1976

Some Night
    book: Harry Delf

ز

music: Harry Delf
lyrics: Harry Delf
staging: W. H. Post and Julian Mitchell
Productions:
Opened September 23, 1918 for 24 performances
Reviews:
Dramatic Mirror 79:507, Oct 5, 1918
New York Times page 11, Sep 17, 1918
IV, page 1, Sep 29, 1918
Theatre Magazine 38:279, Nov 1918

Some Party
arranged: R. H. Burnside
music: Silvio Hein, Percy Wenrich and Gustave Kerker
staging: R. H. Burnside
Productions:
Opened April 15, 1922 for 17 performances
Reviews:
New York Clipper 70:20, Apr 19, 1922
New York Times page 22, Apr 17, 1922

Somebody's Sweetheart
book: Alonzo Price
music: Antonio Bafunno
lyrics: Alonzo Price
staging: Arthur Hammerstein
Productions:
Opened December 23, 1918 for 224 performances
Reviews:
Dramatic Mirror 80:9, Jan 4, 1919
Forum 61:248, Feb 1919
New York Times page 7, Dec 24, 1918
Theatre Magazine 29:78, Feb 1919
29:145, Mar 1919

Something for the Boys
book: Herbert and Dorothy Fields
music: Cole Porter
lyrics: Cole Porter
staging: Hassard Short
sets: Howard Bay
costumes: Billy Livingston
choreography: Jack Cole
Productions:
Opened January 7, 1943 for 422 performances
Reviews:
Catholic World 156:601, Feb 1943
Life 14:79+, Feb 8, 1943
New York Theatre Critics' Reviews 1943:398+
New York Times page 24, Jan 8, 1943
VIII, page 1, Jan 17, 1943
II, page 1, Apr 30, 1944

New Yorker 18:32, Jan 16, 1943
Theatre Arts 27:138-9, Mar 1943
Time 41:58, Jan 18, 1943

Something More!
book:	Nate Monaster, based on Gerald Green's Porto-fino P.T.A.
music:	Sammy Fain
lyrics:	Marilyn and Alan Bergman
staging:	Jule Styne
sets:	Robert Randolph
costumes:	Alvin Colt
choreography:	Bob Herget

Productions:
Opened November 10, 1964 for 15 performances
Reviews:
Dance Magazine 39:18-19, Jan 1965
New York Theatre Critics' Reviews 1964:159+
New York Times II, page 3, Oct 4, 1964
page 36, Nov 11, 1964
page 52, Nov 18, 1964
Time 84:81, Nov 20, 1964

Something's Afoot
book:	James McDonald, David Vos, and Robert Gerlach
music:	James McDonald, David Vos, and Robert Gerlach
lyrics:	James McDonald, David Vos, and Robert Gerlach
additional music:	Ed Linderman
staging:	Tony Tanner
sets:	Richard Seger
costumes:	Walter Watson, Clifford Capone
choreography:	Tony Tanner

Productions:
Opened May 27, 1976 for 61 performances
Reviews:
New York 9:62, Jun 14, 1976
New York Theatre Critics' Reviews 1976:234
New York Times III, page 14, May 28, 1976
II, page 5, Jun 6, 1976
New Yorker 52:79, Jun 7, 1976
Time 107:74, Jun 7, 1976

Sometime
material:	Rida Johnson Young and Rudolf Friml

Productions:
Opened October 4, 1918 for 283 performances
Reviews:
New York Times page 11, Oct 5, 1918
IV, page 2, Oct 13, 1918
Theatre Magazine 38:346, Dec 1918

Somewhere Else
       book: Avery Hopwood
       music: Gustav Luders
       lyrics: Avery Hopwood
       staging: Frank Smithson
Productions:
       Opened January 30, 1913 for 8 performances
Reviews:
       Dramatic Mirror 69:7, Jan 22, 1913
       New York Dramatic News 57:25, Jan 25, 1913
       New York Times page 13, Jan 21, 1913

Song & Dance
       book: Don Black
       music: Andrew Lloyd Webber
       lyrics: Don Black; American adaptation and additional
                      lyrics by Richard Maltby Jr.
       staging: Richard Maltby Jr.
       sets: Robin Wagner
       costumes: Willa Kim
       choreography: Peter Martins
Productions:
       Opened September 18, 1985 for 292 performances
Reviews:
       America 153:283, Nov 2, 1985
       Dance Magazine 59:86, Nov 1985
       Glamour 83:222, Oct 1985
       Nation 241:414+, Oct 26, 1985
       New Leader 68:19, Nov 4-18, 1985
       New York 18:87-8, Sep 30, 1985
       New York Theatre Critics' Reviews 1985:202
       New York Times III, page 19, Sep 19, 1985
       New Yorker 61:111, Sep 30, 1985
       Newsweek 106:75, Sep 30, 1985
       Time 126:88, Sep 30, 1985
       Vogue 175:676-7, Sep 1985

Song Night in the City
       conceived: John Braswell
       songs: Various authors and composers
       staging: John Braswell
Productions:
       (Off-Broadway) Opened April 16, 1980 for 15 performances
No Reviews.

Songbook (see The Harold Arlen Songbook)

Songs and Impressions (see Maurice Chevalier in Songs and Impres-
       sions)

Songs on a Shipwrecked Sofa
  book: James Milton and Polly Pen, based on Mervyn
                   Peake's nonsense poems
  music: Polly Pen
  staged: Andre Ernotte
Productions:
  (Off-Off-Broadway) Opened June 2, 1987
Reviews:
  New York Times III, page 18, Jun 4, 1987
  New Yorker 63:72-3, Jun 15, 1987

Sonny
  book: George V. Hobart
  music: Raymond Hubbell
  staging: George V. Hobart
Productions:
  Opened August 16, 1921 for 31 performances
Reviews:
  Dramatic Mirror 84:265, Aug 20, 1921
  New York Clipper 69:24, Aug 24, 1921
  New York Times page 12, Aug 17, 1921
  Theatre Magazine 34:236, Oct 1921

Sons o'Fun
  book: Ole Olsen, Chic Johnson, Hal Block
  songs: Jack Yellen and Sam E. Fain
  staging: Edward D. Dowling
  sets: Raoul Pene du Bois
  choreography: Robert Alton
Productions:
  Opened December 1, 1941 for 742 performances
Reviews:
  Catholic World 154:474, Jan 1942
  Life 11:44-5, Nov 17, 1941
  Nation 153:621, Dec 13, 1941
  New York Theatre Critics' Reviews 1941:193+
  New York Times page 20, Nov 1, 1941
                   page 28, Dec 2, 1941
  Time 38:73, Dec 15, 1941

Sons o'Guns
  book: Fred Thompson
  music: J. Fred Coots
  lyrics: Arthur Swanstrom and Benny Davis
  staging: Bobby Connelly
  choreography: Albertina Rasch
Productions:
  Opened November 26, 1929 for 295 performances
Reviews:
  New York Times page 30, Nov 27, 1929
                   X, page 2, Dec 15, 1929

VIII, page 1, Jan 12, 1930
Theatre Magazine 51:49, Jan 1930

Soon
  book: Joseph Martinez Kookoolis and Scott Fagan;
                     adapted by Martin Duberman
  music: Joseph Martinez Kookoolis and Scott Fagan
  lyrics: Scott Fagan
  staging: Gerald Freedman
  sets: Kert Lundell
  costumes: David Chapman
  choreography: Fred Benjamin
Productions:
  Opened January 12, 1971 for 3 performances
Reviews:
  New York Theatre Critics' Reviews 1971:393
  New York Times page 29, Jan 13, 1971
              page 43, Jan 14, 1971
  New Yorker 46:66, Jan 23, 1971

Sophie
  book: Phillip Pruneau
  music: Steve Allen
  lyrics: Steve Allen
  staging: Jack Sydow
  sets: Robert Randolph
  costumes: Fred Voelpel
  choreography: Donald Saddler
Productions:
  Opened April 15, 1963 for 8 performances
Reviews:
  New York Theatre Critics' Reviews 1963:344+
  New York Times page 32, Apr 16, 1963
              page 28, Apr 19, 1963
  Newsweek 61:54, Apr 29, 1963
  Theatre Arts 47:66, Jun 1963

Sophisticated Ladies
  conceived: Donald McKayle, based on the music of Duke
                  Ellington
  music and
    lyrics: Duke Ellington and others
  staging: Michael Smuin
  sets: Tony Walton
  costumes: Willa Kim
  choreography: Donald McKayle and Michael Smuin, Henry LeTang
Productions:
  Opened March 1, 1981 for 767 performances
Reviews:
  Dance Magazine 55:54-7, Mar 1981
                 55:166, May 1981
                 55:112, Nov 1981

614 / The Sound of Music

Down Beat 48:11-12, Jun 1981
Essence 12:12+, Sep 1981
Los Angeles 27:232+, Mar 1982
Nation 232:378+, Mar 28, 1981
New Leader 64:19, Apr 6, 1981
New York 14:43-4, Mar 16, 1981
New York Theatre Critics' Reviews 1981:330
New York Times III, page 13, Mar 2, 1981
            II, page 1, Mar 8, 1981
New Yorker 57:61, Mar 16, 1981
Newsweek 97:103, Mar 16, 1981
Saturday Review 8:79, May 1981
Theatre Crafts 23:36-8+, May 1989
Time 117:82, Mar 16, 1981
        117:59, Apr 27, 1981

The Sound of Music
    book: Howard Lindsay and Russel Crouse, suggested
                   by Maria Augusta Trapp's The Trapp Family
                   Singers
    music: Richard Rodgers
    lyrics: Oscar Hammerstein II
    staging: Vincent J. Donehue
    sets: Oliver Smith
    costumes: Lucinda Ballard
    choreography: Joe Layton
Productions:
    Opened November 16, 1959 for 1,443 performances
    Opened April 26, 1967 for 23 performances
    (Off-Broadway) Opened July 8, 1971
    (Off-Off-Broadway) Opened September 20, 1979
    (Off-Off-Broadway) Opened June 1980
Reviews:
    America 102:402, Jan 2, 1960
    Catholic World 191:19-22, Apr 1960
    Christian Century 76:1407-8, Dec 2, 1959
    Dance Magazine 41:38+, Jun 1967
    Life 47:137-46, Nov 23, 1959
    Musical America 79:15, Dec 1, 1959
    New Republic 141:25-6, Dec 28, 1959
    New York Theatre Critics' Reviews 1959:227+
    New York Times VI, pages 22-23, Nov 1, 1959
                    II, page 1, Nov 15, 1959
                    page 40, Nov 17, 1959
                    II, page 1, Nov 22, 1959
                    page 22, May 19, 1961
                    page 41, May 19, 1965
                    page 27, Jan 16, 1967
                    page 52, Apr 27, 1967
                    page 23, Jul 12, 1971
                    XXII, page 18, Feb 20, 1977
                    III, page 13, Jun 30, 1980

New Yorker 35:106+, Nov 28, 1959
Newsweek 54:100+, Nov 30, 1959
Saturday Review 42:28-9, Dec 5, 1959
Theatre Arts 44:65-9, Jan 1960
      46:57-9+, Nov 1962
Theatre Crafts 20:22-3+, May 1986
Time 74:64, Nov 30, 1959

South Pacific

book:	Oscar Hammerstein II and Joshua Logan, based on James A. Michener's Tales of the South Pacific
music:	Richard Rodgers
lyrics:	Oscar Hammerstein II
staging:	Joshua Logan
sets:	Jo Mielziner
costumes:	Motley
choreography:	Joshua Logan

Productions:

Opened April 7, 1949 for 1,925 performances
Opened May 4, 1955 for 15 performances
Opened April 24, 1957 for 23 performances
Opened April 26, 1961 for 23 performances
Opened June 2, 1965 for 15 performances
Opened June 12, 1967 for 104 performances

Reviews:

America 93:221+, May 21, 1955
     105:355, May 20, 1961
     117:63, Jul 15, 1967
     119:55, Jul 20, 1968
American Mercury 73:114-18, Dec 1951
Business World pages 96-8+, Jun 18, 1949
Catholic World 169:145-6, May 1949
Commonweal 50:69, Apr 29, 1949
Coronet 26:10-11, Jul 1949
     29:44-52, Mar 1951
Good Housekeeping 129:4+, Dec 1949
Harper's Bazaar 83:83, Jun 1949
Life 26:93-6, Apr 18, 1949
    30:63-5, Jan 29, 1951
Los Angeles 30:42+, Jul 1985
Musical America 69:13, May 1949
Nation 168:480, Apr 23, 1949
New Republic 120:27-8, Apr 25, 1949
New York 20:92+, Mar 23, 1987
New York Theatre Critics' Reviews 1949:312+
                          1987:370
New York Times II, page 1, Apr 3, 1949
           page 30, Apr 8, 1949
           II, page 1, Apr 17, 1949

                    II, page 1, May 1, 1949
                    II, page 1, Jun 5, 1949
                    II, page 1, Jul 3, 1949
                    page 26, Apr 25, 1950
                    page 36, Apr 26, 1950
                    page 1, May 2, 1950
                    page 32, Oct 24, 1950
                    page 30, Jul 10, 1951
                    II, page 1, Sep 2, 1951
                    II, page 3, Nov 11, 1951
                    page 17, Jan 29, 1952
                    page 9, Jan 31, 1952
                    page 16, Sep 15, 1952
                    II, page 3, Nov 2, 1952
                    page 41, Dec 11, 1953
                    page 83, Jan 17, 1954
                    page 39, May 5, 1955
                    II, page 1, Sep 23, 1956
                    page 35, Apr 25, 1957
                    page 26, Apr 27, 1961
                    page 25, Jun 3, 1965
                    page 56, Jun 13, 1967
                    page 60, Sep 18, 1967
                    page 54, Jun 30, 1968
                    II, page 11, Mar 2, 1987
New York Times Magazine pages 22-3, Mar 27, 1949
                    page 56+, Nov 27, 1949
New Yorker 25:54+, Apr 16, 1949
           41:130+, Jun 12, 1965
Newsweek 33:78-9, Apr 11, 1949
Saturday Review 32:47-8, Mar 26, 1949
                32:28-30, Apr 30, 1949
                33:4, Jan 14, 1950
                51:35, Jul 20, 1968
Theatre Arts 33:15, Jun 1949
             34:42-3, Jun 1950
             41:16, Jul 1957
Time 53:77, Apr 18, 1949
     65:91, Mar 28, 1955

A Space Oddity (see 2,008 1/2)

Speed Gets the Poppies
      book: Lila Levant
      music: Lorenzo Fuller
      lyrics: Lorenzo Fuller and Lila Levant
      staging: Charles Abbott
      sets: Milton Duke
      costumes: Milton Duke
      choreography: Charles Abbott
Productions:
   (Off-Broadway) Opened July 25, 1972 for 7 performances

Reviews:
    New York Times page 21, Jul 26, 1972

Spice of 1922
    book: Jack Lait
    staging: Allen K. Foster
Productions:
    Opened July 6, 1922 for 73 performances
Reviews:
    Life (New York) 80:18, Aug 3, 1922
    New York Clipper 70:20, Jul 12, 1922
    New York Times page 12, Jul 7, 1922
    Theatre Magazine 36:151+, Sep 1922

Spiro Who?
    book: William Meyers
    music: Phil Ochs
    staging: Bernard Barrow
    sets: Eldon Elder
    costumes: Winn Morton
Productions:
    (Off-Broadway) Opened May 18, 1969 for 41 performances
Reviews:
    New York Times page 55, May 19, 1969
                    II, page 3, Jun 15, 1969
                    page 35, Jun 20, 1969

Split Lip
    book: John Cromwell
    music: Lee Pockriss
    staging: Gene Frankel
    choreography: Doug Rogers
Productions:
    (Off-Off-Broadway) Opened May 14, 1974
Reviews:
    New York Times page 49, May 16, 1974

Spook Scandals
    conceived: Jerry Sylvon
    music: Sergio De Karlo
    staging: Jerry Sylvon
    choreography: Paul Haakon, Marta Nita and Paul Reyes
Productions:
    Opened December 8, 1944 for 2 performances
No Reviews.

Spotlight
    book: Richard Seff, based on a story by Leonard Starr
    music: Jerry Bressler
    lyrics: Lyn Duddy
    staged: David Black

sets: Robert Randolph
costumes: Robert Mackintosh
choreography: Tony Stevens
Productions:
Closed prior to Broadway opening (Washington, D.C., January 1978)
Reviews:
New York Times III, page 15, Jan 11, 1978

Spring Is Here
    book: Owen Davis
    music: Richard Rodgers
    lyrics: Lorenz Hart
    staging: Alexander Leftwich
    choreography: Bobby Connelly
Productions:
Opened March 11, 1929 for 104 performances
Reviews:
Catholic World 129:205-6, May 1929
Life (New York) 93:25, Apr 12, 1929
New York Times page 26, Mar 12, 1929
Outlook 151:508, Mar 27, 1929
Theatre Magazine 49:47, May 1929
Vogue 73:150, May 11, 1929

The Spring Returneth
    material: Alfred Allegro
    staging: William Vaughan
Productions:
(Off-Broadway) Opened February 9, 1939 for 3 performances
No Reviews.

Springtime of Youth
    book: Based on the book by Bernhauser and Rudolph
                   Schanzer
    music: Sigmund Romberg and Walter Rollo
    lyrics: Harry B. Smith, Cyrus Wood, Matthew Woodward
    staging: John Harwood
Productions:
Opened October 26, 1922 for 68 performances
Reviews:
New York Clipper 70:20, Nov 1, 1922
New York Times page 15, Oct 27, 1922

Stag Movie
    book: David Newburge
    music: Jacques Urbont
    lyrics: David Newburge
    staging: Bernard Barrow
    sets: David Chapman
    costumes: David Toser
    choreography: Doug Rogers

Productions:
(Off-Broadway) Opened January 3, 1971 for 88 performances
Reviews:
New York Times page 39, Jan 4, 1971

Staggerlee
    book: Vernel Bagneris
    music: Allen Toussaint
    lyrics: Allen Toussaint and Vernel Bagneris
    staging: Vernel Bagneris
    sets: Akira Yoshimura
    costumes: JoAnn Clevenger
    choreography: Pepsi Bethel
Productions:
(Off-Broadway) Opened March 18, 1987 for 118 performances
Reviews:
New York 20:97, Mar 30, 1987
New York Times III, page 25, Mar 19, 1987
New Yorker 63:93, Mar 30, 1987
Rolling Stone page 18, May 21, 1987

Standup Shakespeare
    conceived: Ray Leslee and Kenneth Welsh
    words: William Shakespeare
    music: Ray Leslee
    staging: Mike Nichols
    sets: John Arnone
    costumes: Cynthia O'Neal
Productions:
(Off-Broadway) Opened April 4, 1987 for 2 performances
Reviews:
New York Times III, page 16, Apr 6, 1987
New Yorker 63:75, Apr 20, 1987

Star and Garter
    assembled: Michael Todd
    music and
      lyrics: Irving Berlin, Al Dubin, Will Irwin, Harold Rome, Lester Lee, Irving Gordon, Alan Roberts, Harold Arlen, Frank McCue, Doris Tauber, Dorival Caymmi, Jerry Seelen, Jerome Brainin, Johnny Mercer, Sis Wilner, Al Stillman
    staging: Hassard Short
    sets: Harry Horner
    costumes: Irene Sharaff
Productions:
Opened June 24, 1942 for 609 performances
Reviews:
Life 13:60+, Jul 27, 1942
Nation 155:18, Jul 4, 1942
New York Theatre Critics' Reviews 1942:262+

New York Times page 26, Jun 25, 1942
                 VIII, page 1, Sep 13, 1942
    Newsweek 20:60, Jul 6, 1942
    Time 40:54, Jul 6, 1942

The Star Gazer
    book: Cosmo Hamilton
    music: Franz Lehar
    lyrics: Matthew C. Woodward
Productions:
    Opened November 26, 1917 for 8 performances
Reviews:
    Dramatic Mirror 77:5, Dec 8, 1917
    New York Times page 14, Nov 27, 1917

Stardust
    conceived: Albert Harris
    music: Duke Ellington, Benny Goodman, Will Hudson,
                   and other collaborators of Mitchell Parish
    lyrics: Mitchell Parish
    staging: Albert Harris
    sets: David Jenkins
    costumes: Mardi Philips
    choreography: Patrice Soriero
Productions:
    (Off-Off-Broadway) Opened November 11, 1986 for 59 performances
    Opened February 19, 1987 for 102 performances
Reviews:
    New Leader 70:21, Mar 9, 1987
    New York 20:111, Mar 2, 1987
    New York Theatre Critics' Reviews 1987:383
    New York Times III, page 26, Nov 12, 1986
    New Yorker 63:76, Mar 2, 1987

Starlight Express
    music: Andrew Lloyd Webber
    lyrics: Richard Stilgoe
    staging: Trevor Nunn
    design: John Napier
    choreography: Arlene Phillips
Productions:
    Opened March 15, 1987 for 761 performances
Reviews:
    America 156:427, May 23, 1987
    Dance Magazine 61:86-7, Apr 1987
    Nation 244:516, Apr 18, 1987
    New Leader 70:21, Apr 6, 1987
    New York 20:66-8, Mar 9, 1987
               20:96-7, Mar 30, 1987
    New York Theatre Critics' Reviews 1987:328
    New York Times III, page 17, Mar 16, 1987

New Yorker 63:93, Mar 30, 1987
Popular Mechanics 164:85, Dec 1987
Theatre Crafts 19:18-21+, Feb 1985
           21:8, Mar 1987
           22:42-9, Jan 1988
Time 129:83, Mar 30, 1987
U S News and World Report 102:72-3, Mar 16, 1987
Vogue 174:127, Sep 1984

Starmites
  book: Stuart Ross and Barry Keating
  music: Barry Keating
  lyrics: Barry Keating
  staging: Larry Carpenter
  sets: Lowell Detweiler
  costumes: Susan Hirschfeld
  choreography: Michele Assaf
Productions:
  (Off-Off-Broadway) Opened October 23, 1980
  (Off-Off-Broadway) Opened April 26, 1987
  Opened April 27, 1989 for *40 performances (still running 6/1/89)
Reviews:
  Nation 248:862-3, Jun 19, 1989
  New York 22:88, May 8, 1989
  New York Theatre Critics' Reviews 1989:292
  New York Times page 73, Nov 9, 1980
              III, page 16, Apr 29, 1987
              III, page 3, Apr 28, 1989

Stars in Your Eyes (Swing to the Left)
  book: J. P. McEvoy
  music: Arthur Schwartz
  lyrics: Dorothy Fields
  staging: Joshua Logan
  sets: Jo Mielziner
  costumes: John Hambleton
  choreography: Carl Randall
Productions:
  Opened February 9, 1939 for 127 performances
Reviews:
  Catholic World 149:88-9, Apr 1939
  Commonweal 29:525, Mar 3, 1939
  Life 6:66-9, Feb 27, 1939
  Nation 148:245, Feb 25, 1939
  New Republic 98:102-3, Mar 1, 1939
  New York Times page 18, Feb 10, 1939
              X, page 1, Mar 5, 1939
  Stage 16:4+, Feb 1939
  Theatre Arts 23:242-3, Apr 1939
  Time 33:54-5, Feb 20, 1939

Stars on Ice
assembled:	Sonja Henie and Arthur M. Wirtz
music:	Paul McGrane and Paul Van Loan
lyrics:	Al Stillman
staging:	William H. Burke and Catherine Littlefield
sets:	Bruno Maine
costumes:	Lucinda Ballard
choreography:	Catherine Littlefield

Productions:
Opened July 2, 1942 for 830 performances
Reviews:
Catholic World 155:727, Sep 1942
Commonweal 36:328, Jul 24, 1942
New York Times page 12, Jul 3, 1942
page 13, Jun 25, 1943
II, page 2, Oct 10, 1943
Newsweek 20:67, Jul 13, 1942
Theatre Arts 26:630, Oct 1942

Starting Here, Starting Now
book:	Richard Maltby Jr.
music:	David Shire
lyrics:	Richard Maltby Jr.
staging:	Richard Maltby Jr.
costumes:	Stanley Simmons
choreography:	Ethel Martin

Productions:
(Off-Broadway) Opened March 7, 1977 for 120 performances
Reviews:
New York 10:86, May 23, 1977
New York Times page 25, Mar 8, 1977
III, page 34, Mar 25, 1977

Stein, Gertrude (see Gertrude Stein)

Step Lively, Boy
book:	Vinnette Carroll; based on a play by Irwin Shaw
music:	Micki Grant
lyrics:	Micki Grant
staging:	Vinnette Carroll

Productions:
(Off-Off-Broadway) Opened February 7, 1973
No Reviews.

Step This Way (The Girl Behind the Counter)
book:	Edgar Smith
music:	E. Ray Goetz and Bert Grant
lyrics:	E. Ray Goetz
staging:	Frank McCormack
choreography:	Jack Mason

Productions:
Opened May 29, 1916 for 88 performances

Reviews:
Dramatic Mirror 75:8, Jun 3, 1916
New York Times page 7, May 30, 1916
Theatre Magazine 24:11, Jul 1916

Stepping Stones
book: Anne Caldwell and R. H. Burnside
music: Jerome Kern
lyrics: Anne Caldwell
staging: R. H. Burnside
Productions:
Opened November 6, 1923 for 241 performances
Opened September 1, 1924 for 40 performances
Reviews:
New York Times page 14, Nov 7, 1923
                VI, page 8, Dec 16, 1923
                page 8, Aug 20, 1924
Theatre Magazine 39:58, Jan 1924

Sterling Silver
music: Frederick Silver
lyrics: Frederick Silver
staging: Sue Lawless
sets: Kenneth Foy
costumes: David Toser
choreography: Bick Goss
Productions:
(Off-Broadway) Opened March 7, 1979 for 6 performances
No Reviews.

Stomp
devised: The Combine
Productions:
(Off-Broadway) Opened November 16, 1969 for 161 performances
Reviews:
Commonweal 91:534-5, Feb 13, 1970
Dance Magazine 44:93, Feb 1970
New York Times page 32, Oct 31, 1969
                page 60, Nov 17, 1969
                II, page 1, Nov 23, 1969
                page 23, Jan 24, 1970
Newsweek 74:86+, Dec 1, 1969
         74:138-9, Dec 8, 1969

Stoones, Harry (see Another Evening with Harry Stoones)

Stop! Look! Listen!
book: Harry B. Smith
music: Irving Berlin
lyrics: Irving Berlin
staging: R. H. Burnside

Productions:
  Opened December 25, 1915 for 105 performances
Reviews:
  Dramatic Mirror 75:9, Jan 1, 1916
  Green Book 15:447-8, Mar 1916
  Life (New York) 67:26, Jan 2, 1916
  New York Dramatic News 62:18, Jan 1, 1916
  New York Times II, page 15, Dec 25, 1915
                 II, page 9, Mar 12, 1916
  Opera Magazine 3:29-31, Feb 1916
  Stage 15:41, Aug 1938
  Theatre Magazine 23:66, Feb 1916
                   23:180, Feb 1916

Stop the World--I Want to Get Off
  book: Leslie Bricusse and Anthony Newley
  music: Leslie Bricusse and Anthony Newley
  lyrics: Leslie Bricusse and Anthony Newley
  staging: Anthony Newley
  sets: Sean Kenny
  choreography: John Broome and Virginia Mason
Productions:
  Opened October 3, 1962 for 555 performances
  Opened August 3, 1978 for 30 performances
  (Off-Off-Broadway) Opened November 1, 1984
Reviews:
  America 107:1231, Dec 8, 1962
  Catholic World 196:200, Dec 1962
  Commonweal 77:201, Nov 16, 1962
  Dance Magazine 36:24-5+, Dec 1962
  Life 53:117, Nov 30, 1962
  Nation 195:246-7, Oct 20, 1962
  New York 11:67+, Aug 21, 1978
  New York Theatre Critics' Reviews 1962:260+
                                    1978:225
  New York Times page 39, Sep 17, 1962
                 page 45, Oct 4, 1962
                 VI, page 36, Oct 7, 1962
                 II, page 1, Oct 14, 1962
                 III, page 4, Aug 4, 1978
                 XXI, page 19, Nov 11, 1984
  New York Times Magazine page 36, Oct 7, 1962
  New Yorker 38:180, Oct 13, 1962
             54:48, Aug 14, 1978
  Newsweek 60:68, Oct 15, 1962
  Reporter 27:42, Dec 20, 1962
  Saturday Review 45:37, Oct 20, 1962
  Theatre Arts 46:11, Nov 1962
  Time 80:67, Oct 12, 1962
       112:68, Aug 14, 1978

Strada, La   (see La Strada)

Stranger Here Myself
    by: Angelina Reaux
    songs: Kurt Weill
    staging: Christopher Alden
    sets: Paul Steinberg
Productions:
    (Off-Broadway) Opened August 11, 1988 for 19 performances
Reviews:
    New York Times III, page 3, Aug 12, 1988

The Straw Hat Revue
    conceived by: Max Liebman
    assembled by: Max Liebman
    sketches: Max Liebman and Samuel Locke
    music: Sylvia Fine and James Shelton; special music by
                     Glenn Bacon
    lyrics: Sylvia Fine and James Shelton
    staging: Max Liebman
    sets: Edward Gilbert
    choreography: Jerome Andrews
Productions:
    Opened September 29, 1939 for 75 performances
Reviews:
    Catholic World 150:216, Nov 1939
    Commonweal 30:563, Oct 13, 1939
    New York Times page 10, Sep 30, 1939
                      IX, page 3, Oct 29, 1939
                      IX, page 8, Nov 12, 1939
    Theatre Arts 23:860-2, Dec 1939
    Time 34:49, Oct 9, 1939

Street Scene
    book: Elmer Rice, based on his nonmusical play Street
                     Scene
    music: Kurt Weill
    lyrics: Langston Hughes
    staging: Charles Friedman
    sets: Jo Mielziner
    costumes: Lucinda Ballard
    choreography: Anna Sokolow
Productions:
    Opened January 9, 1947 for 148 performances
    (Off-Broadway) Season of 1958-59
    Opened February 24, 1966 for 6 performances
Reviews:
    Catholic World 164:453, Feb 1947
    Commonweal 45:397, Jan 31, 1947
    Life 22:78, Feb 24, 1947
    Musical Courier 135:52, Feb 1, 1947

Musical America 79:3+, May 1959
                79:29-30, Oct 1959
New Republic 116:40, Feb 10, 1947
New York Theatre Critics' Reviews 1947:490+
New York Times II, page 3, Jan 5, 1947
                page 17, Jan 10, 1947
                II, page 2, Jan 19, 1947
                II, page 7, Jan 26, 1947
                II, page 3, Feb 2, 1947
                VI, page 28, Feb 2, 1947
                II, page 1, May 4, 1947
                page 24, May 12, 1947
New Yorker 22:44+, Jan 18, 1947
Newsweek 29:84, Jan 20, 1947
Saturday Review 30:24-6, Feb 1, 1947
Theatre Arts 31:12-13+, Mar 1947
Time 49:69, Jan 20, 1947

Street Singer
     book: Cyrus Wood and Edgar Smith
     music: John Gilbert, Nicholas Kempner, Sam Timberg
     lyrics: Graham John
     staging: Busby Berkeley
Productions:
Opened September 17, 1929 for 191 performances
Reviews:
New York Times page 35, Sep 18, 1929
Outlook 153:192, Oct 2, 1929
Theatre Magazine 50:72, Nov 1929

Streetheat
     conceived: Michele Assaf and Rick Atwell
     songs: Various authors and composers
     staging: Rick Atwell
     sets: Franne Lee
     costumes: Franne Lee
     choreography: Rick Atwell
Productions:
Opened January 27, 1985 for 20 performances
Reviews:
Dance Magazine 57:120, Dec 1983

The Streets of New York
     book: Barry Alan Grael; based on the play by Dion
                       Boucicault
     music: Richard B. Chadosh
     lyrics: Barry Alan Grael
     staging: Joseph Hardy
     sets: Howard Becknell
     costumes: W. Thomas Seitz
     choreography: Neal Kenyon

Productions:
(Off-Broadway)   Opened October 29, 1963 for 318 performances
Reviews:
America 109: 644, Nov 16, 1963
New York Times page 47, Oct 30, 1963
New Yorker 39: 95-6+, Nov 9, 1963
Newsweek 62: 72, Nov 18, 1963

Streets of Paris

sketches:	Charles Sherman, Tom McKnight, Mitchell Hodges, S. Jay Kaufman, Edward Duryea Dowling, James LaVer, Frank Eyton, Lee Brody
music:	James McHugh
lyrics:	Harold J. Rome and Al Dubin
staging:	Edward Duryea Dowling and Dennis Murray
sets:	Lawrence L. Goldwasser
costumes:	Irene Sharaff
choreography:	Robert Alton

Productions:
Opened June 19, 1939 for 274 performances
Reviews:
Commonweal 30: 278, Jul 7, 1939
Life 7: 32+, Jul 17, 1939
Nation 149: 110, Jul 22, 1939
New York Theatre Critics' Reviews 1940: 484+
New York Times page 25, Jun 20, 1939
              IX, page 1, Jun 25, 1939
              IX, page 4, Dec 17, 1939
Newsweek 14: 28, Jul 3, 1939
Time 34: 42, Jul 3, 1939

Strider

book:	Mark Rozovsky, adapted from Leo Tolstoy's story Kholstomer: The Story of a Horse
English stage version:	Robert Kalfin and Steve Brown, based on a translation by Tamara Bering Sunguroff
music:	Mark Rozovsky and S. Vetkin, adapted with additional music by Norman L. Berman
lyrics:	Uri Riashentsev (original Russian) and Steve Brown (English)
staging:	Robert Kalfin and Lynne Gannaway
design:	Wolfgang Roth
costumes:	Andrew B. Marlay

Productions:
(Off-Broadway)   Opened May 31, 1979 for 189 performances
Opened November 21, 1979 for 214 performances
Reviews:
New Republic 181: 26-8, Dec 8, 1979
New York 12: 74, Jun 18, 1979
New York Theatre Critics' Reviews 1979: 188

New York Times III, page 7, Jun 1, 1979
            III, page 23, Oct 24, 1979
            III, page 6, Nov 23, 1979
Newsweek 94:141, Dec 3, 1979
Time 114:60, Aug 27, 1979

Strike Me Pink

book:	Ray Henderson and Lew Brown, additional dialogue by Mack Gordon
music:	Ray Henderson
lyrics:	Lew Brown
staging:	Ray Henderson and Lew Brown
sets:	Henry Dreyfuss
choreography:	Seymour Felix

Productions:
Opened March 4, 1933 for 105 performances
Reviews:
    Nation 136:356, Mar 29, 1963
    New Outlook 161:46, Apr 1933
    New York Times page 16, Mar 6, 1933
                 IX, page 2, Apr 9, 1933
    Stage 10:19-22, Apr 1933
    Time 21:40, Mar 13, 1933

Strike up the Band

book:	Morrie Ryskind, based on George S. Kaufman's libretto
music:	George Gershwin
lyrics:	Ira Gershwin
staging:	Alexander Leftwich
choreography:	George Hale

Productions:
Opened January 14, 1930 for 191 performances
Reviews:
    Christian Century 48:899-901, Jul 8, 1931
    High Fidelity 34:MA22, Dec 1984
    Life (New York) 95:18, Feb 7, 1930
    Nation 130:226, Feb 19, 1930
    New York Times VIII, page 4, Dec 29, 1929
                 page 29, Jan 15, 1930
    Outlook 154:191, Jan 29, 1930
    Theatre Magazine 51:48, Mar 1930
    Vogue 75:106+, Mar 1, 1930

Strings

book:	Samuel Taylor
music:	Richard Rodgers
lyrics:	Richard Rodgers
staging:	Ric Michaels
sets:	Billy Puzzo
costumes:	Sally Krell
choreography:	Lynn Gannaway

Productions:
   (Off-Broadway) Opened March 9, 1972
No Reviews.

Strip!
by:	Duane Mazey
music:	Norman Bergman
lyrics:	Norman Bergman
staging:	Phil Oesterman

Productions:
   (Off-Broadway) Opened June 30, 1987 for 8 performances
No Reviews.

Strip Girl
book:	Henry Rosendahl
music:	Harry Archer
lyrics:	Jill Rainsford
staging:	Jose Ruben
sets:	Cirker and Robbins

Productions:
   Opened October 19, 1935 for 33 performances
Reviews:
   New York Times page 22, Oct 21, 1935

The Student Gypsy, or The Prince of Liederkranz
book:	Rick Besoyan
music:	Rick Besoyan
lyrics:	Rick Besoyan
staging:	Rick Besoyan
sets:	Raoul Pene du Bois
costumes:	Raoul Pene du Bois
choreography:	Ray Harrison

Productions:
   Opened September 30, 1963 for 16 performances
Reviews:
   New York Theatre Critics' Reviews 1963:266+
   New York Times page 34, Oct 1, 1963
                page 51, Oct 10, 1963
   Newsweek 62:77, Oct 14, 1963
   Theatre Arts 47:13, Dec 1963

The Student Prince
book:	Dorothy Donnelly
music:	Sigmund Romberg
lyrics:	Dorothy Donnelly
staging:	J. C. Huffman

Productions:
   Opened December 2, 1924 for 608 performances
   Opened January 29, 1931 for 42 performances
   Opened June 8, 1943 for 153 performances
   (Off-Broadway) Opened July 13, 1961 for 13 performances

(Off-Broadway) Opened May 11, 1976 for 18 performances
(Off-Broadway) Opened October 18, 1978 for 42 performances
(Off-Broadway) Opened May 6, 1981 for 28 performances
(Off-Broadway) Opened June 3, 1981 for 14 performances
Reviews:
American Mercury 4:248-9, Feb 1925
Commonweal 38:252, Jun 25, 1943
New York Theatre Critics' Reviews 1943:320
New York Times page 25, Dec 3, 1924
              page 18, Jan 30, 1931
              VIII, page 3, Feb 1, 1931
              page 16, Jun 9, 1943
              page 14, Jul 14, 1961
              page 37, May 12, 1976
Newsweek 21:104, Jun 21, 1943
Theatre Magazine 41:14-15, Feb 1925

Subways Are for Sleeping
    book: Betty Comden and Adolph Green, suggested by
                    Edmund G. Love's novel
    music: Jule Styne
    lyrics: Betty Comden and Adolph Green
    staging: Michael Kidd
    sets: Will Steven Armstrong
    costumes: Freddy Wittop
    choreography: Michael Kidd and Marc Breaux
Productions:
Opened December 27, 1961 for 205 performances
Reviews:
America 106:737, Mar 3, 1962
Dance Magazine 36:13, Mar 1962
New York Theatre Critics' Reviews 1961:135+
New York Times II, page 3, Dec 17, 1961
              page 22, Dec 28, 1961
              page 27, Jun 21, 1962
New Yorker 37:56, Jan 6, 1962
Newsweek 59:44, Jan 8, 1962
Theatre Arts 46:60, Mar 1962
Time 79:52, Jan 5, 1962

Suds: The Rocking 60's Musical Soap Opera
    conceived: Melinda Gilb, Steve Gunderson and Bryan Scott
    written: Melinda Gilb, Steve Gunderson and Bryan Scott
    songs: Various authors and composers
    staging: Will Roberson
    sets: Alan Okazaki
    costumes: Gregg Barnes
    choreography: Javier Velasco
Productions:
    (Off-Broadway) Opened September 25, 1988 for 81 performances

Reviews:
New York Times III, page 20, Sep 28, 1988
New Yorker 64:84-5, Oct 10, 1988

Sue, Dear
book: Bide Dudley, Joseph Herbert and C. S. Montayne
music: Frank H. Grey
lyrics: Bide Dudley
staging: Joseph Herbert and Jack Mason
Productions:
Opened July 10, 1922 for 96 performances
Reviews:
New York Clipper 70:20, Jul 12, 1922
New York Times page 16, Jul 11, 1922

Sue Lawless and Ted Pugh (see An Evening with Sue and Pugh)

Sugar
book: Peter Stone; based on the screen play Some Like
                 It Hot by Billy Wilder and I. A. L. Diamond
                 (based on a story by Robert Thoeren)
music: Jule Styne
lyrics: Bob Merrill
staging: Gower Champion
sets: Robin Wagner
costumes: Alvin Colt
choreography: Gower Champion
Productions:
Opened April 9, 1972 for 505 performances
Reviews:
America 126:462, Apr 29, 1972
Harper's 105:84, Mar 1972
Life 72:28, May 12, 1972
New Republic 166:35, Apr 29, 1972
New York Theatre Critics' Reviews 1972:320
New York Times page 47, Apr 10, 1972
              II, page 1, Apr 16, 1972
              II, page 1, Apr 23, 1972
New Yorker 48:109, Apr 15, 1972
Newsweek 79:50, Apr 24, 1972
Saturday Review 55:65, May 6, 1972
Time 99:66, Apr 24, 1972

Sugar Babies
conceived: Ralph G. Allen and Harry Rigby
sketches: Ralph G. Allen, based on traditional material
staging: Ernest Flatt
sets: Raoul Pene du Bois
costumes: Raoul Pene du Bois
choreography: Ernest Flatt
Productions:
Opened October 8, 1979 for 1,208 performances

Reviews:
>America 141:281, Nov 10, 1979
Horizon 22:56-63, Oct 1979
Los Angeles 29:48+, Mar 1984
Nation 229:442, Nov 3, 1979
New York 12:97-8, Oct 22, 1979
New York Theatre Critics' Reviews 1979:133
New York Times II, page 5, Oct 21, 1979
New Yorker 55:142, Oct 22, 1979
Newsweek 94:129-30, Oct 22, 1979
Saturday Review 7:43, Jan 5, 1980
Time 114:98, Oct 22, 1979

Sugar Hill
>book: Charles Tazewell
music: Jimmy Johnson
lyrics: Jo Trent

Productions:
>Opened December 25, 1931 for 11 performances

Reviews:
>New York Times page 15, Dec 26, 1931

Summer on Parade
>book: Arthur C. Leach
music: Irving Bilbo and Jerry Lang

Productions:
>(Off-Broadway) Opened January 22, 1934

No Reviews.

Summer Share   (see Romance Romance)

The Summer Widowers
>words: Glen Macdonough
music: A. Baldwin Sloan
staging: Ned Wayburn

Productions:
>Opened June 4, 1910 for 140 performances

Reviews:
>Dramatic Mirror 63:6, Jun 11, 1910
Green Book Album 4:681, Oct 1910
                5:304, Feb 1911
Hampton 25:526, Oct 1910
Metropolitan Magazine 32:678-9, Aug 1910
Theatre Magazine 12:3-4, Jul 1910

The Sun Dodgers
>book: Edgar Smith
music: E. Ray Goetz and A. Baldwin Sloane
lyrics: E. Ray Goetz and A. Baldwin Sloane
staging: Ned Wayburn

Productions:
>Opened November 30, 1912 for 29 performances

Reviews:
   Blue Book 16:908-11, Mar 1913
   Dramatic Mirror 68:6, Dec 4, 1912
                   68:2, Dec 18, 1912
   Green Book 9:367, Feb 1913
   Harper's Weekly 56:19, Dec 7, 1912
   New York Dramatic News 56:19, Dec 7, 1912
   Theatre Magazine 17:4, Jan 1913

Sun Showers
   staging: Frederick Stanhope
Productions:
   Opened February 5, 1923 for 40 performances
Reviews:
   New York Clipper 71:14, Feb 14, 1923
   New York Times page 14, Feb 6, 1923

Sunday in the Park With George
   book: James Lapine
   music: Stephen Sondheim
   lyrics: Stephen Sondheim
   staging: James Lapine
   sets: Tony Straiges
   costumes: Patricia Zipprodt and Ann Hould-Ward
Productions:
   Opened May 2, 1984 for 604 performances
Reviews:
   America 151:15, Jul 7-14, 1984
   Art in America 72:165-6, Summer 1984
   Atlantic 255:46-7, Jan 1985
   Chicago 33:112+, May 1984
   Horizon 27:15, Nov 1984
            28:14, May 1985
   Life 7:96-8+, Jul 1984
   Nation 238:650-1, May 26, 1984
   New Leader 67:23, Jun 11, 1984
   New Republic 190:25-6, Jun 18, 1984
   New York 17:79-80, May 14, 1984
   New York Theatre Critics' Reviews 1984:282
   New York Times III, page 21, May 3, 1984
                    II, page 7, May 13, 1984
                    II, page 1, Jun 10, 1984
                    VI, page 52, Oct 21, 1984
   New York Times Magazine pp52-4+, Oct 21, 1984
   New Yorker 60:128, May 14, 1984
   Newsweek 103:83-4, May 14, 1984
   Theatre Crafts 18:24-9+, Aug/Sep 1984
                  21:48-55+, Nov 1987
   Time 123:75, May 14, 1984

Sunday Night Varieties
   conceived: Nat Lichtman

sketches:	Berenice Kazounoff and Sylvia Fine
lyrics:	John La Touche and David Gregory
sets:	Nat Lichtman

Productions:
  (Off-Broadway) Opened April 9, 1939
No Reviews.

Sunkist
book:	Fanchon and Marco
lyrics:	Fanchon and Marco

Productions:
  Opened May 23, 1921 for (27) performances
Reviews:
  New York Times page 20, May 24, 1921

Sunny
book:	Otto Harbach and Oscar Hammerstein II
music:	Jerome Kern
lyrics:	Otto Harbach and Oscar Hammerstein II

Productions:
  Opened September 22, 1925 for 517 performances
Reviews:
  New Republic 44:303, Nov 11, 1925
  New York Times page 29, Sep 10, 1925
                page 22, Sep 23, 1925
                page 29, Dec 6, 1926
  Theatre Magazine 42:16, Dec 1925

Sunny Days
book:	Clifford Grey and William Cary Duncan; adapted from M. Hennequin and P. Veber's A Kiss in the Taxi
music:	Jean Schwartz
lyrics:	Clifford Grey and William Cary Duncan
staging:	Hassard Short

Productions:
  Opened February 8, 1928 for 101 performances
  Opened October 1, 1928 for 32 performances
Reviews:
  New York Times page 29, Feb 9, 1928
                VIII, page 2, May 20, 1928
                page 34, Oct 2, 1928
  Theatre Magazine 47:41, Apr 1928

Sunny River
book:	Oscar Hammerstein II
music:	Sigmund Romberg
lyrics:	Oscar Hammerstein II
staging:	Oscar Hammerstein II
sets:	Stewart Chaney
costumes:	Irene Sharaff
choreography:	Carl Randall

Productions:
Opened December 4, 1941 for 36 performances
Reviews:
Catholic World 154:474, Jan 1942
New York Theatre Critics' Reviews 1941:186+
New York Times page 28, Dec 5, 1941
Newsweek 18:72, Dec 15, 1941

Sunset
by:	Gary William Friedman
music:	Gary William Friedman
lyrics:	Will Holt
staging:	Andre Ernotte
sets:	Kate Edmunds
costumes:	Patricia Zipprodt
choreography:	Buzz Miller

Productions:
(Off-Broadway) Opened November 7, 1983 for one performance
No Reviews.

The Sunshine Girl
book:	Paul A. Rubens and Cecil Raleigh
music:	Paul A. Rubens
staging:	J. A. E. Malone

Productions:
Opened February 3, 1913 for 160 performances
Reviews:
Blue Book 17:246-9, Jun 1913
Dramatic Mirror 69:6, Feb 5, 1913
                    69:2, Feb 19, 1913
                    69:2, Mar 5, 1913
Green Book 9:560-2+, Apr 1913
Munsey 47:985, Sep 1912
        49:154, Apr 1913
New York Dramatic News 57:13, Feb 8, 1913
New York Times page 11, Feb 4, 1913
Red Book 21:113+, May 1913
Theatre Magazine 17:66-7, Mar 1913
                  18:24, Jul 1913
                  18:93, Sep 1913

The Sunshine Train
conceived:	William E. Hunt
staging:	William E. Hunt
sets:	Philip Gilliam

Productions:
(Off-Broadway) Opened June 15, 1972 for 224 performances
No Reviews.

Surprise Package
book:	Tom Hill

music: Frances Ziffer, Hortense Belson and Hardy
                        Wieder
Productions:
(Off-Broadway) Season of 1952-53
No Reviews.

The Survival of St. Joan
    book: James Lineberger
    music: Hank and Gary Ruffin
    lyrics: James Lineberger
    staging: Chuck Gnys
    sets: Peter Harvey
    costumes: Peter Harvey
Productions:
(Off-Broadway) Opened February 28, 1971 for 17 performances
No Reviews.

Surviving Death in Three Acts
    book: Nancy Fales
    music: George Miller
    staging: Nancy Fales and Gail Julian
Productions:
(Off-Off-Broadway) Opened May 7, 1973
No Reviews.

Susanna and the Elders   (see Ballet Ballads)

Susanna, Don't You Cry
    book: Sarah Newmeyer and Clarence Loomis
    music: Melodies of Stephen Foster; special music by
                        Haus Spialek
    lyrics: Sarah Newmeyer and Clarence Loomis
    staging: Jose Ruben
    sets: Robert Edmund Jones
Productions:
Opened May 22, 1939 for 4 performances
Reviews:
    Musical Courier 119:7, Jun 1, 1939
    New York Times X, page 7, Apr 16, 1939
                    page 27, May 23, 1939
    Newsweek 13:34, Jun 5, 1939

Suzette
    book: Roy Dixon
    music: Arthur Gutman
Productions:
Opened November 24, 1921 for 4 performances
Reviews:
    New York Times page 18, Nov 25, 1921

Sweeney Todd, the Demon Barber of Fleet Street
    book: Hugh Wheeler, based on a version of Sweeney

Todd by Christopher Bond

music:	Stephen Sondheim
lyrics:	Stephen Sondheim
staging:	Harold Prince
sets:	Eugene Lee
costumes:	Franne Lee
choreography:	Larry Fuller

Productions:

Opened March 1, 1979 for 557 performances

Reviews:

America 140:260, Mar 31, 1979

American Record Guide 42:54+, Jul 1979

California 6:149+, Oct 1981

Commonweal 106:338-9, Jun 8, 1979
             116:566-7, Oct 20, 1989

Horizon 22:20-5, Apr 1979
      29:31-2, Dec 1986

Los Angeles 24:260+, Sep 1979
      26:348+, Aug 1981

Nation 228:315-16, Mar 24, 1979

New Leader 62:21-2, Mar 26, 1979

New Republic 180:124-5, Mar 24, 1979

New York 12:74-5, Mar 19, 1979
      17:82-3, Oct 29, 1984
      22:82+, Oct 2, 1989

New York Theatre Critics' Reviews 1979:350
                            1989:237

New York Times III, page 1, Mar 2, 1979
            II, page 1, Mar 11, 1979
            III, page 16, Mar 29, 1979
            III, page 8, May 1, 1979
            page 26, Jul 6, 1980
            XXI, page 17, Dec 7, 1980

New Yorker 55:107, Mar 12, 1979

Newsweek 93:101+, Mar 12, 1979

People 11:104-5, Jun 4, 1979

Saturday Review 6:33, Apr 28, 1979

Stereo Review 43:7, Aug 1979

Time 113:82-3, Mar 12, 1979
     134:76, Sep 25, 1989

Sweet Adeline

book:	Oscar Hammerstein II
music:	Jerome Kern
lyrics:	Oscar Hammerstein II
staging:	Reginald Hammerstein and Danny Dare
choreography:	Danny Dare

Productions:

Opened September 3, 1929 for 234 performances

Reviews:

Arts and Decoration 32:67, Nov 1929

Catholic World 131:81, Apr 1930
Commonweal 10:564, Oct 2, 1929
Life (New York) 94:23, Sep 27, 1929
Nation 129:310-11, Sep 18, 1929
New York Times VIII, page 3, Aug 25, 1929
                  page 33, Sep 23, 1929
Theatre Magazine 50:45, Nov 1929
Vogue 74:63+, Oct 26, 1929

Sweet and Low
    book: David Freedman
    music: Billy Rose
    lyrics: David Freedman
    staging: Alexander Leftwich
Productions:
    Opened November 17, 1930 for 184 performances
Reviews:
    Nation 131:632, Dec 3, 1930
    New York Times page 28, Nov 18, 1930

Sweet Charity
    book: Neil Simon; based on the screenplay Nights of
                   Cabiria by Federico Fellini, Tullio Pinelli and
                   Ennio Flaiano
    music: Cy Coleman
    lyrics: Dorothy Fields
    staging: Bob Fosse
    costumes: Irene Sharaff
    sets: Robert Randolph
    choreography: Bob Fosse
Productions:
    Opened January 29, 1966 for 608 performances
    Opened April 27, 1986 for 368 performances
Reviews:
    America 114:452, Apr 2, 1966
    Commonweal 84:57, Apr 1, 1966
    Dance Magazine 40:24, May 1966
                    60:72-3, Jun 1986
                    60:60-1, Jul 1986
    Jet 69:55, Sep 23, 1985
        70:54-5, May 19, 1986
    Life 60:99-100, Mar 25, 1966
    Los Angeles 30:50+, Sep 1985
    Nation 202:248-9, Feb 28, 1966
    New York 7:76+, Apr 22, 1974
               19:139-40, May 12, 1986
    New York Theatre Critics' Reviews 1966:384
                               1986:309
    New York Times page 22, Jan 31, 1966
                II, page 1, Feb 6, 1966
                page 29, Jun 30, 1967

page 13, Jul 1, 1967
page 17, Jul 21, 1967
page 34, Oct 13, 1967
III, page 19, Apr 28, 1986
New Yorker 41:84, Feb 5, 1966
Newsweek 67:88, Feb 14, 1966
107:78, May 12, 1986
Saturday Review 49:44, Feb 12, 1966
Time 87:46, Feb 4, 1966
127:97, May 12, 1986
Vogue 147:58, Mar 15, 1966

Sweet Feet
    book: Dan Graham
    music: Don Brockett
    lyrics: Don Brockett
    staging: Don Brockett
    sets: James French
    costumes: Tom Fallon
Productions:
    (Off-Broadway) Opened May 25, 1972 for 6 performances
Reviews:
    New York Times page 17, May 26, 1972

Sweet Little Devil
    book: Frank Mandel and Laurence Schwab
    music: George Gershwin
    lyrics: B. G. DeSylva
Productions:
    Opened January 21, 1924 for 120 performances
Reviews:
    New York Times page 15, Jan 22, 1924
    Theatre Magazine 39:70, Mar 1924

Sweet Miami
    book: Stuart Bishop
    music: Ed Tyler
    lyrics: Ed Tyler
    staging: Louis MacMillan
    sets: Stuart Slade
    costumes: André
Productions:
    (Off-Broadway) Opened September 25, 1962 for 22 performances
Reviews:
    New York Times page 33, Sep 26, 1962
    New Yorker 38:183-4, Oct 13, 1962

Sweet Potato   (see Noel Coward's Sweet Potato)

Sweet Will
    book: Lance Mulcahy

music: Lance Mulcahy
lyrics: From the works of William Shakespeare
staging: John Olon
sets: Desmond Heeley
choreography: Dennis Dennehy
Productions:
  (Off-Broadway) Opened January 5, 1986 for 9 performances
Reviews:
  New York Times III, page 12, Jan 6, 1986

The Sweetheart Shop
  book: Anne Caldwell
  music: Hugo Felix
  lyrics: Anne Caldwell
  sets: Edgar MacGregor
Productions:
  Opened August 31, 1920 for 55 performances
Reviews:
  Dramatic Mirror 82:782, Apr 24, 1920
                  page 420, Sep 4, 1920
  New York Clipper 68:27, Sep 15, 1920
  New York Times page 13, Sep 1, 1920
  Theatre Magazine 32:281, Nov 1920
                  32:334, Nov 1920

Sweetheart Time
  book: Harry B. Smith; based on Never Say Die
  music: Walter Donaldson and Joseph Meyer
  lyrics: Ballard Macdonald and Irving Caesar
Productions:
  Opened January 19, 1926 for 143 performances
Reviews:
  New York Times page 23, Jan 20, 1926
  Theatre Magazine 43:18, Apr 1926

Sweethearts (1913)
  book: Harry B. Smith and Fred De Gresac
  music: Victor Herbert
  lyrics: Robert B. Smith
  staging: Frederick G. Latham
Productions:
  Opened September 8, 1913 for 136 performances
  Opened January 21, 1947 for 288 performances
Reviews:
  Blue Book 18:221-4, Dec 1913
  Dramatic Mirror 69:2, Apr 9, 1913
                  69:1, Apr 30, 1913
                  70:7, Sep 10, 1913
                  70:2, Oct 1, 1913
  Green Book 10:870-71, Nov 1913
            10:967, Dec 1913

Munsey Magazine 50:295-6, Nov 1913
New Republic 116:44, Feb 3, 1947
New York Dramatic News 58:20, Sep 13, 1913
New York Theatre Critics' Reviews 1947:479
New York Times page 7, Sep 9, 1913
                 II, page 2, Jan 19, 1947
                 page 31, Jan 22, 1947
                 II, page 1, Feb 2, 1947
                 II, page 1, Jul 6, 1947
                 page 39, Dec 9, 1947
Newsweek 29:71, Feb 3, 1947
Theatre Arts 31:24, Mar 1947
        31:17-18, Apr 1947
Theatre Magazine 18:xii-xiii, Oct 1913
              50:72, Nov 1929
Time 49:72, Feb 3, 1947

Sweethearts (1986)
    book: Uncredited, based on a collection of the famous
                          solos and duets of Jeanette MacDonald and Nelson
                          Eddy
    music: Various composers
    lyrics: Various authors
    costumes: Josie Garner
Productions:
    (Off-Broadway) Opened May 7, 1986 for 56 performances
    (Off-Broadway) Opened December 7, 1988 for 54 performances
Reviews:
    New York Times III, page 15, May 15, 1986
                     III, pag 22, Dec 8, 1988
                     XXII, page 13, Jul 16, 1989

Swing
    conceived: Elizabeth Swados
    music: Elizabeth Swados, Andrew Julian Meyers,
                      Preston Fulwood Jr., David Levitt, and Connie
                      Alexander
    staging: Elizabeth Swados
Productions:
    (Off-Off-Broadway) Opened October 24, 1987
Reviews:
    New York Times III, page 17, Oct 26, 1987

Swing It
    book: Cecil Mack and Milton Reddie
    music: Eubie Blake
    lyrics: Cecil Mack and Milton Reddie
    staging: Cecil Mack and Jack Mason
    sets: Walter Walden and Victor Zanoff
    costumes: Maxine and Alexander Jones

Productions:
    Opened July 22, 1937 for 60 performances
Reviews:
    New York Times page 17, Jul 22, 1937

Swing to the Left   (see Stars in Your Eyes)

Swingin' the Dream
    book: Gilbert Seldes and Erik Charell, based on Shake-
                    speare's A Midsummer Night's Dream
    music: Jimmy Van Heusen
    lyrics: Eddie de Lange
    staging: Erik Charell
    sets: Herbert Andrews and Walter Jageman, based on
                    Walt Disney cartoons
    choreography: Agnes deMille and Herbert White
Productions:
    Opened November 29, 1939 for 13 performances
Reviews:
    Catholic World 150:471, Jan 1940
    New York Times page 24, Nov 30, 1939
                   page 66, Dec 10, 1939
    Theatre Arts 24:93, Feb 1940
    Time 34:50, Dec 11, 1939

Sybil
    book: Max Brody and Frank Martos; English version by
                    Harry Graham
    music: Victor Jacobi
    staging: Fred G. Latham
Productions:
    Opened January 10, 1916 for 168 performances
Reviews:
    Dramatic Mirror 75:7, Jan 15, 1916
                    75:2, Jan 29, 1916
                    75:2, Feb 5, 1916
                    75:4, Mar 18, 1916
                    75:2, Apr 1, 1916
    Green Book 15:446, Mar 1916
    Munsey 57:500, Apr 1916
            58:315, Jul 1916
    New York Dramatic News 62:18, Jan 15, 1916
    New York Times page 11, Jan 11, 1916
    Theatre Magazine 23:125-6, Mar 1916
                     23:135, Mar 1916

-T-

T.N.T.   (Tricephalous Neurosyllogistic Training)
    book: Richard Morrock

music: Richard Morrock
lyrics: Richard Morrock
staging: Frank Carucci
sets: Ernest Allen Smith
costumes: Susan J. Wright
choreography: Mary Lou Crivello
Productions:
(Off-Broadway) Opened April 22, 1982 for 6 performances
No Reviews.

The Taffetas
conceived: Rick Lewis
music: Various composers
lyrics: Various authors
staging: Steven Harris
sets: Evelyn Sakash
costumes: David Graden
choreography: Tina Paul
Productions:
(Off-Broadway) Opened October 12, 1988 for 95 performances
(Off-Broadway) Opened February 1, 1989 for 165 performances
Reviews:
America 159:321, Oct 29, 1988
People 31:133, Apr 3, 1989

Take a Bow
music: Ted Murray and Benny Davis
staging: Wally Wanger
sets: Kaj Velden
costumes: Ben Wallace
choreography: Marjorie Fielding
Productions:
Opened June 15, 1944 for 12 performances
Reviews:
New York Theatre Critics' Reviews 1944:167
New York Times page 15, Jun 16, 1944

Take a Chance
book: B. G. DeSylva and Laurence Schwab, additional dialogue by Sid Silvers
music: Nacio Herb Brown and Richard Whiting, additional songs by Vincent Youmans
lyrics: B. G. De Sylva
staging: Edgar MacGregor
sets: Cleon Throckmorton
choreography: Bobby Connelly
Productions:
Opened November 26, 1932 for 243 performances
Reviews:
New Outlook 161:47, Jan 1933
New York Times page 11, Nov 18, 1932
III, page 2, Dec 4, 1932

Take It from Me
      book: Will B. Johnstone
      music: Will R. Anderson
      lyrics: Will B. Johnstone
      staging: Fred A. Bishop, Joe C. Smith and Joseph Gaites
Productions:
      Opened March 31, 1919 for 96 performances
Reviews:
      Forum 61:30, May 1919
      Life (New York) 73:663, Apr 17, 1919
      New York Times page 9, Apr 1, 1919
      Theatre Magazine 29:275-6, May 1919
                        29:293, May 1919

Take It from the Top
      staging: Maurice Edwards
      sets: Duane Camp
Productions:
      (Off-Broadway) Opened November 22, 1967 for 15 performances
No Reviews.

Take Me Along
      book: Joseph Stein and Robert Russell, based on
                         Eugene O'Neill's Ah, Wilderness!
      music: Robert Merrill
      lyrics: Robert Merrill
      staging: Peter Glenville
      sets: Oliver Smith
      costumes: Miles White
      choreography: Onna White
Productions:
      Opened October 22, 1959 for 448 performances
      (Off-Off-Broadway) Opened March 23, 1984
      Opened April 14, 1985 for one performance
      (Off-Off-Broadway) Opened January 8, 1987
Reviews:
      America 102:255, Nov 21, 1959
      Commonweal 71:240, Nov 20, 1959
      Dance Magazine 33:24-5, Dec 1959
      Life 47:117-20, Nov 2, 1959
      New York 18:93-4, Apr 29, 1985
      New York Theatre Critics' Reviews 1959:244+
                                        1985:313
      New York Times page 22, Oct 23, 1959
                     II, page 1, Nov 1, 1959
                     page 50, Dec 14, 1960
                     II, page 2, Mar 16, 1984
                     III, page 24, Apr 4, 1984
                     III, page 16, Aug 15, 1985
                     III, page 23, Jan 14, 1987
      New Yorker 35:134-5, Oct 31, 1959
                 61:126+, Apr 22, 1985

Newsweek 54:94, Nov 2, 1959
Saturday Review 42:40, Nov 14, 1959
Theatre Arts 43:13, Dec 1959
Time 74:30+, Nov 2, 1959

Take the Air
    book: Anne Caldwell and Gene Buck
    music: Dave Stamper
    lyrics: Anne Caldwell and Gene Buck
    staging: Alexander Leftwich and Gene Buck
Productions:
    Opened November 22, 1927 for 206 performances
Reviews:
    Life (New York) 90:21, Dec 29, 1927
    New York Times page 28, Nov 23, 1927
                    VIII, page 4, Feb 12, 1928
    Vogue 71:70, Jan 15, 1928

Taking My Turn
    conceived: Robert H. Livingston
    music: Gary William Friedman
    lyrics: Will Holt
    staging: Robert H. Livingston
    sets: Clarke Dunham
    costumes: Judith Dolan
    choreography: Douglas Norwick
Productions:
    (Off-Broadway) Opened June 9, 1983 for 345 performances
Reviews:
    New York 16:72-3, Jun 27, 1983
    New York Times III, page 3, Jun 10, 1983
    New Yorker 59:76, Jun 20, 1983

Tales of Rigo
    book: Maurice V. Samuels; based on a story by Hyman
                      Adler
    music: Ben Schwartz
    lyrics: Ben Schwartz
    staging: Clarence Derwent
Productions:
    Opened May 30, 1927 for 20 performances
No Reviews.

Talk About Girls
    book: William Cary Duncan; based on a play by John
                      Hunter Booth
    music: Harold Orlob and Stephen Jones
    lyrics: Irving Caesar
    staging: John Harwood
Productions:
    Opened June 14, 1927 for 13 performances

Reviews:
  Life (New York) 80:19, Jun 30, 1927
  New York Times page 31, Jun 15, 1927
  Theatre Magazine 46:18, Aug 1927

Tallulah
  book: Tony Lang
  music: Arthur Siegel
  lyrics: Mae Richard
  staging: David Holdgrive
  sets: John Falabella
  costumes: John Falabella
  choreography: David Holdgrive
Productions:
  (Off-Off-Broadway) Opened June 13, 1983
  (Off-Broadway) Opened October 30, 1983 for 42 performances
Reviews:
  New York 16:101, Nov 14, 1983
  New York Theatre Critics' Reviews 1983:82
  New York Times III, page 21, Jun 15, 1983
             III, page 14, Oct 31, 1983

Tambourines to Glory
  book: Langston Hughes, adapted from his novel
  music: Jobe Huntley
  lyrics: Langston Hughes
  staging: Nikos Psacharapoulos
  sets: John Conklin
  costumes: John Conklin
Productions:
  Opened November 2, 1963 for 24 performances
Reviews:
  New York Theatre Critics' Reviews 1963:207+
  New York Times page 47, Nov 4, 1963
             page 46, Nov 12, 1963
             page 28, Nov 15, 1963
             page 43, Nov 22, 1963

Tangerine
  book: Philip Bartholomae
  music: Carlo Sanders
  lyrics: Howard Johnston
  staging: George Marion and Bert French
Productions:
  Opened August 9, 1921 for 337 performances
Reviews:
  Dramatic Mirror 84:229, Aug 13, 1921
  Life (New York) 78:18, Aug 25, 1921
  New York Clipper 69:24, Aug 17, 1921
  New York Times page 8, Aug 10, 1921
             page 16, Sep 5, 1921

Theatre Magazine 34:213, Oct 1921
34:234, Oct 1921

Tango Apasionado

conceived: Graciela Daniele
book: Graciela Daniele and Jim Lewis, adapted from the works of Jorge Luis Borges
music: Astor Piazzolla
lyrics: William Finn
staging: Graciela Daniele
sets: Santo Loquasto
costumes: Santo Loquasto
choreography: Graciela Daniele

Productions:
(Off-Off-Broadway) Opened October 28, 1987 for 56 performances
Reviews:
New York 20:115-16, Nov 23, 1987
New York Times III, page 15, Nov 10, 1987
New Yorker 63:103-4, Dec 21, 1987

Tantalizing Tommy

book: Michael Morton and Paul Gavault
music: Dr. Hugo Felix
lyrics: Adrian Ross
staging: George Marion

Productions:
Opened October 1, 1912 for 31 performances
Reviews:
Blue Book 16:16-19, Nov 1912
Dramatic Mirror 68:7, Sep 11, 1912
68:6, Oct 9, 1912
Harper's Weekly 56:20, Oct 12, 1912
Leslie's Weekly 115:411, Oct 24, 1912
Munsey 48:525, Dec 1912
New York Dramatic News 56:24-5, Oct 12, 1912
Theatre Magazine 16:xv, Nov 1912
17:23, Jan 1913

The Tap Dance Kid

book: Charles Blackwell, based on the novel Nobody's Family Is Going to Change by Louise Fitzhugh
music: Henry Krieger
lyrics: Robert Lorick
staging: Vivian Matalon
sets: Michael Hotopp and Paul dePass
costumes: Ann Emonts
choreography: Danny Daniels

Productions:
Opened December 21, 1983 for 669 performances
Reviews:
Dance Magazine 58:85-7, Mar 1984
58:58-60, Apr 1984

Los Angeles 30:46+, Nov 1985
New York 17:57, Jan 9, 1984
New York Theatre Critics' Reviews 1983:52
New York Times III, page 11, Dec 22, 1983
New Yorker 59:81, Jan 2, 1984
Newsweek 103:96, Jan 9, 1984
Time 123:90, Jan 2, 1984

Tatterdemalion   (see King of Schnorrers)

Tattle Tales
    book: Frank Fay and Nick Copeland
    music and
      lyrics: Howard Jackson, Edward Ward, Leo Robin, Ralph Rainger, George Waggoner, Willard Robison, Edward Eliscu, Eddie Beinbryer, William Walsh
    staging: Frank Fay
Productions:
    Opened June 1, 1933 for 28 performances
Reviews:
    New Outlook 162:43, Jul 1933
    New York Times page 22, Jun 2, 1933

The Tattooed Countess
    book: Coleman Dowell; based on Carl Van Vechten's novel
    music: Coleman Dowell
    lyrics: Coleman Dowell
Productions:
    (Off-Broadway) Opened Season of 1960-61
Reviews:
    New York Times page 40, May 4, 1961
                   page 27, May 6, 1961

Ted Pugh   (see An Evening with Sue and Pugh)

Teddy & Alice
    book: Jerome Alden
    music: John Philip Sousa and Richard Kapp
    lyrics: Hal Hackady
    artistic
      consultant: Alan Jay Lerner
    staging: John Driver
    sets: Robin Wagner
    costumes: Theoni V. Aldredge
    choreography: Donald Saddler
Productions:
    Opened November 12, 1987 for 77 performances
Reviews:
    America 157:430, Dec 5, 1987
    New York 20:115, Nov 23, 1987

New York Theatre Critics' Reviews 1987:124
New York Times III, page 3, Nov 13, 1987
New Yorker 63:153, Nov 23, 1987

Telecast
book: Barry Harman
music: Martin Silvestri
lyrics: Barry Harman
staging: Barry Harman and Wayne Cilento
choreography: Wayne Cilento
Productions:
(Off-Broadway)   Opened February 15, 1979 for 113 performances
No Reviews.

Telemachus Friend
book: Sally Dixon Weiner; based on the O. Henry
                  short story
Productions:
(Off-Broadway)   Opened April 17, 1972
No Reviews.

The Telephone   (Presented with The Medium)
book: Gian-Carlo Menotti
music: Gian-Carlo Menotti
lyrics: Gian-Carlo Menotti
staging: Gian-Carlo Menotti
sets: Horace Armistead
costumes: Horace Armistead
Productions:
Opened May 1, 1947 for 212 performances
Opened December 7, 1948 for 40 performances
Opened July 19, 1950 for 110 performances
Reviews:
Catholic World 165:265-6, Jun 1947
               171:469, Sep 1950
Musical Courier 135:16, Mar 1, 1947
               138:5, Nov 15, 1948
Nation 164:637, May 24, 1947
New York Theatre Critics' Reviews 1947:379
                                  1950:280
New York Times page 28, May 2, 1947
               II, page 2, May 11, 1947
               page 26, Apr 30, 1948
               page 41, Dec 8, 1948
New Yorker 23:50+, May 10, 1947
Newsweek 29:76, Mar 3, 1947
Saturday Review 30:22-4, May 31, 1947
School and Society 66:66, Jul 26, 1947
                  69:86, Jan 29, 1949
Theatre Arts 31:60, May 1947
Time 49:65, Mar 3, 1947

Tell Her the Truth
book: R. P. Weston and Bert Lee, adapted from Fred-
                  erick Isham and James Montgomery's Nothing
                  But the Truth
music: Jack Waller and Joseph Tunbridge
lyrics: R. P. Weston and Bert Lee
staging: Morris Green and Henry Thomas
Productions:
Opened October 28, 1932 for 11 performances
Reviews:
New York Times page 18, Oct 29, 1932
             page 20, Nov 7, 1932

Tell Me More
book: Fred Thompson and William K. Wells
music: George Gershwin
lyrics: B. G. DeSylva and Ira Gershwin
Productions:
Opened April 13, 1925 for 32 performances
Reviews:
Life (New York) 85:18, May 28, 1925
New York Times page 27, Apr 14, 1925
Theatre Magazine 42:16, Jul 1925

A Temporary Island
book: Halsted Welles
songs: Lorenzo Fuller
music: Lehman Engel
staging: Halsted Welles
sets: Lawrence Goldwasser
costumes: Mildred Sutherland
Productions:
Opened March 14, 1948 for 6 performances
Reviews:
New Republic 118:30, Mar 29, 1948
New York Times page 27, Mar 15, 1948
Theatre Arts 32:32, Spring 1948

Ten Percent Revue
words: Tom Wilson Weinberg
music: Tom Wilson Weinberg
staging: Scott Green
costumes: Kevin-Robert
choreography: Tee Scatuorchio
Productions:
(Off-Broadway) Opened April 13, 1988 for 239 performances
Reviews:
New York Times III, page 26, Apr 14, 1988

Tenderloin
book: George Abbott and Jerome Weidman, based on
                  the novel by Samuel Hopkins Adams

music: Jerry Bock
lyrics: Sheldon Harnick
staging: George Abbott
sets: Cecil Beaton
costumes: Cecil Beaton
choreography: Joe Layton

Productions:
Opened October 17, 1960 for 216 performances
(Off-Off-Broadway) Opened November 6, 1975

Reviews:
America 104:354+, Dec 3, 1960
Christian Century 77:1382, Nov 23, 1960
Dance Magazine 34:33, Dec 1960
Nation 191:353, Nov 5, 1960
New York Theatre Critics' Reviews 1960:205+
New York Times page 47, Oct 18, 1960
              page 28, Nov 4, 1960
              page 30, Apr 13, 1961
              page 26, Nov 11, 1975
New Yorker 36:86, Oct 29, 1960
Newsweek 56:84, Oct 31, 1960
Saturday Review 43:39, Nov 5, 1960
Theatre Arts 44:12, Dec 1960
Time 76:68, Oct 31, 1960

Texas, Li'l Darlin'

book: John Whedon and Sam Moore
music: Robert Edmund Dolan
lyrics: Johnny Mercer
staging: Paul Crabtree
sets: Theodore Cooper
costumes: Eleanor Goldsmith
choreography: Al White, Jr.

Productions:
Opened November 25, 1949 for 221 performances

Reviews:
Catholic World 170:309, Jan 1950
Commonweal 51:293, Dec 16, 1949
New York Theatre Critics' Reviews 1949:214+
New York Times page 10, Nov 26, 1949
              page 19, Jul 11, 1951
New Yorker 25:70-1, Dec 3, 1949
Newsweek 34:84, Dec 5, 1949
Theatre Arts 34:9, Feb 1950
Time 54:66, Dec 5, 1949

That 5 A.M. Jazz

music: Will Holt
lyrics: Will Holt
staging: Michael Kahn
sets: Lloyd Burlingame
choreography: Sandra Devlin

Productions:
    (Off-Broadway)   Opened October 19, 1964 for 94 performances
Reviews:
    New York Times page 42, Oct 20, 1964
    New Yorker 40:129, Oct 31, 1964

That Hat!
    book: Adapted by Cy Young from the French farce
                         Le Chapeau de Paille d'Italie
    music and
      lyrics: Adapted by Cy Young
    staging: Dania Krupska
    sets: Bill Hargate
    costumes: Bill Hargate
    choreography: Dania Krupska
Productions:
    (Off-Broadway)   Opened September 23, 1964 for one performance
Reviews:
    New York Times page 45, Sep 24, 1964
                    page 33, Sep 25, 1964

That's Entertainment
    music: Howard Dietz and Arthur Schwartz
    lyrics: Howard Dietz and Arthur Schwartz
    staging: Paul Aaron
    sets: David F. Segal
    costumes: Jane Greenwood
    choreography: Larry Fuller
Productions:
    Opened April 14, 1972 for 4 performances
Reviews:
    New York Theatre Critics' Reviews 1972:317
    New York Times page 19, Apr 15, 1972
    New Yorker 48:108, Apr 22, 1972

Theater Songs   (see Leonard Bernstein's Theater Songs)

There You Are
    book: Carl Bartfield
    music: William Heagney
    lyrics: William Heagney and Tom Connell
    staging: Horace Sinclair
Productions:
    Opened May 16, 1932 for 8 performances
Reviews:
    New York Times page 25, May 17, 1932

They Don't Make 'em Like That Anymore
    sketches: Hugh Martin and Timothy Gray
    music: Hugh Martin and Timothy Gray
    lyrics: Hugh Martin and Timothy Gray

staging: Timothy Gray
sets: Don Gordon
costumes: E. Huntington Parker
Productions:
  (Off-Broadway) Opened June 8, 1972 for 32 performances
Reviews:
  New York Times page 44, Jun 12, 1972

They're Playing Our Song

book: Neil Simon
music: Marvin Hamlisch
lyrics: Carole Bayer Sager
staging: Robert Moore
sets: Douglas W. Schmidt
costumes: Ann Roth
choreography: Patricia Birch
Productions:
  Opened February 11, 1979 for 1,082 performances
  (Off-Off-Broadway) Opened January 9, 1986
Reviews:
  Los Angeles 23:220+, Dec 1978
               24:201, Jan 1979
  Nation 228:252, Mar 3, 1979
  New West 4:75, Jan 1, 1979
  New York 12:102-3, Feb 26, 1979
  New York Theatre Critics' Reviews 1979:374
  New York Times III, page 11, Feb 12, 1979
                   II, page 3, Feb 18, 1979
                   III, page 16, Jan 13, 1986
  New Yorker 55:78, Feb 26, 1979
  Newsweek 93:76, Feb 26, 1979
  Saturday Review 6:38, Apr 14, 1979
  Time 113:82, Feb 26, 1979

The Thing Itself

book: Arthur Sainer
music: Jim Kurtz, Meredith Monk, Robert Cosmo Savage
                  and David Tice
staging: Crystal Field
Productions:
  (Off-Off-Broadway) Opened November 30, 1972
No Reviews.

The Third Little Show

assembled by: Dwight Deere Wiman
music: Noel Coward, Henry Sullivan, Michael Cleary,
                  Morris Hamilton, Burton Lane, Herman Hupfeld,
                  Ned Lehak, William Lewis, Jr.
lyrics: Noel Coward, Earle Crooker, Max and Nathaniel
                  Lief, Grace Henry, Harold Adamson, Herman Hup-
                  feld, Edward Eliscu, Ted Fetter
staging: Alexander Leftwich

Productions:
    Opened June 1, 1931 for 136 performances
Reviews:
    Bookman 73:632-3, Aug 1931
    Catholic World 133:463, Jul 1931
    Commonweal 14:188, Jun 17, 1931
    Life (New York) 97:19, Jun 26, 1931
    New York Times VIII, page 2, May 10, 1931
                    page 34, Jun 2, 1931
    Outlook 158:219, Jun 17, 1931

13 Daughters
    book: Eaton Magoon (additional book material by Leon
                     Tokatyan)
    music: Eaton Magoon
    lyrics: Eaton Magoon
    staging: Billy Matthews
    sets: George Jenkins
    costumes: Alvin Colt
    choreography: Rod Alexander
Productions:
    Opened March 2, 1961 for 28 performances
Reviews:
    New York Theatre Critics' Reviews 1961:350+
    New York Times page 17, Mar 3, 1961
                    page 30, Mar 23, 1961
    New Yorker 37:112, Mar 11, 1961

This Is the Army
    sketches: James McColl, based on the musical show Yip,
                     Yip, Yaphank
    music: Irving Berlin
    lyrics: Irving Berlin
    staging: Ezra Stone
    sets: John Koenig
    costumes: John Koenig
    choreography: Robert Sidney and Nelson Barclift
Productions:
    Opened July 4, 1942 for 113 performances
Reviews:
    American Mercury 55:450-1, Oct 1942
    Catholic World 155:726, Sep 1942
    Collier's 110:14-15+, Oct 17, 1942
    Commonweal 36:303-4, Jul 17, 1942
    Life 13:72-5, Jul 20, 1942
    New York Theatre Critics' Reviews 1942:256+
    New York Times VIII, page 1, Jun 14, 1942
                    page 28, Jul 5, 1942
                    VII, page 1, Jul 12, 1942
                    VII, page 6, Jul 12, 1942
                    VIII, page 1, Aug 16, 1942
                    VIII, page 8, Sep 13, 1942

New York Times Magazine pages 6-7, Jul 12, 1942
page 20, Nov 21, 1943
Newsweek 20:52+, Jul 13, 1942
Theatre Arts 26:546, Sep 1942
26:608+, Oct 1942
Time 40:36, Jul 13, 1942

Thoughts
book and
music: Lamar Alford
lyrics: Lamar Alford; additional lyrics by Megan Terry
                 and Jose Tapla
staging: Michael Schultz
sets: Stuart Wurtzel
costumes: Joseph Thomas
choreography: Jan Mickens
Productions:
(Off-Broadway) Opened March 19, 1973 for 24 performances
Reviews:
New York Times page 25, Feb 5, 1973
page 29, Mar 20, 1973
II, page 3, Apr 1, 1973
New Yorker 49:77, Mar 31, 1973

Three Cheers
book: Anne Caldwell and R. H. Burnside
music: Raymond Hubbell
lyrics: Anne Caldwell
staging: R. H. Burnside
choreography: Dave Bennett
Productions:
Opened October 15, 1928 for 210 performances
Reviews:
New York Times page 28, Oct 16, 1928
IX, page 1, Oct 21, 1928
Outlook 150:1086, Oct 31, 1928
Theatre Magazine 48:46, Dec 1928
Vogue 72:146, Dec 8, 1928

3 for Tonight
special
material: Robert Wells
music: Walter Schumann
lyrics: Robert Wells
staging: Gower Champion
Productions:
Opened April 6, 1955 for 85 performances
Reviews:
America 93:165, May 7, 1955
Catholic World 181:226, Jun 1955
Commonweal 62:105, Apr 29, 1955

Life 38:129-30+, Apr 25, 1955
Nation 180:354-5, Apr 23, 1955
New York Theatre Critics' Reviews 1955:337+
New York Times II, page 3, Apr 3, 1955
      page 23, Apr 7, 1955
      II, page 1, Apr 17, 1955
New Yorker 31:74+, Apr 16, 1955
Newsweek 44:90+, Dec 13, 1954
Saturday Review 38:25, Apr 23, 1955
Theatre Arts 39:20-1, 93, Jun 1955
Time 65:72, Apr 18, 1955
Vogue 125:122, Apr 1, 1955

3 Guys Naked From the Waist Down

book:	Jerry Colker
music:	Michael Rupert
lyrics:	Jerry Colker
staging:	Andrew Cadiff
sets:	Clarke Dunham
costumes:	Tom McKinley
choreography:	Don Bondi

Productions:
  (Off-Broadway) Opened February 5, 1985 for 160 performances
Reviews:
  New Republic 192:27-8, Apr 1, 1985
  New York Theatre Critics' Reviews 1985:347
  New York Times III, page 17, Feb 6, 1985
  New Yorker 60:110, Feb 18, 1985

Three Little Girls

book:	Herman Feiner and Bruno Hardt-Warden, adapted by Marie Hecht and Gertrude Purcell
music:	Walter Kollo
lyrics:	Harry B. Smith
staging:	J. J. Shubert

Productions:
  Opened April 14, 1930 for 104 performances
Reviews:
  Life (New York) 95:18, May 2, 1930
  New York Times page 29, Apr 15, 1930
  Theatre Magazine 51:48, Jun 1930

Three Musketeers

book:	William Anthony McGuire, adapted from the story by Alexandre Dumas
music:	Rudolf Friml
lyrics:	P. G. Wodehouse and Clifford Grey
staging:	William Anthony McGuire

Productions:
  Opened March 13, 1928 for 318 performances
  (Off-Off-Broadway) Opened May 8, 1975
  Opened November 11, 1984 for 9 performances

Reviews:
New York 17:76, Nov 26, 1984
New York Theatre Critics' Reviews 1984:170
New York Times IX, page 1, Mar 4, 1928
               IX, page 2, Mar 4, 1928
               page 28, Mar 14, 1928
               IX, page 1, Mar 25, 1928
               page 23, May 16, 1975
               I, page 13, Nov 12, 1984
New Yorker 60:184, Nov 19, 1984

Three Postcards
     book: Craig Lucas
     music: Craig Carnelia
     lyrics: Craig Carnelia
     staging: Norman Rene
     sets: Loy Arcenas
     costumes: Walter Hicklin
     choreography: Linda Kostalik-Boussom
Productions:
     (Off-Broadway) Opened May 14, 1987 for 22 performances
Reviews:
New York 20:108+, May 25, 1987
New York Theatre Critics' Reviews 1987:192
New York Times III, page 3, May 15, 1987
New Yorker 63:87, May 25, 1987
Time 129:71, May 25, 1987

The Three Romeos
     book: R. H. Burnside
     music: Raymond Hubbell
     lyrics: R. H. Burnside
     staging: R. H. Burnside
Productions:
     Opened November 13, 1911 for 56 performances
Reviews:
Blue Book 14:469-71, Jan 1912
Dramatic Mirror 66:10, Nov 15, 1911
                    66:2, Nov 22, 1911
                    66:2, Dec 6, 1911
Life (New York) 58:902-3, Nov 23, 1911
New York Times page 13, Nov 14, 1911
Theatre Magazine 14:xv, Dec 1911

Three Showers
     book: William Cary Duncan
     music: Creamer and Layton
     lyrics: Creamer and Layton
Productions:
     Opened April 5, 1920 for 48 performances
Reviews:
Dramatic Mirror 82:681, Apr 10, 1920

New York Clipper 68:14, Apr 14, 1920
New York Times page 18, Apr 6, 1920
Theatre Magazine 31:402, May 1920
            31:407, May 1920

Three to Make Ready

book:	Nancy Hamilton
music:	Morgan Lewis
lyrics:	Nancy Hamilton
staging:	John Murray Anderson
sets:	Donald Oenslager
costumes:	Andre
choreography:	Robert Sidney

Productions:
  Opened March 7, 1946 for 327 performances
Reviews:
  Catholic World 163:72-3, Apr 1946
  Commonweal 43:572-3, Mar 22, 1946
  Life 20:67-70, Mar 25, 1946
  Musical Courier 133:14, Apr 15, 1946
  New York Theatre Critics' Reviews 1946:434+
  New York Times page 16, Mar 8, 1946
                II, page 1, Mar 17, 1946
                II, page 1, May 19, 1946
                II, page 2, Oct 27, 1946
  New Yorker 22:44+, Mar 16, 1946
  Newsweek 27:92, Mar 18, 1946
  Theatre Arts 30:261-2, May 1946
  Time 47:56, Mar 18, 1946

Three Waltzes

book:	Clare Kummer and Rowland Leigh, adapted from Paul Knepler and Armin Robinson's play
music:	Johann Strauss, Sr., Johann Strauss, Jr., Oscar Strauss
lyrics:	Clare Kummer, Edwin Gilbert
staging:	Hassard Short
sets:	Watson Barratt
costumes:	Connie dePinna
choreography:	Chester Hale

Productions:
  Opened December 25, 1937 for 122 performances
Reviews:
  Commonweal 27:300, Jan 7, 1938
  New York Times page 15, Nov 15, 1937
                page 10, Dec 27, 1937
  One Act Play Magazine 1:849, Jan 1938
  Stage 15:51, Feb 1938
  Theatre Arts 22:100, Feb 1938
  Time 31:24, Jan 3, 1938

Three Wishes for Jamie

    book: Charles O'Neal and Abe Burrows, based on
                             Charles O'Neal's novel
    music: Ralph Blane
    lyrics: Ralph Blane
    staging: Abe Burrows
    sets: George Jenkins
    costumes: Miles White
    choreography: Ted Cappy, Herbert Ross, Eugene Loring
Productions:

    Opened March 21, 1952 for 91 performances
Reviews:

    Catholic World 175:148, May 1952
    Commonweal 56:14, Apr 11, 1952
    Life 32:119+, Apr 14, 1952
    New York Theatre Critics' Reviews 1952:332+
    New York Times page 9, Mar 22, 1952
    New Yorker 28:62, Mar 29, 1952
    Newsweek 39:84, Mar 31, 1952
    Saturday Review 35:27, Apr 5, 1952
    Theatre Arts 36:91, May 1952
    Time 59:69, Mar 31, 1952

The Threepenny Opera

    book: Marc Blitzstein; based on the play by Bertolt
                             Brecht
    music: Kurt Weill
    lyrics: Marc Blitzstein
Productions:

    (Off-Broadway) Opened March 1954 for 2,611 performances
    (Off-Off-Broadway) Opened October 13, 1972
    Opened May 1, 1976 for 307 performances
    (Off-Broadway) Opened June 28, 1977 for 27 performances
Reviews:

    America 134:484-inside back cover, May 29, 1976
              161:382, Nov 25, 1989
    Catholic World 179:226, Jun 1954
    Commentary 62:67-9, Dec 1976
    Commonweal 60:118, May 7, 1954
    Coronet 49:18, Dec 1960
    Dance Magazine 50:73, Aug 1976
    Gentlemen's Quarterly 59:280-3+, Dec 1989
    Harper's Bazaar 122:180-1+, Oct 1989
    Los Angeles 23:208+, Feb 1978
    Maclean's 99:66, Nov 3, 1986
    Mother Jones 14:52-3, Nov 1989
    Musical America 74:14, Apr 1954
    Nation 178:265-6, Mar 27, 1954
           222:636-7, May 22, 1976
           249:767-8, Dec 18, 1989
    National Review 41:53-4, Nov 24, 1989

New Republic 153:35, Aug 7, 1965
              174:24, Feb 28, 1976
              174:18-19, May 22, 1976
              201:29-30, Dec 11, 1989
New York 9:71+, May 17, 1976
         22:50-1, Sep 11, 1989
         22:126+, Nov 20, 1989
New York Theatre Critics' Reviews 1976:250
                              1989:171
New York Times II, page 3, Mar 7, 1954
                  page 26, Mar 11, 1954
                  II, page 1, Mar 21, 1954
                  II, page 7, Apr 4, 1954
                  page 38, Sep 21, 1955
                  page 83, Feb 12, 1956
                  VI, page 24, Feb 16, 1958
                  page 32, Sep 14, 1959
                  page 13, Oct 10, 1959
                  page 44, Sep 15, 1960
                  page 46, Sep 20, 1960
                  page 15, Feb 4, 1961
                  page 30, Apr 13, 1961
                  page 41, Sep 21, 1961
                  page 58, Dec 6, 1961
                  page 33, Oct 24, 1972
                  page 42, May 3, 1976
                  III, page 3, Sep 17, 1976
                  III, page 3, Jul 8, 1977
New Yorker 30:62+, Mar 20, 1964
           41:172-3, Mar 20, 1965
           52:103, May 10, 1976
           65:112-13, Nov 20, 1989
Newsweek 46:54, Oct 3, 1955
         87:96, May 17, 1976
Opera News 41:32-33, Jul 1976
People 32:77, Nov 20, 1989
Saturday Review 37:22, Mar 27, 1954
                 37:21, Apr 17, 1954
                 39:47, Sep 15, 1956
                 41:64-5, Oct 25, 1958
                 48:22, Mar 27, 1965
Time 63:46, Mar 22, 1954
    107:58, May 17, 1976
Vogue 179:424-5, Nov 1989

Three's a Crowd
    book: Howard Dietz
    music: Arthur Schwartz and others
    lyrics: Howard Dietz
    staging: Hassard Short
    choreography: Albertina Rasch

Productions:
   Opened October 15, 1930 for 272 performances
Reviews:
   Bookman 72:411-12, Dec 1930
   Catholic World 132:721-2, Mar 1931
   Life (New York) 96:21, Oct 31, 1930
   Nation 131:480, Oct 29, 1930
   New York Times IX, page 4, Oct 5, 1930
                    page 28, Oct 16, 1930
                    VIII, page 1, Oct 26, 1930
   Theatre Magazine 53:42, Jan 1931
                    53:20, Feb 1931
   Vogue 76:76+, Dec 8, 1930

Through the Years
   book: Brian Hooker, based on Jane Cowl's Smilin'
                      Through
   music: Vincent Youmans
   lyrics: Edward Heyman
   staging: Edgar McGregor
   choreography: Jack Haskell and Max Scheck
Productions:
   Opened January 28, 1932 for 20 performances
Reviews:
   New York Times VIII, page 3, Jan 3, 1932
                    page 23, Feb 13, 1932

Thumbs Up
   sketches: H. I. Phillips, Harold Atteridge, Alan Baxter,
                      Ballard McDonald, Earle Crooker
   music: James Hanley and Henry Sullivan
   lyrics: H. I. Phillips, Harold Atteridge, Alan Baxter,
                      Ballard McDonald, Earle Crooker
   staging: John Murray Anderson
   sets: Ted Weidhaas, James Reynolds, Raoul Pene du
                      Bois
   choreography: Robert Alton
Productions:
   Opened December 27, 1934 for 156 performances
Reviews:
   Catholic World 140:723, Mar 1935
   Commonweal 21:346, Jan 18, 1935
   New York Times VIII, page 2, Feb 3, 1934
                    IX, page 1, Aug 18, 1934
                    page 24, Dec 28, 1934
   Newsweek 5:26, Jan 5, 1935

Ti-Jean and His Brothers
   book: Derek Walcott
   music: Andre Tanker
   lyrics: Derek Walcott and Andre Tanker

staging: Derek Walcott
sets: Edward Burbridge
choreography: George Faison
Productions:
(Off-Broadway)   Opened July 20, 1972 for 15 performances
Reviews:
New York Times page 20, Jul 28, 1972
II, page 1, Aug 6, 1972

Tick-Tack-Toe
written: Herman Timberg
staging: Herman Timberg
Productions:
Opened February 23, 1920 for 32 performances
Reviews:
Dramatic Mirror 82: 415-16, Mar 6, 1920
New York Clipper 68: 19, Mar 1920
New York Times page 11, Feb 24, 1920
Theatre Magazine 31: 273, Apr 1920

Tickets, Please!
sketches: Harry Herrmann, Edmund Rice, Jack Roche,
                  Ted Luce
music and
  lyrics: Lyn Duddy, Joan Edwards, Mel Tolkin, Lucille
                  Kallen, Clay Warnick
staging: Mervyn Nelson
sets: Ralph Alswang
costumes: Peggy Morrison
choreography: Joan Mann
Productions:
Opened April 27, 1950 for 245 performances
Reviews:
Catholic World 171: 227, Jun 1950
New Republic 122: 20, May 15, 1950
New York Theatre Critics' Reviews 1950: 300+
New York Times page 25, Apr 28, 1950
                  II, page 1, May 7, 1950
                  II, page 1, Aug 6, 1950
New Yorker 26: 52, May 6, 1950
Newsweek 35: 80, May 8, 1950
Theatre Arts 34: 16, Jul 1950
Time 55: 48, May 8, 1950

Tickle Me
book: Otto Harbach, Oscar Hammerstein II, Frank
                  Mandel
music: Herbert Stothart
lyrics: Otto Harbach, Oscar Hammerstein II, Frank
                  Mandel
staging: William Collier
choreography: Bert French

Productions:
Opened August 17, 1920 for 207 performances
Reviews:
    Dramatic Mirror page 327, Aug 21, 1920
    New York Clipper 68:19, Aug 25, 1920
    New York Times page 12, Aug 19, 1920
    Theatre Magazine 32:240, Oct 1920

Tickles by Tucholsky
    conceived: Moni Yakim
    original
      material: Kurt Tucholsky, translated and adapted by
                  Louis Golden and Harold Poor
    staging: Moni Yakim
    sets: Don Jensen
    costumes: Christina Giannini
Productions:
    (Off-Broadway) Opened April 26, 1976 for 16 performances
Reviews:
    New York 9:72, May 17, 1976
    New York Times page 31, Apr 27, 1976

La Tierra de la Alegria (see The Land of Joy)

The Tiger Rag
    book: Seyril Schochen; based on the Oedipus legend
    music: Kenneth Gaburo
    lyrics: Seyril Schochen
Productions:
    (Off-Broadway) Opened Season of 1960-61
Reviews:
    New York Times page 20, Feb 17, 1961

Tillie's Nightmare
    book: Edgar Smith
    music: A. Baldwin Sloane
    staging: Ned Wayburn
Productions:
Opened May 5, 1910 for 77 performances
Reviews:
    Dramatic Mirror 63:6, May 14, 1910
    Leslie's Weekly 110:591, Jun 18, 1910
    Life (New York) 55:922, May 19, 1910
    Metropolitan Magazine 32:540-41, Jul 1910
    Pearson 24:92, Jul 1910
             24:94-5, Jul 1910
    Theatre Magazine 11:174, Jun 1910
                  11:187, Jun 1910

Timbuktu!
    book: Luther Davis, based on the musical Kismet by

Charles Lederer and Luther Davis from the play by Edward Knoblock

music and
lyrics: Robert Wright and George Forrest, from themes of Alexander Borodin and African folk music
staging: Geoffrey Holder
sets: Tony Straiges
costumes: Geoffrey Holder
choreography: Geoffrey Holder
Productions:
Opened March 1, 1978 for 221 performances
Reviews:
Encore 7:26-7, Apr 3, 1978
Los Angeles 24:203, Jan 1979
New Leader 61:28, Mar 27, 1978
New York 11:89-90, Mar 20, 1978
New York Theatre Critics' Reviews 1978:365
New York Times III, page 15, Mar 2, 1978
             II, page 3, Mar 12, 1978
Newsweek 91:95, Mar 13, 1978
Saturday Review 5:26, Apr 29, 1978
Theatre Crafts 12:13-15+, May 1978
Time 111:75, Mar 13, 1978

A Time for Singing
book: Gerald Freedman and John Morris; based on Richard Llewellyn's novel How Green Was My Valley
music: John Morris
lyrics: Gerald Freedman
staging: Gerald Freedman
sets: Ming Cho Lee
costumes: Theoni V. Aldredge
choreography: Donald McKayle
Productions:
Opened May 21, 1966 for 41 performances
Reviews:
America 114:881-2, Jun 25, 1966
Commonweal 84:370, Jun 17, 1966
Dance Magazine 40:25, Jul 1966
New York Theatre Critics' Reviews 1966:305
New York Times page 48, May 23, 1966
             page 28, Jun 20, 1966
New Yorker 42:79, May 28, 1966
Newsweek 67:89, Jun 6, 1966
Saturday Review 49:34, Jun 11, 1966

Time, Gentlemen Please
staging: Don Gammell and Fred Stone
sets: Thea Neu
costumes: Reginald Woolley
choreography: Tony Bateman

Productions:
   (Off-Broadway)   Opened November 4, 1961 for 336 performances
No Reviews.

The Time, the Place, and the Girl
   book: Will Morrissey, John Neff, William B. Friedlander,
                    based on the musical by Will M. Hough, Frank R.
                    Adams, and Joe Howard, originally produced in
                    Chicago in 1906
   music: Joe Howard
   lyrics: Will Morrissey, John Neff, William B. Friedlander,
                    based on the musical by Will M. Hough, Frank R.
                    Adams, and Joe Howard, originally produced in
                    Chicago in 1906
   staging: William B. Friedlander
   sets: Karl Amend
   costumes: Paul DuPont
   choreography: Carl Randall
Productions:
   Opened October 21, 1942 for 13 performances
Reviews:
   New York Theatre Critics' Reviews 1942:198+
   New York Times page 24, Oct 22, 1942

Times Square Two   (see An Evening with the Times Square Two)

Timon of Athens
   book: based on William Shakespeare's play
   music: Jonathon Tunick
   staging: Gerald Freedman
   sets: Ming Cho Lee
   costumes: Theoni V. Aldredge
   choreography: Joyce Trisler
Productions:
   (Off-Broadway)   Opened June 25, 1971 for 19 performances
Reviews:
   New York Times page 22, Jul 2, 1971
                    II, page 1, Jul 11, 1971

Tintypes
   conceived: Mary Kyte with Mel Marvin and Gary Pearle
   songs: Various authors and composers from the Gay
                    Nineties to World War I
   staging: Gary Pearle
   sets: Tom Lynch
   costumes: Jess Goldstein
   choreography: Mary Kyte
Productions:
   (Off-Broadway)   Opened April 17, 1979 for 134 performances
   Opened October 23, 1980 for 93 performances
Reviews:
   Dance Magazine 54:94, Jul 1980

Los Angeles 26:316, May 1981
New York 13:58, Nov 10, 1980
New York Theatre Critics' Reviews 1980:138
New York Times III, page 8, Apr 22, 1980
               III, page 3, Oct 24, 1980
               II, page 3, Nov 2, 1980
New Yorker 56:110+, May 5, 1980
           56:164, Nov 3, 1980
Newsweek 96:77, Nov 3, 1980
Theatre Crafts 20:25+, May 1986
Time 116:64, Nov 24, 1980

Tip-Toes
    book: Guy Bolton and Fred Thompson
    music: George Gershwin
    lyrics: Ira Gershwin
    staging: John Harwood
Productions:
Opened December 28, 1925 for 194 performances
(Off-Broadway) Opened March 24, 1979 for 19 performances
Reviews:
New York 12:93-4, Apr 9, 1979
New York Clipper 68:28, Oct 13, 1920
New York Times page 20, Dec 29, 1925
              page 27, Sep 1, 1926
              III, page 22, May 3, 1978
              III, page 7, Mar 27, 1979
New Yorker 55:99, Apr 9, 1979
           55:150+, Apr 9, 1979
Saturday Review 5:35, Sep 16, 1978
Theatre Magazine 32:424, Dec 1920
Vogue 67:102+, Feb 15, 1926

Tip Top
    book: Anne Caldwell and R. H. Burnside
    music: Ivan Caryll
    lyrics: Anne Caldwell and R. H. Burnside
Productions:
Opened October 5, 1920 for 246 performances
Reviews:
Dramatic Mirror page 665, Oct 9, 1920
Life (New York) 76:724, Oct 21, 1920
New York Clipper 68:28, Oct 13, 1920
New York Times page 13, Oct 6, 1920
              page 17, Apr 12, 1921
              VI, page 1, Apr 17, 1921
Theatre Magazine 32:424, Dec 1920

'Tis of Thee
    assembled: Alfred Hayes
    sketches: Sam Locke

music: Alex North and Al Moss, additional music and
                    lyrics by Peter Barry, David Gregory, Richard
                    Levine
staging: Nat Lichtman
sets: Carl Kent
choreography: Esther Junger
Productions:
   Opened October 26, 1940 for one performance
Reviews:
   New York Theatre Critics' Reviews 1940:240+
   New York Times page 21, Oct 28, 1940
   Stage 1:20, Nov 1940

To Be or Not to Be--What Kind of a Question Is That?
   book: H. Ritterman and Zvi Reisel
   music: Eli Rubinstein
   lyrics: Max Meszel
   staging: Marvin Gordon
   sets: Ami Shamir
Productions:
   (Off-Broadway) Opened October 19, 1970 for 23 performances
Reviews:
   New York Times page 39, Oct 20, 1970

To Broadway with Love
   conceived: Morton Da Costa
   music: Philip J. Lang, Jerry Bock and Sheldon Harnick
   staging: Morton Da Costa
   sets: Peter Wolf
   costumes: Freddy Wittop
Productions:
   (Off-Broadway) Opened April 21, 1964 for 97 performances
Reviews:
   America 111:55-6, Jul 11, 1964
   Dance Magazine 38:21+, Jul 1964
   Life 56:17, May 22, 1964
   Newsweek 63:60, May 11, 1964

To Live Another Summer, to Pass Another Winter
   book: Hayim Hefer
   music: Dov Seltzer; additional music by David Krivoshei,
                    Alexander Argov and Naomi Shemer
   lyrics: Hayim Hefer; additional lyrics by Naomi Shemer
   staging: Jonathon Karmon
   sets: Neil Peter Jampolis
   costumes: Lydia Pincus Ganay
   choreography: Jonathon Karmon
Productions:
   Opened October 21, 1971 for 173 performances
Reviews:
   New York Theatre Critics' Reviews 1971:226

New York Times page 29, Oct 22, 1971
                 II, page 3, Oct 31, 1971
                 page 41, Nov 3, 1971
                 page 7, Nov 7, 1971
Time 98:95, Nov 1, 1971

To the Water Tower
    music: Tom O'Horgan
    staging: Paul Sills
    sets: Ralph Alswang
Productions:
    (Off-Broadway) Opened April 4, 1963 for 210 performances
Reviews:
    New Republic 148:28-9, May 11, 1963

To Whom It May Concern
    book: Carol Hall
    music: Carol Hall
    lyrics: Carol Hall
    staging: Geraldine Fitzgerald
    choreography: Michael O'Flaherty
Productions:
    (Off-Broadway) Opened December 16, 1985 for 106 performances
Reviews:
    Dance Magazine 60:103, Mar 1986
    New York Times III, page 18, Dec 18, 1985

Todd, Michael   (see Michael Todd)

Together Again for the First Time
    conceived: Barry Kleinbort and Colin Romoff, with Jo Sulli-
                    van and Emily Loesser
    music: Various composers
    lyrics: Various authors
    staging: Barry Kleinbort
    sets: Phillip Baldwin
    costumes: William Ivey Long
    choreography: Donald Saddler
Productions:
    (Off-Broadway) Opened February 27, 1989 for 30 performances
Reviews:
    New York Times III, page 16, Mar 2, 1989

'Toinette
    book: J. I. Rodale; based on Molière's The Imaginary
                    Invalid
    music: Deed Meyer
    lyrics: Deed Meyer
    staging: Curt Conway
Productions:
    (Off-Broadway) Opened November 20, 1961 for 31 performances

Reviews:
    New York Times page 46, Nov 21, 1961
                    page 40, Nov 28, 1961
                    page 42, Nov 28, 1961
                    page 38, Dec 19, 1961
    New Yorker 37:121, Dec 2, 1961

Tomfoolery
    words: Tom Lehrer, adapted by Cameron Mackintosh and
                    Robin Ray
    music: Tom Lehrer
    staging: Gary Pearle and Mary Kyte
    sets: Tom Lynch
    costumes: Ann Emonts
Productions:
    (Off-Broadway) Opened December 14, 1981 for 120 performances
Reviews:
    Los Angeles 31:62, Mar 1986
    New York 15:99-100, Dec 28, 1981-Jan 4, 1982
    New York Times III, page 9, Dec 15, 1981
    People 17:44+, Jan 11, 1982
    Time 118:73, Dec 28, 1981

Tonight's the Night
    book: Fred Thompson
    music: Paul Rubens
    staging: Austen Hurgon
Productions:
    Opened December 24, 1914 for 108 performances
Reviews:
    Current Opinion 58:98-9, Feb 1915
    Dramatic Mirror 72:8, Dec 30, 1914
                    73:2, Jan 13, 1915
                    73:2, Feb 3, 1915
                    73:2, Feb 17, 1915
    Munsey 54:543, Apr 1915
    Nation 99:783-4, Dec 31, 1914
    New York Times page 11, Dec 25, 1914
    Theatre Magazine 21:57+, Feb 1915

Too Many Girls
    book: George Marion, Jr.
    music: Richard Rodgers
    lyrics: Lorenz Hart
    staging: George Abbott
    sets: Jo Mielziner
    costumes: Raoul Pene du Bois
    choreography: Robert Alton
Productions:
    Opened October 18, 1939 for 249 performances
    (Off-Off-Broadway) Opened March 12, 1987

Reviews:
   Catholic World 150:338, Dec 1939
   Commonweal 31:96, Nov 17, 1939
   Life 7:78-80, Oct 23, 1939
   Nation 244:480-1, Apr 11, 1987
   New Republic 101:16, Nov 8, 1939
   New York Theatre Critics' Reviews 1940:467+
   New York Times page 26, Oct 19, 1939
                  IX, page 1, Oct 29, 1939
                  I, page 63, Mar 22, 1987
   Theatre Arts 23:861, Dec 1939
   Time 34:42, Oct 30, 1939

Toot Sweet
   music: Richard A. Whiting
   lyrics: Raymond B. Eagan
   staging: Will Morrissey
Productions:
   Opened May 7, 1919 for 45 performances
Reviews:
   Life (New York) 73:904, May 22, 1919
   New York Times page 19, May 8, 1919
   Theatre Magazine 29:343-4, Jun 1919
                    30:17, Jul 1919

Toot-Toot
   book: Edgar Allan Woolf; adapted from Excuse Me by
                   Rupert Hughes
   music: Jerome Kern
   lyrics: Berton Braley
   staging: Edgar Allan Woolf and Edward Rose
Productions:
   Opened March 11, 1918 for 40 performances
Reviews:
   Dramatic Mirror 78:32, Jan 5, 1918
                   78:5, Mar 23, 1918
                   78:4, Apr 6, 1918
   New York Times page 11, Mar 12, 1918
                   IV, page 10, Mar 24, 1918
   Theatre Magazine 27:220, Apr 1918
                    27:289, May 1918

Top Banana
   book: H. S. Kraft
   music: Johnny Mercer
   lyrics: Johnny Mercer
   staging: Jack Donohue
   sets: Jo Mielziner
   costumes: Alvin Colt
   choreography: Ron Fletcher
Productions:
   Opened November 1, 1951 for 350 performances

Reviews:
Catholic World 174:228, Dec 1951
Commonweal 55:173-4, Nov 23, 1951
Life 31:75-6+, Dec 3, 1951
New York Theatre Critics' Reviews 1951:180+
New York Times page 19, Nov 2, 1951
II, page 1, Nov 18, 1951
New Yorker 27:64+, Nov 10, 1951
Newsweek 38:92, Nov 12, 1951
Theatre Arts 35:3, Dec 1951
36:81, Jan 1952
Time 58:59, Nov 12, 1951

Top-Hole
book: Eugene Conrad and George Dill; revised by
                Gladys Unger
music: Jay Gorney
lyrics: Owen Murphy
Productions:
Opened September 1, 1924 for 104 performances
Reviews:
New York Times page 23, Sep 2, 1924
Theatre Magazine 40:72, Nov 1924

Top-Notchers
assembled: Clifford C. Fischer
Productions:
Opened May 29, 1942 for 48 performances
Reviews:
New York Times page 8, May 30, 1942
(Also see Keep 'em Laughing)

Top Speed
book: Guy Bolton
music: Harry Ruby
lyrics: Bert Kalmar
staging: John Harwood
choreography: John Boyle
Productions:
Opened December 25, 1929 for 102 performances
Reviews:
Life (New York) 95:20, Jan 17, 1930
New York Times IX, page 4, Nov 17, 1929
page 20, Dec 26, 1929
Theatre Magazine 51:63, Feb 1930
Vogue 75:122, Feb 15, 1930

Topics of 1923
book: Harold Atteridge and Harry Wagstaff Gribble
music: Jean Schwartz and Alfred Goodman
lyrics: Harold Atteridge
staging: J. C. Huffman

Productions:
  Opened November 20, 1923 for 143 performances
Reviews:
  New York Times page 23, Nov 21, 1923
  Theatre Magazine 39:16, Jan 1924

Toplitzky of Notre Dame
  book: George Marion, Jr.
  music: Sammy Fain
  lyrics: Jack Barnett
  staging: Jose Ruben
  sets: Edward Gilbert
  costumes: Kenn Barr
  choreography: Robert Sidney
Productions:
  Opened December 26, 1946 for 60 performances
Reviews:
  Catholic World 164:455, Feb 1947
  New York Theatre Critics' Reviews 1946:201+
  New York Times II, page 4, Dec 22, 1946
                  page 13, Dec 27, 1946
                  page 19, Feb 16, 1947
  New Yorker 22:48+, Jan 11, 1947
  Newsweek 29:64, Jan 6, 1947
  Theatre Arts 31:17, Mar 1947
  Time 49:56, Jan 6, 1947

Topsy and Eva
  book: Catherine Chisholm Cushing
  music: Duncan Sisters
  lyrics: Duncan Sisters
  staging: Oscar Eagle
Productions:
  Opened December 23, 1924 for 159 performances
Reviews:
  New York Times page 11, Dec 24, 1924
  Theatre Magazine 41:16, Mar 1925
                  42:31, Jul 1925

Touch
  book: Kenn Long and Amy Salz
  music: Kenn Long and Jim Crozier
  lyrics: Kenn Long
  staging: Amy Salz
  sets: Robert U. Taylor
Productions:
  (Off-Broadway) Opened November 8, 1970 for 422 performances
Reviews:
  Nation 211:542, Nov 23, 1970
  New York Times page 52, Nov 9, 1970
  New Yorker 46:132, Dec 12, 1970

Touch and Go

sketches:	Jean Kerr and Walter Kerr
music:	Jay Gorney
lyrics:	Jean Kerr and Walter Kerr
staging:	Walter Kerr
sets:	John Robert Lloyd
choreography:	Helen Tamiris

Productions:

Opened October 13, 1949 for 176 performances

Reviews:

Catholic World 170:228, Dec 1949
Commonweal 51:159, Nov 11, 1949
Life 27:52, Oct 24, 1949
New York Theatre Critics' Reviews 1949:250+
New York Times page 34, Oct 14, 1949
II, page 1, Oct 30, 1949
II, page 1, Nov 6, 1949
page 9, May 20, 1950
New Yorker 25:60+, Oct 22, 1949
Newsweek 34:84, Oct 24, 1949
Saturday Review 33:4-5, Jan 14, 1950
Theatre Arts 33:13, Dec 1949
Time 54:57, Oct 24, 1949

Tour de Four

conceived:	Tom Eyen
sketches:	John Aman, Larry Alexander, Gary Popkin and others
music:	John Aman, Larry Alexander, Gary Popkin and others
lyrics:	John Aman, Larry Alexander, Gary Popkin and others
staging:	Tom Eyen
costumes:	Edward Charles

Productions:

(Off-Broadway) Opened June 18, 1963 for 16 performances

Reviews:

New York Times page 41, Jun 19, 1963

Tovarich

book:	David Shaw, based on the play by Robert E. Sherwood and Jacques Deval
music:	Lee Pockriss
lyrics:	Anne Crosswell
staging:	Peter Glenville
sets:	Rolf Gerard
costumes:	Motley
choreography:	Herbert Ross

Productions:

Opened March 18, 1963 for 264 performances

Reviews:

America 108:651, May 4, 1963

Commonweal 78:224, May 17, 1963
National Review 14:535-7, Jul 2, 1963
Nation 196:334, Apr 20, 1963
New York Theatre Critics' Reviews 1963:308+
New York Times page 5, Jan 23, 1963
      page 5, Mar 20, 1963
      page 40, Nov 11, 1963
New Yorker 39:108+, Mar 30, 1963
Newsweek 61:78, Apr 1, 1963
Saturday Review 46:40, Apr 6, 1963
Theatre Arts 47:14-15+, May 1963
Time 81:46, Mar 29, 1963

Town Topics (see Ned Wayburn's Town Topics)

Tragedie de Carmen, La (see La Tragedie de Carmen)

The Transposed Heads
 adapted: Julie Taymor and Sidney Goldfarb, from Thomas
         Mann's novella
 music: Elliot Goldenthal
 lyrics: Sidney Goldfarb
 staging: Julie Taymor
 sets: Based on a concept by Alexander Okun
 costumes: Carol Oditz
 choreography: Margo Sappington, Julie Taymor and the Company
         (Indian choreography by Swati Gupte Bhise and
         Rajika Puri)
Productions:
 (Off-Off-Broadway) Opened May 10, 1984
 (Off-Broadway) Opened October 31, 1986 for 4 performances
Reviews:
 New York Times III, page 24, May 23, 1984
        I, page 13, Nov 1, 1986

Treasure Girl
 book: Fred Thompson and Vincent Lawrence
 music: George Gershwin
 lyrics: Ira Gershwin
 staging: Bertram Harrison
 choreography: Bobby Connelly
Productions:
 Opened November 8, 1928 for 68 performances
Reviews:
 Life (New York) 92:11, Nov 12, 1928
 New York Times page 22, Nov 9, 1928
 Outlook 150:1195, Nov 21, 1928
 Vogue 72:82, Dec 22, 1928

A Tree Grows in Brooklyn
 book: Betty Smith and George Abbott, based on Betty
         Smith's novel

music: Arthur Schwartz
lyrics: Dorothy Fields
staging: George Abbott
sets: Jo Mielziner
choreography: Herbert Ross
Productions:
Opened April 19, 1951 for 270 performances
(Off-Broadway) Opened April 15, 1966 for 14 performances
Reviews:
Catholic World 173:229, Jun 1951
Commonweal 54:88, May 4, 1951
Life 30:97-8+, May 7, 1951
Musical America 71:34, Jul 1951
Nation 172:403, Apr 28, 1951
New Republic 124:20, May 14, 1951
New York Theatre Critics' Reviews 1951:291+
New York Times II, page 3, Apr 15, 1951
              page 24, Apr 20, 1951
              II, page 1, Apr 29, 1951
New Yorker 27:56+, Apr 28, 1951
Newsweek 37:53, Apr 30, 1951
Saturday Review 34:23-4, May 5, 1951
Time 57:89, Apr 30, 1951

Treemonisha
conceived: Frank Corsaro, from the opera by Scott Joplin
music: Scott Joplin
lyrics: Scott Joplin
staging: Frank Corsaro
sets: Franco Colavecchia
costumes: Franco Colavecchia
choreography: Louis Johnson
Productions:
Opened October 21, 1975 for 64 performances
Reviews:
New York Review of Books 22:34+, Jan 22, 1976
New York Theatre Critics' Reviews 1975:189
Rolling Stone 202:110, Dec 18, 1975

The Trials of Oz
book: Geoff Robertson
songs: Buzzy Linehart, Mick Jagger, John Lennon and
               Yoko Ono
staging: Jim Sharman
sets: Mark Ravitz
costumes: Joseph G. Aulisi
Productions:
(Off-Broadway) Opened December 19, 1972 for 15 performances
Reviews:
New York Times page 51, Mar 14, 1972
               page 54, Dec 20, 1972
               II, page 1, Jan 7, 1973

Tricephalous Neurosyllogistic Training   (see T.N.T.)

Tricks
     book: Jon Jory; based on Molière's Les Fourberies de
                        Scapin
     music: Jerry Blatt
     lyrics: Lonnie Burstein
     staging: Jon Jory
     sets: Oliver Smith
     costumes: Miles White
     choreography: Donald Saddler
Productions:
     Opened January 8, 1973 for 8 performances
Reviews:
     New York Theatre Critics' Reviews 1973:391
     New York Times page 29, Jan 9, 1973
     New Yorker 48:59, Jan 20, 1973

A Trip to Japan
     book: R. H. Burnside
     music: Manuel Klein
     lyrics: Manuel Klein
     staging: R. H. Burnside
Productions:
     Opened September 4, 1909 for 447 performances
Reviews:
     Leslie's Weekly 109:415, Oct 28, 1909

Trixie True, Teen Detective
     book: Kelly Hamilton
     music: Kelly Hamilton
     lyrics: Kelly Hamilton
     staging: Bill Gile
     sets: Michael J. Hotopp and Paul De Pass
     costumes: David Toser
     choreography: Arthur Faria
Productions:
     (Off-Broadway) Opened December 4, 1980 for 86 performances
Reviews:
     New York Times III, page 3, Dec 5, 1980
                     II, page 3, Dec 14, 1980

Trois Jeunes Filles Nues
     book: Yves Mirande and Albert Willemetz
     music: Raoul
     lyrics: Yves Mirande and Albert Willemetz
Productions:
     Opened March 4, 1929 for 40 performances
Reviews:
     New York Times page 28, Mar 5, 1929
     Theatre Magazine 50:41, Jul 1929

Trouble in Tahiti (part of a bill titled All in One)
    book: Leonard Bernstein
    music: Leonard Bernstein
    lyrics: Leonard Bernstein
    staging: David Brooks
Productions:
    Opened April 19, 1955 for 47 performances
    (Off-Off-Broadway) Opened April 23, 1965 for 14 performances
Reviews:
    America 93:192, May 14, 1955
    Catholic World 181:227, Jun 1955
    Commonweal 62:255, Jun 10, 1955
    Nation 180:410, May 7, 1955
    New Republic 132:22, May 2, 1955
    New York Theatre Critics' Reviews 1955:325
    New York Times page 40, Apr 20, 1955
                    II, page 1, Apr 24, 1955
    New Yorker 31:69-71, Apr 30, 1955
    Saturday Review 38:26, May 14, 1955
    Theatre Arts 39:26, May 14, 1955
    Time 65:78, May 2, 1955

Trumpets of the Lord
    book: Vinnette Carroll; based on James Weldon John-
                    son's God's Trombones
    music: Based on gospel hymns
    lyrics: Based on gospel hymns
    staging: Donald McKayle
    sets: Ed Wittstein
    costumes: Normand Maxton
Productions:
    (Off-Broadway) Opened December 21, 1963 for 160 performances
    Opened April 29, 1969 for 7 performances
Reviews:
    New York Times page 22, Dec 23, 1963
                    page 37, Apr 30, 1969
                    page 53, May 1, 1969
    New Yorker 39:60-1, Jan 4, 1964

Tumble In
    book: Otto Hauerbach; adapted from Mary R. Rinehart
                    and Avery Hopwood's Seven Days
    music: Rudolf Friml
    lyrics: Rudolf Friml
    staging: Bertram Harrison
Productions:
    Opened March 24, 1919 for 128 performances
Reviews:
    New York Times page 11, Mar 25, 1919
    Theatre Magazine 29:274, May 1919
                    29:277, May 1919

Tunes from Blackness   (see Ain't Supposed to Die a Natural Death)

Tuscaloosa's Calling Me ... but I'm Not Going!
   book: Bill Heyer, Hank Beebe, and Sam Dann
   music: Hank Beebe
   lyrics: Bill Heyer
   staging: James Hammerstein and Gui Andrisano
   sets: Charles E. Hoefler
   costumes: Rome Heyer
Productions:
   (Off-Broadway) Opened December 1, 1975 for 205 performances
Reviews:
   New York 8:100+, Dec 15, 1975
   New York Times page 45, Dec 2, 1975
                     II, page 5, Jan 25, 1976
                     III, page 2, May 21, 1976
                     XXII, page 24, Dec 10, 1978

Twinkle, Twinkle
   book: Harlan Thompson
   music: Harry Archer
   lyrics: Harlan Thompson
   additional
     material: Bert Kalmar and Harry Ruby
   staging: Frank Craven, Julian Alfred and Harry Puck
Productions:
   Opened November 16, 1926 for 167 performances
No Reviews.

2 by 5
   conceived: Seth Glassman
   music: John Kander
   lyrics: Fred Ebb
   staging: Seth Glassman
   sets: Dan Leigh
   costumes: Dan Leigh
Productions:
   (Off-Broadway) Opened October 19, 1976 for 57 performances
Reviews:
   America 135:373, Nov 27, 1976
   New York Times page 52, Oct 19, 1976

Two by Two
   book: Peter Stone; based on the play The Flowering
                     Peach by Clifford Odets
   music: Richard Rodgers
   lyrics: Martin Charnin
   staging: Joe Layton
   sets: David Hays
   costumes: Fred Voelpel
Productions:
   Opened November 10, 1970 for 351 performances

Reviews:
America 124:124-5, Feb 6, 1971
Commonweal 93:397, Jan 22, 1971
Commentary 51:80, Feb 1971
New York Theatre Critics' Reviews 1970:160
New York Times page 52, Jun 16, 1970
page 26, Aug 11, 1970
II, page 1, Nov 8, 1970
page 37, Nov 11, 1970
page 52, Nov 12, 1970
II, page 1, Nov 22, 1970
II, page 8, Dec 20, 1970
page 15, Jul 23, 1971
II, page 27, Aug 15, 1971
New Yorker 46:103, Nov 21, 1970
Newsweek 76:137, Nov 23, 1970
Saturday Review 53:12, Nov 28, 1970
Time 96:100, Nov 23, 1970

Two for the Show
sketches: Nancy Hamilton
music: Morgan Lewis
lyrics: Nancy Hamilton
staging: John Murray Anderson
sets: Raoul Pene du Bois
costumes: Raoul Pene du Bois
choreography: Robert Alton
Productions:
Opened February 8, 1940 for 124 performances
Reviews:
Catholic World 150:731-2, Mar 1940
Commonweal 31:386, Feb 23, 1940
New York Theatre Critics' Reviews 1940:394+
New York Times page 14, Feb 9, 1940
IX, page 1, Feb 18, 1940
IX, page 2, Feb 18, 1940
Theatre Arts 24:237-8, Apr 1940

Two for Tonight
sketches: Ralph Berton and Mitchell Hodges
music: Eugene Berton, Ralph Berton, Berenice Kazounoff
                 and John Latouche
lyrics: Eugene Berton, Ralph Berton, Berenice Kazounoff
                 and John Latouche
Productions:
(Off-Broadway) Opened December 28, 1939
No Reviews.

Two Gentlemen of Verona
adapted: John Guare and Mel Shapiro; based on the play
                 by William Shakespeare

music: Galt MacDermot
lyrics: John Guare
staging: Mel Shapiro
sets: Ming Cho Lee
costumes: Theoni V. Aldredge
choreography: Jean Erdman
Productions:
  Opened December 1, 1971 for 627 performances
  (Off-Broadway) Opened July 22, 1971 for 14 performances
Reviews:
  America 125:534-5, Dec 18, 1971
  Commentary 53:85-7, Apr 1972
  Nation 213:668, Dec 20, 1971
  New York Theatre Critics' Reviews 1971:172
  New York Times page 40, Jul 29, 1971
                  II, page 1, Aug 8, 1971
                  II, page 3, Aug 22, 1971
                  page 65, Dec 2, 1971
                  page 30, Dec 3, 1971
                  II, page 3, Dec 12, 1971
                  II, page 1, Dec 26, 1971
                  II, page 1, Feb 27, 1972
                  II, page 21, Oct 8, 1972
  New Yorker 47:101, Dec 11, 1971
  Newsweek 78:114, Dec 13, 1971
  Saturday Review 55:38, Jan 8, 1972
                  54:18, Aug 21, 1971
  Time 98:48, Dec 13, 1971
  Vogue 158:124, Dec 1971

Two if by Sea
  book: Priscilla B. Dewey and Charles Werner Moore
  music: Tony Hutchins
  lyrics: Priscilla B. Dewey
  staging: Charles Werner Moore
  sets: John Doepp
  costumes: Julie Weiss
  choreography: Edward Roll
Productions:
  (Off-Broadway) Opened February 6, 1972 for one performance
Reviews:
  New York Times page 35, Feb 7, 1972

Two Is Company
  book: Edward A. Paulton and Adolf Philipp; from Paul
                  Herve's My Friend Emily
  music: Jean Briquet and Adolf Philipp
  staging: Adolf Philipp
Productions:
  Opened September 22, 1915 for 29 performances

Reviews:
    Dramatic Mirror 74:8, Sep 29, 1915
                  74:2, Oct 30, 1915
    Green Book 14:970-1, Dec 1915
    New York Dramatic News 61:19, Oct 2, 1915
    Opera Magazine 2:31, Nov 1915
    Theatre Magazine 22:224, Nov 1915
                  22:234, Nov 1915

Two Little Brides

book:	Arthur Anderson, James T. Powers and Harold Atteridge; from the German of Willner and Wilhelm, adapted by Gustave Kerker
lyrics:	Arthur Anderson, James T. Powers and Harold Atteridge
staging:	J. C. Huffman

Productions:
    Opened April 23, 1912 for 63 performances
Reviews:
    Blue Book 15:686-9, Aug 1912
    Dramatic Mirror 67:6, May 1, 1912
    Green Book 8:12-14+, Jul 1912
              8:135, Jul 1912
    Life (New York) 59:975, May 9, 1912
    Red Book 19:764-5+, Aug 1912
    Theatre Magazine 15:x, Jun 1912
                15:172, Jun 1912

Two Little Girls in Blue

book:	Fred Jackson
music:	Vincent Youmans and Paul Lannin
lyrics:	Arthur Francis (Ira Gershwin)
staging:	Ned Wayburn

Productions:
    Opened May 3, 1921 for 135 performances
Reviews:
    Dramatic Mirror 83:715, Apr 23, 1921
                83:769, May 7, 1921
    New York Clipper 69:19, May 11, 1921
    New York Times page 10, May 4, 1921
    Theatre Magazine 34:30, Jul 1921

Two on the Aisle

sketches:	Betty Comden, Adolph Green, Nat Hiken, William Friedberg
music:	Jule Styne
lyrics:	Betty Comden, Adolph Green, Nat Hiken, William Friedberg
staging:	Abe Burrows
sets:	Howard Bay
costumes:	Joan Personette
choreography:	Genevieve Pitot

Productions:
    Opened July 19, 1951 for 281 performances
Reviews:
    Catholic World 173:469-70, Sep 1951
    Commonweal 54:405-6, Aug 3, 1951
    Harper's 203:100-1, Sep 1951
    Life 31:111-12, Sep 10, 1951
    Nation 173:78, Jul 28, 1951
    New Republic 125:21, Sep 17, 1951
    New York Theatre Critics' Reviews 1951:246+
    New York Times page 13, Jul 20, 1951
                    II, page 1, Jul 29, 1951
                    VI, page 14, Aug 5, 1951
    New York Times Magazine page 14, Aug 5, 1951
    New Yorker 27:48+, Jul 28, 1951
    Newsweek 38:47, Jul 30, 1951
    Theatre Arts 35:6, 22-3+, Sep 1951
    Time 58:47, Jul 30, 1951

2,008-1/2 (A Space Oddity)
    book: Tom Eyen
    music: Gary William Friedman
    lyrics: Tom Eyen
    staging: Tom Eyen
Productions:
    (Off-Off-Broadway) Opened February 10, 1974
Reviews:
    New York Times page 39, Feb 12, 1974

Two's Company
    sketches: Charles Sherman and Peter De Vries
    music: Vernon Duke
    lyrics: Ogden Nash and Sammy Cahn
    staging: John Murray Anderson
    sets: Ralph Alswang
    costumes: Miles White
    choreography: Jerome Robbins
Productions:
    Opened December 15, 1952 for 90 performances
Reviews:
    Catholic World 176:389, Feb 1953
    Collier's 130:20-1, Nov 29, 1952
    Commonweal 57:376-7, Jan 16, 1953
    Life 33:24, Dec 29, 1952
    Nation 175:613, Dec 27, 1952
    New York Theatre Critics' Reviews 1952:157+
    New York Times page 43, Dec 16, 1952
                    II, page 3, Dec 21, 1952
    New Yorker 28:44, Dec 27, 1952
    Newsweek 40:40, Dec 29, 1952
    Saturday Review 36:52, Jan 3, 1953
    Time 60:54, Dec 29, 1952

-U-

Uhuruh
   book: Danny Duncan
   music: Danny Duncan
   lyrics: Danny Duncan
   staging: Danny Duncan
   costumes: Richmond Curry
   choreography: Danny Duncan
Productions:
   (Off-Broadway) Opened March 20, 1972 for 8 performances
Reviews:
   New York Times page 35, Mar 21, 1972

Umbrellas of Cherbourg
   book: Jacques Demy, based upon his film, and trans-
                     lated by Sheldon Harnick in association with
                     Charles Burr
   music: Michel Legrand
   staging: Andrei Serban
   sets: Michael Yeargan
   costumes: Jane Greenwood
Productions:
   (Off-Broadway) Opened February 1, 1979 for 36 performances
Reviews:
   Los Angeles 25:318+, Aug 1980
   Nation 228:221-2, Feb 24, 1979
   New West 5:SC-26, Jul 14, 1980
   New York 12:70+, Feb 19, 1979
   New York Theatre Critics' Reviews 1979:325
   New York Times III, page 3, Feb 2, 1979
                 II, page 3, Feb 11, 1979
   New Yorker 54:45, Feb 12, 1979
   Newsweek 93:62, Feb 12, 1979

Under Many Flags
   book: Carroll Fleming
   music: Manuel Klein
   lyrics: Manuel Klein
   staging: Carroll Fleming
Productions:
   Opened August 31, 1912 for 445 performances
Reviews:
   Dramatic Mirror 68:11, Sep 19, 1912
   Munsey 48:347-9, Nov 1912
   Theatre Magazine 16:xv, Oct 1912

Under the Counter
   book: Arthur Macrae
   music: Manning Sherwin
   lyrics: Harold Purcell

```
        staging:        Jack Hulbert
        sets:           Clifford Pember
        costumes:       Clifford Pember
        choreography:   Jack Hulbert
Productions:
    Opened October 3, 1947 for 27 performances
Reviews:
    Catholic World 166:172, Nov 1947
    Nation 165:481, Nov 1, 1947
    New York Theatre Critics' Reviews 1947:320+
    New York Times II, page 3, Sep 28, 1947
                    page 10, Oct 4, 1947
    New Yorker 23:52, Oct 11, 1947
    Newsweek 30:81, Oct 13, 1947
```

Unfair to Goliath

```
        book:           Ephraim Kishon
        music:          Menachem Zur
        lyrics:         Herbert Appleman
        staging:        Ephraim Kishon and Herbert Appleman
        sets:           C. Murawski
        costumes:       Pamela Scofield
Productions:
    (Off-Broadway)  Opened January 25, 1970 for 73 performances
Reviews:
    America 122:228, Feb 28, 1970
    New York Times page 28, Jan 16, 1970
                    page 27, Jan 26, 1970
                    page 35, Mar 31, 1970
    New Yorker 45:76, Feb 7, 1970
```

The Unsinkable Molly Brown

```
        book:           Richard Morris
        music:          Meredith Willson
        lyrics:         Meredith Willson
        staging:        Dore Schary
        sets:           Oliver Smith
        costumes:       Miles White
        choreography:   Peter Gennaro
Productions:
    Opened November 3, 1960 for 532 performances
Reviews:
    America 104:353-4, Dec 3, 1960
    Christian Century 77:1441-2, Dec 7, 1960
    Dance Magazine 34:33, Dec 1960
    Life 49:141-3+, Dec 5, 1960
    Nation 191:421, Nov 26, 1960
    New York Theatre Critics' Reviews 1960:184+
    New York Times VI, page 41, Oct 23, 1960
                    page 28, Nov 4, 1960
    New Yorker 36:103, Nov 12, 1960
```

Newsweek 56:61, Nov 14, 1960
Saturday Review 43:38, Nov 19, 1960
Theatre Arts 45:58-9, Jan 1961
Time 76:84, Nov 14, 1960

Unsung Cole
   conceived: Norman L. Berman
   music: Cole Porter
   lyrics: Cole Porter
   staging: Norman L. Berman
   sets: Peter Harvey
   costumes: Carol Oditz
   choreography: Dennis Grimaldi
Productions:
   (Off-Broadway) Opened June 23, 1977 for 75 performances
Reviews:
   New York Theatre Critics' Reviews 1977:210
   New York Times III, page 3, Jun 24, 1977
   Newsweek 90:70, Aug 1, 1977
   Time 110:61, Jul 4, 1977

Up and Down Broadway
   book: Edgar Smith
   music: Jean Schwartz
   lyrics: William Jerome
   staging: William J. Wilson
Productions:
   Opened July 18, 1910 for 72 performances
Reviews:
   Cosmopolitan 49:612, Oct 1910
   Dramatic Mirror 64:10, Jul 30, 1910
   Theatre Magazine 12:xiv, Sep 1910
                12:85, Sep 1910

Up Eden
   book: Robert Rosenblum and Howard Schuman
   music: Robert Rosenblum; adapted from Mozart's Cosi
                 fan Tutte
   lyrics: Robert Rosenblum and Howard Schuman
   staging: John Bishop
   sets: Gordon Micunis
   costumes: Gordon Micunis
   choreography: Patricia Birch
Productions:
   (Off-Broadway) Opened November 27, 1968 for 7 performances
Reviews:
   New York Times page 42, Nov 27, 1968
   New Yorker 44:142, Dec 7, 1968

Up from Paradise
   book: Arthur Miller

music: Stanley Silverman
lyrics: Arthur Miller
staging: Ran Avni
Productions:
  (Off-Off-Broadway) Opened October 25, 1983
Reviews:
  New York 16: 97-8, Nov 7, 1983
  New York Times III, page 22, Oct 26, 1983
  New Yorker 59: 150-1, Nov 7, 1983

Up in Central Park

book: Herbert and Dorothy Fields
music: Sigmund Romberg
lyrics: Herbert and Dorothy Fields
staging: John Kennedy
sets: Howard Bay
costumes: Grace Houston and Ernest Schraps
choreography: Helen Tamiris
Productions:
  Opened January 27, 1945 for 504 performances
  Opened May 19, 1947 for 16 performances
Reviews:
  Catholic World 160: 549-50, Mar 1945
  Commonweal 41: 448, Feb 16, 1945
  Harper's Bazaar 79: 91, Feb 1945
  Life 18: 41-2+, Feb 19, 1945
      18: 80, Apr 9, 1945
  New York Theatre Critics' Reviews 1945: 280+
  New York Times II, page 1, Jan 21, 1945
                page 17, Jan 29, 1945
                II, page 4, Feb 4, 1945
                II, page 1, May 18, 1947
                page 29, May 20, 1947
                II, page 1, May 25, 1947
                page 31, May 27, 1947
  New Yorker 20: 40+, Feb 3, 1945
  Newsweek 25: 83, Feb 12, 1945
  Theatre Arts 29: 333, Jan 1945
             29: 205+, Apr 1945
             29: 651, Nov 1945
             31: 37, Jun 1947
  Time 45: 60, Feb 5, 1945

Up in One (see Peter Allen Up In One)

Up She Goes

book: Frank Craven; adapted from Too Many Cooks
music: Harry Tierney
lyrics: Joseph McCarthy
staging: Frank Craven and Bert French
Productions:
  Opened November 6, 1922 for 256 performances

Reviews:
   New York Clipper 70:20, Nov 15, 1922
   New York Times page 14, Nov 7, 1922

Ups-a-Daisy
   book: Clifford Grey and Robert A. Simon
   music: Lewis E. Gensler
   lyrics: Clifford Grey
   staging: Edgar MacGregor and Earl Lindsey
Productions:
   Opened October 8, 1928 for 64 performances
Reviews:
   Life (New York) 92:21, Nov 2, 1928
   New York Times page 34, Oct 9, 1928

Upstairs at O'Neals'
   conceived: Martin Charnin
   songs: Martin Charnin and various authors and com-
                       posers
   staging: Martin Charnin
   sets: Ray Recht
   costumes: Zoran
   choreography: Ed Love
Productions:
   (Off-Broadway) Opened October 29, 1982 for 308 performances
Reviews:
   New York 15:82, Nov 29, 1982
   New York Times III, page 20, Oct 29, 1982
                    III, page 1, Nov 19, 1982
   New Yorker 59:113, Mar 7, 1983

Uptown ... It's Hot!   (American popular music from the 1930s to the 1980s)
   conceived: Maurice Hines
   songs: Various authors and composers
   staging: Maurice Hines
   sets: Tom McPhillips
   costumes: Ellen Lee
   choreography: Maurice Hines
Productions:
   Opened January 29, 1986 for 24 performances
Reviews:
   Down Beat 53:12, Apr 1986
   Essence 16:35, Mar 1986
   Horizon 29:37-40, Jan/Feb 1986
   New York 19:57, Feb 10, 1986
   New York Theatre Critics' Reviews 1986:384
   New York Times III, page 13, Jan 29, 1986

Urban Blight
   conceived: John Tillinger

```
    sketches:       Various authors
    music:          David Shire
    lyrics:         Richard Maltby Jr.
    additional
      song:         Edward Kleban
    staging:        John Tillinger and Richard Maltby Jr.
    sets:           Heidi Landesman
    costumes:       C. L. Hundley
    choreography:   Charles Randolph-Wright
Productions:
    (Off-Broadway)  Opened June 19, 1988 for 12 performances
Reviews:
    New York Times II, page 5, Jun 19, 1988
                   III, page 13, Jun 20, 1988
```

The Utter Glory of Morrissey Hall

```
    book:           Clark Gesner and Nagle Jackson
    music:          Clark Gesner
    lyrics:         Clark Gesner
    staging:        Nagle Jackson
    sets:           Howard Bay
    costumes:       David Graden
    choreography:   Buddy Schwab
Productions:
Opened May 13, 1979 for one performance
Reviews:
    New York Theatre Critics' Reviews 1979:235
    New York Times III, page 13, May 14, 1979
    New Yorker 55:105, May 21, 1979
```

-V-

The Vagabond King

```
    book:           Brian Hooker and W. H. Post; based on J. H.
                    McCarthy's If I Were King
    music:          Rudolf Friml
    lyrics:         Brian Hooker and W. H. Post
    staging:        Max Figman
Productions:
    Opened September 21, 1925 for 511 performances
    Opened June 29, 1943 for 56 performances
    (Off-Broadway)  Opened December 3, 1975 for 42 performances
    (Off-Broadway)  Opened January 12, 1977 for 13 performances
    (Off-Broadway)  Opened August 17, 1977 for 14 performances
    (Off-Broadway)  Opened October 1, 1986 for 14 performances
Reviews:
    Catholic World 157:521-2, Aug 1943
    New York Theater Critics' Reviews 1943:311
    New York Times page 23, Sep 22, 1925
                   VIII, page 2, Jan 17, 1926
```

page 20, Jun 2, 1943
page 24, Jun 30, 1943
page 58, Dec 11, 1975
Newsweek 22:66, Jul 12, 1943
Theater Magazine 47:44, Dec 1925
48:13, Jan 1926
Woman's Home Companion 53:141, Feb 1926

Valmouth

book:	Sandy Wilson; based on the novel by Ronald Firbank
music:	Sandy Wilson
lyrics:	Sandy Wilson
staging:	Vida Hope
sets:	Tony Walton
costumes:	Tony Walton
choreography:	Harry Naughton

Productions:
(Off-Broadway) Opened October 6, 1960 for 14 performances
Reviews:
New York Times page 29, Oct 7, 1960
page 46, Oct 18, 1960
New Yorker 34:168-9, Nov 1, 1958
36:75-6, Oct 15, 1960

Value of Man   (see $ Value of Man)

The Vamp

book:	John Latouche and Sam Locke, based on a story by John Latouche
music:	James Mundy
lyrics:	John Latouche
staging:	David Alexander
sets:	Raoul Pene du Bois
costumes:	Raoul Pene du Bois
choreography:	Robert Alton

Productions:
Opened November 10, 1955 for 60 performances
Reviews:
Catholic World 182:310, Jan 1956
Commonweal 63:285, Dec 16, 1955
Look 19:108+, Nov 29, 1955
New York Theatre Critics' Reviews 1955:210+
New York Times II, page 1, Nov 6, 1955
page 30, Nov 11, 1955
New Yorker 31:121, Nov 19, 1955
Newsweek 46:68, Nov 21, 1955
Saturday Review 38:26, Nov 26, 1955
Theatre Arts 40:20-1, Jan 1956
Time 66:110+, Nov 21, 1955

The Vanderbilt Revue
  assembled by: Lew Fields
  sketches: Kenyon Nicholson, Ellis O. Jones, Sig Herzig,
                   E. North
  music and
    lyrics: Dorothy Fields, Jimmy McHugh, Jacques Fray,
                   Mario Braggiotti, E. Y. Harburg
  staging: John E. Lonergan, Jack Haskell, Theodore J.
                   Hammerstein
Productions:
  Opened November 5, 1930 for 13 performances
Reviews:
  Bookman 72:409, Dec 1930
  New York Times VIII, page 3, Oct 26, 1930
                 page 22, Nov 6, 1930

Vanities (see Earl Carroll Vanities)

Veils
  book: Irving Kaye Davis
  music: Donald Heywood
  staging: Edward Elsner
Productions:
  Opened March 13, 1928 for 4 performances
Reviews:
  Theatre Magazine 47:40-41, May 1928

The Velvet Lady
  book: Fred Jackson; adapted by Henry Blossom
  music: Victor Herbert
  lyrics: Henry Blossom
  staging: Edgar MacGregor and Julian Mitchell
Productions:
  Opened February 3, 1919 for 136 performances
Reviews:
  Dramatic Mirror 80:48, Jan 11, 1919
  New York Times page 11, Feb 4, 1919
  Theatre Magazine 29:135, Mar 1919
                   29:143, Mar 1919

Vera Violetta
  book: Leonard Liebling and Harold Atteridge; from the
                   German of Leo Stein
  music: Edmund Eysler
Productions:
  Opened November 20, 1911 for 112 performances
Reviews:
  Dramatic Mirror 66:7, Nov 22, 1911
  Green Book 7:232-6+, Feb 1912

Very Good, Eddie
  book: Philip Bartholomae and Guy Bolton

music: Jerome Kern
lyrics: Schuyler Green
Productions:
Opened December 23, 1915 for 341 performances
Opened December 21, 1975 for 304 performances
Reviews:
Dance Magazine 50:83, Apr 1976
Dramatic Mirror 75:8, Jan 1, 1916
Green Book 15:445-6, Mar 1916
Los Angeles 26:410+, Dec 1981
Nation 222:28-9, Jan 3, 1976
New Republic 174:20-1, Feb 7, 1976
New York 9:70, Jan 12, 1976
New York Dramatic News 62:17, Jan 1, 1916
New York Theatre Critics' Reviews 1975:120
New York Times page 28, Oct 28, 1975
                   page 41, Dec 22, 1975
                   II, page 5, Jan 4, 1976
Opera Magazine 3:30-1, Mar 1916
Theater Magazine 23:64-5, Feb 1916
Time 107:61, Jan 12, 1976

Very Warm for May
book: Oscar Hammerstein II
music: Jerome Kern
lyrics: Oscar Hammerstein II
staging: Oscar Hammerstein II and Vincente Minnelli
sets: Vincente Minnelli
choreography: Albertina Rasch
Productions:
Opened November 17, 1939 for 59 performances
Reviews:
Catholic World 150:470, Jan 1940
Commonweal 31:137, Dec 1, 1939
New York Times IX, page 2, Nov 12, 1939
                   page 23, Nov 18, 1939
Theatre Arts 24:19, Jan 1940
Time 34:60, Nov 27, 1939

The Vi-Ton-Ka Medicine Show
book: Glenn Hinson, assembled from elements of the
                    traditional American medicine show
music: Various composers
lyrics: Various authors
staging: Brooks McNamara
sets: Marco A. Martinez-Galarce
Productions:
(Off-Broadway) Opened October 4, 1983 for 18 performances
No Reviews.

Via Galactica
book: Christopher Gore and Judith Ross

music: Galt MacDermot
lyrics: Christopher Gore
staging: Peter Hall
sets: John Bury
costumes: John Bury
Productions:
Opened November 28, 1972 for 7 performances
Reviews:
America 127:570, Dec 30, 1972
New York Theatre Critics' Reviews 1972:174
New York Times II, page 1, Feb 27, 1972
           page 42, Sep 26, 1972
           page 33, Nov 29, 1972
           page 52, Nov 30, 1972
           II, page 5, Dec 10, 1972
New Yorker 48:109, Dec 9, 1972
Opera News 37:24, Jan 20, 1973

Victor Borge's One-Man Show   (see Comedy in Music)

Vintage '60
sketches: Jack Wilson, Alan Jeffreys, Maxwell Grant
added material: David Rogers, Mickey Deems, Mark Bucci,
                 Sheldon Harnick, David Baker, Phil Green,
                 Tommy Garlock, Fred Ebb, Paul Klein, William
                 Lanteau, Alice Clark, David Morton, Lee Gold-
                 smith, Michael Ross, Barbara Heller, Fay DeWitt,
                 Ronald Axe, William Link, Richard Levinson
staging: Jonathan Lucas
sets: Fred Voelpel
costumes: Fred Voelpel
choreography: Jonathan Lucas
Productions:
Opened September 12, 1960 for 8 performances
Reviews:
New York Theatre Critics' Reviews 1960:247+
New York Times page 41, Sep 13, 1960
           page 44, Sep 21, 1960
New Yorker 36:97, Sep 24, 1960
Newsweek 56:109, Sep 26, 1960
Theatre Arts 44:10, Nov 1960

Virginia
book: Laurence Stallings and Owen Davis
music: Arthur Schwartz
lyrics: Albert Stillman
staging: Leon Leonidoff
sets: Lee Simonson
costumes: Irene Sharaff
choreography: Florence Rogge
Productions:
Opened September 2, 1937 for 60 performances

Reviews:
    Catholic World 146:86, Oct 1937
    Commonweal 26:478, Sep 17, 1937
    Nation 145:303, Sep 18, 1937
    New York Times page 13, Sep 3, 1937
                    XI, page 1, Sep 12, 1937
                    page 29, Oct 5, 1937
    Newsweek 10:25, Sep 13, 1937
    Stage 14:34-5, Sep 1937
    Theatre Arts 21:836-7, Nov 1937

Viva O'Brien
    book: William K. and Eleanor Wells
    music: Marie Grever
    lyrics: Raymond Leveen
    staging: Robert Milton
    sets: Clark Robinson
    costumes: John N. Booth, Jr.
    choreography: Chester Hale
Productions:
    Opened October 9, 1941 for 20 performances
Reviews:
    New York Theatre Critics' Reviews 1941:271+
    New York Times page 27, Oct 10, 1941

Viva Reviva
    book: Eve Merriam
    music: Amy D. Rubin
    lyrics: Eve Merriam
    staging: Graciela Daniele
    sets: Kate Carmel
    costumes: Kate Carmel
Productions:
    (Off-Off-Broadway) Opened October 13, 1977 for 11 performances
Reviews:
    New York Times III, page 22, Oct 19, 1977

Vogues of 1924
    book: Fred Thompson and Clifford Grey
    music: Herbert Stothart
Productions:
    Opened March 27, 1924 for (92) performances
Reviews:
    American Mercury 2:118-19, May 1924
    New York Times page 14, Mar 28, 1924
                    page 18, Apr 12, 1924
                    page 9, Apr 22, 1924
    Theatre Magazine 39:14-16, Jun 1924

-W-

Wait a Minim!
     book: Leon Gluckman
     staging: Leon Gluckman
     sets: Frank Rembach and Leon Gluckman
     costumes: Heather MacDonald-Rouse
     choreography: Frank Staff and Kendrew Lascelles
Productions:
     Opened March 7, 1966 for 456 performances
Reviews:
     America 114:604, Apr 23, 1966
     Commonweal 84:154, Apr 22, 1966
     Dance Magazine 40:24, May 1966
     Life 61:26, Oct 14, 1966
     National Review 18:1062-5, Oct 18, 1966
     Nation 202:374, Mar 28, 1966
     New York Theatre Critics' Reviews 1966:335
     New York Times page 43, Mar 8, 1966
                      page 46, Mar 9, 1966
                      II, page 1, Mar 20, 1966
                      page 54, Mar 30, 1967
     New Yorker 42:160, Mar 19, 1966
     Newsweek 67:98, Mar 21, 1966
     Saturday Review 49:45, Mar 26, 1966
     Time 87:80, Mar 18, 1966
     Vogue 147:145, May 1966

Wake up and Dream
     book: J. H. Turner
     music: Cole Porter
     lyrics: Cole Porter
     staging: Frank Collins
     choreography: Tilly Losch, Jack Buchanan, Max Rivers
Productions:
     Opened December 30, 1929 for 136 performances
Reviews:
     Life (New York) 95:20, Jan 24, 1930
     Nation 130:106, Jan 22, 1930
     New York Times X, page 1, Apr 14, 1929
                      page 14, Dec 31, 1929
                      VIII, page 1, Jan 5, 1930
     Theatre Magazine 51:63, Feb 1930
     Vogue 75:122, Feb 15, 1930

Walk a Little Faster
     sketches: S. J. Perelman and Robert MacGunigle
     music: Vernon Duke
     lyrics: E. Y. Harburg
     staging: E. M. Woolley (Monty Woolley)
     sets: Boris Aronson
     choreography: Albertina Rasch

Productions:
  Opened December 7, 1932 for 119 performances
Reviews:
  New Outlook 161:47, Jan 1933
  New Republic 73:189, Dec 28, 1932
  New York Times page 24, Dec 8, 1932
  Vogue 81:56+, Feb 1, 1933

Walk Down Mah Street!
  music: Norman Curtis; special material by James Taylor,
                  Gabriel Levenson and the members of The Next
                  Stage Theater Company
  lyrics: Patricia Taylor Curtis
  staging: Patricia Taylor Curtis
  sets: Jack Logan
  costumes: Bob Rodgers
Productions:
  (Off-Broadway) Opened June 12, 1968 for 135 performances
Reviews:
  New York Times page 54, Jun 13, 1968
  New Yorker 44:59, Jun 22, 1968

Walk with Music
  book: Guy Bolton, Parke Levy, Allen Lipscott, based on
                  Stephen Powys' Three Blind Mice
  music: Hoagy Carmichael
  lyrics: Johnny Mercer
  staging: R. H. Burnside
  sets: Watson Barratt
  costumes: Tom Lee
  choreography: Anton Dolin and Herbert Harper
Productions:
  Opened June 4, 1940 for 55 performances
Reviews:
  Catholic World 151:472, Jul 1940
  New York Theatre Critics' Reviews 1940:290+
  New York Times page 33, Jun 5, 1940

Walking Happy
  book: Roger O. Hirson and Ketti Frings; based on
                  Harold Brighouse's play Hobson's Choice
  music: James Van Heusen
  lyrics: Sammy Cahn
  staging: Cy Feuer
  sets: Robert Randolph
  costumes: Robert Fletcher
  choreography: Danny Daniels
Productions:
  Opened November 26, 1966 for 161 performances
Reviews:
  America 116:160, Jan 28, 1967

Dance Magazine 41:76-7, Jan 1967
Nation 204:29, Jan 2, 1967
New York Theatre Critics' Reviews 1966:225
New York Times page 47, Nov 28, 1966
           II, page 3, Dec 11, 1966
           II, page 3, Dec 18, 1966
           page 35, Feb 7, 1967
Newsweek 68:100, Dec 12, 1966
Time 88:60, Dec 9, 1966

The Wall Street Girl

book:	Margaret Mayo and Edgar Selwyn
music:	Karl Hoschna
lyrics:	Hapgood Burt
staging:	Charles Winninger and Gus Sohlke

Productions:
Opened April 15, 1912 for 56 performances
Reviews:
Blue Book 14:692-5, Feb 1912
Dramatic Mirror 67:7, Apr 17, 1912
                  67:7, Apr 24, 1912
Green Book 8:133, Jul 1912
Munsey 47:468, Jun 1912
New York Dramatic News 55:19, Apr 20, 1912
Red Book 19:766-8, Aug 1912
Theatre Magazine 15:xvi, May 1912

Waltz of the Stork

book:	Melvin Van Peebles
music:	Melvin Van Peebles
lyrics:	Melvin Van Peebles
additional music and lyrics:	Ted Hayes and Mark Barkan
staging:	Melvin Van Peebles
sets:	Kert Lundell
costumes:	Bernard Johnson

Productions:
Opened January 5, 1982 for 160 performances
Reviews:
New York Theatre Critics' Reviews 1982:398
New York Times III, page 16, Jan 6, 1982
New Yorker 57:85, Jan 11, 1982
People 17:57-8+, Feb 15, 1982

Wanted

book:	David Epstein
music:	Al Carmines
lyrics:	Al Carmines
staging:	Lawrence Kornfeld
sets:	Paul Zalon
costumes:	Linda Giese

Productions:
   (Off-Broadway)   Opened January 19, 1972 for 79 performances
   (Off-Broadway)   Opened Season of 1971-72
Reviews:
   New York Theatre Critics' Reviews 1972:339
   New York Times page 52, Jan 20, 1972
                II, page 9, Jan 30, 1972
   New Yorker 47:74, Jan 29, 1972
   Newsweek 79:83, Jan 31, 1972

The Warrior Ant
   book: Lee Breuer
   music: Bob Telson
   lyrics: Lee Breuer
   staging: Lee Breuer
Productions:
   (Off-Off-Broadway)   Opened October 1988
Reviews:
   New York Times III, page 11, Oct 24, 1988
   New York Times Magazine pages 92-3+, Oct 16, 1988

Wars of the World
   conceived: Arthur Voegtlin
   music: Manuel Klein
   lyrics: Manuel Klein
   dialogue: John P. Wilson
   staging: William J. Wilson
Productions:
   Opened September 5, 1914 for 229 performances
Reviews:
   Green Book 12:1065, Dec 1914
   Munsey 53:356, Nov 1914
   New York Dramatic News 60:33, Jan 2, 1915
   Theatre Magazine 20:151, Oct 1914
                20:193, Oct 1914

Watch Your Step
   book: Harry B. Smith
   music: Irving Berlin
   lyrics: Irving Berlin
   staging: R. H. Burnside
Productions:
   Opened December 8, 1914 for 175 performances
Reviews:
   Dramatic Mirror 72:8, Dec 16, 1914
   Green Book 13:301, Feb 1915
                13:575-6, Mar 1915
   Munsey 55:99, Jun 1915
   New Republic 1:27, Jan 9, 1915
   New York Dramatic News 60:18, Dec 19, 1914
   New York Times page 13, Dec 1, 1914

Stage 15:41, Aug 1938
Theatre Magazine 21:9, Jan 1915
21:67, Feb 1915
22:78, Aug 1915

The Water Carrier
    book: Jacob Prayer
    music: Alexander Olshanetsky
Productions:
    (Off-Broadway) Opened December 24, 1936
No Reviews.

Waters, Ethel (see At Home with Ethel Waters)

Wayburn, Ned (see Ned Wayburn)

We Live and Laugh
    material: Alfred Kreymborg, J. L. Peretz and others
    staging: Judah Bleich and Zvee Scooler
Productions:
    Opened May 8, 1936
Reviews:
    New York Times page 9, May 10, 1936

The Wedding Night (see Oh, I Say!)

Weekend
    book: Roger Lax
    music: Roger Lax
    lyrics: Roger Lax
    staging: David H. Bell
    sets: Ursula Belden
    costumes: Sally Lesser
    choreography: David H. Bell
Productions:
    (Off-Broadway) Opened October 24, 1983 for 8 performances
Reviews:
    New York Times III, page 11, Oct 25, 1983

Weill, Kurt (see Kurt Weill)

Welcome to the Club
    book: A. E. Hotchner
    music: Cy Coleman
    lyrics: Cy Coleman and A. E. Hotchner
    staging: Peter Mark Schifter
    sets: David Jenkins
    costumes: William Ivey Long
    choreography: Patricia Birch
Productions:
    Opened April 13, 1989 for 12 performances

Reviews:
New York 22:140, Apr 24, 1989
New York Theatre Critics' Reviews 1989:297
New York Times III, page 3, Apr 14, 1989
New Yorker 65:82-3, Apr 24, 1989

We're Civilized?

book: Alfred Aiken
music: Ray Haney
lyrics: Alfred Aiken
staging: Martin B. Cohen
sets: Jack H. Cornwell
costumes: Sonia Lowenstein
choreography: Bhaskar

Productions:
(Off-Broadway) Opened November 8, 1962 for 22 performances
Reviews:
New York Times page 30, Nov 9, 1962
New Yorker 38:148, Nov 17, 1962

West Side Story

book: Arthur Laurents
music: Leonard Bernstein
lyrics: Stephen Sondheim
staging: Jerome Robbins
costumes: Irene Sharaff
choreography: Jerome Robbins and Peter Gennaro

Productions:
Opened September 26, 1957 for 732 performances
Opened April 27, 1960 for 249 performances
Opened April 8, 1964 for 31 performances
Opened June 24, 1968 for 89 performances
Opened February 14, 1980 for 333 performances
(Off-Off-Broadway) Opened July 13, 1982
Reviews:
America 98:90, Oct 19, 1957
        119:54, Jul 20, 1968
Catholic World 186:224-5, Dec 1957
Christian Century 75:561-2, May 7, 1958
Dance Magazine 31:14-19, Aug 1957
               31:12-13, Nov 1957
               39:35-8, Apr 1965
               39:40-1, Nov 1965
               42:18, Aug 1968
               54:26-7, May 1980
Encore 9:38, Apr 1980
Fortune 101:73, May 19, 1980
Good Housekeeping 145:40, Sep 1957
Life 43:103-4+, Sep 16, 1957
Musical America 77:11, Nov 1, 1957
Nation 185:250-1, Oct 12, 1957

New Republic 137:21, Sep 9, 1957
New York 13:82, Mar 3, 1980
New York Theatre Critics' Reviews 1957:252+
                                  1960:275+
                                  1980:366
New York Times VI, page 28, Aug 25, 1957
               VI, page 60, Sep 8, 1957
               page 14, Sep 27, 1957
               II, page 1, Oct 6, 1957
               II, page 9, Oct 13, 1957
               II, page 15, Oct 27, 1957
               page 31, Apr 28, 1960
               II, page 1, May 8, 1960
               II, page 5, Dec 11, 1960
               page 24, Apr 9, 1964
               page 50, Nov 18, 1964
               page 12, Dec 31, 1964
               page 32, Jun 25, 1968
               II, page 20, Sep 1, 1968
               II, page 5, Sep 8, 1968
               III, page 3, Feb 15, 1980
               XXI, page 17, Aug 15, 1982
New York Times Magazine pages 60-1, Sep 8, 1957
New Yorker 33:64, Oct 5, 1957
Newsweek 50:102, Oct 7, 1957
         52:28, Dec 29, 1958
         95:90, Feb 25, 1980
Reporter 17:38, Nov 14, 1957
Saturday Review 40:22, Oct 5, 1957
                51:41+, Jul 13, 1968
Theatre Arts 41:22-3, Sep 1957
             41:16-17, Dec 1957
Time 70:48-9, Oct 7, 1957
     115:63, Feb 25, 1980
     115:59-60, Mar 3, 1980

Wet Paint
    staging: Michael Ross
    sets: David Moon
    costumes: Mostoller
    choreography: Rudy Tronto
Productions:
    (Off-Broadway) Opened April 12, 1965 for 16 performances
Reviews:
    New York Times page 33, Apr 13, 1965
    New Yorker 41:85-6, Apr 24, 1965

What a Killing
    book: Fred Hebert
    music: George Harwell
    lyrics: George Harwell and Joan Anania

Productions:
   (Off-Broadway)   Opened Season of 1960-61
Reviews:
   New York Times page 41, Mar 28, 1961

What Makes Sammy Run?
   book: Budd and Stuart Schulberg, based on the novel
                      by Budd Schulberg
   music: Ervin Drake
   lyrics: Ervin Drake
   staging: Abe Burrows
   sets: Herbert Senn and Helene Pons
   costumes: Noel Taylor
   choreography: Matt Mattox
Productions:
   Opened February 27, 1964 for 540 performances
Reviews:
   America 110:465, Mar 28, 1964
   Life 57:30, Sep 25, 1964
   New York Theatre Critics' Reviews 1964:328+
   New York Times II, page 3, Feb 9, 1964
                   page 19, Feb 28, 1964
   Saturday Review 47:34, Apr 11, 1964
   Time 83:50, Mar 6, 1964

What's a Nice Country Like You Doing in a State Like This?
   conceived: Ira Gasman, Cary Hoffman, and Bernie Travis
   music: Cary Hoffman
   lyrics: Ira Gasman
   staging: Miriam Ford
   sets: Billy Puzzo
   costumes: Danny Morgan
   choreography: Miriam Ford
Productions:
   (Off-Broadway)   Opened April 19, 1973 for 543 performances
   (Off-Off-Broadway)   Opened October 21, 1984 for 31 performances
   (Off-Broadway)   Opened July 31, 1985 for 252 performances
Reviews:
   New York 6:80, Jun 11, 1973
           7:84, Apr 8, 1974
           17:81, Nov 5, 1984
   New York Times page 21, Apr 21, 1973
                   page 34, Mar 26, 1974
                   III, page 16, Oct 22, 1984
   New Yorker 49:81, May 5, 1973
              60:156, Nov 5, 1984

What's in a Name?
   book: John Murray Anderson, Anna Wynne O'Ryan and
                      Jack Yellen
   music: Milton Ager

lyrics: John Murray Anderson, Anna Wynne O'Ryan and Jack Yellen
Productions:
Opened March 19, 1920 for 87 performances
Reviews:
Dramatic Mirror 82:576, Mar 27, 1920
Life (New York) 75:664, Apr 8, 1920
New York Clipper 68:14, Mar 24, 1920
New York Times page 14, Mar 20, 1920
Theatre Magazine 31:405, May 1920
                              31:460, May 1920
                              32:375, Dec 1920

What's Up
book: Alan Jay Lerner and Arthur Pierson
music: Frederick Loewe
lyrics: Alan Jay Lerner and Arthur Pierson
staging: George Balanchine and Robert H. Gordon
sets: Boris Aronson
costumes: Grace Houston
Productions:
Opened November 11, 1943 for 63 performances
Reviews:
Catholic World 158:395, Jan 1944
Commonweal 39:144, Nov 26, 1943
New York Theatre Critics' Reviews 1943:229+
New York Times page 24, Nov 12, 1943
                     II, page 1, Nov 21, 1943

When Claudia Smiles
book: Anne Caldwell; based on a play by Leo Ditrichstein
songs: Anne Caldwell
Productions:
Opened February 2, 1914 for 56 performances
Reviews:
Dramatic Mirror 71:2, Feb 18, 1914
                       71:7, Dec 4, 1914
Life (New York) 63:318-19, Feb 19, 1914
Munsey Magazine 51:584-5, Apr 1914
New York Times page 9, Feb 4, 1914
Theatre Magazine 19:115, Mar 1914

When Dreams Come True
book: Philip Bartholomae
music: Silvio Hein
lyrics: Philip Bartholomae
staging: Frank Smithson and Philip Bartholomae
Productions:
Opened August 18, 1913 for 64 performances
Reviews:
Blue Book 17:441-4, Jul 1913

Dramatic Mirror 70:6, Aug 20, 1913
              70:2, Oct 1, 1913
Green Book 10:8-9, Jul 1913
          10:120, Jul 1913
Munsey Magazine 50:94-5, Oct 1913
New York Dramatic News 58:21-2, Aug 23, 1913
New York Times page 9, Aug 19, 1913
Theatre Magazine 18:xi, Aug 1913
                18:101, Sep 1913
                18:xiii-xiv, Oct 1913
                18:117, Oct 1913

When Sweet Sixteen
book:	George V. Hobart
music:	Victor Herbert
lyrics:	George V. Hobart
staging:	R. H. Burnside

Productions:
Opened September 14, 1911 for 12 performances
Reviews:
Blue Book 13:19-21, May 1911
Dramatic Mirror 66:10, Sep 20, 1911
Green Book Album 5:928, May 1911
New York Times page 9, Sep 15, 1911

When the Owl Screams
music:	Tom O'Horgan
staging:	Paul Sills
sets:	Ralph Alswang

Productions:
(Off-Broadway) Opened September 12, 1963 for 141 performances
No Reviews.

When You Smile
book:	Tom Johnstone and Jack Alicoate
music:	Tom Johnstone
lyrics:	Phil Cook
staging:	Oscar Eagle

Productions:
Opened October 5, 1925 for 49 performances
Reviews:
New York Times page 31, Oct 6, 1925

Where's Charley?
book:	George Abbott, based on Brandon Thomas's Charley's Aunt
music:	Frank Loesser
lyrics:	Frank Loesser
staging:	George Abbott
sets:	David Ffolkes
costumes:	David Ffolkes
choreography:	George Balanchine and Fred Danielli

Productions:
   Opened October 11, 1948 for 792 performances
   Opened January 29, 1951 for 48 performances
   Opened May 25, 1966 for 15 performances
   Opened December 20, 1974 for 76 performances
   (Off-Off-Broadway) Opened March 10, 1983
Reviews:
   Catholic World 168:242, Dec 1948
   Collier's 122:26-7, Dec 11, 1948
   Commonweal 49:94, Nov 5, 1948
   Dance Magazine 40:27, Jul 1966
                  49:34+, Mar 1975
   Life 25:85-8, Nov 8, 1949
       60:18, Jun 17, 1966
   Nation 167:503, Oct 30, 1948
   New Republic 119:28, Nov 1, 1948
   New York 8:56, Jan 20, 1975
   New York Theatre Critics' Reviews 1948:197+
                                     1974:114, 118
   New York Times II, page 1, Oct 10, 1948
                   page 33, Oct 12, 1948
                   II, page 1, Oct 24, 1948
                   II, page 2, Apr 3, 1949
                   II, page 3, Nov 20, 1949
                   II, page 1, Aug 20, 1950
                   page 57, May 26, 1966
                   page 19, Dec 20, 1974
                   II, page 5, Dec 29, 1974
                   III, page 26, Mar 16, 1983
                   III, page 1, Mar 18, 1983
   New Yorker 24:52, Oct 23, 1948
              50:52, Dec 30, 1974
   Newsweek 32:87, Oct 25, 1948
   Saturday Review 31:26-7, Nov 6, 1948
   Theatre Arts 33:17, Jan 1949
   Time 52:63, Oct 25, 1948
   Vogue 112:154, Dec 1948

The Whirl of New York
   book: Hugh Morton and Edgar Smith
   music: Gustav Kerker, Al Goodman and Lew Pollack
   lyrics: Hugh Morton and Edgar Smith
   staging: Lew Morton
Productions:
   Opened June 13, 1921 for (3) performances
Reviews:
   New York Clipper 69:20, Jun 22, 1921
   New York Times page 18, Jun 14, 1921
   Theatre Magazine 34:126, Aug 1921
                    34:169, Aug 1921

Whirl of Society

book:	Harrison Rhodes
music:	Louis A. Hirsch
lyrics:	Harold Atteridge
staging:	J. C. Huffman

Productions:

Opened March 5, 1912 for 136 performances

Reviews:

Blue Book 15:697-700, Aug 1912

New York Dramatic News 55:13, Mar 16, 1912

The Whirl of the World

dialogue:	Harold Atteridge
music:	Sigmund Romberg
lyrics:	Harold Atteridge
staging:	William J. Wilson

Productions:

Opened January 10, 1914 for 161 performances

Reviews:

Dramatic Mirror 71:22, Jan 14, 1914

New York Dramatic News 60:4, Nov 7, 1914

New York Times II, page 15, Jan 11, 1914

Theatre Magazine 19:100, Feb 1914

Whispers on the Wind

book:	John B. Kuntz
music:	Lor Crane
lyrics:	John B. Kuntz
staging:	Burt Brinckerhoff
sets:	David F. Segal
costumes:	Joseph G. Aulisi

Productions:

(Off-Broadway) Opened June 3, 1970 for 15 performances

Reviews:

New York Times page 50, Jun 4, 1970

New Yorker 46:90+, Jun 13, 1970

White, George (see George White)

White Eagle

book:	Brian Hooker and W. H. Post, based on Edwin Milton Royle's The Squaw Man
music:	Rudolf Friml
lyrics:	Brian Hooker and W. H. Post
staging:	Richard Boleslavsky

Productions:

Opened December 26, 1927 for 48 performances

Reviews:

New York Times page 24, Dec 27, 1927

VIII, page 4, Jan 1, 1928

Theatre Magazine 47:62, Mar 1928

White Horse Inn
    book: Hans Mueller, suggested by Oskar Blumenthal
                       and G. Kandelburg, adapted by David Freedman
    music: Ralph Benatsky
    lyrics: Irving Caesar
    staging: Erick Charell
    sets: Ernst Stern
    costumes: Irene Sharaff
    choreography: Max Rivers
Productions:
    Opened October 1, 1936 for 223 performances
Reviews:
    Catholic World 144:215, Nov 1936
    Collier's 98:64-6, Nov 7, 1936
    Commonweal 34:590, Oct 16, 1936
    Literary Digest 122:31-2, Oct 17, 1936
    New Republic 88:314, Oct 21, 1936
    New York Times X, page 1, Aug 16, 1936
                     page 28, Oct 2, 1936
                     X, page 2, Oct 11, 1936
    Newsweek 8:28-9, Oct 10, 1936
    Theatre Arts 20:848-9, Nov 1936
    Time 28:53, Oct 12, 1936

White Lights
    book: Paul Gerard Smith and Leo Donnelly
    music: J. Fred Coots
    lyrics: Al Dubin and Dolf Singer
Productions:
    Opened October 11, 1927 for 31 performances
Reviews:
    New York Times page 30, Oct 12, 1927
    Theatre Magazine 46:43, Dec 1927

White Lilacs
    book: Harry B. Smith, based on the life of Frederic
                     Chopin from the German original by Sigurd
                     Johannsen
    music: Karl Hajos, based on melodies by Chopin
    lyrics: Harry B. Smith
    staging: J. J. Shubert and George Marion
Productions:
    Opened September 10, 1928 for 136 performances
Reviews:
    New York Times page 31, Sep 11, 1928
                     X, page 5, Oct 14, 1928
                     page 25, Oct 22, 1928
    Theatre Magazine 48:80, Nov 1928

White Nights
    book: Paul Zakrzewski; based on the short story by
                     Dostoyevsky

music: Wally Harper
lyrics: Paul Zakrzewski
staging: Paul Zakrzewski
Productions:
    (Off-Off-Broadway)   Opened February 6, 1974
No Reviews.

Who Cares
    sketches: Edward Clarke Lilley, Bertrand Robinson, Ken-
                    neth Webb, John Cantwell
    music: Percy Wenrich
    lyrics: Harry Clarke
    staging: George Vivian, Edward Clarke Lilley, William
                    Holbrook
Productions:
    Opened July 8, 1930 for 32 performances
Reviews:
    Life (New York) 96:16, Aug 1, 1930
    New York Times page 27, Jul 9, 1930
    Theatre Magazine 52:26, Aug 1930

Who Did It?
    book: Stephen Gardner Champlin
Productions:
    Opened June 9, 1919 for 8 performances
Reviews:
    New York Times page 13, Jun 10, 1919
                    page 22, Jun 18, 1919
    Theatre Magazine 30:81, Aug 1919

Whoopee
    book: William Anthony McGuire, based on Owen Davis's
                    The Nervous Wreck
    music: Walter Donaldson
    lyrics: Gus Kahn
    staging: William Anthony McGuire and Seymour Felix
Productions:
    Opened December 4, 1928 for 379 performances
    Opened February 14, 1979 for 204 performances
Reviews:
    Nation 228:284, Mar 17, 1979
    New Leader 62:22, Mar 12, 1979
    New York 12:100+, Mar 5, 1979
    New York Theatre Critics' Reviews 1979:370
    New York Times X, page 2, Nov 11, 1928
                    X, page 4, Dec 9, 1928
                    page 18, Sep 23, 1929
                    III, page 4, Jul 21, 1978
                    III, page 15, Feb 15, 1979
                    II, page 3, Feb 25, 1979
                    III, page 15, Mar 27, 1979

New Yorker 55:78, Feb 26, 1979
Outlook 152:434, Jul 10, 1929
Theatre Magazine 49:50, Feb 1929
Time 113:82, Feb 26, 1979

Whoop-Up

book: Cy Feuer, Ernest H. Martin, and Dan Cushman,
                   based on "Stay Away Joe" by Dan Cushman
music: Moose Charlap
lyrics: Norman Gimbel
staging: Cy Feuer
sets: Jo Mielziner
costumes: Anna Hill Johnstone
choreography: Onna White

Productions:
Opened December 22, 1958 for 56 performances
Reviews:
America 100:558-9, Feb 7, 1959
Catholic World 188:506, Mar 1959
Dance Magazine 33:18, Feb 1959
New York Theatre Critics' Reviews 1958:161+
New York Times II, page 1, Feb 8, 1958
                  page 2, Dec 23, 1958
New Yorker 34:50+, Jan 3, 1959
Saturday Review 42:67, Jan 10, 1959
Theatre Arts 43:9, Mar 1959

Whores, Wars, and Tin Pan Alley

songs: Kurt Weill
Productions:
(Off-Broadway) Opened June 16, 1969 for 72 performances
Reviews:
New York Times page 37, Jun 17, 1969

Who's Who

assembled by: Leonard Sillman
sketches: Leonard Sillman and Everett Marcy
music: Baldwin Bergersen, James Shelton, Irvin
                   Graham, Paul McGrane
lyrics: June Sillman, Irvin Graham, James Shelton
staging: Leonard Sillman
sets: Mercedes
costumes: Billy Livingston

Productions:
Opened March 1, 1938 for 23 performances
Reviews:
New York Times page 16, Mar 2, 1938
                  page 24, Mar 20, 1938

Who's Who, Baby?

book: Gerald Frank; based on Guy Bolton and P. G.
                   Wodehouse's Who's Who?

music: Johnny Brandon
lyrics: Johnny Brandon
staging: Marvin Gordon
sets: Alan Kimmel
costumes: Alan Kimmel
choreography: Marvin Gordon
Productions:
   (Off-Broadway) Opened January 29, 1968 for 16 performances
Reviews:
   New York Times page 28, Jan 26, 1968
                  page 36, Jan 30, 1968
                  page 38, Feb 10, 1968
   New Yorker 43:90-1, Feb 10, 1968

Why Do I Deserve This?
   sketches: Kay and Lore Lorentz, Eckart Hachfeld and
                 Martin Morlock
   music: Werner Kruse, Emil Schuchardt and Fritz Maldener
   lyrics: Wolfgang Franke and Mischa Leinek
   staging: Kay Lorentz
   sets: Fritz Butz
   costumes: Fritz Butz
Productions:
   (Off-Broadway) Opened January 18, 1966 for 12 performances
Reviews:
   New York Times page 31, Jan 19, 1966

Why I Love New York
   book: Al Carmines
   music: Al Carmines
   lyrics: Al Carmines
   staging: Leonard Peters
Productions:
   (Off-Off-Broadway) Opened October 10, 1975
Reviews:
   New York Times page 25, Oct 17, 1975

The Wife Hunters
   book: Edgar Allan Woolf
   music: Anatol Friedland and Malvin Franklin
   lyrics: David Kempner
   staging: Ned Wayburn
Productions:
   Opened November 2, 1911 for 36 performances
Reviews:
   Dramatic Mirror 66:7, Nov 8, 1911
                   66:4, Nov 29, 1911
   Green Book 7:19-22+, Jan 1912
   Theatre Magazine 14:xiii, Dec 1911
                    14:187, Dec 1911

Wild and Wonderful
    book: Phil Phillips
    music and   Bob Goodman; from an original work by Bob
      lyrics: Brotherton and Bob Miller
    staging: Burry Fredrik
    sets: Stephen Hendrickson
    costumes: Frank Thompson
    choreography: Ronn Forella
Productions:
    Opened December 7, 1971 for one performance
Reviews:
    New York Theatre Critics' Reviews 1971:170
    New York Times page 71, Dec 8, 1971
                     page 64, Dec 9, 1971

The Wild Rose
    book: Otto Harbach and Oscar Hammerstein II
    music: Rudolf Friml
    lyrics: Otto Harbach and Oscar Hammerstein II
    staging: William J. Wilson
Productions:
    Opened October 20, 1926 for 61 performances
Reviews:
    New York Times page 23, Oct 21, 1926
    Theatre Magazine 45:16, Jan 1927

The Wildcat (1921)
    book: Manuel Penella
    staging: Manuel Penella
Productions:
    Opened November 26, 1921 for 74 performances
Reviews:
    Dramatic Mirror 84:809, Dec 3, 1921
    New York Clipper 69:20, Nov 30, 1921
    New York Times page 16, Nov 28, 1921
    Theatre Magazine 35:99, Feb 1922

Wildcat (1960)
    book: N. Richard Nash
    music: Cy Coleman
    lyrics: Carolyn Leigh
    staging: Michael Kidd
    sets: Peter Larkin
    costumes: Alvin Colt
    choreography: Michael Kidd
Productions:
    Opened December 16, 1960 for 171 performances
Reviews:
    America 104:546, Jan 21, 1961
    Coronet 49:16, Apr 1961
    Nation 191:531, Dec 31, 1960

New York Theatre Critics' Reviews 1960:134+
New York Times page 20, Dec 17, 1960
             page 39, Feb 7, 1961
New Yorker 36:38, Dec 24, 1960
Newsweek 56:53, Dec 26, 1960
Saturday Review 43:28, Dec 31, 1960
Theatre Arts 45:9-10, Feb 1961

Wildflower
    book: Otto Harbach and Oscar Hammerstein II
    music: Herbert Stothart and Vincent Youmans
    lyrics: Otto Harbach and Oscar Hammerstein II
    staging: Oscar Eagle
    choreography: David Bennett
Productions:
    Opened February 7, 1923 for 477 performances
Reviews:
    Life (New York) 81:18, Mar 1, 1923
    New York Clipper 71:14, Feb 14, 1923
    New York Times page 17, Feb 8, 1923
    Theatre Magazine 38:16, Aug 1923

Will the Mail Train Run Tonight
    book: Malcolm L. La Prade; based on a play by Hugh
                  Nevill
    music: Alyn Hein
    lyrics: Malcolm L. La Prade
    staging: Jon Baisch
    sets: Gene Czernicki
    costumes: Joe Crosby
    choreography: Lynne Fippinger
Productions:
    (Off-Broadway) Opened January 9, 1964 for 8 performances
Reviews:
    New York Times page 18, Jan 10, 1964

Williams & Walker
    written: Vincent D. Smith, based on the Ziegfeld Follies
    songs: Various Progressive Era authors and composers
    staging: Shauneille Perry
    sets: Marc D. Malamud
    costumes: Judy Dearing
    choreography: Lenwood Sloan
Productions:
    (Off-Broadway) Opened March 9, 1986 for 77 performances
Reviews:
    New York Theatre Critics' Reviews 1986:280
    New York Times III, page 14, Mar 11, 1986
    New Yorker 62:102, Mar 17, 1986

Willie the Weeper (see Ballet Ballads)

Wind in the Willows
  book: Jane Iredale, adapted from the book by Kenneth
                  Grahame
  music: William Perry
  lyrics: Roger McGough and William Perry
  staging: Tony Stevens
  sets: Sam Kirkpatrick
  costumes: Freddy Wittop
  choreography: Margery Beddow
Productions:
  Opened December 19, 1985 for 4 performances
Reviews:
  New York Theatre Critics' Reviews 1985:120
  New York Times I, page 15, Dec 21, 1985

Wings
  book: Robert McLaughlin and Peter Ryan, based on
                  Aristophanes's The Birds
  music: Robert McLaughlin and Peter Ryan
  lyrics: Robert McLaughlin and Peter Ryan
  staging: Robert McLaughlin
  sets: Karl Eigsti
  costumes: Shadow
  choreography: Nora Christiansen
Productions:
  (Off-Broadway) Opened March 16, 1975 for 9 performances
Reviews:
  New York Times page 34, Mar 17, 1975

The Wings of the Dove
  book: Ethan Ayer, based on Henry James' novel
  music: Douglas Moore
  lyrics: Ethan Ayer
  staging: Christopher West
  sets: Donald Oenslager
  costumes: Patton Campbell
  choreography: Robert Joffrey
Productions:
  (Off-Broadway) Opened October 12, 1961 for 3 performances
No Reviews.

A Winsome Widow
  book: Raymond Hubbell; based on A Trip to Chinatown
                  by Charles H. Hoyt
  music: Raymond Hubbell
  lyrics: Raymond Hubbell
Productions:
  Opened April 11, 1912 for 172 performances
Reviews:
  Blue Book 15:452-7, Jul 1912
  Dramatic Mirror 67:6, Apr 17, 1912

67:2, May 1, 1912
67:2, May 8, 1912
67:4, Jun 19, 1912
Green Book 8:4-7+, Jul 1912
8:136, Jul 1912
8:326-7, Aug 1912
Leslie's Weekly 115:760, Jul 4, 1912
Munsey Magazine 47:467-8, Jun 1912
New York Dramatic News 55:18, Apr 20, 1912
Red Book 19:574-6, Jul 1912
Theatre Magazine 15:140, May 1912

Wish You Were Here

book: Arthur Kober and Joshua Logan, based on
    Arthur Kober's play Having Wonderful Time
music: Harold Rome
lyrics: Harold Rome
staging: Joshua Logan
sets: Jo Mielziner
costumes: Robert Mackintosh
choreography: Joshua Logan
Productions:
    Opened June 25, 1952 for 598 performances
Reviews:
    Catholic World 175:388, Aug 1952
    Commonweal 56:366-7, Jul 18, 1952
    Life 33:79-80, Jul 21, 1952
    Nation 175:18, Jul 5, 1952
    New York Theatre Critics' Reviews 1952:266+
    New York Times VI, page 22, Jun 15, 1952
    II, page 1, Jun 22, 1952
    page 26, Jun 26, 1952
    II, page 1, Aug 31, 1952
    II, page 1, Feb 22, 1953
    II, page 1, Jul 12, 1953
    page 83, Oct 11, 1953
    II, page 3, Oct 18, 1953
    New Yorker 28:45, Jul 5, 1952
    28:56, Dec 20, 1952
    Newsweek 40:70, Jul 7, 1952
    Saturday Review 35:24, Jul 12, 1952
    35:5, Aug 16, 1952
    Theatre Arts 36:14, Jul 1952
    36:28-9, Aug 1952
    Time 60:60, Jul 7, 1952

The Wiz

book: William F. Brown
music: Charlie Smalls
lyrics: Charlie Smalls
staging: Geoffrey Holder

```
    sets:              Tom H. John
    costumes:          Geoffrey Holder
    choreography:      George Faison
Productions:
    Opened January 5, 1975 for 1,672 performances
    Opened May 24, 1984 for 13 performances
Reviews:
    Dance Magazine 49: 34+, Mar 1975
    Ebony 30: 114-16+, Oct 1975
    Essence 5: 11, Mar 1975
           6: 32+, Sep 1975
    Los Angeles 21: 193, Aug 1976
    New West 2: SC-19, Aug 1, 1977
    New York 8: 51, Jan 27, 1975
            10: 114, Jun 27, 1977
            17: 79, Jun 4, 1984
    New York Theatre Critics' Reviews 1975: 390
                                       1984: 268
    New York Times page 32, Jan 6, 1975
                    II, page 5, Jan 12, 1975
                    II, page 1, Jul 20, 1975
                    II, page 5, Dec 28, 1975
                    II, page 5, Jan 18, 1976
                    III, page 4, Apr 1, 1977
                    III, page 3, May 25, 1984
    New Yorker 50: 64, Jan 13, 1975
    Newsweek 85: 82, Jan 20, 1975
    Time 105: 76, Jan 20, 1975
```

The Wizard of Oz

```
    book:              Michel M. Grilikhes, adapted from the stories of
                       L. Frank Baum
    original music:    Harold Arlen (from the movie)
    original lyrics:   E. Y. Harburg (from the movie)
    original inci-
      dental
      music:           Herbert Stothart
    staging:           Michel M. Grilikhes
    sets:              Stephen Ehlers
    costumes:          Bill Campbell
    choreography:      Onna White
Productions:
    Opened March 22, 1989 for 39 performances
Reviews:
    New York Times III, page 3, Mar 24, 1989
```

Woman of the Year

```
    book:              Peter Stone, based on the M-G-M film by Ring
                       Lardner Jr. and Michael Kanin
    music:             John Kander
    lyrics:            Fred Ebb
```

staging: Robert Moore
sets: Tony Walton
costumes: Theoni V. Aldredge
choreography: Tony Charmoli
Productions:
Opened March 29, 1981 for 770 performances
Reviews:
America 144:487, Jun 13, 1981
Dance Magazine 55:72-3, Jun 1981
                57:142-3, May 1983
Nation 232:611-12, May 16, 1981
New Leader 64:19, Apr 20, 1981
New York 14:14-15, Feb 9, 1981
         14:46, Apr 13, 1981
New York Theatre Critics' Reviews 1981:302
New York Times III, page 15, Mar 30, 1981
              II, page 3, Apr 5, 1981
              III, page 19, Apr 9, 1981
              III, page 3, Dec 11, 1981
              III, page 11, Feb 28, 1983
New Yorker 57:121, Apr 6, 1981
Newsweek 97:81, Apr 13, 1981
Saturday Review 8:63, Jun 1981
Time 117:89, Apr 13, 1981
     120:62, Aug 16, 1982

The Wonder Bar
book: Irving Caesar and Aben Kandel; adapted from
                  the German of Geza Herczeg and Karl Farkas
music: Robert Katscher
staging: William Mollison
Productions:
Opened March 17, 1931 for 76 performances
Reviews:
Bookman 73:408-9, Jun 1931
Drama 21:6+, May 1931
Life (New York) 97:20, Apr 17, 1931
New York Times VIII, page 3, Mar 8, 1931
              VIII, page 1, Mar 22, 1931
              page 35, Jun 2, 1931
Theatre Arts 15:366-7+, May 1931
Vanity Fair 36:52, Jun 1931

The Wonder Years
book: David Levy, David Holdgrive, Steve Liebman and
                  Terry LaBolt; based on an idea by Leslie Eber-
                  hard
music: David Levy
lyrics: David Levy
staging: David Holdgrive
sets: Nancy Thun

costumes: Richard Schurkamp
choreography: David Holdgrive
Productions:
  (Off-Broadway)   Opened May 25, 1988 for 23 performances
Reviews:
  Los Angeles 31:216, Sep 1986
  New York Times I, page 47, May 29, 1988

Wonderful Town
  book: Joseph Fields and Jerome Chodorov, based on
                   the play My Sister Eileen by Joseph Fields and
                   Jerome Chodorov and the stories of Ruth McKen-
                   ney
  music: Leonard Bernstein
  lyrics: Betty Comden and Adolph Green
  staging: George Abbott
  sets: Raoul Pene du Bois
  costumes: Raoul Pene du Bois
  choreography: Donald Saddler
Productions:
  Opened February 25, 1953 for 559 performances
  Opened March 5, 1958 for 16 performances
  Opened February 13, 1963 for 16 performances
  Opened May 17, 1967 for 23 performances
  (Off-Off-Broadway) Opened March 10, 1977
Reviews:
  America 88:661, Mar 14, 1953
  Catholic World 177:67-8, Apr 1953
  Commonweal 57:603-4, Mar 20, 1953
  Dance Magazine 32:15, Apr 1958
                 41:70-1, Jul 1967
  Life 34:134-5, Mar 16, 1953
  Look 17:84-5, Mar 10, 1953
  Los Angeles 20:141+, Aug 1975
  Nation 176:232, Mar 14, 1953
          249:611, Nov 20, 1989
  New York Theatre Critics' Reviews 1953:344+
  New York Times II, page 1, Feb 22, 1953
                    page 33, Feb 26, 1953
                    II, page 1, Mar 8, 1953
                    II, page 1, Apr 5, 1953
                    II, page 7, May 10, 1953
                    II, page 1, May 9, 1954
                    page 33, May 17, 1955
                    page 32, Mar 6, 1958
                    page 10, Feb 15, 1963
                    page 56, May 18, 1967
                    page 16, Mar 12, 1977
  New Yorker 29:59, Mar 7, 1953
  Newsweek 41:59, Mar 9, 1953
  Saturday Review 36:36, Mar 14, 1953
                  36:6, May 9, 1953

Theatre Arts 37:16-17, May 1953
           37:18-21, Aug 1953
Time 61:96+, Mar 9, 1953
      61:40-2+, Mar 30, 1953

Woof, Woof
   book: Estelle Hunt, Sam Summers, Cyrus Wood
   music: Edward Pola and Eddie Brandt
   lyrics: Edward Pola and Eddie Brandt
   staging: Leonide Massine
Productions:
   Opened December 25, 1929 for 45 performances
Reviews:
   New York Times page 20, Dec 26, 1929
   Theatre Magazine 51:63, Feb 1930

Words and Music (1917)
   by: E. R. Goetz and R. Hitchcock
   staging: Leon Errol
Productions:
   Opened December 24, 1917 for 24 performances
Reviews:
   Dramatic Mirror 78:5, Jan 5, 1918
   New York Times page 13, Dec 25, 1917
   Theatre Magazine 27:88, Feb 1918

Words and Music (1974)
   words: Sammy Cahn
   music: various composers
   lyrics: Sammy Cahn
   staging: Jerry Adler
   sets: Robert Randolph
Productions:
   Opened April 16, 1974 for 128 performances
Reviews:
   America 130:344, May 4, 1974
   Nation 218:666-7, May 25, 1974
   New York 7:80, May 6, 1974
   New York Theatre Critics' Reviews 1974:307
   New York Times page 35, Apr 17, 1974
                    II, page 1, Apr 28, 1974
                    page 20, Aug 1, 1974
   New Yorker 50:63, Apr 29, 1974
   Playboy 21:22, Aug 1974

Working
   book: adapted by Stephen Schwartz from the book by
                   Studs Terkel
   songs: Craig Carnelia, Micki Grant, Mary Rodgers and
                   Susan Birkenhead, Stephen Schwartz and James
                   Taylor

        staging: Stephen Schwartz
        sets: David Mitchell
        costumes: Marjorie Slaiman
        choreography: Onna White
Productions:
    Opened May 14, 1978 for 25 performances
Reviews:
    Commonweal 105:498, Aug 4, 1978
    Harper's 257:78-9, Dec 1978
    Horizon 21:28-33, Apr 1978
    Los Angeles 25:258+, Oct 1980
    Nation 226:676, Jun 3, 1978
    New Leader 61:24, Jun 5, 1978
    New York 11:77-8, May 29, 1978
    New York Theatre Critics' Reviews 1978:274
    New York Times III, page 15, May 15, 1978
                    II, page 3, May 28, 1978
    New Yorker 54:84, May 29, 1978
    Saturday Review 5:24, Jul 8, 1978
    Time 111:83, May 29, 1978

Working 42nd Street at Last   (see Kaye Ballard: Working 42nd Street
    at Last)

The World of Charles Aznavour
    music: Charles Aznavour
    lyrics: Charles Aznavour
    sets: Ralph Alswang
Productions:
    Opened October 14, 1965 for 29 performances
Reviews:
    New York Times page 49, Oct 15, 1965
    Time 86:102+, Oct 22, 1965
(also see Aznavour and Charles Aznavour)

The World of Kurt Weill in Song
    written: Will Holt
    music: Kurt Weill
    staging: Will Holt
Productions:
    (Off-Broadway) Opened June 6, 1963 for 245 performances
Reviews:
    Saturday Review 48:38, Jan 23, 1965

A World of Pleasure
    book: Harold Atteridge
    music: Sigmund Romberg
    lyrics: Harold Atteridge
    staging: J. C. Huffman
    choreography: Jack Mason and Theodore Kosloff
Productions:
    Opened October 14, 1915 for 116 performances

Reviews:
    Dramatic Mirror 74:8, Oct 23, 1915
                   74:2, Nov 13, 1915
    Green Book 15:70-72, Jan 1916
    Life (New York) 66:808, Oct 28, 1915
    New York Dramatic News 61:17, Oct 23, 1915
    Theatre Magazine 22:282, Dec 1915

Worlds of Oscar Brown, Jr.
    created: Oscar Brown, Jr.
    performed: Oscar Brown, Jr.
Productions:
    (Off-Broadway) Opened February 18, 1965 for 55 performances
Reviews:
    New York Times page 25, Feb 19, 1965

The Would-Be Gentleman
    book: Bobby Clark; adapted from Molière's Le Bourgeois
                      Gentilhomme
    music: Jerome Moross; adapted from the original by
                      Lully
    staging: John Kennedy
    sets: Howard Bay
    costumes: Irene Sharaff
Productions:
    Opened January 9, 1946 for 77 performances
Reviews:
    Nation 162:108, Jan 26, 1946
    New York Theatre Critics' Reviews 1946:490
    New York Times II, page 1, Jan 6, 1946
                   page 29, Jan 10, 1946
                   page 18, Jan 18, 1946
                   II, page 1, Jan 20, 1946
    Newsweek 27:87, Jan 21, 1946
    Saturday Review 29:28-30, Feb 9, 1946
    Theatre Arts 30:137+, Mar 1946
    Time 47:79, Jan 21, 1946
    Vogue 107:100, Feb 15, 1946

Wynn, Ed   (see Ed Wynn)

                            -Y-

The Yankee Girl
    book: George V. Hobart
    music: Silvio Hein
    lyrics: George V. Hobart
    staging: Ned Wayburn
Productions:
    Opened February 10, 1910 for 92 performances

Reviews:
    Theatre Magazine 11:xi, Mar 1910

The Yankee Princess
    book: William Le Baron; adapted from Die Bajadere by
                   Julius Brammer and Alfred Grunwald
    music: Emmerich Kalman
    lyrics: B. G. DeSylva
    staging: Fred G. Latham and Julian Mitchell
Productions:
    Opened October 2, 1922 for 80 performances
Reviews:
    New York Clipper 70:20, Oct 11, 1922
    New York Times page 22, Oct 3, 1922
    Theatre Magazine 36:377, Dec 1922

Yeah Man
    book: Leigh Whipper and Billy Mills
    music: Al Wilson, Charles Weinberg, Ken Macomber
    lyrics: Al Wilson, Charles Weinberg, Ken Macomber
    staging: Walter Campbell
Productions:
    Opened May 26, 1932 for 4 performances
Reviews:
    New York Times page 27, May 27, 1932

The Yearling
    book: Herbert Martin and Lore Noto; based on the
                   novel by Marjorie Kinnan Rawlings
    music: Michael Leonard
    lyrics: Herbert Martin
    staging: Lloyd Richards
    sets: Ed Wittstein
    costumes: Ed Wittstein
    choreography: Ralph Beaumont
Productions:
    Opened December 10, 1965 for 3 performances
Reviews:
    New York Theatre Critics' Reviews 1965:221
    New York Times page 19, Aug 27, 1965
                   page 25, Dec 11, 1965
                   page 55, Dec 13, 1965

Yes, Yes, Yvette
    book: James Montgomery and William Cary Duncan;
                   based on a story by Frederick S. Isham
    music: Philip Charig and Ben Jerome
    lyrics: Irving Caesar
    staging: H. H. Freeze
Productions:
    Opened October 3, 1927 for 40 performances

Reviews:
>   New York Times page 25, May 14, 1927
>   page 32, Oct 4, 1927

Yip Yip Yaphank
>   words: Irving Berlin
>   music: Irving Berlin

Productions:
>   Opened August 19, 1918 for 32 performances

Reviews:
>   Dramatic Mirror 79:301, Aug 31, 1918
>   Green Book 19:398-9+, Mar 1918
>   New York Times page 7, Jul 27, 1918
>   page 7, Aug 20, 1918
>   page 12, Sep 11, 1918
>   Stage 15:40, Aug 1938
>   Theatre Magazine 28:222-3, Oct 1918

Yokel Boy
>   book: Lew Brown and Charles Tobias
>   music: Sam Stept
>   lyrics: Lew Brown and Charles Tobias
>   staging: Lew Brown
>   sets: Walter Jagemann
>   costumes: Frances Feist and Veronica
>   choreography: Gene Snyder

Productions:
>   Opened July 6, 1939 for 208 performances

Reviews:
>   New York Theatre Critics' Reviews 1940:481+
>   New York Times page 12, Jul 12, 1939
>   page 16, Aug 17, 1939
>   Time 34:66, Jul 17, 1939

You Never Know
>   book: Rowland Leigh, adapted from the original by
>   Robert Katscher, Siegfried Geyer, Karl Farkas
>   music: Cole Porter
>   lyrics: Cole Porter
>   staging: Rowland Leigh
>   sets: Watson Barratt and Albert Johnson
>   choreography: Robert Alton

Productions:
>   Opened September 21, 1938 for 78 performances
>   (Off-Broadway) Season of 1969-70
>   (Off-Broadway) Opened March 12, 1973 for 8 performances

Reviews:
>   Catholic World 148:215, Nov 1938
>   New York Times page 16, Mar 4, 1938
>   page 26, Sep 22, 1938
>   page 31, Mar 13, 1973

Theatre Arts 22:783, Nov 1938
Time 31:38, Apr 11, 1938

You Said It
book:	Jack Yellen and Sid Silvers
music:	Harold Arlen
lyrics:	Jack Yellen
staging:	John Harwood and Danny Dare

Productions:
Opened January 29, 1931 for 192 performances
Reviews:
Life (New York) 97:18, Feb 6, 1931
New York Times page 21, Jan 20, 1931

You'll See Stars
book:	Herman Timberg
music:	Leo Edwards
lyrics:	Herman Timberg
staging:	Herman Timberg and Dave Kramer
choreography:	Eric Victor

Productions:
Opened December 29, 1942 for 4 performances
Reviews:
New York Theatre Critics' Reviews 1942:122+
New York Times page 26, Jan 1, 1943

Young Abe Lincoln
book:	Richard N. Bernstein and John Allen
music:	Victor Ziskin
lyrics:	Joan Javits and Arnold Sungaard

Productions:
(Off-Broadway) Season of 1960-61
Reviews:
New York Times page 36, Apr 26, 1961
page 27, May 6, 1961

The Young Turk
book:	Aaron Hoffman
music:	Max Hoffman
lyrics:	Harry Williams
staging:	Herbert Gresham

Productions:
Opened January 31, 1910 for 32 performances
Reviews:
Dramatic Mirror 63:8, Feb 12, 1910
Theatre Magazine 11:xii, Mar 1910

Your Arms Too Short to Box With God
conceived:	Vinnette Carroll, from the Book of Matthew
music:	Alex Bradford
lyrics:	Alex Bradford

```
     additional
       music and
         lyrics:        Micki Grant
      staging:          Vinnette Carroll
      sets:             William Schroder
      costumes:         William Schroder
       choreography:    Talley Beatty
Productions:
   Opened December 22, 1976 for 429 performances
   Opened June 2, 1980 for 149 performances
   Opened September 9, 1982 for 70 performances
Reviews:
   America 136:60, Jan 22, 1977
   Christianity Today 20:16-17, Jan 30, 1976
   Dance Magazine 51:39-40, May 1977
   Ebony 35:122+, Oct 1980
   Los Angeles 25:210, Jan 1980
   Nation 224:61, Jan 15, 1977
   New York 10:63, Jan 10, 1977
   New York Theatre Critics' Reviews 1976:52
                                     1980:223
                                     1982:212
   New York Times page 20, Dec 23, 1976
                    page 13, Jan 15, 1977
                    III, page 7, Jun 3, 1980
                    III, page 3, Sep 10, 1982
   New Yorker 52:60, Jan 3, 1977
   Newsweek 89:66, Jan 10, 1977
   Time 109:55, Jan 24, 1977
```

Your Own Thing

```
   book:            Donald Driver; suggested by William Shakespeare's
                    Twelfth Night
   music:           Hal Hester and Danny Apolinar
   lyrics:          Hal Hester and Danny Apolinar
   staging:         Donald Driver
   sets:            Robert Guerra
   costumes:        Albert Wolsky
    choreography:   Charles Schneider
Productions:
   (Off-Broadway) Opened January 13, 1968 for 933 performances
Reviews:
   Commonweal 87:623-4, Feb 23, 1968
   Dance Magazine 42:26-7, Apr 1968
   Mademoiselle 67:116-17, Jun 1968
   Nation 206:220, Feb 12, 1968
   New York Theatre Critics' Reviews 1968:270
   New York Times page 33, Jan 15, 1968
                    II, page 3, Jan 28, 1968
                    II, page 7, Feb 25, 1968
                    page 23, Feb 8, 1969
                    page 39, Mar 29, 1969
```

New Yorker 43:86, Jan 27, 1968
Saturday Review 51:39, Feb 10, 1968
Time 91:45, Jan 26, 1968
Vogue 151:46, Apr 15, 1968

You're a Good Man, Charlie Brown
    book: Clark Gesner; based on the comic strip "Peanuts"
                      by Charles M. Schulz
    music: Clark Gesner
    lyrics: Clark Gesner
    staging: Joseph Hardy
    sets: Alan Kimmel
    costumes: Alan Kimmel
Productions:
    (Off-Broadway) Opened March 7, 1967 for 1,597 performances
    Opened June 1, 1971 for 32 performances
Reviews:
    Christian Century 84:1561, Dec 6, 1967
    Nation 204:444-5, Apr 3, 1967
    New Republic 19:976-8, Sep 5, 1967
    New York Theatre Critics' Reviews 1971:255
    New York Times page 51, Mar 8, 1967
                  page 44, Mar 9, 1967
                   II, page 1, Apr 9, 1967
                   II, page 1, Sep 3, 1967
                  page 46, Mar 8, 1968
                  page 13, Feb 13, 1971
                  page 16, May 1, 1971
                  page 48, May 6, 1971
                  page 33, Jun 2, 1971
                  page 56, Jun 23, 1971
    New Yorker 43:121-3, Mar 18, 1967
    Newsweek 69:109, Mar 20, 1967
    Saturday Review 50:42, Apr 1, 1967
    Time 89:62, Mar 17, 1967

You're in Love
    book: Otto Hauerbach and Edward Clark
    music: Rudolf Friml
    lyrics: Otto Hauerbach and Edward Clark
    staging: Edward Clark
Productions:
    Opened February 6, 1917 for 167 performances
Reviews:
    Dramatic Mirror 77:5, Feb 10, 1917
                   77:7+, Feb 17, 1917
                   77:4, Mar 3, 1917
    New York Dramatic News 63:27, Dec 16, 1918
    New York Times page 11, Feb 7, 1917
    Theatre Magazine 25:151-2, Mar 1917
                   25:231, Apr 1917

Yours, Anne
  book: Enid Futterman, based on Anne Frank: The
                 Diary of a Young Girl and the play by Frances
                 Goodrich and Albert Hackett
  music: Michael Cohen
  lyrics: Enid Futterman
  staging: Arthur Masella
  sets: Franco Colavecchia
  costumes: Judith Dolan
Productions:
  (Off-Broadway) Opened October 13, 1985 for 57 performances
Reviews:
  New York 18:98+, Oct 28, 1985
  New York Theatre Critics' Reviews 1985:170
  New York Times III, page 16, Oct 14, 1985

Yours Truly
  book: Clyde North
  music: Raymond Hubbell
  lyrics: Anne Caldwell
  staging: Paul Dickey and Ralph Reader
Productions:
  Opened January 25, 1927 for 129 performances
  Opened March 12, 1928 for 16 performances
Reviews:
  Life (New York) 89:21, Feb 24, 1927
  New York Times page 16, Jan 26, 1927
  Theatre Magazine 45:19, Apr 1927

Yves Montand (see An Evening with Yves Montand)

Yvette
  book: Benjamin Thorne Gilbert
  music: Frederick Herendeen
  lyrics: Frederick Herendeen
  staging: M. Ring
Productions:
  Opened August 10, 1916 for 4 performances
Reviews:
  Dramatic Mirror 76:8, Aug 19, 1916
  New York Times page 7, Aug 11, 1916
                 page 9, Aug 12, 1916

-Z-

Ziegfeld Follies of 1910
  book: Harry B. Smith
  music: Gus Edwards
  staging: Julian Mitchell
  sets: John H. Young and Ernest Albert
  costumes: Crage, Berlin, Tappé and W. H. Matthews, Jr.

Productions:
    Opened June 20, 1910 for 88 performances
Reviews:
    Leslie's Weekly 111:11, Jul 7, 1910
                111:31, Jul 14, 1910
                111:55, Jul 21, 1910
    Metropolitan Magazine 32:674-5, Aug 1910
    Theatre Magazine 12:35+, Aug 1910

Ziegfeld Follies of 1911
    book: George V. Hobart
    music: Maurice Levi, Raymond Hubbell, Jerome Kern,
                   and Irving Berlin
    staging: Julian Mitchell
    sets: Ernest Albert and Unitt and Wickers
    costumes: Matthews and Tryce
Productions:
    Opened June 26, 1911 for 80 performances
Reviews:
    Blue Book 13:1124-9, Oct 1911
    Dramatic Mirror 65:14, Jun 28, 1911
                    66:9, Jul 12, 1911
                    66:4, Jul 19, 1911
    Green Book Album 6:452-7, Sep 1911
    Red Book 17:955, Sep 1911
    Stage 13:56+, Aug 1936
    Theatre Magazine 14:40, Aug 1911
                     14:46+, Aug 1911

Ziegfeld Follies of 1912
    book: Harry B. Smith
    music: Raymond Hubbell
    lyrics: Harry B. Smith
    staging: Julian Mitchell
    sets: Ernest Albert
    costumes: Callot of Paris, Schneider and Anderson
Productions:
    Opened October 21, 1912 for 88 performances
Reviews:
    Blue Book 16:452-7, Jan 1913
    Dramatic Mirror 68:6, Oct 23, 1912
    Green Book 9:18-20+, Jan 1913
    Harper's Weekly 56:20, Nov 2, 1912
    Munsey 48:528-9, Dec 1912
    New York Dramatic News 56:21, Oct 26, 1912

Ziegfeld Follies of 1913
    book: George V. Hobart
    music: Raymond Hubbell, Gene Buck, and Dave Stamper
    lyrics: George V. Hobart
    staging: Julian Mitchell

sets: John H. Young, Gates and Morange, Ernest
                   Albert
costumes: Schneider and Anderson
Productions:
   Opened June 16, 1913 for 96 performances
Reviews:
   Blue Book 17:868-71, Sep 1913
   Dramatic Mirror 70:2, Jul 2, 1913
   Green Book 10:373-75, Sep 1913
              10:430-32, Sep 1913
              11:212-18, Feb 1914
   Munsey 50:92, Oct 1913
   New York Times page 11, Jun 17, 1913

Ziegfeld Follies of 1914
   book: Goerge V. Hobart
   music: Raymond Hubbell and David Stamper
   lyrics: George V. Hobart; additional lyrics by Gene
                   Buck
   staging: Florenz Ziegfeld, Jr. and Leon Errol
   sets: John H. Young and Ernest Albert
   costumes: Cora McGeachey and W. H. Matthews, Jr.
Productions:
   Opened June 1, 1914 for 112 performances
Reviews:
   Dramatic Mirror 71:8, Jun 3, 1914
   Green Book 12:322-5, Aug 1914
   Munsey 53:90-92, Oct 1914
   New York Times page 11, Jun 2, 1914
   Theatre Magazine 20:37, Jul 1914

Ziegfeld Follies of 1915
   book: Channing Pollock, Rennold Wolf and Gene Buck
   music: Louis Hirsch and David Stamper
   lyrics: Channing Pollock, Rennold Wolf and Gene Buck
   staging: Julian Mitchell and Leon Errol
   sets: Joseph Urban
   costumes: Lucille and Tappé
Productions:
   Opened June 21, 1915 for 104 performances
Reviews:
   Dramatic Mirror 73:8, Jun 23, 1915
   Green Book 14:388-403, Sep 1915
              14:874-5, Nov 1915
   Harper's Bazaar 50:48, Jul 1915
   New Republic 3:366, Jul 31, 1915
   New York Times page 15, Jun 22, 1915
   Strand 50:208-15, Sep 1915
   Theatre Magazine 22:66, Aug 1915

Ziegfeld Follies of 1916
   book: George V. Hobart and Gene Buck

music: Louis Hirsch, Jerome Kern and Dave Stamper
lyrics: George V. Hobart and Gene Buck
staging: Ned Wayburn
sets: Joseph Urban
costumes: Lucille
Productions:
Opened June 12, 1916 for 112 performances
Reviews:
Dramatic Mirror 75:8, Jun 17, 1916
Green Book 16:418-19, Sep 1916
New York Times page 9, Jun 13, 1916
Theatre Magazine 24:11+, Jul 1916
                24:71, Aug 1916

Ziegfeld Follies of 1917

book: Gene Buck and George V. Hobart
music: Raymond Hubbell and Dave Stamper
lyrics: Gene Buck and George V. Hobart
additional
  sketches: Ring Lardner
staging: Ned Wayburn
sets: Joseph Urban
costumes: Lucille, Callot of Paris, Bendel
Productions:
Opened June 12, 1917 for 111 performances
Reviews:
Dramatic Mirror 77:5+, Jun 23, 1917
                77:7, Jun 23, 1917
New Republic 11:278, Jul 17, 1917
New York Times page 11, Jun 13, 1917
                VIII, page 5, Jun 17, 1917
Theatre Magazine 26:55, Jul 17, 1917
                26:87, Aug 1917

Ziegfeld Follies of 1918

book: Rennold Wolf and Gene Buck
music: Louis A. Hirsch, Victor Jacobi, Dave Stamper,
                Irving Berlin
lyrics: Rennold Wolf and Gene Buck
staging: Ned Wayburn
sets: Joseph Urban
costumes: Lucille
Productions:
Opened June 18, 1918 for 151 performances
Reviews:
Dramatic Mirror 78:921, Jun 29, 1918
Green Book 20:388-99, Sep 1918
New York Times page 9, Jun 19, 1918
Theatre Magazine 28:112, Aug 1918

Ziegfeld Follies of 1919

book: Gene Buck, Dave Stamper, Rennold Wolf

music: Victor Herbert, Harry Tierney, Joseph J. Mc-
                    Carthy, and Irving Berlin
lyrics: Gene Buck, Dave Stamper, Rennold Wolf
staging: Ned Wayburn
sets: Joseph Urban
costumes: Lucille and Mme. Frances
Productions:
  Opened September 1919 for 171 performances
Reviews:
  Arts and Decoration 11: 302, Oct 1919
  Theatre Magazine 30: 77, Aug 1919
                    30: 81, Aug 1919
                    30: 159, Sep 1919

Ziegfeld Follies (1920)
  sketches: W. C. Fields, George V. Hobart, James Mont-
                    gomery
  music/lyrics: Irving Berlin, Dave Stamper, Gene Buck, Joseph
                    McCarthy, Harry Tierney, Victor Herbert
  staging: Edward Royce
Productions:
  Opened June 22, 1920 for 123 performances
Reviews:
  New York Clipper 68: 14, Mar 17, 1920
  New York Times page 14, Jun 23, 1920

Ziegfeld Follies (1921)
  book: Willard Mack, Raymond Hitchcock, Channing
                    Pollock, Ralph Spence
  music: Victor Herbert, Rudolf Friml, Dave Stamper
  lyrics: Gene Buck, B. G. DeSylva, Brian Hooker
  staging: Edward Royce
Productions:
  Opened June 21, 1921 for 119 performances
Reviews:
  Life (New York) 78: 18, Jul 14, 1921
  New York Clipper 69: 20, Jun 29, 1921
  New York Times page 8, Jun 17, 1921
                    page 10, Jun 22, 1921
  Theatre Magazine 34: 168, Sep 1921

Ziegfeld Follies of 1922
  book: Ring Lardner, Gene Buck and Ralph Spence
  music: Victor Herbert, Louis A. Hirsch and Dave
                    Stamper
  staging: Ned Wayburn
  sets: Joseph Urban and Herman Rosse
  costumes: James Reynolds, Cora McGeachey, Alice O'Neill,
                    Ben Ali Haggin, Tappé, and Charles LeMaire
  choreography: Michel Fokine
Productions:
  Opened June 5, 1922 for 333 performances

Reviews:
    Bookman 55:601-2, Aug 1922
    Life (New York) 79:18, Jun 29, 1922
    New York Clipper 70:20, Jun 14, 1922
    New York Times page 18, Jun 6, 1922
    Theatre Magazine 36:95, Aug 1922
               36:135, Sep 1922

Ziegfeld Follies (1923)
    sketches: Eddie Cantor and Gene Buck
    music: Victor Herbert, Rudolf Friml, Dave Stamper
    lyrics: Gene Buck
    staging: Ned Wayburn
Productions:
    Opened October 20, 1923 for 233 performances
Reviews:
    Dial 76:618, Dec 1923
    Life (New York) 82:18, Nov 8, 1923
    New York Times page 17, Oct 22, 1923
               VIII, page 1, Oct 28, 1923
               page 25, Mar 18, 1924
    Theatre Magazine 38:19, Dec 1923

Ziegfeld Follies of 1924
    book: Will Rogers and William Anthony McGuire
    music: Victor Herbert, Raymond Hubbell, Dave
                      Stamper, Harry Tierney, and Dr. Albert Sirmay
    lyrics: Gene Buck and Joseph J. McCarthy
    staging: Julian Mitchell
    sets: Joseph Urban and John Wenger
    costumes: Erté of Paris, James Reynolds, Alice O'Neill
Productions:
    Opened June 24, 1924 for 401 performances
Reviews:
    Life (New York) 84:18, Jul 17, 1924
    New York Times page 25, Jun 19, 1924
               page 17, Jun 22, 1924
               page 26, Jun 25, 1924
               page 19, Mar 11, 1925
               page 9, Jun 6, 1925
    Theatre Magazine 40:15, Sep 1924
    World's Work 48:595, Oct 1924

Ziegfeld Follies (1927)
    sketches: Harold Atteridge and Eddie Cantor
    music: Irving Berlin
    lyrics: Irving Berlin
    staging: Florenz Ziegfeld, Sammy Lee, Zeke Colvan
Productions:
    Opened August 16, 1927 for 167 performances
Reviews:
    Independent 119:362, Oct 8, 1927

Life 90:21, Sep 1, 1927
New York Times VII, page 1, Aug 7, 1927
                page 27, Aug 17, 1927
                VII, page 1, Aug 28, 1927
                VII, page 2, Sep 18, 1927
Vogue 70:96, Oct 15, 1927

Ziegfeld Follies, 1931
    assembled by: Florenz Ziegfeld
    contributors: Gene Buck, Mark Hellinger, J. P. Murray, Barry
                     Trivers, Ben Oakland, Walter Donaldson, Dave
                     Stamper, Hugo Reisenfeld, Mack Gordon, Harry
                     Revel, Dmitri Tiomkin
    staging: Florenz Ziegfeld and Gene Buck
    choreography: Bobby Connelly and Albertina Rasch
Productions:
Opened July 1, 1931 for 165 performances
Reviews:
New Republic 67:262-3, Jul 22, 1931
New York Times page 30, Jul 2, 1931
                VIII, page 2, Aug 16, 1931
Outlook 158:343, Jul 15, 1931

Ziegfeld Follies (1934)
    sketches and   Vernon Duke, Samuel Pokrass, Billy Hill, H. I.
       songs: Phillips, Fred Allen, Harry Tugend, Ballard Mc-
                     Donald, David Freedman
    lyrics: E. Y. Harburg
    staging: Edward C. Lilley
    sets: Watson Barratt and Albert R. Johnson
    choreography: Robert Alton
Productions:
Opened January 4, 1934 for 182 performances
Reviews:
Commonweal 19:441, Feb 16, 1934
Nation 138:310, Mar 14, 1934
New Outlook 163:48, Feb 1934
New York Times X, page 1, Jan 21, 1934
                IX, page 1, Nov 11, 1934
Review of Reviews 89:40, Feb 1934
Time 23:40, Jan 15, 1934
Vanity Fair 42:38-9, Mar 1934

Ziegfeld Follies (1936)
    book: Ira Gershwin and David Freedman
    music: Vernon Duke
    lyrics: Ira Gershwin and David Freedman
    staging: John Murray Anderson
    sets: Vincente Minnelli
    costumes: Vincente Minnelli
    choreography: Robert Alton

Productions:
   Opened January 30, 1936 for 115 performances
Reviews:
   Nation 142:231, Feb 19, 1936
   New York Times page 10, Dec 31, 1935
                   IX, page 3, Jan 5, 1936
                   page 17, Jan 31, 1936
   Time 27:47, Feb 10, 1936

Ziegfeld Follies of 1936-1937

book:	Ira Gershwin and David Freedman
music:	Vernon Duke
lyrics:	Ira Gershwin and David Freedman
staging:	John Murray Anderson
sets:	Vincente Minnelli
costumes:	Vincente Minnelli
choreography:	Robert Alton

Productions:
   Opened September 4, 1936 for 112 performances
Reviews:
   New York Times page 37, Sep 15, 1936

Ziegfeld Follies (1943)

sketches:	Lester Lee, Jerry Seelen, Bud Pearson, Les White, Joseph Erens, Charles Sherman, Harry Young, Lester Lawrence, Baldwin Bergersen, Ray Golden, Sid Kuller, William Wells, Harold Rome
music:	Ray Henderson and Dan White
lyrics:	Jack Yellen and Buddy Burston
staging:	John Murray Anderson
sets:	Watson Barratt
costumes:	Miles White
choreography:	Robert Alton

Productions:
   Opened April 1, 1943 for 553 performances
Reviews:
   New York Theatre Critics' Reviews 1943:338+
   New York Times page 16, Apr 2, 1943
                   II, page 1, Apr 11, 1943
   Newsweek 21:84, Apr 12, 1943
   Theatre Arts 27:331, Jun 1943

Ziegfeld Follies (1957)

sketches:	Arnie Rosen, Coleman Jacoby, David Rogers, Alan Jeffreys, Maxwell Grant
music/lyrics:	Jack Lawrence, Richard Myers, Howard Dietz, Sammy Fain, David Rogers, Colin Romoff, Dean Fuller, Marshall Barer, Carolyn Leigh, Philip Springer
staging:	John Kennedy

sets: Raoul Pene du Bois
costumes: Raoul Pene du Bois
choreography: Frank Wagner
Productions:
Opened March 1, 1957 for 123 performances
Reviews:
America 97:311, Jun 8, 1957
Catholic World 185:147-8, May 1957
Commonweal 66:36, Apr 12, 1957
Life 42:89-90+, Mar 18, 1957
Nation 184:242, Mar 16, 1957
New York Theatre Critics' Reviews 1957:327+
New York Times page 19, Mar 2, 1957
New Yorker 33:64, Mar 9, 1957
Newsweek 49:66, Mar 11, 1957
Theatre Arts 41:18, May 1957
Time 69:80, Mar 11, 1957

Ziegfeld Midnight Frolic
music: Gene Buck and Dave Stamper
lyrics: Gene Buck and Dave Stamper
staging: Leon Errol
Productions:
Opened November 17, 1921 for 123 performances
Reviews:
New York Times page 11, Nov 19, 1921

Ziegfeld Midnight Frolic, Second Edition
music: Dave Stamper
lyrics: Gene Buck
staging: Ned Wayburn
Productions:
Opened October 2, 1919 for 88 performances
Reviews:
New York Clipper 68:14, Mar 24, 1920
New York Times page 15, Oct 4, 1919
Theatre Magazine 32:106, Sep 1920
                   32:334, Nov 1920

Ziegfeld's American Revue of 1926   (see No Foolin')

Zizi
sketches: Roland Petit
songs: Jean Ferrat, Michel Legrand, and others
staging: Roland Petit
costumes: Yves Saint-Laurent
choreography: Roland Petit
Productions:
Opened November 21, 1964 for 49 performances
Reviews:
Dance Magazine 39:19, Jan 1965

New York Theatre Critics' Reviews 1964:135
New York Times page 51, Nov 23, 1964
Newsweek 64:93, Nov 30, 1964
Saturday Review 48:32, Jan 2, 1965

Zorbá
book:	Joseph Stein; adapted from Zorba the Greek by Nikos Kazantzakis
music:	John Kander
lyrics:	Fred Ebb
staging:	Harold Prince
sets:	Boris Aronson
costumes:	Patricia Zipprodt
choreography:	Ronald Field

Productions:
Opened November 17, 1968 for 305 performances
Opened October 16, 1983 for 354 performances
Reviews:
America 119:632, Oct 14, 1968
California 8:120, Jul 1983
Dance Magazine 43:93, Jan 1969
                58:79-80, Jan 1984
Los Angeles 28:48, Jul 1983
New Leader 66:22, Oct 31, 1983
New York 16:58+, Oct 31, 1983
New York Theatre Critics' Reviews 1968:174
                                   1983:146
New York Times page 58, Nov 4, 1968
              page 58, Nov 18, 1968
              II, page 1, Nov 24, 1968
              page 28, Aug 5, 1969
              page 43, Nov 12, 1969
              III, page 15, Oct 17, 1983
New Yorker 44:124+, Nov 23, 1968
           59:147, Oct 24, 1983
Newsweek 72:105, Dec 2, 1968
Saturday Review 51:36, Dec 7, 1968
Time 92:71, Nov 29, 1968

The Zulu and the Zayda
book:	Howard Da Silva and Felix Leon; based on a story by Dan Jacobson
music:	Harold Rome
lyrics:	Harold Rome
staging:	Dore Schary
sets:	William and Jean Eckart
costumes:	Frank Thompson

Productions:
Opened November 10, 1965 for 179 performances
Reviews:
New York Theatre Critics' Reviews 1965:278

New York Times page 59, Nov 11, 1965
page 36, Apr 6, 1966

LONG RUN MUSICALS

Performances	Show	Season
12,106*	(OB) The Fantasticks	1959-1960
5,856*	Oh! Calcutta! (Also see 704 perf. and 610 perf.)	1976-1977
5,756*	A Chorus Line	1975-1976
3,486	42nd Street	1980-1981
3,388	Grease	1971-1972
3,242	Fiddler on the Roof	1964-1965
2,844	Hello Dolly!	1963-1964
2,777*	Cats	1982-1983
2,717	My Fair Lady	1955-1956
2,611	(OB) The Threepenny Opera	1953-1954
2,377	Annie	1976-1977
2,332	(OB) Forbidden Broadway	1981-1982
2,328	Man of La Mancha	1965-1966
2,212	Oklahoma!	1942-1943
2,209	(OB) Little Shop of Horrors	1982-1983
2,124	(OB) Godspell (Also see 527 perf.)	1970-1971
1,944	Pippin	1972-1973
1,925	South Pacific	1948-1949
1,920	The Magic Show	1973-1974
1,847	(OB) Jacques Brel Is Alive and Well and Living in Paris	1967-1968
1,774	Dancin'	1977-1978
1,761	La Cage aux Folles	1983-1984
1,750	Hair	1967-1968
1,672	The Wiz	1974-1975
1,639	Best Little Whorehouse in Texas	1978-1979
1,604	Ain't Misbehavin'	1977-1978
1,597	(OB) You're a Good Man, Charlie Brown	1966-1967
1,595*	Me and My Girl	1986-1987
1,567	Evita	1979-1980
1,522	Dreamgirls	1981-1982
1,508	Mame	1965-1966
1,443	The Sound of Music	1959-1960
1,431*	(OB) Nunsense	1985-1986

*Still Running on June 1, 1989

(OB) Off-Broadway Production

Performances	Show	Season
1,417	How to Succeed in Business Without Really Trying	1961-1962
1,404	Hellzapoppin	1938-1939
1,375	The Music Man	1957-1958
1,372	(OB) One Mo' Time	1979-1980
1,348	Funny Girl	1963-1964
1,327	(OB) Let My People Come	1973-1974
1,281	Promises, Promises	1968-1969
1,246	The King and I (Also see 696 perf.)	1950-1951
1,217	1776	1968-1969
1,208	Sugar Babies	1979-1980
1,200	Guys and Dolls	1950-1951
1,165	Cabaret	1966-1967
1,165	(OB) I'm Getting My Act Together and Taking It On the Road	1977-1978
1,147	Annie Get Your Gun	1945-1946
1,143	(OB) Little Mary Sunshine	1959-1960
1,114	(OB) El Grande de Coca-Cola	1972-1973
1,108	Pins and Needles	1937-1938
1,082	They're Playing Our Song	1978-1979
1,070	Kiss Me, Kate	1948-1949
1,065	Don't Bother Me, I Can't Cope	1971-1972
1,063	The Pajama Game	1953-1954
1,050	Shenandoah	1974-1975
1,019	Damn Yankees	1954-1955
1,005	Big River	1984-1985
964	A Funny Thing Happened on the Way to the Forum	1961-1962
933	(OB) Your Own Thing	1967-1968
931	(OB) Curly McDimple	1967-1968
928	(OB) Leave It to Jane	1959-1960
924	Bells Are Ringing	1956-1957
920	Beatlemania	1976-1977
898	Chicago	1975-1976
896	Applause	1969-1970
892	Can-Can	1952-1953
890	Carousel	1944-1945
889	Hats Off To Ice	1944-1945
888	Fanny	1954-1955
882	Follow the Girls	1943-1944
873	Camelot	1960-1961
872	I Love My Wife	1976-1977
871	(OB) The Mad Show	1965-1966
868*	Les Miserables	1986-1987
861	No! No! Nanette	1970-1971
854	Barnum	1979-1980
849	Comedy in Music	1953-1954
847	Raisin	1973-1974
835	La Plume De Ma Tante	1958-1959

Performances	Show	Season
831	(OB) Scrambled Feet	1979-1980
830	Stars On Ice	1942-1943
795	Fiorello!	1959-1960
792	Where's Charley?	1948-1949
774	Oliver!	1962-1963
770	Woman of the Year	1980-1981
767	My One and Only	1982-1983
767	Sophisticated Ladies	1980-1981
766	Bubbling Brown Sugar	1975-1976
763	(OB) The Boy Friend	1957-1958
761	Starlight Express	1986-1987
747	Joseph and the Amazing Technicolor Dreamcoat	1981-1982
742	Sons O'Fun	1941-1942
740	Candide	1973-1974
740	Gentlemen Prefer Blondes	1949-1950
739	Nine	1981-1982
734	Call Me Mister	1945-1946
732	West Side Story	1957-1958
728	(OB) Dime A Dozen	1962-1963
727	High Button Shoes	1947-1948
725	Finian's Rainbow	1946-1947
720	Jesus Christ Superstar	1971-1972
719	Carnival!	1960-1961
705	Company	1969-1970
704	(OB) Oh! Calcutta! (Also see 5,856 perf. and 610 perf.)	1969-1970
702	Gypsy	1958-1959
696	The King and I (Also see 1,246 perf.)	1976-1977
693	Li'l Abner	1956-1957
688	Purlie	1969-1970
676	The Most Happy Fella	1955-1956
675*	Anything Goes	1987-1988
674	(OB) Club	1976-1977
669	Tap Dance Kid	1983-1984
655*	Into the Woods	1987-1988
654	Bloomer Girl	1944-1945
644	Call Me Madame	1950-1951
627	Two Gentlemen of Verona	1971-1972
626	(OB) Oil City Symphony	1987-1988
620	(OB) The Game Is Up	1964-1965
610	(OB) Oh! Calcutta! (Also see 5,856 perf. and 704 perf.)	1970-1971
609	Star and Garter	1942-1943
608	Mystery of Edwin Drood	1985-1986
608	Sweet Charity	1965-1966
608	The Student Prince	1924-1925
607	Bye Bye Birdie	1959-1960
604	Irene (1973)	1972-1973

Performances	Show	Season
604	Sunday in the Park With George	1983-1984
600	(OB) Beehive	1985-1986
600	Flower Drum Song	1958-1959
600	A Little Night Music	1972-1973
598	Wish You Were Here	1952-1953
592	Blossom Time	1921-1922
588	Day in Hollywood/Night in the Ukraine	1979-1980
586	The Me Nobody Knows	1970-1971
583	Kismet	1953-1954
581	Brigadoon	1946-1947
580	No Strings	1961-1962
575	(OB) Dames at Sea	1968-1969
573	Pump Boys and Dinettes	1981-1982
572	Show Boat	1927-1928
570	Sally	1920-1921
568	Golden Boy	1964-1965
567	One Touch of Venus	1943-1944
563*	Phantom of the Opera	1987-1988
560	I Do! I Do!	1966-1967
560*	Sarafina!	1987-1988
559	Wonderful Town	1952-1953
557	Rose-Marie	1924-1925
557	Sweeney Todd, The Demon Barber of Fleet Street	1978-1979
555	Jamaica	1957-1958
555	Stop the World--I Want to Get Off	1962-1963
553	Ziegfeld Follies (1943)	1942-1943
551	Good News	1927-1928
551	Peter Pan, Or the Boy Who Wouldn't Grow Up	1979-1980
547	Let's Face It	1941-1942
543	Milk and Honey	1961-1962
543	(OB) What's a Nice Country Like You Doing in a State Like This?	1972-1973
540	Pal Joey	1951-1952
540	What Makes Sammy Run?	1963-1964
532	The Unsinkable Molly Brown	1960-1961
531	The Red Mill	1945-1946
527	Godspell (Also see 2,124 perf.)	1976-1977
524	Irma La Douce	1960-1961
521	Follies (1971)	1970-1971
518	Lew Leslie's Blackbirds of 1928	1927-1928
517	Sunny	1925-1926
511	Half a Sixpence	1964-1965
511	The Vagabond King	1925-1926
509	The New Moon	1928-1929
507	The Rothchilds	1970-1971
505	On Your Toes	1982-1983
505	Sugar	1970-1971

Performances	Show	Season
504	Shuffle Along	1920-1921
504	Up in Central Park	1944-1945
503	Carmen Jones	1943-1944
501	Panama Hattie	1940-1941

PULITZER PRIZE MUSICALS

1931-1932	Of Thee I Sing
1949-1950	South Pacific
1959-1960	Fiorello!
1961-1962	How to Succeed in Business Without Really Trying
1975-1976	A Chorus Line
1984-1985	Sunday in the Park With Goerge

TONY AWARD MUSICALS

The Antoinette Perry (Tony) Awards were established in 1947.

1947	no award
1948	no award
1949	Kiss Me, Kate
1950	South Pacific
1951	Guys and Dolls
1952	The King and I
1953	Wonderful Town
1954	Kismet
1955	The Pajama Game
1956	Damn Yankees
1957	My Fair Lady
1958	The Music Man
1959	Redhead
1960	(tie) Fiorello! and The Sound of Music
1961	Bye Bye Birdie
1962	How to Succeed in Business Without Really Trying
1963	A Funny Thing Happened on the Way to the Forum
1964	Hello, Dolly!
1965	Fiddler on the Roof
1966	Man of La Mancha
1967	Cabaret
1968	Hallelujah, Baby!
1969	1976
1970	Applause
1971	Company

1972	Two Gentlemen of Verona
1973	A Little Night Music
1974	Raisin
1975	The Wiz
1976	A Chorus Line
1977	Annie
1978	Ain't Misbehavin'
1979	Sweeney Todd, the Demon Barber of Fleet Street
1980	Evita
1981	42nd Street
1982	Nine
1983	Cats
1984	La Cage aux Folles
1985	Big River
1986	The Mystery of Edwin Drood
1987	Les Miserables
1988	The Phantom of the Opera
1989	Jerome Robbins' Broadway

NEW YORK DRAMA CRITICS' CIRCLE AWARD MUSICALS

First award for "Best Musical Production" granted in 1945-1946.

1945-1946	Carousel
1946-1947	Brigadoon
1947-1948	no award
1948-1949	South Pacific
1949-1950	The Consul
1950-1951	Guys and Dolls
1951-1952	Pal Joey
1952-1953	Wonderful Town
1953-1954	The Golden Apple
1954-1955	The Saint of Bleecker Street
1955-1956	My Fair Lady
1956-1957	The Most Happy Fella
1957-1958	The Music Man
1958-1959	La Plume de Ma Tante
1959-1960	Fiorello!
1960-1961	Carnival
1961-1962	How to Succeed in Business Without Really Trying
1962-1963	no award
1963-1964	Hello Dolly!
1964-1965	Fiddler on the Roof
1965-1966	Man of La Mancha
1966-1967	Cabaret
1967-1968	Your Own Thing
1968-1969	1776
1969-1970	Company

1970-1971	Follies
1971-1972	Two Gentlemen of Verona
1972-1973	A Little Night Music
1973-1974	Candide
1974-1975	A Chorus Line
1975-1976	Pacific Overtures
1976-1977	Annie
1977-1978	Ain't Misbehavin'
1978-1979	Sweeney Todd, the Demon Barber of Fleet Street
1979-1980	Evita
1980-1981	no award
1981-1982	no award
1982-1983	Little Shop of Horrors
1983-1984	Sunday in the Park With Goerge
1984-1985	no award
1985-1986	no award
1986-1987	Les Miserables
1987-1988	Into the Woods
1988-1989	no award

INDEX OF AUTHORS, COMPOSERS, LYRICISTS

INDEX OF ORIGINAL WORKS AND AUTHORS